The University of Chicago School Mathematics Project

Transition Mathematics

Authors

Zalman Usiskin

and

James Flanders
Cathy Hynes
Lydia Polonsky
Susan Porter
Steven Viktora

About the Cover

If a person runs at a constant speed, then the graph of the
ordered pairs (time, distance) is a line. This example combines algebra
and geometry with applied arithmetic–
a major theme of this book.

Scott, Foresman and Company

Editorial Offices: Glenview, Illinois   Regional Offices: Sunnyvale, California •
Tucker, Georgia • Glenview, Illinois • Oakland, New Jersey • Dallas, Texas

Acknowledgments

Authors

Zalman Usiskin
Professor of Education, The University of Chicago

James Flanders
UCSMP

Cathy Hynes
Mathematics Teacher, The University of Chicago Laboratory Schools

Lydia Polonsky
UCSMP

Susan Porter
Mathematics Teacher, Evanston Township H.S., Evanston, Illinois

Steven S. Viktora
Chairman, Mathematics Department, Kenwood Academy, Chicago Public Schools

UCSMP Production and Evaluation:

Series Editors: Zalman Usiskin, Sharon L. Senk

Technical Coordinator: Susan Chang

Director of the Field Trial Evaluation: Kathryn Sloane

Director of the Nationwide Evaluation: Sandra Mathison

Assistant to the Directors: Penelope Flores

Teacher's Edition Additional Author: Sharon Mallo
Lake Park H.S. East, Roselle, Illinois

Editorial Development and Design

Scott, Foresman staff, Kristin Nelson Design

We wish to acknowledge the generous support of the **Amoco Foundation** in helping to make it possible for these materials to be developed and tested, and the additional support of the **Carnegie Corporation of New York** in the nationwide field-testing of these materials.

It takes many people to put together a project of this kind and we cannot thank them all by name. We wish particularly to acknowledge James Schultz and Glenda Lappan of the UCSMP Advisory Board, who commented on early versions of the manuscript; Carol Siegel, who coordinated the use of these materials in schools; Edgar Arredondo, Janine Crawley, Maryann Kannappan, and Mary Lappan of our technical staff.

We wish to acknowledge and give thanks to the following teachers who taught preliminary versions of *Transition Mathematics*, participated in the pilot or formative research, and contributed many ideas to help improve this book:

Chris Coley
Parkside Community Academy
Chicago, Illinois

Alice Ekstrom
Lively Junior High School
Elk Grove, Illinois

Pat Finegan
Glenbrook South High School
Glenview, Illinois

Jonelle Glass
McClure Junior High School
Western Springs, Illinois

Rose Gunn
Grove Junior High School
Elk Grove, Illinois

Wilhelm Lilly
Kenwood Academy
Chicago Public Schools

Sharon Mallo
Mead Junior High School
Elk Grove Village, Illinois

Doc Mutchmore
Glenbrook South High School
Glenview, Illinois

Candace Schultz
Wheaton-Warrenville Middle School
Wheaton, Illinois

We also wish to acknowledge the following schools which used an earlier version of *Transition Mathematics* in a nationwide study and whose comments, suggestions, and performance guided the changes made for this version.

Powell Junior High School
Littleton, Colorado

16th St. Middle School
St. Petersburg, Florida

Walt Disney Magnet School
Gale Academy
Hubbard High School
Von Steuben High School
Chicago, Illinois

Hillcrest High School
Country Club Hills, Illinois

Friendship Junior High School
Des Plaines, Illinois

Bremen High School
Midlothian, Illinois

Holmes Junior High School
Mt. Prospect, Illinois

Sundling Junior High School
Winston Park Junior High School
Palatine, Illinois

Adams Junior High School
Schaumburg, Illinois

Edison Junior High School
Wheaton, Illinois

Golden Ring Middle School
Sparrows Point High School
Baltimore, Maryland

Walled Lake Central High School
Walled Lake, Michigan

Columbia High School
Columbia, Mississippi

Oak Grove High School
Hattiesburg, Mississippi

Roosevelt Middle School
Taylor Middle School
Albuquerque, New Mexico

Gamble Middle School
Schwab Middle School
Cincinnati, Ohio

Tuckahoe Middle School
Richmond, Virginia

Jason Lee School
Shumway Junior High School
Vancouver, Washington

We wish to acknowledge the hundreds of other schools and thousands of other students who have used earlier versions of these materials.

UCSMP Transition Mathematics

The University of Chicago School Mathematics Project (UCSMP) is a long-term project designed to improve school mathematics in grades K-12. UCSMP began in 1983 with a 6-year grant from the Amoco Foundation. Additional funding has come from the Ford Motor Company, the Carnegie Corporation of New York, the National Science Foundation, the General Electric Foundation, GTE, and Citicorp.

The project is centered in the Departments of Education and Mathematics of the University of Chicago, and has the following components and directors:

Resources	Izaak Wirszup, Professor Emeritus of Mathematics
Primary Materials	Max Bell, Professor of Education
Elementary Teacher Development	Sheila Sconiers, Research Associate in Education
Secondary	Sharon L. Senk, Assistant Professor of Mathematics and Education, Syracuse University (on leave) Zalman Usiskin, Professor of Education
Evaluation	Larry Hedges, Professor of Education Susan Stodolsky, Professor of Education

From 1983-1987, the director of UCSMP was Paul Sally, Professor of Mathematics. Since 1987, the director has been Zalman Usiskin.

The text *Transition Mathematics* was developed by the Secondary Component (grades 7-12) of the project, and constitutes the first year in a six-year mathematics curriculum devised by that component. As texts in this curriculum complete their multi-stage testing cycle, they are being published by Scott, Foresman and Company. The schedule for first publication of the texts follows. Titles for the last two books are tentative.

Transition Mathematics	spring, 1989
Algebra	spring, 1989
Geometry	spring, 1990
Advanced Algebra	spring, 1989
Functions, Statistics, and Trigonometry, with Computers	spring, 1991
Precalculus and Discrete Mathematics	spring, 1991

A first draft of *Transition Mathematics* was written and piloted during the 1983-84 school year. After a major revision, a field trial edition was used in twelve schools in 1984-85. A second revision was given a comprehensive nationwide test during 1985-86. Results are available by writing UCSMP. A hardcover project edition incorporated changes based on results of testing and comments from many students and teachers. The Scott, Foresman and Company edition is based on improvements suggested by the authors, editors, and some of the many teacher and student users of earlier editions.

Comments about these materials are welcomed. Address queries to Mathematics Product Manager, Scott, Foresman and Company, 1900 East Lake Avenue, Glenview, Illinois 60025, or to UCSMP, The University of Chicago, 5835 S. Kimbark, Chicago, IL 60637.

This book is designed for the course immediately preceding first-year algebra. Its content and questions have been carefully sequenced to provide a smooth path from arithmetic to algebra, and from the visual world and arithmetic to geometry. It is for this reason that this book is entitled *Transition Mathematics.*

Transition Mathematics differs from other books for this course in six major ways. First, it has **wider scope**, including substantial amounts of geometry integrated with the arithmetic and algebra that is customary. This is to correct the present situation in which many students who finish algebra find themselves without enough prior knowledge to succeed in geometry. Also, some students never get as far as geometry yet need to be able to deal with measurements and the geometry of objects.

Second, **reading and problem solving** are emphasized throughout. The lessons are written for students and each contains questions covering that reading. They must learn to read mathematics in order to become able to use mathematics outside of school. Our testing shows students can and should be expected to read. Every lesson also contains problem-solving questions applying the mathematics. Like skills, problem solving must be practiced; when practiced it becomes far less difficult. Some problem-solving techniques are so important that at times they (rather than the problems) should be the focus of instruction; consequently, an entire chapter is devoted to these techniques.

Third, there is a **reality orientation** towards both the selection of content and the approaches allowed the student in working out problems. Being able to do arithmetic is of little ultimate use to an individual unless he or she can apply that content. Each arithmetic operation is studied in detail for its applications to real-world problems. Real-life situations motivate ideas and provide additional settings for practice.

Fourth, fitting the reality orientation, students are expected to use current **technology**. Calculators are assumed throughout this book because virtually all individuals who use mathematics today find it helpful to have them. Scientific calculators are recommended because they use an order of operations closer to that found in algebra and have numerous keys that are helpful in understanding concepts at this level. Computer exercises show how the computer can be used as a helpful tool in doing mathematics.

Fifth, **four dimensions of understanding** are emphasized: skill in carrying out various algorithms; developing and using mathematical properties and relationships; applying mathematics in realistic situations; and representing or picturing mathematical concepts. We call this the SPUR approach: **S**kills, **P**roperties, **U**ses, **R**epresentations. On occasion, a fifth dimension of understanding, the historical dimension, is discussed.

Sixth, the **instructional format** is designed to maximize the acquisition of both skills and concepts. The book is organized around lessons meant to take one day to cover. Ideas introduced in a lesson are reinforced through "Review" questions in the immediately succeeding lessons. This daily review feature allows students several nights to learn and practice important concepts and skills. The lessons themselves are sequenced into carefully constructed chapters. At the end of each chapter, a carefully focused Progress Self-Test and a Chapter Review, each keyed to objectives in all the dimensions of understanding, are then used to solidify performance of skills and concepts from the chapter so that they may be applied later with confidence. Finally, to increase retention, important ideas are reviewed in "Review" questions of later chapters.

CONTENTS

Welcome to *Transition Mathematics*. We hope you enjoy this book; it was written for you. Its goals are to solidify the arithmetic you already know and to prepare you for algebra and geometry.

You need to have some tools to do any mathematics. The most basic tools are paper, pencils, and erasers (everyone makes mistakes sometimes). For this book, you will also need the following drawing equipment:

> *ruler* (to draw and measure along lines, with both centimeter and inch markings)
> *compass* (to draw circles)
> *protractor* (to draw and measure angles)

It is best if both the ruler and protractor are transparent plastic.

You will also need a scientific calculator in many places in this book, beginning in Chapter 1. Scientific calculators differ widely in the range of keys they have. If you are going to buy or borrow a calculator, it should have the following keys: x^y or y^x (powering), $\sqrt{x}$ (for square root), $x!$ (factorial), $\pm$ or $+/-$ (for negative numbers), π (pi), and $1/x$ (reciprocals), and it should write very large or very small numbers in scientific notation. We recommend a *solar-powered* calculator so that you do not have to worry about batteries, though some calculators have batteries which can last for many years and work in dim light. A good calculator can last for many years.

There is another important goal of this book: to assist you to become able to learn mathematics on your own, so that you will be able to deal with the mathematics you see in newspapers, magazines, on television, on any job, and in school. The authors, who are all experienced teachers, offer the following advice.

1. You can watch basketball hundreds of times on television. Still, to learn how to play basketball, you must have a ball in your hand and actually dribble, shoot, and pass it.

   Mathematics is no different. You cannot learn much mathematics just by watching other people do it. You must participate. Some teachers have a slogan:

   > *Mathematics is not a spectator sport.*

2. You are expected to read each lesson. Read slowly, and keep a pencil with you as you check the mathematics that is done in the book. Use the Glossary or a dictionary to find the meaning of a word you do not understand.

3. If you cannot answer a question immediately, don't give up! Read the lesson again; read the question again. Look for examples. If you can, go away from the problem and come back to it a little later. Do not be afraid to ask questions and to talk to others when you do not understand something. You are expected to learn many things by reading, but school is designed so that you do not have to learn everything by yourself.

We hope you join the many thousands of students who have enjoyed this book. We wish you much success.

CHAPTER 1

Decimal Notation

The chart below shows how the ten **digits**

| 0 | 1 | 2 | 3 | 4 | 5 | 6 | 7 | 8 | 9 |

have developed over the years. Notice that the Greeks and Romans did not write numbers the way we do. Instead they used the letters of their alphabets. The Romans used fewer letters than the Greeks. For larger numbers, the Romans used L for fifty, C for one hundred, D for five hundred, and M for one thousand. From about 100 B.C. until about 1400 A.D., Europeans most often wrote numbers using Roman numerals.

In the years 600–900 A.D., the Hindus developed the decimal system. The **decimal system** is the system in which *any* whole number can be written with just ten symbols. The Arabs wrote about this system. Europeans did not learn about it until 1202 A.D., when Leonardo of Pisa, an Italian mathematician also known as Fibonacci, translated an Arabic manuscript into Latin.

The Development of Arabic Numerals

Greeks	α	β	γ	δ	ε	ζ	η	θ	ι
Romans	I	II	III	IV	V	VI	VII	VIII	IX
976 A.D.	I	ح	ح	۲	ٮ	ٮ	٦	8	9
10th century	Τ	ω	Ν	Ρ	Ψ	Ο	Ѵ	Ʒ	S
1077 A.D.	۱	ح	ż	₮	۶	٤	Λ	8	2
11th century ②	I	۲	Hb	B	Ч	Ь	∧	8	٦
11th century	I	۲	Σ	ﻌﻌ	Ψ	۴	Λ	8	9
12th century	I	۲	۴	۶	۷	Ь	ν	8	ϑ
1200 A.D.	I	۲	໗	؟	۹	Ь	∧	8	١
15th century ●	I	۲	۶	۶	۹	Ρ	∧	8	١
1490 A.D.	o	١	2	3	٤	ﬁ	6	٨	8	٩
1522 A.D.	o	١	٢	3	4	5	6	7	8	9

1-1

Decimals for Whole Numbers

In the decimal system, the smallest ten **whole numbers** need only one digit. Today we write them as 0, 1, 2, 3, 4, 5, 6, 7, 8, and 9. But look again at the chart on page 3. Notice that the symbols we use today did not all appear until the late 1400s.

Two digits are needed to write the next ninety whole numbers as decimals.

   10   11   12   . . .   19   20   21   . . .   99

Notice that we call the whole numbers *decimals* even though there are no decimal points.

The next nine hundred whole numbers can be written with three digits.

   100   101   102   . . .   200   201   . . .   999

By using more digits, very large numbers can be written. The census estimate of the U.S. population on July 1, 1980, was 226545805 people. To make this easier to read, groups of digits are separated by commas.

In decimal notation:
2 2 6, 5 4 5, 8 0 5

In English words:
Two hundred twenty-six million, five hundred forty-five thousand, eight hundred five.

Notice that decimal notation is shorter than English words.

Each digit in a decimal has a **place value.** Here are the place values for the nine digits of the number that represents the U.S. population.

2 2 6 , 5 4 5 , 8 0 6

hundred millions
ten millions
millions
hundred thousands
ten thousands
thousands
hundreds
tens
ones

The U.S. population is an example of a **count.** The most basic use of numbers is as counts. For every count there is a **counting unit.** Counts are always whole numbers, never fractions between whole numbers. Here are some examples.

Phrase	Count	Counting unit
0 eight-legged insects	0	eight-legged insects
28 letters in "antidisestablishmentarianism"	28	letters
U.S. population of 226,545,805	226,545,805	people

Questions

1. What letter did the Greeks use to denote the number one?

2. How did the Romans denote the number two?

3. What letter did the Romans use to stand for the number of fingers on one normal human hand?

4. What letter did the Romans use to stand for the number of fingers on two hands?

5. What people invented the decimal system?

6. When was the decimal system invented?

7. Name the smallest whole number.

8. Who was Fibonacci, what did he do that relates to the decimal system, and when did he do it?

9. About when did all the symbols for the numbers zero through nine appear as we know them?

In 10–12, written in the decimal system, how many whole numbers have

10. one digit?

11. two digits?

12. three digits?

In 13–18, consider the number 568,249. Name the digit in each place.

13. thousands

14. ones

15. hundreds

16. tens

17. ten thousands

18. hundred thousands

19. A number is written as a decimal. Must there be a decimal point?

20. Name one advantage of writing numbers as decimals rather than using English words.

21. A count is always what kind of number?

22. Name something for which the count is between one million and one billion.

23. Consider the U.S. population in 1980.
    a. Name the count.
    b. Name the counting unit.

24. Give an example of a count that is larger than the 1980 U.S. population.

25. Consider the number of stars on a U.S. flag.
    a. Name the count.
    b. Name the counting unit.

26. The book of the Old Testament called Numbers gets its name because it begins with a census of the adult males of the tribes of Israel. The ancients did not have our numerals. So they wrote out the population in words. ''. . . of the tribe of Reuben, were forty and six thousand and five hundred.'' Write this number as a decimal.

27. Federal aid is often given on the basis of population: the greater the population, the greater the aid. According to these 1980 Census data,
   a. which of the four metropolitan areas would get the most aid?
   b. which of the four metropolitan areas would get the least aid?

Salinas-Monterey, California	290,444
Appleton-Oshkosh, Wisconsin	291,325
McAllen-Edinburg, Texas	283,229
Pensacola, Florida	289,782

Monterey, California

28. Tell why the counts in Question 27 are estimates, even on the day they were made.

In 29–31, write as a decimal.

29. 6 hundred million

30. ten thousand

31. five hundred six

32. In decimal notation, what is the smallest five-digit whole number?

33. In decimal notation, write the number that is one less than ten thousand.

Exploration

34. In Europe, the decimal numeral for seven is sometimes written as shown in the cartoon. Why is this done?

HE'S NEVER BEEN THE SAME SINCE RETURNING FROM EUROPE!

7 7 7 7   7

1-2

Decimals for Numbers Between Whole Numbers

Measuring is as common and important a use of numbers as counting. A **unit of measure** can always be split into smaller parts. This makes measures different from counts.

For instance, you can split up measures of time. Suppose someone runs 200 meters and is timed in between 21 and 22 seconds. This time **interval** is pictured on the **number line** below. The marks on the number line are called *tick marks*. The interval on this number line is one second, the distance between two tick marks.

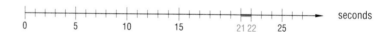

To get more accuracy, blow up the number line between 21 and 22. Then split that interval into ten parts. The interval on the new number line is **one tenth** of a second. The location of the dot shows that the time we are graphing is between 21.8 and 21.9 seconds.

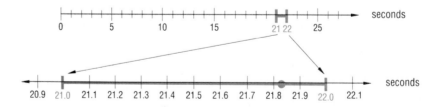

In early 1984, a U.S. women's record in the 200-meter dash was set by Evelyn Ashford. Her time of 21.83 is what is being graphed. To graph 21.83, split the interval between 21.8 and 21.9 into ten parts. The interval on the new number line is one **one-hundredth** of a second.

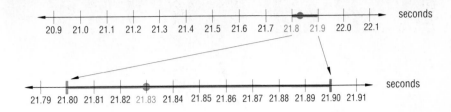

In 21.83, the digit 8 is in the **tenths place.** The digit 3 is in the **hundredths place.** For more accuracy, still more places to the right of the decimal can be used. For instance, here is the famous number pi, written π. The number π is the circumference of (distance around) a circle whose diameter is 1.

$$\pi = 3.1415926\ldots$$

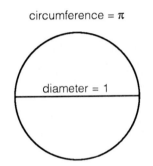

circumference = π

diameter = 1

3 . 1 4 1 5 9 2 6 ...

tenths
hundredths
thousandths
ten-thousandths
hundred-thousandths
millionths
ten-millionths
etc.

The names of the places to the right of the decimal point are similar to the names of the places to the left. Think of the ones place and the decimal point as the center. Then there is perfect balance of names to the right and to the left.

Today's uses often require many decimal places. Some instruments need to be accurate to within millionths of an inch. (That's much less than the thickness of this page.) Computers work at speeds often measured in billionths of a second.

Decimal places were first extended to the right by Simon Stevin, a Flemish mathematician, in 1585. Before then, fractions were used. Decimals are now more common than fractions for measurements. One reason is that they are easier to put in order and compare.

Example 1   Which is larger, 3.01 or 2.999?

Solution   Align the decimal points. "Align" means to put one above the other.

$$3.01$$
$$2.999$$

Start at the left of each number. 3 is larger than 2, so 3.01 is larger.

Example 2   Which is the largest?   0.0073   0.007294   0.00078

Solution 1   Again, align the decimal points.

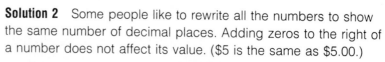

$$0.0073$$
$$0.007294$$
$$0.00078$$

The bottom number is smallest because it has 0 thousandths while the others have 7 thousandths. To find which of the first two is larger, compare the ten thousandths place. The 3 is larger than the 2, so the top number is largest.

Solution 2   Some people like to rewrite all the numbers to show the same number of decimal places. Adding zeros to the right of a number does not affect its value. ($5 is the same as $5.00.)

$$0.007300$$
$$0.007294$$
$$0.000780$$

Now it is easy to tell that the top number is largest.

In Example 2, a zero appears to the left of the decimal point of each number. This is often done to make it easier to order numbers. It also draws attention to the decimal point and corresponds to the display on most calculators. Notice that two different solutions are given to answer the question of Example 2. When there is more than one way of getting the answer to a question, you should try to learn all the ways.

Some of the questions for this lesson are review. Review questions are very important. You should seek help from friends or your teacher if you cannot do them. The lesson numbers in parentheses following review questions tell where the idea of the question is explained.

Covering the Reading

In 1–4, consider the number 21.83.

1. Between what two consecutive whole numbers is this number?

2. What digit is in the tenths place?

3. What digit is in the hundredths place?

4. What special event does 21.83 seconds measure?

In 5–10, consider the number 654,987.123456789. What digit is in each place?

5. thousandths   **6.** tenths

7. hundredths   **8.** ten thousandths

9. millionths   **10.** hundred thousandths

11. What digit is in the millionths place of π?

12. Name a kind of measurement that can require accuracy to billionths.

13. Who invented the idea of extending decimal places to the right, and when?

14. Name one advantage of decimals over fractions.

In 15–18, tell which of the three given numbers is largest and which is smallest.

15. 0.033, 0.015, 0.024   **16.** 6.783, .6783, 67.83

17. 0.98, 0.8, 0.9   **18.** 4.398, 4.4, 4.4001

19. a. What is the name of the number that is the circumference of a circle with diameter 1?
    b. Give the first five decimal places of this number. (''Decimal places'' refer to places to the *right* of the decimal point.)

In 20–25, use the number line drawn here. The tick marks are equally spaced. Which letter (if any) corresponds to the given number?

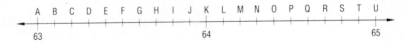

20. 63.4   **21.** 64.0   **22.** 64.3

23. 64.8   **24.** 64.80   **25.** 64.08

26. What is the difference between a count and a measure?

Here are examples showing decimals translated into English.

3.5	three and five tenths
3.54	three and fifty-four hundredths
3.549	three and five hundred forty-nine thousandths

In 27–30, use the above examples to help translate the given number into English.

27. 5.9 **28.** 324.66 **29.** 0.024 **30.** 1.414

31. In the decimal for one thousandth, how many zeros are between the decimal point and the one?

32. To find a number between 8.2 and 8.3, write them as 8.20 and 8.30. Then any decimal beginning with 8.21, 8.22, and so on up to 8.29 is between them. Use this idea to find a number between 44.6 and 44.7.

33. A store sells 5 pairs of socks for $16. Mel wants 1 pair and divides 16 by 5, using a calculator. The calculator shows 3.2. What should Mel pay?

34. In 1988, Florence Griffith-Joyner (pictured below) set a women's world record of 10.49 seconds in the 100-meter dash. If this record was lowered by a tenth of a second, what would the new record be?

In 35 and 36, order the numbers from smallest to largest.

35. three thousandths
four thousandths
three millionths

36. sixty-five thousandths
sixty-five thousand
sixty five

37. In the summer of 1988 Florence Griffith-Joyner ran 200 meters in 21.77 seconds. Is this faster or slower than the 1984 time of Evelyn Ashford?

In 38 and 39, write as a decimal. *(Lesson 1-1)*

38. four hundred million

39. thirty-one thousand sixty-eight

40. Consider the number 587,402,139. What number is in each place?
(Lesson 1-1)
a. thousands   **b.** hundred thousands
c. ten millions   **d.** ones

41. Based on population, which area will get the most federal aid?
(Lesson 1-1)
Kansas City, Missouri-Kansas (population 1,327,000)
Seattle-Everett, Washington (1,606,765)
Miami, Florida (1,625,979)
Denver, Colorado (1,619,921)

42. Written as a decimal, the number one million is a 1 followed by how many zeros? *(Lesson 1-1)*

43. In "76 trombones," name the count and the counting unit.
(Lesson 1-1)

44. a. What is the largest number of places to the right of the decimal point that your calculator will display?
b. If your calculator has a key for π, what does it display when you press that key?

1-3

Estimating by Rounding Up or Rounding Down

In many types of situations, an **estimate** may be preferred over an exact value.

1. An exact value may *not be worth the trouble* it would take to get it.
   Example: There were about 3500 people at that concert.

2. An estimate is often *easier to work with* than the exact value.
   Example: Instead of multiplying $169.95, let's use $170.

3. It may be *safer* to use an estimate than to try to use an exact value.
   Example: The trip will cost at least $1800, so we will budget $2000 to play it safe.

4. An exact *value may change* from time to time, forcing an estimate.
   Example: I estimate that the coin will land heads 5 times in 10 tosses.

5. Predictions of the future or notions about the past usually are estimates, since *exact values may be impossible to obtain*.
   Example: One estimate of the world population in the year 2000 is 7 billion.

The most common method of estimating is **rounding.** There are three kinds of rounding: **rounding up, rounding down,** and rounding to the nearest. Here are some examples of rounding up and rounding down. (In Lesson 1-4, rounding to the nearest is discussed.) Rounding is almost always done with a particular decimal place in mind.

Example 1   A certain type of label is sold in packages of 100. If you need 1325 labels, how many labels must you buy?

Solution   You must buy more labels than you need. So you need to round *up* to the next 100. Since 1325 is between 1300 and 1400, round up to 1400.

Example 2   A store sells six cans of orange juice for $1.39. You want one can. So you divide 1.39 by 6 to get the cost. Your calculator shows 0.2316666. What will you probably have to pay for the can?

Solution   The store will probably round *up* to the next penny. Pennies are hundredths of dollars, so look at the hundredths place in 0.2316666. The hundredths place is 3. That means that 0.2316666 is between 0.23 and 0.24. You will probably have to pay $0.24, which is 24¢.

Example 3   Some calculators round *down*, or **truncate,** all long decimals to the preceding millionth (the sixth decimal place). What will such a calculator show for π = 3.1415926535...?

Solution   The sixth decimal place is 2. The calculator will show 3.141592.

Questions

Covering the Reading

1. Give an example of a situation where an estimate should be preferred over an exact value.

2. Name five reasons why estimates are often preferred over exact values.

3. The most common way of estimating is by __?__.

4. Name three types of rounding.

5. A certain type of label is sold in packages of 100. If you need 1721 labels, how many labels must you buy?

6. Some special pencils are sold in packages of 10. A teacher needs one pencil for each student in a class of 32. How many pencils must be bought?

7. A store sells three cans of soup for $1. You want one can. So you divide $1.00 by 3 to get the cost. Your calculator shows 0.333333. How much will you probably have to pay for the can?

8. A store sells a dozen eggs for $1.09. You want a half dozen. To find out how much you will pay, you divide $1.09 by 2 on your calculator. The calculator shows 0.545. How much will you have to pay?

9. If a calculator rounds down to the preceding millionth, what will it show for 0.0123456?

Applying the Mathematics

10. When a decimal is truncated, what happens to it?

11. Suppose a calculator rounds down to the preceding hundred-millionth (the eighth decimal place). What will it show for 0.97531246809?

12. Round $1795 **a.** up to the next ten dollars, and **b.** down to the preceding ten dollars.

13. Round 5280, the number of feet in a mile, **a.** up to the next 1000, and **b.** down to the preceding 1000.

14. Round 30.48, the number of centimeters in a foot, as follows:
    a. up to the next tenth.   **b.** down to the preceding tenth.

15. Round $30.48 as follows:
    a. up to the next ten dollars.
    b. down to the preceding ten dollars.

16. Round 1.609344, the number of kilometers in a mile, **a.** up to the next thousandth, and **b.** down to the preceding thousandth.

In 17–20, tell whether a high or a low estimate would be preferred.

17. You are estimating how large a birthday cake to order for a party.

18. You estimate how much money you should take on a trip.

19. You estimate how much weight an elevator can carry without being overloaded.

20. You estimate how many minutes it will take to do your math homework.

Review

In 21 and 22, order the numbers from smallest to largest.
(Lesson 1-2)

21. 5.1, 5.01, 5.001

22. .29, 0.3, .07

23. Which number does not equal 0.86? *(Lesson 1-2)*
    0.860   .86   .086

In 24 and 25, find a number that is between the two given numbers. *(Lesson 1-2)*

24. 5.8 and 5.9

25. 5.9 and 6

In 26 and 27, use this number line. *(Lesson 1-2)*

```
    Z  Y  X  W  V  U  T  S  R  Q  P  O  N  M  L  K  J  I
  ←─┼──┼──┼──┼──┼──┼──┼──┼──┼──┼──┼──┼──┼──┼──┼──┼──┼──┼─→
              2              3              4
```

26. What is the interval on the number line?

27. Which letter on the number line corresponds to the given number?
a. 3.0   **b.** 2.8   **c.** 1.4

28. Write this number as a decimal: four million, thirty thousand.
(Lesson 1-1)

Exploration

29. The men's world record in the mile (as of December 1988) was set by the British runner, Steve Cram, in 1985. It is usually written as 3:46.32. Translate the number 3:46.32 into English.

30. What is a dictionary definition of the word *truncate*?

31. On this and other computer questions in this book, it is possible that your computer will not act as other computers. If you get a strange message or no response, ask your teacher for help.
a. Put your computer in programming mode, and type ?INT(4.57). The ? is short for PRINT. You could also type PRINT INT(4.57). Now press the RETURN key. What does the computer print?
b. Try part **a** with the following: ?INT(115.68), ?INT(789), ?INT(30000.12345), and ?INT(.995). Based on what the computer prints, what does INT() do to the number inside the parentheses?

1-4

Estimating by Rounding to the Nearest

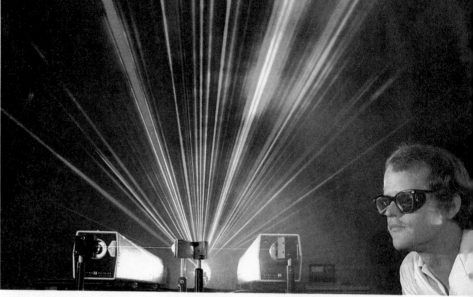

Lasers, like the one above, travel at the speed of light.

If 38 is rounded *up* to the next ten, the result is 40. If 38 is rounded *down* to the preceding ten, the result is 30. The number 40 is nearer to 38 than 30, so 40 is a better estimate of 38. When 38 is rounded to 40, we say that 38 has been **rounded to the nearest** 10.

Example 1   The speed of light is nearly 186,281.7 miles per second. Round this quantity to the nearest
a. mile per second
b. ten miles per second
c. hundred miles per second
d. thousand miles per second
e. ten thousand miles per second.

Solutions
a. 186,281.7 is between 186,281 and 186,282. Because .7 is greater than .5, the number 186,281.7 is nearer to 186,282.
b. 186,281.7 is between 186,280 and 186,290. Because 81.7 is closer to 80 than to 90, the rounded value is nearer 186,280.
c. 186,281.7 is between 186,200 and 186,300 and is closer to 186,300.
d. The answer is 186,000.
e. The answer is 190,000.

The more accuracy that is needed, the closer one would want to be to the original value.

Example 2   To calculate interest at 8.237%, the number 0.08237 may be used as a multiplier. Round this number to the nearest **a.** tenth, **b.** hundredth, **c.** thousandth, and **d.** ten thousandth.

Solutions

a. 0.08237 is between 0.0 and 0.1. It is nearer to 0.1, so that's the answer.

b. 0.08237 is between 0.08 and 0.09 and is nearer to 0.08.

c. 0.08237 is between 0.082 and 0.083 and is closer to 0.082.

d. 0.08237 is between 0.0823 and 0.0824 and is nearer to 0.0824.

Example 3 Paula must multiply $10.49 by 7 to find the cost of seven tapes. She rounds $10.49 to the nearest ten cents, $10.50, to estimate.

Actual cost: $\begin{array}{r} \$10.49 \\ \times\ 7 \\ \hline \$73.43 \end{array}$ Paula's estimate: $\begin{array}{r} \$10.50 \\ \times\ 7 \\ \hline \$73.50 \end{array}$

In Example 3, Paula can get a quick estimate by rounding $10.49 to the nearest dollar, $10. She can then estimate the cost in her head.

If the digit to the right of the place to be rounded to is a 5, there may be a choice in rounding. For instance, to round $10.50 to the nearest dollar, either $10 or $11 can be a correct answer. When there are many numbers with 5s to be rounded, it makes sense to round up half the time and round down the other half of the time.

Questions

Covering the Reading

1. Round 43 as follows: **a.** up to the next ten, **b.** down to the preceding ten, and **c.** to the nearest ten.

2. Round 0.547 as follows: **a.** up to the next hundredth, **b.** down to the preceding hundredth, and **c.** to the nearest hundredth.

3. Round 88.8888 to the nearest **a.** hundredth, **b.** tenth, **c.** one, **d.** ten, and **e.** hundred.

4. To estimate the cost of 4 records at $4.69 each, you might round $4.69 to the nearest ten cents. What do you get for the rounded value?

5. To estimate the cost of 4 records at $4.69 each, you might round $4.69 to the nearest dollar. What is your rounded value?

6. Estimate the cost of 6 shirts at $19.95 each by rounding to the nearest dollar and then multiplying.

7. Round the speed of light to the nearest hundred thousand miles per second.

8. When is there a choice in rounding to the nearest?

9. The number 0.0525 is used in some calculations of interest on savings. Round this number to the nearest thousandth.

10. When there are many numbers ending in 5 to be rounded, what is the sensible thing to do?

11. The U.S. Internal Revenue Service allows taxpayers to round all amounts to the nearest dollar. But half dollars must be rounded up. In figuring income tax, to what value can you round each amount?
   a. $89.46   b. $165.50
   c. $100.91   d. $5324.28

12. Round 2.54, the number of centimeters in an inch, to the nearest tenth.

13. Round 328.35, the average consumer price index in December, 1986, to the nearest whole number.

14. Round 3.666666 to the nearest a. tenth, b. hundredth, c. thousandth, and d. ten-thousandth.

15. Round 12.5300 to the nearest hundredth.

16. You buy items costing $4.99, $6.99, and $8.99 in a store.
   a. Add these numbers.
   b. How close would you be if you rounded each given number to the nearest dollar and then added?

17. Consider the addition problem $2.898765489 + 8.1898989898$.
   a. Estimate the answer by rounding both numbers to the nearest whole number and adding the estimates.
   b. How could you get a better estimate?

In 18–21, what is the answer rounded to the nearest whole number? (Hint: You should be able to do these mentally.)

18. $6 \times \$3.99$

19. $11.95 divided by 2

20. $920.9994 - 0.0003992$

21. $2.0123456789 + 3.0123456789$

22. A number is rounded to the nearest hundred. The resulting estimate is 9,600.
   a. What is the smallest value the original number might have had?
   b. What is the largest value the original number might have had?

Review

In 23–25, find a number that is between the two given numbers. *(Lesson 1-2)*

23. 3.2 and 3.4   **24.** 6.3 and 6.29   **25.** 14.23 and 14.230

26. Write one thousand, five hundred six and three tenths as a decimal. *(Lesson 1-2)*

27. John bought a dozen eggs. In "a dozen eggs," what is the count and what is the counting unit? (Watch out!) *(Lesson 1-1)*

28. If a calculator shows that you should pay $1.534 for something, what will a store probably charge you? *(Lesson 1-3)*

29. Round 1.008 as follows: **a.** up to the next hundredth, and **b.** down to the preceding hundredth. *(Lesson 1-3)*

30. Truncate 3.775 to one decimal place. *(Lesson 1-3)*

31. The number ten million consists of a one followed by how many zeros? *(Lesson 1-1)*

Exploration

32. a. Find the number that satisfies all of these conditions.
   Condition 1: When rounded up to the next hundred, the number becomes 600.
   Condition 2: When rounded down to the preceding ten, the number becomes 570.
   Condition 3: When rounded to the nearest ten, the number is increased by 4.
   Condition 4: The number is a whole number.
   b. Are any of the conditions not needed?

1-5

Negative Numbers

On every item a store sells, the store can make money, lose money, or break even. Here are some of the possibilities.

In English	In mathematics
make $3	3
make $2	2
make $1	1
break even	0
lose $1	-1
lose $1.50	-1.5
lose $2	-2
lose $3	-3

The numbers along the number line describe the situation without using words. Higher numbers on the line are larger and mean more profits. Lower numbers mean lower profits. The - (negative) sign stands for **opposite of.** The opposite of making $1.50 is losing $1.50. So the opposite of 1.50 is -1.50, and vice versa. The numbers with the - sign are called **negative numbers.**

There are three common ways in which the - sign for negatives is said out loud.

-3: negative 3   correct
-3: opposite of 3   correct
-3: minus 3   very commonly used, but can be confusing, since there is no subtraction here.

Most people know negative numbers from temperatures. But they are found in many other situations. On TV bowling, -12 means ''behind by 12 pins.'' The symbol +12, called **positive** 12, means ''ahead by 12 pins.'' The numbers 12 and +12 are identical. (In this book we use +12 as little as we can. The + sign can get confused with addition.)

On a horizontal number line, negative numbers are almost always placed at the left. The numbers identified on the number line drawn here are the **integers.** The **positive integers** are the numbers 1, 2, 3, ... The positive integers are sometimes called the **natural numbers.** The **negative integers** are -1, -2, -3, ... *Zero* is an integer but is neither positive nor negative.

negative numbers   positive numbers

Negative numbers can be used when a situation has two opposite directions. Either direction may be picked as positive. The other is then negative. Zero stands for the starting point. The table below gives some situations that often use negative numbers.

Situation	Negative	Zero	Positive
savings account	withdrawal	no change	deposit
time	before	now	after
games	behind	even	ahead
business	loss	break even	profit
elevation	below sea level	sea level	above sea level

Example 1 The shore of the Dead Sea in Israel, the lowest land on Earth, is 1286 feet below sea level. This can be represented by -1286 feet.

Example 2 Suppose time is measured in seconds. Then 4.3 seconds before the launch of a space shuttle is given by -4.3 seconds. Rounded to the nearest second, that is -4 seconds. One *minute* after the launch is 60 seconds. The time of launch is 0 seconds.

Questions

1. Translate -4 into English in two different ways.

2. You withdraw $25 from a savings account. Is this transaction considered positive, or is it considered negative?

3. Next to a bowler's name on TV is the number -8. Is the bowler ahead or behind?

4. On a horizontal number line, negative numbers are usually to the __?__ of positive numbers.

5. On a vertical number line, negative numbers are usually __?__ positive numbers.

6. Graph -7, -3, -9.6, 0, and 2 on a horizontal number line.

7. Graph a profit of $4, a loss of $7, breaking even, and a profit of $10 on a vertical number line.

In 8–10, three words or phrases relating to a situation are given. Which would usually be considered positive? which negative? which zero?

8. Football: losing yardage, gaining yardage, no gain

9. Time: tomorrow, today, yesterday

10. Stock market: no change, gain, loss

11. What numbers are the integers?

12. Which of the following numbers is not an integer? 5   0   -5   .5

13. Another name for *positive integer* is __?__.

14. Give an example of an integer that is neither positive nor negative.

15. Give an example of a negative number that is not an integer.

16. Suppose time is measured in days and 0 stands for today.
    a. What number stands for yesterday?
    b. What number stands for tomorrow?
    c. What number stands for the day before yesterday?
    d. What number stands for the day after tomorrow?

17. You guess how many points your school's basketball team will score in its next game. What number could stand for:
    a. a guess 3 points too high?
    b. a guess ten points too low?
    c. a perfect guess?

In 18–21, use the number line drawn here. Which letter corresponds to the given number?

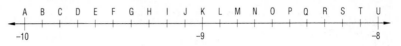

18. -9.1   **19.** -8.4   **20.** -9.0   **21.** -10.1

22. Pick the two numbers that are equal: -43.3, -43.03, -43.30, 43.3

23. Which numbers are not natural numbers? -1   0 $\frac{1}{2}$ 1   2

In 24–27, round to the nearest integer.
24. -1.75   **25.** -3.9   **26.** -43.06   **27.** -0.53

Review

28. Order from smallest to largest: 439   349   394   493. *(Lesson 1-1)*

29. Order from smallest to largest: 5.67   5.067   5.607   5.60. *(Lesson 1-2)*

30. Write as a decimal: four hundred sixty-two thousand and one tenth. *(Lesson 1-2)*

31. What number is in the thousands place of 24,680.13579? *(Lesson 1-2)*

32. What number is in the thousandths place of 24,680.13579? *(Lesson 1-2)*

33. Round $28.47 as follows: **a.** up to the next dollar, **b.** down to the preceding dollar, and **c.** to the nearest dollar. *(Lessons 1-3, 1-4)*

34. Suppose the points are equally spaced on the number line drawn here. If *E* is 1 and *L* is 2, what number corresponds to *C*? *(Lesson 1-2)*

Exploration

35. Use an almanac to find the place in the United States with the lowest elevation. What number represents this elevation?

36. Find an example of negative numbers that is not given in this lesson.

1-6

Symbols for Inequality

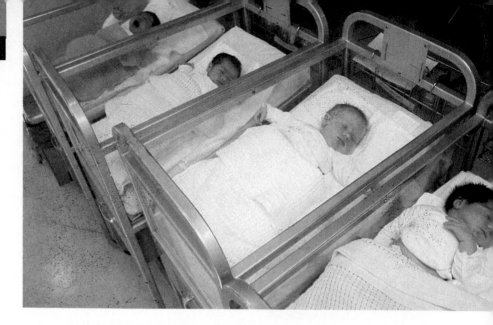

Counts are frequently compared. For instance, in 1970 there were about 3,256,000 births in the United States. In 1977 there were about 3,326,000 births. To indicate that there were fewer births in 1970, we write

$$3,256,000 < 3,326,000.$$

The symbol $<$ means **is less than.** The symbol $>$ means **is greater than,** so we could also write

$$3,326,000 > 3,256,000.$$

The symbols $<$ and $>$ are examples of **inequality symbols.** These symbols always point to the smaller number. Comparison of populations is useful in knowing whether more schools or hospitals should be built, or how many people could buy a particular item, or watch a television program.

Measures can also be compared. You probably have compared your height and weight to those of other people. Mario is 5'6" tall. Setsuko is 4'10" tall. You can conclude:

Mario is taller than Setsuko.
$$5'6" > 4'10"$$
Setsuko is shorter than Mario.
$$4'10" < 5'6"$$

Numbers can be compared, whether they are positive, negative, or zero. For instance, a temperature of 0°C is colder than one of 4°C. In symbols,

$$0 < 4.$$

A temperature of -7°C is colder than either of these temperatures.

$$-7 < 0$$
$$-7 < 4$$

Numbers on a number line are easy to compare. Smaller numbers are usually to the *left* of, or *below* larger numbers. The numbers -7, 0, and 4 are graphed on the vertical and the horizontal number lines below.

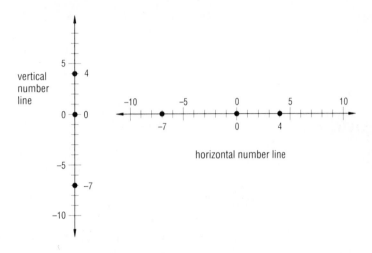

When numbers are in order, inequalities can be combined. For the number lines pictured here, you could write either -7 < 0 < 4 or 4 > 0 > -7.

Caution: Even though 10 is greater than 5, -10 is less than -5. In symbols, -10 < -5. This is because -10 could mean a lower temperature or bigger loss than -5.

Caution: Do not use > and < in the same sentence. For instance, do not write 5 > 3 < 4.

Questions

Covering the Reading

1. Give an example of an occasion when it would be useful to compare counts.

2. What is the meaning of the symbol <?

3. What is the meaning of the symbol >?

In 4–7, rewrite the sentence using inequality symbols.

4. -5 is less than -3.

5. 6 is greater than -12.

6. 4′11″ is shorter than 5′.

7. 0 is between -2 and 2. (Use two symbols.)

In 8–10, write a sentence with the same meaning, using the other inequality symbol.

8. $2 < 2.1$

9. $18 > 0$

10. $0.43 < 0.432 < 0.44$

In 11–13, translate into English words.

11. $-3 < 3$ **12.** $17 > -1.5$ **13.** $-4 < -3 < -2$

In 14–16, translate into mathematics, using a $>$ or $<$ sign.

14. A temperature of $-6°F$ is colder than a temperature of $15°F$.

15. The wrestler Andre the Giant, whose height is $7'4''$, is taller than the basketball player Kareem Abdul-Jabbar, whose height is $7'2''$.

16. That school has 125 ninth-graders and 119 tenth-graders. There are more ninth-graders.

17. On a horizontal number line, larger numbers are to the __?__ of smaller numbers.

18. On a vertical number line, larger numbers are __?__ smaller numbers.

Applying the Mathematics

In 19 and 20, translate into mathematics.

19. A profit of $8000 is better than a loss of $2000.

20. An elevation 300 ft below sea level is higher than an elevation 400 ft below sea level.

In 21–26, choose the correct symbol: $<$, $=$, or $>$.

21. .305 __?__ .3046   **22.** .0008 __?__ 0.008

23. 6.01 __?__ 6.000001   **24.** -14 __?__ -14.5

25. -99.5 __?__ 9.95   **26.** -3.20 __?__ -3.2

In 27 and 28, put the three numbers into one sentence with two inequality symbols.

27. 62.1, 6.21, 0.621   **28.** -4.1, -41, and 4.1

29. The thermometer pictured below shows Joanne's body temperature on three consecutive days of a cold. Put the three numbers into one sentence connected by inequality symbols.

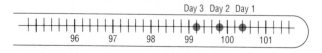

30. Consider the number 8249.0351. Name the digit in each place. *(Lesson 1-2)*
    a. thousands   **b.** thousandths
    c. hundreds   **d.** hundredths

31. Order 0.07243, 0.07249, and 0.0782 from smallest to largest. *(Lesson 1-2)*

32. Name all the whole numbers less than 5. *(Lesson 1-1)*

33. Name all the integers between -4 and 3. *(Lesson 1-5)*

34. Suppose time is measured in years and 0 stands for this year. What number stands for:
    a. next year?   **b.** last year?
    c. 2010?   **d.** 1925? *(Lesson 1-5)*

In 35 and 36, estimate each sum to the nearest whole number. *(Lesson 1-4)*

35. 70.0392 + 6.98234   **36.** $14.95 + $2.99 + $7.89

37. Round 6.28318... (the number that is 2 times π) to the nearest thousandth. *(Lesson 1-4)*

38. Write twenty-two and ninety-five hundredths in decimal notation. (This was the winning time in seconds in the 1982 World Rubik's Cube competition.) *(Lesson 1-2)*

39. The inequality signs < and > were first used by Thomas Harriot, an English mathematician, in 1631. Find out something else about this person.

1-7

Knowing Your Calculator

Calculators make it easy to do arithmetic quickly and accurately. But they cannot help unless you know how and why to use them. Different calculators may give different answers even when the same buttons are pushed. With this book it is best if you have a **scientific calculator.** (On page 1, there is a description of this kind of calculator.) You should have a calculator with you as you read this lesson.

When a calculator turns on, 0 or 0. will appear in the **display.** We show this as ⌈ **0.** ⌉

As you press keys (this is called **entering** or **keying in**), the display changes. For instance, here is how to do the addition problem 2 + 5 on a calculator.

	Display shows
Press 2.	⌈ 2. ⌉
Now press +.	⌈ 2. ⌉
Next press 5.	⌈ 5. ⌉
Now press =.	⌈ 7. ⌉

The set of instructions in the left column above is called the **key sequence** for this problem. We write the key sequence for this problem using boxes for everything pressed but the numbers.

$$2 \quad \boxed{+} \quad 5 \quad \boxed{=}$$

Sometimes we put in the display values underneath the last key pressed.

Key sequence: 2 ⌈+⌉ 5 ⌈=⌉

Display: ⌈ 2. ⌉ ⌈ 2. ⌉ ⌈ 5. ⌉ ⌈ 7. ⌉

The next key sequence is for the calculation of $85 + 9 \times 2$.

Key sequence: 85 $[+]$ 9 $[\times]$ 2 $[=]$

Display: $[$ *85.* $]$ $[$ *85.* $]$ $[$ *9.* $]$ $[$ *9.* $]$ $[$ *2.* $]$ $[$ *103.* $]$

If your calculator first added 85 and 9, and then multiplied by 2, it gave you the answer 188. If you got 188, your calculator is probably not a scientific calculator.

Calculators also differ in the way they round decimals to the right of a decimal point. This usually does not make much of a difference, but you should know what your calculator does. To check your calculator, try this experiment.

This book's calculator symbol for division is $[\div]$.
Key in 2 $[\div]$ 3 $[=]$.

The actual answer to 2 divided by 3 is 0.666666666666666..., where the digit 6 repeats forever. No calculator can list all the digits. So the calculator must be programmed to round. (Calculators *are* computers; each key triggers a program.) If the last digit your calculator displays is a 7, your calculator rounds up.
If the last digit your calculator displays is a 6, your calculator truncates.

All scientific calculators have a way to enter negative numbers. This is done by a key that looks like $[+/-]$ or $[\pm]$. For example, 7 $[\pm]$ keys in -7.

Most scientific calculators have a way of entering the number π. If you have a π key, simply press it. However, on some calculators, you must press two keys to display π. If there is a small π written next to a key, two keys are probably needed. In this case, press $[inv]$, $[2nd]$ or $[F]$ before pressing the key with the π next to it.

Questions

Covering the Reading

1. What is a key sequence?

2. *True or false* If you follow the same key sequence on two different calculators, you will always get the same answer.

3. Do the following key sequence on your calculator. Write down what is in the display after each key is pressed.
   Key sequence: 8 $[+]$ 7.2 $[\times]$ 10 $[=]$
   Display: $[$ $]$ $[$ $]$ $[$ $]$ $[$ $]$ $[$ $]$ $[$ $]$

4. What is the key sequence for the problem $15 - 27$?

5. Display π on your calculator. Compare your value with the value of π given in Lesson 1-2. Does your calculator truncate, or does it round to the nearest?

6. What number does the key sequence 87 $\boxed{\pm}$ yield?

7. How many decimal places does your calculator display? Perform the following key sequence to find out.

13717421 $\boxed{\div}$ 333 $\boxed{\div}$ 333667 $\boxed{=}$

Applying the Mathematics

In 8–12, do the arithmetic problem on your calculator.

8. 3.5625×512

9. $0.9 + 0.99 + 0.999$

10. $6 \times \pi$

11. -412 divided by -2

12. $8.3 \times 5.1 - 3.71$

13. What is the largest number in decimal notation that your calculator can display?

14. What is the smallest positive number in decimal notation that your calculator can display?

15. What is the smallest negative number in decimal notation that your calculator can display?

16. Which is larger, $\pi \times \pi$ or 10?

17. All calculators have a way of allowing you to correct a mistake in an entry. You press a key to replace one entry with another. On your calculator, what is this key called?

18. All calculators have a way of starting from scratch with a new calculation. How is this done on your calculator?

19. **a.** Order ⁻1, ⁻2, and ⁻1.5 from smallest to largest.
    b. Write the numbers in part **a** on one line with inequality signs between them. *(Lesson 1-6)*

20. **a.** Order from largest to smallest: .3, .33, .303. *(Lesson 1-2)*
    b. Write the three numbers in part **a** on one line with inequality signs between them. *(Lesson 1-6)*

21. Place the correct sign <, =, or > in the sentence:
⁻4 __?__ ⁻10. *(Lesson 1-6)*

22. You run a race in 53.7 seconds. Someone beats you by two tenths of a second. What was that person's time? *(Lesson 1-2)*

23. You run a race in 53.7 seconds. Round your time to the nearest second. *(Lesson 1-4)*

24. Estimate 896.5555555555 + 7.96113 to the nearest hundred. *(Lesson 1-4)*

25. Find a number between ⁻4.632 and ⁻4.631. *(Lesson 1-2)*

26. Translate into English: 3,412,670. *(Lesson 1-1)*

27. Three hundred thousand is written as a three followed by how many zeros? *(Lesson 1-1)*

28. What number is three less than three hundred thousand? *(Lesson 1-1)*

29. Key in 5 ÷ 0 = on your calculator.
    a. What is displayed?
    b. What does the display mean?
    c. Why did this happen?

30. **a.** Put your computer in programming mode, and type ?78/0. Now press the RETURN key. What does the computer print?
    b. Try the same with ?0/0. What happens?
    c. What other things that you might type in will give the same result?

1-8

Decimals for Simple Fractions

A symbol of the form $\frac{a}{b}$ or a/b is a **fraction** with a **numerator** a and **denominator** b. The fraction bar — or slash / indicates division.

$$\frac{a}{b} = a/b = a \div b$$

In the language of division, the number a is the **dividend,** b is the **divisor,** and $\frac{a}{b}$ is the **quotient.** In $\frac{2}{3}$, 2 is the numerator or dividend, and 3 is the denominator or divisor. The fraction itself is the quotient, the result of dividing 2 by 3.

The fraction bar was first used by the Arabs and later by Fibonacci, but it was not widely used until the 1500s. A curved slash, $a\int b$, was first used by the Mexican Manuel Antonio Valdes in 1784. In the 1800s this developed into the slash in a/b.

A **simple fraction** is a fraction with an integer in its numerator and a nonzero integer in its denominator. (Zero cannot be in the denominator of a fraction.) Here are some simple fractions. Notice that the opposite of a simple fraction is a simple fraction.

$$\frac{3}{4} \qquad 3/4 \qquad \frac{-72}{-8} \qquad \frac{3}{11} \qquad -\frac{3}{11} \qquad \frac{0}{135} \qquad \frac{-4}{180}$$

Fractions are very useful because they are related to division. But fractions are harder to order, round, add, and subtract than decimals. So it often helps to find a decimal that equals a given fraction. This is easy to do, particularly with a calculator.

Example 1   Find the decimal equal to $\frac{7}{4}$.

Solution   Key in: 7 ⟮÷⟯ 4 ⟮=⟯. The calculator displays the exact answer, 1.75.

Example 2 Find a decimal equal to $-\frac{3}{5}$.

Solution Find the decimal equivalent of $\frac{3}{5}$ first, then take the opposite. Key in: 3 ⌷÷⌷ 5 ⌷=⌷ ⌷±⌷. The calculator displays -0.6.

Example 3 Find the decimal equal to 3/11.

Solution Key in: 3 ⌷÷⌷ 11 ⌷=⌷. What the calculator shows depends on the way it rounds and the number of decimal places it displays. You might see 0.27272727 or 0.2727273 or 0.2727272, or something like this with fewer or more decimal places. This suggests that the 27 repeats again and again. That is the case.

$$3/11 = 0.27272727272727272727272727272727\ldots,$$

where the 27 repeats forever. For practical purposes an abbreviation is needed. It has become the custom to write

$$3/11 = 0.\overline{27}.$$

The bar over the 27 indicates that the 27 repeats forever. The digits under the bar are the **repetend** of this **infinite repeating decimal.**

Long division can verify that a decimal repeats. Here we again work out 3/11, this time using long division.

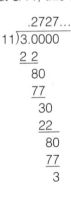

```
        .2727...
    11)3.0000
        2 2
         80
         77
         30
         22
         80
         77
          3
```

Notice that the remainders, after subtraction, alternate between 8 and 3. This shows that the digits in the quotient repeat forever.

Example 4 Find the decimal equal to $\frac{87}{70}$.

Solution Key in: 87 $\div$ 70 $=$.
The author's calculator displays 1.242857142.

That is all you are expected to do at this time. You cannot tell from this whether or not the decimal repeats. Actually it does, with the six-digit repetend 428571.

$$\frac{87}{70} = 1.2\overline{428571}$$

All simple fractions are equal to ending or repeating decimals. It takes experience to know when the decimal repeats. It will help you throughout this book if you know the decimals for some of the more common simple fractions between 0 and 1.

Fourths and Eighths	Thirds and Sixths	Fifths and Tenths
$\frac{1}{8} = 0.125$	$\frac{1}{6} = 0.1\overline{6}$	$\frac{1}{10} = 0.1$
$\frac{1}{4} = \frac{2}{8} = 0.25$	$\frac{1}{3} = \frac{2}{6} = 0.\overline{3}$	$\frac{1}{5} = \frac{2}{10} = 0.2$
$\frac{3}{8} = 0.375$	$\frac{3}{6} = 0.5$	$\frac{3}{10} = 0.3$
$\frac{2}{4} = \frac{4}{8} = 0.5$	$\frac{2}{3} = \frac{4}{6} = 0.\overline{6}$	$\frac{2}{5} = \frac{4}{10} = 0.4$
$\frac{5}{8} = 0.625$	$\frac{5}{6} = 0.8\overline{3}$	$\frac{5}{10} = 0.5$
$\frac{3}{4} = \frac{6}{8} = 0.75$		$\frac{3}{5} = \frac{6}{10} = 0.6$
$\frac{7}{8} = 0.875$		$\frac{7}{10} = 0.7$
		$\frac{4}{5} = \frac{8}{10} = 0.8$
		$\frac{9}{10} = 0.9$

Some fractions are whole numbers in disguise.

Example 5 Find the decimal equal to $\frac{91}{13}$.

Solution Key in 91 $\div$ 13 $=$.

The calculator displays 7.

In Example 5, we say that 91 is **evenly divisible** by 13. Sometimes we merely say that 91 is **divisible** by 13. The number 13 is called a **factor** of 91. The other factors of 91 are 1, 7, and 91.

1. Consider the fraction $\frac{15}{8}$.
   a. What is its numerator?
   b. What is its denominator?
   c. What is the sign for division?
   d. Does it equal 15/8 or 8/15?
   e. Does it equal $8 \div 15$?
   f. Does it equal $15 \div 8$?
   g. What is the divisor?
   h. What is the dividend?
   i. Find the decimal equal to it.

2. Before the 1500s, who used the fraction bar?

3. Who first developed a slash symbol for fractions, and when?

4. Which of the following are simple fractions?

   a. $\frac{15}{8}$ b. $\frac{-7}{1}$ c. $\frac{3 \cdot 5}{2 \cdot 3}$ d. $6\frac{2}{3}$ e. -5/6

5. Why is it helpful to be able to find a decimal for a fraction?

In 6–10, find the decimal for each fraction.

6. 3/20   7. 23/20   8. -23/20

9. 4/7   10. 1/27

11. In $86.\overline{27}$, what is the repetend?

12. In $0.39\overline{8}$, what is the repetend?

In 13–15, write the first ten decimal places.

13. $9.8\overline{7}$

14. $0.\overline{142857}$

15. $-5.\overline{4}$

16. If you do not know the decimals for these fractions, you should learn them now. Try to find each decimal without looking at the preceding page.

   a. $\frac{1}{10}$ b. $\frac{2}{10}$ c. $\frac{3}{10}$ d. $\frac{4}{10}$ e. $\frac{5}{10}$

   f. $\frac{6}{10}$ g. $\frac{7}{10}$ h. $\frac{8}{10}$ i. $\frac{9}{10}$ j. $\frac{1}{5}$

   k. $\frac{2}{5}$ l. $\frac{3}{5}$ m. $\frac{4}{5}$ n. $\frac{1}{2}$ o. $\frac{1}{4}$

   p. $\frac{3}{4}$ q. $\frac{3}{8}$ r. $\frac{5}{8}$ s. $\frac{7}{8}$ t. $\frac{1}{3}$

   u. $\frac{2}{3}$ v. $\frac{4}{6}$ w. $\frac{1}{6}$ x. $\frac{5}{6}$

In 17–22, give a simple fraction for each decimal. Try to find each fraction without looking at page 36.

17. 0.4   **18.** .25   **19.** $.\overline{3}$

20. 0.60   **21.** 0.7   **22.** $.\overline{666}$

23. 92/23 = 4. So we say that 23 is a __?__ of 92.

24. The factors of 12 are 1, 2, 3, 6, 12 and what other number?

25. Give the factors of 30.

Applying the Mathematics

26. Carpenters often measure in sixteenths of an inch.
    a. Change 3/16″ to a decimal.
    b. Is 3/16″ shorter or longer than 1/5″?

27. Rewrite 1/14 as a decimal rounded to the nearest thousandth.

28. Order 3/10, 1/3, and 0.33 from smallest to largest.

29. Order $\frac{2}{9}$, $\frac{2}{11}$, and $\frac{2}{7}$ from smallest to largest.

Review

30. Find a number between 0.036 and 0.0359. *(Lesson 1-2)*

31. Which is larger, 34.000791 or 34.0079? *(Lesson 1-2)*

32. Translate into mathematics: In football, a loss of 2 yards is better than a loss of 3 yards. *(Lesson 1-6)*

33. What temperature is shown by this thermometer? *(Lesson 1-2)*

34. Round 9.8978675645 to the nearest ten-thousandth. *(Lesson 1-4)*

Exploration

35. a. Find the decimals for 1/9, 2/9, 3/9, 4/9, 5/9, 6/9, 7/9, and 8/9.
    b. Based on the pattern you find, what fraction should equal $.\overline{9}$?
    c. Is the cartoon true?

Nothing can ever come between us.

36. a. Write down the decimals for $\frac{1}{2}$, $\frac{1}{3}$, $\frac{1}{4}$, $\frac{1}{5}$, and $\frac{1}{6}$.
    b. Find the decimals for $\frac{1}{7}$, $\frac{1}{8}$, $\frac{1}{9}$, $\frac{1}{10}$, $\frac{1}{11}$, and $\frac{1}{12}$.
    c. If you keep going, to what number are these decimals getting closer and closer?

37. Explore the decimals for all simple fractions between 0 and 1 whose denominator is 7. Use your results to give the first twelve decimal places for each of these fractions.

1-9

Decimals for Mixed Numbers

The number $2\frac{3}{4}$ consists of an integer and a fraction. It is called a **mixed number** (though more accurately it should be called a mixed numeral). This mixed number is the sum of the integer 2 and the fraction $\frac{3}{4}$. Only the plus sign is missing.

Mixed numbers are common in measurement. The blue line segment below is about $2\frac{3}{4}$ inches long. (Is it obvious to you that $2\frac{3}{4}$ is between 2 and 3?)

The way we have shown the fractions suggests how the decimal for a mixed number can be found. First calculate the decimal for the simple fraction. Then add that decimal to the integer.

Example Express $2\frac{3}{4}$ in decimal notation.

Solution 1 Remember or calculate: $\frac{3}{4} = 0.75$

Now add. $\qquad 2\frac{3}{4} = 2 + \frac{3}{4} = 2 + 0.75 = 2.75$

Solution 2 On a scientific calculator, you can key in 2 $\boxed{+}$ 3 $\boxed{\div}$ 4 $\boxed{=}$. On simpler calculators, the division must be done first, then the 2 must be added.

Solution 3 Fourths are quarters. Two and three-fourths is like two dollars and three quarters. Two dollars and three quarters is $2.75, which includes the correct decimal.

Questions

Covering the Reading

1. Consider the mixed number $10\frac{3}{4}$.
   a. Between what two integers is this number?
   b. Identify the integer part of this mixed number.
   c. Rewrite this number in decimal notation.
   d. Graph this number on a number line.

2. Repeat Question 1 for the number $4\frac{2}{3}$.

3. What is it about the mixed number of Question 1 that enables a person to think about it in terms of money?

In 4–7, change each mixed number to a decimal. (The fraction parts are ones you should know, so try to do these without a calculator.)

4. $2\frac{1}{2}$ 5. $7\frac{2}{5}$ 6. $1\frac{3}{10}$ 7. $17\frac{5}{6}$

In 8–11, change each mixed number to a decimal.

8. $5\frac{1}{8}$ 9. $12\frac{3}{16}$ 10. $4\frac{1}{11}$ 11. $20\frac{8}{15}$

Applying the Mathematics

12. To find the decimal for a negative mixed number, first calculate the decimal for the corresponding positive mixed number. Then put in the negative sign. Use this idea to find a decimal for the number $-1\frac{4}{5}$.

13. A stock goes up $4\frac{1}{4}$ dollars a share. What is this in dollars and cents? (Most stock prices are measured in eighths.)

14. A stock goes down $1\frac{7}{8}$. What is this in dollars and cents?

15. Order from the smallest to largest: $2\frac{3}{5}$; $3\frac{2}{5}$; $5\frac{2}{3}$.

16. Mouse A is $2\frac{3}{10}$ inches long. Mouse B is $2\frac{1}{4}$ inches long. Which mouse is longer?

17. Round $12\frac{8}{15}$ to the nearest thousandth.

18. The Preakness, a famous horse race, is $1\frac{3}{16}$ miles long. Convert this length to a length in decimals.

19. A shelf is measured to be $35\frac{11}{32}$ inches long. Is this shorter or longer than $35\frac{1}{3}$ inches?

20. Give the decimal for each number. *(Lesson 1-8)*
    a. $\frac{1}{6}$ **b.** $\frac{2}{6}$ **c.** $\frac{3}{6}$ **d.** $\frac{4}{6}$ **e.** $\frac{5}{6}$

    f. $\frac{1}{8}$ **g.** $\frac{2}{8}$ **h.** $\frac{3}{8}$ **i.** $\frac{4}{8}$ **j.** $\frac{5}{8}$

21. Consider the number 215,386.945706. Name the digit in the ten thousands place. *(Lesson 1-2)*

22. Consider the following sentences. Each human hand has 27 small bones. Together the hands have over 1/4 of the 206 bones in the whole body. *(Lesson 1-1)*
    a. Name the counts.
    b. Name the counting units.

23. In decimal notation, write the integer that is one less than one million. *(Lesson 1-1)*

24. Name one advantage of decimals over fractions. *(Lesson 1-8)*

25. **a.** Which is larger, -4.3 or -4.4?
    b. Find a number between -4.3 and -4.4. *(Lesson 1-5)*

26. Find a number between 2 and 2.1. *(Lesson 1-2)*

27. Estimate 16.432893542050 + 83.5633344441 to the nearest integer. *(Lesson 1-4)*

28. Translate into English: 0 > -6. *(Lesson 1-6)*

29. Order -9.99, 9.99, and 9 using the inequality symbol <.
    (Lesson 1-6)

30. *True or false* 5 = 5.0 *(Lesson 1-6)*

31. What digit is in the eleventh decimal place in $7.8\overline{142}$? *(Lesson 1-8)*

In 32 and 33, find all the factors of the number. *(Lesson 1-8)*

32. 36 **33.** 39

34. Examine a stock market page from a daily newspaper. Approximately how many mixed numbers are there on the page?

35. How many decimal places does your computer show when it does computation?
    a. Type ?3/4 and press RETURN. What does the computer print, 0.75 or .75?
    b. Type ?2/3 and press RETURN. How many decimal places does the computer print? Does the computer round to the nearest, or does it round down?
    c. Instruct the computer to print decimals for $\frac{1}{7}$ and $\frac{8}{7}$. For which number does the computer show more decimal places?

Equal Fractions

Jane was practicing with her calculator. She discovered that when she changed $\frac{3}{4}$, $\frac{6}{8}$, and $\frac{12}{16}$ to decimals, she got 0.75 each time. This shows that

$$\frac{3}{4} = \frac{6}{8} = \frac{12}{16}.$$

These are examples of **equal fractions.** It is easy to find other fractions equal to a given fraction. Just pick a number and multiply the numerator and denominator by that number.

■ ■ ■ ■ ■ ■ ■ ■

Example 1 Find two other fractions equal to $\frac{2}{3}$.

Solution Multiply the numerator and denominator by 2.
$$\frac{2 \times 2}{3 \times 2} = \frac{4}{6}$$

Check Division shows that $\frac{4}{6} = 0.\overline{6}$ and $\frac{2}{3} = 0.\overline{6}$. So $\frac{4}{6} = \frac{2}{3}$.

To find a second fraction equal to $\frac{2}{3}$, pick another number to multiply by. We use 10.
$$\frac{2 \times 10}{3 \times 10} = \frac{20}{30}$$

Check $\frac{20}{30} = 0.\overline{6}$ also, so $\frac{2}{3} = \frac{20}{30}$.

Consider the fraction 6/15. Suppose we divide its numerator and denominator by 3. This gives the fraction 2/5.

$$\frac{6}{15} \quad \begin{matrix} \text{Divide 6 by 3.} \\ \text{Divide 15 by 3.} \end{matrix} \quad \frac{6/3}{15/3} = \frac{2}{5}$$

Now 6/15 = 0.4 and 2/5 = 0.4. So dividing numerator and denominator by 3 yields an equal fraction. This is true in general.

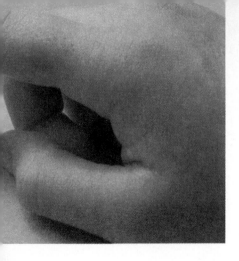

Equal Fractions Property:

If the numerator and denominator of a fraction are both multiplied (or divided) by the same nonzero number, then the resulting fraction is equal to the original one.

Of the many fractions equal to 6/15, the one with the smallest whole numbers is 2/5. We say that 6/15, written in **lowest terms,** equals 2/5. To write a fraction in lowest terms, look for a factor of both the numerator and denominator.

Example 2   Write 20/35 in lowest terms.

Solution   5 is a factor of both 20 and 35. It is the largest whole number that divides both 20 and 35. Divide both numerator and denominator by 5.

$$\frac{20}{35} = \frac{20/5}{35/5} = \frac{4}{7}$$

Check   You should verify that 4/7 and 20/35 equal the same decimal.

There are many ways to simplify a fraction. All correct ways lead to the same answer.

Example 3   Simplify $\frac{60}{24}$. (To simplify means to write in lowest terms.)

Solution 1   Vince saw that 4 is a factor of both 60 and 24. Here is his work.

$$\frac{60}{24} = \frac{60/4}{24/4} = \frac{15}{6}$$

Since 3 is a factor of both 15 and 6, $\frac{15}{6}$ is not in lowest terms. Vince needed a second step.

$$\frac{15}{6} = \frac{15/3}{6/3} = \frac{5}{2}$$

$\frac{5}{2}$ is in lowest terms. So $\frac{60}{24} = \frac{5}{2}$.

Solution 2 Heather knew that 3 is a factor of both 60 and 24. Here is her work.

$$\frac{60}{24} = \frac{60/3}{24/3} = \frac{20}{8}$$

Now she saw that 2 is a factor of 20 and 8.

$$\frac{20}{8} = \frac{20/2}{8/2} = \frac{10}{4}$$

Dividing numerator and denominator again by 2, she got the same answer Vince got.

Solution 3 Karen did more in her head than either Vince or Heather. She thought: the factors of 24 are

1 2 3 4 6 8 12 24.

Of these, 24 is not a factor of 60, but 12 is. So 12 is the **greatest common factor** of 24 and 60. Then she divided the numerator and denominator by this number. Here is Karen's work.

$$\frac{60}{24} = \frac{60/12}{24/12} = \frac{5}{2}$$

Questions

Covering the reading

1. *Multiple choice* Which of the following is not equal to $\frac{3}{4}$?

    (a) $\frac{6}{8}$ (b) $\frac{8}{12}$ (c) 0.75   (d) All of (a) to (c) are equal.

2. The letter P corresponds to the point at 7/2 on the number line below. Find two other fractions equal to 7/2.

In 3 and 4, which fraction, if any, is not equal to the others?

3. $\frac{24}{36}$ $\frac{48}{72}$ $\frac{4.8}{7.2}$ $\frac{24 \text{ million}}{36 \text{ million}}$

4. $\frac{8}{12}$ $\frac{3}{4}$ $\frac{15}{20}$ $\frac{30,000}{40,000}$

5. Find a fraction equal to 21/12 that has a bigger numerator.

6. How can you tell when a fraction is in lowest terms?

7. **a.** Write the factors of 48.
   b. Write the factors of 60.
   c. Name all common factors of 48 and 60.
   d. Name the greatest common factor of 48 and 60.
   e. Write $\frac{48}{60}$ in lowest terms.

In 8–11, **a.** name a common factor of the numerator and denominator, and **b.** rewrite in lowest terms.

8. $\frac{21}{12}$ 9. $\frac{15}{20}$

10. $\frac{180}{16}$ 11. $\frac{240}{72}$

In 12 and 13, find mixed numbers equal to the given numbers.

12. $11\frac{5}{12}$ 13. $37\frac{3}{7}$

14. What equality of fractions is pictured below?

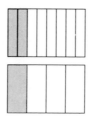

15. Use the idea of Question 14 to picture the equality $\frac{6}{9} = \frac{2}{3}$.

16. As you know, $13/1 = 13$. Find three other fractions equal to 13.

17. Find a fraction equal to 8 that has 3 in its denominator.

In 18 and 19, write the number as a fraction in lowest terms.
18. fourteen eighths   19. seventy-five hundredths

In 20–22, round *up* to the nearest hundredth. *(Lessons 1-3, 1-8, 1-9)*
20. $4\frac{2}{17}$ 21. 0.00785   22. 43/50

23. Find three different numbers between 0 and -1. *(Lesson 1-5)*

24. Which is larger, $\frac{9}{16}$ or $\frac{4}{7}$? *(Lesson 1-8)*

In 25–27, estimate to the nearest tenth. *(Lessons 1-4, 1-7)*
25. four thousand sixty-two times three thousandths

26. $\pi \times$ -567.34

27. $18 + 1.8 - 0.18$

28. Write $5\frac{13}{16}$ as a decimal. *(Lesson 1-9)*

29. Try to find a decimal for each fraction without using a calculator or looking it up. *(Lesson 1-8)*
a. 4/10   **b.** 5/8   **c.** 3/4   **d.** 1/3   **e.** 5/6

In 30 and 31, give the factors of the number. *(Lesson 1-8)*

30. 24   **31.** 51.

32. *True or false*   Sixteen and twenty are both factors of eighty. *(Lesson 1-8)*

Exploration

33. To rewrite fractions in lowest terms, you usually must find factors of the numbers in the numerator and denominator. There are easy ways to tell whether 2, 3, 5, and 9 are factors of numbers.
a. What about the digits of an integer tells you whether 2 is a factor of it?
b. What about the digits of an integer tells you whether 5 is a factor of it?
c. 3 is a factor of an integer exactly when the sum of the digits of the integer is divisible by 3. Which of the following numbers is *not* divisible by 3?   321   2856   198   4444
d. 9 is a factor of an integer exactly when the sum of the digits of the integer is divisible by 9. Which of the following numbers is *not* divisible by 9?   198   44442   267   87561
e. Find a 5-digit number that is divisible by 5 and 9, but not by 2.

Summary

Today by far the most common way of writing numbers is in the decimal system. In this chapter, decimals are used for whole numbers, for numbers between whole numbers, for negative numbers, for fractions, and for mixed numbers.

Decimals are easy to order. This makes it easy to estimate them. We estimated decimals by rounding up, rounding down, and rounding to the nearest decimal place. Decimals are also easy to graph on a number line. All calculators represent numbers as decimals. So, if you can write numbers as decimals, then you can make the calculator work for you. By changing fractions to decimals, they can be ordered and you can tell whether two fractions are equal.

Vocabulary

You should be able to give a general description
and a specific example of each
of the following ideas.

Lesson 1-1
digit
decimal system, decimal notation
whole number
ones place, tens place, hundreds place,
    thousands place, and so on
count, counting unit

Lesson 1-2
measure, unit of measure, interval
number line
tenths place, hundredths place, thousandths place,
    and so on

Lesson 1-3
estimate
rounding up, rounding down
truncate

Lesson 1-4
rounding to the nearest

Lesson 1-5
negative number, opposite
integer, positive integer, negative integer
natural number

Lesson 1-6
inequality symbols
$<$ (is less than), $>$ (is greater than)

Lesson 1-7
scientific calculator
display ( )
enter, key in, key sequence
$\pm$ or +/−
inv, 2nd, F

Lesson 1-8
fraction, simple fraction
numerator, denominator
dividend, divisor, quotient
infinite repeating decimal, repetend
evenly divisible, divisible, factor

Lesson 1-9
mixed number, mixed numeral

Lesson 1-10
equal fractions
Equal Fractions Property
lowest terms
greatest common factor

Progress Self-Test

Take this test as you would take a test in class. You will need a calculator. Then check your work with the solutions in the Selected Answers section in the back of the book.

In 1–4, write as a decimal.

1. seven hundred thousand
2. forty-five and six tenths
3. $\frac{1}{4}$
4. $15\frac{13}{16}$
5. What number is in the hundredths place of 1234.5678?
6. Write 0.003 in English.
7. Consider the four numbers .6, .66, .$\overline{6}$, and .606. Which is largest?
8. Consider the four numbers $\frac{1}{2}, \frac{2}{5}, \frac{1}{3}, \frac{3}{10}$. Which is smallest?
9. Round 98.76 down to the preceding tenth.
10. Round 98.76 to the nearest integer.
11. Translate into mathematics: An elevation 80 ft below sea level is higher than an elevation 100 ft below sea level.

In 12 and 13, use the number line pictured.

12. Which letter corresponds to the position of $\frac{1}{2}$?
13. Which letter corresponds to the position of -1.25?
14. Give a number between 16.5 and 16.6.
15. Give a number between -2.39 and -2.391.

In 16–18, which symbol, <, =, or >, goes between the numbers?

16. 0.45 _?_ 0.4500000001
17. -9.24 _?_ -9.240
18. -4 _?_ -5

19. What fraction equals 0.6?
20. Give an example of a number that is not an integer.
21. A store sells grapes on sale at 69¢ a pound. You need a quarter pound. So you divide by 4 on your calculator. The display shows 0.1725. What will you have to pay?
22. Estimate 3.012012012 + 9.0888888888888 to the nearest integer.
23. Indicate the key sequence for doing 3.456 × 2.345 on a calculator.
24. Use your calculator to estimate 6 × π to the nearest integer.
25. What is the repetend of the repeating decimal 4.5677777777…?
26. Graph the numbers 7, 7.7, and 8 on the same number line.
27. Graph these temperatures on the same vertical number line: 5°, -4°, 0°.
28. Give a situation where an estimate must be used because an exact value cannot be obtained.
29. Write a sentence containing a count and a counting unit. Underline the count once and the counting unit twice.
30. Which is largest? one tenth, one millionth, one billionth, one thousandth
31. Find all the factors of 18.
32. Find a fraction equal to 6 with 5 in its denominator.
33. Rewrite 12/21 in lowest terms.
34. *Multiple choice* When was the decimal system developed?
    (a) between 2000 B.C. and 1000 B.C.
    (b) between 1 A.D. and 1000 A.D.
    (c) between 1000 B.C. and 1 B.C.
    (d) between 1000 A.D. and today

Chapter Review

Questions on **SPUR** Objectives

SPUR stands for **S**kills, **P**roperties, **U**ses, and **R**epresentations. The Chapter Review questions are grouped according to the SPUR Objectives for this chapter.

SKILLS deal with the procedures used to get answers.

Objective A: *Translate back and forth from English into the decimal system.*
(Lessons 1-1, 1-2)

1. Write four thousand three as a decimal.

2. Write seventy-five hundredths as a decimal.

3. Write one hundred twenty million as a decimal.

4. Write three and six thousandths as a decimal.

5. Translate 500,400 into English.

6. Translate 0.001 into English.

Objective B: *Order decimals and fractions.*
(Lessons 1-2, 1-5, 1-8, 1-9)

7. Which of these numbers is largest, which smallest?
   400,000,000   400,000,001
   .40000000000001   0.4

8. Order from smallest to largest:
   0   -0.2   0.2   0.19

9. Order from smallest to largest:
   -586.36   -586.363   -586.34

10. Order $\frac{1}{7}$, $\frac{1}{11}$, and $\frac{1}{9}$ from smallest to largest.

11. Order $\frac{2}{3}$, $\frac{6}{10}$, and 0.66 from smallest to largest.

12. Order from smallest to largest: $3\frac{1}{3}$, $2\frac{2}{3}$, $4\frac{1}{6}$

13. Order from smallest to largest:
    5.3, 5.$\overline{3}$, 4.33

Objective C: *Give a number that is between two decimals. (Lessons 1-2, 1-5)*

14. Give a number between 73 and 73.1.

15. Give a number between -1 and -2.

16. Give a number between 6.99 and 7.

17. Give a number between 3.40 and 3.$\overline{40}$.

Objective D: *Round any decimal up or down or to the nearest value of a decimal place.*
(Lessons 1-3, 1-4)

18. Round 345.76 down to the preceding tenth.

19. Round 5.8346 up to the next hundredth.

20. Round 39 down to the preceding ten.

21. After six decimal places, Joan's calculator truncates. What will her calculator display for 0.59595959595959…?

22. Round 34,498 to the nearest thousand.

23. Round 6.81 to the nearest tenth.

24. Round 5.55 to the nearest integer.

Objective E: *Estimate answers to arithmetic calculations to the nearest integer. (Lesson 1-4)*

25. Estimate 58.9995320003 + 2.86574309 to the nearest integer.

26. Estimate 6 × 7.99 to the nearest integer.

Objective F: *Use a calculator to perform arithmetic operations.* *(Lesson 1-7)*

27. Find 35.68×123.4.

28. Find $555 + 5.55 + .555 + 0.50$.

29. Find $73 - \pi$ to the nearest ten-thousandth.

Objective G: *Convert simple fractions and mixed numbers to decimals.* *(Lessons 1-8, 1-9)*

30. Give the decimal for $\frac{11}{5}$.

31. Give the decimal for -16/3.

32. Change $6\frac{4}{7}$ to a decimal.

33. Change $5\frac{1}{4}$ to a decimal.

Objective H: *Know by memory the common decimals and fractions between 0 and 1.* *(Lesson 1-8)*

34. Give the decimal for $\frac{3}{4}$.

35. Give the decimal for $\frac{2}{3}$.

36. Give the decimal for 1/5.

37. Give the decimal for 1/6.

38. Give a simple fraction for .8.

39. Give a simple fraction for $.\overline{3}$.

40. Give a simple fraction for 0.25.

PROPERTIES deal with the principles behind the mathematics.

Objective I: *Use the $<$ and $>$ symbols correctly between numbers.* *(Lesson 1-6)*

41. Choose the correct symbol $<$, $=$, or $>$:
2.0 __?__ 0.2

42. Choose the correct symbol $<$, $=$, or $>$:
0.1 __?__ $0.\overline{1}$

43. Write the numbers $\frac{2}{3}$, .6, and .667 on one line with the correct symbols between them.

Objective J: *Correctly use the raised bar symbol for repeating decimals.* *(Lesson 1-8)*

44. Give the 13th decimal place in $.\overline{1428}$.

45. Write the repeating decimal 468.5686868... using the repetend symbol.

Objective K: *Use the Equal Fractions Property to rewrite fractions.* *(Lesson 1-10)*

46. Find another fraction equal to $\frac{2}{7}$.

47. Find the factors of 42.

48. Rewrite $\frac{80}{60}$ in lowest terms.

USES deal with applications of mathematics in real situations.

Objective L: *Round to estimate a given number in a real situation.* *(Lessons 1-3, 1-4)*

49. A sign gives a city's population as 29,451. Round the population to the nearest thousand.

50. To quickly estimate the cost of 5 records at $8.95 each, what rounding should you do?

51. A store sells 6 granola bars for $2.99. You want 1 bar. Dividing on your calculator gives 0.498333. What will the bar cost you?

Objective M: *Give situations where estimates are preferred over exact values. (Lesson 1-3)*

52. Give a situation where an estimate would be used for a safety reason.

53. Name a reason other than safety for needing an estimate.

Objective N: *Correctly interpret situations with two directions as positive, negative, or corresponding to zero. (Lessons 1-5, 1-6)*

54. 350 feet below sea level corresponds to what number?

55. Translate into mathematics: A loss of $75,000 is worse than a gain of $10,000.

56. An auto mechanic estimates how much it will cost to fix your car. What number could stand for: **a.** an estimate $25 too low? **b.** an estimate $40 too high? **c.** an estimate equal to the cost?

REPRESENTATIONS deal with pictures, graphs, or objects that illustrate concepts.

Objective O: *Graph a decimal on a number line. (Lessons 1-2, 1-5).*

57. Graph the numbers 0, 2, and -3 on the same number line.

58. Graph 6, 6.4, and 7 on the same number line.

59. Represent on the same vertical number line: -3°, 1°, and -5°.

Objective P: *Read a number line. (Lessons 1-2, 1-5)*

In 60 and 61, use this number line.

60. What is its unit?

61. The dot is the graph of what number?

In 62 and 63, use this number line.

62. What is its unit?

63. The dot corresponds to what number?

Objective Q: *Indicate key sequences for doing an arithmetic problem on a calculator. (Lessons 1-7, 1-8)*

64. What is the key sequence for entering -5?

65. Give the key sequence for converting $\frac{77}{8.2}$ to a decimal.

HISTORY

Objective R: *Give peoples and rough dates for key ideas in the development of arithmetic. (Lessons 1-1, 1-2, 1-8)*

66. What people invented the decimal system?

67. *Multiple choice* Our symbols for 0,1,2,3,4,5,6,7,8, and 9 did not all appear until about what date?
(a) 2000 B.C.   (b) 1000 A.D.
(c) 1400 A.D.   (d) 1900 A.D.

Large and Small Numbers

Decimal and fraction notations work well for most numbers in everyday use. But a trillion is a large number, which as a decimal is 1,000,000,000,000. With so many digits, this decimal is difficult to work with. So there are other notations that make things easier. One of these other notations is in the newspaper headline in the cartoon.

In this chapter, you will study notations that are particularly useful for work with large and small numbers.

"BY THE WAY, WHAT COMES AFTER A TRILLION?"

The photograph shows the tracks of tiny atomic particles traveling through liquid helium. The mass of an atomic particle is a very small number usually written in scientific notation.

2-1

Multiplying by 10

Consider the whole number 25,794. The 4 is in the ones place. The 9 is in the tens place (so it stands for 90). The 7 is in the hundreds place (so it stands for 700). The 5 is in the thousands place (so it stands for 5000). And the 2 is in the ten-thousands place (so it stands for 20,000). In this way, each place value is ten times the value of the place to its right. This makes it easy to multiply the number by 10. Here is the result when 25,794 is multiplied by 10. Notice that after multiplying, zero is in the ones place.

$$2\,5{,}7\,9\,4$$
$$2\,5{,}7\,9\,4 \times 1\,0 = 2\,5\,7{,}9\,4\,0$$

There is another way to think about this. Write 25,794 with a decimal point and a zero following it. (Remember that you can always insert a decimal point followed by zeros to the right of a whole number without changing its value. For example, $5 = $5.00)

$$2\,5{,}7\,9\,4\,.\,0$$
$$2\,5{,}7\,9\,4.0 \times 1\,0 = 2\,5\,7{,}9\,4\,0\,.$$

To multiply a number in decimal notation by 10, move the decimal point one place to the right.

For example, $62.58 \times 10 = 625.8$ and $.0034 \times 10 = .034$.

This simple idea is very powerful. Suppose you want to multiply a number by 100. Since $100 = 10 \times 10$, multiplying by 100 is like multiplying by 10 and then multiplying by 10 again. So move the decimal point *two* places to the right. For example, $59.072 \times 100 = 5907.2$.

The same idea can be extended to multiply by 1000, 10,000, and so on.

$$10 \times 47.3 = 473.$$
$$100 \times 47.3 = 4730.$$
$$1000 \times 47.3 = 47,300.$$
$$10,000 \times 47.3 = 473,000.$$

So, if you want to multiply by the decimal 1 followed by some zeros (10, 100, 1000, . . .), move the decimal point as many places to the right as there are zeros.

As you know, the numbers 10, 100, 1000, and so on have the short *word names* ten, hundred, thousand. Here are some other numbers that have short word names.

Decimal	Word name
1,000,000	million
1,000,000,000	billion
1,000,000,000,000	trillion
1,000,000,000,000,000	quadrillion
1,000,000,000,000,000,000	quintillion

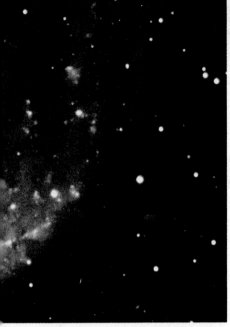

The distance from Earth to a galaxy of stars such as this spiral galaxy is measured in terms of light-years. One light-year is equal to about ten trillion kilometers.

Now look at the cartoon on page 53. The newsboy is holding up a newspaper mentioning a debt limit of 1.2 trillion dollars. The phrase 1.2 trillion means 1.2 *times* a trillion. Since a trillion has 12 zeros, move the decimal point 12 places to the right.

$$1.2 \text{ trillion} = 1.2 \times 1,000,000,000,000$$
$$= 1,200,000,000,000$$

Notice how much shorter and clearer 1.2 trillion is than 1,200,000,000,000. For these reasons, it is common to use word names for large numbers in sentences and charts.

Example A newspaper report in 1988 listed 6.851 million people as unemployed in August. Write this number in decimal notation (without words).

Solution 6.851 million = 6.851 × 1,000,000
= 6,851,000

Check This is easy to check. You would expect 6.851 million to be between 6 million and 7 million.

1. In the number 81,345, the place value of the digit 1 is ___?___ times the place value of the digit 3.

In 2–5, multiply each number by 10.

2. 634   **3.** 2.4   **4.** 0.08   **5.** 47.21

6. Give a general rule for multiplying a decimal by 10.

7. Give a general rule for multiplying a decimal by 100.

In 8–11, multiply each number by 100.

8. 113   **9.** .05   **10.** 7755.2   **11.** 6.301

12. Give a general rule for multiplying a decimal by 1000.

13. Give a general rule for multiplying a decimal by 10,000.

In 14–17, calculate.

14. $1.43 \times 10,000$ **15.** 32×1000

16. 1000×46.314 **17.** $0.095 \times 10,000$

In 18–23, give the word name for the decimal 1 followed by:

18. 3 zeros   **19.** 6 zeros

20. 9 zeros   **21.** 12 zeros

22. 15 zeros   **23.** 18 zeros

The quotes in 24–26 are from the *Chicago Sun–Times* of August 28, 1988. Write the underlined numbers in decimal notation.

24. "Estimates of the winter wheat crop have been increased to 2.02 billion bushels."

25. "There are 1.35 million dollars in scholarships and grants that go unused each year because parents and students don't know that they exist."

26. "Last year some 88 million people shopped by mail or phone ... sales for the year range from $22.2 billion to $33.6 billion."

27. How can rounding be used to help you check your answer to Question 16?

28. 98.765 times what number equals 98,765?

In 29–32, use this graph to estimate the world population for the given year to the nearest tenth of a billion. Write this number in decimal notation.

29. 1950   **30.** 1960   **31.** 1970   **32.** 1980

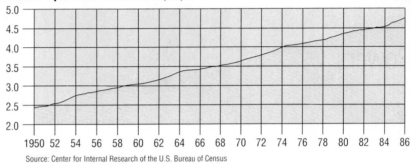

World Population in billions of people

Source: Center for Internal Research of the U.S. Bureau of Census

In 33–35, write the number as it might appear in a magazine or newspaper.

33. 230,000,000 people   **34.** $15,600,000 in the budget

35. 26,500,000,000,000 miles to the nearest star

36. What is the answer to the question in the cartoon on page 53?

Review

37. The letters are equally spaced on the number line above. *(Lessons 1-2, 1-8)*
   a. What number corresponds to F?
   b. What number corresponds to B?
   c. What letter corresponds to $\frac{3}{5}$?

38. Change to decimals: *(Lesson 1-8)*
   a. $\frac{1}{8}$ **b.** $\frac{1}{10}$ **c.** $\frac{1}{50}$ **d.** $\frac{1}{100}$

39. Round 2.6494 *down* to thousandths. *(Lesson 1-3)*

40. Translate into mathematics: Negative ten is less than nine. *(Lessons 1-5, 1-6)*

Exploration

41. Locate, in a newspaper or magazine, at least two numbers written with a decimal followed by a word name (like those in the example in this lesson). Copy the complete sentences that contain the numbers.

42. In England, the word *billion* does not always mean the number 1 followed by 9 zeros. What number does the word *billion* often represent in England?

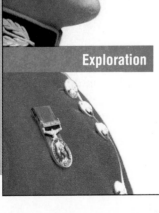

2-2

Powers

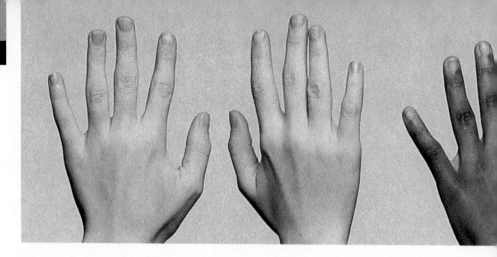

In Lesson 2-1, you multiplied by 100. This was explained as multiplying by 10, followed by multiplying by 10. This repeated multiplication is so common that there is a shorthand for it. We write

$$10^2$$

(say "10 to the 2nd **power**") to mean 10×10, or 100. In 10^2, the number 10 is called the **base.** The number 2 is called the **exponent.** Similarly, 10^3 (say "10 to the 3rd power") means $10 \times 10 \times 10$, or 1000, and 10^4 (say "10 to the 4th power") means $10 \times 10 \times 10 \times 10$, or 10,000. In this book, only integers will be used as exponents.

There can be powers of any number.

    3 to the 2nd power $= 3^2 = 3 \times 3 = 9$
    8 to the 3rd power $= 8^3 = 8 \times 8 \times 8 = 512$
    1.3 to the 5th power $= 1.3^5 = 1.3 \times 1.3 \times 1.3 \times 1.3 \times 1.3$
                       $= 3.71293$
    1 to the 7th power $= 1^7 = 1 \times 1 \times 1 \times 1 \times 1 \times 1 \times 1 = 1$

It is useful to know some powers of small numbers without having to calculate them every time. Here are the smallest positive integer powers of 2: $2^2 = 4$, $2^3 = 8$, $2^4 = 16$, $2^5 = 32$, $2^6 = 64$, $2^7 = 128$, $2^8 = 256$, $2^9 = 512$, and $2^{10} = 1024$. If you do not know the powers of 2, you have to calculate them. But the powers of 10 are very special in the decimal system. You can calculate them in your head.

Above we found that $10^2 = 100$, $10^3 = 1000$, and $10^4 = 10,000$. The next power, 10^5, is found by multiplying 10,000 by 10. It is 100,000. So, when written as decimals, 10^2 is a 1 followed by 2 zeros, 10^3 is a 1 followed by 3 zeros, and so on. Then 10^{12} is a 1 followed by 12 zeros. So 10^{12} is another way of writing one trillion.

You have now studied three different ways of representing the place values in the decimal system.

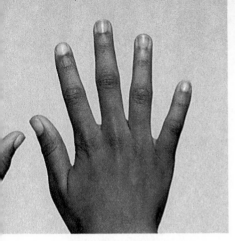

Historically we use 10 as a base because we have ten fingers.

Power of 10	Word name	Written as decimal
10^1	ten	10
10^2	hundred	100
10^3	thousand	1000
10^6	million	1,000,000
10^9	billion	1,000,000,000
10^{12}	trillion	1,000,000,000,000
10^{15}	quadrillion	1,000,000,000,000,000
10^{18}	quintillion	1,000,000,000,000,000,000

You already know a quick way to multiply by 10, 100, 1000, and so on. It is just as quick to multiply by these numbers when they are written as powers.

$$53 \times 10^5 = 53 \times 100,000 = 5,300,000$$
$$2.38 \times 10^4 = 2.38 \times 10,000 = 23,800.$$

The decimal point moves to the right one place for each power of 10.

To multiply by a positive integer power of 10:

Move the decimal point to the right the same number of places as the value of the exponent.

Powers of small numbers can be quite large. $9^8 = 43,046,721$. Only powers of 10 and a few powers of small numbers are easy to calculate by hand. Usually it is quicker and more accurate to use a calculator. A scientific calculator has a special key labeled $\boxed{x^y}$ or $\boxed{y^x}$, the powering key. (If this label is in small print above or below a key, you will need to press $\boxed{\text{inv}}$ or $\boxed{\text{2nd}}$ or $\boxed{\text{F}}$ before pressing the powering key.) For example, to evaluate 5^7:

Key sequence: 5 $\boxed{y^x}$ 7 $\boxed{=}$

Display: $\boxed{5.}$ $\boxed{5.}$ $\boxed{7.}$ $\boxed{78125.}$

$$5^7 = 78,125.$$

Note: Whether the key is labeled $\boxed{x^y}$ or $\boxed{y^x}$, the base is entered before the exponent.

Questions

Covering the Reading

1. Consider 4^6. **a.** Name the base. **b.** Name the exponent. **c.** This number is __?__ to the __?__th __?__.

2. Calculate 3^2, 3^3, 3^4, 3^5, and 3^6.

3. Give the values of 2^2, 2^3, 2^4, 2^5, and 2^6.

4. Calculate 7^6.   **5.** Calculate 2^{20} and 20^2.   **6.** Calculate 1^{984}.

7. Calculate 1.08^3. (This kind of calculation is found in money matters.)

8. In decimal notation, 10^7 is a 1 followed by __?__ zeros.

9. Write 10^6 in two ways: **a.** as a decimal, and **b.** as a word name.

10. Write one thousand in two ways:
a. as a decimal, and **b.** as a power of 10.

11. Write as a power of 10. **a.** million; **b.** billion; **c.** trillion.

12. According to the table in this lesson, 10 to the first power equals what number?

13. Write 5×10^2 as a decimal.

14. Write 3.7×10^4 as a decimal.

15. What is the general rule for multiplying by a positive integer power of 10?

16. If you multiply by 10 to the first power, you should move the decimal point how many places to the right?

17. a. Give the next number in this pattern of powers: 256, 64, 16, __?__.
b. What powers of what number are given in part **a**?

Applying the Mathematics

18. What is the number that is 1 less than 10^3?

19. Which is larger, 2^3 or 3^2?

20. The table in this lesson skips from 10^3 to 10^6. Fill in the two rows that are missing.

21. Ten million is the __?__ power of 10.

22. *Multiple choice* $3^{10} - 2^{10}$ is between
(a) 1 and 100. (b) 100 and 10,000. (c) 10,000 and 1,000,000.

23. a. Enter the key sequence 3 $\boxed{\times}$ 2 $\boxed{y^x}$ 5 $\boxed{=}$ on your calculator. What number results?
b. Some calculators do the multiplication first, then take the power. Other calculators take the power first, then multiply. What did your calculator do first?

24. *True or false* $2^{10} > 10^3$.

25. In the early 1980s, a puzzle known as Rubik's Cube was popular. The object in this puzzle is to rearrange a cube to its original position. There are 43,252,003,274,489,856,000 possible positions. Write this number in English. (This shows how much easier decimal notation is than English words.)

Review

26. A census report of August 30, 1988 said the world had grown by 1.8 billion people since 1960. Write 1.8 billion as a decimal. *(Lesson 2-1)*

27. You buy 3 records at $6.95 each. What multiplication should you do to estimate the cost to the nearest dollar? *(Lesson 1-4)*

28. Give the positive or negative decimal suggested by each situation.
a. Walter Payton ran for thirteen yards on the first play of the game.

b. The deepest lake in the world, Lake Baykal in Siberia, has a point that is fourteen hundred eighty-five meters below sea level.
c. Absolute zero is four hundred fifty-nine and sixty-seven hundredths degrees Fahrenheit below zero. *(Lesson 1-5)*.

29. What number results from this key sequence? *(Lesson 1-7)*
$$8 \; \div \; 9 \; \div \; 4 \; \times \; 200 \; =$$

30. What digit is in the thousandths place when $\frac{15}{7}$ is rewritten as a decimal? *(Lessons 1-2, 1-8)*

31. Multiply mentally: **a.** $100 \times 10{,}000$; **b.** $180 \times 10{,}000$; **c.** 20×400. *(Lesson 2-1)*

Exploration

32. A *googol* is one of the largest numbers that has a name. Look in a dictionary or other reference book to find out something about this number.

33. On computers, to calculate 3^5, you need to type a symbol, usually, either ^ or ** between the 3 and the 5. Test your computer.
a. What do you have to type in order to get the computer to calculate 3^5? (Remember: You need to type ? or a similar command so that the computer will know you want to see the calculation.)
b. Use the computer to calculate 6^7. Compare the answer to the one given on your calculator.

2-3

Scientific Notation for Large Numbers

Light travels at a speed of about 186,281.7 miles per second. Since there are 60 seconds in a minute, light travels 60 × 186,281.7 miles per minute. This works out to 11,176,902 miles per minute. (You should check this on your calculator.) To find out how far light travels in an hour, you must multiply by 60 again.

$$60 \times 11,176,902 = 670,614,120 \text{ miles}$$

There are now three possible things your calculator will do.
1. It may display all 9 digits.

$$\boxed{670614120.}$$

2. It may display an error message. The number is too big. The E tells you there is an error and the calculator will refuse to do anything until you clear the number.

$$\boxed{E\ 6.7061412} \qquad \boxed{6.7061412\ E} \qquad \boxed{ERROR}$$

3. It may display the number in **scientific notation.**

$$\boxed{6.7061412\ 08} \qquad \boxed{6.7061\quad 8} \qquad \boxed{6.7061\ \times 10\quad 08}$$

Scientific notation is the way that scientific calculators display very large and very small numbers. The display usually looks like one of those shown here. Each of these stands for the number 6.7061412×10^8 or a rounded value of that number. The user is expected to know that the 8 (or 08) stands for 10^8. So to convert the number into decimal notation, move the decimal point 8 places to the right. (The display at the right above contains × 10 and is clearest.)

If you multiply this number by 24, scientific calculators will give you the scientific notation for 16,094,738,880.

$$\boxed{1.60947\quad 10}$$

This is the number of miles light travels in a day. The calculator will round the decimal to a fixed number of places. So 16,094,738,880 is approximately 1.60947×10^{10}.

In scientific notation, an integer power of 10 is multiplied by a number greater than or equal to 1 and less than 10.

Here are some numbers written as decimals and in scientific notation.

Decimal notation	Scientific notation
340.67	3.4067×10^2
2,380,000,000	2.38×10^9
60 trillion	6×10^{13}

Here is how to convert decimals into scientific notation.

Example 1   The distance from Earth to the Sun is about 150,000,000 km. Write this number in scientific notation.

Solution   First, move the decimal point to get a number between 1 and 10. In this case, the number is 1.5 and this tells you the answer will look like this:
$$1.5 \times 10^{exponent}$$
The exponent of 10 is the number of places you must move the decimal in 1.5 to the *right* in order to get 150,000,000. You must move it 8 places, so the answer is
$$1.5 \times 10^8.$$

Example 2   The population of the world passed 5.1 billion in 1989. This number is 5,100,000,000 and has too many digits for most calculators. Write it in scientific notation so that it can be entered into a calculator and used.

Solution   Since 1 billion $= 10^9$, 5.1 billion $= 5.1 \times 10^9$.
So the number is 5.1×10^9 in scientific notation.

■ ■ ■ ■ ■ ■ ■ ■

Example 3 Enter 5.1 billion on your calculator.

Solution First write 5.1 billion in scientific notation. This is done in Example 2. From the answer to Example 2, key in

$$5.1 \boxed{EE} 9 \text{ or } 5.1 \boxed{exp} 9.$$

■ ■ ■ ■ ■ ■ ■ ■

Example 4 Write 45678 in scientific notation.

Solution Ask yourself: 45,678 equals 4.5678 times what power of 10? The answer to the question is 4. So
$$45678 = 4.5678 \times 10^4.$$

Like calculators, computers use scientific notation for large numbers. Some computer printers cannot write exponents as numbers above the line. So the number 5.1 billion may be written as 5.1 E 9. In this case the E means "exponent of 10" and does not mean that an error has been made.

Questions

Covering the Reading

1. 2.6×10^{13} miles is the approximate distance to the nearest star (other than the Sun), Alpha Centauri. Write this number as a decimal.

2. 1.6×10^5 kg is the approximate weight of the largest blue whale ever measured. Write this number as a decimal.

3. In scientific notation, a number greater than or equal to __?__ and less than __?__ is multiplied by an integer __?__ of 10.

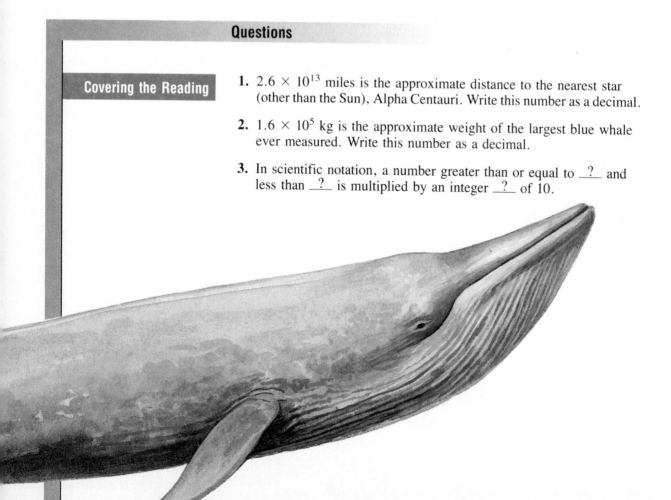

In 4–11, rewrite the number in scientific notation.

4. 800

5. 804

6. 3,500,000 square miles, the approximate land area of the U.S.

7. 5,880,000,000,000,000,000,000 tons, the approximate mass of Earth.

8. 57.54 million people, the number of passengers handled by Chicago's O'Hare Airport in 1987.

9. 1.2 trillion dollars, a ceiling (1985) on the national debt. (Recall the cartoon on page 53.)

10. 63.21

11. 765.4

12. What key sequence can you use to display 6.75×10^{11} on your calculator?

In 13–15, what does your calculator display for each number?

13. 49×10^{14}

14. 60 trillion

15. 3,800,000,000,000

Applying the Mathematics

16. The number of miles light travels in a day is given in this lesson. How many miles does light travel in a 365-day year?

17. How many seconds are there in a 365-day year?

18. a. Using scientific notation, what is the largest number you can display on your calculator? **b.** What is the smallest number you can display? (Hint: The smallest number is negative.)

19. Which is larger, 1×10^{10} or 9×10^{9}?

Review

20. Calculate the first, second, and third powers of 8. *(Lesson 2-2)*

In 21 and 22, calculate mentally. *(Lesson 2-1)*

21. $0.0006 \times 10{,}000$

22. 523×100

23. Arrange from smallest to largest: $14\frac{3}{5}$, 14.6, $14.\overline{61}$, $14.\overline{6}$. *(Lessons 1-8, 1-9)*

24. Name a fraction whose decimal is 0.9. *(Lesson 1-8)*

25. On this number line, what letter corresponds to each number? *(Lessons 1-2, 1-8)*

a. $\frac{3}{5}$ **b.** $-\frac{3}{5}$ **c.** .8   **d.** -.8

26. Batting "averages" in baseball are calculated by dividing the number of hits by the number of at-bats and usually rounding to the nearest thousandth. In 1970, Alex Johnson and Carl Yastrzemski had the top two batting averages in the American League. *(Lesson 1-4)*
a. Johnson had 202 hits in 614 at-bats. What was his average?
b. Yastrzemski had 186 hits in 566 at-bats. What was his average?
c. Who was the batting champion?

27. Write 10^9 **a.** as a decimal, and **b.** using a word name. *(Lesson 2-2)*

Exploration

28. The decimal for 1/17 repeats after 16 digits. Calculators do not display this many digits. However, it is still possible to find all the digits in the repetend.
a. Find the first six places of the decimals for 2/17, 3/17, and so on up to 16/17.
b. Each of these decimals contains 6 consecutive digits of the 16-digit repetend. Use this information to work out the entire repetend.
c. Did you need to get the decimals to all 16 fractions to work this out?

29. Kathleen entered 531×10^{20} on her calculator using the key sequence

$$531 \qquad \boxed{\text{EE}} \qquad 20.$$

$$\boxed{531} \quad \boxed{531 \quad 00} \quad \boxed{531 \quad 20}$$

Then she pressed $\boxed{=}$.
a. What is now displayed? b. What has happened?

30. a. Type ?2*3 on your computer and press RETURN. What does the computer print? What is the computer doing?
b. Increase the number of zeros in the 2 or 3 of part **a** by one, so that you have either ?20*3 or ?2*30. What does the computer print this time?
c. Continue increasing the number of zeros until the computer is forced to print an answer in its form of scientific notation. How does your computer write numbers in scientific notation?
d. What is the largest number your computer will itself print that is not in scientific notation?

2-4

Multiplying by $\frac{1}{10}$ or .1

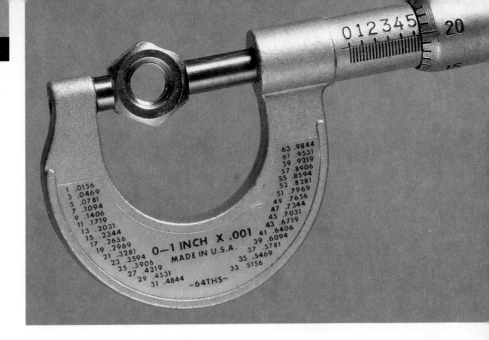

The numbers 10, 100, 1000, and so on, get larger and larger. By contrast, the numbers 1/10, 1/100, and 1/1000 get smaller and smaller. This can be seen by looking at the decimals for them.

$$\frac{1}{10} = .1 = \text{one tenth}$$

$$\frac{1}{100} = .01 = \text{one hundredth}$$

$$\frac{1}{1000} = .001 = \text{one thousandth}$$

$$\frac{1}{10,000} = .0001 = \text{one ten-thousandth}$$
and so on.

To multiply a decimal by 10, remember that you can move the decimal point one place to the *right*. Multiplication by 1/10 undoes multiplication by 10. So, to multiply by 1/10, you can move the decimal point one place to the *left*.

$$\frac{1}{10} \times 15.283 = 1.5283$$

You can estimate to check. A tenth of $15 is $1.50.

Multiplying by 1/100 is equivalent to multiplying by 1/10 and then multiplying by 1/10 again. So, to multiply by 1/100, move the decimal point *two* places to the *left*.

$$\frac{1}{100} \times 15.283 = 0.15283$$

The pattern continues. Multiplication by 1/1000 is equivalent to multiplying by 1/10 three times. So move the decimal point three places to the left.

$$\frac{1}{1000} \times 15.283 = 0.015283$$

On a calculator, you might want to use decimals instead of fractions. Of course the same pattern holds.

$$.1 \times 12345 = 1234.5$$
$$.01 \times 12345 = 123.45$$
$$.001 \times 12345 = 12.345$$
$$.0001 \times 12345 = 1.2345$$
and so on.

You may wish to check these multiplications on your calculator.

Questions

Covering the Reading

In 1–4, write as a decimal.

1. one tenth

2. 1/100

3. one thousandth

4. 1/10,000

In 5–8, give a general rule for multiplying a decimal by the given number.

5. .1

6. 1/10

7. .01

8. 1/10,000

In 9–18, write the answer as a decimal.

9. $\frac{1}{10} \times 46$

10. $46 \times \frac{1}{10}$

11. $.1 \times 46$

12. $46 \times .1$

13. $\frac{1}{100} \times 6$

14. $\frac{1}{100} \times 5.93$

15. 0.01×770

16. $.001 \times .03$

17. $\frac{1}{10,000} \times 52$

18. $250,000 \times .0001$

19. Multiplying by 1/100 is like multiplying by 1/10 and then multiplying by __?__.

20. To multiply by 1/1000 using a calculator, what decimal should you use?

Applying the Mathematics

21. The number 15.283 is multiplied by 1/10, 1/100, and 1/1000 in this lesson. Continue that pattern for three more multiplications.

22. The number 12345 is multiplied by .1, .01, .001, and .0001 in this lesson. Give the next multiplication in this pattern.

23. Give an example showing that multiplication by 1/10 undoes multiplication by 10.

24. By what number can you multiply 46.381 to get 0.46381?

25. Betty weighs 87.5 pounds. She weighed about a tenth of that at birth. To the nearest pound, what did she weigh at birth?

26. Multiply $\frac{1}{10^3}$ by 43.87.

27. Write the three underlined numbers as decimals. *(Lessons 1-1, 1-9)* The number of students enrolled in grades 9–12 grew from nine million six hundred ninety thousand in 1960 to fourteen million six hundred seventy thousand in 1980. An estimate for 1990 is twelve and a half million.

28. Write the underlined numbers of Question 27 in scientific notation. *(Lesson 2–3)*

29. Consider the number $59\frac{5}{11}$. *(Lessons 1-4, 1-9)*
   a. Between what two integers is this number?
   b. Rewrite this number as a decimal.
   c. Round this decimal to the nearest millionth.

30. a. Order the numbers $^-1.4$, $^-14$, and 0.14 from smallest to largest. *(Lesson 1-5)*.
   b. Put them in a sentence with two inequality symbols in it. *(Lesson 1-6)*
   c. Graph them on the same number line. *(Lesson 1-2)*

31. As of 1988, the best-selling record album of all time worldwide had sold over 39 million copies. Write this number in scientific notation. *(Lesson 2-3)*

32. Which is larger, 8×3 or 8^3? *(Lesson 2-2)*

33. Change each fraction to a decimal: **a.** 1/5; **b.** 1/2; **c.** 3/5; **d.** 5/6 *(Lesson 1-8)*

34. Write one quintillion **a.** as a decimal, and **b.** as a power of ten. *(Lesson 2-2)*

35. In the previous lessons, the largest power of 10 named has been quintillion. But there are larger powers of 10 with names. Look up the given word in a dictionary. (You may need a large dictionary.) Write the number as a decimal and as a power of 10.
   a. sextillion **b.** octillion **c.** nonillion **d.** decillion

36. Use your answer to Question 35. Write six octillionths as a decimal.

2-5

Percent

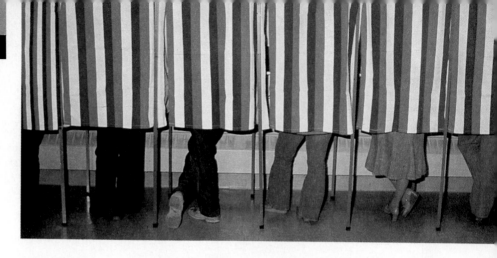

The symbol % is read **percent.** The percent symbol is very common. Here are four examples of its use.

All items in the sale are 20% off.

Only 73% of the registered voters voted in the election.

That savings account gives a $5\frac{1}{4}\%$ interest rate.

A baby weighs about 200% more at the age of one year than it does at birth.

The percent sign % means hundredths. So to change a percent to a decimal, just multiply the number in front of the percent sign by $\frac{1}{100}$. Since $\frac{1}{100} = .01$, you can multiply instead by .01 if you wish. The examples use the above percents.

Example 1 Rewrite 20% as a decimal.

Solution $20\% = 20 \times \frac{1}{100} = .20 = .2$
Recall that $.2 = \frac{1}{5}$. So $20\% = \frac{1}{5}$ too.
20% off is the same as $\frac{1}{5}$ off.

Example 2 Rewrite 73% as a decimal.

Solution $73\% = 73 \times .01 = .73$
Here we multiplied by .01.
Multiplying by $\frac{1}{100}$ would give the same answer.
Use whichever is easier for you.

Example 3 Rewrite $5\frac{1}{4}\%$ as a decimal.

Solution   First change the fraction to a decimal.
$5\frac{1}{4}\% = 5.25\%$
Now multiply by .01 instead of using the % sign.
$= 5.25 \times .01 = 0.0525$
The number 0.0525 is the number you can multiply by to determine the amount of interest in this kind of savings account.

Example 4 Rewrite 200% as a decimal.

Solution $200\% = 200 \times \frac{1}{100} = 2$
Percents of increase (or decrease) use tricky language. A baby that weighs 200% more than it did at birth has increased 2 times its weight. So its final weight is 3 times what it weighed at birth—the original weight *plus* the increase.

In Example 1, 20% was seen to equal the commonly found simple fraction $\frac{1}{5}$. Other percents equal common fractions. Some of these are graphed on the number line below. You should learn these.

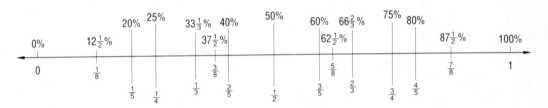

In Example 4, 200% was found to equal the integer 2. $100\% = 1$. Here is another number line with some other percents indicated on it.

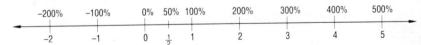

The idea of percent is old. The word *percent* comes from the Latin words *per centum,* meaning "through 100." (Sometimes it is useful to think of percent as "out of 100.") The symbol for percent is much newer. In 1650 the symbol $\frac{o}{o}$ was used. People have used the symbol % only in the last 100 years. Many writers still write "per cent" as two words. (Either one word or two words is correct.)

1. The symbol % is read __?__.

2. The symbol % means __?__.

3. To change a % to a decimal, __?__ the number in front of the % symbol by __?__.

4. Give a sentence using the % symbol that might be in a store ad.

In 5–16, change to a decimal.

5. 80%	**6.** 50%	**7.** 5%
8. 2%	**9.** 1.5%	**10.** 5.75%
11. 300%	**12.** 150%	**13.** 105%
14. 10.6%	**15.** $8\frac{1}{2}\%$	**16.** $8\frac{1}{3}\%$

In 17–24, change to a decimal and to a simple fraction.

17. 25%	**18.** 75%
19. 20%	**20.** 10%
21. $33\frac{1}{3}\%$	**22.** $66\frac{2}{3}\%$
23. $87\frac{1}{2}\%$	**24.** 40%

25. According to the number line in the lesson, which is larger, 2/3 or 5/8?

26. What is a typical interest rate on a savings account?

In 27–30, change to a decimal and to a percent.

27. 1/2	**28.** 3/5
29. 7/8	**30.** 3/10

31. About how old is the symbol %?

In 32 and 33, rewrite each underlined number as either a fraction or a decimal.

32. The teachers wanted a 7% raise and the school board offered 4%.

33. In 1983, the president of Brazil's central bank said, "We cannot live with 150% inflation."

34. *Multiple choice* 0.3 =
(a) 300%   (b) 30%   (c) 3%   (d) 0.3%

35. *Multiple choice* $0.\overline{3}$ is closest to
(a) 333%   (b) 33%   (c) 3%   (d) .3%

36. Between what two integers is 250%? (Hint: Change 250% to a decimal.)

37. Between what two integers is 5.625%

38. Change 0.1% to a decimal and to a fraction.

39. Convert 1/25 to a percent by first changing it to a decimal.

40. According to the graph below:
   a. Which automaker had the biggest percent increase in sales?
   b. Which automaker had the biggest percent decrease in sales?

New Car Sales in percent change, 1986-1987

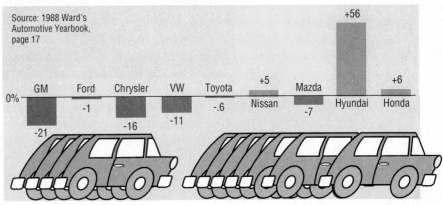

Source: 1988 Ward's Automotive Yearbook, page 17

   c. Which automaker had an increase, but the smallest percent increase in sales?
   d. Which automakers were the closest to each other in percent change of sales?
   e. What percent would indicate no change in sales?

Review

41. Multiply 2.3 by:
   a. 1000; **b.** 10; **c.** 10^4; **d.** 1/100; **e.** 0.0001. *(Lessons 2-1, 2-2, 2-4)*

42. Write 72,400,000 in scientific notation. *(Lesson 2-3)*

43. Which number is smallest: 9×10^4, 8.2×10^5, or 3.01×10^9? *(Lesson 2-3)*

Exploration

44. Money rates are often given as percents. Find the following rates by looking in a daily newspaper or weekly magazine.
   a. the prime interest rate charged by banks to good credit risks
   b. a local mortgage rate on a new home purchase
   c. the interest rate on an account at a local savings institution

2-6

Percent of a Quantity

You have learned to convert percents and fractions to decimals. You have learned to put some decimals in scientific notation. The purpose of all this rewriting is to give you *flexibility*. Sometimes it's easier to use fractions. Sometimes decimals are easier. Sometimes percent or scientific notation is needed.

But why does all of this work? Why can you use .01 in place of $\frac{1}{100}$, or 3×10^6 instead of 3 million, or 0.4 instead of $\frac{2}{5}$ or 40%? The reason is due to a general idea called the **Substitution Principle.**

Substitution Principle

If two numbers are equal, then one can be substituted for the other in any computation without changing the results of the computation.

The Substitution Principle is used in many places. Here it is used to find percents of. The phrase "percent of" is a signal to multiply.

■ ■ ■ ■ ■ ■ ■ ■

Example 1 Suppose 30% of (thirty percent of) the 2000 students in a high school are freshmen. How many students is this?

Solution   30% of 2000 students

Change "of" to "times." $= 30\% \times 2000$ students
Now use the Substitution Principle,
rewriting 30% as .3 $= .3 \times 2000$ students
                                                    $= 600$ students

74

Example 2 Suppose 100% of the 2000 students live within the school district. How many students is this?

Solution   100% of 2000 students

Change "of" to "times."   = 100% × 2000 students

Now use the Substitution Principle,
rewriting 100% as 1.   = 1 × 2000 students

                                              = 2000 students

So *all* of the students live in the school district.

From Example 2, you can see that "100% of" means "all of." Since 0% = 0, 0% of the students is 0 × 2000 students. So "0% of" means "none of." You know that 50% is equal to $\frac{1}{2}$. So "50% of" means "half of."

Percents are commonly used, and you must be able to work with them.

Example 3 To save money for college, parents put $1500 in a savings certificate that earns 8.25% interest yearly. How much will this certificate earn the first year?

Solution 8.25% of $1500 is the amount of interest. Calculate as follows.

                                              8.25% of $1500

                                          = 8.25% × $1500

Change 8.25% to a decimal.   = 0.0825 × $1500

                                          = $123.75, the amount earned.

Notice that the steps are the same in Examples 1, 2, and 3. Only the numbers are more complicated in Example 3. With a calculator, you do not have to worry about complicated numbers.

Example 4 A sofa sells for $569.95. It is put on sale at 20% off. How much will you save if you buy the sofa during the sale? What will the sale price be?

Solution   You save 20% of $569.95.

$$20\% \times \$569.95$$
$$= .2 \times \$569.95$$
$$= \$113.99$$

Subtraction tells you what the sale price will be.

$569.95	original price
− 113.99	amount saved
$455.96	sale price

Without a calculator, you might choose to estimate the answer to Example 4. Estimate $569.95 as $570. Because $570 is so close to the actual price, the estimate should be very accurate.

$$20\% \text{ of } \$570$$
$$= 20\% \times \$570$$
$$= .2 \times \$570$$
$$= \$114, \text{ only one penny off the actual amount saved!}$$

This estimate also checks the calculation in Example 4.

Questions

Covering the Reading

1. Why is it useful to have many ways of writing numbers?

2. State the Substitution Principle.

3. *True or false?*   (Hint: Recall that $20\% = \frac{1}{5}$ and $30\% = \frac{3}{10}$.)
   a. You can substitute $\frac{1}{5}$ for 20% in *any* computation and the answer will not be affected.
   b. $20\% + 30\% = \frac{1}{5} + \frac{3}{10}$
   c. $20\% \times \$6000 = \frac{1}{5} \times \$6000$

4. a. In calculating 30% of 2000, when is the Substitution Principle used?
   b. Calculate 30% of 2000.

5. Match each percent at left with the correct phrase at right.
100% of	none of
50% of	all of
0% of	half of

In 6–9, calculate.

6. 50% of 6000

7. 100% of 12

8. 0% of 50

9. 150% of 30

10. A sofa sells for $899.

    a. To estimate how much the sofa would cost at 30% off, what value can be used in place of $899?

    b. Estimate the price at a "30% off" sale.

11. Estimate how much you can save if a $10.95 record is put on sale at 25% off.

In 12 and 13, what does each remark mean?

12. "We are with you 100%!"   **13.** "Let's split it 50-50."

In 14 and 15, take the U.S. population to be about 250,000,000.

14. In your head, figure out what 10% of the U.S. population is. Use this to figure out **a.** 20%, **b.** 30%, **c.** 40%, and **d.** 50% of the population.

15. The U.S. population is now increasing at the rate of about 1.6% a year. How many people is this?

16. In Bakersfield, California, it rains on about 10% of the days in a year. About how many days is this?

17. In store A you see a $600 stereo at 25% off. In store B the same stereo normally costs $575 and is on sale at 20% off. Which store has the lower sale price?

18. Team E wins 48% of its games. Does team E win or lose more often?

19. Should you prefer to buy something at half price or at 40% off?

20. Which is larger, 250% of 10, or 300% of 8?

21. An interest penalty is charged on credit card purchases if you do not pay on time. Suppose you have $1000 in overdue bills. If the penalty is 1.5% per month, how much interest will you have to pay?

22. The population of Los Angeles, California, was about 100,000 in 1900 and increased 1800% from 1900 to 1950. How many people is that increase?

Review

23. The highest mountain in the world is Mt. Everest in the Himalayas. Its peak is about 29,028 feet above sea level and is on the Tibet-Nepal border. *(Lessons 1-4, 1-5)*
a. Should you call its height 29,028 feet, or -29,028 feet?
b. Round the height to the nearest 100 feet.
c. Round the height to the nearest 1000 feet.
d. Round the height to the nearest 10,000 feet.

24. Write in decimal notation. *(Lessons 1-1, 1-9, 2-2)*
a. three billion four hundred thousand
b. 5^4
c. 8.3 million
d. 2.56×10^8
e. $4\frac{4}{5}$

25. Give the value of $\pi/4$ truncated to ten-thousandths. *(Lessons 1-2, 1-3)*

26. Multiply 56 by: **a.** 1 **b.** .1 **c.** .01 **d.** .001. *(Lesson 2-4)*

27. Change to a percent: **a.** 1/4 **b.** 1/3 **c.** 5/4 *(Lesson 2-5)*

28. Write as a power of 10: **a.** quadrillion **b.** ten thousand. *(Lesson 2-2)*

29. Write $\frac{48}{100}$ in lowest terms. *(Lesson 1-10)*

Exploration

30. a. Find a use of percent in a newspaper or magazine.
b. Make up a question about the information you have found.
c. Answer the question you have made up.

2-7

Fractions, Decimals, and Percents

Every fraction can be converted to a decimal. So can every percent. It is also easy to convert the other way, from decimals into fractions, or decimals into percent.

If a **terminating** (ending) **decimal** has only a few decimal places, just read the decimal in English and write the fraction.

Example 1   Convert 4.53 to a fraction.

Solution   Read "four and fifty-three hundredths." That tells you $4.53 = 4\frac{53}{100}$.

Suppose the decimal cannot be easily read. First write it as a fraction over 1. Then multiply numerator and denominator by a power of 10 large enough to get rid of the decimal point in the numerator. This is an application of the Equal Fractions Property.

Example 2   Write 0.036 as a fraction in lowest terms.

Solution   Write 0.036 as $\frac{0.036}{1}$.

Multiply numerator and denominator by 1000 to get $\frac{36}{1000}$. To write $\frac{36}{1000}$ in lowest terms, notice that 4 is a factor of both the numerator and denominator. Divide each by 4.

$$0.036 = \frac{36}{1000} = \frac{9}{250}$$

Check   Convert $\frac{9}{250}$ to a decimal using a calculator. You should get 0.036.

Using the idea from Example 2, you can convert a fraction with decimals in it to a simple fraction.

Example 3 Find a fraction equal to $\frac{2.5}{35}$ that has integers in its numerator and denominator.

Solution Multiply the numerator and denominator by 10. This moves the decimal point one place to the right in both the numerator and denominator.

$$\frac{2.5}{35} = \frac{25}{350}$$

Since 25 is a factor of 25 and 350, we get $\frac{2.5}{35} = \frac{1}{14}$.

Now consider percents. Remember that to convert a percent to a decimal, just move the decimal point two places to the left. For example, $53\% = 0.53$, $1800\% = 18$, and $6.25\% = 0.0625$.

To convert decimals to percents, just reverse the procedure. Move the decimal point two places to the right. Here are a few examples.

$$0.46 \quad = 46\%$$
$$3 \quad\quad = 300\%$$
$$0.0007 = 0.07\%$$

To convert fractions to percents, convert them to decimals first. Then convert the decimals to percents.

Example 4 A worker receives time-and-a-half for overtime. What percent of a person's pay is this?

Solution Time-and-a-half $= 1\frac{1}{2} = 1.50 = 150\%$

Example 5 A photographer reduces the dimensions of photos to 5/8 their original size. A final dimension is what percent of a corresponding original dimension?

Solution $5/8 = 0.625 = 62.5\%$

In 1–3, **a.** write the decimal in English and **b.** convert the decimal to a fraction.

1. 8.27   **2.** 630.5   **3.** 0.001

4. The probability of a single birth being a boy is about .52. Convert this number to a percent.

In 5 and 6, convert to a percent.

5. 0.724   **6.** 8

7. 3.14 is an approximation to π. Convert this number to a fraction.

8. Write 2.35 as a fraction in lowest terms.

9. About 1/4 of all families with two children are likely to have two girls. What percent of families is this?

10. The cost of living in 1988 was about $3\frac{1}{3}$ times what it was in 1970. What percent is this?

11. Write 4.2/1.04 as a fraction in lowest terms.

12. Ariel put 6.5 gallons of gasoline in a 12-gallon gas tank. So the tank is 6.5/12 full. What simple fraction of the tank is this?

13. A money market account at a local bank pays 6.75% interest. What fraction is this?

In 14–17, complete the table. Put fractions in lowest terms.

Fraction	Decimal	Percent
1/2	0.5	50%
14. ?	?	9.8%
15. ?	3.2	?
16. 5/16	?	?
17. ?	0.27	?

18. Find twelve percent of ten thousand. *(Lessons 1-1, 2-6)*

19. Would you prefer to buy something at 30% off or 1/3 off? *(Lesson 2-6)*

In 20–22, calculate. *(Lessons 2-1, 2-2, 2-6)*
20. 1918.37 × 10,000   **21.** 14% of 231   **22.** 3^5

In 23 and 24, give the word name for the decimal. *(Lesson 2-1)*
23. One followed by nine zeros

24. One followed by fifteen zeros

25. Order from smallest to largest: .011, 1/10, 1/100. *(Lessons 1-2, 1-8)*

In 26–28, rewrite the number in scientific notation. *(Lesson 2-3)*
26. 3,320,000 square miles, the approximate area of the Sahara desert

27. 27,878,400 square feet, the number of square feet in a square mile

28. 525,600 minutes, the number of minutes in a 365-day year

29. Leslie used 30% of her $5.00 allowance to buy a magazine. How much did the magazine cost? *(Lesson 2-6)*

In 30–32, write the numbers as decimals. *(Lessons 1-1, 2-2, 2-5)*
30. fifty-million fifty

31. 2.4×10^5

32. 3200%

33. Examine this sequence of numbers.
0.5
0.2 5
0.1 2 5
0.0 6 2 5
0.0 3 1 2 5
0.0 1 5 6 2 5
0.0 0 7 8 1 2 5
0.0 0 3 9 0 6 2 5
0.0 0 1 9 5 3 1 2 5
a. Find a pattern and describe it in words.
b. What is the next number in the sequence?

More Powers of 10

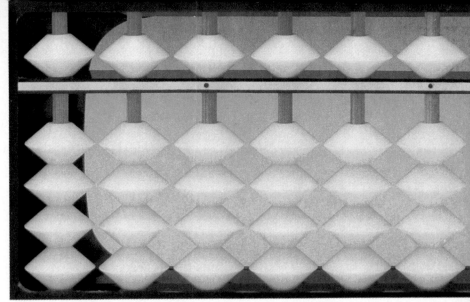

Different versions of this Japanese abacus are still used in some countries for computation. Its operation is based on the powers of 10.

A number that is written with an exponent, like 4^3 or 10^9, is said to be in **exponential form.** Exponential form is a short way of writing some large numbers. For example, $2^{20} = 1048576$. The decimal 1,048,576 is longer than the exponential form 2^{20} for the same number. Powers of 10 such as 100, 1000, and 10,000 are easily written in exponential form as 10^2, 10^3, and 10^4. Thus exponential form makes it possible to rewrite *large* numbers in the shorter scientific notation. Now we consider how to use exponential form to write *small* numbers.

Examine this pattern closely. The numbers in each row going across are equal. Guess what should be the next entry going down in each column.

$$10^6 = 1,000,000 = \text{million}$$
$$10^5 = 100,000 \quad = \text{hundred thousand}$$
$$10^4 = 10,000 \quad = \text{ten thousand}$$
$$10^3 = 1,000 \quad = \text{thousand}$$
$$10^2 = 100 \quad = \text{hundred}$$
$$10^1 = 10 \quad = \text{ten}$$

In the left column, the exponents decrease by 1, so the next entry should be 10^0. In the middle column, each number is 1/10 the number above it. So the next number should be 1/10 of 10, which is 1. The right column gives the place values. Next to the tens place is the ones place. Here is the next row.

$$10^0 = 1 \quad = \text{one}$$

Thus *10 to the zero power is equal to 1.* This is a fact that surprises many people. Check it on your calculator. Also check the zero power of other numbers on your calculator.

If the pattern is continued, negative exponents appear in the left column. This is exactly what is needed in order to represent small numbers.

$$10^{-1} = 0.1 \qquad = \text{one tenth} \qquad\qquad = \tfrac{1}{10}$$

$$10^{-2} = 0.01 \qquad = \text{one hundredth} \qquad = \tfrac{1}{100}$$

$$10^{-3} = 0.001 \qquad = \text{one thousandth} \qquad = \tfrac{1}{1000}$$

$$10^{-4} = 0.0001 \quad = \text{one ten-thousandth} \qquad = \tfrac{1}{10,000}$$

$$10^{-5} = 0.00001 = \text{one hundred-thousandth} = \tfrac{1}{100,000}$$

and so on.

The names of the negative powers of 10 follow closely those for the positive powers.

10^1 = ten	10^{-1} = one tenth
10^2 = one hundred	10^{-2} = one hundredth
10^3 = one thousand	10^{-3} = one thousandth
10^6 = one million	10^{-6} = one millionth
10^9 = one billion	10^{-9} = one billionth
10^{12} = one trillion	10^{-12} = one trillionth
10^{15} = one quadrillion	10^{-15} = one quadrillionth
10^{18} = one quintillion	10^{-18} = one quintillionth

Recall that to multiply a decimal by 0.1 or $\tfrac{1}{10}$, just move the decimal point one unit to the left. Since $10^{-1} = 0.1$, the substitution principle tells us that again, to multiply by 10^{-1}, just move the decimal point one unit to the left.

$$829.43 \times 10^{-1} = 82.943$$

To multiply a decimal by 0.01 or 1/100, you know you only have to move the decimal point two units to the left. Since $10^{-2} = 0.01$, the same goes for multiplying by 10^{-2}.

$$829.43 \times 10^{-2} = 8.2943$$

Do you see the simple pattern?

To multiply by a negative integer power of 10:

> Move the decimal point to the left as many places as indicated by the exponent.

■ ■ ■ ■ ■ ■ ■ ■

Example 1 Write 72×10^{-5} as a decimal.

Solution To multiply by 10^{-5}, move the decimal point five places to the left. So $72 \times 10^{-5} = 72.0 \times 10^{-5} = .00072$.

Example 2 Write 6 trillionths as a decimal.

Solution 6 trillionths = 6×10^{-12} = 0.00000 00000 06.
(When a decimal has many digits, we put spaces between groups of five digits to make it easier to count the digits.)

Questions

Covering the Reading

1. Which one of these numbers is written in exponential form?
   a. 2/3   b. million   c. 2×10^6 d. 7^3 e. 1.45

2. Write $10 \times 10 \times 10 \times 10$ in exponential form.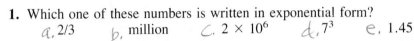

3. Give the place value name for these powers.
   a. 10^5 b. 10^4 c. 10^3 d. 10^2 e. 10^1

4. Continue the pattern of Question 3 to give the place value name for:
   a. 10^0 b. 10^{-1}

5. Press these keys on your calculator. 10 $\boxed{y^x}$ 0 $\boxed{=}$
   What have you calculated and what is the result?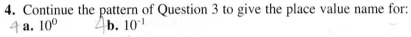

6. Write as a decimal a. 10^{-2} b. 10^{-3}

7. Tell whether the number is positive, negative, or equal to zero.
   a. 10^0 b. 10^{-1}

8. 10^7 = ten million. What is a word name for 10^{-7}?

In 9–11, write as a power of 10.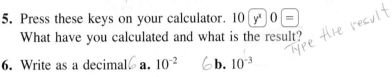

9. one thousandth   10. one millionth   11. one trillionth

In 12–17, write as a decimal.

12. 3×10^{-2}

13. 3.45×10^{-4}

14. 41.3×10^0

15. four thousandths

16. sixty billionths

17. five millionths

18. What is the general rule for multiplying by a negative power of 10?

Applying the Mathematics

19. *Multiple choice* Which number does not equal the others?
    (a) 1%   (b) .01   (c) 1/100   (d) 10^{-2}
    (e) one hundredth   (f) All of (a) through (e) are equal.

20. 64 can be written in exponential form because $4^3 = 64$.
    Write in exponential form.
    a. 81   b. 144   c. 32

21. Write 10×10^{-7} as a decimal.

22. a. Calculate $10^4 \times 10^{-4}$.
   b. What is a hundred times one one-hundredth?
   c. Make a general conclusion from parts **a** and **b.**

23. Arrange from smallest to largest: 1, 10^{-5}, 0, 10^2.

24. An electron microscope can magnify an object 10^5 times. The length of a poliomyelitis virus is 1.2×10^{-8} meter. Multiply this length by 10^5 to find how many meters long the virus would appear to be when viewed through this microscope.

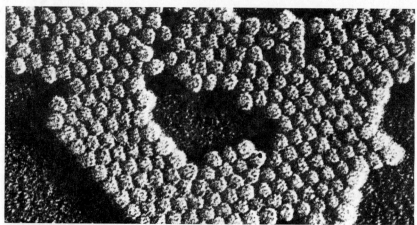

Poliomyelitis virus under magnification

Review

In 25 and 26, change the decimal to **a.** a fraction and **b.** a percent. *(Lesson 2-7)*

25. 12.45

26. 0.1875

27. In store C you see a $50 tape marked 30% off. In store D you can buy this tape for $35. Which store gives the better buy? *(Lesson 2-6)*

28. It rains or snows on about 42% of the days of the year in Seattle, Washington. About how many days per year is this? *(Lesson 2-6)*

29. Change 30%:
   a. to a decimal   **b.** to a simple fraction *(Lesson 2-5)*

30. 512 is what power of 2? *(Lesson 2-2)*

31. 93,000,000 miles is the approximate distance from Earth to the Sun. Write this number in scientific notation. *(Lesson 2-3)*

Exploration

32. Large computers are able to do computations in nanoseconds. Look in a dictionary for the meaning of *nanosecond*.

2-9

Scientific Notation for Small Numbers

Compartments in the outer shell of this dirigible were filled with hydrogen so that it would float in the heavier air.

The mass of one atom of hydrogen, the lightest element, has been found to be

.00000 00000 00000 00000 00016 75 gram.

(By comparison, a piece of notebook paper weighs more than a gram!) A number this small is quite difficult to read and compute with, in decimal notation. To help you with the reading, we have put a space after every fifth digit of the decimal. But the number can be written in scientific notation. In scientific notation such numbers are easier to deal with.

A small number written in scientific notation is a number greater than or equal to 1 and less than 10, multiplied by a negative integer power of 10.

For instance, 1.91×10^{-5} is a small number written in scientific notation. The same ideas are involved in putting small numbers into scientific notation as were used with large numbers.

▪ ▪ ▪ ▪ ▪ ▪ ▪ ▪ ▪ ▪

Example 1 Write the mass of one atom of hydrogen, given above, in scientific notation.

Solution First place the decimal point between the 1 and the 6. This gives you 1.675, a number between 1 and 10. Now find the power of 10 by counting the number of places you must move the decimal to the *left* to change 1.675 into .00000 00000 00000 00000 00016 75. (The movement to the left is in the negative direction and signals the negative exponent.) The move is 24 places to the left. So the mass, in scientific notation, is

$$1.675 \times 10^{-24} \text{ grams.}$$

Example 2   Change 3.97×10^{-8} to a decimal.

Solution   Recall that, to multiply by 10^{-8}, move the decimal point 8 places to the left.
$$3.97 \times 10^{-8} = 0.00000\ 00397$$

Example 3   Enter 0.00000 00000 6993 into a calculator.

Solution   This decimal is too long to fit on the display. So convert into scientific notation. Starting at 6.993, you must move the decimal point 11 places to the left to get the given number. So 0.00000 00000 6993 = 6.993×10^{-11}. To enter that number on your calculator, use the key sequence
$$6.993\ \boxed{\text{EE}}\ 11\ \boxed{\pm}.$$

Questions

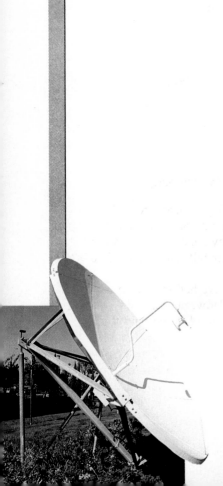

Covering the Reading

1. A small number in scientific notation is a number greater than or equal to __?__ and less than __?__ multiplied by a __?__ power of __?__.

2. Why are small numbers often written in scientific notation?

3. Give an example of a small quantity that is usually written in scientific notation.

4. Write a key sequence that will display 1.675×10^{-24} on your calculator.

5. What number in scientific notation is given by this key sequence?
$$6.008\ \boxed{\text{EE}}\ 5\ \boxed{\pm}$$

In 6–8, rewrite the number in scientific notation.

6. 0.00008052 second, the time needed for TV signals to travel 15 miles

7. 0.28 second, a time needed for sound to travel the length of a football field.

8. 0.00000 00000 00000 00000 0396 gram, the weight of one atom of uranium.

9. Suppose a decimal is multiplied by a negative power of 10. Should its decimal point be moved to the right or to the left?

In 10–12, rewrite the numbers as decimals.

10. 1×10^{-8} centimeter, the angstrom (a unit of measure)

11. 2×10^{-7} meter, the length of the longest known virus

12. 2.82×10^{-11} centimeter, the radius of an electron

13. Using your calculator, find the first six places of the decimal for 1/102.

14. Write the number in *decimal* notation given by the key sequence 4.675 $\boxed{\text{EE}}$ 7 $\boxed{\pm}$.

15. Change $\dfrac{3 \times 10^{-8}}{6 \times 10^{-7}}$ to a decimal.

In 16 and 17, choose one of the symbols $<$, $=$, or $>$.

16. 5.37×10^{-5} __?__ 5.37×10^{-4}

17. 49×10^{-9} __?__ 4.9×10^{-8}

18. Write 4,500,000,000 in scientific notation. *(Lesson 2-3)*

19. Write as a power of 10.
a. one million **b.** one millionth *(Lesson 2-8)*

20. Calculate 5 to the 7th power. *(Lesson 2-2)*

21. The Skunks baseball team lost 60% of its games. Did the team win or lose more often? *(Lesson 2-6)*

22. a. What fraction is equal to 75%? **b.** What is 75% of 400?
(Lessons 2-5, 2-6)

In 23–25, write as a decimal. *(Lessons 1-9, 2-5)*

23. 3% **24.** $-19\frac{7}{10}$ **25.** 150%

26. Between what two integers is 3.4% ? (Watch out!) *(Lesson 2-5)*

27. Newspaper columnist Georgie Anne Geyer once wrote about receiving a tax bill for $0.01. The payment was due June 30, 1984.
a. If Ms. Geyer did not pay her bill by June 30th, she would have to pay a penalty of 10% of her bill. How much is this? *(Lesson 2-6)*
b. Also, if she paid late, she would have had to pay an additional interest penalty of 1% of her bill. How much is this? *(Lesson 2-6)*
c. What would be the exact total she owed if she paid the bill late?
d. Round your answer to part **c** to the nearest penny. *(Lesson 1-4)*

28. The narrowest street in the world is in Great Britain. It has a width of $19\frac{5}{16}$ inches. *(Lessons 1-9, 1-8)*
   a. Between what two whole number widths does this width lie?
   b. If you are 19.3 inches wide, could you walk down this street?

In 29 and 30, tell whether a high or a low estimate would be preferred.

29. An airline estimates how much baggage an airplane can carry without being overloaded. *(Lesson 1-3)*

30. A caterer estimates how much food to prepare for a graduation party. *(Lesson 1-3)*

31. Order from smallest to largest: -.6, -.66, -.666, -.656, -2/3. *(Lessons 1-5, 1-8)*

32. Change 76.23 to:
   a. a percent   **b.** a fraction *(Lesson 2-7)*

Exploration

33. a. On your calculator, what is the smallest positive number that can be displayed?
   b. What is the largest negative number that can be displayed?

34. a. Type ?0.25*0.3 on your computer and press RETURN. What does the computer print? What is the computer doing?
   b. Put a zero before the 2 or 3 of part **a**, so that you have either ?0.025*0.3 or ?0.25*0.03. What does the computer print this time?
   c. Continue increasing the number of zeros until the computer is forced to print an answer in its form of scientific notation. How does your computer write small numbers in scientific notation?
   d. What is the smallest positive number your computer will itself print that is not in scientific notation?

Summary

In Chapter 1, you learned three advantages of the decimal system. (1) All of the most common numbers can be written as decimals. (2) Decimals are easy to order. (3) Decimals are used by calculators to represent numbers. In this chapter, another advantage is discussed. (4) Large and small numbers can easily be written as decimals.

The decimal system is based on the number 10. So when numbers are written as decimals, it is easy to multiply by powers of 10. The numbers 10, 100, 1000, ... (or 10^1, 10^2, 10^3, ...) are positive integer powers of 10. The numbers 1/10, 1/100, 1/1000, ... or their decimal equivalents 0.1, 0.01, 0.001, ... (or 10^{-1}, 10^{-2}, 10^{-3}, ...) are negative integer powers of 10. The number one is the zero power of 10.

Percent means multiply by 1/100, so decimals can easily be converted to %. Percents are usually small numbers. To find a percent of a number, multiply the percent by that number. Percents, decimals and fractions are all used often and sometimes interchangeably. So it is useful to be able to convert from one form into another.

Large and small numbers are also often written in exponential form. Scientific notation combines exponential form with decimal notation. It is a standard way used all over the world to express very large or very small numbers.

Vocabulary

You should be able to give a general description and a specific example of each of the following ideas.

Lesson 2-1
million, billion, trillion, and so on

Lesson 2-2
base, exponent, power
, x^y

Lesson 2-3
scientific notation for large numbers

Lesson 2-5
percent, %

Lesson 2-6
Substitution Principle

Lesson 2-7
terminating decimal

Lesson 2-8
exponential form
millionth, billionth, trillionth, and so on

Lesson 2-9
scientific notation for small numbers

Progress Self-Test

Take this test as you would take a test in class. Then check your work with the solutions in the Selected Answers section in the back of the book.

In 1–10, write as a single decimal.

1. $100,000,000 \times 23.51864$
2. 34% of 600
3. 32 billionths
4. 824.59×0.00001
5. $\frac{1}{1000} \times 77$
6. 3456.8910×10^5
7. 2.816×10^{-3}
8. 10^{-7}
9. 8%
10. 6^3

In 11–14, consider 125^6.

11. 125 is called the __?__ and 6 the __?__.
12. What key sequence can you use to calculate this on your calculator?
13. What is the resulting display?
14. Give a decimal estimate for 125^6.

In 15 and 16, write in scientific notation.

15. 21,070,000,000
16. 0.00000 008

In 17 and 18, write the key sequence necessary to enter the number on your calculator.

17. 4.5×10^{13}
18. 0.00000 01234 56

19. Order from smallest to largest: 4^4 5^3 3^5
20. Between what two integers is 40%?
21. Rewrite 4.73 as
    a. a simple fraction
    b. a percent
22. As a fraction, $33\frac{1}{3}\% = $ __?__.

23. A recent survey of 150 chefs reported that 30% of the chefs thought broccoli is the top vegetable. How many chefs is this?

24. A stereo system is on sale at 25% off. If the regular price is $699, to the nearest dollar what is the sale price?
25. Julio correctly answered 80% of the items on a 20-item test. How many did he miss?
26. Why is this number not in scientific notation: 22.4×10^3?
27. What power of 10 equals one million?
28. According to the Substitution Principle, $\frac{3}{5} - \frac{1}{10} = $ __?__ % $-$ __?__ %.
29. It is estimated that a swarm of 250 billion locusts descended on the Red Sea in 1889. Write this number in scientific notation.

Chapter Review

Questions on **SPUR** Objectives

SPUR stands for **S**kills, **P**roperties, **U**ses, and **R**epresentations.
The Chapter Review questions are grouped according to the
SPUR Objectives for this chapter.

SKILLS deal with the procedures used to get answers.

■ **Objective A:** *Multiply by 10, 100, 1000, ...*
(Lesson 2-1)

1. $32 \times 10,000 = $?
2. $100 \times 7.5 = $?
3. $1,000,000 \times 0.025 = $?
4. What number is 3.5 multiplied by to get 3500?

■ **Objective B:** *Change word names for numbers to decimals. (Lessons 2-1, 2-8)*

5. Write the June, 1984, trade deficit of $10 billion as a decimal.
6. Write 4.6 millionths as a decimal.

■ **Objective C:** *Convert powers to decimals.*
(Lesson 2-2)

7. Convert 4^3 to a decimal.
8. Convert 12^8 to a decimal.

■ **Objective D:** *Give decimals and English word names for positive and negative integer powers of 10. (Lessons 2-2, 2-8)*

9. $10^5 = $?
10. In English, 10^9 is ?.
11. $10^{-4} = $?
12. In English, 10^{-2} is ?.
13. One trillion is what power of ten?
14. 0.0001 is what power of ten?

■ **Objective E:** *Multiply by 0.1, 0.01, 0.001, ..., and 1/10, 1/100, 1/1000, ... (Lesson 2-4)*

15. $2.73 \times 0.00000\ 001 = $?
16. $495 \times 0.1 = $?

17. $75 \times \frac{1}{1000} = $?
18. $2.1 \times \frac{1}{100} = $?

■ **Objective F:** *Multiply by powers of 10.*
(Lessons 2-2, 2-8)

19. $3 \times 10^7 = $?
20. $0.42 \times 10^5 = $?
21. $7.34 \times 10^0 = $?
22. $68.3 \times 10^{-4} = $?

■ **Objective G:** *Convert large and small numbers into scientific notation. (Lessons 2-3, 2-9)*

23. Write 480,000 in scientific notation.
24. Write 9,000,000,000,000,000 in scientific notation.
25. Write 0.00013 in scientific notation.
26. Write 0.7 in scientific notation.

■ **Objective H:** *Convert percents to decimals.*
(Lesson 2-5)

27. Write 15% as a decimal.
28. Write 5.25% as a decimal.
29. Write 9% as a decimal.
30. Write 200% as a decimal.

■ **Objective I:** *Know common fraction and percent equivalents. (Lesson 2-5)*

31. Change 1/2 to a percent.
32. Change 4/5 to a percent.
33. What fraction equals 30%?
34. What fraction equals $66\frac{2}{3}\%$?

Objective J: *Find percents of numbers.*
(Lesson 2-6)

35. What is 50% of 150?
36. What is 3% of 3?
37. What is 100% of 6.2?
38. What is 7.8% of 3500?

Objective K: *Convert terminating decimals to fractions or percents.* *(Lesson 2-7)*

39. Find a simple fraction equal to 5.7.
40. Find the simple fraction in lowest terms equal to 0.892.
41. Convert 0.86 to percent.
42. Convert 3.2 to percent.
43. Convert $\frac{3}{7}$ to percent.
44. Convert $\frac{11}{8}$ to percent.

PROPERTIES deal with the principles behind the mathematics.

Objective L: *Know and apply the Substitution Principle.* *(Lesson 2-6)*

45. State the Substitution Principle.
46. How is the Substitution Principle used in evaluating 75% of 40?
47. Name two numbers that could be substituted for 50%.
48. According to the Substitution Principle,
$\frac{1}{2} + \frac{1}{4} = \underline{\ ?\ }\% + \underline{\ ?\ }\%$.

Objective M: *Identify numbers as being written in scientific notation.* *(Lessons 2-3, 2-9)*

49. Why is 23×10^4 not in scientific notation?
50. In scientific notation, a number greater than or equal to $\underline{\ ?\ }$ and less than $\underline{\ ?\ }$ is multiplied by an $\underline{\ ?\ }$ power of 10.

USES deal with applications of mathematics in real situations.

Objective N: *Find percents of quantities in real situations.* *(Lesson 2-6)*

51. At a "40%-off" sale, what will you pay for $26.50 slacks?
52. George Bush received about 53.9% of the votes cast in the 1988 presidential election. About 89,000,000 votes were cast. About how many votes did Bush get?
53. The value of a one-carat flawless diamond reached $64,000 in 1980. By July of 1988, the price had dropped 34% of its former value. What was the value in 1988?

Objective O: *Translate actual quantities into and out of scientific notation.* *(Lessons 2-3, 2-9)*

54. The number of non-human living things on Earth is estimated at 3×10^{33}. Write this number as a decimal.

55. A piece of paper is about 0.005 inches thick. What is that in scientific notation?

94

■ **Objective P:** *Indicate key sequences and displays on a calculator for large and small numbers.*
(Lessons 2-3, 2-9)

56. What key sequence will enter 32 billion on your calculator?

57. What key sequence will enter one trillionth on your calculator?

58. What key sequence will enter 2^{45} on your calculator?

59. What does your calculator display for the number of Question 58?

60. If a calculator displays $\boxed{4.73 \quad 08}$, what decimal is being shown?

61. Estimate 1357975×24681086 using a calculator.

62. Estimate $.0025 \times .00004567$ using a calculator.

63. What key sequence will enter 3×10^{21} on your calculator?

Measurement

fathom

yard

hand

cubit

foot

The first units of length were based on the human body. Some of these units are shown on the photograph on the opposite page. For instance, a "hand" was the width of a person's palm. So the size of a hand differed from place to place. These rough units were sufficient for most purposes. But for accurate building, more accurate units were needed. So units began to be *standardized*.

According to tradition, the *yard* originally was the distance from the tip of the nose of King Henry I of England (who reigned from 1100 to 1135) to the tips of his fingers. The *foot* is supposedly based on the foot of Charlemagne (who ruled France and neighboring areas from 768 to 814).

3-1

Measuring Length

Around the year 1600, scientific experimentation began and more accurate measurement was necessary. Scientists from different countries needed to be able to communicate with each other about their work. With the manufacturing of lenses and clocks, accurate measurement was needed outside of science. About 1760, the industrial revolution began. Hand tools were replaced by power-driven machines. Accurate consistent measurement was needed everywhere.

The writers of the U.S. Constitution in 1787 recognized the need for standardized units. One article in the Constitution reads:

> *The Congress shall have power ... to fix the standard of weights and measures.*

In 1790, Thomas Jefferson proposed to Congress a measuring system based on the number 10. This would closely relate the measuring system to the decimal system. Five years later the metric system, based on the number 10, was established in France. We could have been the first country with this system. But we were emotionally tied to England, at that time an enemy of France. So we adopted the English system of measurement instead. Not until 1866 did the metric system become legal in the United States.

At first the metric system was used mainly in science. But as years go by, it is used in more and more fields and in more and more countries. Even England now has converted to the metric system. The old "English system" or "British Imperial system" has evolved into the **U.S. system** or the **customary system of measurement.** Today in the U.S. we measure in both the metric and U.S. systems.

In all systems of measurement, units of length are basic. For the metric system, the base unit of length is the meter. A **centimeter** is $\frac{1}{100}$ or .01 of a meter. For the U.S. system, the base of unit of length is the **inch.**

one inch   one centimeter

The ruler pictured below has centimeters on the top and inches on the bottom.

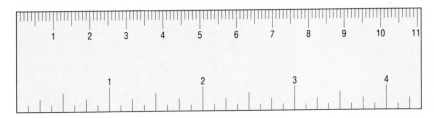

On the ruler, each centimeter is divided into 10 parts. (Each part is a millimeter.) So it is easy to measure in centimeters. The three segments drawn below have lengths of about 6, 6.3, and 7 centimeters.

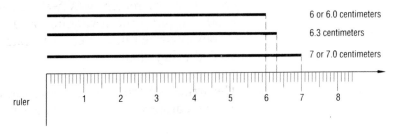

On rulers, inches are usually divided into halves, fourths, and eighths. Look at the part of the ruler drawn below. The longest tick marks between the inches are for half inches. The next longest are for fourths not already marked as $\frac{2}{4}$, $\frac{4}{4}$, and so on. The shortest are for eighths not already marked as $\frac{2}{8}$, $\frac{4}{8}$, and so on. The segments drawn here have lengths of about 1, $1\frac{1}{2}$, $1\frac{3}{4}$, and $1\frac{5}{8}$ inches.

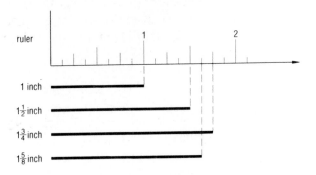

Look at the segment that is $1\frac{3}{4}$ inches long. You can see that its length is between 1 and 2 inches. The $\frac{3}{4}$ is not so easily seen. It comes as follows. There are 8 intervals between 1 inch and 2 inches. So each interval equals $\frac{1}{8}$ of an inch. The segment extends to the 6th tick mark. That is $\frac{6}{8}$ of an inch past 1 inch. So its length is $1\frac{6}{8}$ inches. Reduced to lowest terms, this is $1\frac{3}{4}$ inches.

When you measure, you may have a choice of unit. Units can be divided to give you greater accuracy in your measurement. For instance, lengths are often measured in sixteenths or thirty-seconds of an inch. In industry lengths may be measured to hundredths or thousandths or even smaller parts of an inch. Whatever unit you work with, you are rounding to the nearest. Whatever you choose as your rounding unit (tenth of a centimeter, for example) indicates how accurate your measurement is.

Example 1 Find the length of this small paper clip **a.** to the nearest centimeter, and **b.** to the nearest tenth of a centimeter.

Solution

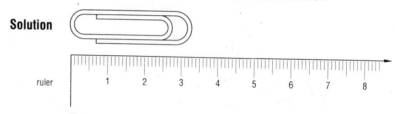

ruler

a. 3 centimeters, to the nearest centimeter
b. 3.3 centimeters, to the nearest tenth of a centimeter

Example 2 Find the height of this photograph **a.** to the nearest $\frac{1}{2}$ inch, **b.** to the nearest $\frac{1}{4}$ inch, and **c.** to the nearest $\frac{1}{8}$ inch.

Solution **a.** 2 in., **b.** $2\frac{1}{4}$ in., **c.** $2\frac{1}{8}$ in.

1. The first units of length were based on __?__.

2. The heights of horses are sometimes measured in hands. What was the way that the length called a hand was originally determined?

3. The yard originally was the distance from the __?__ to the __?__ of what king of England?

4. Whose foot is said to have been the foot from which today's foot originated?

5. Why did units become standardized?

6. About when did accurate lengths become needed everywhere?

In 7–10, *true* or *false*?

7. Thomas Jefferson wanted the U.S. to adopt the English system of measurement.

8. The metric system was established in 1795.

9. The metric system became legal in the U.S. over 100 years ago.

10. Congress has the power to set standards for measurement in the U.S.

11. The English system of measurement now is called by other names. What are those names and why was the name changed?

12. The base unit of length in the metric system is the __?__.

Charlemagne

In 13–15, use this ruler to find the length of the segment. Write the length in lowest terms.

ruler

13. ————————————————

14. ——————————————

15. ——————

In 16–18, measure the length of each segment:
    a. to the nearest tenth of a centimeter.
    b. to the nearest eighth of an inch.

16. ————————————————————

17.

18.

Applying the Mathematics

19. Measure the length and the width of this page to the nearest tenth of a centimeter.

20. Measure your height:
    a. to the nearest inch.
    b. to the nearest centimeter.

21. Draw a vertical segment with length 3.5 inches.

22. Draw a horizontal segment with length 12.4 centimeters.

Review

23. What is the Substitution Principle? *(Lesson 2-6)*

24. Use the number line drawn here. The letters refer to points that are equally spaced. *(Lesson 1-2)*

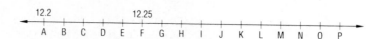

    a. What number corresponds to *E*?
    b. What number corresponds to *N*?
    c. What letter corresponds to 12.3?
    d. 12.213 is between which two points?

25. Some people believe that if a sports team or individual appears on the cover of *Sports Illustrated*, then the team or individual becomes jinxed and will suffer a decline in performance. Researchers at the University of Southern California examined 271 covers. They found that 57.6% of the cover subjects improved in performance.
   a. Did more cover subjects improve or decline in performance? *(Lesson 2-5)*
   b. How many of the 271 cover subjects improved in performance? *(Lesson 2-6)*

26. Which is larger—5 to the 6th power, or 6 to the 5th power? *(Lesson 2-2)*
27. Write 28.2 million (the number of clerks and salesworkers thought in 1988 to be needed in 1995) as a decimal. *(Lesson 2-1)*

In 28 and 29, find equal fractions with 5 in the denominator. *(Lesson 1-10)*

28. 16   29. $\frac{35}{25}$

30. $\frac{1}{3}$ is how many percent? *(Lesson 2-5)*

31. *Multiple choice* Estimate $35.17 - 6.2$. *(Lesson 1-4)*
   (a) 28.97   (b) 34.55   (c) 3.455   (d) 29.15

Exploration

32. There are many units of length that have specialized uses. Find out something about each of these specialized units of length.
   a. pica **b.** ell **c.** link **d.** chain

33. *Your* ''inch'' is the length of your thumb, from the tip to the joint in the middle. How close is your inch to an actual inch?

34. Look at the picture that opens this chapter. Find out what the lengths of **a.** a fathom, and **b.** a cubit, are today.

3-2

The Customary System of Measurement

In the customary, or U.S., system of measurement, there are many units. Few people know all of them. So people refer to tables to check relationships between unfamiliar units. Still, because some units are so often used, you should know some relationships by heart.

Common units in the customary system of measurement

For length:	12 inches = 1 foot (ft)
	3 feet = 1 yard (yd)
	5280 feet = 1 mile (mi)
For weight:	16 ounces = 1 pound (lb)
	2000 pounds = 1 short ton
For capacity (liquid or dry volume):	2 pints = 1 quart (qt)
	4 quarts = 1 gallon (gal)

The abbreviation for inch is *in.* (with the period). The abbreviation for ounce is *oz* without a period. Except for the inch, it is now recommended that periods not be used in abbreviations for units of measure. (Periods get confused with decimals.)

The above relationships make it possible to convert from one unit to another.

Example 1   Convert 3 gallons to quarts.

Solution   Use the Substitution Principle.
Since   1 gallon = 4 quarts,
3 × 1 gallon = 3 × 4 quarts
= 12 quarts.

104

Example 2   How many feet are in 1.7 miles?

> **Solution**   Since   1 mi = 5280 ft,
>   1.7 × 1 mi = 1.7 × 5280 ft
>   = 8976 feet.

Questions

Covering the Reading

In 1–3, consider the customary system of measurement.
1. Name four units of length.

2. Name three units in which a volume of milk could be measured.

3. Name three units of weight.

In 4–10, copy and complete each relationship.
4. 1 ft = _?_ in.   5. 1 gallon = _?_ quarts

6. 1 yd = _?_ ft   7. 1 quart = _?_ pints

8. 1 mi = _?_ ft   9. 1 lb = _?_ oz

10. 1 short ton = _?_ pounds

In 11–15, convert:
11. 0.62 mi to feet

12. 4 yards to feet

13. 7 tons to pounds

14. 2.2 pounds (the approximate number of pounds in a kilogram) to ounces

15. 8.3 gallons to quarts

Applying the Mathematics

16. In some cities, a block is $\frac{1}{8}$ mile long. Convert this to feet.

17. In the U.S. system, a *rod* is defined as 5.5 yards. How many feet are in a rod?

18. In Great Britain, one *gross ton* = 2240 pounds. The longest passenger liner ever built, the *Norway,* weighs about 70,200 gross tons. How many pounds is this?

19. How many feet are in 440 yards, a common distance in many school running events?

20. How many inches are in 1 mile?

21. You have a 1-pint measuring vessel. How many times would you have to use it to fill a 10-gallon tank?

22. Name an appropriate unit for measuring each thing.
  a. the distance around a city block
  b. the weight of an elephant
  c. the amount of gas in a car gas tank

23. Refer to the cartoon below. What should the chief cook tell Zero?

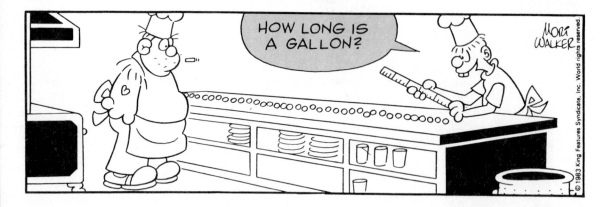

24. Measure this segment **a.** to the nearest $\frac{1}{8}$ of an inch, and **b.** to the nearest centimeter. *(Lesson 3-1)*

25. Measure the length of a dollar bill **a.** to the nearest inch, **b.** to the nearest fourth of an inch, and **c.** to the nearest eighth of an inch. *(Lesson 3-1)*

26. Write in scientific notation. *(Lessons 2-3, 2-9)*
a. 105,000,000 the estimated population of Nigeria in 1986
b. 0.013837 in., the length of 1 point in typesetting

27. Calculate. *(Lessons 2-1, 2-4)*
a. 0.052×100 **b.** $3.446 \times .0001$
c. $15.36 \times .1$ **d.** $640 \times 10,000$

28. 0% of the 500 students in a school are traveling to a game by bus. How many students is this? *(Lesson 2-6)*

29. All systems of measurement in common use in the world today have the same units for time.
1 hour = 60 minutes, 1 minute = 60 seconds.
a. How many seconds are in an hour?
b. How many seconds are in a day?
c. How many seconds are in a year?
d. How many minutes are in a year?
e. If your heart beats 70 times a minute, how many times does it beat in a year?
f. If a heart beats 70 times a minute, how many times will it beat in 78 years, the average lifetime of a woman in the U.S.?

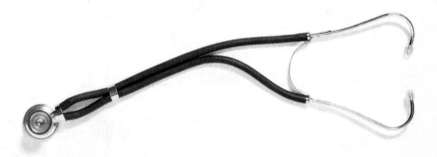

30. An old song goes, ''I love you, a bushel and a peck, a bushel and a peck and a hug around your neck, a hug around your neck and a barrel and a heap, a barrel and a heap and I'm talking in my sleep about you ...'' Three units of capacity of fruits and grains are in the words to the song. What are they and how are they related?

3-3

The Metric System of Measurement

The U.S. system of measurement has three major weaknesses. First, the many units have names that do not help you know how the units are related. Second, the units are multiples of each other in no consistent manner. To see this, look again at the list of relationships in Lesson 3-2. You see the numbers 12, 3, 5280, 16, 2000, 2, and 4. No two are alike. Third, in the decimal system these numbers are not so easy to work with as powers of 10 such as 100, 1000, 10,000, or .1, .01, and .001.

Other older measurement systems had the same weaknesses. So in the late 1700s a movement arose to design a better measurement system. The system devised is called **the international or metric system of measurement.** It is based on the decimal system and is by far the most widely used system of measurement in the world.

In the metric system, prefixes have fixed meanings related to place values in the decimal system. The table on page 109 identifies many of the prefixes. The three most common are kilo-, centi-, and milli-.

kilo-   means 1000

centi-   means $\frac{1}{100}$, or .01

milli-   means $\frac{1}{1000}$, or .001

The basic unit of length is the **meter.** Other units of length are multiples of the meter. (See the table for descriptions of these units.)

1 kilometer   = 1 km = 1000 meters

1 centimeter = 1 cm = $\frac{1}{100}$, or .01 meter

1 millimeter = 1 mm = $\frac{1}{1000}$, or .001 meter

Units of mass are multiples of the **gram.** In everyday usage, the gram is also used to measure weight.

$$1 \text{ kilogram} = 1 \text{ kg} = 1000 \text{ grams}$$
$$1 \text{ milligram} = 1 \text{ mg} = \frac{1}{1000}, \text{ or } .001 \text{ gram}$$

The **liter** and milliliter are used to measure capacity or volume. Soft drinks today are often sold in 2-liter bottles. Smaller amounts are measured in milliliters.

$$1 \text{ milliliter} = 1 \text{ mL} = \frac{1}{1000}, \text{ or } .001 \text{ liter}$$

All conversions within the metric system can be done without a calculator because the multiples are powers of 10.

The International or Metric System of Measurement

Table of Prefixes

place value	thousands	hundreds	tens	ones	tenths	hundredths	thousandths
power of 10	10^3	10^2	10^1	10^0	10^{-1}	10^{-2}	10^{-3}
unit of length	kilometer	hectometer	dekameter	meter	decimeter	centimeter	millimeter
unit of mass	kilogram	hectogram	dekagram	gram	decigram	centigram	milligram
unit of capacity	kiloliter	hectoliter	dekaliter	liter	deciliter	centiliter	milliliter

Some other Prefixes:

place value	trillions	billions	millions	millionths	billionths	trillionths
power of 10	10^{12}	10^9	10^6	10^{-6}	10^{-9}	10^{-12}
prefix	tera-	giga-	mega-	micro-	nano-	pico-

Some common units:

Length:
- **kilometer (km)** - used for distances between towns and cities. 1 km ≈ 0.62 mi
- **meter (m)** - used for measuring rooms, heights, and fabrics. A doorknob is about 1 m high.
- **centimeter (cm)** - used for measuring small items. The diameter of an aspirin tablet is about 1 cm.
- **millimeter (mm)** - used for measuring very small items. The thickness of a dime is about 1 mm.

Mass:
- **kilogram (kg)** - used for measuring meat and body weight. A quart of milk weighs about 1 kg.
- **gram (g)** - used for measuring very light items. An aspirin weighs about 1 g.
- **milligram (mg)** - used in measuring vitamin content in food. A speck of sawdust weighs about 1 mg.

Capacity:
- **liter (L)** - used for measuring milk and other liquids. 1 liter ≈ 1.06 qt.
- **milliliter (mL)** - used for measuring small amounts such as perfume. 1 teaspoon ≈ 5 mL

Example 1   How many meters are in 3.46 kilometers?

>   **Solution**   3.46 kilometers = 3.46 × 1 km
>   = 3.46 × 1000 m   *Substitution Principle*
>   = 3460 m

Example 2   Change 89 milligrams to grams.

>   **Solution**   89 milligrams = 89 × 1 mg
>   = 89 ×.001 g
>   = 0.089 g

Many of the questions refer to the table on page 109. You should study it before reading the questions.

Questions

Covering the Reading

1. Name two weaknesses of the U.S. system of measurement.

2. Another name for the metric system is __?__.

3. Name three common units of length in the metric system.

4. Name three common units of mass in the metric system.

5. Name two common units of capacity in the metric system.

In 6–8, give the meaning of the prefix.
6. kilo-   7. milli-   8. centi-

In 9–11, give the abbreviation for each unit.
9. centimeter   10. kilogram   11. milliliter

In 12–17, convert.
12. 90 cm to meters   13. 345 mL to liters

14. 5 kg to grams   15. 10 km to meters

16. 48 mm to meters   17. 60 mg to grams

18. Name something weighing approximately
    a. 1 kg, **b.** 1 g, **c.** 1 mg.

19. Name something about as long as: **a.** 1 m; **b.** 1 km; **c.** 1 mm.

20. Name something with about as much liquid in it as a liter.

In 21–23, give the power of 10 associated with each prefix.
21. centi-   22. milli-   23. kilo-

In 24–26, choose the one best answer.

24. A high-school freshman might weigh:
    (a) 50 g (b) 50 mg (c) 50 kg (d) 500 g

25. A high-school freshman might be how tall?
    (a) .7 m (b) 1.7 m (c) 2.2 m (d) 5.6 m

26. A common dimension of camera film is:
    (a) 35 km (b) 35 cm (c) 35 m (d) 35 mm

27. Should most students be able to walk one kilometer in an hour?

28. The atomic bomb that exploded on Hiroshima had a force equivalent to 20 kilotons of TNT. How many tons is this?

29. The most powerful bomb ever exploded (by the Soviet Union in a test in 1961) had a force of 57 megatons of TNT. How many tons is this?

30. A millisecond is how many seconds?

31. The United States was the first country in the world (1786) to have a money system based on decimals. In our system:
    $$1 \text{ dollar} = 100 \text{ cents}$$
    or equivalently, $1 \text{ cent} = \frac{1}{100}$, or .01, dollar.
    a. Convert 56¢ to dollars.
    b. Convert $13.49 to cents.
    c. On September 17, 1983, UPI reported that a truck loaded with 7.6 million new pennies overturned on Interstate 80 in the mountains north of Sacramento, California. How many dollars is that?

32. Write $\frac{2}{1000}$ cm, the diameter of a cloud droplet, as a decimal. *(Lesson 1-8)*

33. Order from smallest to largest: 10^{-4}, 0, $\frac{1}{100}$. *(Lessons 2-4, 2-8)*

34. Order from smallest to largest: 5^2, 2^5, 10^1 *(Lesson 2-2)*

35. Complete each with the correct symbol $<$, $=$, or $>$. *(Lessons 1-6, 3-2)*
   a. $2\frac{1}{2}$ pints __?__ 4 quarts   **b.** $3\frac{1}{2}$ feet __?__ 2 yards
   c. 2850 feet __?__ 1 mile   **d.** 1 lb __?__ 16 oz

36. Which measurement is more accurate, one made to the nearest $\frac{1}{16}$ of an inch, or one made to the nearest $\frac{1}{10}$ of an inch? *(Lessons 1-8, 3-1)*

37. Measure the segment at the left to the nearest 0.1 cm *(Lesson 3-1)*

38. In a recent survey, 85% of teenagers responding owned bicycles, 80% owned cameras, 72% had designer clothes, and 52% owned TV sets. If there are 30 students in a class that is representative of all teenagers who responded, how many would you expect to own:
   a. bicycles; **b.** cameras; **c.** designer clothes? (2-6)

39. Almost every country in the world today has a decimal money system. Given is a relationship between monetary units. Name a country in which these units are used.
   a. 1 franc = 100 centimes   **b.** 1 centavo = 100 pesos
   c. 1 kopeck = 100 rubles   **d.** 1 yuan = 100 fen
   e. 1 dinar = 1000 fils   **f.** 1 rupee = 100 paise
   g. 1 cedi = 100 pesewas

40. The computer program below instructs a computer to convert a length in miles to one in feet. The line numbers 10, 20, and so on at left must be typed. The computer executes the program in the order of the line numbers, which can be any positive integers.
   a. Type in the following.

```
NEW
10      PRINT "WHAT IS LENGTH IN MILES?"
20      INPUT NMILES
30      NFEET = 5280*NMILES
40      PRINT "THE NUMBER OF FEET IS " NFEET
50      END
```

   To see what you have typed, LIST and press RETURN. You can change one line by typing it over. You need not type the entire program again.
   b. To run your program, type RUN and press RETURN. The computer will execute line 10 and ask you to input a number. Input 5 and press RETURN. The computer will then execute the rest of the program. What does the computer print?
   c. Run the program a few times, with values of your own choosing. Write down the values you input and the answers the computer gives.

3-4

Converting Between Systems

Because using the metric system is so easy, country after country in the world has adopted it. In the United States, science, medicine, and photography are almost all metric. Carpentry and other building trades usually use the U.S. system. The trend is to use metric units more often as time goes by. Some automobiles are manufactured with parts that conform to metric units. Others use customary units. Auto mechanics need tools for each system.

With two systems in use today, it is occasionally necessary to change from units in one system to units in another. This change is called *converting between systems*. Converting between systems is like converting within one system. However, the numbers are more complicated.

There are five conversions you should know. One of these is exact.

    1 inch = 2.54 centimeters (exactly)

This conversion is exact because the inch is now officially based on the centimeter. The other four conversions are approximate, so we use the sign ≈. This sign means **is approximately equal to.**

    1 meter   ≈ 39.37 inches
    1 kilometer ≈ 0.62 miles
    1 kilogram ≈ 2.2 pounds
    1 liter   ≈ 1.06 quarts

Because these conversions are not equal, you cannot use the Substitution Principle. However, there is an **Estimation Principle** that serves the same purpose.

Estimation Principle:

If two numbers are nearly equal, then when one is substituted for the other in a computation, the results of the computations will be nearly equal.

Example 1   Convert 50 kilograms into pounds.

Solution   50 kilograms = 50 × 1 kilogram
$\approx$ 50 × 2.2 pounds   Estimation Principle
$\approx$ 110 pounds   (Substitute 2.2 pounds for 1 kilogram.)

Example 2   How many centimeters are in 1 foot?

Solution   On page 113, there is no direct conversion given from feet to centimeters. But there is a conversion from inches to centimeters. So change feet to inches. Then convert.
1 foot = 12 inches
= 12 × 1 inch
= 12 × 2.54 centimeters   Substitution Principle
= 30.48 centimeters   (Substitute 2.54 cm for 1 inch.)

In Example 2, the Estimation Principle is not needed because the conversion from inches to centimeters is exact.

Questions

1. Name two professions in which a person in the U.S. would use the metric system more than the U.S. system.

2. Name two professions in which a person in the U.S. would use U.S. units more than metric units.

3. What does the sign $\approx$ mean?

4. What metric unit is a little larger than two pounds?

5. What U.S. unit is most like a liter?

6. One relationship between the U.S. and metric system is exact. What relationship is it?

In 7–10, give a relationship between:

7. kilograms and pounds   **8.** meters and inches

9. liters and quarts   **10.** kilometers and miles

11. a. State the estimation principle. **b.** Give an example of its use.

In 12–15, convert.

12. 6 meters to inches   **13.** 1.8 liters to quarts

14. 0.45 kilograms to pounds   **15.** 5 inches to centimeters

Applying the Mathematics

In 16-20, which is larger?

16. a pound or a kilogram   **17.** a quart or a liter

18. a meter or a yard   **19.** a centimeter or an inch

20. a kilometer or a mile

21. a. Write $\frac{5}{16}$ as a decimal. **b.** A person needs a drill bit with a diameter of approximately $\frac{5}{16}$ in. If a bit with a metric measure must be used, what diameter is needed?

22. An adult human brain weighs about 1.5 kg. Convert this to ounces.

23. The St. Gotthard Tunnel in Switzerland is the longest car tunnel in the world. Its length is 16.4 km. How many miles is this?

24. $\frac{4}{9}$ is a little less than a half. $\frac{7}{13}$ is a little more than a half. So a reasonable estimate for $\frac{4}{9} + \frac{7}{13}$ is ___?___.

In 25 and 26, use the Estimation Principle to estimate each result to the nearest integer.

25. $\frac{19}{20} + \frac{19}{18}$ **26.** $\frac{1}{1000} + \frac{1}{100}$

27. How many inches are in a yard? *(Lesson 3-2)*

28. A bucket holds 8 gallons. How many quarts will it hold? *(Lesson 3-2)*

29. A 5-lb bag of cat food has how many ounces of food in it? *(Lesson 3-2)*

30. How many grams are in 4 kilograms? *(Lesson 3-3)*

31. Measure this segment to the nearest millimeter. *(Lessons 3-1,3-3)*

32. One centimeter is what percent of a meter? *(Lessons 2-7,3-3)*

33. What is 50% of 50? *(Lesson 2-6)*

34. Convert 0.136 to a fraction in lowest terms. *(Lesson 2-7)*

35. On every cereal box, the amount of protein per serving is listed.
   a. Find a cereal box and how much protein per serving is listed.
   b. Is this amount given in U.S. units, metric units, or both?
   c. Is the weight of the box given in U.S. units, metric units, or both?

36. Examine the computer program in Question 40 of Lesson 3-3. Modify that program so that it converts a length in inches to a length in centimeters. Run your program a few times with values of your own choosing.

Measuring Angles

Think of rays of light coming from the sun. Each **ray** has the same starting point, called its **endpoint.** Each ray goes forever in a particular direction. Only a part of any ray can be drawn.

Identified below are rays *SB* and *SA*, written $\overrightarrow{SB}$ and $\overrightarrow{SA}$. Two other rays are not identified.

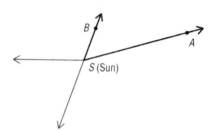

The union of two rays with the same endpoint is an **angle.** The rays are the **sides of the angle.** The endpoint is the **vertex of the angle.** The sides of an angle go on forever; you can draw only part of them.

$\angle$ is the symbol for angle. This symbol was first used by William Oughtred in 1657.

The angle above may be written as $\angle S$, $\angle ASB$, or $\angle BSA$. When three letters are used, the middle letter is the vertex. If an angle shares its vertex with any other angle, you must use three letters to name it. For instance, in the first drawing above, you should not name any angle $\angle S$. Which angle you meant would not be clear.

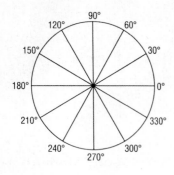

Over 2500 years ago, the Babylonians wrote numbers in a system based on the number 60. So they measured with units based on 60. Even today we use Babylonian ideas to measure time. That is why there are 60 minutes in an hour and 60 seconds in a minute. We also use Babylonian ideas in measuring angles.

The Babylonians divided a circle into 360 equally spaced units, which we call **degrees.** (The number 360 = 6 × 60 and is an estimate of the number of days in a year.)

An instrument that looks like half of the circle at left is the **protractor.** The protractor is the most common instrument used for measuring angles. Many protractors look like the one drawn below. Because protractors cover only half of a circle, the degree measures on the outside go only from 0° to 180°.

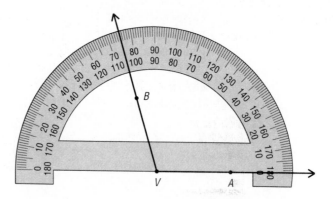

Every protractor has a segment connecting the 0° mark on one side to the 180° mark on the other. This segment is on the *base line* of the protractor. The middle point of this segment is called the *center* of the protractor. In the drawings above and on page 119 this point is named *V*. *V* is usually marked by a hole, an arrow, or a + sign. There are almost always two curved scales on the outside of the protractor. One goes from 0° to 180°. The other goes from 180° to 0°.

To measure an angle with a protractor:

(1) Put the center of the protractor on the vertex of the angle.

(2) Turn the protractor so that one side of the angle is on the base line and the other side of the angle is beneath the curved scales.

(3) The measure of the angle is one of the two numbers crossed by the other side of the angle. Which of the two numbers? The first side of the angle crossed one of the scales at 0°. Pick the number on that scale.

On page 118, the measure of angle *AVB* is 105°. We write m∠*AVB* = 105°. Below, m∠*CVD* = 55°.

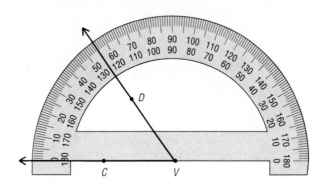

Questions

Covering the Reading

In 1–3, use the angle at left.

1. Name the sides.

2. Name the vertex.

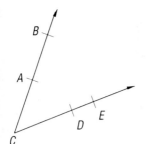

3. Which of the following are correct names for the angle?
   (a) ∠*ACE* (b) ∠*C* (c) ∠*ECA* (d) ∠*CBD*
   (e) ∠*ECB* (f) ∠*DBC* (g) ∠*ACD* (h) ∠*ACB*

4. Why did the Babylonians measure with units based on 60?

5. Name two things measured today using ideas of the Babylonians.

In 6–9, use the drawing.

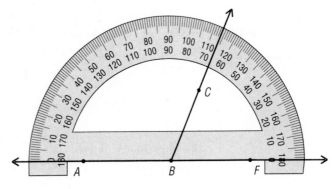

6. Name the base line of this protractor.

7. What point is at the center of this protractor?

8. What is the measure of ∠*ABC*?

9. What is the measure of ∠*CBF*?

10. m∠*AVB* stands for the __?__ of __?__ *AVB*.

In 11–14, use a protractor. Measure the angle to the nearest degree. (You may have to copy the angles and extend their sides.)

11.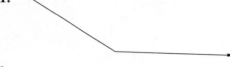

12.

13. 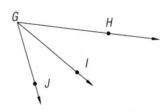   **14.**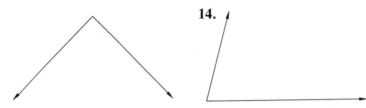

15. Who first used the symbol ∠ for an angle and when was this done?

16. Point X is on $\overrightarrow{UV}$ drawn here. *True* or *false*: $\overrightarrow{UX}$ is the same ray as $\overrightarrow{UV}$.

17. Which angle below has the largest angle measure, ∠JGI, ∠IGH, or ∠JGH?

18. How many angles with vertex E are drawn below? (Be careful. Many students' answers are too low.)

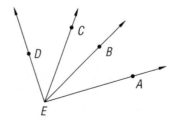

120

19. Draw a 60° angle.   **20.** Draw a 160° angle.

In 21–24, copy the drawing at right, but make your drawing larger. Using your protractor, draw the ray with endpoint P in the given direction.

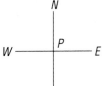

21. A tornado is seen 10° South of West.

22. A UFO is seen 5° East of North.

23. A whale is sighted 15° South of East.

24. A tanker is observed 20° North of West.

Review

25. While driving through Canada, Kirsten saw the sign below. About how many miles away was Toronto? *(Lesson 3-4)*

26. Convert 12 liters into quarts. *(Lesson 3-4)*

27. Convert 82 mm to meters. *(Lesson 3-3)*

28. In the metric system, the amount of water in a bathtub could be measured in __?__. *(Lesson 3-3)*

29. In the U.S. system, the amount of water in a bathtub could be measured in __?__. *(Lesson 3-2)*

30. Write 41.6 million in scientific notation. *(Lesson 2-3)*

31. Roy found that 51 out of 68 people he polled liked the posters he made. Rewrite $\frac{51}{68}$ as a fraction in lowest terms. *(Lesson 1-10)*

Exploration

32. Angles are not always measured in degrees. Two other units for measuring angles are the grad and the radian. Find out something about at least one of these units.

3-6

Kinds of Angles

Angles can be classified by their measures. If the measure of an angle is 90°, the angle is called a **right angle.** Some right angles are drawn below. The sides of this page form right angles at the corners. Many streets intersect at right angles.

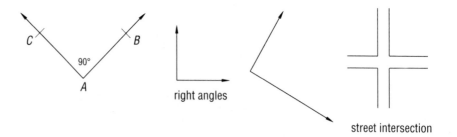

right angles

street intersection

Rays, segments, or lines that form right angles are called **perpendicular.** Above, $\overrightarrow{AC}$ is perpendicular to $\overrightarrow{AB}$. The streets drawn above are also perpendicular. Each long side of this page is perpendicular to each short side.

If the measure of an angle is between 0° and 90°, the angle is called an **acute angle.** An **obtuse angle** is an angle whose measure is between 90° and 180°. Most of the time you can tell whether an angle is acute or obtuse just by looking. If you are unsure, you can measure.

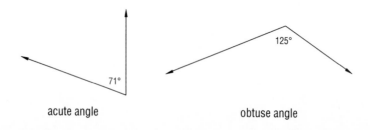

acute angle

obtuse angle

A **triangle** gets its name because it contains parts of three angles. The triangle *PQR* drawn here has angles *P*, *Q*, and *R*. Angle *P* is obtuse while angles *Q* and *R* are acute. △*AOK* below (△ is the symbol for triangle) is called a **right triangle** because one of its angles is a right angle.

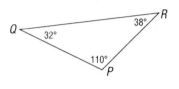

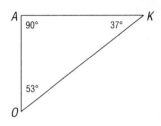

Questions

Covering the Reading

In 1–5, give a definition for the phrase.

1. acute angle

2. obtuse angle

3. right angle

4. right triangle

5. perpendicular lines

In 6–9, an angle has the given measure. Is it acute, right, or obtuse?

6. 40°　　　　**7.** 9°　　　　**8.** 140°　　　　**9.** 90°

In 10–13, without measuring, tell whether the angle looks acute, right, or obtuse.

10.　　　　**11.**　　　　**12.**　　　　**13.**

14. *Multiple choice*　Which triangle looks like a right triangle?

(a)　　　　(b)　　　　(c)　　　　(d)

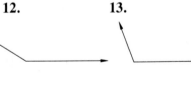

15. In which choice of Question 14 do two segments seem to be perpendicular?

In 16 and 17, use the figure. **a.** Tell whether the angle is acute or obtuse. **b.** Give the measure of the angle.

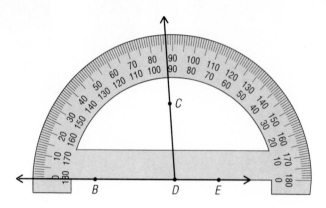

16. ∠CDE   **17.** ∠CDB

18. Find two examples of right angles different from those mentioned in this lesson.

In 19–21, the picture is a closeup of the markings on a giraffe. **a.** Tell whether the angle is acute, right, or obtuse. **b.** Measure the angle.

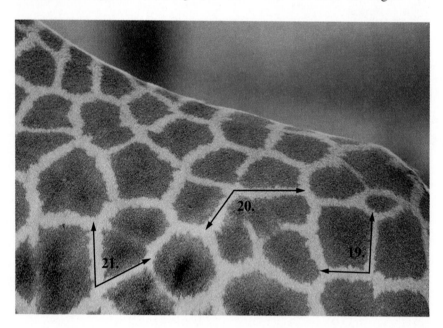

22. Name the type of angle and give the measure of the angle formed by the minute and hour hands of a watch at:
a. 1:00 **b.** 4:00 **c.** 9:00 **d.** 6:30 (Be careful!)

23. Copy the line. Then draw a line perpendicular to the given line.
a.   **b.**

24. Find the measures of the three angles of △XYZ. (Hint: Copy the triangle and extend the lines of the sides before measuring.)

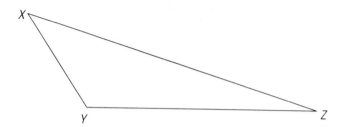

Review

25. Tungsten wire four ten-thousandths of an inch in diameter is used to make filaments for light bulbs. *(Lessons 1-8, 2-9)*
   a. Write this number as a decimal.
   b. Write this number in scientific notation.

26. According to one survey, teenage boys spend an average of 32% of their allowance on food. Teenage girls spend 26% on the average. If a boy and girl each receive $20, how much more does the boy spend on food? *(Lesson 2-6)*

27. Measure the longest side of triangle *XYZ* above: **a.** to the nearest $\frac{1}{2}$ inch, **b.** to the nearest $\frac{1}{4}$ inch. *(Lesson 3-1)*

28. Complete each statement by using a reasonable metric unit.
   a. In one day we rode 40 _____ on our bikes. *(Lesson 3-3)*
   b. A cup can hold about 0.24 _____ of water.
   c. The meat she ate weighed 350 _____.

29. Use <, =, or > to complete each relationship. *(Lessons 1-6, 3-3, 3-4)*
   a. 2 meters _____ 1 yard
   b. 1 kg _____ 10,000 g
   c. 1 kg _____ $4\frac{2}{3}$ lb
   d. 2 liter _____ 1 gal
   e. 2 in. _____ 5.08 cm
   f. 1000 mm _____ 1 m

Exploration

30. A person has acute appendicitis.
   a. What does this mean?
   b. Does this use of the word "acute" have any relation to the idea of acute angle?

31. a. Look up the meaning of the word "obtuse" in the dictionary. What non-mathematical meaning does this word have?
   b. Is the non-mathematical meaning related to the idea of obtuse angle?

32. a. Name a street intersection near your home or school in which the streets do not intersect at right angles.
   b. Approximately what are the measures of the angles formed by the streets?
   c. These kinds of intersections are usually not as safe as right-angle intersections. Is anything done at the intersection you name, to increase its safety?

Measuring Area

Area measures the space inside a two-dimensional (flat) figure. You can think of area as measuring how much is shaded within the figures drawn here.

Regardless of how a figure is shaped, it is customary to measure its area in square units. Recall that a **square** is a four-sided figure with four right angles and four sides of equal length. The common units for measuring area are squares with sides of unit length.

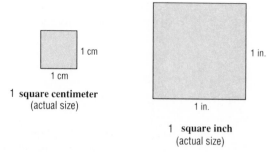

1 cm

1 cm

1 **square centimeter**
(actual size)

1 in.

1 in.

1 **square inch**
(actual size)

A **square kilometer** is a square with each side having a length of one kilometer.

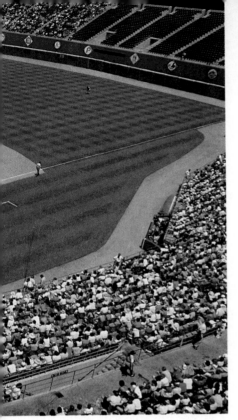

Notice how different area is from length. Each of these figures has shaded area equal to 2 square centimeters. But the lengths of their sides are quite different.

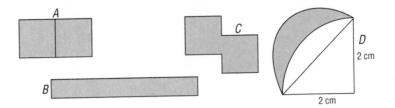

There are three ways to find areas of figures. One way is to count. This will work in Figure A. Another way is to cut and rearrange parts of figures. This will work in figures B and C. But if a figure is complicated, like the shaded part of D, formulas are needed. The simplest formula is that for the area of a square.

Each side has length 5 units.
Counting shows that there are 25 square units.

Each side has length 5.5 units.
Counting shows 25 whole square units,
10 half squares (which equal 5 whole squares)
and an extra quarter square.
This totals 30.25 square units.

Notice that $5^2 = 25$ and $5.5^2 = 30.25$.

The area of a square equals the second power of the length of one of its sides.

For this reason, 5 to the second power, 5^2, is often read "5 squared." Also, for this reason, we write square inches as in.^{2}, square centimeters as cm^2, and square kilometers as km^2.

■ ■ ■ ■ ■ ■ ■ ■ ■

Example Find the area of a city block 220 yards on a side.

Solution Area = $(220 \text{ yd})^2$
= 220 yd × 220 yd
= 48,400 square yards
= 48,400 yd^2

1. What does area measure in a figure?

2. Suppose length is measured in centimeters. Area will most likely be measured in what units?

3. What is a square?

4. Which of the following seem to picture squares?

(a)   (b)   (c)   (d)

5. Give an example of a square you might find outside a mathematics class.

6. A square is a _____-dimensional figure.

7. Name three ways to find the area of a figure.

In 8–10, the length of a side of a square is given. Find the area of the square. Be sure to include the correct unit.

8.   **9.**   **10.**

 2 cm   75 feet   6 km

11. Find the area of a square that is 1.5 inches on a side.

12. 40^2 may be read ''40 to the second power'' or ''40 __?__.''

13. The area of the figure drawn below at the left is how many square inches?

1 sq in. (not to scale)

14. **a.** Make an accurate drawing of 1 square in.
     b. Shade 0.5 sq in.
     c. On another drawing, shade $\frac{1}{4}$ sq in.
     d. On still another drawing, shade 0.6 sq in.

15. Remember there are 3 feet in a yard.
     a. Picture a square yard and split it up into square feet.
     b. How many square feet are in a square yard?

16. A baseball diamond is really square in shape. The distance from home to first is 90 feet. What is the area of the square?

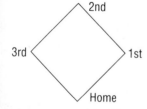

17. The area of a room would most likely be measured in what unit of measure: **a.** in the metric system? **b.** in the U.S. system?

An acre is a unit equal to 43,560 square feet. Use this fact in Questions 18 and 19.

18. How many square feet are in 10 acres?

19. How many square feet are in a half-acre lot?

Review

20. Complete the statement with $<$ or $>$. $13.26 \underline{?} 13\frac{4}{13}$. *(Lessons 1-6, 1-9)*

21. Round 2^{30} to the nearest million. *(Lessons 1-4, 2-2)*

22. Which is larger, 0 or 10^0? *(Lesson 2-8)*

23. A school has 600 students. *(Lesson 2-6)*
　　a. Ten percent of the students is how many students?
　　b. Use your answer in **a.** to find 20%, 40%, and 70% of the student body without doing another percent calculation.

24. Measure the length of this printed line (from the M in "Measure" to the " sign in "Measure") to the nearest half centimeter. *(Lesson 3-1)*

25. The length of the U.S. Grand Prix race is 322.6 kilometers. About how long is this in miles? *(Lesson 3-4)*

26. Sixty kilograms is about how many pounds? *(Lesson 3-4)*

27. Sixty kilograms is about how many grams? *(Lesson 3-3)*

28. Measure this angle to the nearest degree. *(Lesson 3-5)*

29. An angle has measure 19°. Is it acute, right, or obtuse? *(Lesson 3-6)*

Exploration

30. Before exponents appeared as raised decimal numbers, some people wrote them as Roman numerals on the same line as the base. In this notation, 2 to the fifth power would be 2V. Modern exponent symbols first appeared in 1637 in a book by René Descartes. Find out something else about this famous mathematician and philosopher.

31. Most scientific calculators have a $\boxed{x^2}$ key. (On some calculators you must press $\boxed{\text{inv}}$ or $\boxed{\text{F}}$ before pressing this key.) Explore what this key does.

3-8

Measuring Volume

Volume measures space inside a three-dimensional or solid figure. Think of volume as measuring the amount a box, jar, or other container can hold. Or think of volume as telling you how much material is in something that is solid. Whatever the shape of a figure, its volume is usually measured in **cubic units.** A **cube** is a figure with six faces, each face being a square. Sugar cubes, number cubes, and dice are examples. The most common units for measuring volume are cubes with edges of unit length.

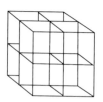

1 cubic inch

In a **cubic meter,** each edge has length 1 meter. Each face is a square with area 1 square meter.

1 cubic centimeter

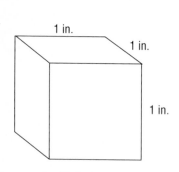

Volume can be calculated by counting cubes, by cutting and pasting cubic units together, or with the help of formulas. At left is a cube with edges of length 2 units. The picture is partially transparent and shows that 8 unit cubes make up the bigger cube.

Notice that volume is quite different from area. If the outside surface of the cube at left is covered by plastic squares, the amount of plastic is found by adding areas. The volume, however, tells how much sand can be poured into the cube.

There are two layers. The top layer has 2×2 or 4 cubes. So does the bottom layer. In all there are $2 \times 2 \times 2$ or 2^3, or 8 cubes. In general:

> The volume of a cube equals the third power of the length of one of its edges.

For this reason, 2^3, 2 to the third power, is often read "2 cubed." Also, for this reason, we write cubic inches as in.^{3}, cubic centimeters as cm^3, cubic meters as m^3, and so on.

You have already learned that the liter is a metric unit of capacity. Capacity is another word for volume. So the **liter** is a unit of volume. It is defined as the volume of a cube that is 10 centimeters on each side.

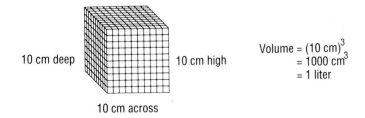

10 cm deep   10 cm high

Volume $= (10 \text{ cm})^3$
$= 1000 \text{ cm}^3$
$= 1$ liter

10 cm across

Soft drinks are often sold in 2-liter bottles. These have a volume of 2000 cm^3.

Questions

Covering the Reading

1. What does volume measure in a 3-dimensional figure?

2. Suppose length is measured in meters. Volume will most likely be measured in what unit?

3. What is a cube?

4. Give an example of a cube you might find outside a math class.

5. A cube is a _?_-dimensional figure.

6. Name three ways to find the volume of a figure.

7. What does the volume of a cube equal?

8. Draw a cube.

In 9–11, find the volume of a cube with an edge of the given length. Use the correct unit in your answer.

9. 4 inches   10. 40 cm   11. 7 yards

12. A liter is defined as the volume of a cube with an edge of length _?_.

13. How many cubic centimeters equal one liter?

14. A 2-liter bottle has a volume of _?_ cubic centimeters.

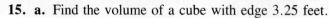

Applying the Mathematics

15. a. Find the volume of a cube with edge 3.25 feet.
   b. The correct answer to part **a** is in millionths of a cubic foot. This is too precise for many uses. Round the answer to the nearest hundredth for a more realistic measure.

16. Remember that there are 12 inches in a foot. You may want to draw a picture to help with these questions.
   a. How many square inches are there in a square foot?
   b. How many cubic inches are there in a cubic foot?

17. Calculate six cubed plus five squared.

18. Arrange from smallest to largest: 1 liter, 89 cubic centimeters, and the volume of a cube with edge 9 cm.

You have learned that the liter (a unit of capacity) and the centimeter (a unit of length) are related. In the metric system, these two units are also related to the mass of water. Specifically,
   1 cm³ of water equals 1 mL of water and weighs 1 gram.

In 19 and 20, use the above information.

19. How much does a liter of water weigh?

20. Suppose an aquarium is a cube 50 cm on a side.
   a. How much water will it hold?
   b. How much will the water weigh in kilograms?
   c. How much will the water weigh in pounds?

Review

21. In the last 6 months of 1987, *TV Guide* sold 16,969,260 copies, the most of any magazine. *(Lessons 1-4, 2-3)*
   a. Round this number to the nearest hundred thousand.
   b. Estimate how many copies would be sold over the entire year.
   c. Write your estimate in scientific notation.

22. *Multiple choice*   A 10-year-old boy who weighs 75 kg is likely to be:
   (a) underweight. (b) about the right weight. (c) overweight.
   (Lesson 3-3)

23. Write 3.4×10^{-4} as **a.** a decimal **b.** a fraction in lowest terms.
   (Lessons 2-7, 2-8)

24. Which is not an integer: -4, $\frac{8}{4}$, 5^2, 0, or $\frac{1}{2}$?
   (Lessons 1-5, 1-8, 2-2)

10 cm

25. Give the area of the square drawn at left. *(Lesson 3-7)*

26. 10^3 meters is how many kilometers? *(Lessons 2-2, 3-3)*

Exploration

27. You receive a letter from your long-lost aunt and uncle in Japan. They invite you to see their villa, which covers an area of 250 hectares. Is this a lot of land?

Summary

The most common uses of numbers are as counts or measures. In this chapter, measures of length, area, volume or capacity, angle measure, and mass or weight are discussed.

There are two systems of measurement in use today in the United States. One is the metric system. Two basic units in the metric system are the meter for length and the kilogram for mass. The other system is called the U.S. or customary system. It uses inches, feet, and so on, for length; ounces, pound, and so on, for weight;

and pints, quarts, gallons, and so on for capacity. The metric system is generally easier to work with because its units are related to each other by powers of 10; so it is closely related to the decimal system.

Units for area are usually squares based on units of length. Units for volume are usually cubes based on units of length. The degree, the common unit for angle measure, is based on splitting the circle. It is used in both the metric system and the U.S. system. Angles can be classified by their measure.

Vocabulary

You should be able to give a general description and a specific example of each of the following ideas.

Lesson 3-1
centimeter, inch

Lesson 3-2
foot (ft), yard (yd), mile (mi), inch (in.)
ounce (oz), pound (lb), short ton
pint, quart (qt), gallon (gal)

Lesson 3-3
international or metric system of measurement
milli-, centi-, kilo-
meter (m)
gram (g)
liter (L)

Lesson 3-4
is approximately equal to ($\approx$)
Estimation Principle

Lesson 3-5
ray, $\overrightarrow{AB}$, endpoint of ray, vertex of an angle
angle, sides of an angle, $\angle ABC$, m$\angle ABC$
degree (°)
protractor

Lesson 3-6
right angle, acute angle, obtuse angle
perpendicular
right triangle

Lesson 3-7
area
square, square units
in.^{2}, cm^2, km^2, and so on

Lesson 3-8
volume
cube, cubic units
in.^{3}, cm^3, m^3, and so on

Progress Self-Test

Take this test as you would take a test in class. You will need a protractor, a ruler, and a calculator. Then check your work with the solutions in the Selected Answers section in the back of the book.

1. Measure this segment to the nearest eighth of an inch.

   _____

2. Draw a segment with length 6.4 centimeters.

3. Give the exact relationship between inches and centimeters.

4. Name the appropriate metric unit for measuring the weight or mass of a person.

5. How many feet are there in $\frac{3}{4}$ of a mile?

6. How many quarts are there in 1 gallon?

7. A kiloton is how many tons?

8. 1103 mg = _?_ g.

9. 5 centimeters = _?_ meters.

10. 3.2 meters ≈ _?_ inches.

11. 4 kilometers ≈ _?_ miles.

12. Measure angle C to the nearest degree.

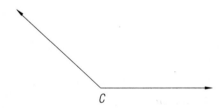

13. Measure ∠ MNL to the nearest degree.

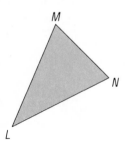

14. An acute angle has measure between _?_ and _?_ degrees.

15. An angle has measure 90°. Is this angle right, acute, or obtuse?

16. Draw an angle with a measure of 123°.

17. Find the area of square with side 4.5 inches.

18. If the side of a square is measured in cm, the area will probably be measured in _?_.

19. How are liters and cubic centimeters related?

20. Which angles of the triangle below seem to be acute, which right, which obtuse?

21. Give the volume of the cube drawn below.

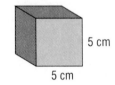

22. A rug is in the shape of a square 6 feet on a side. How many square yards are in the rug?

23. To convert kilograms to pounds, what estimate can be used?

24. Which is larger, 10 quarts or 9 liters?

25. The U.S. system is derived from a measuring system from what country?

Chapter Review

Questions on **SPUR** Objectives

SPUR stands for **S**kills, **P**roperties, **U**ses, and **R**epresentations.
The Chapter Review questions are grouped according to the
SPUR Objectives for this chapter.

SKILLS deals with the procedures used to get answers.

▐ **Objective A:** *Measure lengths to the nearest inch, half inch, quarter inch, or eighth of an inch, or to the nearest centimeter or tenth of a centimeter.* *(Lesson 3-1)*

1. Measure the length of this horizontal segment to the nearest quarter inch.

———————————

2. Measure the length of the above segment to the nearest tenth of a centimeter.

3. Measure the length of the segment below to the nearest centimeter.

4. Measure the length of the segment below to the nearest eighth of an inch.

▐ **Objective B:** *Measure an angle to the nearest degree using a protractor.* *(Lesson 3-5)*

5. Measure angle B below.

6. Measure angle C below.

7. Measure ∠ADC below.

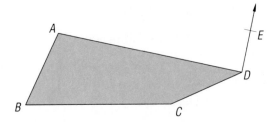

▐ **Objective C:** *Distinguish between acute, right, and obtuse angles by sight.* *(Lesson 3-6)*

Use the figure under Objective B.

8. Which angles seem to be acute?

9. Does ∠CDE seem to be obtuse, acute, or right?

10. Name all angles that seem to be right angles.

▐ **Objective D:** *Find the area of a square, given the length of one side.* *(Lesson 3-7)*

11. Find the area of the square below.

12. Find the area of a square with side 6.5 in.

13. If length is measured in meters, area is most easily measured in what unit?

▐ **Objective E:** *Find the volume of a cube, given the length of one side.* *(Lesson 3-8)*

14. Find the volume of a cube with one side of length 4 mm.

15. To the nearest integer, find the volume of a cube with edge of length 3.75 in.

PROPERTIES deal with the principles behind the mathematics.

■ **Objective F:** *Know the relationships in the U.S. system within units of length, weight, and capacity.* *(Lesson 3-2)*

16. Give a relationship between pints and quarts.

17. How many ounces are in 1 pound?

18. How are feet and miles related?

■ **Objective G:** *Know the relationships in the metric system within units of length, weight, and capacity.* *(Lessons 3-3, 3-8)*

19. What is the meaning of the prefix milli-?

20. How are centimeters and liters related?

21. 1 kilogram = _?_ grams.

■ **Objective H:** *Know the relationships between important units in the metric and U.S. systems of measurement.* *(Lesson 3-4)*

22. Give an approximate relationship between pounds and kilograms.

23. How are centimeters and inches related?

24. Which is larger, a mile or a kilometer?

25. Which is larger, a meter or a yard?

■ **Objective I:** *State and apply the Estimation Principle.* *(Lesson 3-4)*

26. State the Estimation Principle.

27. To convert liters to quarts, what estimate can be used?

USES deal with applications of mathematics in real situations.

■ **Objective J:** *Give appropriate units for measuring mass, length, and capacity in the U.S. or metric system of measurement.* *(Lessons 3-2, 3-3)*

28. Give an appropriate unit in each system for measuring the distance from New York to London, England.

29. Give an appropriate unit in the metric system for measuring the length of your foot.

30. Give an appropriate unit in the metric system for measuring the weight of a postage stamp.

31. Give an appropriate unit in the U.S. system for measuring the capacity of a fish tank.

■ **Objective K:** *Convert within the U.S. system of measurement.* *(Lesson 3-2)*

32. How many inches are in 2.5 yards?

33. Convert 7.3 gallons to quarts.

34. How many pounds are there in 3 short tons?

35. How many feet are in 660 yards?

■ **Objective L:** *Convert within the metric system.* *(Lesson 3-3)*

36. Convert 200 cm to meters.

37. Convert 5 km to meters.

38. Convert 265 ml to liters.

39. Convert 60 mg to g.

■ **Objective M:** *Convert between the U.S. and metric systems.* *(Lesson 3-4)*

40. How many centimeters are in 2 feet?

41. In a guide book the distance between Paris and London is given as 872 km. How many miles is this?

42. How many quarts are in 6.8 liters?

43. Convert 100 kg to pounds.

Objective N: *Identify and measure angles in pictures.* *(Lessons 3-5, 3-6)*

44. Measure $\angle ADC$ to the nearest degree.

45. Name an obtuse angle in this drawing.

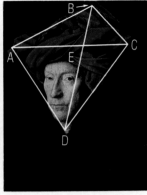

Jan van Eyck, *Portrait of a Man in a Red Turban*

Objective O: *Find areas of squares or volumes of cubes in real contexts.* *(Lessons 3-7, 3-8)*

46. A square table has a side of length 2.5 feet. Will a square tablecloth with an area of 6 square feet cover the table?

47. How much paint can be put into a cubic container 12 cm on a side?

REPRESENTATIONS deal with pictures, graphs, or objects that illustrate concepts.

Objective P: *Draw a line segment of a given length.* *(Lesson 3-1)*

48. Draw a line segment with length 3.5 cm.

49. Draw a line segment with length $2\frac{1}{4}$ inches.

50. Draw a vertical line segment with length 4.375 inches.

Objective Q: *Draw an angle with a given measure.* *(Lesson 3-5)*

51. Draw an angle with a measure of 90°, in which neither side lies on a horizontal line.

52. Draw an angle with a measure of 37°.

53. Draw an angle with a measure of 145°.

HISTORY

Objective R: *Give countries and approximate dates of origin of current measuring ideas.* *(Lessons 3-1, 3-3, 3-5)*

54. When and where did the metric system originate?

55. How was the length of a yard first determined?

56. Our system for measuring angles is based on measuring done by what people?

Uses of Variables

Descartes

Some number patterns are difficult to describe in words. To make things easier, mathematicians invent symbols and define new words. The table below shows some of the more important symbols of arithmetic.

Operation	Symbol	Name for symbol	Inventor of symbol (Year)	Name for result
addition	+	plus	Johann Widman (1498)	sum
subtraction	−	minus	Johann Widman (1498)	difference
multiplication	×	times	William Oughtred (1631)	product
	•	dot	Gottfried Leibniz (1698)	product
	*	asterisk		product
division	− as in $\frac{2}{3}$	bar or vinculum	al-Hassar (1050)	fraction
	$\overline{)}$	into	Michael Stifel (1544)	quotient
	÷	divided by	Johann Rahn (1659)	quotient
	: as in 2:3	colon	Gottfried Leibniz (1684)	ratio
	/ as in 2/3	slash	Manuel A. Valdes (1784)	fraction
powering	3 as in 2^3	exponent	René Descartes (1637)	power
	↑ as in 2 ↑ 3	up arrow	?	power
	** as in 2**3	double asterisk	?	power

Used in arithmetic and on calculators: +   −   ×   ÷   exponent
Used in algebra: +   −   •   bar   exponent
Used in computer languages: +   −   *   /   ** or ↑ or ^ (not listed above)
$\overline{)}$ is used only in long division;   : is used for ratios and instead of ÷ in some countries

4-1

Order of Operations

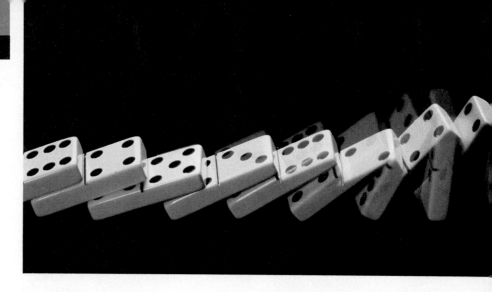

Names or symbols for numbers and operations make up **numerical expressions.** The **value** of a numerical expression is found by working out the arithmetic. Working out the arithmetic is called **evaluating the expression.** For example, the seven expressions here all have the same value, 2.

$$2, \quad 5 - 3, \quad \tfrac{20}{10}, \quad 5 \times 2 - 8, \quad 2^1, \quad 347.8 - 345.8, \quad 10^0 + 10^0$$

On page 139 is a table of symbols for the operations of arithmetic and algebra. Although there are many symbols, each symbol has a precise meaning. This is important, because the meaning of a numerical expression should be the same for everybody.

But recall Lesson 1-7, where you were asked to evaluate $85 + 9 \times 2$ on your calculator. You keyed in:

$$85 \; \boxed{+} \; 9 \; \boxed{\times} \; 2 \; \boxed{=}.$$

If you have a scientific calculator, the calculator multiplied first and displayed 103 as the value. A nonscientific calculator will probably add first; it will wind up with 188.

That can be confusing. Here is another confusing situation. Suppose you have \$25, spend \$10, and then spend \$4. You will wind up with

$$25 - 10 - 4 \text{ dollars.}$$

The situation tells you that the value of this expression is \$11. But someone else evaluating $25 - 10 - 4$ might first subtract the 4 from the 10. This would leave $25 - 6$, or \$19.

Calculating powers can also be confusing. Consider the expression 2×3^4. Some people might do the multiplication first, getting 6^4, which equals 1296. Others might first calculate the 4th power of 3, getting 2×81, which equals 162. These values aren't even close to each other.

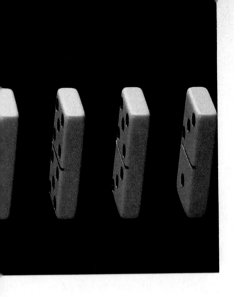

To avoid confusion, rules are needed. These rules tell the order in which operations should be done. These rules have been developed only in this century, but they are now used worldwide.

Order of Operations:

1. Calculate all powers in order, from left to right.
2. Then do multiplications or divisions in order, from left to right.
3. Then do additions or subtractions in order, from left to right.

Example 1 Evaluate $3 + 4 \times 5$.

Solution Multiply before adding. $3 + 4 \times 5 = 3 + 20 = 23$.

Example 2 Evaluate $8 \times 12 - 3 \times 12$.

Solution Do *both* multiplications before the subtraction. Work from left to right.

$$8 \times 12 - 3 \times 12$$
$$= \quad 96 \quad - \quad 36$$
$$= \qquad 60$$

Example 3 Evaluate $100 \div 20 \times 2$.

Solution Multiplications and divisions have equal priority. So work from left to right. This means do the division first.

$$100 \div 20 \times 2$$
$$= \quad 5 \quad \times 2$$
$$= \qquad 10$$

Example 4   Which value is correct for the expression 2×3^4 discussed on page 140?

Solution   Calculate the power before doing the multiplication.

$$2 \times 3^4$$
$$= 2 \times 81$$
$$= 162$$

In 3×10^6, the rules for order of operations say to calculate the power first. This is exactly what you would do in scientific notation. So scientific notation follows these rules.

You should check whether your calculator follows all the rules for order of operations. The following example combines three operations and provides a good test of your calculator.

Example 5   Evaluate $10 + 3 \times 4^2$.

Solution   First evaluate the power. $10 + 3 \times 4^2 = 10 + 3 \times 16$
Now multiply. $= 10 + 48$
Now add. $= 58$

Questions

Covering the Reading

1. $13.004 - 3.976$ is an example of a __?__ expression.

2. What is the value of the expression in Question 1?

3. Finding the value of an expression is called __?__ the expression.

4. Why is there a need to have rules for order of operations?

In 5–8, an expression contains only the two given operations. Which one should you perform first?

5. division and addition

6. a power and subtraction

7. multiplication and division

8. addition and subtraction

In 9–14, evaluate each expression.

9. $55 - 4 \times 7$

10. $6 + .03 \times 10$

11. $200 \div 10 \div 2$

12. $1 \div 9 + 1 \div 7$

13. $1000 - 3 \times 17^2$

14. $4^2 + 8^3$

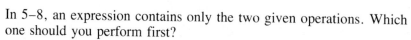

In 15–22, the table on the first page of this chapter will help you.

15. Name three symbols that are used for multiplication, and tell where each is used most often.

16. Translate "three divided by nine" into symbols in 5 different ways.

17. How many years ago were the symbols we use for addition and multiplication invented?

18. When you add, what is the result called?

19. When you subtract, what is the result called?

20. When you multiply, what is the result called?

21. When you divide, what is the result called?

22. Why do mathematicians invent symbols?

Applying the Mathematics

23. Calculate the sum of 11 and 4.2.

24. Calculate the product of 6 and 0.3.

25. Calculate 2 divided by 4.

26. Calculate the difference when 0.87 is subtracted from 500.

In 27–30, each expression is written in a computer language. Evaluate.

27. 2 * 3 + 8

28. 120 − 3 * 4/4

29. 200/2 * 10 − 4

30. 17 + 16 * 3 ↑ 2

31. *Multiple Choice* Which is largest?
(a) the sum of .1 and .2
(b) the product of .1 and .2
(c) .1 divided by .2
(d) the second power of .1

32. Find two numbers whose sum is less than their product.

33. In which expression below does order of operations make *no* difference?

87 − 12 + 3   87 + 12 − 3

34. Does the angle below appear to be acute, right, or obtuse? *(Lesson 3-6)*

35. Measure the angle to the nearest degree. *(Lesson 3-5)*

36. Draw a line segment whose length is 14.3 cm. *(Lesson 3-1)*

37. Write 0.00000 00000 06543 in scientific notation. *(Lesson 2-9)*

38. Some insurance companies give a discount of 15% on homeowner's or renter's insurance if smoke detectors are installed. Suppose you need 3 smoke detectors at $14.99 each. If the insurance bill is $250 a year, will you save money by installing smoke detectors? (They should be installed whether or not you save money.) *(Lesson 2-6)*

39. Find the volume of a cube with an edge of length 5 inches. *(Lesson 3-8)*

40. Mathematics is a worldwide language. Mathematicians from different countries usually use the same symbols. Name some symbols outside mathematics that are used throughout the world.

41. What is, or was, Esperanto?

42. a. Ask a computer to evaluate the expressions of Questions 27–30 on page 143. (Hint: For Question 27, you should type ?2*3 + 8 and press RETURN.)
   b. Does your computer follow the rules for order of operations stated in this lesson? If not, what rules does it seem to follow?

4-2

Describing Patterns with Variables

A **pattern** is a general idea for which there are many examples. An example of a pattern is called an **instance**. Here are three instances of a pattern with percent.

$$5\% = 5 \times .01$$
$$43.2\% = 43.2 \times .01$$
$$78\% = 78 \times .01$$

In Lesson 2–6, this pattern was described using English words:

The percent sign % means to multiply the number in front of it by $\frac{1}{100}$.

But there is a simpler way to describe this pattern.

$$n\% = n \cdot .01$$

The letter n is called a **variable.** *A variable is a symbol that can stand for any one of a set of numbers or other objects.* Here n can stand for any number. Variables are usually letters. Using $\times$ for multiplication would be confused with using the letter X. So the raised dot $\cdot$ is used instead.

Descriptions with variables have two major advantages over descriptions using words. They look like the instances. Also, they are shorter than the verbal descriptions.

Here are three instances of another pattern.

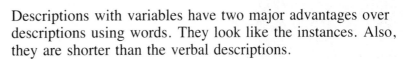

$$\frac{3}{3} = 1 \qquad \frac{657.2}{657.2} = 1 \qquad \frac{2/5}{2/5} = 1$$

A description using words for the pattern is: If a number is divided by itself, the quotient is equal to one. Another description is: If the numerator and denominator of a fraction are the same number, the value of the fraction is 1. The description with variables is shorter and looks like the instances.

$$\frac{t}{t} = 1$$

We could have used any other letter or symbol in place of t.

Some patterns need more than one variable to be described. Here is a pattern that requires two different variables. You've seen this pattern before.

$$1.43 + 2.9 = 2.9 + 1.43$$
$$12 + 37 = 37 + 12$$
$$\frac{8}{3} + \frac{7}{5} = \frac{7}{5} + \frac{8}{3}$$

Description using variables:
$$a + b = b + a$$

A correct description of a pattern must work for *all* instances. This pattern works for all numbers. It works whether you use decimals or fractions. It is so important that it has a special name you may already know: the commutative property of addition. You will study this property in the next chapter.

Patterns with words can also be described with variables. Here are four instances of a pattern.

One person has 2 eyes.
Two people have four eyes in all.
Three people have 6 eyes in all.
Four people have 8 eyes in all.

To describe this pattern with variables, rewrite the instances in a convenient way.

1 person has $2 \cdot 1$ eyes.
2 people have $2 \cdot 2$ eyes in all.
3 people have $2 \cdot 3$ eyes in all.
4 people have $2 \cdot 4$ eyes in all.

Now a description is easy. It will look like the instances. Let p be any natural number.

p people have $2 \cdot p$ eyes in all.

Elementary algebra is the study of variables and the operations of arithmetic with variables. Algebra is generally considered to have begun in 1591. In that year, François Viète (Fraw swah Vee yet), a French mathematician, first used variables to describe patterns. Viète's work quickly led to a great deal more mathematics being invented. Within 100 years, the ideas behind almost all of algebra and calculus has been discovered. (Notice how many symbols in the chart opening this chapter were invented in the 1600s.) For this reason, Viète is sometimes called the "father of algebra."

Questions

1. What is a variable?

2. What use of variables is explained in this lesson?

3. Name two advantages of using variables to describe patterns.

In 4–7, give three instances of the pattern being described by variables.

4. $x/x = 1$

5. $n\% = n \cdot .01$

6. p people have $2 \cdot p$ eyes.

7. $x + y = y + x$

8. Who was the first person to use variables to describe patterns?

9. What does elementary algebra study?

10. Who is sometimes called the "father of algebra"?

11. *Multiple Choice* Algebra was developed about how many years ago?
    (a) 100   (b) 200   (c) 400   (d) 1700

In 12–14, give three instances of each pattern.

12. $12 + y = 5 + y + 7$

13. $6 \cdot a + 13 \cdot a = 19 \cdot a$

14. If your book is d days overdue, your fine will be $20 + d \cdot 5$ cents.

In 15–17, three instances of a general pattern are given. Describe the pattern using variables. Only one variable is needed for each description.

15. $10 \cdot 0 = 0$
    $8.9 \cdot 0 = 0$
    $\frac{15}{5} \cdot 0 = 0$

16. $5 \cdot 40 = 3 \cdot 40 + 2 \cdot 40$
    $5 \cdot \frac{3}{8} = 3 \cdot \frac{3}{8} + 2 \cdot \frac{3}{8}$
    $5 \cdot 0.2995 = 3 \cdot 0.2995 + 2 \cdot 0.2995$

17. In 3 years, we expect $3 \cdot 100$ more students and $3 \cdot 5$ more teachers.
    In 4 years, we expect $4 \cdot 100$ more students and $4 \cdot 5$ more teachers.
    In 1 year, we expect 100 more students and 5 more teachers.

18. Give three instances of the pattern $a \cdot b = b \cdot a$.

19. Three instances of a pattern are given. Describe the pattern using two variables.
$$\frac{1}{3} + \frac{5}{3} = \frac{1 + 5}{3}$$
$$\frac{11}{3} + \frac{46}{3} = \frac{11 + 46}{3}$$
$$\frac{0}{3} + \frac{7}{3} = \frac{0 + 7}{3}$$

20. Li noticed that $3 + .5$ is not an integer, $4 + .5$ is not an integer, and $7.8 + .5$ is not an integer.
   a. Describe a general pattern of these three instances.
   b. Find an instance where the general pattern is not true.
   c. Explain why the pattern is not always true.

Review

In 21–26, evaluate. *(Lessons 2-2, 2-5, 4-1)*

21. $25\% \times 60 + 40$ **22.** $7 \times 2 \times 8 - 7 \times 2$

23. $60 + 40 \div 4 + 4$ **24.** $12.5 - 11.5 \div 5$

25. $12 - 3^2$ **26.** $170 - 5^3$

In 27 and 28, translate into mathematical symbols. Then evaluate. *(Lessons 1-2, 4-1)*

27. fifty divided by one ten-thousandth

28. the product of five hundred and five hundredths

29. 300 centimeters is how many meters? *(Lesson 3-3)*

Exploration

30. Show that the pattern $x^2 > x$ is false by finding an instance that is not true.

In 31–34, for each sequence of numbers: **a.** Find a pattern. **b.** Describe the pattern you have found in words or with variables. **c.** Write the next term according to your pattern.

31. 6, 12, 18, 24, 30, . . .   **32.** 1, 4, 9, 16, 25, . . .

33. 5, 6, 9, 10, 13, 14, . . .   **34.** $\frac{1}{3}, \frac{8}{3}, \frac{27}{3}, \frac{64}{3}, \frac{125}{3}, \ldots$

4-3

Translating Expressions

Translation from one language to another is an important communication skill.

Recall from Lesson 4-1 that $4 + 52$, $9 - 6 \cdot 7$, and $\frac{1}{6}$ are examples of numerical expressions. If an expression contains a variable alone or with number and operation symbols, it is called an **algebraic expression.** Here are some algebraic expressions.

$$t \qquad 3 \cdot a^2 \qquad \frac{z + 400.3}{5} \qquad m - n + m$$

The value of an algebraic expression depends on what is substituted for the variables.

You know how to translate English into numerical expressions.

English expression	numerical expression
the sum of three and five	$3 + 5$
the product of two tenths and fifty	$.2 \times 50$

In the same way, English expressions can be translated into algebraic expressions.

English expression	algebraic expression
the sum of a number and five	$n + 5$
the product of length and width	$\ell \cdot w$

However, many English expressions can translate into the same algebraic expression. The following chart shows some common English expressions and their translations. Notice that in subtraction you must be careful about the order of the numbers.

English expression	algebraic expression
a number *plus* five the *sum* of a number and 5 a number *increased* by five five *more than* a number *add* five to a number	$a + 5$ or $5 + a$

a number *minus* eight
subtract 8 from a number
8 *less than* a number
a number *decreased by* 8

$\longrightarrow$ $h - 8$

eight *minus* a number
subtract a number from 8
8 *less* a number
8 *decreased by* a number

$\longrightarrow$ $8 - n$

Example 1   A person's annual salary is S. It is increased by $700. What is the new salary?

Solution $S + \$700$

Often you have a choice of what letter to use for a number. We used the letter S in Example 1 because the word "salary" begins with that letter.

Example 2   Esther is five years younger than her sister Ann. If Ann's age is A, what expression stands for Esther's age?

Solution   Esther's age is five less than Ann's.
Five less than A is $A - 5$.

Here are some English expressions for multiplication and division. In division as in subtraction, you must be careful about the order of the numbers.

English expression   **algebraic expression**
two *times* a number
the *product* of two and a number $\longrightarrow$ $2 \cdot m$ or $m \cdot 2$
twice a number

six *divided by* a number
a number *into* six $\longrightarrow$ $\dfrac{6}{u}$

a number *divided by* six
six *into* a number $\longrightarrow$ $\dfrac{u}{6}$

150

Some English expressions combine operations.

■ ■ ■ ■ ■ ■ ■ ■■

Example 3 Translate "five times a number, increased by 3."

> **Solution** Let n stand for the number.
> Five times n is $5 \cdot n$.
> $5 \cdot n$ increased by 3 is $5 \cdot n + 3$, or $3 + 5 \cdot n$.

In Example 3, suppose there were no comma after the word "number." The expression "five times a number increased by 3" would then be ambiguous. *Ambiguous* means the expression has more than one possible meaning. We would not know whether to increase by 3 or to multiply by 5 first.

One of the most important abilities to have in mathematics is the ability to translate from English into mathematics. In this book, in every chapter, you will work at increasing that ability.

Questions

Covering the Reading

1. What is the difference between a numerical expression and an algebraic expression?

In 2–11, let n stand for the number. Then translate the English into an algebraic expression.

2. twice the number

3. three more than the number

4. the number multiplied by four

5. the number less five

6. six less the number

7. seven less than the number

8. eight into the number

9. the number divided by nine

10. the number increased by ten

11. eleven decreased by the number

12. What is the meaning of the word "ambiguous"?

13. Give an example of an English expression that is ambiguous.

In 14 and 15, give three possible English expressions for the algebraic expression.

14. $x + 10$ **15.** $2 - y$

16. Translate "a number times six, decreased by five" into an algebraic expression.

Applying the Mathematics

17. Tell why "fourteen less five plus three" is ambiguous.

In working with a number between 0 and 1, the word "of" is often a signal to multiply. In 18–19, translate into a variable expression. Use t to stand for the number.

18. half of the number

19. 6% of the number

20. Write two algebraic expressions for "a number times itself" using two different operations.

21. A person's salary is currently C dollars a week. Write an expression for the new salary if:
   a. the person gets a raise of $50 a week.
   b. the salary is lowered by $12 a week.
   c. the salary is tripled.

22. "Trebled" means "multiplied by three."
   a. What does "quintupled" mean?
   b. What is a word for "multiplying by four"?

23. Translate the following different ideas into mathematics.
   a. Six is less than a number.
   b. six less than a number
   c. six less a number

24. Why is the "quotient of 2 and 4" an ambiguous phrase?

25. Measure this segment to the nearest eighth of an inch. *(Lesson 3-1)*

26. Give three instances of this pattern. *(Lesson 4-2)*
$$7 \cdot x - 6 \cdot x = x$$

27. Three instances of a general pattern are given. Describe the pattern using one variable. *(Lesson 4-2)*
1 million/1 = 1 million
$10^2/1 = 10^2$
8.3/1 = 8.3

28. Three instances of a general pattern are given. Describe the pattern using two variables. *(Lesson 4-2)*
$$4 + 5 + 12 - 5 = 4 + 12$$
$$\tfrac{1}{2} + 5 + \tfrac{1}{3} - 5 = \tfrac{1}{2} + \tfrac{1}{3}$$
$$1.7 + 5 + 6 - 5 = 1.7 + 6$$

29. It is about 1110 km by air from Paris to Rome. In miles, how far is it? *(Lesson 3-4)*

30. The USSR won about 21% of the 138 medals awarded at the 1988 Winter Olympic Games. This was the most medals awarded to one country during those games. How many medals did the USSR win? *(Lesson 2-6)*

31. a. Draw a triangle with three acute angles.
b. Draw a triangle with a right angle.
c. Draw a triangle with an obtuse angle. *(Lesson 3-6)*

32. Find the volume of a cubical box with 10-foot sides. *(Lesson 3-8)*

33. Write 10^{-5} as **a.** a decimal and **b.** a percent. *(Lessons 2-7, 2-8)*

In 34–37, for each sequence of numbers: **a.** Find a pattern. **b.** Describe the pattern you have found in words or with variables. **c.** Write the next term according to your pattern.

34. 2, 5, 8, 11, 14, . . . **35.** 1, 3, 6, 10, 15, 21, . . .

36. 1, 1, 2, 3, 5, 8, 13, . . . **37.** 4, 7, 13, 25, 49, . . .

4-4

Evaluating Algebraic Expressions

A library charges 20¢ if a book is not returned on time. Added to the fine is 5¢ for each day overdue. Now let n be the number of days overdue. Then the fine is

$20 + 5 \cdot n$ cents.

The fine can now be calculated for *any number* of days overdue. For a book 13 days overdue, just replace n by 13. The fine is

$20 + 5 \cdot 13$ cents,

which computes to 85¢.

We say that 13 days is the **value of the variable** n. We can write $n = 13$. The quantity 85¢ is the **value of the expression.** We have evaluated the expression by letting $n = 13$ and finding the value of the resulting expression.

Example

	Expression	Value of variable	Value of expression
1	$25 - 3 \cdot n$	2	$25 - 3 \cdot 2 = 19$
2	$25 - 3 \cdot n$	8	$25 - 3 \cdot 8 = 1$
3	$x - 9$	500	$500 - 9 = 491$
4	$x - 9$	9.243	$9.243 - 9 = 0.243$
5	$y^4 + 5$	30	$30^4 + 5 = 810,000 + 5$ $= 810,005$
6	$36 - 2^p$	3	$36 - 2^3 = 36 - 8 = 28$

We have been using a dot to stand for multiplication. When one of the numbers being multiplied is a variable, the dot is usually not used.

With · for multiplication	Without ·
$6 \cdot t$	$6t$
$25 - 3 \cdot n$	$25 - 3n$
$4 \cdot A + 5 \cdot B$	$4A + 5B$

The rules for order of operations apply even when the multiplication symbol is absent.

Example

	Expression	Value of variable	Value of expression
7	$6y$	4	$6 \cdot 4 = 24$
8	$20 + 5n$	60	$20 + 5 \cdot 60 = 320$
9	πr^2	5	$\pi \cdot 5^2 = \pi \cdot 25$ $\approx 3.14 \cdot 25$ ≈ 78.5
10	$4A + 3B$	$A = 10, B = 7$	$4 \cdot 10 + 3 \cdot 7 = 61$

In Example 10 the expression contains more than one variable. So you need a value for each variable to get a numerical value for the expression.

Questions

1. *Multiple choice* If $n = 3$, then $5 \cdot n =$
(a) 53   (b) 8   (c) 15   (d) none of these

In 2–5, consider the expression $5 \cdot n$ from Question 1. Identify the:

2. variable

3. value of the variable

4. expression

5. value of the expression

6. What is the more usual way for writing $5 \cdot n$?

7. Do the rules for order of operations apply to variables?

In 8–10, suppose that a book is n days overdue and the fine is $20 + 5n$ cents. Calculate the fine for a book that is:

8. 1 day overdue

9. 6 days overdue

10. 20 days overdue

11. Which example of this lesson calculates the fine for a book that is 60 days overdue?

In 12–15, evaluate each expression when d is 5.

12. $d + d$

13. $88 - 4d$

14. $2 + 3d$

15. $d\%$

In 16–19, give the value of each expression when $m = 5$ and $x = 9$.

16. $4m + 7x$

17. $2mx$

18. $1.6x + m^3$

19. πx^2

Applying the Mathematics

20. Let A be an age between 1 and 7 years. A boy of age A weighs, on the average, about $17 + 5A$ pounds.
 a. What is the average weight for 6-year-old boys?
 b. What is the average weight for 2-year-old boys?
 c. For each additional year of age, by how much does the average weight change?

21. Suppose x is 100 and y is 25.
 a. Evaluate $xy - yx$.
 b. Will the answer to part **a** change if the values of x and y are changed? Why or why not?

22. a. Evaluate $2v + 1$ when v is 1, 2, 3, 4, and 5.
 b. Your answers to part **a** should form a pattern. Describe the pattern in English.

In 23–25, **a.** translate into an algebraic expression. **b.** Evaluate that expression when the number has the value 10.

23. eight less than five times a number

24. the product of a number and 4, increased by nine

25. the third power of a number

Review

In 26 and 27, three instances of a pattern are given. Describe the pattern using one variable. *(Lesson 4-2)*

26.
$$5 + 0 = 5$$
$$43.0 + 0 = 43.0$$
$$1/2 + 0 = 1/2$$

27.
$$1 \times 60\% = 60\%$$
$$1 \times 2 = 2$$
$$1 \times 1 = 1$$

28. Four horses have 4 · 4 legs, 2 · 4 ears, and 4 tails. *(Lesson 4-2)*
   a. Six horses have 4 · 6 legs, 2 · ___?___ ears, and ___?___ tails.
   b. Eleven horses have ___?___ legs, ___?___ ears, and ___?___ tails.
   c. *h* horses have ___?___ legs, ___?___ ears, and ___?___ tails.

29. *Multiple choice*   Which is largest? *(Lesson 4-3)*
   (a) the sum of 10 and 1   (b) the product of 10 and 1
   (c) 10 divided by 1   (d) 10 to the first power

30. What is the metric prefix meaning $\frac{1}{1000}$? *(Lesson 3-3)*

31. Which two of these refer to the same numbers? *(Lessons 1-1, 1-5)*
   (a) the whole numbers   (b) the natural numbers
   (c) the integers   (d) the positive integers

32. Convert $\frac{2.4}{10.24}$ into a simple fraction in lowest terms. *(Lesson 2-7)*

Exploration

33. A library decides to charge *m* cents for an overdue book and *A* more cents for every day the book is overdue. What will be the fine for a book that is *d* days overdue?

34. Computers can evaluate algebraic expressions. Here is a program that evaluates a particular expression.

```
10   PRINT "GIVE VALUE OF YOUR VARIABLE"
20   INPUT X
30   V = 30 * X − 12
40   PRINT "VALUE OF EXPRESSION IS", V
50   END
```

   a. What expression does the above program evaluate?
   b. What value does the computer give if you input 3.5 for X?
   c. Modify the program so that it evaluates the expression
      $25X + X^4$ and test your program when X = 1, X = 2, and X = 17. What values do you get?

4-5

Parentheses

These chicks are working from inside their shells to free themselves. This is akin to what is done when working with parentheses.

Consider the expression $3 + 4 \cdot 5$. By order of operations, the multiplication will be done first.

$$3 + 4 \cdot 5$$
$$= 3 + 20$$
$$= 23$$

But what if you want to do the addition first? Then you can use **parentheses.**

Parentheses have priority.

$$(3 + 4) \cdot 5$$
$$= (7) \cdot 5$$
$$= 35$$

Parentheses around a single number can always be dropped. $(7) = 7$. Many students and teachers find it useful to write the steps of calculations vertically as we have in the examples below. This helps them avoid errors and makes their work easy to follow.

■ ■ ■ ■ ■ ■ ■ ■

Example 1   Simplify $7 + 9 \cdot (2 + 3)$.

Solution   Work inside parentheses first.
$$= 7 + 9 \cdot (5)$$
$$= 7 + 9 \cdot 5$$
Now the usual order of operations applies.
$$= 7 + 45$$
$$= 52$$

■ ■ ■ ■ ■ ■ ■ ■ ■

Example 2   Evaluate $36 - (17 - n)$ when $n = 4$.

Solution   First substitute 4 for n. $36 - (17 - 4)$
Work inside parentheses. $= 36 - (13)$
Drop the parentheses. $= 36 - 13$
                                                                $= 23$

Parentheses even have priority over taking powers.

■ ■ ■ ■ ■ ■ ■ ■ ■

Example 3   Evaluate $6 + 5 \cdot (4x)^3$ when $x = 2$.

Solution   First substitute 2 for x. $6 + 5 \cdot (4 \cdot 2)^3$
Work inside parentheses. $= 6 + 5 \cdot (8)^3$
Powering comes next. $= 6 + 5 \cdot 512$
Multiplication comes next. $= 6 + 2560$
Addition comes last. $= 2566$

The dot for multiplication is usually deleted with parentheses.
For the expression of Example 3, it is more common to see
$6 + 5(4x)^3$. The 5 next to the parentheses signals multiplication.

■ ■ ■ ■ ■ ■ ■ ■ ■

Example 4   Evaluate $(y + 15)(11 - 2y)$ when $y = 3$.

Solution 1   Substitute 3 for y. $(3 + 15)(11 - 2 \cdot 3)$
Work inside each ( ), following the usual order of operations.
                                                            $= (18)(11 - 6)$
No operation sign between)(means multiplication.
                                                            $= 18 \cdot 5$
                                                            $= 90$

Most scientific calculators have parentheses keys $\boxed{(}$ and $\boxed{)}$. To
use these keys, just enter the parentheses where they appear in
the problem. But remember the hidden multiplications. Here is
Example 4, done with a calculator.

Solution 2   Key in: $\boxed{(}$ 3 $\boxed{+}$ 15 $\boxed{)}$ $\boxed{\times}$ $\boxed{(}$ 11 $\boxed{-}$ 2 $\boxed{\times}$ 3 $\boxed{)}$ $\boxed{=}$
The problem without calculators is not very difficult. The calculator
solution requires many keystrokes. So unless the numbers are
quite complicated, most people prefer not to use a calculator for
this kind of problem.

It is possible to have parentheses inside parentheses. These are called **nested parentheses.** With nested parentheses, work inside the innermost parentheses first.

Example 5   Simplify $300 - (40 + .6(30 - 8))$

Solution $= 300 - (40 + .6(22))$ Work the inside ( ) first.
$= 300 - (40 + 13.2)$ Multiply before adding.
$= 300 - (53.2)$ Work the remaining ( ).
$= 246.8$ $(53.2) = 53.2$

Some calculators enable you to nest parentheses; some do not. You should explore your calculator to see what it allows.

Questions

Covering the Reading

1. What is one reason for using parentheses?

In 2–5, *true or false*?

2. $5 + 4 \times 3 = (5 + 4) \times 3$ 3. $5 + 4 \times 3 = 5 + (4 \times 3)$

4. $5(3) = 15$ 5. $2 + (4) = 8$

6. *Multiple Choice*   In evaluating an expression with parentheses:
   (a) First do additions or subtractions, from left to right.
   (b) First do multiplications or divisions, from left to right.
   (c) First work inside parentheses.
   (d) First do exponents.
   (e) Work from left to right regardless of the operation.

In 7–11, evaluate.

7. $4 + 3(7 + 9)$ 8. $(12)(3 + 4)$

9. $10 + 20 \div (2 + 3 \cdot 6)$ 10. $40 - (30 - 5)$

11. $(6 + 6)(6 - 6)$

12. Multiplication occurs twice in the expression $2(5 + 4n)$. What are these places?

13. Suppose $n = 8$. Write the key sequence that will evaluate $2(5 + 4n)$ on your calculator.

In 14–17, $a = 2$, $b = 3$, and $c = 5$. Evaluate each expression.

14. $0.30(c - b)$ 15. $(a + b)(7a + 2b)$

16. $(a + 100b) - (7a - 2b)$ 17. $20a + 5(c - 3)$

18. What are nested parentheses?

19. a. To simplify $1000 - (100 - (10 - 1))$, what should you do first?
   b. Simplify $1000 - (100 - (10 - 1))$.

20. Evaluate $2(x + 12) - 3$ when $x = 8$.

21. Evaluate $3 + x(2 + x(1 + x))$ when $x = 5$.

Applying the Mathematics

In 22 and 23, when $n = 3$, do the two expressions have the same value?

22. $4(n + 2)$ and $4n + 8$ **23.** $33 - 7n$ and $(33 - 7)n$

In 24 and 25, let a be 10 and b be 31. Which expression has the larger value?

24. $b - (a - 2)$ or $b - a - 2$

25. $a + 4(b + 3)$ or $(a + 4)b + 3$

26. *Multiple Choice* Begin with a number n. Add 5 to it. Multiply the sum by 4. What number results?
   (a) $n + 5 \cdot 4$
   (b) $4(n + 5)$
   (c) $n + 5 + n \cdot 4$
   (d) $n + 5 + (n + 5)4$

27. *Multiple Choice* Begin with a number t. Multiply it by 3. Add 2 to the product. What number results?
   (a) $5t$ (b) $3 + 2t$ (c) $3(t + 2)$ (d) $3t + 2$

28. Three instances of a pattern are given. Describe the general pattern using three variables.
$$11(3 + 2) = 11 \cdot 3 + 11 \cdot 2$$
$$5(12 + 19.3) = 5 \cdot 12 + 5 \cdot 19.3$$
$$2(0 + 6) = 2 \cdot 0 + 2 \cdot 6$$

29. Evaluate $2(3 + n(n + 1) + 5)$ when $n = 14$.

In 30 and 31, insert parentheses to make the sentence true.

30. $16 - 15 - 9 = 10$ **31.** $16 - 8 - 4 - 2 = 14$

Review

32. In many places in the Midwest, a township is a square 6 miles on a side. What is the area of a township? *(Lesson 3-7)*

In 33 and 34, consider the expression $6T + E + 3F + 2S$.
(Lessons 4-3, 4-4)

33. Evaluate this expression when $T = 3$, $E = 2$, $F = 1$, and $S = 0$.

34. This expression has something to do with scoring in football. The letters T, E, F, and S have been chosen carefully. With these hints:
   a. What precisely do T, E, F, and S stand for?
   b. What does the value of the expression tell you?

35. Three instances of a pattern are given. Describe the general pattern using one variable. *(Lesson 4-2)*
$$3^4 = 3 \cdot 3 \cdot 3 \cdot 3 \qquad 6^4 = 6 \cdot 6 \cdot 6 \cdot 6 \qquad 1^4 = 1 \cdot 1 \cdot 1 \cdot 1$$

36. A person types a line in 5.7 seconds. Another person types it in one tenth of a second faster. What is the second person's time? *(Lesson 1-2)*

Exploration

37. Use the following exercise to find out how many nested parentheses with operations inside your calculator will allow. Key in $100 - (1 - (2 - (3 - (4 \ldots$ and so on. When your calculator shows an error message, the last number keyed is the calculator's limit. What is your calculator's limit?

38. This program finds values of the expression in Example 2 of this lesson.

```
10   PRINT "GIVE VALUE OF YOUR VARIABLE"
20   INPUT N
30   V = 36 − (17 − N)
40   PRINT "VALUE OF EXPRESSION IS", V
50   END
```

   a. Run the program when N = 4 to check that it gives the value of Example 2.
   b. Run the program for at least five other values of N.
   c. Without running this program, how can you predict what the value of the expression will be?

39. Modify the program in Question 38 so that it evaluates the expression of Example 4 for any value of y. (Caution: Be careful to put the multiplication between the parentheses.)

4-6

Formulas

The rectangle drawn here has length about 6.3 cm, width about 2.5 cm, and area about 15.75 cm^2.

6.3 cm

2.5 cm — Area 15.75 cm^2

The length, width, and area are related by a simple pattern.

$$\text{Area} = \text{length times width}$$

Using the variables A for area, ℓ for length, and w for width,

$$A = \ell w.$$

(Remember that multiplication signs are usually not written between variables.) The sentence $A = \ell w$ is a **formula** for the area of a rectangle **in terms of** its length and width.

Formulas are very useful. For instance, the formula $A = \ell w$ works for *any* rectangle. So suppose a rectangular field has a length of 110 ft and a width of 30 ft. Then its area can be calculated using the formula.

$$\begin{aligned} A &= 110 \text{ ft} \cdot 30 \text{ ft} \\ &= 3300 \text{ ft}^2 \end{aligned}$$

In formulas, the *units must be consistent*. If you measure the length of a rectangle in inches and the width in feet, the formula $A = \ell w$ will not work. For instance, suppose a rectangle has width 3 inches and length 4 feet. To calculate the area you would have to either change inches to feet or feet to inches. Also, you must remember that area is measured in square units.

3 in.

4 ft

Area = 3 in. × 4 ft
    = 3 in. × 48 in.
    = 144 in.^{2}

Letters in formulas are chosen carefully. Usually they are the first letter of what they represent. That is why we used A for area, ℓ for length, and w for width. But be careful. In formulas, capital and small letters often stand for *different* things.

■ ■ ■ ■ ■ ■ ■ ■ ■■

Example The area A of the shaded region is $A = S^2 - s^2$. Find the area if $S = 1.75$ in. and $s = 1.25$ in.

Solution Substitute 1.75 in. for S and 1.25 in. for s in the formula. The unit of the answer is square inches.

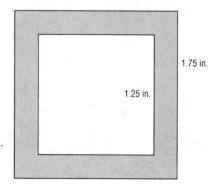

1.75 in.

1.25 in.

$A = S^2 - s^2$
$= (1.75 \text{ in.})^2 - (1.25 \text{ in.})^2$
$= 3.0625 \text{ sq. in.} - 1.5625 \text{ sq. in.}$
$= 1.5 \text{ sq. in.}$

Because capital and small letters can mean different things, in algebra you should not change capital letters to small letters, or vice versa. And you need to learn to write small letters differently from capitals, not just smaller. Do this by putting curves in the small letters. Here are the most confusing letters and one way to write them.

C F I J K L M P S U V W X Y Z

c f i j k l m p s u v w x y z

Questions

Covering the Reading

1. The formula $A = lw$ gives the __?__ of a rectangle in terms of its __?__ and __?__.

2. How do the letters in the formula of Question 1 make that question easier to answer?

164

3. What is the area of a rectangle that is 43 cm long and 0.1 cm wide?

4. a. What is the area of a rectangle that is 3 in. long and 4 ft wide?
   b. What does part **a** tell you about units in formulas?

In 5–7, use the formula $A = S^2 - s^2$

5. Do S and s stand for the same thing?

6. What do S and s stand for?

1.6 cm

0.6 cm

7. Give the area between the two squares drawn at left.

8. In a formula, why should you not change a capital letter to a small letter?

9. a. Write the alphabet from A to Z in capital letters.
   b. Write the alphabet in small letters. Make sure your small letters look different from (not just smaller than) the capital letters.

Applying the Mathematics

In 10–13, use the formula $p = s - c$. This formula relates a store's cost c for an item, the selling price s, and the profit p for this item.

10. This formula gives profit in terms of __?__ and __?__.

11. Why are the letters p, s, and c used in this formula?

12. Calculate p when $s = \$25$ and $c = \$15$.

13. Calculate p when s is $3 and c is 2¢.

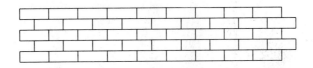

In 14 and 15, use the formula $N = 7LH$. This formula is used by some bricklayers. N is the number of bricks needed in a wall. L is the length of the wall in feet. H is the height of the wall in feet. According to this formula:

14. about how many bricks would a bricklayer need for a wall 10 feet high and 30 feet long?

15. are 1000 bricks enough for a wall $8\frac{1}{2}$ feet high and 20 feet long?

16. A gardener wishes to surround her square garden by a walkway one meter wide. The garden is 5 meters on a side. How much ground will she have to clear?

Review

17. Put into the correct order of operations. *(Lessons 4-1, 4-5)*
    multiplications or divisions from left to right
    powers
    inside parentheses
    additions or subtractions from left to right

In 18–21, evaluate each expression. *(Lessons 4-4, 4-5)*

18. $9 + 5(3 + 2 \cdot 7)$ **19.** $3 + 4 \cdot 5^2$

20. $12 - 4x$ when $x = .5$ **21.** $8/(8/(2 + 6))$

22. Convert 6 kilograms to grams. *(Lesson 3-3)*

23. One liter is how many cubic centimeters? *(Lesson 3-8)*

In 24–27, put one of the symbols $>$, $=$, or $<$ in the blank. *(Lessons 1-6, 1-9, 2-2, 4-4)*

24. $-5 \underline{?} -5.1$ **25.** $4.09 \underline{?} 4\frac{1}{11}$

26. $x + 14 \underline{?} x - 14$ when $x = 20$.

27. $a^3 \underline{?} a^2$ when $a = 0.7$.

28. Change $\frac{8}{4}$, $\frac{9}{4}$, $\frac{10}{4}$, $\frac{11}{4}$, and $\frac{12}{4}$ to decimals. *(Lesson 1-8)*

Exploration

29. a. According to the bricklayer's formula (Questions 14 and 15 above), how many bricks are needed for a square foot of wall?

    b. The bricklayer's formula is related to one of the formulas given in this lesson. Which formula is that, and how are the formulas related?

4-7

Grouping Symbols

Parentheses are the most common **grouping symbols. Brackets** [ ] are grouping symbols sometimes used when there are nested parentheses. Brackets and parentheses mean exactly the same thing.

$5[x + 2y(3 + z)]$ and $5(x + 2y(3 + z))$ are identical.

Many people find brackets clearer than a second pair of parentheses. But some of today's calculators and computer languages do not allow brackets.

Example 1   Simplify $2[4 + 6(3 \cdot 5 - 4)] - 3(30 - 3)$.

Solution   Work within the parentheses inside the brackets first.
$$= 2[4 + 6(15 - 4)] - 3(30 - 3)$$
$$= 2[4 + 6 \cdot 11] - 3(30 - 3)$$
Now there are no nested grouping symbols.
$$= 2[4 + 66] - 3(27)$$
$$= 2(70) - 3(27)$$
$$= 140 - 81$$
$$= 59$$

Another important grouping symbol is the **fraction bar.** You may not have realized that the fraction bar is like parentheses. Here is how it works. Suppose you want to calculate the average of 10, 20, and 36. The average is given by the expression

$$\frac{10 + 20 + 36}{3}.$$

Now suppose you want to write this fraction using the slash /. If you write

$$10 + 20 + 36/3,$$

then, by order of operations, the division will be done first and only the 36 will be divided by 3. So you need to use parentheses.

$$\frac{10 + 20 + 36}{3} = (10 + 20 + 36)/3$$

In this way the slash, /, and the fraction bar, —, are different. (Of course, with something as simple as $\frac{1}{2}$ or 1/2, there is no difference.) You should think of a fraction bar as always having unwritten parentheses. Because the fraction bar is a grouping symbol, you *must* work in the numerator and denominator of a fraction before dividing.

Example 2   Simplify $\dfrac{4 + 9}{2 + 3}$.

Solution   Think $\dfrac{(4 + 9)}{(2 + 3)}$ and get $\dfrac{13}{5}$.

Example 3   Evaluate $\dfrac{4n + 1}{3n - 1}$ when $n = 11$.

Solution 1   Substitute. Then work first in the numerator and denominator.

$$\frac{4 \cdot 11 + 1}{3 \cdot 11 - 1} = \frac{44 + 1}{33 - 1} = \frac{45}{32}$$

Solution 2   Use a calculator to evaluate after substitution. Parentheses must be used to ensure that the entire numerator is divided by the entire denominator. They are emphasized in the key sequence shown here.

$$\boxed{(}\ 4\ \boxed{\times}\ 11\ \boxed{+}\ 1\ \boxed{)}\ \boxed{\div}$$
$$\boxed{(}\ 3\ \boxed{\times}\ 11\ \boxed{-}\ 1\ \boxed{)}\ \boxed{=}$$

You will get 1.40625, the decimal equivalent to $\frac{45}{32}$.

Example 4   Evaluate $x + \dfrac{100(4 + 2x) - 25}{200 - x}$ when $x = 50$.

Solution   First substitute 50 for x whenever x appears.

$$50 + \frac{100(4 + 2 \cdot 50) - 25}{200 - 50}$$

Now work within the parentheses in the numerator.

$$= 50 + \frac{100(104) - 25}{200 - 50}$$

$$= 50 + \frac{10,400 - 25}{150}$$

$$= 50 + \frac{10,375}{150}$$

$$= 50 + 69.1\overline{6}$$

$$= 119.1\overline{6}$$

Summary of Rules for Order of Operations

1. First, do operations within parentheses or other grouping symbols.
    A. If there are nested grouping symbols, work within the innermost symbols first.
    B. Remember that fraction bars are grouping symbols and can be different from /.

2. Within grouping symbols or if there are no grouping symbols:
    A. First, do all powers.
    B. Second, do all multiplications or divisions in order, from left to right.
    C. Then do additions or subtractions in order, from left to right.

Questions

Covering the Reading

1. What are the symbols [ ] called?

2. *True or False* $2[x + 4]$ and $2(x + 4)$ mean the same thing.

3. When are the symbols [ ] usually used?

4. Name three different grouping symbols.

5. When there are grouping symbols within grouping symbols, what should you do first?

In 6–8, simplify.

6. $3[2 + 4(5 - 2)]$

7. $39 - [20 \div 4 + 2(3 + 6)]$

8. $[(3 - 1)^3 + (5 - 1)^4]^2$

9. Write the key sequence for evaluating the expression of Question 6 on your calculator.

10. *Multiple Choice* Written on one line, $\dfrac{20 + 2 \cdot 30}{6 + 4} =$
    (a) $20 + 2 \cdot 30/6 + 4$ (b) $20 + 2 \cdot 30/(6 + 4)$
    (c) $(20 + 2 \cdot 30)/6 + 4$ (d) $(20 + 2 \cdot 30)/(6 + 4)$

In 11 and 12, simplify.

11. $\dfrac{50 + 40}{50 - 40}$

12. $\dfrac{560}{7(6 + 3 \cdot 4.5)}$

13. Write a key sequence for evaluating Question 12 on your calculator.

In 14 and 15, evaluate when $a = 5$ and $x = 4$.

14. $\dfrac{a + 3x}{a + x}$

15. $\dfrac{5x - 2}{(x - 1)(x - 2)}$

Applying the Mathematics

The *average* of three numbers x, y, and z is $\dfrac{x + y + z}{3}$. Use this information in Questions 16–19.

16. Write an expression for the average of a, b, and c.

17. A school district has three elementary schools with 236, 141, and 318 students in them. What is the average number of students per school?

18. A student scores 83, 91, and 89 on 3 tests. What is the average?

19. Grades can range from 0 to 100 on tests. A student scores 85 and 90 on the first two tests.
a. What is the lowest the student can average for all 3 tests?
b. What is the highest the student can average for the 3 tests?

In 20–23, suppose a team wins W games and loses L games. Then its winning percentage is $\dfrac{W}{W + L}$. This number is always converted to a decimal. Then it is rounded to the nearest thousandth. Calculate the winning percentage for each team.

20. the 1988 Super Bowl Champion Washington Redskins, who had a regular season record of 11 wins and 4 losses

21. the 1984 U.S. Olympic Women's basketball team, who won all 6 games they played

22. a volleyball team that wins 7 games and loses 7 games

23. a team that wins 3 and loses 12 games

In 24 and 25, use the formula $T \approx t - \dfrac{2f}{1000}$. This formula estimates the air temperature T at an altitude of f feet when the ground temperature is t. Suppose it is 75° at ground level.

24. Find the temperature at an altitude of 1000 ft.

25. Find the temperature at an altitude of 3000 ft.

26. *Multiple Choice* In a *Bill James Baseball Abstract*, the expression $\dfrac{2(HR \times SB)}{HR + SB}$ is called the Power/Speed number.

A newspaper writer once incorrectly wrote the expression as $2[HR \times SB]/HR + SB$.

What was wrong with the newspaper expression?
(a) It had brackets instead of parentheses.
(b) It should have had parentheses around $HR + SB$.
(c) It had an $\times$ sign for multiplication.
(d) It was written on one line.
(e) It used *HR* and *SB* instead of single letters for variables.

Review

27. Arrange the numbers $7\frac{2}{3}$, $7\frac{3}{5}$, and 7.65 with the symbol $>$ between them. *(Lessons 1-6, 1-9)*

28. The U.S. budget deficit in 1986 is listed in *The World Almanac* as $220,698 million. *(Lesson 1-1, 1-4, 2-3)*
a. Write this number as a decimal.
b. Round this number to the nearest billion.
c. Write the original number in scientific notation.

29. Measure the length and width of a rectangular table to the nearest inch. What is the area of the table? *(Lessons 3-1, 4-6)*

30. Translate into mathematical symbols. *(Lesson 4-3)*
a. the sum of thirty and twenty
b. three more than a number
c. a number decreased by one tenth

Exploration

31. The numerical expression $4 + \frac{4}{4} - 4$ uses four 4s and has a value of 1. Find numerical expressions using only four 4s that have the values of each integer from two to ten. You may use any operations and grouping symbols.

32. This program will calculate the winning percentage using the formula given in Questions 20–23, if you complete Line 30 correctly. Do that and run your program with the values of W and L from Questions 20–23 to check.

```
10   PRINT "WINS"
15   INPUT W
20   PRINT "LOSSES"
25   INPUT L
30   PCT =  ?
40   PRINT "PCT = " PCT
50   END
```

a. Complete line 30 with the correct formula.
b. Run your program with the values of W and L from Question 20 to check.
c. Run your program with values of W and L from the record of a team you know.

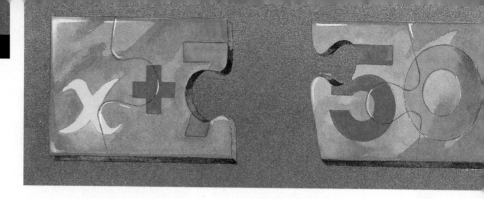

Open Sentences

A sentence with an equal sign = is called an **equation.** Here are some examples of equations.

$$27 = 9(4 - 1) \qquad 1 + 1 = 3 \qquad x + 7 = 50$$

The left equation is true. The middle equation is false. The right equation may be true or false, depending on what you substitute for x. If you substitute 57, the equation is false, because

$$57 + 7 \text{ does not equal } 50.$$

If you substitute 43 for x, the equation is true.

$$43 + 7 = 50$$

The equation $x + 7 = 50$ is an example of an **open sentence.** An open sentence is a sentence with variables that can be true or false, depending on what you substitute for the variables. The **solution** to this open sentence is 43. A solution to an open sentence is a value of a variable that makes the sentence true.

Example 1   Mentally, find the solution to the open sentence $40 - A = 38$.

Solution   Since $40 - 2 = 38$, the number 2 is the solution.

Example 2   *Multiple Choice*   Which number is a solution to $30m = 6$?
(a) 24   (b) 0.5   (c) 5   (d) 0.2

Solution   The answer is the value that works. Substitute to see which one works.
(a) $30 \cdot 24 = 720$, so 24 does not work.
(b) $30 \cdot 0.5 = 15$, so 0.5 does not work.
(c) $30 \cdot 5 = 150$, so 5 does not work.
(d) $30 \cdot 0.2 = 6$, so 0.2 is a solution.
Choice (d) is the correct choice.

One of the most important skills in algebra is finding solutions to open sentences. It is important because open sentences occur often in situations where decisions have to be made.

Example 3 A store is to have an area of 10,000 square feet. But it can only be 80 feet wide. Let ℓ be the length of the store. The value of ℓ is the solution to what open sentence?

Solution Drawing a picture can help.
We know $A = \ell w$. The given information tells us that $A = 10,000$ and $w = 80$. Substituting in the formula, $10,000 = \ell \cdot 80$.

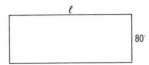

The solution to $10,000 = \ell \cdot 80$ is not obvious. The variable ℓ is called the **unknown.** Finding values of the unknown (or unknowns) that work is called **solving the sentence.** At this point, you are expected to be able to solve only very simple sentences. The solutions are either of the kind you can do in your head (as in Example 1) or you will be given choices (as in Example 2).

Questions

Covering the Reading

1. What is an equation?

2. Give an example of an equation that is false.

3. What is an open sentence?

4. Give an example of an open sentence.

5. Define: solution to an open sentence.

6. What is meant by *solving* an open sentence?

7. *Multiple choice* The solution to $4x + 3 = 12$ is
   (a) 2.25   (b) 0   (c) 2.5   (d) 1

In 8–11, give the solution to each sentence.

8. $18 + A = 19$
9. $2B = 10$
10. $C = 5 - .1$
11. $4 = 3.5 + t$

In 12 and 13, Rhee Taylor wants a store with an area of 1000 square meters. The store can only be 40 meters wide. Rhee wants to know how many meters long the store should be.

12. Solving what equation will give the length l of the store?

13. Which of these lengths is the solution: 25 m, 960 m, 1040 m, or 4000 m?

In 14–17, give one solution to each of these nonmathematical open sentences.

14. __?__ is currently President of the United States.

15. In population, __?__ is a city bigger than Detroit.

16. A trio has __?__ members.

17. An octet has __?__ members.

In 18–21, give at least one solution.

18. There are y millimeters in a meter.

19. x is a negative integer.

20. You move the decimal point two places to the right when multiplying by m.

21. The number one million, written as a decimal, is a 1 followed by z zeros.

22. *Multiple choice* Let n be the number of days a book is overdue. Let F be the fine. Suppose $F = .20 + .05n$ dollars, the situation described in Lesson 4-4. When the fine F is $1.00, what is the number of days overdue?
(a) 20   (b) 15   (c) 16   (d) 25

23. Suppose $y = 2x + 3$. When $x = 4$, what value of y is a solution?

In 24–27, give a solution to each sentence.

24. $n + n = 16$ **25.** $m \cdot m = 16$

26. $z - 4 = 99$ **27.** $y \cdot 25 = 25$

28. In 1987, the world population reached 5.026 billion. *(Lessons 1-4, 2-1, 2-3)*
   a. Round this number to the nearest ten million.
   b. Write your answer to **a** in scientific notation.

In 29 and 30, put the three quantities into one sentence with two inequality signs. *(Lessons 1-6, 3-2, 3-3)*

29. 5 km, 500 m, 50,000 mm   **30.** 2 miles, 5280 ft, 2000 yd

31. The sum of the integers from 1 to n is given by the expression $\dfrac{n(n + 1)}{2}$. *(Lessons 4-4, 4-5, 4-6)*
   a. Evaluate this expression for $n = 5$.
   b. Verify your answer to part **a** by adding the integers from 1 to 5.
   c. Find the sum of the integers from 1 to 100.

32. Evaluate $2x - (y + 3(y + 2))$ when $x = 5.5$ and $y = 0.5$. *(Lesson 4-5)*

33. Evaluate this rather complicated expression. *(Lesson 4-7)*
$$\frac{[6(2 + 4^3)^2 - 3^2]}{40 - 13 \cdot 3}$$

34. Write 0.009:
   a. in scientific notation; **b.** as a fraction. *(Lessons 2-7, 2-9)*

35. Estimate a solution to $(x + 1)(x + 2) = 100$.
   a. between consecutive integers.
   b. between consecutive tenths.
   c. between consecutive hundredths

36. To find the average of the three numbers 83, 91, and 89 in Question 18, Laura typed the following into a computer: ?83 + 91 + 89/3. The answer came out higher than any of the numbers, so Laura knew something was wrong.
   a. What should Laura have typed?
   b. Check your answer by running the correct expression on a computer.

4-9

Inequalities

An **inequality** is a sentence with one of the following symbols.

≠	is not equal to
<	is less than
≤	is less than or equal to
>	is greater than
≥	is greater than or equal to

5 > -7 is an inequality that is true. So is 5 ≥ -7.
An example of an inequality that is false is 3 < 2.
The inequality 50% ≠ 0.5 is also false.

The inequality $x + 2 < 30$ is an open sentence, neither true nor false. The number 20 is a solution, because 20 + 2 < 30. The number 14 is also a solution, since 14 + 2 < 30. However, 28 is not a solution, because 28 + 2 < 30 is not true. Also, 554 is not a solution, because 554 + 2 is not less than 30.

Inequalities that are open sentences usually have many solutions. The solutions are often easier to graph than to list.

Example 1   Graph all solutions to $y < 2$.

Solution   Any number less than 2 is a solution. So there are infinitely many of them. Among the solutions are 0, 1, 1.5, -5, -4.3, and -2,000,000. Below is the graph. The shaded part covers the solutions. The open circle around the mark for 2 tells you that 2 is not a solution. It is not true that 2 < 2.

Remember that the inequality $2 > y$ means the same thing as $y < 2$. So the graph of all solutions to $2 > y$ would look identical to the graph in Example 1.

Example 2 Graph all solutions to $x \geq -1$.

Solution Any number greater than or equal to -1 is a solution. Some solutions are 0, $\frac{1}{2}$, 4, 43, $-\frac{1}{2}$, and 76.2. Below is the graph. The filled-in circle at -1 tells you that -1 is a solution.

Example 3 On some interstate highways, a car's speed must be from 45 mph to 55 mph. Graph all possible legal speeds s.

Solution

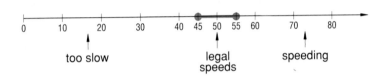

In Example 3, the legal speeds are the solutions to the inequality $45 \leq s \leq 55$. You may read this as "45 is less than or equal to s and s is less than or equal to 55" or "s ranges from 45 to 55." Another way to write this is with $\geq$ signs. $55 \geq s \geq 45$. Some solutions are 48, 50.3, 51, 55, 45, and 49.

Questions

Covering the Reading

1. What is an inequality?

In 2–5, give the meaning of the symbol.

2. $>$ **3.** $\geq$

4. $<$ **5.** $\leq$

6. Write an inequality that means the same thing as $y > 5$.

In 7 and 8, is the sentence an open sentence?

7. $3y \geq 90$ **8.** $2 \leq 9$

In 9–12, *true or false?*

9. $-2 < 1$ **10.** $3 \leq \frac{6}{2}$

11. $-5 \geq 5$ **12.** $6 \neq 5 + 1$

In 13–16, name one solution to each sentence.

13. $A > 5000$ **14.** $n \leq -5$

15. $6\frac{1}{2} < d < 7\frac{1}{4}$ **16.** $55 \geq s \geq 45$

17. *Multiple choice* The solutions to what sentence are graphed here?

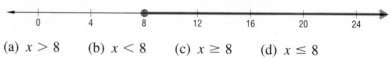

    (a) $x > 8$ (b) $x < 8$ (c) $x \geq 8$ (d) $x \leq 8$

In 18–21, match each sentence with the graph of its solutions.

18. $1 \leq m \leq 4$ **19.** $1 < m < 4$

20. $1 < m \leq 4$ **21.** $1 \leq m < 4$

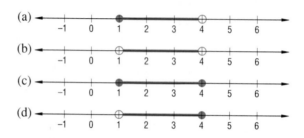

22. The legal speeds s on some interstate highways satisfy what inequality?

23. *Multiple choice* $6 < a \leq 9\frac{2}{3}$ has the same solutions as
    (a) $9\frac{2}{3} < a \leq 6$.   (b) $9\frac{2}{3} > a \geq 6$.
    (c) $9\frac{2}{3} \leq a < 6$.   (d) $9\frac{2}{3} \geq a > 6$.

In 24–26, graph all the solutions to each sentence.

24. $w < \frac{40}{3}$ **25.** $-6 \leq y$ **26.** $-2 < y < 3$

In 27–29: **a.** What inequality describes the situation? **b.** Give three solutions to the inequality. **c.** Graph all possible solutions.

27. The speed limit is 55 mph. A person is driving f miles per hour and is speeding.

28. A person earns d dollars a year. The amount d is less than $25,000 a year.

29. The area is A. Rounded up to the nearest hundred, A is 500.

178

In 30–32, suppose it costs 30¢ for the first minute and 18¢ for each additional minute on a long-distance phone call. Then $c = .30 + .18(m - 1)$, where c is the total cost and m is the number of minutes talked. *(Lesson 4-8)*

30. Calculate c when $m = 6$.

31. What will it cost to talk for 10 minutes?

32. *Multiple choice* For $2.10, how long can you talk?
   (a) 7 minutes   (b) 9 minutes
   (c) 10 minutes   (d) 11 minutes

33. Give three instances of this pattern: There are $6n$ legs on n insects. *(Lesson 4-2)*

34. Three instances of a general pattern are given. Describe the pattern using two variables. *(Lesson 4-2)*
$$\frac{31.4}{2} \cdot \frac{2}{31.4} = 1 \qquad \frac{7}{8} \cdot \frac{8}{7} = 1 \qquad \frac{100}{11} \cdot \frac{11}{100} = 1$$

In 35 and 36, evaluate when $a = 3$, $b = 5$, and $c = 7$. *(Lessons 4-5, 4-7)*

35. $3(c + 10b - a^2)$ **36.** $a[a + b(b + c)]$

37. Scientific calculators often store more digits than they display.
   a. Key in π. Record what you got. Then multiply by 100,000. Now subtract 314,159. Your calculator now displays some digits after those it displayed for π. What are these digits?
   b. Key in $\frac{1}{17}$. Record what you get. Then multiply by 100,000. Now subtract 5882. Compare this result with what you recorded. What extra digits for $\frac{1}{17}$ were stored in the calculator?
   c. Use a similar process to find the digits your calculator stores when you calculate $\frac{1}{13}$.
   d. What is the repetend for $\frac{1}{13}$?

38. Run this program with values of N that you pick.

```
10   PRINT "VALUE OF N"
15   INPUT N
20   IF N >= 8 THEN PRINT "TOO BIG"
25   IF N <= 6 THEN PRINT "TOO SMALL"
30   IF N <> 7 THEN PRINT "NOT CORRECT"
35   IF N = 7 THEN PRINT "JUST RIGHT"
40   END
```

   a. What is the meaning of $>=$ in this program?
   b. What is the meaning of $<=$ in this program?
   c. What is the meaning of $<>$ in this program?

Summary

A variable is a symbol that can stand for any one of a set of numbers or other objects. Usually a variable is a single letter. Algebra is the study of variables and operations on them.

Introduced in this chapter are four uses of variables:
(1) Variables enable *patterns* to be described. For example, *n* people have 2*n* eyes. Descriptions with variables tend to be shorter and look like the instances of the pattern.
(2) Variables describe *properties* of numbers. For example, $a + b = b + a$.
(3) Variables are shorthand for quantities in *formulas*. For example, $A = lw$ is shorthand for area = length × width.

(4) Variables may be *unknowns*. For instance, suppose the area of a rectangle is 4 square meters and a length is 3 meters. Then the width *w* is the solution to the equation $4 = 3w$. The value of *w* can be found by solving this sentence.

Numerical and algebraic expressions may have a number of operations in them. To avoid confusion, rules for order of operations are used worldwide. To operate in a different order than given by these rules, parentheses and other grouping symbols are used.

Vocabulary

You should be able to give a general description and a specific example of each of the following ideas.

Lesson 4-1
symbols $+$, $-$, $\times$, $/$, and so on for operations
numerical expression
value of a numerical expression
evaluating an expression
order of operations

Lesson 4-2
pattern
instance
variable
symbol · for multiplication

Lesson 4-3
algebraic expression
sum, product

Lesson 4-4
value of a variable
value of an expression

Lesson 4-5
parentheses, ( ), nested parentheses

Lesson 4-6
formula
one variable in terms of others

Lesson 4-7
grouping symbols
brackets, [ ]
fraction bar, —

Lesson 4-8
equation
open sentence
solution
unknown
solving an open sentence

Lesson 4-9
inequality
symbols $\leq$, $\geq$, $\neq$

Progress Self-Test

Take this test as you would take a test in class. You will need a ruler. Then check your work with the solutions in the Selected Answers section in the back of the book.

In 1–4, evaluate the expression.

1. $6 + 8 \cdot 7 + 9$

2. $(40 - 5) + (60 - 10)$

3. $75 - 50 - 3 - 1$

4. $5 + 3 \cdot 4^2$

5. Round to the nearest integer: $\dfrac{100 + 2 \cdot 5}{10 + 5}$.

In 6–8, evaluate when $a = 3$, $b = 4$, $x = 10$, and $y = 100$.

6. $x + 3y$

7. $(a + b)(b - a)$

8. $y + 5[y + 4(y + 3)]$

9. *Multiple choice*   Which is a solution to $(4x)^2 = 64$?
   (a) 2   (b) 4   (c) 8   (d) 16

In 10–12, three instances of a pattern are given. Describe the pattern using variables.

10. Use one variable.
$$10 \cdot 5 = 6 \cdot 5 + 4 \cdot 5$$
$$10 \cdot 8.2 = 6 \cdot 8.2 + 4 \cdot 8.2$$
$$10 \cdot 0.04 = 6 \cdot 0.04 + 4 \cdot 0.04$$

11. Use two variables.
$$2 + 8 = 8 + 2$$
$$3.7 + 7.3 = 7.3 + 3.7$$
$$0 + 4 = 4 + 0$$

12. Use one variable.
In one year, we expect the town to grow by 200 people.
In two years, we expect the town to grow by $2 \cdot 200$ people.
In three years, we expect the town to grow by $3 \cdot 200$ people.

In 13 and 14, the formula $c = 20n + 5$ gives the cost of first-class postage in 1988; c is the cost in cents; n is the weight in ounces of the mail, rounded up to the nearest ounce.

13. If $n = 5$, find c.

14. What is the cost of mailing a 9-ounce letter first class? Give your answer in dollars and cents.

In 15–18, translate into a numerical or algebraic expression or sentence.

15. the product of twelve and sixteen

16. forty greater than forty-seven

17. A number is less than zero.

18. a number divided into nine

19. In the formula $p = s - c$, variable __?__ is in terms of __?__ and __?__.

20. In the formula $p = s - c$, calculate p if $s = \$45$ and $c = \$22.37$.

21. *Multiple choice* Written on one line, $\dfrac{W}{W + L}$ is equal to:
   (a) $W/W + L$
   (b) $W/(W + L)$
   (c) $(W/W) + L$
   (d) $(W + L)/W$

22. *Multiple choice* Most of the symbols we now use for arithmetic operations were invented in the years
   (a) before 1 A.D.
   (b) between 1 and 1000 A.D.
   (c) between 1000 and 1800 A.D.
   (d) since 1800 A.D.

23. *Multiple choice* A sentence that means the same as $2 < y$ is
 (a) $2 \leq y$
 (b) $y > 2$
 (c) $y \geq 2$
 (d) $y < 2$

In 24 and 25, find a solution to the given sentence.

24. $6x = 42$

25. $-5 < y < -4$

26. Give an example to show why units in formulas must be consistent.

27. If $x = 7y$ and $y = 3$, what is the value of x?

28. Graph all solutions to $x < 12$.

29. The solutions to what sentence are graphed here?

In 30 and 31, give two instances of the pattern.

30. If your age is A years, your sister's age is $A - 5$ years.

31. $30c/5 = 6c$

Chapter Review

Questions on **SPUR** Objectives

SPUR stands for **S**kills, **P**roperties, **U**ses, and **R**epresentations.
The Chapter Review questions are grouped according to the
SPUR Objectives for this chapter.

SKILLS deal with the procedures used to get answers.

■ **Objective A:** *Use order of operations to evaluate numerical expressions. (Lessons 4-1, 4-7)*

1. Evaluate $235 - 5 \times 4$.

2. Evaluate $32 \div 16 \div 8 \times 12$.

3. Evaluate $2 + 3^4$.

4. Evaluate $4 \times 2^3 + \frac{28}{56}$.

5. Evaluate $5 + 8 \times 3 + 2$.

6. Evaluate $100 - \frac{80}{5} - 1$.

■ **Objective B:** *Evaluate numerical expressions containing grouping symbols. (Lessons 4-5, 4-7)*

7. Evaluate $6 + 8(12 + 7)$.

8. Evaluate $40 - 30/(20 - 10/2)$.

9. Evaluate $1984 - (1947 - 1929)$.

10. Evaluate $(6 + 3)(6 - 4)$.

11. Evaluate $3 + [2 + 4(6 - 3 \cdot 2)]$.

12. Evaluate $4[7 - 2(2 + 1)]$.

13. Evaluate $\dfrac{4 + 5 \cdot 2}{13 \cdot 5}$.

14. Evaluate $\dfrac{3^3}{3^2}$.

■ **Objective C:** *Evaluate algebraic expressions given the values of all variables.*
(Lessons 4-4, 4-5, 4-7)

15. If $x = 4$, then $6x = \underline{\ ?\ }$.

16. If $m = 7$, evaluate $3m + (m + 2)$.

17. Find the value of $2 + a + 11$ when $a = 5$.

18. Find the value of $3x^2$ when $x = 10$.

19. Evaluate $2(a + b - c)$ when $a = 11$, $b = 10$, and $c = 9$.

20. Find the value of $x^3 + 2^y$ when $x = 5$ and $y = 5$.

21. Evaluate $(3m + 5)(2m - 4)$ when $m = 6$.

22. Evaluate $(3m + 5) - (2m + 4)$ when $m = 6$.

23. Evaluate $\dfrac{3a + 2b}{2a + 4b}$ when $a = 1$ and $b = 2.5$.

24. Find the value of $x + [1 + x(2 + x)]$ when $x = 7$.

■ **Objective D:** *Given choices, pick the correct solution or solutions to an open sentence. (Lessons 4-8, 4-9)*

25. *Multiple choice* Which of these is a solution to $3x + 11 = 26$?
    (a) 15 (b) 5 (c) 45 (d) 37

26. *Multiple choice* Which of these is a solution to $y > -5$?
    (a) -4 (b) -5 (c) -6 (d) -7

■ **Objective E:** *Mentally find solutions to equations involving simple arithmetic. (Lesson 4-8)*

27. Find a solution to $3x = 12$.

28. Find a solution to $100 - t = 99$.

29. What is a solution to $y + 8 = 10$?

30. What value of m works in $20 = m \cdot 4$?

■ **Objective F:** *Know the correct order of operations. (Lessons 4-1, 4-5, 4-7)*

31. An expression contains only two operations, a powering and a multiplication. Which should you do first?

32. *True or false*   If an expression contains nested parentheses, you should work the outside parentheses first.

33. *Multiple choice*   Written on one line,
$$\frac{30 + 5}{30 - 5} =$$
(a) $30 + 5/30 - 5$ (b) $(30 + 5)/30 - 5$
(c) $30 + 5/(30 - 5)$ (d) $(30 + 5)/(30 - 5)$

34. *Multiple choice*   Which of the following expressions would have the same value if the grouping symbols were removed?
(a) $10 - (7 - 2)$ (b) $(4 \cdot 87 \cdot 0) + 5$
(c) $10/(5 - 2^2)/2$ (d) $(9 \cdot 3)^2$

PROPERTIES deal with the principles behind the mathematics.

■ **Objective G:** *Given instances of a pattern, write a description of the pattern using variables.* (*Lesson 4-2*)

35. Three instances of a pattern are given. Describe the general pattern using one variable.
$$5 \cdot 12 + 9 \cdot 12 = 14 \cdot 12$$
$$5 \cdot 88 + 9 \cdot 88 = 14 \cdot 88$$
$$5 \cdot \pi + 9 \cdot \pi = 14 \cdot \pi$$

36. Three instances of a pattern are given. Describe the general pattern using three variables.
$$6 + 7 - 8 = 6 - 8 + 7$$
$$10.2 + 0.5 - 0.22 = 10.2 - 0.22 + 0.5$$
$$30\% + 10\% - 20\% = 30\% - 20\% + 10\%$$

37. Three instances of a pattern are given. Describe the general pattern using two variables.
$$\frac{1}{9} + \frac{5}{9} = \frac{1 + 5}{9}; \qquad \frac{0}{9} + \frac{25}{9} = \frac{0 + 25}{9};$$
$$\frac{11}{9} + \frac{44}{9} = \frac{11 + 44}{9}$$

■ **Objective H:** *Give instances of a pattern described with variables.* (*Lesson 4-2*)

38. Give two instances of the pattern $5(x + y) = 5x + 5y$.

39. Give two instances of the pattern $2 + A = 1 + A + 1$.

40. Give two instances of the pattern $ab - c = ba - c$.

USES deal with applications of mathematics in real situations.

■ **Objective I:** *Given instances of a real-world pattern, write a description of the pattern using variables.* (*Lesson 4-2*)

41. Three instances of a pattern are given. Describe the general pattern using variables.
If the weight is 5 ounces, the postage is $5¢ + 20 \cdot 5¢$.
If the weight is 3 ounces, the postage is $5¢ + 20 \cdot 3¢$.
If the weight is 1 ounce, the postage is $5¢ + 20 \cdot 1¢$.

42. Three instances of a pattern are given. Describe the general pattern using variables.
One person has 10 fingers.
Two people have $2 \cdot 10$ fingers.
Seven people have $7 \cdot 10$ fingers.

■ **Objective J:** *Write a numerical expression for an English expression involving arithmetic operations.* (*Lesson 4-3*)

43. Translate into mathematical symbols: the sum of eighteen and twenty-seven.

44. Translate into mathematical symbols: fifteen less than one hundred thousand.

45. Translate into mathematical symbols: the product of four and twenty, decreased by one.

46. Translate into mathematical symbols: seven less six.

Objective K: *Write an algebraic expression for an English expression involving arithmetic operations.* *(Lesson 4-3)*

47. Translate into an algebraic expression: seven more than twice a number.

48. Translate into an algebraic expression: a number divided by six, the quotient decreased by three.

49. Translate into algebra: a number is less than five.

50. Translate into algebra: the product of thirty-nine and a number.

Objective L: *Calculate the value of a variable, given the values of other variables in a formula.* *(Lesson 4-6)*

51. The formula $I = 100m/c$ is sometimes used to measure a person's IQ. The IQ is I, mental age is m, and chronological age is c. What is I if $m = 7$ and $c = 5.5$?

52. The formula $F = 1.8C + 32$ relates Fahrenheit (F) and Celsius (C) temperature. If C is 10, what is F?

53. The formula $A = bh$ gives the area A of a parallelogram in terms of its base b and height h. What is the area of a parallelogram with base 1 foot and height 6 inches?

54. The formula $C = 0.6n + 4$ estimates the temperature C in degrees Celsius when n is the number of cricket chirps in 15 seconds. If a cricket chirps 25 times in 15 seconds, what is an estimate for the temperature?

REPRESENTATIONS deal with pictures, graphs, or objects that illustrate concepts.

Objective M: *Graph the solutions to any inequality of the form $x < a$ and similar inequalities and identify such graphs.* *(Lesson 4-9)*

55. Graph all solutions to $x < 24$.

56. Graph all solutions to $y > 2$.

57. Graph all solutions to $-4 \geq t$.

58. Graph all solutions to $6 \leq d$.

59. The solutions to what sentence are graphed here?

Objective N: *Graph the solutions to any inequality of the form $a < x < b$ and similar inequalities and identify such graphs.* *(Lesson 4-9)*

60. Graph all solutions to $3 < x < 7$.

61. Graph all solutions to $-1 > y \geq -2$.

62. The solutions to what sentence are graphed here?

HISTORY

Objective O: *Give rough dates and names of people for key ideas in arithmetic and algebra notation.* *(Lessons 4-1, 4-2)*

63. Write two arithmetic symbols used by computers but not much elsewhere.

64. *Multiple choice* Who is sometimes considered the "father of algebra"?
(a) Jacques Cousteau
(b) Albert Einstein
(c) François Viète
(d) Augustin-Louis Cauchy

Patterns Leading to Addition

*U*rban areas are cities and suburbs. Less-populated places outside the urban areas are called *rural* areas. The table below gives the 1970 populations of rural and urban areas in all of the regions in the United States. Many of the numbers in the table were calculated by adding other numbers.

Region	Urban	Rural	Total
New England (ME, NH, VT, MA, RI, CT)	9,043,517	2,798,146	11,847,186
Middle Atlantic (NY, NJ, PA)	30,406,301	6,792,739	37,203,339
East North Central (OH, IN, IL, MI, WI)	30,091,847	10,160,629	40,252,678
West North Central (MN, IA, MO, ND, SD, NB, KS)	10,388,913	5,930,274	16,324,389
South Atlantic (DE, MD, DC, VA, WV, NC, SC, GA, FL)	19,523,920	11,147,417	30,671,337
East South Central (KY, TN, AL, MS)	6,987,943	5,815,527	12,804,552
West South Central (AR, LA, OK, TX)	14,028,098	5,292,462	19,322,458
Mountain (MT, ID, WY, CO, NM, AZ, UT, NV)	6,054,979	2,226,583	8,283,585
Pacific (WA, OR, CA, AK, HI)	22,799,412	3,723,219	26,525,774
Totals	149,324,930	53,886,996	203,235,298

Every place in the United States is classified either as urban or rural. Knowing this, you can discover that the Census Bureau made many errors in its tabulation. (The Bureau discovered the errors, but too late.) Addition can help you locate the errors.

In this chapter, you will study many other uses of addition.

The Putting-together Model for Addition

Addition is important because adding gives answers in many actual situations. It is impossible to list all the uses of addition. So we give a general pattern that includes many of the uses. We call this general pattern a model for the operation. In this book, we identify two models for addition: putting-together and slide. Here are five instances of the **Putting-together Model for Addition**.

1. You have 8 cassette tapes. A friend has 5. How many tapes are there in all?

2. Look at the table on the previous page. In 1970, the population of the New England region was 11,847,186 and the population of the Middle Atlantic region was 37,203,339. How many people lived in these regions combined?

3. Suppose a book is purchased for $2.95 and the tax is $0.18. What is the total cost?

4. Taken from my pay is 20% for taxes and 7% for social security. How much is taken altogether?

5. One package weighed $2\frac{1}{2}$ lb and the other weighed $2\frac{3}{4}$ lb. How much did they weigh altogether?

The general pattern is easy to describe using variables.

Putting-together Model for Addition:

A count or measure x is put together with a count or measure y with the same units. If there is no overlap, then the result has count or measure $x + y$.

The numbers in putting-together may be large or small. They may be written as decimals, percents, or fractions.

When the units are not the same, you must make them alike before the addition of the numbers will work. For instance:

6. 2 meters + 46 centimeters
   = 2 meters + 0.46 meter
   = 2.46 meters
7. 8 apples + 14 oranges
   = 8 pieces of fruit + 14 pieces of fruit
   = 22 pieces of fruit

Numbers to be added are called **addends**. If one addend is unknown, the putting-together model can still be used.

8. You weigh 50 kg and a friend weighs x kg. If you step on a scale together, the total weight is $(50 + x)$ kg.

The idea of Example 8 can be applied to weighing a cat that is too small to be weighed on an adult scale. Let c stand for the cat's weight.

9. Suppose a person steps on the scale and weighs 130.5 lb. Together the person and the cat weigh $(c + 130.5)$ lb. Now the person picks up the cat and steps on the scale again. Suppose the total weight is 136.25 lb. Then the cat's weight is the solution to the equation $c + 130.5 = 136.25$.

If you do not know how to solve an equation of this type, you will learn how to do so later in this chapter.

When there is overlap in the addends, simple addition will not give a correct answer. For example, imagine that 50 pages of a book have pictures and 110 pages have tables. You cannot conclude that 160 pages have either pictures or tables. Some pages might have both pictures and tables.

Questions

Covering the Reading

1. What is a model for an operation?

2. What is an addend?

3. What is the Putting-together Model for Addition?

In 4 and 5, give an example of the putting-together model when each addend:

4. has grams as its unit

5. is written using fractions

6. Mary gets on a scale and weighs M kg. Craig gets on a scale and it registers 60 kg. Together they get on the scale and the scale shows 108 kg. Write a sentence relating M, 60, and 108.

7. Carla says you can add apples and oranges. Peter says you cannot. Who is right?

8. Write 3 meters + 4 centimeters as one quantity.

9. Answer the questions given in instances 1-5 on page 188. (In instance 5, you may wish to change the fractions to decimals.)

Applying the Mathematics

10. Together Dan and Diane have $20. Together Diane and Donna have $15. How much do the three of them have in total?

In 11 and 12, give an equation relating the three numbers mentioned.

11. Rich owns 15 tapes. Ruth has r tapes. Together they have 43 tapes.

12. Doris worked $23\frac{1}{2}$ hours last week at the grocery store. David worked 45 hours. Together they worked T hours.

13. Give an inequality relating the three numbers mentioned. The chair will support at most 250 pounds. Mike weighs M pounds. Nina weighs 112 pounds. The chair will hold both of them.

In 14–17, perform the addition.

14. 3 feet + 4 inches = __?__ inches

15. 6 pounds + 13 ounces = __?__ ounces

16. 4 meters + 351 millimeters = __?__ millimeters

17. 100 grams + 2 kilograms = __?__ grams

18. Jane has 2 brothers and 1 sister. Her sister Joan has 2 brothers and 1 sister. How many children are in the family?

19. Michelle has *b* brothers and *s* sisters. How many children are in the family?

20. Of the 25 students in Ms. Jones's class, 9 are on a school team, 10 are in the band or chorus, and 7 are in some other school activity.
 a. Is this possible?
 b. Why or why not?

21. In Springfield last year it rained or snowed on 140 days. The sun shone on *s* days. Can you determine *s* from this information?

In 22–24, refer to the table on the page 187.

22. There are 30 numbers in the table. How many of these numbers are sums of other numbers in the table?

23. Which region has the smallest rural population?

24. Suppose there is an error in the number given for the South Atlantic urban population. If you correct this error, how many other numbers will you have to correct?

Review

25. Which are solutions to $0 \leq x < 50$? *(Lesson 4-9)*
 (a) 35.2   (b) 0   (c) -4   (d) 1/100   (e) 50   (f) 60%

26. Round 99.3% to the nearest whole number. (Hint: Watch out!) *(Lesson 2-5)*

27. Mentally, find the solution to $4 + A = 7$. *(Lesson 4-8)*

28. How many degrees are there in: *(Lessons 3-5, 3-6)*
 a. a right angle?
 b. half a circle?
 c. an acute angle?

29. *True or false?* $-10 \leq -8$ *(Lesson 1-5)*

30. If climbing up 2 meters is represented by the number 2, what number will represent each event? *(Lesson 1-5)*
   a. climbing down 6 meters
   b. staying at the same height

31. Which is larger, $\frac{3}{10}$ or $\frac{29}{97}$? *(Lesson 1-8)*

Exploration

32. Find an error in the table on the first page of this chapter.

33. When 1 cup of sugar is added to 1 cup of water, the result is not 2 cups of the mixture. Why not?

34. In the array of numbers shown here, the whole numbers from 1 to 9 are each used once. The numbers in each row, column, and diagonal add up to 15. The array is called a *magic square*.

2	9	4
7	5	3
6	1	8

Here is the start to a bigger magic square. Enough numbers are given to complete it. Find the missing numbers.

		2	13
5		11	
	6		12
4	15	14	

5-2

Adding Fractions

Nanette put 1/3 cup of milk in a casserole. She forgot and then put in another 1/3 cup of milk. No, no, Nanette! Think of thirds as units. Then by the putting-together model for addition:

$$1 \text{ third} + 1 \text{ third} = 2 \text{ thirds (cups)}$$

$$\frac{1}{3} + \frac{1}{3} = \frac{2}{3} \text{ (cups)}$$

Milton runs to keep in shape. Today he ran 3/4 mile. Yesterday he ran 9/4 miles. Two days ago he ran 10/4 miles. My, my, Milton! The total amount he ran is:

$$3 \text{ fourths} + 9 \text{ fourths} + 10 \text{ fourths} = 22 \text{ fourths (miles)}$$

$$\frac{3}{4} + \frac{9}{4} + \frac{10}{4} = \frac{22}{4} \text{ (miles)}$$

The general pattern is easy to see. To add fractions with the same denominator, add the numerators and keep the denominator the same. Here is the pattern using variables:

Addition of fractions with the same denominator:

$$\frac{a}{c} + \frac{b}{c} = \frac{a + b}{c}$$

Example 1 Simplify $\frac{11}{8} + \frac{5}{8}$.

Solution $\frac{11}{8} + \frac{5}{8} = \frac{11 + 5}{8} = \frac{16}{8}$

Check Check by using decimals.
$\frac{11}{8} = 1.375$, $\frac{5}{8} = 0.625$, and $\frac{16}{8} = 2$.
Does $1.375 + 0.625 = 2$? Yes, so the answer checks.

Example 2 Simplify $\dfrac{3}{x} + \dfrac{5}{x}$.

Solution $\dfrac{3}{x} + \dfrac{5}{x} = \dfrac{3+5}{x} = \dfrac{8}{x}$

Check This should work for any value of x other than zero. So, to check, substitute some value for x. We pick 4, because fourths are terminating decimals.

Does $\frac{3}{4} + \frac{5}{4} = \frac{8}{4}$? Check by rewriting the fractions as decimals. Does $0.75 + 1.25 = 2$? Yes.

Here is a picture of $3/4 + 5/4 = 2$.

3/4   5/4

Bill ate 3 of 8 pieces of one pizza. He ate 2 of 6 pieces of another pizza of the same size. How much did he eat in all?

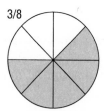 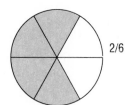

To figure this out requires adding $\frac{3}{8}$ and $\frac{2}{6}$, fractions with different denominators.

$$\tfrac{3}{8} + \tfrac{2}{6}$$

Use the Equal Fractions Property to find equal fractions with the same denominator. Some fractions equal to 3/8 are 6/16, 9/24, 12/32, and so on. Some fractions equal to 2/6 are 4/12, 8/24, and so on. That's enough. Choose the fractions with denominator 24. The number 24 is a **common denominator.**

$$\tfrac{3}{8} + \tfrac{2}{6} = \tfrac{9}{24} + \tfrac{8}{24}$$
$$= \tfrac{17}{24}$$

Bill ate the equivalent of 17/24 of an entire pizza. Since $17/24 = 0.708\ldots \approx 71\%$, we could say that Bill ate about 71% of a pizza.

Example 3   Add $\frac{5}{6} + \frac{1}{2} + \frac{7}{3}$.

Solution   The product of the denominators is 36, but that is much bigger than is needed. Since 6 is a multiple of the other denominators, 6 can be a common denominator.

$$= \frac{5}{6} + \frac{3}{6} + \frac{14}{6}$$
$$= \frac{22}{6}$$

In lowest terms, the answer is $\frac{11}{3}$.

All the examples can be checked by using decimals. For instance, to check Example 3:

$$5/6 \approx 0.83333$$
$$1/2 = 0.5$$
$$7/3 \approx 2.33333$$

So the sum of the fractions should equal about 3.66666. Since 11/3 = 3.66666..., the answer checks.

When adding an integer and a fraction, use the denominator of the fraction as the common denominator.

Example 4   Write $2 + \frac{3}{5}$ as a simple fraction.

Solution   Replace 2 by $\frac{2}{1}$. Then multiply the numerator and denominator of $\frac{2}{1}$ by 5.

$$= \frac{2}{1} + \frac{3}{5}$$
$$= \frac{10}{5} + \frac{3}{5}$$
$$= \frac{13}{5}$$

The sum $2 + \frac{3}{5}$ is often written as $2\frac{3}{5}$ without the + sign. To do Example 4, many people use a shortcut to find the numerator of the simple fraction: multiply 5 by 2, and then add 3.

Questions

Covering the Reading

1. On Monday, Mary ran 7/4 kilometers. On Tuesday, she ran 9/4 km. What is the total number of kilometers Mary ran?

2. Bill used 5/2 cups of flour in one recipe and 3/2 cups of flour in another. How much flour did he use altogether?

3. Terri ate 1/3 of one pizza and 1/4 of another of the same size.
   a. What problem with fractions determines the total that Terri ate?
   b. Name five fractions equal to 1/3.
   c. Name five fractions equal to 1/4.
   d. What is the total amount of pizza that Terri ate?

4. a. To write $\frac{2}{7} + \frac{3}{5}$ as a single fraction, what number can be the denominator of the sum?
   b. Do the addition of part **a**.

5. a. Write $\frac{4}{5} + \frac{3}{10}$ as a single fraction.
   b. Check by using decimals.

In 6–11, simplify.

6. $\frac{50}{11} + \frac{5}{11}$

7. $\frac{13}{x} + \frac{4}{x}$

8. $\frac{8}{9} + \frac{1}{15}$

9. $\frac{5}{8} + \frac{2}{5}$

10. $\frac{11}{7} + \frac{6}{7} + \frac{15}{7}$

11. $\frac{2}{3} + \frac{5}{3} + \frac{5}{6}$

12. a. Write $4 + \frac{2}{5}$ as a simple fraction.
    b. How is $4 + \frac{2}{5}$ usually written?

Applying the Mathematics

13. Two stoplights are 2 km apart. The next stoplight is 1/2 km further. How far apart are the first and third lights?

In 14–17 write the sum as a simple fraction.

14. $4\frac{3}{8} + 2\frac{1}{5}$

15. $4\frac{3}{8} + 2\frac{2}{3}$

16. $\frac{6}{7} + 3\frac{7}{12}$

17. $9.75 + \frac{100}{11} + 3$

18. After a rainstorm, the water level in a swimming pool rose by $1\frac{1}{2}''$. The following day, after another storm, the water level rose $2\frac{1}{4}''$.
    a. What was the total change in the water level?
    b. If the deep end of the pool was originally 9 ft deep, how deep was the water at the end of the second day?

19. The Venturi family ate 6 pieces of a 28-piece loaf of bread at breakfast. They used 12 pieces of the loaf in making sandwiches for lunch. One of them used 2 pieces for an after-school snack. How many pieces of the loaf were eaten altogether? *(Lesson 5-1)*

20. Minnie has 5 brothers and 2 sisters. Her brother Dennis has 4 brothers and 3 sisters. How many children are in the family? *(Lesson 5-1)*

21. A dinosaur known as Brontosaurus weighed about 60,000 pounds. Write this number in scientific notation. *(Lesson 2-3)*

22. Find the measure of angle FUD. *(Lesson 3-5)*

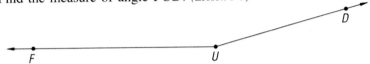

In 23 and 24. **a.** Name one solution to the sentence. **b.** Graph all solutions to the sentence. *(Lesson 4-9)*

23. $x < 3$

24. $-2 \leq y$

25. a. In music, two eighth notes take the same time as a quarter note. What addition of fractions explains this?
b. What amount of time is taken by a sixteenth note followed by another sixteenth note?

two sixteenth notes

5-3

The Slide Model for Addition

Recall that negative numbers are used when a situation has two opposite directions. Examples are deposits and withdrawals in a savings account, ups and downs of temperatures or weight, profits and losses in business, and gains and losses in football or other games. In these situations, you may need to add negative numbers. Here is a situation that leads to the addition problem 10 + -12.

Example 1   Flood waters go up 10 feet and then go back 12 feet. What is the effect of all of this?

Solution   The waters went down 2 feet. 10 + -12 = -2

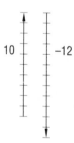

Example 1 is pictured above. Think of the waters sliding up and then sliding back down.

Example 2   Tony spends $4 for dinner and then earns $7 for baby-sitting. What is the net result of this?

Solution   Tony has $3 more than he had before dinner.

Example 2 illustrates the addition problem -4 + 7. The -4 is for spending $4. The 7 is for earning $7. Ending up with $3 more is 3. So -4 + 7 = 3. You can picture this on a number line.

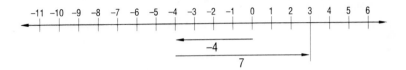

Start at 0. Think of -4 as a slide 4 units to the left. Draw the arrow pointing left. Think of 7 as an arrow going 7 units to the right but starting at -4. Where does the second arrow end? At 3, the sum.

In the **Slide Model for Addition,** positive numbers are shifts or changes or slides in one direction. Negative numbers are slides in the opposite direction. The + sign means "followed by." The sum indicates the net result.

Slide Model for Addition:

If a slide x is followed by a slide y, the result is a slide $x + y$.

Example 3   What is -3 + -2?

Solution   Think of a slide 3 units to the left, followed by a slide 2 more units to the left. The result is a slide 5 units to the left. -3 + -2 = -5.

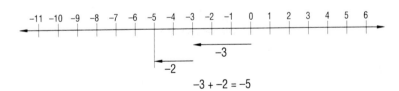

The ⊕ or +/- key on a calculator changes a number to its opposite. The following key sequence can be used to add -3 and -2.

$$3 \;\boxed{+/-}\; \boxed{+}\; 2 \;\boxed{+/-}\; \boxed{=}$$

There can be slides with positive numbers. If the temperature goes up 9° and then goes up 7° more, the result is an increase of 16°. Of course you know this. You have known some instances of the slide model for many years.

Covering the Reading

1. What is the Slide Model for Addition?

In 2–5, what does each phrase mean in the slide model?

2. a positive number   **3.** a negative number

4. the + sign   **5.** the sum

In 6–9, the arrow below represents a slide of 5 on a number line. Using a number line with the same scale, draw an arrow for the given number.

6. -5   **7.** 10   **8.** -10   **9.** 6

10. a. Draw a picture of 5 + -6 using arrows.
    b. 5 + -6 =?

11. a. Draw a picture of -3 + -8 using arrows.
    b. -3 + -8 =?

In 12 and 13, write the key sequence for each addition on a calculator.

12. 24 + -5 (the sum should be 19)

13. -1 + -8 (the sum should be -9)

In 14–18, **a.** what addition is suggested by each situation? **b.** What is the answer to that addition?

14. The temperature falls 5°, then falls 3° more.

15. A person gets a paycheck for $250, then buys a coat for $150.

16. Flood waters gain 15 feet, then go back 17 feet.

Applying the Mathematics

17. A person withdraws $50, then withdraws $40.27.

18. Pat gains 2.3 kg one month, loses 2.3 kg the next.

19. Translate -7 + -5 into a real-life situation and do the addition.

20. Translate $\frac{3}{8} + -\frac{2}{8}$ into a real-life situation and do the addition.

In 21–23, what is the result in each case?

21. A ship goes 40 km in one direction and then goes 60 km in the opposite direction.

22. You walk north 300 feet and then walk south 50 feet.

23. The temperature is at -4° and then falls 3°.

In 24–26, choose the answer from the following choices.
(a) The sum is always positive.
(b) The sum is always negative.
(c) The sum is sometimes positive, sometimes negative.

24. Two negative numbers are added.

25. Two positive numbers are added.

26. A positive and a negative number are added.

Review

27. In the Canadian province of Manitoba, 26% of the people belong to the United Church of Christ, 25% are Roman Catholic, 12% are Anglican, 7% Lutheran, 6% Mennonite, and 6% Ukrainian Catholic.
a. Assuming no one belongs to two churches, what percent of Manitobans do not belong to any of these churches?
b. The population of Manitoba is about 1,070,000. About how many people are Anglicans? *(Lesson 2-6)*

28. The percent p of discount on an item can be calculated by using the formula $p = 100(1 - n/g)$. In this formula, g is the original price, and n is the new price. Find the percent of discount on an item reduced from: **a.** \$2 to \$1. **b.** \$2.95 to \$1.95. *(Lesson 4-6)*

29. Suppose $a = 3.2$ and $x = 1.5$. Evaluate $[40 - (4a - 10)]/(4x)$. *(Lesson 4-6)*

30. Simplify $\frac{11}{6} + \frac{2}{3}$. *(Lesson 5-2)*

31. Name two solutions to $-1 < t < 1$. *(Lesson 4-9)*

32. Steve has h brothers and 4 sisters. There are c children in the family. Give a sentence relating these numbers. *(Lesson 5-1)*

33. a. 6 miles + 1000 feet = __?__ feet *(Lessons 3-2, 5-1)*
b. The sum of 6 miles and 1000 feet is __?__ miles.

Exploration

34. In this lesson, arrows were used to picture addition of negative numbers. Physicists use arrows called *vectors* to add forces. Find out how a physicist would add the two arrows pictured here.

5-4

Zero and Opposites

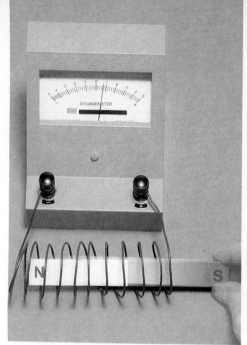
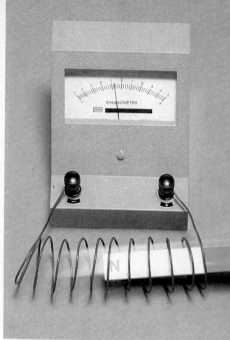

Suppose you have $25. If you get $4 from somewhere, then the amount you will have is $25 + $4, or $29. If you spend $4, the amount you will have is $25 − $4, or $21. If you do nothing, the amount you will have is $25 + $0, or $25. When you add 0 to a number, the value of that number is kept. We say that adding 0 to a number keeps the identity of that number. So 0 is called the **additive identity.**

Additive Identity Property of Zero:

For any number n: $n + 0 = n$.

For example, $-2.4 + 0 = -2.4$, $7777 + 0 = 7777$, and $0 + -18 = -18$.

Remember that 5 and -5 are called *opposites*. This is because if 5 stands for gaining 5 pounds, then -5 stands for its opposite, losing 5 pounds. Now suppose you gain 5 pounds and then lose 5 pounds. In the slide model, the result is found by adding $5 + -5$.

But you know the result! If you gain 5 pounds and then lose 5 pounds, the result is no change in weight. This verifies that

$$5 + -5 = 0.$$

The same thing works regardless of what number you use. The sum of a number and its opposite is 0. In symbols, $-n$ is the opposite of n. The general pattern is called the Property of Opposites.

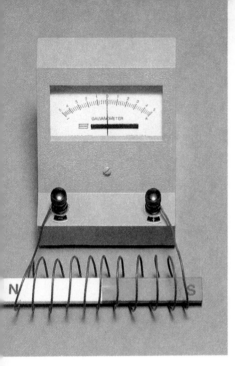

Property of Opposites:

For any number n: $n + -n = 0$.

The word "inverse" means opposite. Because of the property of opposites, the numbers n and $-n$ are called **additive inverses** of each other. For example, the additive inverse of 40 is -40. The additive inverse of -40 is 40. The additive inverse of -6.3 is 6.3. This can be written as $-(-6.3) = 6.3$. The parentheses are used so that it is clear that there are two dashes. Because $0 + 0 = 0$, the opposite of 0 is zero. That is, $-0 = 0$.

The opposite of the opposite of any number is the number itself. We call this the Op-op Property. Your class may wish to make up a different name.

Op-op Property:

For any number n: $-(-n) = n$

To verify the Op-op Property: display any number; then press the $\boxed{+/-}$ key *twice*. After the first pressing, you will get the opposite of the number. After the second pressing, the original number will appear.

Questions

Covering the Reading

1. Why is zero called the additive identity?

2. Add: $0 + 3 + 0 + 4$.　　3. Add: $0 + -3 + 0 + -4$.

4. Another name for additive inverse is ___?___.

In 5–8, give the additive inverse of each number.

5. 70　　　　6. -13　　　　7. $-\frac{1}{2}$　　　　8. $-x$

9. State the Property of Opposites.

10. Describe a real situation that illustrates $7 + -7 = 0$.

11. State the Op-op Property.

In 12–15, an instance of what property is given?

12. $2 + -2 = 0$.

13. $-9.4 = 0 + -9.4$

14. $7 = -(-7)$

15. $0 = 1 + -1$

Applying the Mathematics

In 16–19, perform the additions.

16. $-51 + 51 + 2$

17. $x + 0 + -x$

18. $a + b + -b$

19. $-\frac{8}{3} + -\frac{2}{7} + 0 + \frac{2}{7} + \frac{8}{3} + \frac{14}{11}$

In 20 and 21: **a.** Translate the words into mathematical symbols.
b. An instance of what property is given?

20. Withdraw $25, then make no other withdrawal or other deposit, and you have decreased the amount in your account by $25.

21. Walk 40 meters east, then 40 meters west, and you are back where you started.

In 22–25, simplify.

22. $-(-(-5))$

23. $-(-(-(-6)))$

24. $-(-(-x))$

25. $-(-(-7 + 1))$

26. Suppose you enter the number 5 on your calculator. After pressing the $\boxed{+/-}$ key 50 times, what number will be displayed?

27. If $x = -3$, then $-x = \underline{\ ?\ }$.

28. When $a = -4$ and $b = -5$, then $-(a + b) = \underline{\ ?\ }$.

Review

In 29 and 30: **a.** What is the result for each situation?
b. What addition problem gets that result? *(Lesson 5-3)*

29. The temperature is $-11°$ and then goes up $2°$.

30. You are $150 in debt and take out another loan of $100.

In 31 and 32, give an equation or inequality relating the three numbers. *(Lesson 5-1)*

31. We were at an altitude of t meters. We went down 35 meters in altitude. Our altitude is now 60 meters below sea level.

32. We need $50 to buy that gift for our parents. You have Y dollars. I have $14.50. Together we have more than enough.

33. Put in order, from smallest to largest. *(Lessons 2-2, 2-8)*
3.2×10^4 9.7×10^{-5} 5.1×10^7

34. a. Evaluate $a + c/3 + b$ when $a = 20/3$, $b = 17/6$, and $c = -11$.
(Lesson 5-2)
b. Write your answer to **a** in lowest terms. *(Lesson 1-10)*

35. A rope d inches in diameter can lift a maximum of about
w pounds, where $w = 5000d(d + 1)$. *(Lesson 4-6)*
a. About how many pounds can a rope of diameter 1″ lift?
b. About how many pounds can a rope with a diameter of
one-half inch lift?
c. A rope has diameter $\frac{9}{16}$ inch. Can it lift 5,000 pounds?

Exploration

36. Opposites are common outside of mathematics. You know that
good and bad are opposites, and so are big and little. Find the
four pairs of opposites in the eight animal names given here.

moose	dove	hawk	mouse
tiger	shrimp	bear	bull

5-5

Adding Positive and Negative Numbers

Suppose you want to add -50 and 30. In Lesson 5-2, you learned two ways of doing this. One way is to think of a slide model situation using the numbers -50 and 30.

> I lose $50 and I gain $30.
> How am I doing?

A second way is to draw a number line and arrows. This pictures the addition.

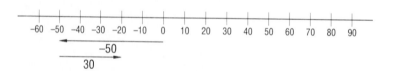

Either way, you should get the answer -20.

If the numbers are complicated, it isn't so easy to think of situations. And it takes a long time to draw a number line and arrows. So it helps to have a rule for adding positive and negative numbers. This rule is described using an idea called the **absolute value of a number.**

When a number is positive, it equals its absolute value. The absolute value of 5 is 5. The absolute value of 3.8 is 3.8. The absolute value of 4 million is 4 million.

The absolute value of a negative number is the opposite of that number. The absolute value of -2 equals 2. The absolute value of -4000 is 4000.

The symbol for absolute value is two vertical lines | |, one on each side of the number. For example |5| = 5; |3.8| = 3.8; |4 million| = 4 million; |-2| = 2; and |-4000| = 4000.

Turns

A *full turn* around in a circle is called one **revolution** or a 360° turn. Pictured are two *quarter turns*. Each is 1/4 of a revolution or 90°.

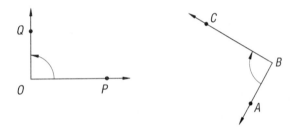

Notice that the turns are in different directions. Consider the turn at left above. Think of standing at point *O* (the center of the turn) and looking at point *P*. Then turn so that you are looking at point *Q*. You have turned *counterclockwise,* the opposite of the way clock hands usually move. Above at right, imagine yourself at point *B*. Look first at point *A*, then turn to look at point *C*. You have turned 90° *clockwise.*

In most of mathematics, the counterclockwise direction is considered positive and the clockwise direction is negative. The turn with center *O* above is a turn of 90°. The turn with center *B* is a turn of -90°.

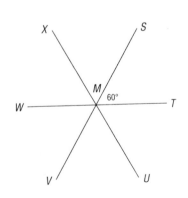

In the picture at left, the six small angles at *M* are drawn to have equal measures. Each angle has measure 60° because each is 1/6 of 360°. Think of standing at *M* and facing point *S*. If you now turn clockwise to face point *U*, you have turned -120°. If you turn from facing *S* to face point *X*, you have turned 60°. The quantities -120° and 60° are called the **magnitudes of the turns.**

For any clockwise turn, there is a counterclockwise turn that winds up in the same place. For instance, the -120° turn from *S* to *U* on page 211 can also be achieved by going 240° counterclockwise. So a turn of -120° is considered identical to a turn of 240°.

You can use protractors to help measure magnitudes of turns. But a protractor cannot tell you the direction of a turn.

Turns are discussed in this chapter because turns provide another use for addition. Pictured below is a 35° turn followed by a 90° turn. The result is a 125° turn. In general, if one turn is followed by another, the magnitude of the result is found by adding the magnitudes of the turns.

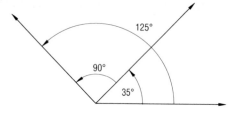

This addition property holds even if the turns are in opposite directions. Below a 60° turn is followed by a -90° turn. The result is a -30° turn (in other words, a turn of 30° clockwise).

$$60 + -90 = -30$$

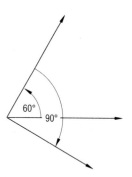

Fundamental Property of Turns:

> If a turn of magnitude x is followed by a turn of magnitude y, the result is a turn of magnitude $x + y$.

Tops, figure skaters, gears, the Earth, pinwheels, and phonograph records turn. All of these objects may turn many revolutions. So it is possible to have turns with magnitudes over 360°. For example, a dancer who spins $1\frac{1}{2}$ times around has spun 540°, since it is the result of a full turn of 360° followed by a half turn of 180°.

Covering the Reading

In 1–4, give the number of degrees in:

1. a full turn

2. one revolution

3. a half turn

4. a quarter turn

5. On page 212, is the 35° turn clockwise or counterclockwise?

6. __?__ turns have positive magnitudes.

7. __?__ turns have negative magnitudes.

In 8–11, all small angles at *O* have the same measure. Think of turns around point *O*. Give the magnitude of:

8. the counterclockwise turn from *D* to *B*.

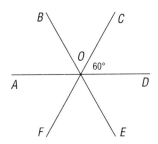

9. the counterclockwise turn from *C* to *F*.

10. the clockwise turn from *D* to *E*.

11. the clockwise turn from *A* to *F*.

12. A turn of -80° winds up in the same place as a turn of what positive magnitude?

In 13–16, give the result of:

13. a 90° turn followed by a 35° turn.

14. a 90° turn followed by a -35° turn.

15. a -5° turn followed by a -6° turn.

16. a 1/4° turn followed by a 1/2° turn.

17. State the Fundamental Property of Turns.

18. An airplane pilot is at point *A* flying toward point *B*. Due to a change in plans, the pilot decides to turn the plane toward point *C*. What is the magnitude of the turn that is needed? (You need to use a protractor.)

•*B*

A•

•*C*

In 19 and 20, the diagrams are pizzas that have been divided equally. What is the measure of an angle at the center of the pizza?

19.   **20.**

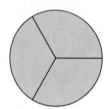   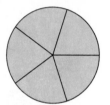

In 21–23, a Ferris wheel is pictured. The spokes are equally spaced.

21. a. What magnitude turn will bring seat *J* to the position of seat *L?*
   b. Where will seat *B* wind up on this turn?

22. a. What magnitude turn will bring seat *K* to the position of seat *G?*
   b. What magnitude turn will bring seat *K* back to its original position?

23. If seat *C* is moved to the position of seat *G*, what seat will be moved to the top?

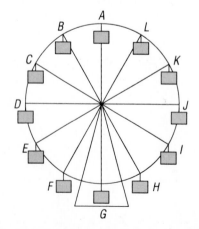

8. In what century were the names commutative and associative first used? (Remember that the years 1901–2000 are the 20th century.)

9. Give a real-world situation that could lead someone to add many positive and negative numbers.

10. On November 1, a person has $400 in a savings account. Here are the transactions for the next two weeks.

DATE	DEPOSIT	WITHDRAWAL
11-03	$102.00	
11-05		$35.00
11-08		75.00
11-11	40.00	
11-12		200.00

   a. What addition can you do to calculate the amount in the account at the end of the day on November 12?

   b. How much is in the account at that time?

Applying the Mathematics

In 11 and 12, simplify.

11. 17 + -1 + -4

12. 0 + -3 + -2 + 4 + -6 + 1

In 13 and 14, add the given numbers.

13. 99, -46, 12, -99, 46, -12

14. $-\frac{3}{8}, -\frac{3}{8}, \frac{40}{3}, -\frac{3}{8}, -\frac{3}{8}, \frac{40}{3}$

15. A family keeps a weekly budget. During a five-week period, they are $12.50 over, $6.30 under, $21 over, $7.05 under, and $9.90 under. How are they doing?

16. A robot turns 50°, -75°, 120°, -103°, and 17°. What is the total turn?

17. The average of *a, b, c,* and *d* is (*a* + *b* + *c* + *d*)/4. Find the average of these daily low temperatures: -1°, 6°, 3°, -4°.

In 18 and 19: **a.** Substitute numbers to show that the property is not always true. **b.** Tell what the property has to do with this lesson.

18. *a* − *b* = *b* − *a*.

19. (*a* − *b*) − *c* = *a* − (*b* − *c*).

In 20 and 21, follow the directions that were given for Questions 4–7 on page 218.

20. 4 + 3x = 3x + 4

21. 8 + (-5 + 5) = 8 + -5 + 5

In 22 and 23, the circles represent Gouda cheeses that have been divided equally.

    a. Find the measure of the smallest angle at the center of the cheese.

    b. Tell whether that angle is acute, obtuse, or right. *(Lessons 3-5, 3-6)*

22.

23.

24. How many degrees are there in a half turn? *(Lesson 5-6)*

25. How many degrees does the second hand of a watch turn in 10 seconds? *(Lesson 5-6)*

26. Refer to the picture of the Ferris wheel in Lesson 5-6. If seat *B* is turned to the position of seat *G,* what seat will be moved to the top? *(Lesson 5-6)*

In 27 and 28, perform the addition. *(Lesson 3-3)*

27. 8 kilograms + 453 grams

28. 1 quart + 1 pint

29. The temperature is $t°$ and goes down 3°. What is the end result? *(Lesson 5-3)*

30. Morrie and Lori together have 7 tickets to a concert. Corey and Lori together have 5 tickets. How many tickets do Corey, Lori, and Morrie have altogether? *(Lesson 5-1)*

31. State the property of opposites. *(Lesson 5-4)*

32. Another term for "additive inverse" is __?__. *(Lesson 5-4)*

33. Mentally solve the equation $x + 45 = 51$. *(Lesson 4-8)*

34. Simplify: -5 + 6(3.7 + 1.3/2) − 4. *(Lesson 4-5)*

35. **a.** Add 203,275 + -89,635 + 265,164 on your calculator.

    b. Turn your calculator 180°. What word does that display spell?

    c. Find two negative numbers and a positive number whose sum on the calculator, when turned 180°, is ShOE.

5-8

Solving
$x + a = b$

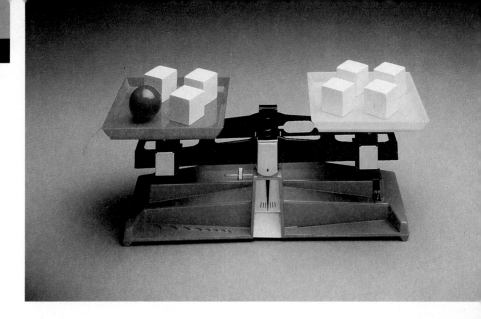

Children in second grade are expected to be able to fill in the blank in

$$\_\_\_ + 3 = 4.$$

In algebra, usually the blank is replaced by a letter. If the sentence involves simple numbers, you should be able to find the solution mentally. For instance, in

$$x + 35 = 48$$

you should know that $x = 13$.

But some equations involve complicated numbers. Other equations involve only variables and no specific numbers at all. It helps to have a systematic way of solving these equations. On one side of both $\_\_\_ + 3 = 4$ and $x + 35 = 48$, a number is being added to an (unknown) variable. On the other side is a single number. They are *equations of the form $x + a = b$.* Think of x as the unknown. Think of a and b as known numbers.

One property of addition is particularly helpful in solving equations. Here is an example. Begin with equal numbers.

$$\tfrac{1}{4} = 0.25$$

If the same number is added to both sides, then the sums will be equal. For instance, if 3 is added to both sides:

$$3 + \tfrac{1}{4} = 3 + 0.25.$$
$$\text{That is,} \quad 3\tfrac{1}{4} = 3.25.$$

Of course, you could add any number to both sides. The sums would still be equal. This property is a special form of the Substitution Principle first mentioned in Lesson 2-6. It has its own name.

Addition Property of Equality:

If $a = b$, then $a + c = b + c$.

The Addition Property of Equality says: If two numbers are equal, then you can add anything you want to both numbers and the sums will be equal. Here is how this property is used in solving equations.

■ ■ ■ ■ ■ ■ ■■

Example 1   Solve $x + -8 = 57$.

>**Solution**   Add 8 to both sides. (That can be done because of the Addition Property of Equality.) Because addition is associative, you do not have to worry about grouping.
>
>$$x + -8 + 8 = 57 + 8$$
>
>Now simplify. Since 8 and -8 are opposites, and 0 is the additive identity,
>
>$$x + 0 = 57 + 8$$
>$$x = 65$$
>
>**Check**   Substitute 65 for x in the original equation.
>Does $65 + -8 = 57$? Yes. So 65 is the solution.

The key thing is to know what number to add to both sides. In Example 1, 8 was added to both sides. This caused the left side to simplify to just x.

In Example 2, no equation is given. An equation has to be figured out from the situation.

■ ■ ■ ■ ■ ■ ■■

Example 2   The temperature was 4° this afternoon and now is -6°. By how much has it changed?

>**Solution**   Let c be the change in temperature. (If c is positive, the temperature has gone up. If c is negative, the temperature has gone down.)
>Then $4 + c = -6$.
>Since 4 is already added to c, we add -4 to both sides. This ensures that c will wind up alone on its side of the equation.
>$$-4 + 4 + c = -4 + -6$$
>$$0 + c = -10$$
>$$c = -10$$
>So the change is -10°. To check, look at the original question. If the temperature was 4° and changes -10°, will it be -6°? Since the answer is yes, -10° is the correct solution.

222

You may be able to solve equations like these in your head. Still, you must learn the general strategy. More complicated problems require it.

In both Examples 1 and 2, after adding the same number to both sides, all you have to do is simplify the sides to find the solution. So there is only one step to remember.

> To solve an equation of the form $x + a = b$, add $-a$ to both sides and simplify.

In solving an equation, the unknown can be on either side. And since addition is commutative, the unknown may be first or second on that side. So all of these four equations have the same solution.

$$x + 43 = -18 \qquad 43 + x = -18 \qquad -18 = x + 43 \qquad -18 = 43 + x$$

When solving an equation, it is important to organize your work carefully. Write each step *underneath* the previous step. Some teachers like students to name properties. Here the equation $x + 43 = -18$ is solved with the properties named where they are used.

$x + 43 = -18$	(original equation)
$x + 43 + -43 = -18 + -43$	Addition Property of Equality
$x + 0 = -18 + -43$	Property of Opposites
$x = -18 + -43$	Additive Identity Property of Zero
$x = -61$	(arithmetic computation)

Check Substitute -61 for x in the original equation.
Does $-61 + 43 = -18$? Yes. So -61 is the solution.

Questions

Covering the Reading

1. Give the solution to $8 + \underline{\quad} = 13$.

2. In algebra, the blank of Question 1 is usually replaced by what?

3. Begin with the equation $4/5 = 0.8$.
   a. Is it true that $6 + 4/5 = 6 + 0.8$?
   b. Is it true that $-1 + 4/5 = -1 + 0.8$?
   c. Is it true that $17.43 + 4/5 = 17.43 + 0.8$?
   d. Parts a to c exemplify what property?

4. Here are steps in the solution of the equation $3.28 = A + \text{-}5$. Give the reason for each step.
  a. $3.28 + 5 = A + \text{-}5 + 5$
  b. $3.28 + 5 = A + 0$
  c. $3.28 + 5 = A$
  d. $\quad\ 8.28 = A$

In 5–8: **a.** To solve the equation, what number could you add to each side of the equation? **b.** Find the solution. **c.** Check your answer.

5. $x + 86 = 230$ **6.** $\text{-}12 + y = 7$

7. $60 = z + \frac{22}{3}$ **8.** $\text{-}5.9 = A + \text{-}3.2.$

9. *Multiple choice* Which equation does not have the same solution as the others?
  (a) $13 + x = \text{-}6$ (b) $\text{-}6 + x = 13$
  (c) $x + 13 = \text{-}6$ (d) $\text{-}6 = x + 13$

10. The temperature was $\text{-}15°$ yesterday and is $\text{-}20°$ today. Let c be the change in the temperature. **a.** What equation can be solved to find c? **b.** Solve that equation. **c.** Check your answer.

11. Suppose the temperature is two degrees below zero. By how much must it change to become three degrees above zero?

Applying the Mathematics

12. If $a = b$, the Addition Property of Equality says that $a + c = b + c$. But it is also true that $c + a = c + b$. Why?

In 13 and 14, you should simplify one side of the equation. Then solve and check.

13. $A + 43 + \text{-}5 = 120$ **14.** $\text{-}35 = 16 + d + 5$

15. A family's income I satisfies the formula $I = F + M + C$, where F is the amount the father earns, M is the amount the mother earns, and C is the amount the children earn. If $I = 40{,}325$, $F = 18{,}800$, and $M = 20{,}500$, how much did the children earn?

16. On Monday, Vito's savings account showed a balance of $103.52. He deposited $35 into the account Tuesday. Wednesday he withdrew $12.50. Thursday he asked the bank to tell him how much was in the account. They said that $130.05 was in the account. What happened is that the bank paid Vito some interest. How much interest?

17. George is G years old. Wilma is W years old.
  a. What will be George's age 10 years from now?
  b. What will be Wilma's age 10 years from now?
  c. If George and Wilma are the same age, how are G and W related?
  d. Translate into mathematics: If George and Wilma are the same age now, then they will be the same age 10 years from now.
  e. Part **d** of this question is an instance of what property?

18. Solve for b: $a + b = c$.

19. Which property is used in getting to each step? *(Lessons 5-4, 5-7)*

$$(5 + 7) + \text{-}5$$

Step 1	$=$	$5 + (7 + \text{-}5)$
Step 2	$=$	$5 + (\text{-}5 + 7)$
Step 3	$=$	$(5 + \text{-}5) + 7$
Step 4	$=$	$0 + 7$
Step 5	$=$	7

20. Simplify: $(4 \cdot 3 - 2 \cdot 1)(4 \cdot 3 + 2 \cdot 1)$. *(Lesson 4-5)*

21. Consider the inequality $x < \text{-}3$. **a.** Name a value of x that is a solution. **b.** Name a value of x that is not a solution. *(Lesson 4-9)*

22. Graph -3, -1, and 2 on a vertical number line. *(Lesson 1-5)*

23. How many zeros follow the 1 in the decimal form of 10^{30}? *(Lesson 2-2)*

24. Approximate 7/16 to the nearest hundredth. *(Lessons 1-4, 1-8)*

25. Draw a picture of a 210° turn. *(Lesson 5-6)*

26. If a $210\frac{1}{2}°$ turn is followed by a $150\frac{1}{8}°$ turn, what results? *(5-2, 5-6)*

27. Draw a line segment with length 73 mm. *(Lessons 3-1, 3-3)*

In 28–30, translate into mathematics. *(Lesson 4-3)*

28. triple a number n

29. five less than a number t

30. a number B divided by twice a second number C

In 31 and 32, translate into English. *(Lesson 3-5)*

31. $\overrightarrow{AB}$

32. $m\angle LNP = 35°$

33. We found this addition example in some scrap paper. Apparently a machine folded this paper funny. Four digits are missing, all in a line! What was the original problem?

34. Run this program at least four times picking four different pairs of values for A and B.

```
10  PRINT "A"
15  INPUT A
20  PRINT "B"
25  INPUT B
30  X = A - B
40  PRINT "X = " X
50  END
```

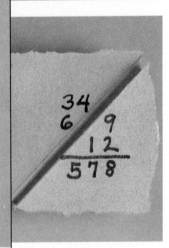

a. What does this program do?
b. Does the program work when A and B are negative numbers?
c. Does the program work when A and B are fractions?
d. Modify the program so that it prints the average of A and B.

Let A and B be any points. There is only one line containing both of them. The line goes on forever. So when it is *drawn*, arrows are put at both ends. This line is written $\overleftrightarrow{AB}$, with the two-sided arrow above the letters.

The points on $\overleftrightarrow{AB}$ that are between A and B, together with the points A and B themselves, make up a **line segment** or **segment**, written as $\overline{AB}$. A and B are the endpoints of $\overline{AB}$.

A **polygon** is a union of segments connected end to end. The segments are called the **sides** of the polygon. Two sides meet at a **vertex** of the polygon. (The plural of vertex is **vertices**.) The number of sides equals the number of vertices. Polygons are classified by that number.

Number of sides	Number of vertices	Type of polygon	Example
3	3	triangle	
4	4	quadrilateral	
5	5	pentagon	
6	6	hexagon	
7	7	heptagon	
8	8	octagon	
9	9	nonagon	
10	10	decagon	

Polygons with more than 10 sides do not always have special names. A polygon with 11 sides is called an 11-gon. A polygon with 42 sides is called a 42-gon. In general, a polygon with *n* sides is called an ***n*-gon.**

Polygons are named by giving their vertices in order around the figure. The boundary of the warehouse pictured at right is quadrilateral *WTUV*. You could also call it polygon *TUVW*, *WVUT*, or five other names. *WTVU* is not a correct name for this polygon because the vertices *W*, *T*, *V*, and *U* are not in order.

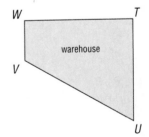

Extend two sides of a polygon drawn from a particular vertex to be rays with the vertex as the endpoint. These rays form an **angle of the polygon**. Every polygon has as many angles as it has sides or vertices. In warehouse polygon *WTUV*, angles *W* and *T* look like right angles. Angle *U* is acute. Angle *V* is obtuse.

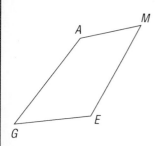

1. The line through points *A* and *B* is written ___?___.

2. The line segment with endpoints *C* and *D* consists of what points?

3. The line segment with endpoints *F* and *E* is written ___?___.

4. Refer to the polygon pictured at left.
  a. Name this polygon.   **b.** Name its sides.   **c.** Name its vertices.
  d. Name its angles.   **e.** What type of polygon is this?

In 5–16, what name is given to a polygon with the given number of sides?

5. 5	**6.** 6	**7.** 7	**8.** 8
9. 9	**10.** 10	**11.** 11	**12.** *n*
13. 3	**14.** 4	**15.** 26	**16.** 4302

17. How many angles does a 12-gon have?

18. A decagon has ___?___ sides, ___?___ angles, and ___?___ vertices.

19. Refer to the figure at left.
  a. Give three possible names for this polygon.
  b. What type of polygon is this?

20. A square is what type of polygon mentioned in this lesson?

21. Temples in the Baha'i religion have 9 sides. Suppose you view a Baha'i temple from directly overhead. The outline of the temple will have what shape?

22. A famous building just outside Washington, D.C., is pictured below. A clue to its name is given by its shape. What is its name?

A **diagonal** of a polygon is a segment that connects two vertices of the polygon but is not a side of the polygon. For example, $\overline{AC}$ and $\overline{BD}$ are the diagonals of quadrilateral *ABCD* drawn below. Use this information in Questions 23 and 24.

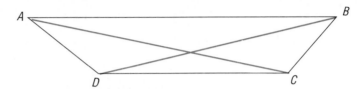

23. **a.** Draw a pentagon *PQRST* and name its diagonals. **b.** How many diagonals does it have?

24. **a.** Draw a hexagon. **b.** How many diagonals does it have?

25. The triangle, quadrilateral, pentagon, and decagon pictured in the table in this lesson are **convex polygons**. The other polygons are not convex. Use this information to pick the correct description of convex polygon from this list. A convex polygon is:
    (a) a polygon in which two sides are parallel.
    (b) a polygon in which there is a right angle.
    (c) a polygon in which no diagonals lie outside the polygon.
    (d) a polygon with a number of sides that is not a prime number.

Review

26. *Multiple choice*   Which equation does not have the same solution as the others? *(Lesson 5-8)*
    (a) $23 = 60 + y$ (b) $y + 60 = 23$
    (c) $23 = y + 60$ (d) $y + 23 = 60$

In 27 and 28, solve and check. *(Lesson 5-8)*

27. $x + 12 = {}^-10$ 28. $300 = 172 + (45 + w)$

29. Given are steps in solving the general equation $a + x = b$ for x. Give the reason why each step is correct. *(Lessons 5-4, 5-8)*
$$a + x = b$$
    Step 1 $-a + a + x = {}^-a + b$
    Step 2 $0 + x = {}^-a + b$
    Step 3 $x = {}^-a + b$

30. A sofa has length s inches. If the sofa were 3 inches longer, it would be 8 feet long. *(Lessons 4-3, 5-8)*
    a. Give an equation that involves the three quantities mentioned in the previous two sentences.
    b. Solve that equation for s.

Exploration

31. A triangle *ABC* can be named in 6 different ways using its vertices: *ABC, ACB, BCA, BAC, CAB,* and *CBA*.
    a. In how many different ways can a quadrilateral be named?
    b. In how many different ways can a pentagon be named?

5-10

Adding Lengths

In driving from Chicago to Louisville, the quickest way is to go through Indianapolis. It is 185 miles from Chicago to Indianapolis. It is 114 miles from Indianapolis to Louisville. How far is it from Chicago to Louisville?

The answer is easy. Just add.

$$185 + 114 = 299$$

It is 299 driving miles from Chicago to Louisville.

The general pattern is easy. If you have two lengths x and y, the total length is $x + y$. This is another instance of the Putting-together Model for Addition.

total length $= x + y$

There are many situations in which more than two lengths are put together. Imagine walking around the building outlined below. You will have walked $40 + 40 + 50 + 10$ meters. This is the idea behind perimeter.

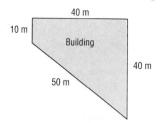

Let the sides of a pentagon have lengths v, w, x, y, and z. If the perimeter is p, then $p = v + w + x + y + z$.

Now suppose $v = 12$, $w = 19$, $x = 15$, $z = 22$, and the perimeter $p = 82$. The situation is pictured below. What is the value of y? You can solve an equation to find out.

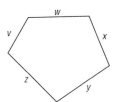 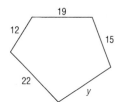

In general: $p = v + w + x + y + z$
In this case: $82 = 12 + 19 + 15 + y + 22$
Simplifying the right side: $82 = 68 + y$
Adding -68 to both sides
and simplifying: $14 = y$

Recall that if A and B are points, we use the following symbols.

$\overleftrightarrow{AB}$ line through A and B
$\overline{AB}$ segment with endpoints A and B
$\overrightarrow{AB}$ ray starting at A and containing B

There is one other related symbol. The **symbol AB** (with nothing over it) stands for the *length of the segment AB*. (It makes no sense to multiply points. So when A and B are points, putting the letters next to each other does not mean multiplication.) Here are some examples of this notation.

The perimeter of triangle PQR is $PQ + QR + RP$.

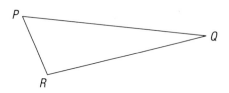

B is on $\overline{AC}$.
$AB + BC = AC$
$12 + 24 = AC$
$36 = AC$

Questions

Covering the Reading

1. Driving along the California coast, San Luis Obispo is between San Francisco and Los Angeles. A map shows that San Francisco is 241 miles from San Luis Obispo. Los Angeles is 195 miles from San Luis Obispo. By this route, how far is it from San Francisco to Los Angeles?

2. The situation in Question 1 is an instance of what model for addition?

In 3–6, *P* and *Q* are points. **a.** Give the meaning of each symbol. **b.** Draw a picture (if possible) of the figure the symbol stands for.

3. $\overleftrightarrow{PQ}$ 4. $\overrightarrow{PQ}$ 5. $\overline{PQ}$ 6. PQ

In 7–10, use the drawing. *B* is on $\overline{AC}$.

7. If $AB = 5$ and $BC = 3$, what is AC?

8. If $AB = x$ and $BC = y$, what is AC?

9. If $AB = x$ and $BC = 3$, what is AC?

10. If $AB = 14.3$ cm, $BC = t$ cm, and $AC = v$ cm, how are 14.3, t, and v related?

11. What is the perimeter of a polygon?

In 12 and 13, give the perimeter of the polygon.

12.
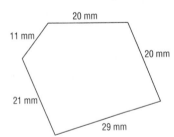

13.
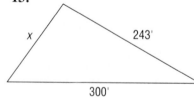

14. In Question 13, suppose the perimeter of the triangle is 689 feet. **a.** What equation can you solve to find *x*? **b.** Solve the equation.

In 15 and 16: **a.** Write an equation that will help answer the question. **b.** Solve the equation.

15. Two sides of a pentagon have length 9 and two sides have length 5. The perimeter of the pentagon is 30. What is the length of the fifth side?

16. A race is to be 10 km long. The organizers want the runners to run over a bicycle path that is 2800 meters long and a final leg that is 650 meters long. How much more of the course must be found?

17. Two sides of a triangle ABC have the same length, and $AB = 40$. The perimeter of triangle ABC is 100. What are the possible lengths for $\overline{BC}$ and $\overline{AC}$?

18. Only one of these is not true. Which one is it?
    (a) $\overleftrightarrow{AB} = \overleftrightarrow{BA}$ (b) $\overrightarrow{AB} = \overrightarrow{BA}$
    (c) $\overline{AB} = \overline{BA}$ (d) $AB = BA$

19. A square has one side of length 5 m. **a.** Is this enough information to find its perimeter? **b.** If so, find it. If not, tell why there is not enough information.

20. Use the drawing below. B is on $\overline{AC}$. If $AC = 1$ ft and $BC = 1$ in., what is AB?

21. Draw a polygon called *NICE* and put $\overrightarrow{CN}$ and $\overline{IE}$ on your drawing.

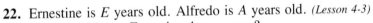

22. Ernestine is E years old. Alfredo is A years old. *(Lesson 4-3)*
    a. How old was Ernestine 4 years ago?
    b. How old was Alfredo 4 years ago?
    c. Translate into mathematics: If Ernestine and Alfredo are the same age now, then they were the same age four years ago.
    d. Part **c** of this question is an instance of what property?

23. The temperature was -22° yesterday and 10° today. Let t be the change in the temperature. **a.** What equation can be used to find t? **b.** Solve the equation. **c.** Check your answer. *(Lesson 5-8)*

24. Suppose the probability of rain is $\frac{1}{50}$. Then the probability of no rain is n, where $\frac{1}{50} + n = 1$. Solve this equation for n. *(Lesson 5-8)*

25. Simplify: **a.** -6 + -(-6); **b.** -(-x) + -(-y). *(Lessons 5-4, 5-5)*

In 26–29, use the drawing.

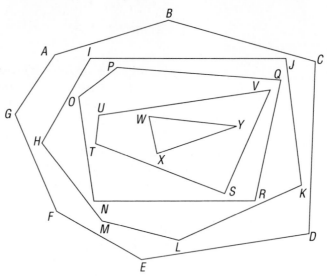

26. Measure the lengths to the nearest millimeter of all sides of the quadrilateral. *(Lesson 3-1)*

27. Which angles of the heptagon seem to be obtuse? *(Lessons 3-6, 5-9)*

28. Which angles of the pentagon seem to be acute? *(Lessons 3-6, 5-9)*

29. Measure angle *TSV*. *(Lesson 3-5)*

In 30 and 31, graph the solutions to each inequality. *(Lesson 4-9)*

30. $x < 5$ **31.** $y \geq -3/2$

32. Solve $-0.3 + A = 6.3$. *(Lesson 5-8)*

Exploration

33. Find the lengths of sides in all triangles satisfying *all* these conditions.
(a) The perimeter is 40.
(b) No side has length under 10.
(c) All sides have different lengths.
(d) The lengths of all sides are integers.
(Hint: Organize your work.)

Summary

A large variety of situations lead to addition. These situations are of two types: putting-together or slide. Some situations can be interpreted as either of these types.

In a putting-together situation, a count or measure x is put together with a count or measure y. If x and y have the same units and there is no overlap, the result has count or measure $x + y$. When the lengths of the sides of a polygon are put together, the result is the perimeter of the polygon. In a putting-together situation, x and y must be positive or zero.

In slide situations, a slide x is followed by a slide y. The result is a slide $x + y$. In slide situations, there may be changes forward or back, up or down, in or out, clockwise or counterclockwise. One direction is positive, the other negative. So in a slide situation, x and y can be positive, zero, or negative.

From these situations, you can see many properties of addition. Zero is the additive identity. Every number has an opposite or additive inverse. Addition is both commutative and associative.

Suppose you know one addend a and the sum b and would like to find the other addend. Then you are trying to find x in an equation $x + a = b$. This sentence can be solved using the Addition Property of Equality and the other properties of addition.

Vocabulary

You should be able to give a general description and a specific example of each of the following ideas.

Lesson 5-1
Putting-together Model for Addition
addend
Lesson 5-2
common denominator
Lesson 5-3
Slide Model for Addition

Lesson 5-4
additive identity
Additive Identity Property of Zero
additive inverse
Property of Opposites, Op-op Property
Lesson 5-5
absolute value, | |
Lesson 5-6
revolution, full turn, quarter turn
clockwise, counterclockwise
magnitude of turn
Fundamental Property of Turns

Lesson 5-7
Commutative Property of Addition
Associative Property of Addition
Lesson 5-8
Addition Property of Equality
situation of the form $x + a = b$
Lesson 5-9
line segment, segment, $\overline{AB}$
$\overleftrightarrow{AB}$
polygon, side, vertex (vertices), angle of polygon
quadrilateral, pentagon, hexagon, ..., n-gon
diagonal of a polygon
convex polygon
Lesson 5-10
perimeter
AB

Progress Self-Test

Take this test as you would take a test in class. Then check your work with the solutions in the Selected Answers section in the back of the book.

In 1–7, simplify.

1. 3 + -10

2. -460 + -250

3. -9.8 + -(-1)

4. $x + y + -x + 4$

5. |-8|

6. |-2| + |1| + |0|

7. -6 + 42 + -11 + 16 + -12

8. Evaluate |-A + 8| when A = -3.

In 9–11, solve.

9. $x + 43 = 31$

10. -25 + y = 12

11. 8 = -2 + z + -5

In 12–15, write as a single fraction in lowest terms.

12. $\frac{53}{12} + \frac{11}{12}$

13. $\frac{5}{x} + \frac{10}{x}$

14. $\frac{17}{9} + \frac{8}{3}$

15. $\frac{1}{4} + \frac{3}{8} + \frac{2}{16}$

In 16 and 17, consider the equation 50 = W + -20.

16. To solve this equation, what number should you add to both sides?

17. What property enables you to add the same number to both sides of an equation?

18. (2 + 3) + 4 = 2 + (3 + 4) is an instance of what property?

19. Give an instance of the Addition Property of Zero.

20. A polygon with 6 sides is called a __?__.

21. A pentagon has two sides of length 3 cm and three sides of length 4 cm. What is its perimeter?

22. *Multiple choice* If L and K are points, which symbol stands for a number?
(a) LK (b) $\overline{LK}$ (c) $\overrightarrow{LK}$ (d) $\overleftrightarrow{LK}$

23. Ms. A's class has m students. Mr. B's class has n students. Together there are 50 students in the classes. How are m, n, and 50 related?

In 24 and 25, Sally was 20 points behind. Now she is 150 points ahead. Let c be the change in Sally's status.

24. What equation can be solved to find c?

25. Solve that equation.

In 26 and 27, use the figure below. A is on $\overline{MP}$.

26. If MA = 16 and AP = 8, what is MP?

M ————————————————— A ————— P

27. If MA = 2.3 and MP = 3, what is PA?

28. Picture the addition problem -3 + 2 on a number line and give the sum.

29. An iron bar is 3 cm longer than 5 meters. In meters, how long is the bar?

30. Is -5.498765432101 + 5.498765432102 positive, negative, or zero?

In 31 and 32, use the figure below. Assume all small angles with vertex O have the same measure.

31. What is m∠VOW?

32. If you are standing at O facing U and turn to X, what is the magnitude of your turn?

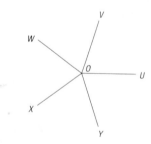

33. What is the result when a 50° clockwise turn is followed by a 250° counterclockwise turn?

34. *Multiple choice* Which is not a side of the polygon $WXYZ$? (a) $\overline{WX}$ (b) $\overline{WY}$ (c) $\overline{WZ}$ (d) Each of (a), (b), (c) is a side.

Chapter Review

Questions on **SPUR** Objectives

SPUR stands for **S**kills, **P**roperties, **U**ses, and **R**epresentations.
The Chapter Review questions are grouped according to the
SPUR Objectives for this chapter.

SKILLS deal with the procedures used to get answers.

■ **Objective A:** *Add any numbers written as decimals or fractions. (Lessons 5-2, 5-3, 5-5)*
In 1–9, add.

1. $-16 + 4$
2. $-7 + -8 + -9$
3. $7 + -2.4 + 5$
4. $-31 + 32$
5. $6/11 + 5/11$
6. $\frac{12}{17} + \frac{-12}{17}$
7. $6 + -\frac{8}{9}$
8. $2/3$ and $6/7$
9. $1/2$, $1/3$, and $1/4$
10. Write $\frac{40}{c} + \frac{-10}{c}$ as a single fraction.

■ **Objective B:** *Calculate absolute value. (Lesson 5-5)*

11. $|-12| = \,?$
12. $|4| = \,?$
13. $|0| + |3| + |-5| = \,?$
14. $-|7| + |4| = \,?$

■ **Objective C:** *Apply properties of addition to simplify expressions. (Lesson 5-4)*

15. $-(-(-17)) = \,?$
16. $-(-4) + 3 = \,?$
17. $-40 + 0 = \,?$
18. $(86 + -14) + (-86 + 14) = \,?$
19. $-(-(0 + \frac{2}{7})) = \,?$
20. $11/4 + y + -11/4 = \,?$
21. When $a = -42$, then $-a + 6 = \,?$
22. If $b = 2$, then $b + -b = \,?$

■ **Objective D:** *Solve equations of the form $x + a = b$. (Lesson 5-8)*

23. Solve $x + -32 = -12$.
24. Solve $6.3 = t + 2.9$.
25. Solve $\frac{10}{3} + y = \frac{1}{3}$.
26. Solve $0 + a = 4 + 1$.
27. Solve $3 + c + -5 = 36$.
28. Solve $-8 = 14 + (d + -6)$.
29. Solve for x: $x + y = 180$.
30. Solve for c: $a + b + c = p$.

■ **Objective E:** *Find the perimeter of a polygon. (Lesson 5–10)*

31. What is the perimeter of a square in which one side has length 3?
32. If $x = 23$, what is the perimeter of the polygon *ABCDE*?

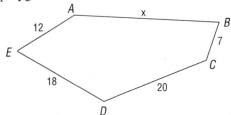

33. Measure the sides of polygon *GHIJ* to find its perimeter to the nearest centimeter.

34. An octagon has 3 sides of length 5 and 4 sides of length 6. What is its perimeter?
35. For polygon *ABCDE* in Question 32, if the perimeter is 82, what equation can be solved to find x?

PROPERTIES deal with the principles behind the mathematics.

■ **Objective F:** *Identify properties of addition.*
(Lessons 5-4, 5-7)

In 36–39, an instance of what property of addition is given?

36. 3.53 meters + 6.74 meters
= 6.74 meters + 3.53 meters

37. Since 30% = 3/10, it is also true that
1/2 + 30% = 1/2 + 3/10.

38. -941 + 941 = 0

39. (1 + 2) + 3 = (2 + 1) + 3

■ **Objective G:** *Classify polygons.* *(Lesson 5-9)*
In 40–42, classify the polygon and tell whether or not it is convex.

40.

41.

42.

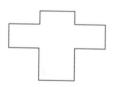

■ **Objective H:** *Identify parts and give names of polygons.* *(Lesson 5-9)*

43. Which is not a correct name for the polygon below?
LAKE, LEAK, KALE, ELAK

44. Name the two diagonals of the polygon below.

45. The polygon below has __?__ vertices and __?__ sides.

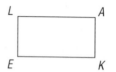

46. Name a side of the polygon *ABCDE*.

USES deal with applications of mathematics in real situations.

■ **Objective I:** *Use the Putting-together Model for Addition to form sentences involving addition.*
(Lessons 5-1, 5-2, 5-8)

47. Bob rode his bicycle a mile and a half to school. Then he rode 3/5 of a mile to his friend's house. Altogether he rode *M* miles. What relationship connects these distances?

48. You have read *x* books this year. A friend has read *y* books. Together you have read 16 books. What relationship connects *x*, *y*, and 16?

49. In the Johannson family, Dad earned *D* dollars last year. Mom earned *M* dollars. The children earned *C* dollars. The total family income was *T* dollars. What sentence relates *D*, *M*, *C*, and *T*?

Objective J: *Apply the putting-together model to relate lengths.* *(Lesson 5-10)*

In 50–52, use the figure at right. B is on $\overline{AC}$.

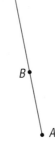

50. What relationship connects AB, BC, and AC?

51. If $AB = x$ and $BC = 3$, what is AC?

52. Let $AC = 10.4$ and $BC = 7.8$.
a. What equation can be used to find AB? **b.** What is AB?

Objective K: *Use the slide model for addition to form sentences involving addition.*
(Lesson 5-3, 5-8)

53. Charyl's stock rose $\frac{3}{8}$ of a point on one day and fell $\frac{1}{4}$ point the next day.
a. What addition gives the total change in Charyl's stock?
b. What is the total change?

54. Bernie gained 5 pounds one week, lost 7 the next, and lost 3 the next.
a. What addition gives the total change in Bernie's weight?
b. What is the total change?

55. A diving team was 250 feet below ground level and then came up 75 feet.
a. What addition tells where the team wound up?
b. Where did they wind up?

56. The temperature was -3° and changed $c°$ to reach -10°. What is c?

REPRESENTATIONS deal with pictures, graphs, or objects that illustrate concepts.

Objective L: *Calculate magnitudes of turns given angle measures or revolutions.* *(Lesson 5-6)*

In 57–59, all small angles at O have the same measure. Think of turns around the point O.

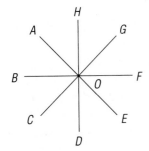

57. What is the magnitude of the turn from F to A?

58. What is the magnitude of the turn from E to C?

59. If you are facing H and turn 315° clockwise, what point will you then be facing?

60. If you turn 90° counterclockwise, and then turn 40° clockwise, what is the result?

Objective M: *Picture addition of positive and negative numbers using arrows on a number line.* *(Lesson 5-3)*

61. Picture the addition -5 + 8 on a number line and give the sum.

62. Picture the addition 17 + -4 on a number line and give the sum.

63. Picture the addition -3.5 + -6.5 on a number line and give the sum.

Problem-Solving Strategies

McGURK'S MOB

To solve a problem is to find a way where no way is known off-hand, to find a way out of a difficulty, to find a way around an obstacle, to attain a desired end that is not immediately attainable, by appropriate means.

—George Polya [1887–1985]

Solving problems is human nature itself.

—Polya

The person who makes no mistakes usually makes nothing.

—Anonymous

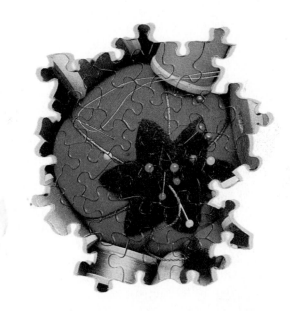

6-1

Being a Good Problem Solver

In Chapter 5, you learned how to solve any equation of the form $a + x = b$ for x. The method was to add $-a$ to each side and then simplify. This method is an example of an algorithm. An **algorithm** is a sequence of steps that leads to a desired result.

Not all algorithms are short. The algorithm called *long division* can involve many steps.

$$
\begin{array}{r}
.75 \\
34\overline{)25.50} \\
\underline{23\ 8} \\
1\ 70 \\
\underline{1\ 70}
\end{array}
$$

You know another algorithm for dividing decimals. It is the calculator algorithm. It is much easier to describe the algorithm for division on a calculator than for long division. The key sequence describes the algorithm.

Key sequence: 25.50   ÷   34   =

Display: `25.50` `25.50` `34` `0.75`

There is another way to think about algorithms. An algorithm is something that a computer could be programmed to do.

An **exercise** is a question that you know how to answer. For you, adding whole numbers is an exercise. You know an algorithm for addition. A **problem** for you is a question you do not know how to answer. It is a question for which you have no algorithm. Many people think that if they do not have an algorithm, then they cannot do a problem. But that isn't true. By following some advice, almost anyone can become a better problem solver.

In this chapter you will learn many strategies for solving problems. But you must do three things.

1. *Take your time.* Few people solve problems fast. (If a person solves a problem fast, then it may not have been a problem for that person!)

2. *Don't give up.* You will never solve a problem if you do not try. Do something! (In the cartoon on page 241, Rick and the man give up too soon.)

3. *Be flexible.* If at first you don't succeed, try another way. And if the second way does not work, try a third way.

George Polya was a mathematician at Stanford University who was famous for his writing about solving problems. He once wrote:

"Solving problems is a practical skill like, let us say, swimming. We acquire any practical skill by imitation and practice. Trying to swim, you imitate what other people do with their hands and feet to keep their heads above water, and, finally, you learn to swim by practicing swimming. Trying to solve problems, you have to observe and to imitate what other people do when solving problems and, finally, you learn to do problems by doing them."

In a famous book called *How to Solve It*, Polya described what good problem solvers do.

- They *read the problem carefully.* They try to understand every word. They make sure they know what is asked for. They reread. They make certain that they are using the correct information. They look up words they do not know.

- They *devise a plan.* Even guesses are planned. They arrange information in tables. They draw pictures. They compare the problem to other problems they know. They decide to try something.

- They *carry out the plan.* They attempt to solve. They work with care. They write things down so they can read them later. If the attempt does not work, they go back to read the problem again.

- They *check work.* In fact, they check their work at every step. They do not check by repeating what they did. They check by estimating, or by trying to find another way of doing the problem.

These are the kinds of strategies you will study in this chapter. You will also learn about some important problems and some fun problems.

1. What is an algorithm?   **2.** Give an example of an algorithm.

3. What is a problem?

4. What is an exercise?

In 5 and 6, refer to the algorithm pictured at right.

$$\begin{array}{r} 34.2 \\ \underline{5.67} \\ 2394 \\ 2052 \\ \underline{1710} \\ 193.914 \end{array}$$

5. What question does this algorithm answer?

6. Write the calculator algorithm that answers the same question.

In 7–9, what problem-solving advice is suggested by each traffic sign?

7.   **8.**   **9.**

SLOW   DETOUR   NO PARKING

10. Who was George Polya?

11. What famous book did Polya write?

In 12 and 13, tell what each person should have done.

12. Monty tried one way to do the problem. When that did not work, he tried the same way again.

13. Priscilla said to herself: "I've never seen any problem like that before. I won't be able to do it."

14. What four things do successful problem solvers do when solving a problem?

15. Marjorie wants to devise a plan to solve a problem. What are some of the things she can do?

16. Adam wrote down an answer very quickly and went on to the next problem. What did he do wrong?

17. Consider the vowels A, E, I, O, U. Make two-letter monograms with these vowels, like AO, UE, II. How many two-letter monograms are there? (Hint: Make an organized list.)

18. You can buy stickers for digits from 0 through 9 at most hardware stores. They can be used for house addresses and room numbers. Suppose you buy stickers for all the digits in all the integers from 1 through 100. **a.** What digit will be used most? **b.** What digit will be used least?

19. Trains leave Union Station every hour from 7 A.M. through 7 P.M. bound for Kroy. How many trains is that in a day?

20. Suppose in Question 19, trains left every *half* hour, from 7 A.M. through 7 P.M. How many trains is that in a day?

21. A cube has how many edges? *(Lesson 3-8)*

22. What is the volume of a cube with an edge of length 5 centimeters? *(Lesson 3-8)*

23. Simplify: $\frac{2}{3} + \frac{5}{7} - \frac{1}{14}$. *(Lessons 5-2, 5-5)*

24. How many feet are in 5 miles? *(Lesson 3-2)*

25. Find the value of $3 + 4a$ when $a = 2.5$. *(Lesson 4-4)*

26. Give the fraction in lowest terms equal to:
a. 10%   **b.** 25%   **c.** 75%   **d.** $66\frac{2}{3}$% *(Lesson 2-5)*

27. One-sixth is equal to __?__ percent. *(Lesson 2-7)*

28. Here are changes in population for the six largest cities in the United States from 1970 to 1980. *(Lessons 5-5, 5-7)*

New York	-823,924
Chicago	-364,185
Los Angeles	155,049
Philadelphia	-261,786
Houston	371,603
Detroit	-310,724

a. Which cities gained in population in that decade?

b. What was the total change in population for the six cities combined?

29. Of the 5.1 billion people on earth, about 1% live in Egypt. How many people is this? *(Lessons 2-1, 2-6)*

Exploration

30. Each letter stands for a different digit in this addition problem. The sum is 10440. Find the digits.

```
        U
      C A N
        D O
    T H I S
    ─────────
    1 0 4 4 0
```

6-2

Read Carefully

To solve a problem, you must understand it. So, if the problem is written down, you must *read it carefully*. To read carefully, there are three things you must do.

1. Know the meaning of all words and symbols in the problem.
2. Sort out information that is not needed.
3. Determine if there is enough information to solve the problem.

Example 1 List the ten smallest positive composite integers.

Strategy To answer this question, you must know the meaning of "positive composite integer." In this book, we have already discussed the positive integers. So the new word here is "composite." Our dictionary has many definitions of "composite," but only one of "composite number." Here is that definition: "Any number exactly divisible by one or more numbers other than itself and 1; opposed to *prime number*." So a composite number is a positive integer that is not prime. Now the problem can be solved.

Solution The positive integers are 1, 2, 3, 4,.... Those that are prime are 2, 3, 5, 7, 11, 13, 17, and so on. The ten smallest composites are the others: 4, 6, 8, 9, 10, 12, 14, 15, 16, 18.

If you do not know the meaning of a word, look it up in a dictionary. Your school may even have a dictionary of mathematical words. Some mathematics books (including this one) have glossaries or indexes in the back that can help you locate words.

Some terms have more than one meaning even in mathematics. The word *divisor* can mean *the number divided by* in a division problem. (In $12 \div 3 = 4$, 3 is the divisor.). But *divisor* also means *a number that divides another number with a zero remainder*. For example, 7 is a divisor of 21. Then *divisor* has the same meaning as *factor*.

Some symbols have more than one meaning. The dash "−" can mean subtraction. It can also mean "the opposite of." However, in phone numbers, like 555—1212, it has no meaning other than to separate the number to make it easier to remember. You must look at the situation to determine which meaning is correct in a given problem.

Here is an example of a problem with too much information. Can you tell what information is not needed?

Example 2   Last year the Williams family joined a reading club. Mrs. Williams read 20 books. Mr. Williams read 16 books. Their son Jed read 12 books. Their daughter Josie read 14 books and their daughter Julie read 7 books. How many books did these children of Mr. & Mrs. Williams read altogether?

Solution   Did you see that the problem asks only about the *children*? The information about the books read by Mr. and Mrs. Williams is not needed. The children read 12 + 14 + 7 books, for a total of 33 books.

Example 3   Read Example 2 again. How many children do the Williamses have?

Solution   Do you think 3? Reread the problem. Nowhere does it say that these are the only children. The Williamses have *at least* 3 children.

Questions

Covering the Reading

1. What three things should you do when you read a problem?

2. Can a word have more than one mathematical meaning?

3. Give an example of a mathematical symbol that has more than one meaning.

4. Which number is not a composite integer?   6   7   8   9   10

5. Which number is not a prime number?   11   13   15   17   19

6. List the ten smallest positive prime numbers.

7. Which number is a divisor of 91?   3   5   7   9   11

8. Which number is a factor of 91? 13 15 17 19 21

In 9–11, refer to Example 2.

9. How many books did Mr. & Mrs. Williams read altogether?

10. What word is a hint that the Williamses have more than three children?

11. Of the three Williams children named, who is youngest?

12. Name three places to look to find a definition of a mathematical term.

Applying the Mathematics

A **natural number** is one of the numbers 1, 2, 3, 4,.... Use this definition in Questions 13–15.

13. *Multiple choice* Which of (a) to (c) is the same as natural number?
(a) whole number (b) integer (c) positive integer (d) none

14. Name all natural numbers that are solutions to $10 > x > 7$.

15. How many natural numbers are solutions of $v < 40$?

16. List all the divisors of 36.

17. In $\frac{24}{35}$ which number is the divisor?

18. Which of the following numbers are prime? 2; 57; 8^6; 5×10^4

In 19–21, give or draw an example of each item.

19. a regular hexagon   **20.** a perfect number

21. a pair of twin primes

In 22 and 23, use the following information. The class in room 25 had 23 students last year and has 27 students this year. The class in room 24 had 25 students last year and has 26 students this year. There are 22 students this year and there were 28 students last year in room 23.

22. What was the total number of students in these classrooms last year?

23. In which year were there more students in these classrooms?

In 24 and 25, use the following information. The class in room a had b students last year and has c students this year. The class in room d had e students last year and has f students this year. There are g students this year and there were h students last year in room i.

24. What was the total number of students in these classrooms last year?

25. In which year were there more students in these classrooms?

26. What are Polya's four steps in problem solving? *(Lesson 6-1)*

27. In a Scrabble® tournament, a person played six different people with the following results: won by 12, lost by 30, won by 65, won by 47, lost by 3, and lost by 91. What was the total point difference between this person and the other six people combined? *(Lesson 5-5)*

28. Simplify: $-(-(-(-y)))$. *(Lesson 5-5)*

29. Simplify: $5 + -(-(-3 + 4 \cdot 2))$. *(Lessons 4-5, 5-4)*

30. Solve for x: $x + 3 + y = y + 8$. *(Lesson 5-8)*

31. Name two segments in the drawing that look perpendicular. *(Lesson 3-6)*

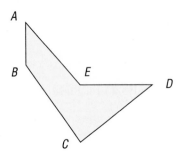

32. List all even prime numbers.

Draw a Picture

You can understand every word in a problem yet still not be able to solve it immediately. One way to devise a plan is to *draw a picture*. Sometimes the picture is obvious, as in Example 1.

Example 1   How many diagonals does a heptagon have?

Strategy   The plan is obvious. Draw a heptagon and draw its diagonals. Count the diagonals as you draw them.

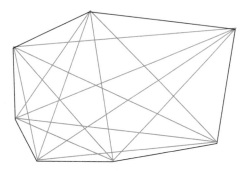

Solution   There are 14 diagonals. (Count them to check.)

Suppose you did not remember that a heptagon has 7 sides. Then you could look back in Chapter 5. Or you could look in a dictionary. The same is true if you forgot what a diagonal is.

Sometimes a problem is not geometric. A drawing can still help.

■ ■ ■ ■ ■ ■ ■ ■ ■ ■

Example 2 Seven teams are to play each other in a tournament. How many games are needed?

Solution Name the teams *A, B, C, D, E, F,* and *G*. Use these letters to name points in a drawing. When *A* plays *D,* draw the segment *AD.* So each segment between two points represents a different game.

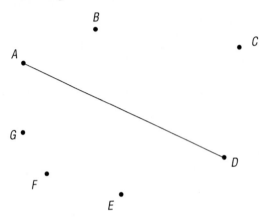

The number of games played is the number of segments that can be drawn. But the segments are the sides and diagonals of a heptagon. Since a heptagon has 7 sides and Example 1 showed that there are 14 diagonals in a heptagon, there are 21 segments altogether. Twenty-one games are needed for the tournament.

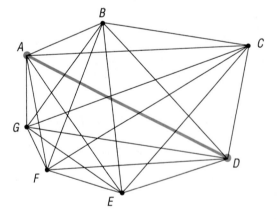

Drawing a picture is a very important problem-solving idea. You may never have thought of picturing teams as we did above. In newspapers and magazines you often see numbers pictured in bar graphs and circle graphs. Chapter 8 in this book is devoted to these kinds of displays.

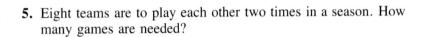

Questions

Covering the Reading

1. How many diagonals does a heptagon have?

2. Seven teams are to play each other in a tournament. How many games are needed?

3. How many diagonals does a quadrilateral have?

4. Four teams are to play each other in a tournament. How many games are needed?

Applying the Mathematics

5. Eight teams are to play each other two times in a season. How many games are needed?

In 6–9, the strategy of this lesson will help.

6. A square dog pen is 10 feet on a side. There is a post in each corner. There are posts every 2 feet on each side. How many posts are there in all?

7. Bill is older than Wanda and younger than Jill. Jill is older than Chris and younger than Pete. Chris is older than Wanda. Bill is younger than Pete. Chris is older than Bill. Who is youngest?

8. Amy is driving along Interstate 55 in Illinois from Collinsville to Joliet. She will pass through Litchfield and then through Atlanta. The distance from Collinsville to Litchfield is half the distance from Litchfield to Atlanta. The distance from Atlanta to Joliet is three times the distance from Collinsville to Litchfield. The distance from Atlanta to Joliet is 114 miles. How far is it from Collinsville to Joliet?

9. The Sherman family has a pool 30 feet long and 25 feet wide. There is a walkway 4.5 feet wide around the pool.
   a. What is the perimeter of the pool?
   b. What is the perimeter of the outside of the walkway?

Review

10. Find the value of $6x^4$ when $x = 3$. *(Lesson 4-4)*

11. List all the natural number factors of 40. *(Lesson 6-2)*

12. Name three places to look if you do not know the meaning of a mathematical term. *(Lesson 6-2)*

13. What number will you get if you follow this key sequence?
    20 $\boxed{y^x}$ 3 $\boxed{\times}$ 2 $\boxed{+}$ $\boxed{(}$ 5 $\boxed{+}$ 4 $\boxed{)}$ $\boxed{=}$ *(Lessons 1-7, 2-2)*

14. List the natural numbers between 8.4 and 4.2. *(Lesson 6-2)*

15. List all prime numbers between 40 and 50. *(Lesson 6-2)*

In 16 and 17, suppose that Sarah has *S* dollars and Dana has *D* dollars. Translate into English. *(Lesson 5-8)*

16. $S = D$ **17.** If $S = D$, then $S + 2 = D + 2$.

18. When $a = -3$ and $b = 6$, what is the value of $-(a + b)$? *(Lessons 4-5, 5-5)*

19. What is the absolute value of -30? *(Lesson 5-5)*

20. Which is larger, 45 centimeters or 800 millimeters? *(Lesson 3-3)*

21. Round 56.831 to the nearest hundredth. *(Lesson 1-4)*

22. Write .00000 0035 in scientific notation. *(Lesson 2-9)*

23. 10 kg is about how many pounds? *(Lesson 3-4)*

24. Give three instances of the following pattern: $x + x + x = 3x$. *(Lesson 4-2)*

Exploration

25. 27 small cubes are arranged to form one big $3 \times 3 \times 3$ cube. Then the entire big cube is dipped in paint. How many small cubes will now be painted on exactly two sides?

26. One local baseball league has 5 teams and another has 6 teams. Each team in the first league is to play each team in the second league. How many games are needed? (Hint: The drawing at left may be helpful.)

LESSON
6-4

Trial and Error

Trial and error is a problem-solving strategy everyone uses at one time or another. In trial and error, you try an answer. (The word "trial" comes from "try.") If the answer is in error, you try something else. You keep trying until you get a correct answer. This is a particularly good strategy if a question has only a few possible answers.

Example 1 Which of the numbers 4, 5, and 6 is a solution to $(n + 3)(n - 2) = 36$?

Strategy This type of equation is not discussed in this book. You probably do not know how to solve it. You have no algorithm. So it is a problem for you. However, since there are only three choices for a value of n, trial and error is a suitable strategy.

Solution Try the numbers one at a time.
Try 4. Does $(4 + 3)(4 - 2) = 36$? Does $7 \cdot 2 = 36$? No.
Try 5. Does $(5 + 3)(5 - 2) = 36$? Does $8 \cdot 3 = 36$? No.
Try 6. Does $(6 + 3)(6 - 2) = 36$? Does $9 \cdot 4 = 36$? Yes.
So 6 is a solution.

Sometimes results of early trials can help in later ones. In Example 2, the first two trials are so easy that they encourage going on to try more complicated figures.

Example 2 A polygon has 9 diagonals. How many sides does the polygon have?

Strategy Combine two strategies. Draw pictures of various polygons with their diagonals. Keep trying until a polygon with 9 diagonals is found. Count the diagonals as you draw them.

Solution

A triangle has 0 diagonals.

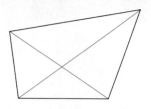

A quadrilateral has 2 diagonals.

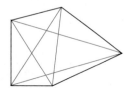

A pentagon has 5 diagonals.

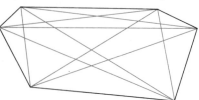

A hexagon has 9 diagonals.

So the polygon with 9 diagonals has 6 sides.

Computers are able to try things very quickly. Even when there is a large number of possible solutions, a computer may use trial and error. In Example 2 we tested the polygons in order of number of sides. Likewise, a computer will search for solutions in an organized way. Trial and error is not a good procedure if the trials are not organized.

Questions

Covering the Reading

1. Describe the problem-solving strategy called "trial and error."

2. When is trial and error a useful strategy?

3. Which of the numbers 4, 5, or 6 is a solution to $(x + 3)(x - 2) = 24$?

4. Which of the numbers 4, 5, or 6 is a solution to $(x + 3)(x - 2) = 14$?

In 5–8, which of the numbers 1, 2, 3, 4, or 5 is a solution?

5. $(x + 7)(x + 2)(x + 3) = 300$

6. $3y - 2 + 5y = 30$

7. $1 + A/3 = 2$

8. $11 - x = 7 + x$

9. What polygon has 5 diagonals?

10. A polygon has 14 diagonals. How many sides does it have?

11. Can a polygon have exactly 10 diagonals?

12. Do computers use trial and error?

In 13–17, trial and error is a useful strategy.

13. Choose one number from each row so that the sum of numbers is 300.

    Row 1:   147   152   128
    Row 2:   132   103   118
    Row 3:   63   35   41

14. Joel was 13 years old in a year in the 1980s when he noticed that his age was a factor of the year. In what year was Joel born?

15. What two positive integers whose sum is 14 have the smallest product?

16. Find all sets of three integers satisfying all of the following conditions: (1) The numbers are different. (2) The sum of the numbers is 0. (3) No number is greater than 4. (4) No number is less than -4.

17. Hidden inside the box are two two-digit numbers. The difference between the numbers is 54. The sum of the digits in each number is 10. What are the two numbers?

18. How many sides are in a dodecagon? *(Lesson 6-2)*

19. Kenneth is older than Ali and Bill. Carla is younger than Ali and older than Bill. Don is older than Carla but younger than Kenneth. Don is Ali's older brother. If the ages of these people are 11, 12, 13, 14, and 15, who is the 13-year-old? *(Lesson 6-3)*

20. List all composite numbers between 11 and 23. *(Lesson 6-2)*

21. What are the rules for order of operations? *(Lesson 4-7)*

22. Evaluate $2xy + x/z$ when $x = 3$, $y = 4$, and $z = 1.5$. *(Lesson 4-4)*

23. Graph all solutions to $x \leq -2$. *(Lesson 4-9)*

24. Add: $\frac{1}{10} + \frac{-2}{7} + \frac{7}{18}$ *(Lessons 5-2, 5-3)*

25. Give an example of the Associative Property of Addition. *(Lesson 5-7)*

26. Give an example of the Substitution Principle. *(Lessons 2-6, 5-8)*

27. To the nearest inch, how many inches are in 2.7 feet? *(Lesson 3-2)*

28. Consider the number 5.843%. *(Lessons 1-2, 1-4, 2-5)*
   a. Convert this number to a decimal.
   b. Round the number in **a** to the nearest thousandth.
   c. Between what two integers is this number?

29. Repeat Question 28 for the number $\frac{99}{70}$. *(Lessons 1-4, 1-8)*

Exploration

30. Put one of the digits 0, 1, 2, 3, 4, 5, 6, 7, 8, 9, in each circle. This will form two five-digit numbers. Make the sum as large as possible. (For example, 53,812 and 64,097 use all the digits, but their sum of 117,909 is easy to beat.)

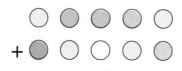

31. Computers are very good at trial and error. Try this program.

```
10   FOR N = 1 TO 100
20   IF (N+3) * (N−2) = 696 THEN PRINT N
30   NEXT N
40   END
```

   a. What does this program find?
   b. Modify the program so that it finds any integer solution between 1 and 50 to the equation x(x + 40) = 329.
   c. Modify the program so that it finds all integer solutions between -100 and 100 to n(n + 18) = 25(3n + 28)/n.

Make a Table

Vadim thought he knew everything about diagonals and polygons. But this question had him stumped.

How many diagonals does a 13-gon have?

He read it carefully. It was easy to understand. He drew a picture of a 13-gon.

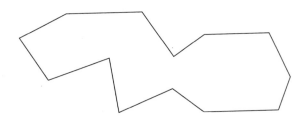

He started drawing diagonals and quickly gave up this approach. He thought about trial and error. He even thought about guessing. He had used all of the strategies of the last three lessons. What could he do?

Sometimes it helps to *make a table*. A table is an arrangement with rows and columns. Making a table is just one way of organizing what you know. Vadim's friend Rose recalled the following information from Lesson 6-2. She made a table with two columns.

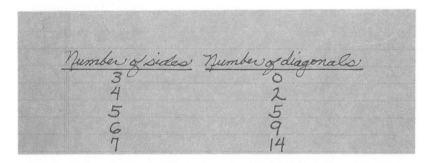

Number of sides	Number of diagonals
3	0
4	2
5	5
6	9
7	14

She noticed that the number of diagonals increases by 2, then 3, then 4, then 5. She thought if the pattern continued, then here would be the next three rows of the table.

8	20
9	27
10	35

She checked her work by drawing an octagon. It did have 20 diagonals. So she continued the pattern and answered Vadim's question. (You are asked to do this yourself in the questions following this lesson.)

In solving problems, there are three reasons for making a table.
    First, a table organizes your thoughts.
    Second, it helps to find patterns.
    Third, it can help you to make a generalization.
A **generalization** is a statement that is true about many instances. The next story is about making a generalization.

Francie lives in Phoenix. She has a telephone in her room. She pays for all long-distance calls she makes. One Sunday she called her cousin Meg in San Diego. They got to talking and Francie forgot about the time. They had talked for at least an hour! She called her long-distance operator for rates and found that it cost $.25 for the first minute and $.18 for each additional minute. She had a problem.

> What is the cost of a one-hour phone call, if the first minute costs $.25 and each additional minute costs $.18?

Francie began by making a table.

Number of minutes talked	Cost of phone call
1	$ .25
2	.43
3	.61
4	.79
5	.97

It wasn't working at all. Yet the pattern was simple. You add .18 to get the next cost. But she wanted to know the cost for 60 minutes. She did not want to add .18 all those times. She would probably make a mistake, even with a calculator.

George helped Francie by rewriting the costs to show a different pattern.

Number of minutes talked	Cost of phone call
1	$.25
2	.25 + .18
3	.25 + 2 • .18
4	.25 + 3 • .18
5	.25 + 4 • .18

"Look across the rows," he said. "See what stays the same and what changes. In the right column, the only number that changes is the number multiplied by .18. It is always one less than the number in the left column. So,

60	.25 + 59 • .18

now you can calculate the cost." Francie did the calculations.

$$.25 + 59 \cdot .18 = 10.87$$

The cost of her phone call was over $10.87! Francie then fainted.

She fainted before George could tell her something else about this. The table makes it possible to write a formula—a general pattern—for the cost.

m	$.25 + (m - 1) \cdot .18$

If Francie spoke for m minutes, it would cost $.25 + (m - 1) \cdot .18$ dollars, not including tax.

The formula enables you to find the cost for any number of minutes easily. It is a generalization made from the pattern the instances formed in the table.

Covering the Reading

In 1–3, use information given in this lesson.

1. How many diagonals does a 10-gon have?

2. How many diagonals does an 11-gon have?

3. Answer the question Vadim could not answer.

In 4–7, refer to the story about Francie in this lesson.

4. If Francie had only talked to her cousin Meg for 5 minutes, what would have been the cost of the phone call?

5. If Francie had talked to her cousin Meg for 30 minutes, what would have been the cost of the call?

6. For a call to Meg that was m minutes long, it cost Francie how much?

7. For a two-hour phone call to Meg, what would it cost Francie?

8. What is a generalization?

9. In the story about Francie, what generalization is made?

Applying the Mathematics

10. Make a table to help answer this question. In a 50-gon, all the diagonals from *one* particular vertex are drawn. How many triangles are formed?

11. Inge wants to call her cousin Erich in Germany. The cost is $1.46 for the first minute and 82¢ for each additional minute.
   a. Make a table indicating the cost for calls of duration 1, 2, 3, 4, and 5 minutes.
   b. What is the cost of a 25-minute call?
   c. What is the cost of a call lasting m minutes?

12. In 1988, it cost 25¢ to mail a one-ounce first-class letter. It cost 20¢ for each additional ounce or part of an ounce up to 11 ounces.
   a. What was the cost to mail a letter weighing 4 ounces?
   b. What was the cost to mail a letter weighing 9.5 ounces?
   c. What was the cost to mail a letter weighing w ounces, if w is a whole number?

Review

13. Use trial and error. I am thinking of a number. When I add the number to 268, I get the same answer as if I had subtracted it from 354. What is the number? *(Lesson 6-4)*

14. One type of polygon is the *undecagon*. How many sides does an undecagon have? *(Lesson 6-2)*

15. $x^y = 343$ and x and y are integers between 1 and 10 Find x and y. *(Lessons 2-2, 6-4)*

16. List all the factors of 54. *(Lesson 1-8)*

17. Mabel was 5 pounds overweight. Now she is 3 pounds underweight. If c is the change in her weight, what is c? *(Lesson 5-8)*

18. Let k be the number of centimeters in one yard. *(Lessons 1-4, 3-4)*
  a. Give the exact value of k.
  b. Round k to the nearest integer.

Exploration

19. Here is a table of some positive integers and their squares.

Integer	Square	Integer	Square
1	1	11	121
2	4	12	144
3	9	13	169
4	16	14	196
5	25	15	225
6	36	16	256
7	49	17	289
8	64	18	324
9	81	19	361
10	100	20	400

  a. Find a pattern that determines the square of 21 without any multiplication or squaring.
  b. What is the units digit in the square of 43,847,217?
  c. Find some other pattern in the table.

20. The table on page 260 of this lesson can be printed by a computer using the following program.

```
10   PRINT "MINUTES", "COST"
20   FOR M = 1 TO 5
30   AMT = .25+(M − 1) * .18
40   PRINT M, AMT
50   NEXT M
60   END
```

  a. Run a program which prints the number of minutes and the cost for from 1 to 10 minutes talking time.
  b. Modify this program to print the left two columns of the table in Question 19.

6-6

Work with a Special Case

Elaine was not sure whether the generalization

$$x(y + z) = xy + xz$$

is true for all numbers x, y, and z. So she substituted 10 for x, 3 for y, and 2 for z. She asked:

Does $10(3 + 2) = 10 \cdot 3 + 10 \cdot 2$?

Following rules for order of operations, she simplified. She asked:

Does $10(5) = 30 + 20$?

The answer is yes. The question is true for this special case. A **special case** is an instance of a pattern used for some definite purpose. Elaine was using a strategy called **testing a special case**.

Special cases help to test whether a property or generalization is true.

Example 1 Is it true that $-(a + b) = -a + -b$ for any numbers a and b?

Strategy Work with a special case. Let $a = 3$ and $b = 2$.
Does $-(3 + 2)$ $=$ $-3 + -2$?
Does $-(5)$ $=$ -5 ?   Yes.

This case may be *too* special. Both numbers are positive. So try another special case, this time substituting a negative number. Let $a = -4$ and $b = 7$. Now substitute.
Does $-(-4 + 7)$ $=$ $-(-4) + -7$?
Does $-(3)$ $=$ $4 + -7$?   Again, yes.
But it wasn't as obvious this time.

You might want to try other special cases.

Solution We have evidence that the property is true. We still do not know for certain.

Suppose you know that only one of a small number of possibilities is true. Then working with a special case can help you decide which one.

Example 2   *Multiple choice*   In an *n*-gon, how many diagonals from one vertex can be drawn?

(a) *n*   (b) *n* − 2   (c) *n* − 3   (d) *n*/2

Strategy   Pick a special case. Let *n* be a small number that is easy to work with. We want a polygon with diagonals, so we need *n* ≥ 4. Reword the question for the special case when *n* is 4.

> **Special case**   *Multiple choice*   In a 4-gon, how many diagonals from one vertex can be drawn?
>
> (a) 4   (b) 4 − 2   (c) 4 − 3   (d) 4/2

Draw a picture to answer the question for the special case.

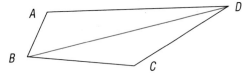

Solution   There is only one diagonal from 1 vertex in a quadrilateral (a 4-gon). Choice (c) is correct for the quadrilateral. So choice (c) *n* − 3 is correct for an *n*-gon.

To check Example 2, try another special case, perhaps a pentagon. With a little knowledge, a special case can go a long way.

Example 3   Bob has forgotten how to divide a decimal by 100. He remembers that you can move the decimal point a certain number of places. But he has forgotten how many places. What can he do?

Strategy   Work with a special case. Pick 400 as the decimal to be divided. (400 is picked because it is easy to divide by 100.)

$$400 \div 100 = 4$$

400 = 400. and 4 = 4., so the decimal point (in 400.) has been moved two places to the left (4.00), past the two zeros.

Solution   To divide by 100, the general pattern is to move the decimal point two places to the left.

It is always a good idea to test more than one special case. In Example 3, you might want to use a calculator and try 123.456 divided by 100. The quotient is 1.23456. This verifies that the answer is correct.

Caution:

Even if several special cases of a pattern are true, the pattern may not always be true.

■ ■ ■ ■ ■ ■ ■■■

Example 4   Is x^2 always greater than or equal to x?

Strategy   Try $x = 6$. $6^2 = 36$, which is bigger than 6.
Test $x = 13$. $13^2 = 169$, which is greater than 13.

So you might think $x^2 \geq x$ is always true.
But now try $x = 0.5$.
$0.5^2 = 0.25$, which is less than 0.5.

Solution x^2 is *not* always greater than or equal to x.

Questions

Covering the Reading

1. What is a special case of a pattern?

In 2–4, consider the pattern $-(a + b) = -a + -b$.

2. Give an instance of this pattern.

3. Let $a = -5$ and $b = -11$. Is this special case true?

4. Let $a = 4.8$ and $b = 3.25$. Is this special case true?

5. *True or false*   If more than two special cases of a pattern are true, then the pattern is true.

6. *True or false*   When a special case of a pattern is not true, then the general pattern is not true.

In 7–11, consider the following pattern: In an *n*-gon, there are $n - 3$ diagonals that can be drawn from one vertex.

7. **a.** When $n = 4$, to what kind of polygon does the pattern refer?
   b. Is the pattern true for that kind of polygon?

8. **a.** When $n = 7$, to what kind of polygon does the pattern refer?
   b. Is the pattern true for that kind of polygon?

9. **a.** What value of n refers to a hexagon?
   b. Is the pattern true for hexagons?

10. a. What value of n refers to a triangle?
   b. Is the pattern true for triangles?

11. Show, by a drawing, that this pattern is true for an octagon.

12. How should you move the decimal point in order to divide a decimal by 1000? (Test a special case if you are not sure of the answer.)

Which direction?

13. How should you move the decimal point in order to divide a decimal by .001? (Test a special case if you are not sure of the answer.)

14. Consider the pattern $x^2 \geq x$.
   a. Give two instances that are true.
   b. Give an instance that is false.
   c. What do parts **a** and **b** tell you about special cases?

Applying the Mathematics

15. Consider the pattern $x \cdot x - x = 0$.
   a. Is this pattern true for the special case $x = 0$?
   b. Is this pattern true for the special case $x = 1$?
   c. Is this pattern true for the special case $x = 2$?
   d. From your answers to parts **a**, **b**, and **c**, do you think the pattern is true for every possible value of x?

16. Consider the pattern $2a + 3b = 6ab$. Test at least two special cases with positive numbers. Decide whether the pattern is
   (a) possibly true, or   (b) definitely not always true.

17. Consider the pattern $-(-m + 9) = m + -9$.
   a. Test a special case with a positive number.
   b. Test the special case with a negative number.
   c. Decide whether the pattern is possibly true or definitely not always true.

Questions 18 and 19 are *multiple choice.* Use special cases to help you select.

18. The sum of all the whole numbers from 1 to n is
(a) $n + 1$ (b) $n + 2$ (c) $n(n + 1)/2$ (d) n^2

19. The sum of the measures of the four angles of any quadrilateral is:
(a) 180   (b) 360   (c) 540   (d) 720

Review

20. The number 17 is a divisor of x and $925 < x < 950$. Find x.
(Lesson 6-4)

21. Five teams are to play each other in a tournament. How many games are needed? *(Lesson 6-3)*

22. Virginia's garden is in the shape of a triangle. Each side of the triangle is 12 feet long. There is a stake at each corner. There are stakes every 3 feet on each side. How many stakes are there in all? *(Lesson 6-4)*

23. A downtown parking lot charges $1.00 for the first hour and $.50 for each additional hour or part of an hour. *(Lesson 6-5)*
a. What will it cost you to park from 9 A.M. to 4:45 P.M.
b. At this rate, what does it cost for h hours of parking?

24. What is an algorithm? *(Lesson 6-1)*

25. Write 1/3 as a decimal and as a percent. *(Lessons 1-8, 2-5)*

26. Solve for x: $14 + x = 14 + {-438}$. *(Lesson 5-8)*

27. $AB + BC + CD + DA$ is called the __?__ of polygon $ABCD$.
(Lesson 5-10)

28. Is $-382{,}471.966638 + 382{,}471.966642$ positive, negative, or zero? *(Lesson 5-5)*

Exploration

29. What five integers between 1 and 101 have the most positive integer divisors?

Try Simpler Numbers

Recall Polya's four main steps in solving a problem.

1. read carefully
2. devise a plan
3. carry out the plan
4. check work

You have learned a number of strategies to help with these steps. Drawing a picture can help you devise a plan and can be used to check work. Trial and error is a good way to solve many problems. Testing a special case is a way to check work.

A strategy called **try simpler numbers** can be used to devise a plan, to solve problems, and to check work. For this reason it is a powerful strategy. Here is an example of how it works.

Example 1 In a delicatessen it costs $2.49 for a half pound of roast beef sliced. The person behind the counter slices .53 pound. What should it cost?

Strategy Try simpler numbers in place of those in the problem to help devise a plan for solving.
Suppose it cost $3.00 for 5 pounds of roast beef and the person sliced 2 pounds.
You could divide $3.00 by 5 to get the price per pound, $.60.
Then multiply by 2 to get the price for 2 pounds, $1.20.

Solution Replace the simpler numbers (chosen in the Strategy above) by the numbers in the problem.
Divide $2.49 by 0.5. (Half = 0.5.)
Then multiply the quotient by .53.
You will get $2.6394; so it should cost $2.64.

Check $2.64 is reasonable, since .53 pound is just over a half pound, and $2.64 is a little more than $2.49.

In most situations, the same operations that you would use with simple numbers will work with more complicated ones. So, if you have complicated numbers, try simpler ones.

Example 2 Steve can bike one mile in 8 minutes. If he can keep up this rate, how far will he ride in 1 hour?

Strategy The numbers are complicated. There are minutes and hours—that makes things more difficult. Modify the problem so that the numbers are simpler and you can answer the question. Then look for a pattern.

Modified problem Steve can bike one mile in <u>10</u> minutes. If he can keep up this rate, how far will he ride in 60 minutes (1 hour)?
Solution The answer to this new problem is 6 miles. (Do you see why?)

Solution The answer 6 to the modified problem is 60 divided by 10. This suggests that the original problem can be solved by division. Dividing the corresponding numbers of the original problem, the number of miles is 60/8. Steve can go 7.5 miles in an hour.

Trying simpler numbers has a bonus. Suppose you can do a problem no matter how complicated the numbers are. This means you have found an algorithm for that type of problem. Then you can describe the answer even when the original information is given with variables. Examples 3 and 4 generalize Example 2.

Example 3 Alice can bike one mile in t minutes. At this rate, how far can she bike in an hour?

Strategy When t is 10, the answer was 60/10. When t is 8, the answer was 60/8.

Solution Therefore, in t minutes, Alice can ride $60/t$ miles.

Example 4   Therese can bike one mile in t minutes. At this rate, how far can she bike in u minutes?

Strategy   Example 3 has simpler numbers. When u was 60, the answer was $60/t$.

Solution   Therese can ride u/t miles.

Questions

Covering the Reading

1. Suppose steak costs $5 a pound. You buy 2 pounds. How much should it cost you?

2. Suppose steak costs $4.49 a pound. The steaks you want weigh a total of 2.61 pounds. How much should it cost you?

3. How are Questions 1 and 2 the same? How are they different?

4. Consider this question. Turkey is $2.29 for a half pound. A shopper buys 1.87 pounds. How much should it cost the shopper?
   a. Change the problem so that it has simpler numbers.
   b. Answer the question for the simpler numbers.
   c. What operations did you use to get the answer to the simpler question?
   d. Use these operations to answer the original question.

5. What strategy is used in Question 4?

6. Follow the directions of Question 4 on the following question: Buzz can bike one mile in 7 minutes. At this rate, how far can he ride in an hour?

7. Kristin can bike one mile in M minutes. At this rate, how far can she bike in 30 minutes?

8. *True or false* A simpler number is always a smaller number.

9. a. If tomatoes are 98¢ a kg, what will $2\frac{1}{2}$ kilograms cost?
   b. If tomatoes are 98¢ per kg, what will k kilograms cost?
   c. If tomatoes cost c¢ per kg, what will k kilograms cost?

10. a. Judy drove 250 miles on 11.2 gallons of gas. How many miles per gallon is her car getting?
   b. Hank drove m miles on 11.2 gallons of gas. How many miles per gallon is his car getting?
   c. Louise drove m miles on g gallons of gas. How many miles per gallon is her car getting?

In 11-13, if you cannot answer the question, try simpler numbers.

11. A roll of paper towels originally had R sheets. If Z sheets are used, how many sheets remain?

12. There are 8 boys and 7 girls at a party. A photographer wants to take a picture of each boy with each girl. How many pictures are required?

13. A coat costs $49.95. You give the clerk G dollars. How much change should you receive?

14. Try at least two special cases with positive and negative numbers to decide whether the pattern is probably always true or definitely not true:
$a + {-b} + {-c} = {-(b + {-a} + c)}$. *(Lesson 6-6)*

15. How should you move the decimal point if you are dividing a decimal by 10^4? *(Lessons 2-4, 6-6)*

16. An *n*-gon has exactly 77 diagonals. What is *n*? *(Lesson 6-5)*

17. $x + 5 \geq 2$, $x < 0$, *x* is an integer, and $-x$ is divisible by 2. Find *x*. *(Lesson 6-4)*

18. When is a question a problem, and when is it an exercise? *(Lesson 6-1)*

19. Write 350,000,000,000 in scientific notation. *(Lesson 2-3)*

20. Write 0.9 in scientific notation. *(Lesson 2-9)*

21. 4 kilograms + 25 grams + 43 milligrams equals how many grams? *(Lesson 5-1)*

22. Would an adult be more likely to weigh 10 kg, 70 kg, or 170 kg? *(Lesson 3-3)*

23. Evaluate a^{b+c} when $a = 5$, $b = 2$, and $c = 4$. *(Lessons 2-2, 4-4)*

Exploration

24. Put one of the digits 0, 1, 2, 3, 4, 5, 6, 7, 8, 9, in each circle. This will form two five-digit numbers. Make the difference as large as possible. (For example, 64097 and 53812 use all the digits, but their difference of 10285 is easy to beat.)

Summary

If you have an algorithm for answering a question, it is an exercise for you. If not, then the question is a problem for you. Problems are frustrating unless you know strategies that can help you approach them. This chapter discusses six general strategies. They are:

1. Read the problem carefully. Look up definitions for any unfamiliar words. Determine if enough information is given. Sort out information that is not needed.
2. Draw an accurate picture.
3. Use trial and error. Use earlier trials to help in choosing better later trials.

4. Make a table. Use the table to organize your thoughts. Use the table to find patterns. Use the table to make generalizations.
5. Use special cases to help decide whether a pattern is true.
6. Try simpler numbers. Generalize to more complicated numbers or variables.

These strategies can help in understanding a problem, in devising a plan, in solving, and in checking. Good problem solvers take their time. They do not give up. They are flexible. And they continually check their work.

Vocabulary

You should be able to give a general description
and a specific example of each
of the following ideas.

Lesson 6-1
algorithm, exercise, problem

Lesson 6-2
prime number, composite number
divisor, factor
natural number

Lesson 6-4
trial and error

Lesson 6-5
table
generalization

Lesson 6-6
special case
testing a special case

Lesson 6-7
simpler number

Progress Self-Test

Take this test as you would take a test in class. Then check your work with the solutions in the Selected Answers section in the back of the book.

1. Name two places to find the meaning of the term "trapezoid."

2. How many diagonals does an octagon have?

3. There are six players in a singles tennis tournament. Each player will compete with each of the others. How many games will be played?

4. What two positive integers whose product is 24 have the smallest sum?

5. *True or false* If you know an algorithm for multiplying fractions, then multiplying fractions is a problem for you.

6. List the prime numbers between 50 and 60.

7. Consider $|x| + |y| = |x + y|$. Find values of x and y that make this false.

8. How much will 1.62 pounds of hamburger cost if the price is $1.49 per pound?

9. *True or false* If a special case of a pattern is true, then the general pattern may still be false.

10. What integer between 5 and 10 is a solution to $(x - 3) + (x - 4) = 9$?

11. Donna has some disks numbered 1, 2, 3, 4, and so on. She arranges them in order in a circle, equally spaced. The last disk is the same space from the first disk. If disk 3 is directly across from disk 10, how many disks are in the circle?

12. When all the possible diagonals are drawn, an n-gon has $n+3$ diagonals. What is n?

13. How many decimal places and in which direction should you move a decimal point in order to divide by .01?

14. Phyllis was given $1000 by her parents to spend during her first year of college. She decided to spend $25 a week. Make a table to show how much she will have left after 1, 2, 3, and 4 weeks.

15. In the situation of Question 14, how much will Phyllis have after 31 weeks?

16. Robert carefully read a problem, prepared a table to help solve the problem, and worked until he reached a conclusion. He wrote his answer and went on to the next problem. What step in good problem solving did Robert omit?

Chapter Review

Questions on SPUR Objectives

SPUR stands for **S**kills, **P**roperties, **U**ses, and **R**epresentations.
The Chapter Review questions are grouped according to the
SPUR Objectives for this chapter.

SKILLS deal with the procedures used to get answers.

Objective A: *Understand the methods followed by good problem solvers. (Lesson 6-1)*

1. *Multiple-choice* Which advice should be followed to become a better problem solver?
   (a) Check work by answering the question the same way you did it.
   (b) Be flexible.
   (c) Skip over words you don't understand as long as you can write an equation.
   (d) none of (a) through (c)

2. If you can apply an algorithm to a problem, then the problem becomes an ___?___.

3. After Nancy multiplies 1487×309 on her calculator, what would be a good way to check her answer?

Objective B: *Determine solutions to sentences by trial and error. (Lesson 6-4)*

4. Which integer between 10 and 20 is a solution to $3x + 15 = 66$?

5. *Multiple choice* Which number is *not* a solution to $n^2 \geq n$?
   (a) 0   (b) 0.5   (c) 1   (d) 2

6. Choose one number from each row so that the sum of the numbers is 255.
88	84	9
69	79	76
108	104	102

7. What number between 1000 and 1050 has 37 as a factor?

PROPERTIES deal with the principles behind the mathematics.

Objective C: *Determine whether a number is prime or composite. (Lesson 6-2)*

8. Is 49 prime or composite? Explain your answer.

9. Is 47 prime or composite? Explain your answer.

10. List all composite numbers n with $20 < n < 30$.

11. List all prime numbers between 30 and 40.

Objective D: *Find the meaning of unknown words. (Lesson 6-2)*

12. What is a tetrahedron?

13. What is a perfect number?

Objective E: *Make a table to find patterns and make generalizations. (Lesson 6-5)*

14. Mandy is saving to buy a present for her parents' anniversary. She has $10 now and adds $5 a week.
    a. How much will she save in 12 weeks?
    b. How much will she save in w weeks?

15. Consider 2, 4, 8, 16, 32, ... (the powers of 2). Make a table listing all the factors of these numbers. How many factors does 256 have?

In Example 2, if the original length was L meters, then there would be $L - 0.4$ meters left. If C meters were cut off, the remaining length would be $L - C$ meters.

Example 3 In the drawing below, what is the measure of $\angle ABC$?

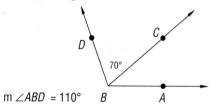

m $\angle ABD$ = 110°

Solution Subtract the measure of $\angle CBD$ from the measure of $\angle ABD$. The difference is 40°.

Example 4 What is the area of the shaded region between the squares?

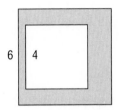

Solution The area of the larger square is 6^2 or 36. The area of the smaller square is 4^2 or 16. Think of cutting away the inner square from the outer. The amount left is $36 - 16$. The shaded area is 20 square units.

In a real situation, the shaded region might be a walkway around a house. The area would tell you how much concrete would be needed to pave the walkway. The shaded region could be a picture frame. The area would be the amount of material needed for the frame.

Questions

Covering the Reading

1. Hungry Heloise ate 8 of the dozen rolls her mother prepared for dinner. How many rolls are left for the others at the table?

2. Hungry Heloise ate A of the dozen rolls her mother prepared for dinner. How many rolls are left for the others at the table?

3. There are 320 passenger seats in one wide-body jet plane. A flight attendant counts 4 vacant seats. How many passengers are on board?

4. There are *S* passenger seats in a wide-body jet plane. A flight attendant counts *V* vacant seats. How many passengers are on board?

5. Questions 1–4 are instances of what model for subtraction?

In 6–9, use the picture below.

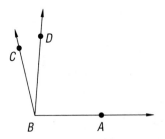

6. If $m\angle ABC = 100°$ and $m\angle DBA = 84°$, what is $m\angle DBC$?

7. If $m\angle ABC = 103°$ and $m\angle DBC = 22°$, what is $m\angle DBA$?

8. $m\angle ABC - m\angle DBC = m\angle$ _?_

9. $m\angle ABC - m\angle DBA = m\angle$ _?_

10. State the Take-Away Model for Subtraction.

In 11–13, use the two squares pictured below.

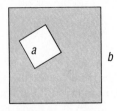

11. What is the area of the shaded region?

12. Find the area of the shaded region if $a = 8$ and $b = 10$.

13. Find the area of the shaded region if $a = 4\frac{1}{2}$ and $b = 6.7$.

In 14–17, use the picture below of towns *A, B, C,* and *D* along a highway.

A   B   C   D

14. Suppose $AD = 10$ km and $AC = 6$ km. **a.** What other distance can be found? **b.** What is that distance?

15. If $DA = 260$ miles and $BD = 147$ miles, find all other lengths that are possible to determine.

16. **a.** $AD - CD = \underline{\ ?\ }$ **b.** $AD - AB - CD = \underline{\ ?\ }$

17. CD is 20% of the length of $\overline{AD}$. AB is 25% of the length of $\overline{AD}$. Then BC is what percent of the length of $\overline{AD}$?

18. According to the National Center for Health Statistics in 1981, on the average, of 100,000 people born in the years 1901–1906, 57,044 were still alive.
    a. How many had died?
    b. How old were those that were still alive?

19. Bill's savings account has $510.75 in it. How much will be left if:
    a. He withdraws $40? **b.** He withdraws *W* dollars?

20. **a.** If the four corner squares of an 8-by-8 checkerboard are cut off, how many squares remain?
    b. If *C* squares of an *n* by *n* checkerboard are cut off, how many squares remain?

21. The weather forecast says there is a 60% chance of rain. What fraction represents the chance of rain? *(Lesson 2-5)*

22. Give the additive inverse of: **a.** 5; **b.** -3.4; **c.** 0. *(Lesson 5-4)*

23. Evaluate $3p + q^4$ if $p = 4$ and $q = 5$. *(Lesson 2-2, 4-4)*

24. *True or false?* $\frac{5}{4} + \frac{5}{4} = \frac{10}{8}$ *(Lesson 5-2)*

25. How are milligrams and grams related? *(Lesson 3-3)*

26. How are grams and pounds related? *(Lesson 3-4)*

27. Try positive and negative numbers to see whether it is true that $-(a + b) = -b + -a$. *(Lesson 6-6)*

28. Solve: $-5 + x = -5$. *(Lesson 5-8)*

29. Give a number that is between 3 and 3.01. *(Lesson 1-2)*

30. Select the largest number: π; $\frac{22}{7}$; 3.14. *(Lesson 1-2)*

Exploration

31. If the same number is added to both numbers in a subtraction, the answer is not changed. For instance, if the question is

$$\begin{array}{r} 4307 \\ -\ 2998 \end{array}$$

you can add 2 to both numbers to get

$$\begin{array}{r} 4309 \\ -\ 3000 \end{array}$$

which is much easier. The answer to both questions is 1309. For each of the subtraction questions below, find a number to add to make the subtraction easier. Then do the subtraction.

a. $\begin{array}{r} 136 \\ -\ 97 \end{array}$ **b.** $\begin{array}{r} 4905 \\ -\ 1996 \end{array}$ **c.** $\begin{array}{r} 1117 \\ -\ 989 \end{array}$

The Slide Model for Subtraction

The temperature is 50° and goes down 12°. What temperature results? This situation can be pictured on a number line. Start at 50° and slide 12° to the left.

The resulting temperature is 38°.

The answer could also be found by subtracting 50 − 12. This subtraction is not take-away, but a second model for subtraction called the **slide model.**

Slide Model for Subtraction:

If a quantity a is decreased by an amount b,
the resulting quantity is $a - b$.

In slide situations, you usually can slide up or down. Results of sliding up are found by addition. Results of sliding down are either found by adding negative numbers or by subtracting.

	By subtraction	By addition	Answer
A person who weighs 60 kg loses 4 kg. What is the resulting weight?	60 kg − 4 kg	60 kg + -4 kg	56 kg
A temperature of -17° falls 20°. What is the resulting temperature?	-17° − 20°	-17° + -20°	-37°

These examples show a basic relationship between subtraction and addition. We call it the **Add-Opp Property of Subtraction.**

Add-Opp Property of Subtraction:

For any numbers a and b
$$a - b = a + \text{-}b.$$
In words, subtracting b is the same as adding the opposite of b.

The Add-Opp Property allows any subtraction to be converted to an addition. This is helpful because you already know how to add both positive and negative numbers.

Example 1   Simplify: -5 − 2.

Solution 1   Use the slide model. Start at -5 and slide down 2. The result is -7.

Solution 2
Use the Add-Opp Property. $\text{-}5 - 2 = \text{-}5 + \text{-}2$
(Instead of subtracting 2, add -2.) $= \text{-}7$

Example 2   Simplify: 40 − 50.79.

Solution   Use the Add-Opp Property.
$40 - 50.79 = 40 + \text{-}50.79 = \text{-}10.79.$

Example 3   Simplify: -6 − -8.

Solution
Use the Add-Opp Property.
(Instead of subtracting -8, add its opposite, 8.)
$$\text{-}6 - \text{-}8 = \text{-}6 + 8$$
$$= 2$$

Example 4   Simplify: $x - \text{-}y$.

Solution   By the Add-Opp Property, $x - \text{-}y = x + y$.

Another reason for using the Add-Opp Property is that addition has the commutative and associative properties. You do not have to worry about order of additions. This is particularly nice if there are more than two numbers involved in the subtractions.

Example 5 Simplify: $-5 - -3 + 8 + -2 - 7 - 4$.

Solution Remember order of operations. Proceed from left to right, converting subtractions to additions.

$$= -5 + 3 + 8 + -2 + -7 + -4$$

Now change order, putting all negatives together.

$$= -5 + -2 + -7 + -4 + 3 + 8$$
$$= \quad\quad -18 \quad\quad + \quad\quad 11$$
$$= \quad\quad\quad\quad -7$$

You have learned three uses of the $-$ sign. Each use has a different English word.

where $-$ sign is found	example	in English
between numbers or variables	$2 - 5$	2 *minus* 5
in front of a positive number	-3	*negative* 3
in front of a variable or	$-x$	*opposite of x*
negative number	$-(-4)$	*opposite of negative* 4

For example, $3 - -y$ is read "three minus the opposite of y."

Questions

1. To picture $3 - 4$ on the number line, you can start at __?__ and draw an arrow __?__ units long pointing to the __?__.

2. State the Slide Model for Subtraction.

In 3–5: **a.** Give a subtraction problem that will answer the question. **b.** Give an addition problem that will answer the question. **c.** Answer the question.

3. The temperature is 74° F and is supposed to drop 20° by this evening. What is the expected temperature this evening?

4. The temperature is -4° C and is supposed to drop 10° by morning. What is the expected morning temperature?

5. A person who weighs 72 kg loses 3 kg. What weight results?

6. State the Add-Opp Property: **a.** in symbols; **b.** in words.

7. $5 - {}^-8 = 5 + \underline{\ ?\ }$.   **8**

8. ${}^-x - {}^-y = {}^-x + \underline{\ ?\ }$.

In 9–16, simplify.

9. ${}^-8 - 45$

10. $83 - 100$

11. $1 - 5$

12. ${}^-22 - 8$

13. $3 - {}^-7$

14. $0 - {}^-41$

15. ${}^-9 - {}^-6$

16. $m - {}^-2$

17. Give two reasons why it is useful to be able to convert subtractions to additions.

18. Consider the expression ${}^-43 - {}^-x$. Which of the three dashes (left, center, or right) is read: **a.** minus; **b.** opposite of; **c.** negative?

19. Translate into English: ${}^-A - {}^-4$.

20. Simplify: $40 - 50 - 20$.

Applying the Mathematics

21. Evaluate $5 - y$:
 a. when $y = 2$;   **b.** when $y = 3$;   **c.** when $y = 4$;
 d. when $y = 5$;   **e.** when $y = 6$;   **f.** when $y = 7$.

22. The formula $p = s - c$ connects profit p, selling price s, and cost c.
 a. Calculate p when $s = \$49.95$ and $c = \$30.27$.
 b. Calculate p when $s = \$49.95$ and $c = \$56.25$.
 c. Your answer to part **b** should be a negative number. What does a negative profit indicate?

23. Calculate $a - b + c - d$ when $a = {}^-1$, $b = {}^-2$, $c = {}^-3$, and $d = {}^-4$.

24. **a.** On your calculator, give a key sequence that will do the subtraction $3 - {}^-4$. **b.** Give a key sequence that will do the subtraction ${}^-5 - {}^-77$.

In 25–28, use trial and error, or test special cases.

25. *Multiple choice*   If $9 = 7 - x$, then $x =$
 (a) 2   (b) 16   (c) ${}^-2$ (d) ${}^-16$

26. *Multiple choice*   A person weighs 165 lb and goes on a diet, losing L lb. The resulting weight is R lb. Then $R =$
 (a) $L - 165$ (b) $165 - L$
 (c) $L - {}^-165$ (d) ${}^-165 - L$

27. *True or false?* **a.** When x is a positive number, $x - x = 0$.
b. When x is a negative number, $x - x = 0$.

28. a. For all numbers x, y, and z, is it true that
$(x - y) - z = x - (y - z)$?
b. Does subtraction have the associative property?

29. a. What relationship among any numbers a and b would have to be true in order for subtraction to be commutative?
b. Is subtraction commutative?

Review

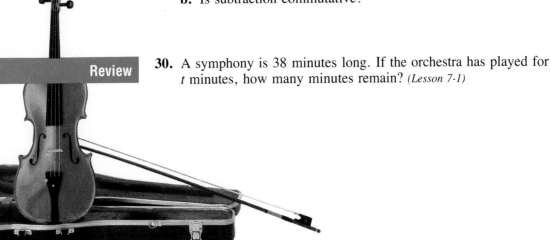

30. A symphony is 38 minutes long. If the orchestra has played for t minutes, how many minutes remain? *(Lesson 7-1)*

31. Let n be a number. What is the number that is four less than n? *(Lesson 4-3)*

32. How many degrees does the minute hand of a watch turn in 1 minute? *(Lesson 5-6)*

33. What property justifies adding the same number to both sides of an equation? *(Lesson 5-8)*

34. In a single elimination tournament a team plays until it is beaten. Eight teams are to play a single elimination tournament. How many games must be played? *(Lesson 6-3)*

Exploration

35. When $m = 3$ and $n = 7$,
$m^n - n^m = 3^7 - 7^3 = 2187 - 343 = 1844$.
a. Find integer values of m and n between 1 and 15 so that $m^n - n^m = 1927$.
b. Find positive integer values of m and n so that the value of $m^n - n^m$ is the current year on the calendar.

7-3

The Comparison Model for Subtraction

The first number in a subtraction problem is called the **minuend.** The second number is the **subtrahend.** The answer is called the **difference.**

$$
\begin{array}{ll}
436.2 & \text{minuend} \\
-\ \ 98.5 & \text{subtrahend} \\
\hline
337.7 & \text{difference}
\end{array}
$$

The term ''difference'' comes from a third model of subtraction, the *comparison* model. Here are two examples.

Example 1 Yvonne is 160 cm tall. Her boyfriend, Ulysses, is 184 cm tall. How much taller is Ulysses than Yvonne?

Solution 184 cm − 160 cm, or 24 cm

Example 2 The highest point in California is the peak of Mount Whitney, 14,494 feet above sea level. The lowest point in California is in Death Valley and is 282 feet below sea level. What is the difference in the elevations of these two points?

Solution The elevation below sea level is represented by the number -282.
14,494 − -282 = 14,494 + 282 = 14,776 feet

The general pattern is called the **comparison model for subtraction.**

Comparison Model for Subtraction:

$x - y$ is how much more x is than y.

A special type of comparison is change. Suppose a school had 1200 students last year and 1150 this year. The change is 1150 − 1200, or -50 students. The negative answer signifies a loss. Notice that the later value comes first, the earlier value second.

---

change = later value − earlier value

Here is an example of change where the minuend and subtrahend are negative.

Example 3   The temperature was -3° earlier today. Now it is -17°. By how much has it changed?

Solution   -17° − -3° = -17° + 3° = -14°. The temperature has gone down 14°.

Another special type of comparison gives the amount of an error. Again, negative numbers may be involved.

---

error in estimate = estimated value − actual value

Example 4   Josie thought the girls' football team would lose their game by 10 points. Instead they won by 6. How far off was Josie?

Solution   A loss by 10 is -10. A win by 6 is 6. The difference is -10 − 6, which equals -10 + -6, or -16. Josie was 16 points too low.

Think of $x - y$. When x is bigger than y, as in $5 - 2$, the difference is a positive number. When x is smaller than y, as in $2 - 5$, the difference is negative. This happens regardless of the numbers used. For instance, look again at Example 4. -10 is less than 6. So -10 − 6 is negative.

What happens if you subtract the numbers in reverse order?

$$6 − -10 = 6 + 10 = 16$$

The difference is now the opposite of -16. This pattern is always true.

This property can help in computation. Suppose you wish to calculate $432 - 999$. Just subtract in reverse order. Since $999 - 432 = 567$, so $432 - 999 = -567$.

Questions

Covering the Reading

In 1–3, consider the subtraction fact $12 - 8 = 4$. Identify the:

1. difference.   2. minuend.   3. subtrahend.

4. State the Comparison Model for Subtraction.

5. Jim weighs 150 pounds but wants to get his weight down to 144 pounds. How much does he need to lose?

6. Nina has $240 saved for a stereo system that costs $395. How much more does she need?

7. The highest elevation in Louisiana is Driskill Mountain, at 535 feet above sea level. The lowest elevation is in New Orleans, at 5 feet below sea level. What is the difference in elevation between these two points?

French Quarter, New Orleans

In 8 and 9, calculate the change in temperature from yesterday to today.

8. Yesterday, 27°; today, 13°.   9. Yesterday, -9°; today, -8°.

Fred thinks that the Dallas Cowboys will win next Sunday's football game by 13 points. In 10 and 11, give the error in his guess if the Cowboys:

10. win by 20.   11. lose by 4.

12. For all numbers x and y: $x - y$ is the opposite of __?__.

13. Since $835 - 467 = 368$, what is $467 - 835$?

14. If $a - b = 40$, then $b - a =$ __?__.

In 15–20, without doing the subtraction, tell whether the difference is positive or negative.

15. $3.498764 - 2.99834657$ **16.** $7.08 - 12$

17. $-100 - -400$ **18.** $65 - -430$

19. $-2 - 1.00004$ **20.** $-0.0094 - 0.0093$

Applying the Mathematics

In 21 and 22, use special cases if you cannot first answer the question.

21. In 1987, the population of Arizona was 437,000 more than in 1980. Suppose the 1987 population was x and the 1980 population was y. How are x, y, and 437,000 related?

Arizona roadrunner

22. Last year the Peas Porridge Co. had a profit of D dollars. This year their profit was E dollars. What is the change in profit from last year to this?

23. Here are census figures for Portland, Oregon.

1950	373,628
1960	373,676
1970	379,967
1980	366,383

a. Calculate the change from each census to the next. You should get two positive numbers and one negative number.
b. Add the three numbers you got in part **a**.
c. What does the sum in part **b** mean?

24. The steps here show that $b - a$ and $a - b$ add to zero. This confirms that $b - a$ and $a - b$ are opposites. Give the property that tells why each step follows from the preceding one.

$$(b - a) + (a - b)$$
Step 1: $= (b + {}^-a) + (a + {}^-b)$
Step 2: $= b + ({}^-a + a) + {}^-b$
Step 3: $= b + 0 + {}^-b$
Step 4: $= b + {}^-b$
Step 5: $= 0$

25. The famous scientist, Marie Curie, was born in 1867 and died in 1934. From this information, how old was she when she died? (Watch out. There are two possible answers)

26. The Roman poet, Livy, was born in 59 B.C. and died in 17 A.D. From this information, how old was he when he died? (Watch out again. There was no year 0. The year 1 A.D. followed 1 B.C.)

27. Try simpler numbers if you cannot get the answer right away.
   a. How many integers are between 100 and 1000, not including 100 or 1000?
   b. How many integers are between two integers *I* and *J*, not including *I* or *J*?

Review

28. Give a calculator sequence to do ⁻1 − ⁻2 − ⁻8. *(Lessons 1-7, 7-2)*

29. Of 100,000 people born in the U.S. in the years 1971–1976, on the average, 98,590 were alive in 1981. **a.** How many had died? **b.** How old were those that were still alive? *(Lesson 7-1)*

30. Solve ⁻*a* + *y* = *b* for *y*. *(Lesson 5-8)*

31. Find the perimeter of the figure at left. *(Lesson 5-10)*

32. Write $\frac{2}{5}$ as a percent. *(Lesson 2-7)*

Exploration

33. Ask five different people not in your class to estimate how many heads will turn up if you toss a penny ten times. Then toss the penny 10 times. Calculate the error for each person. (Remember that your answer should be negative if a guess was too low.)

34. Is *x* − *y* the opposite of *y* − *x* when *x* and *y* are complicated? Test this conjecture using the following computer program. Type in the following program.

```
NEW
10 PRINT "X"
15 INPUT X
20 PRINT "Y"
25 INPUT Y
30 PRINT "Y − X", "X − Y"
35 PRINT Y−X, X−Y
40 END
```

   a. Run the program inputting 5 for X and 3 for Y to test it. Record your results.
   b. What happens when you input 98.7 for X and ⁻3.456 for Y?
   c. Try some numbers of your own choosing and record the results.

7-4

Solving $x - a = b$

The equation $x - 59 = 12$ is an equation of the form $x - a = b$. To solve this equation just convert the subtraction to addition using the Add-Opp Property. Then solve the resulting equation as you did in Chapter 5.

Example 1 Solve $x - 59 = 12$.

Solution
Convert to addition $\qquad\qquad x + \text{-}59 = 12$
Add 59 to both sides. $\quad x + \text{-}59 + 59 = 12 + 59$
Simplify. $\qquad\qquad\qquad\qquad x + 0 = 71$
$\qquad\qquad\qquad\qquad\qquad\qquad x = 71$

Check Substitute 71 for x in the original sentence.
Does $71 - 59 = 12$? Yes. So 71 is the solution.

The equation $x - a = b$ can be used to model many real-life situations.

Example 2 From a large herd of cattle, cowhands drove away 230 cows. There were 575 cows left in the herd. How large was the original herd?

Solution Let C be the number of cows in the original herd. Then by the Take-Away Model of Subtraction, $C - 230 = 575$. Solve this equation.

Convert to addition. $\qquad\qquad C + \text{-}230 = 575$
Add 230 to both sides. $\quad C + \text{-}230 + 230 = 575 + 230$
Simplify. $\qquad\qquad\qquad\qquad\qquad C + 0 = 805$
$\qquad\qquad\qquad\qquad\qquad\qquad\qquad C = 805$

So the herd started with 805 cattle.

Check If there were 805 cows in the original herd and 230 were driven away, would 575 remain? Yes.

Examples 1 and 2 tell *how* to solve a simple subtraction equation. The next example shows *why* the steps work.

Example 3 Solve $x - a = b$ for x, and give a reason why each step follows.

Solution

$$x + \text{-}a = b \qquad \text{(Add-Opp Property of Subtraction)}$$
$$(x + \text{-}a) + a = b + a \qquad \text{(Addition Property of Equality)}$$
$$x + (\text{-}a + a) = b + a \qquad \text{(Associative Property of Addition)}$$
$$x + 0 = b + a \qquad \text{(Property of Opposites)}$$
$$x = b + a \qquad \text{(Additive Identity Property of Zero)}$$

The next example shows an application of $x - a = b$ using the Slide Model for Subtraction.

Example 4 A group of divers paused on a natural plateau below the surface of the sea. After descending 20 meters more, they found themselves 83 meters below sea level. What was the elevation of the plateau?

Solution Let E be the elevation of the plateau (in meters). From the Slide Model for Subtraction, $E - 20 = \text{-}83$. Solve this equation.

Convert to addition.	$E + \text{-}20 = \text{-}83$
Add 20 to both sides.	$E + \text{-}20 + 20 = \text{-}83 + 20$
Simplify.	$E + 0 = \text{-}63$
	$E = \text{-}63$

The plateau was 63 meters below sea level.

Questions

Covering the Reading

1. What is the name of the property that enables $x - a$ to be replaced by $x + {}^-a$?

2. What is the only difference between solving an equation of the form $x - a = b$ and solving an equation of the form $x + a = b$?

In 3–6: **a.** Convert the sentence to one with only addition in it. **b.** Solve.

3. $x - 14 = {}^-2$

4. $73 = y - 28$

5. $a - 6 = 9$

6. $c - 12.5 = 3$

7. Is $^-42$ the solution to $x - 13 = {}^-29$?

8. Is $y = {}^-1$ the solution to $6 = y - {}^-7$?

9. *Multiple choice* If $x - a = b$, then $x =$
   (a) $a - b$ (b) $b - a$ (c) $b + a$ (d) $b + {}^-a$

In 10 and 11, solve and check.

10. $B - {}^-5 = 6$

11. $3.01 = e - 9.2$

In 12 and 13: **a.** Write an equation involving subtraction describing the situation. **b.** Solve the equation. **c.** Answer the question.

12. After descending 75 feet, Monty Climber is at an elevation of 12,450 feet on the mountain. At what elevation was he originally?

Applying the Mathematics

13. A volleyball team gives up 3 points and is now losing by 2 points. How was the team doing before they lost the points?

14. The formula $p = s - c$ relates profit, selling price, and cost. Solve for the selling price s in terms of the profit and the cost.

15. A fish starts at a depth of d feet below the surface of a pond. While searching for food it ascends 4 feet, then descends 12 feet. Its final depth is 15 feet below the surface. What was the fish's initial depth?

16. Solve for s: $s - \frac{1}{8} = \frac{1}{2}$.

Review

17. Calculate $2 - 3 - 10$. *(Lesson 7-2)*

18. Calculate $^-8 - 9$. *(Lesson 7-2)*

19. The highest temperature ever recorded in the United States was 134°F, in Death Valley, California, on July 10, 1913. The lowest temperature ever recorded in the U.S. was -80°F, in Prospect Creek, Alaska, on January 23, 1971.
a. To the nearest year, how many years separate the two dates?
b. What is the difference between the temperatures? *(Lesson 7-3)*

20. A person was born in this century in the year *B* and died in the year *D*. What are the possible ages of this person at the time of death? (Use special cases if you cannot answer quickly.)
(Lessons 6-6, 7-3)

21. An age guesser at a carnival gives a prize if your age is not guessed within (and including) five years. Let *G* be the guess. If a person is 26 years old, describe the values of *G* that will give that person a prize. *(Lessons 4-9, 7-3)*

22. Barry had $312 in his checking account and made out a check for $400. By how much was he overdrawn? *(Lessons 7-1, 7-2)*

23. On personal checks, dollar amounts must be written out in English. Write out $2305 as you would need to for a personal check. *(Lesson 1-1)*

24. If $-x = 17$, what is x? *(Lesson 5-4)*

25. *B* is on $\overline{AC}$. If $AC = 1$ meter and $AB = 30$ cm, what is BC?
(Lesson 7-1)

A   B   C

In 26–31, rewrite as a decimal.

26. $\frac{3}{4}$ *(Lesson 1-8)*   **27.** 150% *(Lesson 2-5)*

28. $\frac{6}{11}$ *(Lesson 1-8)*   **29.** 6.34×10^6 *(Lesson 2-3)*

30. five trillion *(Lesson 2-1)*

31. sixty-four millionths *(Lesson 1-2)*

32. Measure $\angle V$ to the nearest degree. *(Lesson 3-5)*

Exploration

33. a. Replace each letter with a digit to make a true subtraction. Different letters stand for different digits. Each letter stands for the same digit wherever it occurs.

$$
\begin{array}{r}
T\,W\,O \\
-\;O\,N\,E \\
\hline
O\,N\,E
\end{array}
$$

b. There is more than one solution. How many solutions are there?

7-5

Equivalent Sentences and Formulas

Stores use formulas to compute profit. See page 300.

Suppose you have to solve $30 + x = 52$. Using the techniques you have learned, you write down $x = 22$. You have written a sentence **equivalent** to the original. Two sentences are equivalent if they have exactly the same solutions.

Example Which equation is *not* equivalent to the others?

$$x + 3 = 8 \qquad 2x = 10 \qquad \text{-}1 = 4 - x \qquad x - 0.4 = 4.96$$

Solution The first three equations have the single solution 5. The equation at the right has solution 5.36. It is not equivalent to the others.

Of all equations with solution 5, the simplest is $x = 5$.

> The idea in solving equations is to find a sentence of the form $x = $ ___ that is equivalent to the original equation.

You can use equivalent sentences to locate an error in your work. A student wrote what is given here. Not all steps are shown because this student did some steps mentally. Lines are identified for future reference.

Line 1	$A - 35 - 12 = 40$
Line 2	$A - 23 \qquad\quad = 40$
Line 3	$A + \text{-}23 \qquad\quad = 40$
Line 4	$A \qquad\qquad = 40 + 23$
Line 5	$A \qquad\qquad = 63$

There must be an error because 63 does not work in the equation of Line 1.

$$63 - 35 - 12 \neq 40$$

But 63 does work on every other line. So all the other equations are equivalent. This says that the error must be in going from Line 1 to Line 2. Do you see the error? (Hint: It has to do with order of operations.)

In applications it is important to know when you are dealing with **equivalent formulas.** Here is an example. You have seen the formula $p = s - c$. (Profit on an item equals its selling price minus the cost of producing it.) If the selling price is $49.95 and the cost is $30.27, then the profit is $49.95 - $30.27, or $19.68.

Now solve the formula for s. You will get $s = c + p$. (Selling price equals cost plus profit.) The same three numbers work in the formula $s = c + p$.

$$\begin{array}{ccccc} p & = & s & - & c \\ 19.68 & = & 49.95 & - & 30.27 \end{array} \qquad \begin{array}{ccccc} s & = & c & + & p \\ 49.95 & = & 30.27 & + & 19.68 \end{array}$$

The formulas $p = s - c$ and $s = c + p$ are equivalent because the same numbers work in both of them. When you take a formula and solve for a variable in it, you always get an equivalent formula.

Questions

Covering the Reading

1. When are two sentences equivalent?

2. What is the general idea in solving equations?

3. Sentences I, II, and III are equivalent.
   I: $2 - x - 3 = 1$ II: $x + 5 = 3$ III: $x = -2$
   a. Which sentence is the simplest?
   b. What is the solution to sentence I?

In 4–6, find the sentence that is not equivalent to the others.
4. $x = 5$ $5 - x = 10$ $x = -5$

5. $y + 1 = 4$ $4 + 1 = y$ $1 + y = 4$

6. $a + \frac{2}{3} = b$ $a - b = \frac{2}{3}$ $b - a = \frac{2}{3}$

In 7 and 8, an attempt was made to solve the sentence on Line 1. But an error was made. a. Find the one sentence that is not equivalent to the others. b. Between what lines was the error made?

7. Line 1: -6 $= y - 9$
   Line 2: $-6 + 9 = y$
   Line 3: -15 $= y$

8. Line 1: $A - 10 - 5 = 12$
   Line 2: $A - 5$ $= 12$
   Line 3: A $= 17$

9. When are formulas equivalent?

10. Which formula is not equivalent to the others?
    $s = p + c$ $p = s - c$ $p = c - s$

In 11–13, find the simplest sentence equivalent to the given sentence.

11. $x + 40 = 35$

12. $\frac{6}{5} = \frac{2}{3} + A$

13. $y - 1.8 = 8.7$

14. What *one word* could replace the directions to Questions 11–13?

The three numbers 3, 4, and 7 are related in many ways. For example:
$$3 + 4 = 7; \qquad 7 - 4 = 3; \qquad \text{and} \qquad 7 - 3 = 4.$$
Because these sentences use the same numbers, they are called *related facts*. In 15–20, find a fact related to each given fact that does not use the same operation.

15. $80 + 14 = 94$

16. $9 \cdot 79 = 711$

17. $4 + \text{-}5 = \text{-}1$

18. $.3 \cdot .5 = .15$

19. $10 - 23 = \text{-}13$

20. $(\frac{2}{3})/(\frac{4}{5}) = \frac{5}{6}$

21. *Multiple choice* Which sentence is equivalent to $A = \ell w$? (Hint: If you do not know the answer quickly, test a special case.)
(a) $A\ell = w$ (b) $Aw = \ell$
(c) $A/\ell = w$ (d) none of these

22. Solve $x - 11 = \text{-}11$. *(Lesson 7-4)*

23. Solve $8 = y - 40$. *(Lesson 7-4)*

24. Solve for d in terms of c: $c + d = 30$. *(Lesson 5-8)*

25. Booker T. Washington was born in 1856 and died in 1915. How old was he when he died? *(Lesson 7-3)*

Booker Taliaferro Washington (far left) and his two sons

26. In Montreal, Quebec, the average normal high temperature in January is -6°C. The average normal low temperature is -15°C. What is the average range in the temperature on a January day in Montreal? *(Lesson 7-3)*

27. Evaluate $3 - x$ when: **a.** $x = 17$; **b.** $x = -85$. *(Lesson 7-2)*

28. Pick all of the following that are correct names for the angle below. *(Lesson 3-5)*

(a) $\angle O$ (b) $\angle OCW$

(c) $\angle COW$ (d) $\angle WOC$

(e) $\angle C$ (f) $\angle W$

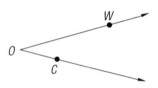

29. How many degrees are in a half turn? *(Lesson 5-6)*

30. Round 357.9124 up to the nearest thousandth. *(Lesson 1-3)*

31. If n stands for a number, what stands for the number that is three less than twice n? *(Lesson 4-3)*

Exploration

32. Write down ten 3-digit numbers that are divisible by 9. Add up the digits in each of these numbers. What pattern do you find?

Solving
$a - x = b$

An equation can be used to find how many tickets have been sold. See Example 2.

The equation $3 - x = 20$ is of the form $a - x = b$. To solve this equation, we can use the same strategy we used to solve $x - a = b$. Because the variable is subtracted, one more step is needed.

Example 1   Solve $3 - x = 20$.

Solution 1

First convert to addition.	$3 + \text{-}x = 20$
Now add -3 to both sides.	$\text{-}3 + 3 + \text{-}x = \text{-}3 + 20$
Simplify.	$\text{-}x = 17$

This equation is easy to solve. Just take the opposite of both sides. $\text{-}(\text{-}x) = \text{-}17$

Simplify. $x = \text{-}17$

Check   Substitute in the original sentence.
Does $3 - \text{-}17 = 20$? Yes.

Solution 2   Another way to solve $3 - x = 20$ is to add x to both sides.

First convert to addition	$3 + \text{-}x = 20$
Now add x to both sides.	$3 + \text{-}x + x = 20 + x$
Simplify.	$3 = 20 + x$

This is an equation you have solved many times before.

Add -20 to both sides.	$\text{-}20 + 3 = \text{-}20 + 20 + x$
Simplify.	$\text{-}17 = 0 + x$
	$\text{-}17 = x$

Look carefully at Solution 2. By adding x to both sides, the equation $3 - x = 20$ was converted to the equivalent equation $3 = 20 + x$. The equation $3 = 20 + x$ is one you know how to solve. This is the most important strategy in solving equations: Do things to both sides so that you wind up with a simpler equivalent equation.

Here is a situation that can lead to an equation of the form $a - x = b$.

Example 2 There were 3500 tickets available for a concert. Only 212 are left. How many tickets have been sold?

Solution This is an instance of the take-away model. Let S be the number of tickets sold. S is taken away from 3500, leaving 212.

$$3500 - S = 212$$

You are asked to solve this equation in the questions that follow.

Questions

Covering the Reading

1. Consider the equation $3 - x = 20$. To solve this equation, you can convert the subtraction to an addition. What sentence results?

In 2–4, consider $-5 = 14 - t$.

2. To solve this equation using the strategy of Example 1, Solution 1, what should be added to both sides?

3. To solve this equation using the strategy of Example 1, Solution 2, what should be added to both sides?

4. Solve the equation using the strategy you like better.

In 5–10, solve and check.

5. $300 - x = -2$ **6.** $61 = 180 - y$

7. $-45 = 45 - z$ **8.** $m - 3.3 = 1$

9. $A - 57 = -110$ **10.** $\frac{2}{3} - B = \frac{88}{9}$

11. a. Solve the equation of Example 2. **b.** Answer the question of Example 2.

Applying the Mathematics

In 12 and 13, the question can lead to an equation of the form $a - x = b$. **a.** Give that equation. **b.** Solve the equation. **c.** Answer the question.

12. The temperature was $14°$ just 6 hours ago. Now it is $3°$ below zero. How much has it decreased?

13. The Himalayan mountain climbers pitched camp at 22,500 feet yesterday. Today they pitched camp at 20,250 feet. How far did they come down the mountain?

In 14–17, solve. You will have to simplify first.

14. $40 - x + 20 = 180$

15. $-6 = -1 - y - 5$

16. $12 - -B = 6$

17. $13 - 5 \cdot 2 = 9 - K - -7$

18. Solve for y: $x = 90 - y$.

19. Give a reason for each step in this detailed solution of $a - x = b$ for x.

Step 1: $a + -x = b$
Step 2: $(a + -x) + x = b + x$
Step 3: $a + (-x + x) = b + x$
Step 4: $a + 0 = b + x$
Step 5: $a = b + x$
Step 6: $-b + a = -b + (b + x)$
Step 7: $-b + a = (-b + b) + x$
Step 8: $-b + a = 0 + x$
Step 9: $-b + a = x$

20. *Multiple choice*   Which of (a) to (c) is not equal to $-b + a$?
(a) $a + -b$ (b) $a - b$
(c) $b + -a$ (d) All equal $-b + a$.

Review

21. What is a simple equation equivalent to $40 = A + 12$? *(Lesson 7-5)*

22. An event occurs half the time. What percent of the time is this? *(Lesson 2-6)*

23. Draw an angle with a measure of $70°$. *(Lesson 3-5)*

24. Draw an angle with a measure of $110°$. *(Lesson 3-5)*

25. a. Draw two perpendicular lines. **b.** What kind of angles are formed? *(Lesson 3-6)*

In 26 and 27: **a.** Write an equation involving subtraction for the situation. **b.** Solve the equation. *(Lessons 7-1, 7-4)*

26. The hot air balloon fell 125 feet from its highest point. The new altitude was 630 ft. How high had it flown?

27. In the 1988 Summer Olympics, an American diver, Greg Louganis, defeated a Chinese diver, Xiong Ni, by one and fourteen-hundredths points. If Ni's total score was 637.47, what was Louganis's score?

28. a. Which of these famous English monarchs had the longest reign? *(Lesson 7-3)*

    King Henry II, who reigned from 1154 to 1189
    King Henry VIII, 1509-1547
    Queen Elizabeth I, 1558-1603
    Queen Victoria, 1837-1901

  b. The present Queen of England, Elizabeth II, ascended to the throne in 1952. In what year could she become the longest-reigning queen? *(Lessons 7-1, 7-4)*

29. Point O is on $\overline{AD}$. You are at O facing A. First you turn from A to B. Then you turn from B to C. Then you turn from C to D. What is the magnitude of the result of these three turns? *(Lesson 5-6)*

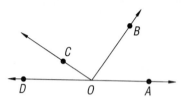

Exploration

30. Suppose $a = 5$, $b = 4$, $c = 3$, $d = 2$, and $e = 1$. Consider the expression $a - b - c - d - e$, in which all the dashes are for subtraction. Now put grouping symbols wherever you want. For instance, you could consider $(a - b) - (c - d) - e$; this gives the values $(5 - 4) - (3 - 2) - 1$, which simplifies to -1. Or consider $a - [b - (c - d)] - e$, which is $5 - [4 - (3 - 2)] - 1$, which simplifies to 1. How many different values of the expression are possible?

Suppose B is on $\overleftrightarrow{AC}$. Think of standing at B. If you turn from C to A, you have turned half a revolution. The magnitude of this turn is half of 360°, or 180°. For this reason, some mathematicians say that there is an angle CBA whose measure is 180°. These mathematicians call $\angle CBA$ a **straight angle.** $\overrightarrow{BA}$ and $\overrightarrow{BC}$ are called **opposite rays** because they have the same endpoint and together they form a line.

Now add a ray $\overrightarrow{BD}$ to the picture. Angles DBC and DBA are formed.

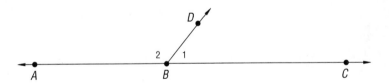

We name them 1 and 2 to make reading easier. These angles are called a **linear pair** because they have a common side ($\overrightarrow{BD}$) and their non-common sides ($\overrightarrow{BA}$ and $\overrightarrow{BC}$) are opposite rays. You should measure these angles. Confirm that m$\angle 1 = 50°$ and m$\angle 2 = 130°$. In fact, because of the Fundamental Property of Turns, the sum of the measures of two angles in a linear pair must be 180°.

If the line containing $\overrightarrow{BD}$ is drawn, angles 3 and 4 are formed.

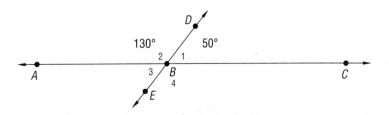

Because angles 1 and 4 form a linear pair, $m\angle 4 = 130°$.
Because angles 2 and 3 form a linear pair, $m\angle 3 = 50°$.
You might want to measure angles 3 and 4 to check this.

Angles 1 and 3 are called **vertical angles.** Two angles are vertical angles when they are formed by intersecting lines, but are not a linear pair. Vertical angles always have the same measure. Angles 2 and 4 are also vertical angles.

In summary, when two lines intersect, four angles are formed. Two of these have one measure, call it x. The other two have measure y. The sum of x and y is 180°. That is, $x + y = 180°$.

All of this is related to subtraction.
Solve the equation $x + y = 180$ for y.
$$\text{-}x + x + y = 180 + \text{-}x$$
$$0 + y = 180 + \text{-}x$$
$$y = 180 + \text{-}x$$
$$y = 180 - x$$

So if you know x, the measure of one angle when two lines intersect, the measures of the other three angles are either x or $180° - x$.
For instance, if $x = 110°$, then $y = 180° - x = 70°$.

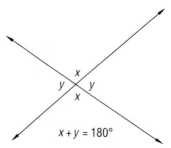

$x + y = 180°$

Two lines intersecting is a common situation. So angles whose measures add to 180° appear often. Such angles are called **supplementary angles.** Supplementary angles do not have to form a linear pair. For instance, any two angles with measures 53° and 127° are supplementary because $53 + 127 = 180$, no matter where the angles are located.

In this picture, two lines intersect to form right angles. Then all four angles have measure 90°. Any two of the angles are supplementary. Recall that the lines are called perpendicular.

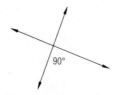

90°

Here is a sketch of part of a map of Chicago. Drexel and Ellis Avenues go north and south from 71st to 72nd streets. Then they bend so that they intersect South Chicago Avenue at right angles.

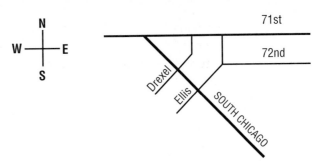

Suppose Drexel did not bend. Then the situation would be as pictured below. A driver going south on Drexel could easily see a car traveling northwest (from C_2 to C_1) on South Chicago. But the driver could not easily see a car going southeast (from C_1 to C_2) on South Chicago. By making the streets perpendicular, a driver can see both directions equally well! The intersection is safer.

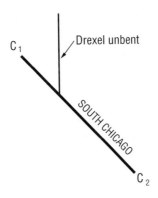

Questions

Covering the Reading

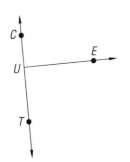

In 1–7, C, U, and T are points on the same line.

1. Angle CUT is sometimes called a __?__ angle.

2. $\overrightarrow{UC}$ and $\overrightarrow{UT}$ are __?__ rays.

3. $\angle CUE$ and $\angle EUT$ form a __?__.

4. $m\angle CUE + m\angle EUT = $ __?__ degrees.

5. If $m\angle CUE = 88°$, then $m\angle EUT = $ __?__.

6. If $m\angle CUE = 90°$, then $\overleftrightarrow{CT}$ and $\overleftrightarrow{UE}$ are __?__.

7. Angles CUE and EUT are __?__ angles.

In 8–12, $\overrightarrow{AB}$ and $\overleftrightarrow{CD}$ intersect at E.

8. Name all pairs of vertical angles.

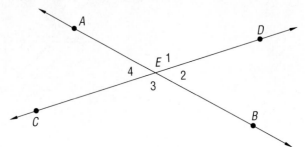

9. Name all linear pairs.

10. Name all pairs of supplementary angles.

11. If m∠1 = 125°, what are the measures of the other angles?

12. Measure angles 1, 2, 3, and 4 (to the nearest degree) with a protractor.

In 13–15, find the unknown angle measures without using a protractor.

13. **14.**

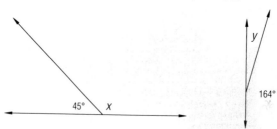

15.

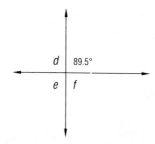

16. Two lines intersect below. If m∠5 = x, find the measure of
a. ∠6; **b.** ∠7; **c.** ∠8.

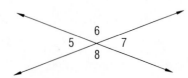

In 17–21, use the map below. Assume all the streets are two-way.

17. *True or false?*   Drexel and South Chicago intersect at right angles.

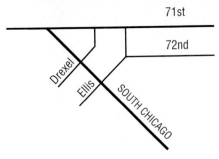

18. *True or false?*   Ellis and 71st intersect at right angles.

19. How many street intersections are pictured on the map?

20. At which intersection is the best visibility of oncoming traffic?

21. At which intersection is the worst visibility of oncoming traffic?

Applying the Mathematics

22. Entrance ramps onto expressways usually form very small angles with the expressway. This is bad for visibility and is quite dangerous. Why aren't entrance ramps perpendicular to expressways?

In 23 and 24, name all linear pairs shown in the figure.

23.

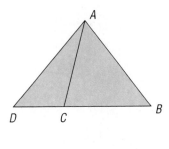

24.

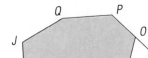

In 25–28, *true or false?*

25. If one angle of a linear pair is an acute angle, then the other angle is obtuse.

26. If one of two vertical angles is acute, the other is obtuse.

27. If two angles are both acute, they cannot be a linear pair.

28. If two angles are supplementary, one must be acute, the other obtuse.

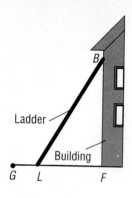

Ladder

Building

G L   F

29. A firefighter places a ladder against a building so that m∠*BLF* = 58°. What is m∠*BLG*?

In 30 and 31, suppose *x* and *y* are measures of two angles. How are *x* and *y* related if:

30. The angles are vertical angles.

31. The angles are supplementary.

32. An angle has measure 40°. A supplement to this angle has what measure?

Review

In 33–36, solve.

33. $180 - x = 23$ *(Lesson 7-6)*

34. $90 - y = 31$ *(Lesson 7-6)*

35. $17 - (2 - 6) + A = 5 - 2(5 + 6)$ *(Lessons 5-8, 7-2)*

36. $4c = 12$ *(Lesson 4-8)*

37. Suppose the sign in the cartoon is true. How much would you pay for a down jacket normally selling for $129.95? *(Lesson 2-6)*

HERMAN®

127.35

"Salesman of the week gets to go to Hawaii."

Exploration

38. In this lesson you learned about supplementary angles. What are **complementary** angles?

312

7-8

Angles and Parallel Lines

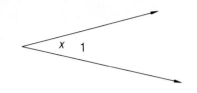

Begin with ∠1 that has measure *x*. Draw the lines *t* and *m* containing its sides. This forms four angles as pictured below. Angle 3, vertical to ∠1, has measure *x*, and the other angles have measure $180 - x$. For example, if $x = 25$, then the original angle has measure 25°. The other angles either measure 25° or $180° - 25°$, which is 155°.

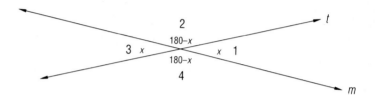

Two lines in a plane are **parallel** if they have no points in common. Now we draw a line *n* parallel to line *m*. It intersects line *t* and helps form angles 5, 6, 7, and 8. Because parallel lines go in the same direction, the measures of the four new angles equal the measures of the four angles that were already there.

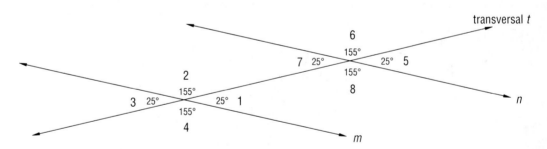

The line that is not parallel is called a **transversal.** The eight angles have names that tell how they are related to the two parallel lines and the transversal.

Name	Angles in above figure	Measures
Corresponding angles	1 and 5, 2 and 6 3 and 7, 4 and 8	equal
Interior angles	1, 2, 7, 8	
Alternate interior angles	2 and 8, 1 and 7	equal
Exterior angles	3, 4, 5, 6	

In work with angles, it helps to use special symbols to indicate when angles have the same measure. Use a single arc when two angles have the same measure. When two other angles are also equal, use a double arc. And so on.

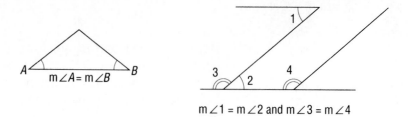

m∠A = m∠B

m∠1 = m∠2 and m∠3 = m∠4

Arrows in the middle of two lines that look parallel mean that they are parallel. The symbol ‖ means *is parallel to*. If lines *m* and *n* are parallel, you can write *m ‖ n*. Here is the drawing of the previous page. The symbols for parallel lines and for angles of equal measure are included. Also identified are the interior and exterior angles.

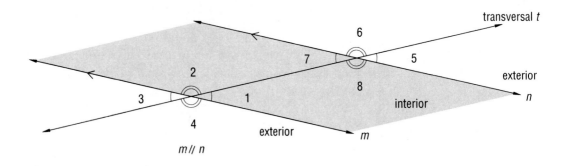

There are also symbols for perpendicularity. In a drawing, the symbol ⌐ shows that lines or line segments are perpendicular. In writing, ⊥ means *is perpendicular to*.

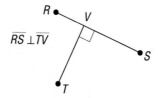

$\overline{RS} \perp \overline{TV}$

In drawings, put the ⌐ symbol on only one of the angles at the point of intersection.

314

Questions

In 1–6, $m \parallel n$. Give the measure of the indicated angle.

1. 1   **2.** 2

3. 3   **4.** 4

5. 5   **6.** 6

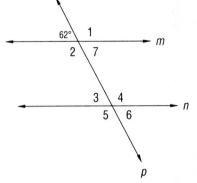

7. In the drawing of Questions 1–6, which line is the transversal?

8. When are two lines parallel?

In 9–18, use the drawing below. Lines r and s are parallel.

9. Name all pairs of corresponding angles.

10. Name the exterior angles.

11. Name the interior angles.

12. Name the two pairs of alternate interior angles.

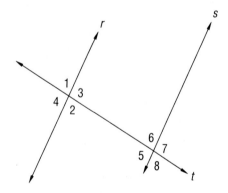

13. Do the corresponding angles 1 and 6 have the same measure?

14. Do the alternate interior angles 3 and 5 have the same measure?

15. If $m\angle 2 = 84°$, give the measure of all other angles.

16. If $m\angle 5 = x$, give the measure of all other angles.

17. If angle 6 is a right angle, which other angles are right angles?

18. If angle 4 has measure t, which angles have measure $180 - t$?

In 19–23, use the drawing below. Consider segments that look perpendicular to be perpendicular. Segments that look parallel are parallel.

19. Copy the drawing and put in the symbols indicating parallel and perpendicular segments.

20. What symbol completes the statement? $\overline{AB}$ _?_ $\overline{CE}$.

21. What symbol completes the statement? $\overline{AB}$ _?_ $\overline{CD}$

22. $m\angle C =$ _?_ degrees   **23.** $m\angle AEC =$ _?_ degrees

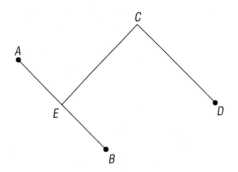

24. At right, $m \parallel n$. Copy the drawing and put in all symbols indicating equal angles.

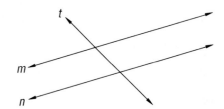

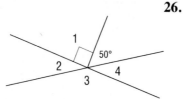

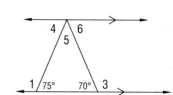

Applying the Mathematics

In 25 and 26, find the measure of each numbered angle.

25.   **26.**

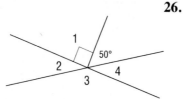

27. Find the sum of the measures of angles 1, 2, 3, and 4 in the drawing below.

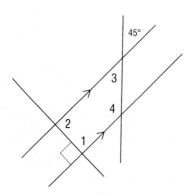

In 28–30, draw an accurate example and identify on your drawing:

28. a linear pair

29. vertical angles

30. supplementary angles that are not a linear pair. *(Lesson 7-7)*

31. Three instances of a pattern are given. Describe the pattern using one variable. *(Lesson 4-2)*
$$73 \cdot 1 = 73 \qquad \tfrac{8}{7} \cdot 1 = \tfrac{8}{7} \qquad -4.02 \cdot 1 = -4.02$$

32. Solve: $m - \tfrac{8}{3} = -3$. *(Lesson 7-4)*

33. Solve for c: $a + b + c = 180$. *(Lesson 5-8)*

34. A savings account contains C dollars. Then $100 is withdrawn and $30.45 is deposited. How much is now in the account? *(Lesson 5-5)*

35. A savings account contains C dollars. Then W dollars are withdrawn and D dollars are deposited. How much is now in the account? *(Lesson 5-5)*

36. Some students think that Question 34 is easier than Question 35. Some students think that Question 35 is easier.
a. Give your opinion. **b.** Give a reason defending your choice.

37. The photograph below pictures balusters (the parallel vertical supports) and a banister (the transversal) on stairs. Give two other places where it is common to find parallel lines and transversals.

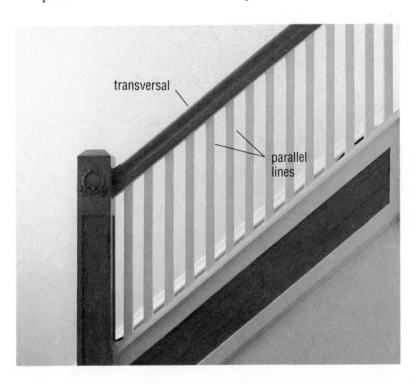

transversal

parallel lines

Special
Quadrilaterals

Here is a drawing of two parallel lines *m* and *n* and a transversal *t*. The pattern of angle measures is shown.

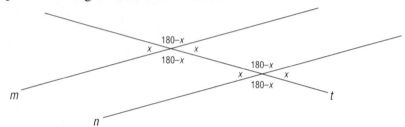

Now we add a fourth line *u* to the picture, parallel to *t*. This forms 8 new angles. Each angle either has measure x or $180 - x$. Also formed is the quadrilateral known as a **parallelogram**. A parallelogram is a quadrilateral with two pairs of parallel sides.

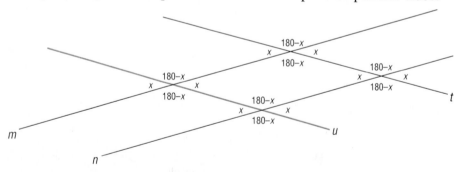

To see the parallelogram better, take it out of the picture. Call it *ABCD*.

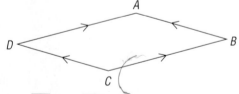

In this parallelogram, $\overline{AB}$ and $\overline{CD}$ are called *opposite sides*. $\overline{AD}$ and $\overline{BC}$ are also opposite sides. Angles *A* and *C* are *opposite angles*. So are angles *B* and *D*. From the parallel lines we know that $m\angle A = m\angle C$ and $m\angle B = m\angle D$. So opposite angles have the same measure. Also, opposite sides have the same length. So $AB = CD$ and $AD = BC$. This is true in any parallelogram.

1. The triangle drawn at the top of page 323 has $m \angle U = 18°$, $m \angle T = 135°$, and $m \angle Q = 27°$. The sum of these measures is 180°.
Multiple choice Which is true?
(a) In some but not all triangles the sum of the measures of the angles is 180°.
(b) In all triangles the sum of the measures of the angles is 180°.
(c) The sum of the measures of the angles of a triangle can be any number from 180° to 360°.

2. Why did the corners of the triangles in the cartoon fit together to make a straight line?

3. What is the Triangle-Sum Property?

In 4–7, two angles of a triangle have the given measures. Find the measure of the third angle.

4. 30°, 60°

5. 117°, 62°

6. 1°, 2°

7. $x°$, $140° - x°$

8. What is the sum of the measures of the four angles of a rectangle?

9. Explain why a triangle cannot have two obtuse angles.

10. Use the drawing below. Find the measures of angles 1 through 8.

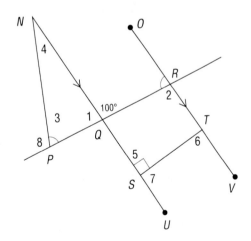

11. In a triangle with a right angle, what is the sum of the measures of the other two angles?

12. In the figure below, $\overline{BA} \perp \overline{AC}$. Angle BAC is bisected (split into two equal parts) by $\overline{AD}$. m$\angle B = 60°$.
Find the measures of angles 1 and 2.

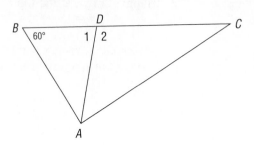

13. *Multiple choice*   Two angles of a triangle have measures x and y. The third angle must have what measure?
(a) $180 - x + y$ (b) $180 + x + y$
(c) $180 + x - y$ (d) $180 - x - y$

14. Find m$\angle ABC$.   **15.** Find m$\angle XYZ$.

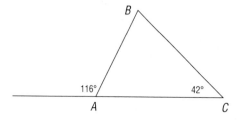
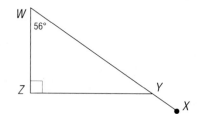

16. In the figure below, $\overline{EH}$ and $\overline{GI}$ intersect at F. Find the measure of as many angles as you can.

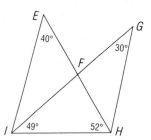

Review

In 17–20, use the drawing at left. What is the meaning of each symbol? *(Lesson 7-8)*

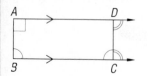

17. the arrows on segments $\overline{AD}$ and $\overline{BC}$

18. the sign that looks like an L by angle A

19. the single arcs by points B and C

20. the double arcs by points C and D

In 21 and 22: **a.** translate into English; **b.** draw a picture. *(Lesson 7-8)*

21. $\overleftrightarrow{AB} \parallel \overrightarrow{CD}$

22. $\overleftrightarrow{EF} \perp \overline{GH}$

23. **a.** *True or false?*   A square is a special type of rectangle.
b. *True or false?*   A square is a special type of rhombus.
(Lesson 7-9)

24. Four people went to a health club. Here are their weights on February 1 and March 1. **a.** How much did each person's weight change? **b.** Who gained the most? **c.** Who lost the most? *(Lesson 7-3)*

	February 1	March 1
Richard	65.3 kg	62.8 kg
Marlene	53.4 kg	54.3 kg
Evelyn	58.6 kg	55.1 kg
Daniel	71.1 kg	72.0 kg

25. Evaluate $a - b + c - d$ when $a = 0$, $b = -10$, $c = -100$, and $d = -1000$. *(Lesson 7-2)*

26. Evaluate $a - b + c - d$ when $a = -43$, $b = 2$, $c = 5$, and $d = 11$. *(Lesson 7-2)*

27. Solve: $-5 = 15.4 - x$. *(Lesson 7-6)*

28. Solve: $x - 3 = -3$. *(Lesson 7-4)*

Exploration

29. Here is a quadrilateral that is not a parallelogram. **a.** Measure the four angles. **b.** What is the sum of the measures?

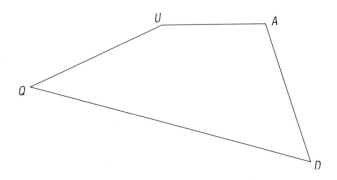

30. *Multiple choice*   The sum of the measures of the angles of an *n*-gon is:
(a) $180n$ (b) $180(n + 1)$
(c) $180(n - 2)$ (d) $180(n + 3)$

Summary

Subtraction arises from take-away, slide, or comparison situations. In take-away situations, $x - y$ stands for the amount left after y has been taken away from x. In the linear pair pictured here, $m\angle BDA$ can be thought of as the amount left after x has been taken from 180°. So $m\angle BDA = 180 - x$. Measures of linear pairs add to 180°.

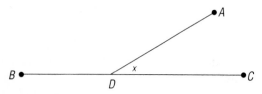

In slide situations, $x - y$ is the result after x has been decreased by y. Earlier this was described as an addition slide situation $x + -y$. $x - y = x + -y$ always.

In comparison situations, $x - y$ is how much more x is than y. Special kinds of comparison are change and error. The word *difference* for the answer to a subtraction problem comes from this kind of subtraction.

All of these situations can lead to equations of the form $x - a = b$ or $a - x = b$.

By extending $\overline{AD}$ at left, vertical angles are formed. Then adding a line parallel to $\overline{BC}$ forms eight angles. Adding a line parallel to $\overline{AD}$ forms a parallelogram. All of the angles formed have measures x or $180 - x$. Special kinds of parallelograms are rectangles, rhombuses, and squares, so these ideas have many uses.

Vocabulary

You should be able to give a general description and a specific example for each of the following ideas.

Lesson 7-1
Take-Away Model for Subtraction

Lesson 7-2
Slide Model for Subtraction
Add-Opp Property of Subtraction

Lesson 7-3
minuend, subtrahend, difference
Comparison Model for Subtraction

Lesson 7-5
equivalent sentences
equivalent formulas

Lesson 7-7
straight angle, opposite rays
linear pair, vertical angles
supplementary angles

Lesson 7-8
parallel lines, transversal
corresponding angles
interior angles
alternate interior angles
exterior angles
||, ⊥
symbols in figures for parallel, perpendicular,
   and angles of equal measure

Lesson 7-9
parallelogram
rectangle, rhombus, square

Lesson 7-10
Triangle-Sum Property

Progress Self-Test

Take this test as you would take a test in class. Then check your work with the solutions in the Selected Answers section in the back of the book.

1. Picture the subtraction $-6 - 22$ on a number line and give the result.

2. Simplify $45 - 110$.

3. Evaluate $5 - x + 2 - y$ when $x = 13$ and $y = -11$.

4. Solve: $y - 14 = -24$

5. Solve: $-50 = 37 - x$

6. Solve: $g - 3.2 = -2$

7. Solve for a: $c - a = b$

In 8 and 9, use the figure below. $m\angle ABD = 25°$.

8. $m\angle ABE = \underline{\ ?\ }°$ 9. $m\angle CBD = \underline{\ ?\ }°$

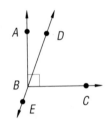

In 10–12, use the figure below. $m \parallel n$

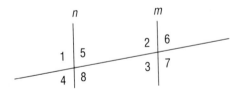

10. If $m\angle 5 = 74°$, then $m\angle 7 = \underline{\ ?\ }°$.

11. Which angles have measures equal to the measure of angle 6?

12. Which angles are supplementary to angle 5?

13. Why can't a triangle have three right angles?

14. Two angles of a triangle have measures $55°$ and $4°$. What is the measure of the third angle?

15. What other angle in the figure below has the same measure as angle E?

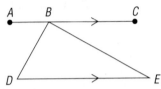

16. In parallelogram $WXYZ$ (not drawn), if $m\angle W = 50°$, what is $m\angle X$?

17. Of parallelograms, rectangles, rhombuses, and quadrilaterals, which have all sides equal in length?

18. Convert all subtractions to additions: $x - y - -5$.

19. Which formula is not equivalent to the others?
    (a) $180 = x + y$ (b) $180 - y = x$
    (c) $x - y = 180$ (d) $180 - x = y$

20. Valleyview H. S. scored V points against Newtown H. S. Newtown scored N points and lost by L points. How are V, N, and L related?

21. A piece 0.4 meters long was cut from a board 5 meters long. What was the length of the board that remained?

22. Ray is Z inches tall. Fay is 67 inches tall. How much taller is Ray than Fay?

After dropping $7°$, the temperature is now $-3°$. Use this information in 23 and 24.

23. Solving what equation will tell what the temperature was?

24. Solve that equation.

25. Below are two squares. The outer square is 8 meters on a side. The inner square is 4 meters on a side. Find the area of the shaded region.

Chapter Review

Questions on **SPUR** Objectives

SPUR stands for **S**kills, **P**roperties, **U**ses, and **R**epresentations.
The Chapter Review questions are grouped according to the
SPUR Objectives for this chapter.

SKILLS deal with the procedures used to get answers.

■ **Objective A:** *Subtract any numbers written as decimals.* (*Lesson 7-2*)

1. Simplify $40 - 360$.
2. Simplify $-4 + -12$.
3. Evaluate $x - y - z$ when $x = 10.5$, $y = 3.8$, and $z = -7$.
4. Evaluate $a - (b - c)$ when $a = -2$, $b = -3$, and $c = 4$.

■ **Objective B:** *Solve sentences of the form $x - a = b$.* (*Lesson 7-4*)

5. Solve: $x - 64 = 8$.
6. Solve: $6 = y - \frac{1}{5}$.
7. Solve: $-4.2 = V - -3$.
8. Solve: $2 + m - 5 = 4$.
9. Solve for c: $e = c - 45$.

■ **Objective C:** *Solve sentences of the form $a - x = b$.* (*Lesson 7-6*)

10. Solve: $200 - b = 3$.
11. Solve: $-28 = 28 - z$.
12. Solve: $223 - x = 215$.
13. Solve: $\frac{4}{9} - y = \frac{5}{18}$.
14. Solve for y: $180 - y = x$.

■ **Objective D:** *Find measures of angles in figures with linear pairs, vertical angles, or perpendicular lines.* (*Lesson 7-7*)

In 15–18, use the figure below to determine the measures.

15. $m \angle 1 = \underline{\ ?\ }$ degrees

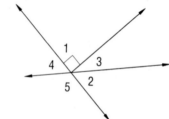

16. If $m \angle 2 = 60°$, then $m \angle 4 = \underline{\ ?\ }$.
17. If $m \angle 4 = x°$, $m \angle 5 = \underline{\ ?\ }$.
18. If $m \angle 5 = 125°$, then $m \angle 3 = \underline{\ ?\ }$.

■ **Objective E:** *Find measures of angles in figures with parallel lines and transversals.* (*Lesson 7-8*)

In 19–22, use the figure below.

19. Which angles have the same measure as $\angle 6$?

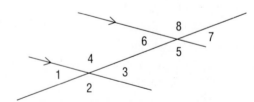

20. If $m \angle 3 = 43°$, then $m \angle 7 = \underline{\ ?\ }°$.
21. If $m \angle 2 = y°$, then $m \angle 7 = \underline{\ ?\ }°$.
22. If $m \angle 8 = 135°$, then $m \angle 1 = \underline{\ ?\ }°$.

Objective F: *Use the Triangle-Sum Property to find measures of angles. (Lesson 7-10)*

23. Two angles of a triangle have measures 118° and 24°. What is the measure of the third angle?

24. Two angles of a triangle have measures $y°$ and $150° - y°$. What is the measure of the third angle?

25. If $\overline{AB} \perp \overline{BC}$ and m$\angle ECF = 40°$, find m$\angle A$.

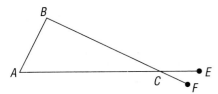

26. Use the figure for Question 25. If $\overline{AB} \perp \overline{BC}$ and m$\angle A = 72°$, find m$\angle ECB$.

Objective G: *Find measures of angles and sides in special quadrilaterals without measuring. (Lesson 7-9)*

27. A rhombus has one side of length 2.5 cm. Is this enough to find its perimeter?

28. Each angle of a rectangle has measure ___?___ .

29. In parallelogram $ABCD$, if $DC = 4$ and $BC = 6$, find AB.

30. In parallelogram $ABCD$, if m$\angle D = 105°$, find m$\angle A$.

PROPERTIES deal with the principles behind the mathematics.

Objective H: *Apply the properties of subtraction. (Lessons 7-2, 7-3)*

31. According to the Add-Opp Property, $7 - 3 = 7 + $ ___?___ .

32. If $967 - 432 = 535$, then $432 - 967 = $ ___?___ .

Objective I: *Distinguish equivalent from non-equivalent sentences and formulas. (Lesson 7-5)*

33. Which sentence is not equivalent to the others?
$a - c = b$ $a - b = c$ $a + c = b$
$b + c = a$

34. Which sentence is not equivalent to the others?
$x - 8 = 3$ $3 - 8 = x$ $-x + 3 = -8$
$-8 + x = 3$

Objective J: *Know relationships among angles formed by intersecting lines. (Lesson 7-7)*

35. Angles 1 and 2 form a linear pair. If m$\angle 1 = 40°$, what is m$\angle 2$?

36. Angles 1 and 2 are vertical angles. If m$\angle 1 = 40°$, what is m$\angle 2$?

37. Angles 1 and 2 are supplementary. If m$\angle 1 = x°$, what is m$\angle 2$?

Objective K: *Know relationships among angles formed by two parallel lines and a transversal. (Lesson 7-8)*

In 38–41, use the figure below.

38. Angles 2 and ___?___ are corresponding angles.

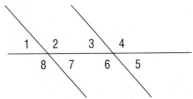

39. Name the exterior angles.

40. Angles 3 and ___?___ are alternate interior angles.

41. Name four angles supplementary to angle 8.

Objective L: *Apply the definitions of parallelogram, rectangle, rhombus, and square to determine properties of these figures. (Lesson 7-9)*

In 42–45, consider parallelograms, rectangles, rhombuses, and squares.

42. In which of these figures are all sides equal in length?

43. In which of these figures are all angles equal in measure?

44. In which of these figures are both pairs of opposite sides equal in length?

45. In which of these figures are both pairs of opposite angles equal in measure?

Objective M: *Explain the consequences of the Triangle-Sum Property. (Lesson 7-10)*

46. Why can't a triangle have two 100° angles?

47. Can a triangle have three acute angles? Explain your answer.

USES deal with applications of mathematics in real situations.

Objective N: *Use the Take-Away Model for Subtraction to form sentences involving subtraction. (Lessons 7-1, 7-4, 7-6)*

48. A one-hour TV program allows $9\frac{1}{2}$ minutes for commercials. How much time is there for the program itself?

49. A 2000 square-foot house was built on a lot of A square feet. Landscaping used the remaining 3500 square feet. How big was the original lot?

50. Anne must keep $100 in a bank account. The account had x dollars in it. Then Anne withdrew y dollars. There was just enough left in the account. How are x, y, and 100 related?

51. A, B, C, D, and E are points in order on a line. If $AE = 50$, $BC = 12$, and $CE = 17$, what is AB?

Objective O: *Use the Slide Model for Subtraction to form sentences involving subtraction. (Lesson 7-2)*

52. O'Hare airport in Chicago is often 5°F colder than downtown Chicago. Suppose the record low for a day is -13°F and was recorded downtown. What was the possible temperature at O'Hare?

53. The famous actor Henry Fonda died in 1982 at the age of 77. Knowing only this information, in what two years might he have been born?

54. *Multiple choice* A person weighs 70 kg and goes on a diet, losing x kg. The resulting weight is y kg. Then $y =$
(a) $x - 70$ (b) $70 - x$
(c) $x - {-70}$ (d) $-70 - x$

■ **Objective P:** *Use the Comparison Model for Subtraction to form sentences involving subtraction. (Lesson 7-3)*

55. The average number of 16- to 19-year-olds working in 1960 was about 4.1 million. By 1987 the number had increased to about 6.6 million. About how many more teen-agers were working in 1987 than in 1960?

56. Yvette believes that her team will win its next game by 12 points. But they lose by 1 point. How far off was Yvette?

57. An airline fare of F dollars is reduced by R. The lower fare is L dollars. How are F, R, and L related?

REPRESENTATIONS deal with pictures, graphs, or objects that illustrate concepts.

■ **Objective Q:** *Picture subtraction of positive and negative numbers on a number line. (Lesson 7-2)*

58. Picture the subtraction $-5 - 3$ on a number line and give the result.

59. Picture the subtraction $8 - 10$ on a number line and give the result.

Displays

To *display* means to show. The most common ways of displaying numbers are in graphs and tables. Below, a day in the life of a high school freshman is displayed in three different ways. In this chapter, you will study various kinds of displays.

A Day in the Life of F. R. Eshman

Table

Sleep	8 hr.
Eat	1.5 hr
At School	7 hr
Going to/from school	1 hr
Homework	2 hr
School activity	2 hr
Relaxation time	2.5 hr

Circle Graph

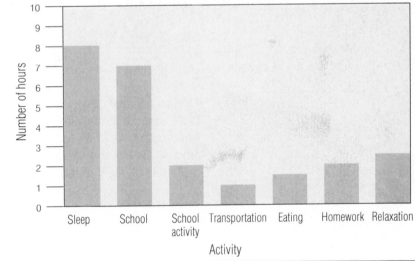

Relaxation time (2.5 hr)
Homework (2 hr)
School activity (2 hr)
At school (7 hr)
Eating (1.5 hr)
Going to/from school (1 hr)
Sleep (8 hr)

Bar Graph

Number of hours (y-axis, 0 to 10)

Sleep — 8
School — 7
School activity — 2
Transportation — 1
Eating — 1.5
Homework — 2
Relaxation — 2.5

Activity (x-axis)

Bar Graphs

According to the 1980 U.S. Census, about 3.4 million people of Asian or Pacific Islander ancestry were living in the U.S. in 1980. This number includes 812,000 Chinese; 782,000 Filipinos; 716,000 Japanese; 357,000 Koreans; 245,000 Vietnamese; 230,000 Pacific Islanders; and 140,000 of other nationalities.

The preceding paragraph shows numerical information in **prose** writing. Prose allows a person to insert opinions and extra information. It is the usual way you are taught to write.

Numbers in paragraphs are not always easy to follow. Many people prefer to see numbers displayed. One common display is the **bar graph**.

Example 1 Display the above numerical information in a bar graph.

Solution Step 1: Every bar graph is based on a number line. Draw a number line with a *uniform scale*. A uniform scale is one where numbers that are equally spaced differ by the same amount. Below, the *interval* of the scale is 100,000 people. This interval is chosen so that all of the numbers will fit on the graph.

Step 2: Graph each of the numbers.

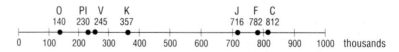

Step 3: Draw a segment from 0 to each number. Each segment is a *bar* of the bar graph. Then raise each bar above the number line.

Step 4: Identify the bars and put their length by them. Finally, label the entire graph so that someone else will know what you have graphed.

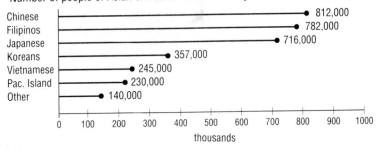

Number of people of Asian or Pacific Island ancestry in the U.S. in 1980

Chinese	812,000
Filipinos	782,000
Japanese	716,000
Koreans	357,000
Vietnamese	245,000
Pac. Island	230,000
Other	140,000

thousands

The number line underneath the bar graph serves as a scale. It is not always drawn, but for now you should draw it.

A single bar graph takes up more space than prose. To save space, two related bar graphs can be combined into one.

Example 2 Display the information below in a double bar graph.

Six Largest Cities in the United States

City	1970 Population	1984 Population
New York City	7,896,000	7,165,000
Chicago	3,369,000	2,992,000
Los Angeles	2,812,000	3,097,000
Philadelphia	1,950,000	1,647,000
Detroit	1,514,000	1,089,000
Houston	1,234,000	1,706,000

Solution

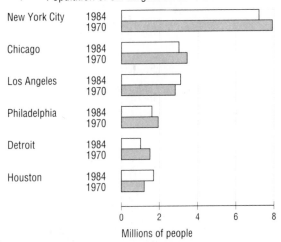

Population of Six Largest Cities in the U.S.

Millions of people

Independence Hall, Philadelphia

Below is a bar graph that appeared in *USA Today* January 12, 1984. This bar graph has several features to notice. The bars are vertical. There is no written scale, but horizontal lines are drawn for every billion dollars. The bars are drawn in two directions because both positive and negative numbers are being graphed.

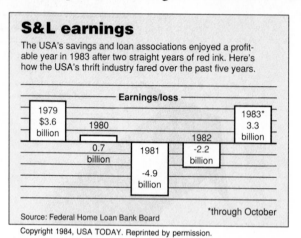

S&L earnings

The USA's savings and loan associations enjoyed a profitable year in 1983 after two straight years of red ink. Here's how the USA's thrift industry fared over the past five years.

Earnings/loss

1979 $3.6 billion	1980		1983* 3.3 billion
0.7 billion	1981	1982 -2.2 billion	
	-4.9 billion		

Source: Federal Home Loan Bank Board

*through October

To make bar graphs, you must have several skills. Obviously you need to be able to use a ruler. You have to know subtraction and order of numbers well enough to construct a uniform scale. You must be able to estimate. And you have to be able to translate number words into decimals.

Questions

Covering the Reading

In 1–3, use the bar graph of F. R. Eshman's day, page 335.

1. What is the interval of the scale of the bar graph?

2. Are the bars on this graph horizontal or vertical?

3. F. R. Eshman could spend more time on homework. Where could the time come from?

In 4–6, use the bar graph of Example 1.

4. What is the interval of the scale of the bar graph?

5. Are the bars on this graph horizontal or vertical?

6. In 1980, were there more people of Filipino or Japanese ancestry living in the U.S.?

In 7–9, use the bar graph of Example 2.

7. Which of the cities gained in population from 1970 to 1984?

8. In which city did the population decrease the most from 1970 to 1984?

9. What is the interval of the scale of this bar graph?

In 10–12, use the bar graph of S & L earnings on page 338.

10. What is the interval of the scale?

11. a. Which year from 1979 to 1983 was the worst year for savings and loan associations?
b. What were the earnings that year?

12. a. Which year from 1979 to 1983 was the best year for savings and loan associations?
b. What were the earnings that year?

13. On this graph, are the bars vertical or horizontal?

Applying the Mathematics

In 14–17: **a.** Is the scale uniform? **b.** If the scale is uniform, what is its interval? If the scale is not uniform, where is it not uniform?

14.

```
 0   2   4   6   8   10  12  14  16  18
```

15.
```
 4   7   10  13  16  19  22  25  28  31
```

16.
```
 0   1.0  1.05  1.1  1.15  1.2  1.25  1.3  1.35  1.4
```

17.
```
 0   2   4       6       8       10
```

In 18 and 19, suppose a bar graph had bars of lengths 3.39, 3.4, 3.391, and 3.294.

18. Which number will have the longest bar?

19. Which two bars will differ the most in length?

In 20 and 21, some information is given. To put the information into a bar graph, what might be a good interval to use?

20. Annual average unemployment rate in the United States: 1983, 9.6%; 1984, 7.5%; 1985, 7.2%; 1986, 7.0%

21. Popular vote in the Presidential election of 1860: Abraham Lincoln, 1,866,352 votes; Stephen A. Douglas, 1,375,157 votes; John C. Breckinridge, 845,763 votes; John Bell, 589,581 votes.

22. Here are the number of miles of coastline of those states bordering on the Gulf of Mexico: Alabama, 53; Florida, 770; Louisiana, 397; Mississippi, 44; Texas, 367. **a.** If you wanted to put this information into a bar graph, what might be a good interval to use? **b.** Put this information into a bar graph.

23. The record high and low Fahrenheit temperatures in selected states are: Alaska, 100° and -80°; California, 134° and -45°; Hawaii, 100° and 12°. Put this information into a double bar graph.

24. Which of the states in Question 23 has the greatest difference between high and low temperatures? What is that difference? *(Lesson 7-3)*

25. The number -2.2 billion appears in a bar graph in this lesson. Write this number as a decimal. *(Lesson 2-1)*

26. Use the information of Question 20. If there were 100,000,000 people in the U.S. work force in 1985, how many people were unemployed? *(Lesson 2-6)*

27. Round the numbers of Question 21 to the nearest hundred thousand. *(Lesson 1-4)*

28. How many degrees are in: **a.** half a circle; **b.** one third of a circle; **c.** one fifth of a circle? *(Lesson 3-5)*

29. What is 40% of 360? *(Lesson 2-6)*

30. **a.** Solve the equation $105 + 45 + x = 180$.
b. Write a problem about triangles that can lead to that equation.
   (Lessons 5-8, 7-10)

31. As Example 2 shows, New York has the largest population of any city in the United States. **a.** Are there any cities in the world larger than New York? **b.** If so, make a list of these cities. If not, give the name and approximate population of the largest city in each of the following: Asia, Africa, Europe, Central or South America.

32. There is software that enables a computer to display a bar graph on a monitor. If you have access to a computer, find the name of such software. If the software is available, use it to draw the bar graph on page 335 of this chapter.

8-2

Coordinate Graphs

The Art Institute, Chicago

Some patterns involve many *pairs* of numbers. A bar for each pair would take up too much space. **Coordinate graphs** are used instead.

Example 1 At left is a table of temperatures for a very cold January morning in Chicago. Put this information onto a coordinate graph.

Solution Here is the coordinate graph.

Time of day	Temperature (°F)
1 A.M.	-2
2 A.M.	-2
3 A.M.	-2
4 A.M.	-1
5 A.M.	0
6 A.M.	-2
7 A.M.	-1
8 A.M.	0
9 A.M.	3
10 A.M.	7
11 A.M.	11
12 noon	18

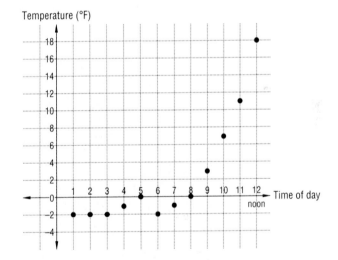

Examine the graph carefully. Notice that there are two number lines. The horizontal number line represents the time of day and goes from 1 to 12 (from 1 A.M. to 12 noon). The vertical number line represents temperature and goes from -4°F to 18°F. Its interval is chosen as 2° so that all the temperatures will fit on the graph. Each line of the table is a pair of numbers, and each pair of numbers corresponds to one point on the coordinate graph.

The coordinate graph has advantages over the table. It pictures change. As the temperature rises, so do the points on the graph. Also, you can insert points between the times on the coordinate graph without making it larger.

When a pair of numbers is being graphed as a point, the numbers are put in parentheses with a comma between them. For instance, the left point on the graph in Example 1 is (1, -2). This means at 1:00 A.M. the temperature was -2°F. The next three points are (2, -2), (3, -2), and (4, -1). The point furthest to the right is (12, 18). So at 12:00 noon the temperature was 18°F.

The symbol (a, b) is called an **ordered pair.** a is called the **first coordinate** of the ordered pair; b is the **second coordinate.** *Order makes a difference.* In Example 1, the first coordinate is the number for the time of day and the second coordinate is the number for the temperature at that time. At 9 A.M. a temperature of 3° is graphed as the point (9, 3). This is not the same as a temperature of 9° at 3:00 A.M., which would be graphed as the point (3, 9).

What are the coordinates of the points A, B, and C in the graph below?

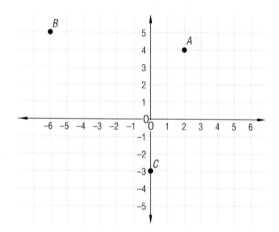

Solution Find the first coordinate of A by looking at the horizontal number line. A is above the 2. The second coordinate is found by looking at the vertical number line. A is to the right of the 4. So A = (2, 4).

B is above the -6, so the first coordinate of B is -6. B is to the left of the 5, so the second coordinate of B is 5. B = (-6, 5).

C is below the 0 on the horizontal number line. C is at the -3 on the vertical number line. So C = (0, -3).

Example 3   Graph the points (-1, -3) and (7, 0) on a coordinate graph.

Solution   To graph (-1, -3), go left to -1 on the horizontal number line. Then go down to -3. That point is *V* on the graph below.

To graph (7, 0), go right to 7 on the horizontal number line. Then stay there! The 0 tells you not to go up or down. This is point *T* on the graph.

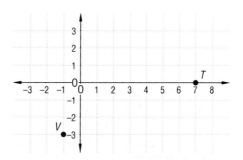

When variables stand for coordinates, it is customary to let *x* stand for the first coordinate and *y* stand for the second coordinate. For this reason, the first coordinate of a point is called the **x-coordinate**. The second coordinate is called the **y-coordinate**. For example, the point (-20, 4.5) has *x*-coordinate -20 and *y*-coordinate 4.5. The horizontal number line is called the **x-axis**. The vertical number line is the **y-axis**. The *x*-axis and the *y*-axis intersect at a point called the origin. The origin has coordinates (0, 0).

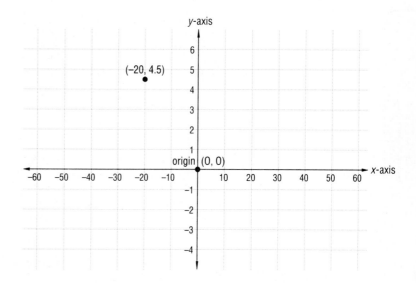

1. Trace the drawing below. Label the *x*-axis, *y*-axis, origin, and the point (2, 4).

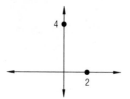

In 2–13, use the drawing below. The intervals on the graph are one unit. What letter names each point?

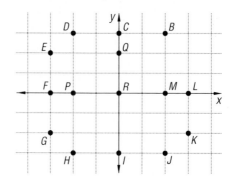

2. (2, 3)	**3.** (-3, 2)	**4.** (-2, 0)	**5.** (0, 3)
6. (0, -3)	**7.** (-2, -3)	**8.** (0, 0)	**9.** (-3, 0)
10. (3, -2)	**11.** origin	**12.** (3, 0)	**13.** (2, -3)

In 14 and 15, draw axes like those shown below. Plot the given points on your graph. Call the points *A*, *B*, *C*, and *D*.

14. (25, 10), (25, 5), (25, 0), (25, -5)

15. (-5, -5), (-10, -10), (-15, -15), (15, 15)

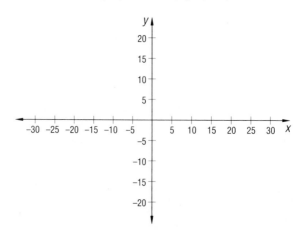

In 16 and 17, refer to Example 1.

16. **a.** From 3 A.M. to 5 A.M. in the table, did the temperature go up or down?
    b. How is this shown in the graph?

17. Estimate the temperature at 11:30 A.M.

18. Display the information given in the table on a graph like that below.

Time of day	Temperature (°C)
1 A.M.	3
2 A.M.	-1
3 A.M.	-4
4 A.M.	-1
5 A.M.	0
6 A.M.	0
7 A.M.	2
8 A.M.	3
9 A.M.	5
10 A.M.	6
11 A.M.	8
12 noon	10

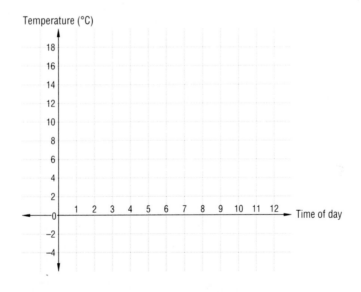

19. The x-coordinate of (-3, -1) is __?__.

20. The point (0, 3) is on the __?__-axis.

21. The point (0, 0) is called the __?__.

22. The second coordinate of a point is also called the __?__-coordinate.

23. The x-axis contains the point (-4, __?__).

24. The two coordinates of a point are always placed inside __?__ with a __?__ between them.

The four areas of a graph determined by the axes are called **quadrants** I, II, III, and IV, as shown at right.

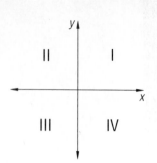

In 25–28, tell in which quadrant the given point lies.

25. (-50, 400) **26.** (78, -78)

27. (-.005, -4) **28.** (14, 13)

In 29–32, use the idea of Questions 25-28. Between which two quadrants does the point lie?

29. (0, -4000) **30.** (1 millionth, 0)

31. (-30.43, 0) **32.** (0, -989)

In 33–36, use the idea of Questions 25-28. In which quadrant is the point (x, y) if:

33. x and y are both negative.

34. x is positive and y is negative.

35. x is negative and y is positive.

36. x and y are both positive.

37. Convert this scale from miles to feet. *(Lesson 3-2)*

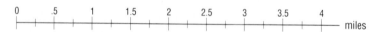

38. In Question 20 of the last lesson you picked an interval for a graph of the average annual unemployment rate in the United States. Here is the information again. Put it into a bar graph. 1983, 9.6%; 1984, 7.5%; 1985, 7.2%; 1986, 7.0%. *(Lesson 8-1)*

39. Draw a picture of two parallel lines and a transversal. Label one pair of alternate interior angles. *(Lesson 7-8)*

40. If one of two vertical angles has measure 20°, what is the measure of the other angle? *(Lesson 7-7)*

41. Evaluate $y - x$ when $y = -\frac{13}{16}$ and $x = -\frac{17}{32}$. *(Lesson 7-2)*

42. If $a + b = 9$, find a when $b = 15$. *(Lesson 5-8)*

Exploration

43. Most business sections of newspapers contain coordinate graphs. Cut out an example of a coordinate graph either from a newspaper or a magazine.
  a. What information is graphed?
  b. Are the scales on the axes uniform?
  c. If so, what are their intervals?

In a triangle, the sum of the measures of all three angles is 180°. In a *right triangle*, one angle has measure 90°. So the measures of the other two angles must add to 90°. Suppose these other angle measures are x and y. Seven pairs of possible values of x and y are in the table below. The ordered pairs are graphed below the table.

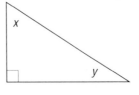

x	y
10	80
20	70
35	55
52	38
45	45
80	10
62.8	27.2

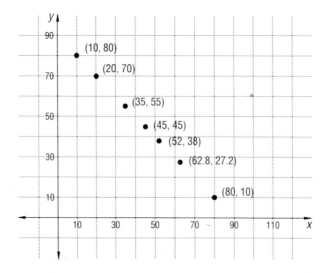

The *x*-coordinates and *y*-coordinates of all these points satisfy the equation $x + y = 90$. The seven points lie on a line. This line is the *graph of the solutions* to $x + y = 90$.

Of course there are many other pairs of numbers that work in $x + y = 90$. Some of them, like 110 and -20, involve negative numbers. Below, the entire line is graphed. The arrows on the line indicate that the line goes on forever in both directions.

Graph of *x* + *y* = 90

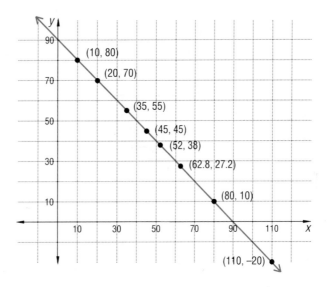

Every sentence with two variables has a graph. These graphs can be beautiful curves, but some of the simplest graphs are lines.

Example 1 Graph all solutions to the equation $x - y = 4$.

Solution Find some pairs of numbers that work in the equation. Keep track of the numbers you find by putting them in a table.

If $x = 6$, then $6 - y = 4$. So $y = 2$.
If $x = 4$, then $4 - y = 4$. So $y = 0$.
If $x = -1$, then $-1 - y = 4$. Solving
 this equation, $y = -5$.

x	*y*
6	2
4	0
-1	-5

The graph is on the next page.

Now graph the points (x, y) that you found. For the equations in this lesson, the graph is a line unless you are told otherwise. You should use at least three points in your table. Two points enable the line to be drawn. The third point is a check.

x	y
6	2
4	0
-1	-5

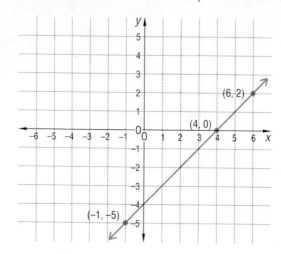

You may have to solve an equation to find a pair of numbers that works.

Example 2 Find a pair of numbers that works in the equation $-7 = -x - y$.

Solution Pick a value for x, say 6. Substitute 6 for x and solve for y.

$$-7 = -6 - y$$
$$-7 + y = -6 + -y + y$$
$$-7 + y = -6$$
$$7 + -7 + y = 7 + -6$$
$$y = 1$$

So when $x = 6$, $y = 1$. Thus $(6, 1)$ is one point on the graph of $-7 = -x - y$. Substituting other numbers for x and solving for y will give the coordinates of other points that work.

Questions

Covering the Reading

1. Name three pairs of numbers that work in $x + y = 90$.

2. When all pairs of numbers that work in $x + y = 90$ are graphed, they lie on a ___?___.

3. Suppose x and y are measures of the two acute angles in a right triangle. How are x and y related?

350

4. Name three pairs of numbers that work in $x - y = 4$.

5. The graph of $x - y = 4$ is a __?__.

6. If $x + y = 10$ and $x = 2$, then $y =$ __?__.

In 7 and 8, an equation and a value of x are given.
  a. Find the corresponding value of y.
  b. Tell what point these values determine on the line.

7. $x - y = 5$; $x = 3$ **8.** $x = 6 - y$; $x = 40$

In 9 and 10, graph all solutions to each equation.

9. $x + y = 10$ **10.** $x - y = 6$

11. *Multiple choice* The point $(2, 3)$ is not on which line?
(a) $x - y = -1$ (b) $-5 = -x - y$
(c) $x - y = 1$ (d) $y - x = 1$

12. *Multiple choice* Which graph pictures the solutions to $x + y = 10$?

(a)
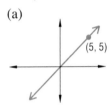

(b)
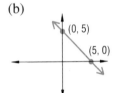

(c)
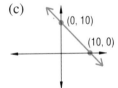

(d)
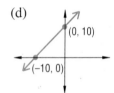

In 13 and 14: **a.** Write an equation that relates x and y.
b. Graph all pairs of values of x and y that work in the equation.

13. Margie had x dollars beginning the day. She spent y dollars. She wound up with $8.

14. There are 60 students, x of them in this classroom, y of them next door.

If you need to find many points in a graph, it is a good idea first to solve for one of the variables. In 15 and 16: **a.** Solve the equation for y. **b.** Use the solved equation to find three pairs of values of x and y that work in the equation.

15. $y + x = -7$

16. $-x - y = 0$

Review

17. In which quadrant is the point $(-800, 403.28)$? *(Lesson 8-2)*

18. Between which two quadrants is the point $(-3, 0)$? *(Lesson 8-2)*

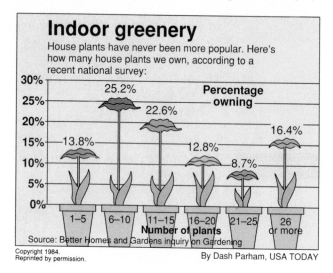

Indoor greenery
House plants have never been more popular. Here's how many house plants we own, according to a recent national survey:

Percentage owning

25.2%, 22.6%, 16.4%, 13.8%, 12.8%, 8.7%

Number of plants: 1–5, 6–10, 11–15, 16–20, 21–25, 26 or more

Source: Better Homes and Gardens inquiry on Gardening
Copyright 1984.
Reprinted by permission.
By Dash Parham, USA TODAY

19. According to the above graph:
a. What percent of people own more than 20 house plants?
b. What percent of people have no house plants? *(Lesson 8-1)*

20. Two angles of a triangle have measures 5° and 10°. What is the measure of the third angle of the triangle? *(Lesson 7-10)*

21. Suppose a savings account gives 5.25% interest per year. How much interest a year should you expect on $200? *(Lesson 2-6)*

22. How are quarts and liters related? *(Lesson 3-4)*

23. An integer is a *palindrome* if it reads the same forward and backward. For example, 252, 12,321, and 18,466,481 are palindromes. How many palindromes are there between 10 and 1000? *(Lesson 6-1)*

Exploration

24. In Question 14, $x + y = 60$. **a.** Name a pair of values of x and y that satisfy this equation but do not have meaning in the real situation. **b.** Describe all values of x which have meaning in the real situation.

25. A table like that on page 348 in this lesson can be printed by a computer using the following program.

a. Type and run this program, and describe the result.

```
10      PRINT "X", "Y"
20      FOR X = 10 TO 80
30      Y = 90 - X
40      PRINT X, Y
50      NEXT X
60      END
```

b. Change line 20 as indicated here.

```
20      FOR X = 10 TO 80 STEP 10
```

How does the change affect what the computer does and what is printed?

c. Change the program so that it prints different tables of coordinates of points on the line. Record the changes you made and describe the tables printed.

8-4

Why Graph?

In Lesson 8-3, you saw how a graph can picture relationships between numbers. For this reason, graphs are very important in mathematics. But graphs are used for other reasons.

You can find coordinate graphs in many newspapers. Here is a graph similar to one that may appear in your local newspaper. Before reading on, can you tell what the three broken lines represent?

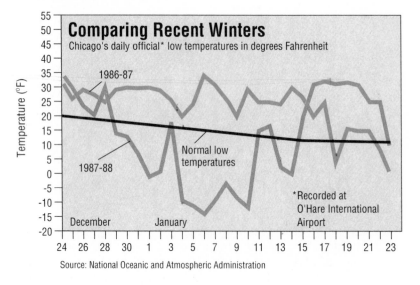

Source: National Oceanic and Atmospheric Administration

The line that starts near 20 on the vertical axis shows normal low temperatures for Chicago. The green broken line, starting at 32, shows temperatures for the winter of 1986-87. The red broken line, starting at 34, shows temperatures for the winter of 1987-88. This is much more information than could be put in a paragraph or table of the same size.

The above graph compares information and shows trends. Which winter was warmer, 1987-88 or 1986-87? How did each winter compare with the normal? Which month is usually colder—December or January? You can answer these questions just by looking at the graph.

In applications, as in the temperature graph, it is very important to select a useful scale on each axis. The scales may intersect at a point other than (0, 0). They may have different units. But in almost all simple graphs, each scale is uniform.

A barrel is pictured at right. Suppose you wanted to describe this picture to someone over the phone. You might use angle measures and segment lengths. But it is easier just to put the figure on a graph and tell someone the coordinates of the key points.

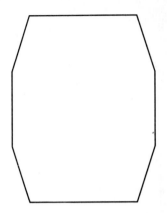

We put the origin at the center of the barrel because the barrel is symmetric.

Now, to describe the barrel over a phone, you can say that the barrel is pictured as a polygon with vertices (-4, -2), (-3, -5), (3, -5), and so on.

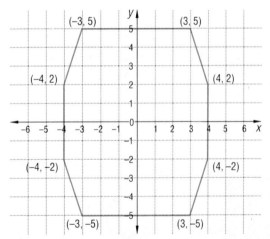

The same idea is used in many computer programs to store drawings or geometric figures in a computer.

You now have seen four reasons for using graphs.
Graphs can picture relationships between numbers.
Graphs can show a lot of information in a small space.
Graphs can show trends.
Graphs can describe drawings and geometric figures.

Covering the Reading

In 1–9, refer to the temperature graph on page 354.

1. Which December–January period was colder in Chicago, 1986-87 or 1987-88?

2. On January 18, give **a.** the normal low temperature, **b.** the low temperature in 1987, and **c.** the low temperature in 1988.

3. Repeat Question 2 for January 4.

4. Was either winter period warmer than the normal?

5. Which month is usually colder, December or January?

6. On December 24, 1983, an all-time low temperature of -25° set a record for any day in Chicago. Which of the days listed came closest to that record?

7. What is the interval of the scale on the horizontal axis?

8. What is the interval of the scale on the vertical axis?

9. At what point do the axes intersect?

10. Which of the four reasons for graphs apply to the graph on page 354?

11. Which of the four reasons for graphs apply to the graph of the barrel?

12. How are drawings and geometric figures stored in many computers?

Applying the Mathematics

13. Graph the following 12 points. Then connect them *in order* by a smooth curve. What figure seems to be formed?
(13, 0), (12, 5), (5, 12), (0, 13), (-5, 12), (-12, 5), (-13, 0), (-12, -5), (-5, -12), (0, -13), (5, -12), (12, -5), (13, 0)

14.

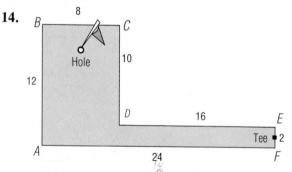

Outlined above is a miniature golf hole. All the angles are right angles. Lengths of sides are given. Suppose this outline were graphed with A at (0, 0) and B on the y-axis. **a.** Give the coordinates of points B, C, D, E, and F. **b.** Give the coordinates of the tee. **c.** Estimate the coordinates of the hole.

15. Given are the latitude and longitude of five European cities. Use these numbers as coordinates in graphing. Use axes like those at right, but make your drawing bigger. (If correct, your drawing will show how these cities are located relative to each other.)

City	North Latitude	East Longitude
London	51°	0°
Paris	49°	2°
Berlin	53°	13°
Rome	42°	12°
Warsaw	52°	21°

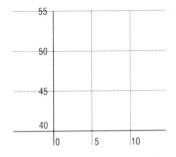

Review

16. Refer to the barrel drawn in this lesson. **a.** What kind of polygon is this barrel? **b.** The angles of this polygon are all what kind of angle? **c.** If you drew the eight lines containing the sides of the polygon, how many pairs of parallel lines would you have? **d.** If you drew the eight lines containing the sides of the polygon, how many pairs of perpendicular lines would you have? (*Lessons 3-6, 5-9, 7-8*)

17. Graph all pairs of solutions to the equation $x - y = 3$. (*Lesson 8-3*)

18. The temperature x near the floor is 5° cooler than the temperature y near the ceiling.
a. Find an equation that relates x and y.
b. Graph five pairs of values of x and y that work in that equation. (*Lessons 4-3, 8-3*)

19. A point is 2 units above (3, 6). What are the coordinates of the point? (*Lesson 8-2*)

Exploration

20. A *lattice point* is a point whose coordinates are both integers. Below a circle is graphed. **a.** How many lattice points are inside the circle? **b.** How many lattice points are on the circle?

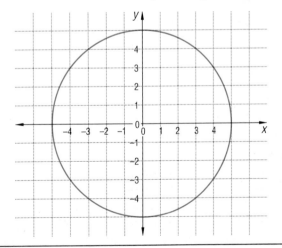

Translations (Slides)

If you change coordinates of the points in a figure, the figure will be altered. Adding the same number to the coordinates yields a **translation image** or **slide image** of the original figure.

Imagine beginning with triangle *MNO*. Add 3 to each first coordinate. Then graph the new points. You get a triangle 3 units to the right of *MNO*. We call this △*M'N'O'* (read "triangle *M* prime, *N* prime, *O* prime").

This procedure replaces (0, 0) by (3, 0), (2, 4) by (5, 4) and (-4, 6) by (-1, 6). Each **image** point is 3 units to the right of the **preimage** point.

In general, if you add *h* to each first coordinate, you will get a slide image of the original figure that is *h* units to the right. (If *h* is negative, then you will go "negative right," which is left.)

This is a two-dimensional picture of the slide model for addition that you studied in Chapter 5.

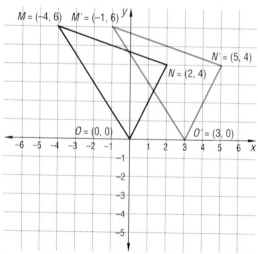

What happens if you add a particular number to the *second* coordinate? It's just what you might expect. The preimage slides up or down.

Below a third triangle is now on the graph. It is the image of $\triangle M'N'O'$ when -5 is added to the second coordinate. We call the image $M*N*O*$ (*M* star, *N* star, *O* star).

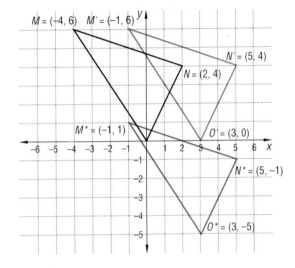

In general, if you add k to the second coordinate of all points in a figure, you will slide the figure k units up. (If k is negative, as it is here, then the slide is "negative up," which is down.)

Congruent figures are figures with the same size and shape. A translation image is always congruent to its preimage. The three triangles above are congruent.

Questions

Covering the Reading

In 1–4, what happens to the graph of a figure when:
1. 3 is added to the first coordinate of every point on it?

2. 10 is added to the second coordinate of every point on it?

3. -7 is added to the second coordinate of every point on it?

4. 6 is subtracted from the first coordinate of every point on it?

5. Another name for slide is __?__.

6. When you change the coordinates of points of a figure, the original figure is called the __?__ and the resulting figure is called its __?__.

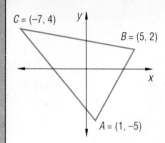

$C = (-7, 4)$

$B = (5, 2)$

$A = (1, -5)$

In 7 and 8, graph the triangle *ABC* shown at left. Then, on the same axes, graph its image under the translation that is described.

7. Add 2 to the first coordinate of each point.

8. Add -3 to the first coordinate and 5 to the second coordinate of each point.

In 9 and 10, tell what happens to the graph of a figure when:

9. *k* is added to the second coordinate of each point and *k* is positive.

10. *h* is added to the first coordinate of each point and *h* is negative.

11. Congruent figures have the same ⟨?⟩ and ⟨?⟩.

12. *True or false*   A figure and its slide image are always congruent.

Applying the Mathematics

13. a. Draw quadrilateral *PQRS* with *P* = (0, 0), *Q* = (5, 0), *R* = (5, 3), and *S* = (0, 4). **b.** On the same axes, draw its image when 3 is subtracted from each first coordinate and 2 is subtracted from each second coordinate. **c.** The preimage and image are ⟨?⟩.

14. Triangle *A′B′C′* is a slide image of triangle *ABC*. *A* = (0, 0), *B* = (3, 0), *C* = (0, -4), and *C′* = (-1, 5). What are the coordinates of *A′* and *B′*?

15. a. Give three instances of the following general pattern: Under a particular transformation, the image of (x, y) is $(x + 4, y - 5)$.
b. Draw the three points and their images.

16.

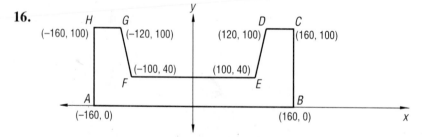

Polygon *ABCDEFGH* outlines a top view of a school building. The architect wishes to send this outline by computer to a builder. The builder may not understand negative numbers, so the architect slides the graph so that the image of point *A* is at the origin. The image is drawn here.

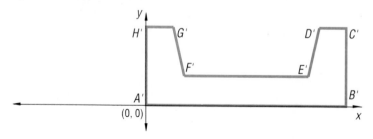

What will be the coordinates of *B′*, *C′*, *D′*, *E′*, *F′*, *G′*, and *H′*?

12. The point (2, 4) is reflected over the *x*-axis. What are the coordinates of its image? (Hint: Draw a picture.)

13. a. Graph the quadrilateral with vertices (1, 2), (3, 4), (4, -2), and (5, 0). **b.** Change each first coordinate to its opposite and graph the quadrilateral with the new vertices. **c.** The preimage is reflected over what line?

14. a. Give three instances of the following general pattern: Under a particular transformation, the image of (*x*, *y*) is (*y*, *x*).
b. Draw the three points and their images.

In 15–18, trace the figure. What word results when the figure is reflected over the given line?

15.

16.

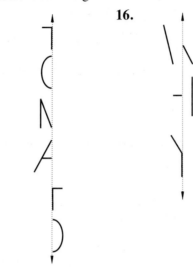

17.

18.

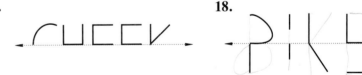

Review

19. The picture of the letter L below is to be stored in a computer with point *A* having coordinates (0, 0) and point *B* on the *x*-axis. Give the coordinates of the other points. *(Lesson 8-4)*

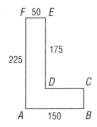

20. Graph the line with equation $x - y = 10$. *(Lesson 8-3)*

21. Use this bar graph that appeared in *USA Today* on July 27, 1984.

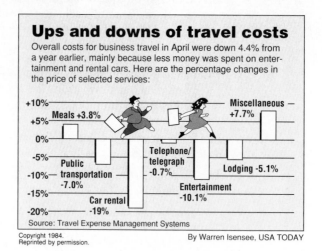

Ups and downs of travel costs

Overall costs for business travel in April were down 4.4% from a year earlier, mainly because less money was spent on entertainment and rental cars. Here are the percentage changes in the price of selected services:

Meals +3.8%
Miscellaneous — +7.7%
Telephone/telegraph -0.7%
Public transportation -7.0%
Lodging -5.1%
Entertainment -10.1%
Car rental -19%

Source: Travel Expense Management Systems

Copyright 1984.
Reprinted by permission.

By Warren Isensee, USA TODAY

a. What interval is used in the scale?
b. By how much more did car rentals decrease than public transportation?
c. Which travel cost area decreased the least? *(Lesson 8-1)*

22. Make up some scrambled words like those in Questions 15-18.

LESSON
8-7

Line Symmetry

Suppose triangle *ABC* is reflected over line *BD*. The image of *A* is *C*. The image of *C* is *A*. And the image of *B* is *B* itself. So the entire triangle coincides with its reflection image. We say that the triangle is **symmetric with respect to line *BD***. It has **line symmetry**.

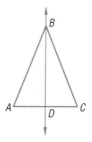

Symmetry lines do not have to be horizontal or vertical. Below at left is a rhombus *PQRS*. This figure has two symmetry lines. You can check this by folding the rhombus over either of these lines.

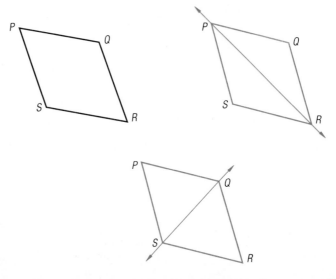

Perhaps the line *m* shown below at left is another symmetry line for *PQRS*. To test this, reflect *PQRS* over *m*. The image *P'Q'R'S'* is shown in blue below at right.

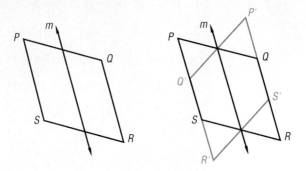

Since *P'Q'R'S'* does not coincide with the original rhombus, *m* is not a symmetry line.

Line symmetry is found in many places. Here are some common figures and their lines of symmetry.

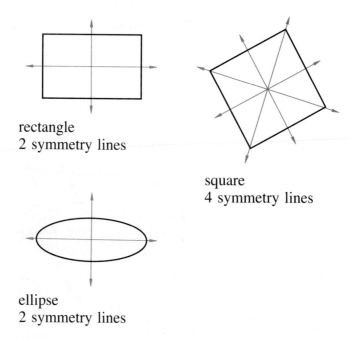

rectangle
2 symmetry lines

square
4 symmetry lines

ellipse
2 symmetry lines

Any line through the center of a circle is a line of symmetry. So a circle has infinitely many symmetry lines.

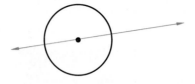

a circle with its center
and one of its symmetry lines

1. When does a figure have line symmetry?

2. How many lines of symmetry does a rhombus have?

3. Draw a figure with no lines of symmetry.

4. Draw a figure that has exactly one symmetry line.

5. Draw a figure that has exactly two lines of symmetry.

6. Draw a figure that has a symmetry line that is neither horizontal nor vertical.

7. How many symmetry lines does a circle have?

In 8–10, examine these capital letters.

ABCDEFGHIJKLMNOPQRSTUVWXYZ

8. Which letters have a horizontal line of symmetry?

9. Which letters have a vertical line of symmetry?

10. Which letters have a symmetry line that is neither horizontal nor vertical?

Symmetry occurs often in nature. In 11 and 12, how many lines of symmetry does each of these pictures have?

11.

12.

In 13–16, draw all symmetry lines for these figures.

13.
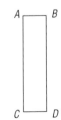

14.
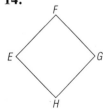

15.   **16.**

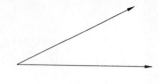

In 17 and 18, part of a symmetric figure is shown. All lines drawn are symmetry lines. Draw in the rest of the figure.

17.   **18.**

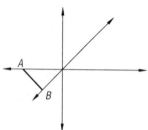

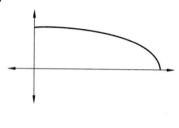

In 19 and 20, draw a hexagon with:

19. no lines of symmetry.

20. two lines of symmetry.

Review

21. Here are 1987 circulations of four of the best-selling magazines in the United States. Draw a bar graph with this information. *(Lesson 8-1)*

Magazine	Circulation
Better Homes and Gardens	8,091,751
The National Geographic	10,764,998
Reader's Digest	16,609,847
TV Guide	16,800,441

22. a. Graph the quadrilateral with vertices (2, -3), (6, -1), (0, 0), and (-4, -2). **b.** Translate (slide) this quadrilateral up four units. *(Lessons 8-2, 8-5)*

23. Graph the line with equation $x + y = -4$. *(Lesson 8-3)*

24. The point (-3, 8) is reflected over the x-axis. What is its image? *(Lesson 8-6)*

25. Find the value of $a + 3(b + 4(c + 5))$ when $a = 1$, $b = 2$, and $c = 3$. *(Lesson 4-5)*

26. A figure has **rotation symmetry** if it coincides with an image under a rotation or turn. For instance, all parallelograms have rotation symmetry. Under a 180° rotation (half turn) about point *O*, *ABCD* coincides with its image.

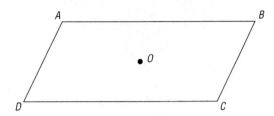

Tell whether the figure below has rotation symmetry. If so, give the magnitude of the smallest rotation under which the figure coincides with its image.

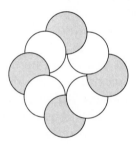

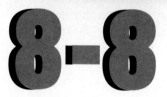

8-8

Tessellations

Pictured here are honey bees in their beehive. Each hexagon behind the bees is a cell in which the bees store honey. Bees are naturally talented at making such cells, so the pattern of hexagons is close to perfect. The pattern of hexagons is an example of a *tessellation*.

A **tessellation** is a filling up of a two-dimensional space by congruent copies of a figure that do not overlap. The figure is called the **fundamental region** or *fundamental shape* for the tessellation. Tessellations can be formed by combining translation, rotation, and reflection images of the fundamental region.

In the beehive the fundamental region is a *regular hexagon*. A **regular polygon** is a convex polygon whose sides all have the same length and whose angles all have the same measure. A regular polygon with six sides is a regular hexagon.

Only two other regular polygons tessellate. They are the square and the *equilateral triangle*. Pictured here are parts of tessellations using them. A fundamental region is shaded in each drawing.

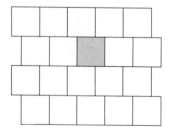

Variations of these regular polygons can also tessellate. If you modify one side of a regular fundamental region, and then modify the opposite side in the same way, the resulting figure will tessellate. (It is very much like balancing an equation as you solve it—always do the same thing to both sides.)

Example Modify a square to create a new tessellation.

Solution Start with the square at left. Change one side. Then copy the change to the opposite side. At right is a picture of the new tessellation.

Many other shapes can be fundamental regions for tessellations. The Dutch artist, Maurits Escher, became famous for the unusual shapes he used in tessellations.
Here is a part of one of his drawings.

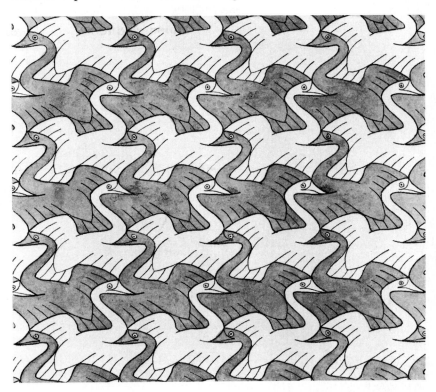

Some shapes do not tessellate. For instance, there can be no tessellation using only congruent regular *pentagons*. (You may want to try, but you will not succeed.)

1. What is a tessellation?

2. What is the fundamental region for a tessellation?

3. In a beehive, what figure is the fundamental region?

4. What is a regular polygon?

5. Name three regular polygons that tessellate.

6. Can a polygon that is not a regular polygon tessellate?

7. If a figure is not a polygon, can it be a fundamental region for a tessellation?

8. Draw a tessellation with equilateral triangles.

9. Draw a tessellation with a modified square different from the one pictured in the Example on page 373.

In 10–13, trace the figure onto hard cardboard. Make a tessellation using the figure as a fundamental region. Figure 13 is from the drawings of Maurits Escher.

10.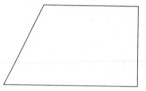

11.

12.

13.

14. **a.** Stop signs on highways are in the shape of what regular polygon? **b.** Can this shape be a fundamental shape for a tessellation?

15. Pictured here is a postage stamp from the Polynesian kingdom of Tonga. **a.** Why are most postage stamps shaped like rectangles? **b.** Why do you think Tonga has stamps shaped like ellipses?

16. How many degrees are in each angle of an equilateral triangle? (Hint: What is the sum of the measures of the angles?)

17. Another name for *regular quadrilateral* is __?__.

18. Graph the line with equation $y = x + 5$. *(Lesson 8-3)*

19. Draw the reflection image of triangle *ABC* over line *m*. *(Lesson 8-6)*.

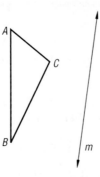

In 20 and 21, draw all symmetry lines for the given figure. *(Lesson 8-7)*

20.

21.

22. A quadrilateral is symmetric with respect to the *y*-axis. Two of the vertices of the quadrilateral are (4, 8) and (-2, 5). What are the other two vertices? *(Lessons 8-6, 8-7)*

23. Write 0.00000 002 in scientific notation. *(Lesson 2-9)*

24. Solve for *C*: $A + B + C + D = 360$. *(Lesson 5-8)*

25. *Multiple choice* Which could be an expression for the measure of one angle of a regular *n*-gon? *(Lesson 6-6)*
(a) $180n(n - 2)$ (b) $360/n$
(c) $180(n - 2)/n$ (d) $180/n$

26. Tiles on floors or ceilings usually form tessellations. Find at least two examples. Sketch the shape of the fundamental region in each.

27. If you visit the Alhambra you will see many examples of tessellations. **a.** Where is the Alhambra? **b.** What is it? **c.** Who built it? **d.** When was it built?

Summary

This chapter is concerned with two kinds of displays. The first kind is the display of numerical information. Bar graphs compare quantities by using segments or bars of lengths on a specific scale. The scale uses the idea of a number line.

Combining two number lines (usually one horizontal, one vertical), pairs of numbers can be pictured on a coordinate graph. These graphs enable a great amount of information to be pictured in a small space. They can show trends and relationships between numbers. Some simple relationships, such as those pairs of numbers satisfying $x + y = k$ or $x - y = k$, have graphs that are lines.

Relationships between geometric figures can also be displayed. A figure can be put on a coordinate graph. By changing the coordinates of points on the figure, an image of the figure can be drawn. By adding the same numbers to the coordinates, a slide or translation image results.

Coordinates are not necessary for figures and images. Any figure can be reflected over a line that acts like a mirror. The image is called a reflection image. If the figure coincides with its image, then it is said to be symmetric with respect to that line.

Reflections and translations are examples of transformations. So are the rotations you studied in an earlier chapter. Under these kinds of transformations, figures are congruent to their images. By taking a figure and congruent images, beautiful designs known as tessellations can be constructed.

Vocabulary

You should be able to give a general description
and a specific example for each
of the following ideas.

Lesson 8-1
bar graph
uniform scale, interval on scale

Lesson 8-2
coordinate graph
ordered pair, x-coordinate, y-coordinate
x-axis, y-axis, origin
quadrant

Lesson 8-5
translation image, slide image
preimage point, image point
congruent figures

Lesson 8-6
reflection image, reflecting line, mirror
coincide
transformation

Lesson 8-7
line symmetry, symmetry with respect to a line
symmetric figure

Lesson 8-8
tessellation
fundamental region
regular polygon

Progress Self-Test

Take this test as you would take a test in class. Then check your work with the solutions in the Selected Answers section in the back of the book.

In 1–3, use the graph below.

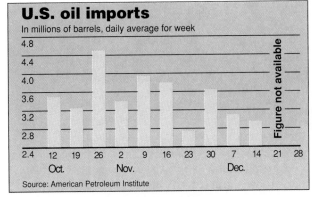

U.S. oil imports
In millions of barrels, daily average for week

Source: American Petroleum Institute

1. In which week of November were the most barrels of oil imported into the U.S.?

2. About how many barrels of oil per day were imported into the U.S. during the week of December 14?

3. What is the interval of the scale on the vertical axis of this graph?

4. A Thanksgiving meal in 1988 cost the typical person about 45¢ for green beans, 75¢ for a beverage, 30¢ for cranberries, 18¢ for sweet potatoes, and 99¢ for turkey. Put this information into a bar graph.

In 5–7, use the graph below. The interval of each scale is 1 unit.

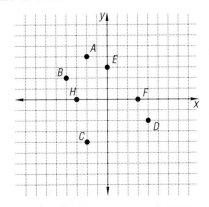

5. a. What letter names the point (0, 3)?
   b. What letter names the point (-2, 4)?

6. Which point or points are on the y-axis?

7. Which point or points are on the line $x + y = -2$?

8. Point Q has coordinates (2, 5). What are the coordinates of the point that is ten units above Q?

9. Graph the line with equation $x - y = 2$.

In 10 and 11, use the graph of the miniature golf hole at below left. All angles are right angles. The intervals on the axes are uniform.

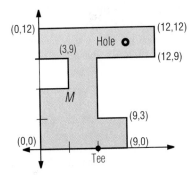

10. Give the coordinates of point M.

11. Estimate the coordinates of the hole.

12. Draw a quadrilateral with no lines of symmetry.

13. Draw a figure with exactly two lines of symmetry.

14. Draw all lines of symmetry of square $ABCD$.

15. Trace triangle *GHI* and line *m*. Draw the reflection image of triangle *GHI* over line *m*.

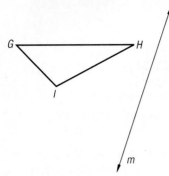

16. Draw part of a tessellation that uses triangle *GHI* as its fundamental region.

17. It costs 25¢ to mail a letter weighing 1 oz, 45¢ for a 2-oz letter, 65¢ for a 3-oz letter, and 85¢ for a 4-oz letter. Graph the ordered pairs suggested by this information.

18. *V* is the reflection image of *W* over line *l*. If m∠*UVW* = 72°, what is m∠*W*?

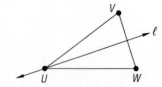

19. Give a reason for having graphs.

20. When are two figures congruent?

16. Find the area of the shaded region between rectangles *MNOP* and *RSTQ*.

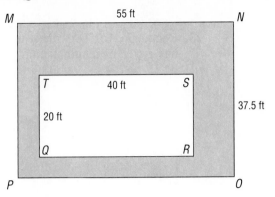

17. *True or false?* If $x = 7.6092$, then $3(x + 4) = (x + 4) \cdot 3$.

18. Find the area of the rectangle with vertices (2, 4), (5, 4), (5, 10), and (2, 10).

19. Multiply the numbers in both orders. Are the products equal?
a. 357 and 246; **b.** 1/2 and 2/5 (convert to decimals);
c. 67.92 and 0.00043.

Review

20. Solve the equation $x + \frac{22}{7} = -\frac{3}{2}$. *(Lesson 5-8)*

21. With your protractor, draw an angle with measure 40°. *(Lesson 3–5)*

22. One kilogram equals approximately how many pounds? *(Lesson 3–4)*

23. Evaluate $14 - 3(x + 3y)$ when $x = -2$ and $y = 5$. *(Lesson 4–5)*

24. Consider 48.49:
a. Round to the nearest integer. *(Lesson 1–4)*
b. Rewrite as a simple fraction. *(Lesson 2–7)*

25. The Northwest Ordinance of 1787 divided many areas of the central United States into square-shaped townships 6 miles on a side.
a. What is the perimeter of such a township? *(Lesson 5–10)*
b. What is the area? *(Lesson 3–7)*

26. There were about 2,380,000 high school graduates in the United States in 1986. Of these, about 58% went to a 2-year or 4-year college. How many college students is this? *(Lesson 2–6)*

27. How much bigger is the volume of a cube with edge 3.01 cm than the volume of a cube with edge 3 cm? *(Lesson 3–8)*

Exploration

28. Rectangle *ABCD* is made up entirely of squares. The black square has a side of length 1 unit. What is the area of *ABCD?*

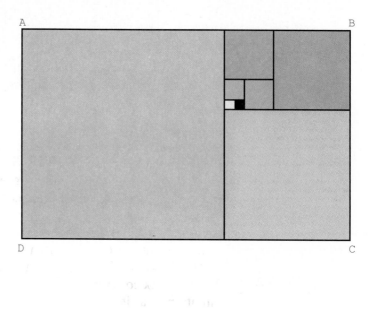

9-2

Surface Area

The cereal box at the left is an example of a **rectangular solid.**
The box has six sides, called *faces*. Each face is a rectangle.
(In a drawing, you view some faces at an angle. So all of the
faces don't seem to be rectangles.)

Rectangular solids like this cereal box are often constructed by
cutting a pattern out of a flat piece of cardboard. This process is
pictured below. The dotted segments show where folds are made.
The folds become the edges of the box. (For a real box, the
situation is a little more complicated. But the same idea is used.)

The flat pattern   After one fold

The **surface area** of a solid is the sum of the areas of its faces.
For the cereal box, the surface area tells you how much cardboard is needed to make the box. The cereal box has six faces:
top, bottom, right, left, front, and back. The flat pattern has six
rectangles.

A typical cereal box is 24 cm high, 16 cm wide, and 5 cm deep.
These are its dimensions.

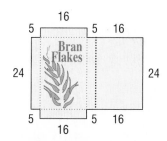

It may be easier to see the dimensions by separating the rectangles in the flat pattern. Adding the six areas gives the total surface area.

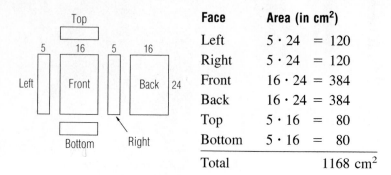

Face	Area (in cm²)	
Left	5 · 24	= 120
Right	5 · 24	= 120
Front	16 · 24	= 384
Back	16 · 24	= 384
Top	5 · 16	= 80
Bottom	5 · 16	= 80
Total		1168 cm²

Example Find the surface area of a rectangular solid 10 in. high, 4 in. wide, and 3 in. deep.

Solution First, draw a picture. You may want to separate the faces as shown here.

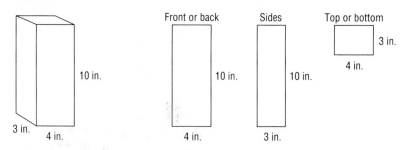

Now, just add the areas of the faces. The surface area is

$$10 \cdot 4 + 10 \cdot 4 + 10 \cdot 3 + 10 \cdot 3 + 4 \cdot 3 + 4 \cdot 3$$
$$= 40 + 40 + 30 + 30 + 12 + 12$$
$$= 164 \text{ square inches.}$$

Questions

Covering the Reading

1. A cereal box is an example of a figure called a __?__.

2. Each face of a rectangular solid is a __?__.

3. How many faces does a rectangular solid have?

4. What is the surface area of a solid?

In 5 and 6:
   a. Sketch a rectangular solid with the given dimensions.
   b. Draw a flat pattern out of which the solid could be made.
   c. Find the surface area of the solid.

5. dimensions 9 cm, 12 cm, and 7 cm

6. dimensions 3″, 3″, and 3″

7. Find the surface area of this rectangular solid.

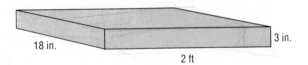

18 in.   3 in.   2 ft

8. A rectangular solid has length ℓ, width w, and height h. What is its surface area?

9. A shirt to be given as a gift is put into a box . The dimensions of the box are 14″, 9″, and 2.5″. What is the least amount of wrapping paper needed to wrap the gift? (You are allowed to use a lot of tape.)

10. Pat Tern wanted to make a rectangular box out of cardboard. She drew the following flat pattern. Correct the error in this pattern by moving one rectangle.

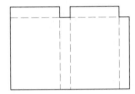

11. Using a sheet of notebook paper, a ruler, tape, and scissors, construct a box out of paper. You may pick whatever dimensions you wish.

12. Suppose that the Bran Flakes box mentioned in this lesson is made from a single rectangular sheet of cardboard. **a.** What are the smallest dimensions that sheet of cardboard could have? **b.** How much material will be wasted in making the box?

13. Here is a flat pattern for a cube. All sides of the squares have length 5. What is the surface area of the cube?

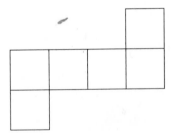

14. The bottom of a box has dimensions 24 cm and 20 cm. The box is 10 cm high and has no top. What is the surface area of the box?

15. How many ellipses are pictured? *(Lesson 9–1)*

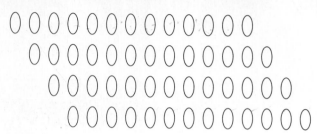

16. Simplify:
a. $xy - xy$;
b. $0.12 \cdot 3.4 + 3.4 \cdot 0.12 - 0.12 \cdot 3.4$. *(Lesson 9–1)*

17. What property guarantees that $x + 45$ equals $45 + x$? *(Lesson 5–7)*

18. Simplify: $\frac{1}{6} - \frac{3}{18} - \frac{2}{3} + \frac{5}{9}$. *(Lesson 7–2)*

19. Give three true statements relating the numbers 57, 91, and 34. *(Lesson 7–5)*

20. Solve for y: $x - y = 34$. *(Lesson 7–6)*

21. Let n be a number. Translate into mathematics:
a. 2 less than a number.
b. 2 is less than a number.
c. 2 less a number. *(Lesson 4–3)*

22. What is the perimeter of a rectangle with length 40 and width 60? *(Lesson 5–10)*

23. What is the volume of the cube constructed in Question 13 above? *(Lesson 3–8)*

24. In Question 13 a pattern was given for a cube. Here is a different pattern. (Patterns are different if they are not congruent.)

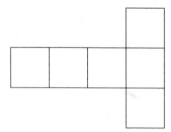

Draw all possible different patterns for a cube.

9-3

Volumes of Rectangular Solids

Whereas surface area measures the boundary of a solid, **volume** measures the space inside. Volume gives the capacity of containers ranging in size from atoms to objects even larger than the Earth. Knowing volume can help in finding weight, mass, pressure, and many other physical properties.

The volume of a rectangular solid can sometimes be calculated by counting. At other times a formula is needed.

Example 1 Find the volume of the rectangular solid pictured below. (The solid has been opened up to show the unit cube compartments.)

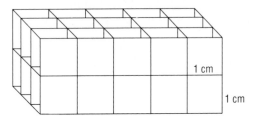

1 cm

1 cm

Solution 1 When the dimensions are integers, the unit cubes fit evenly into the solid. If the dimensions are small, you can count the cubes. There are 15 cubes on each level. The volume is therefore 30 cm^3, 30 cubic centimeters.

Solution 2 This solid has height 2 cm, length 5 cm, and depth 3 cm. The volume is the product of these three dimensions.

$$\text{Volume} = 5 \text{ cm} \cdot 3 \text{ cm} \cdot 2 \text{ cm}$$
$$= 30 \text{ cm}^3$$

The volume of a rectangular solid is always the product of its three dimensions, even when the dimensions are not integers.

Example 2 Find the volume *V* of a rectangular solid 5.3 cm long, 2.7 cm high, and 3.1 cm deep.

Solution

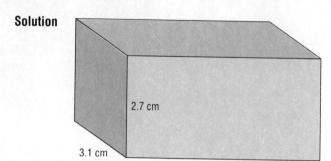

2.7 cm

3.1 cm

5.3 cm

$$V = 5.3 \text{ cm} \cdot 3.1 \text{ cm} \cdot 2.7 \text{ cm} = 44.361 \text{ cm}^3$$

In Example 2, the product of 3.1 cm and 5.3 cm is the area of the bottom or *base* of the box. So the volume is the product of the area of the base and the height.

Let *V* be the volume of a rectangular solid with dimensions *a*, *b*, and *c*.

Then $V = abc$.

Or $V = Bh$,

where *B* is the area of the base and *h* is the height.

By flipping a rectangular solid over on its side, any two dimensions can become the length and width of the base.

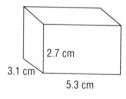

2.7 cm

3.1 cm

5.3 cm

5.3 cm

3.1 cm

2.7 cm

$V =$ Bh

$= (5.3 \text{ cm} \cdot 3.1 \text{ cm}) \cdot 2.7 \text{ cm}$

$=$ 16.43 cm^2 $\cdot 2.7 \text{ cm}$

$=$ 44.361 cm^3

$V =$ hB

$= 5.3 \text{ cm} \cdot (3.1 \text{ cm} \cdot 2.7 \text{ cm})$

$= 5.3 \text{ cm} \cdot$ 8.37 cm^2

$=$ 44.361 cm^3

The volume is the same regardless what face is the base. This verifies that multiplication is associative.

Associative Property of Multiplication:

For any numbers a, b, and c: $a(bc) = (ab)c = abc$.

Because multiplication is both commutative and associative, numbers can be multiplied in any order without affecting the product. These properties can shorten multiplications.

Example 3 Multiply in your head: $35 \cdot 25 \cdot 4 \cdot 4 \cdot 25$.

Solution Notice that $4 \cdot 25 = 100$. Multiply these first.
Think:
$$35 \cdot 25 \cdot 4 \cdot 4 \cdot 25$$
$$= 35 \cdot (25 \cdot 4) \cdot (4 \cdot 25)$$
$$= 35 \cdot \quad 100 \quad \cdot \quad 100$$
$$= 350,000.$$

Questions

Covering the Reading

1. Name two ways of finding the volume of a rectangular solid.

In 2–4, give the volume of a rectangular solid with the given dimensions.

2. height 6 cm, width 3 cm, and depth 4 cm

3. width 12 in., height 6 in., and depth 2.25 in.

4. height 10 meters, width w meters, and depth d meters

In 5–7, give the volume of a rectangular solid in which:

5. the area of the base is 40 square centimeters and the height is 4 cm.

6. the base has one side of length 10 inches, another side 2 inches longer, and the height is 1.5 in.

7. the base has area A and the height is h.

8. State the Associative Property of Multiplication.

9. Give an instance of the Associative Property of Multiplication.

In 10–12, use the properties of multiplication to do these problems mentally. No calculator or pencil-and-paper figuring allowed.

10. $5 \cdot 437 \cdot 2$

11. $6 \cdot 7 \cdot 8 \cdot 9 - 9 \cdot 8 \cdot 7 \cdot 6$

12. 50% of 67 times 2

13. The floor of a rectangularly shaped room is 9 feet by 12 feet. The ceiling is 8 feet high. How much air is in the room?

14. Give two possible sets of dimensions for a rectangular solid whose volume is 144 cubic units.

15. a. Draw a rectangular solid whose volume is 8 cm^3 and has all dimensions the same. **b.** What is this rectangular solid called? **c.** Draw a second rectangular solid whose volume is 8 cm^3 but whose dimensions are not equal.

16. Give **a.** the volume and **b.** the surface area of this box.

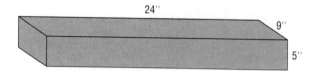

17. A computer has a display screen that can show up to 364 rows and 720 columns of dots. How many dots can be on that screen? *(Lesson 9-1)*

18. A rectangular solid has width W centimeters, length L centimeters, and depth D centimeters. What is the surface area of the solid? *(Lesson 9-2)*

19. Solve the equation $83 - x = 110$. *(Lesson 7-6)*

20. In the triangle below:

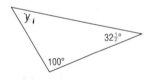

a. What is the value of y? *(Lesson 7-10)*
b. How many angles are acute?
c. How many angles are obtuse? *(Lesson 3-6)*

21. a. Press the following keys on a calculator. *(Lesson 1-7)*

[2] [3] [.] [4] [×] [5] [.] [6] [7] [=]

b. Press the following keys.

[5] [.] [6] [7] [×] [2] [3] [.] [4] [=]

c. Compare the displays you get for **a** and **b**. What property have you verified? *(Lesson 9-1)*

In 22–24, put one of the signs $<$, $=$, or $>$ in the blank. *(Lesson 1-6)*

22. -4 – 4 __?__ -4 + 4

23. -7.352 __?__ -7.351

24. 2/3 __?__ .66666666

25. a. In which quadrant is the point (4, -1)?
   b. Give an equation for a line that goes through (4, -1).
      (Lessons 8-3, 6-1)

26. If $n = 10$, what is the value of $(3n + 5)(2n - 3)$? *(Lesson 4-5)*

27. 2.6 kilometers is how many meters? *(Lesson 3-3)*

28. What digit is in the thousandth place of 54,321.09876? *(Lesson 1-2)*

29. To divide a decimal by .001, how many places should you move the decimal point, and in what direction? *(Lesson 6-6)*

Exploration

30. a. How many entries are needed to complete this multiplication table?

$\times$	3.0	3.2	3.4	3.6	3.8	4.0
7.0						
7.2						
7.4						
7.6						
7.8						
8.0						

   b. Fill in the table.
   c. Find at least two patterns in the numbers you put into the table.

Dimensions and Units

The size of a line segment is given by its length.

Rectangles and other polygons are two-dimensional. There are two common ways of measuring these figures. Perimeter measures the boundary (in black below). Area measures the space inside the figure (shown below with hearts).

Area and perimeter are quite different. The perimeter of the rectangle pictured below is 6 + 100 + 6 + 100, or 212 *feet*. That's how far you have to go to walk around the rectangle. Perimeter is measured in units of length.

100 ft

6 ft

Area measures how much space is taken up by the rectangle. The area of the rectangle above is 600 *square feet*.

The area of the rectangle below is 6 cm · 3 cm, or 18 cm². Its perimeter is 6 cm + 3 cm + 6 cm + 3 cm, or 18 cm. Area and perimeter can never actually be equal because the units are different. In a situation like this one, the area and perimeter are called *numerically equal*.

6 cm

3 cm

In lakes, perimeter measures shoreline. Area measures fishing room. Lake Willy-Nilly does not have much fishing room despite a lot of shoreline. It has a small area compared to its perimeter.

Lake Willy-Nilly

There are three different ways to measure the size of a three-dimensional figure. Consider the shoebox below. We can measure the total length of its edges. Like perimeter, this is one-dimensional. We can measure its surface area. That is two-dimensional. Or we can measure its volume. That is three-dimensional.

The shoebox has edges of lengths 14 inches, 5 inches, and 7 inches. There are four edges of each length. (Some are hidden from view.) The total length of all edges is
$4 \cdot 5'' + 4 \cdot 7'' + 4 \cdot 14'' = 104$ *inches.*

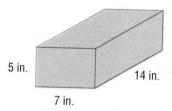

5 in.

14 in.

7 in.

The surface area of this shoebox is found by adding the areas of the six rectangular faces. You should check that it is 406 *square inches.*

The volume of this box measures the space occupied by the box. It is 5 in. · 7 in. · 14 in., or 490 *cubic inches.*

Surface area and volume have different units. They measure different things, as the next example shows.

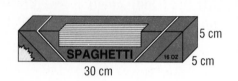

Example　The spaghetti box and teabag box have 750 cubic centimeters of volume each. Which box requires more cardboard?

5 cm
5 cm
30 cm

10 cm
10 cm
7.5 cm

Solution　The surface area of the spaghetti box is
$30 \cdot 5 + 30 \cdot 5 + 30 \cdot 5 + 30 \cdot 5 + 5 \cdot 5 + 5 \cdot 5$, or 650 cm².

The surface area of the box of teabags is
$10 \cdot 10 + 10 \cdot 10 + 10 \cdot 7.5 + 10 \cdot 7.5 + 10 \cdot 7.5 + 10 \cdot 7.5$, or 500 cm².

The spaghetti box needs more cardboard to hold the same volume as the teabag box. (This is because the spaghetti box is long and thin.)

To summarize: Length, perimeter, and edge length are 1-dimensional. Area and surface area are 2-dimensional, and usually measured in square units. Volume is 3-dimensional, and usually measured in cubic units.

Questions

Covering the Reading

In 1–4, suppose that length is measured in centimeters. In what unit would you expect each to be measured?

1. perimeter
2. volume

3. area
4. surface area

5. __?__ measures the space inside a 2-dimensional figure.

6. __?__ measures the space inside a 3-dimensional figure.

7. __?__ measures the distance around a 2-dimensional figure.

8. __?__ measures the surface of a 3-dimensional figure.

9. Suppose the area of Lake Willy-Nilly is measured in square miles.
　a. In what unit would you expect its shoreline to be measured?
　b. In what unit would you expect its fishing room to be measured?

400

10. Draw a lake that has lots of perimeter but very little area.

11. Each side of a square has length 4. *True or false:* The perimeter and area of the square are equal.

12. Give an example of two rectangular solids with the same volume but with different surface areas.

13. Find the area of each face of the shoebox in this lesson.

14. A small box has dimensions 11 mm, 12 mm, and 13 mm. Find: **a.** the total length of its edges; **b.** its surface area; **c.** its volume.

Applying the Mathematics

15. A box has dimensions ℓ, w, and h. What is the total length of its edges?

16. A rectangle has a perimeter of over 100 inches. But its area is less than 1 square inch. **a.** Is this possible? **b.** If so, give dimensions of such a rectangle. If not, tell why it is not possible.

In 17–19, tell whether the idea concerns surface area or volume.

17. the amount of wrapping paper needed for a gift

18. how many paper clips a small box can hold

19. the weight of a rock

20. An *acre* is a unit of area in the U.S. system. 640 acres = 1 square mile. A farm is measured in acres. *Multiple choice* What is being measured about this farm? (a) its land area; (b) its perimeter; (c) its volume

21. Recall that a liter is a metric unit equal to 1000 cm^3. *Multiple choice* What does a liter measure? (a) length; (b) area; (c) volume

Review

22. Trace the drawing. Then reflect triangle *ABC* over the line *m*. *(Lesson 8-6)*

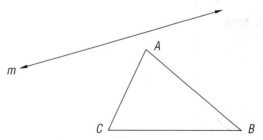

23. Find the area of the quadrilateral with vertices (4, -8), (-3, -8), (-3, 11), and (4, 11). *(Lessons 8-2, 9-1)*

24. Graph the line with equation $y = x$. *(Lesson 8-3)*

25. How many feet are in 3 miles? *(Lesson 3-2)*

26. In this figure, $\angle 2$ is a right angle and m$\angle 1 = 140°$. What is m$\angle 3$? *(Lesson 7-8)*

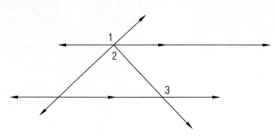

27. The point (8, -4) is translated 10 units down. What is its image? *(Lesson 8-5)*

28. a. Rewrite 3 trillion in scientific notation.
b. Rewrite 3 trillionths in scientific notation. *(Lessons 2-3, 2-8)*

29. Rewrite each number as a percent. **a.** 1/3; **b.** 2/3; **c.** 4/5. *(Lessons 1-8, 2-5)*

30. Graph all solutions to the inequality $x > 4$. *(Lesson 4-9)*

31. In this program to calculate and print the surface area and volume of a box, there are two incomplete lines.

```
10 PRINT "SIDES OF BOX"
15 INPUT A,B,C
20 PRINT "VOLUME", "SURFACE AREA"
30 VOL = ____
40 SA = ____
50 PRINT VOL,SA
60 END
```

a. Fill in the blanks to make this program give correct values for VOL and SA.
b. What will the computer print if A = 2, B = 3, and C = 4?
c. Run the completed program with values of your own choosing to test it. *(Lessons 9-2, 9-3)*

Exploration

32. The "D" in 3-D movies is short for "dimensional." **a.** Are these movies actually three dimensional? **b.** When you watch a 3-D movie in a theater, you must wear special glasses. How do these glasses work?

More Properties of Multiplication

Even using a calculator, you may make a mistake in computation. So you should always learn ways to check problems. The worst way to check is to do a problem over the same way you did it the first time. You are likely to make the same mistake twice.

Properties of multiplication can help you check your work. For instance, to check the answer 2513 to the multiplication $7 \cdot 359$, you can use the commutative property and multiply in the reverse order. Doing $359 \cdot 7$, you should also get 2513.

When one factor in a multiplication problem is a small positive integer, you can check the answer using repeated addition. For example, you can check $7 \cdot 359 = 2513$ by doing the addition

$$359 + 359 + 359 + 359 + 359 + 359 + 359.$$

You should again get 2513. Obviously, if neither factor is a small positive integer, this check is too difficult. Repeated addition also does not work if both numbers are fractions or if both numbers are negative. You may have used repeated addition when you first learned to multiply. Many people continue to use repeated addition whenever they can.

Repeated addition model for multiplication:

If n is a positive integer, then
$$nx = \underbrace{x + x + \ldots + x}_{n \text{ addends}}$$

Specifically:
$$1x = x$$
$$2x = x + x$$
$$3x = x + x + x$$
$$4x = x + x + x + x$$
and so on.

Example 1   What is the perimeter of a square with side length s?

Solution   The perimeter is $s + s + s + s$.
By repeated addition, this equals $4s$.

Example 2   What is the perimeter of a rectangle with length ℓ and width w?

Solution: The perimeter $= \ell + w + \ell + w$.

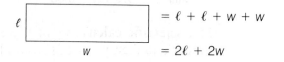

$= \ell + \ell + w + w$ (Commutative and Associative properties of Addition)

$= 2\ell + 2w$ (Repeated Addition Model for Multiplication)

From Examples 1 and 2 come the formulas $p = 4s$ for the perimeter of a square and $p = 2\ell + 2w$ for the perimeter of a rectangle.

Since $1x = 1 \cdot x = x \cdot 1 = x$, multiplying a number by 1 does not change its value. For this reason, the number 1 is called the *multiplicative identity*. It has the same role in multiplication that 0 has in addition.

Additive Identity Property of Zero:

For any number n: $n + 0 = 0 + n = n$.

Multiplicative Identity Property of One:

For any number n: $n \cdot 1 = 1 \cdot n = n$.

Recall that 4 and -4 are additive inverses or opposites because their sum is 0, the additive identity. Similarly, the numbers 3 and $\frac{1}{3}$ are called **multiplicative inverses** or **reciprocals**, because their product is 1, the multiplicative identity.

Property of Opposites:

For any number n: $n + \text{-}n = 0$.

Property of Reciprocals:

For any nonzero number n: $n \cdot \frac{1}{n} = 1$.

For example, the reciprocal of 6 is $\frac{1}{6}$, because $6 \cdot \frac{1}{6} = 1$. Notice that *the reciprocal of a number is 1 divided by that number*.

Example 3 Write the reciprocal of 12.5 as a decimal.

> **Solution** The reciprocal of 12.5 is $\dfrac{1}{12.5}$. A calculator shows that quotient to equal 0.08.
>
> **Check** Does $12.5 \cdot 0.08 = 1$? Yes.

Most scientific calculators have a reciprocal key $\boxed{1/n}$. Enter a number and then press this key. The reciprocal of the number you entered should be displayed.

Questions

Covering the Reading

1. Carlisle pressed the key sequence $3.00 \boxed{\times} 67.8 \boxed{=}$. **a.** Write two key sequences Carlisle could use to check his answer. **b.** Do your key sequences give the same answer?

2. Heather presses $16 \boxed{1/n}$. **a.** What will the calculator do? **b.** How can she check her answer?

3. Using repeated addition, check by hand whether $4 \cdot 953 = 3712$.

4. **a.** Name the multiplicative identity.
   b. Name the additive identity.

5. **a.** State the Multiplicative Identity Property of One.
   b. State the Additive Identity Property of Zero.

6. For the number 20, give: **a.** its reciprocal; **b.** its opposite;
   c. its additive inverse; and **d.** its multiplicative inverse.

7. Repeat Question 6 for the number x.

In 8–10, simplify by using multiplication in place of the repeated addition.

8. $x + x + x$ 9. $\ell + w + \ell + w$

10. $25 + 20 + 20 + 25 + 20 + 20 + 25 + 20 + 25$

11. What could the variables used in Question 9 represent?

In 12 and 13, change the multiplications to additions.

12. $6y$

13. $2x + 4z$

14. Orange juice is $1.19 per can in a grocery store. A shopper buys 6 cans. Name two ways the shopper can figure out the total cost.

15. Orange juice is $1.19 per can in a grocery store. A shopper buys c cans. What is the total cost?

16. Simplify: $4e - e$. (Hint: Change everything to additions.)

17. *Multiple choice* Which does **not** equal the multiplicative identity?
(a) $\frac{7}{7}$ (b) $.6 \cdot \frac{5}{3}$ (c) $x - x$ (d) $.3 + .7$

18. Which pairs of numbers are reciprocals?
(a) 100 and 0.01   (b) 2 and 1/2
(c) 2.5 and 2/5   (d) 7/4 and 4/7
(e) 3.5 and 3/5   (f) 16 and -16
(g) 1.5 and $0.\overline{6}$ (h) 3 and .3

19. Which of the pairs of numbers in Question 18 are opposites?

20. What simple sentence is being described? "The sum of the multiplicative identity and the additive identity is the multiplicative identity."

21. Rewrite 12.5 and its reciprocal as simple fractions.

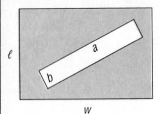

22. A rectangle with dimensions a and b is inside a rectangle with dimensions ℓ and w.
   a. What is the area of the shaded region?
   b. Suppose you tilt the smaller rectangle (as pictured at left). Does this change the area between the two rectangles? *(Lessons 7-1, 9-1)*

23. Name the general property. *(Lessons 5-7, 9-3, 7-2)*
   a. $a + (b + c) = (a + b) + c$
   b. $6.4 \cdot (3.7 \cdot 900) = (6.4 \cdot 3.7) \cdot 900$
   c. $35 + {}^-78 = 35 - 78$

24. A box has dimensions $2'$, $3'$, and $4'$. *(Lessons 9-2, 9-3)*
   a. Find the area and perimeter of the largest face of the box.
   b. Find the surface area and volume of the box.

25. How far off is the person's estimate? *(Lesson 7-3)*
   a. A person estimates that a team will win by 4 points, but the team wins by 5.
   b. A person estimates that a team will win by *w* points, but the team wins by *z* points.

26. *True or false?* $1.005 \cdot 2.34567893456 > 2.34567893456$.
   (Lesson 4-9)

27. Find the measures of the numbered angles, given that $m \parallel n$.
   (Lesson 7-8)

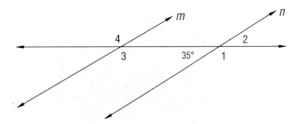

28. Enter 5 on your calculator. Press the reciprocal key $\boxed{1/n}$ twice.
   a. What number is displayed? **b.** What has happened? **c.** What will happen if you press the reciprocal key 75 times? **d.** Make a generalization.

9-6

Size Changes — Expansions

As the zebra colt grows, its size expands.

Suppose the segment below has length L.

L ———

Place a copy next to it. The total length is $L + L$ or $2L$. Multiplying by 2 lengthens the segment. The new segment is twice the length of the original.

2L ————————

Place another copy. The length is $2L + L$ or $3L$. Multiplying by 3 expands the segment even more.

3L ——————————

Example 1 Consider the segment above with length L. Draw a segment 2.5 times as long.

Solution Measure the segment with length L. Its length is 0.5″. Multiply 0.5 by 2.5.

$$2.5 \cdot 0.5 \text{ inches} = 1.25 \text{ inches}$$

The desired segment is 1.25 inches, or $1\frac{1}{4}$ inches long. Draw it.

2.5L ——————————

Check Notice that $2.5L$ should be halfway between $2L$ and $3L$. It is.

These examples show that multiplying by a number can change the size of things. The number is called the **size change factor**. Above, the size change factors are 2, 3, and then 2.5.

With coordinates it is even easier to change the size of things. We begin with a quadrilateral (in black). Then multiply both coordinates of all vertices by 2. The image is in blue. It has the same shape as the preimage. But its sides are 2 times as long.

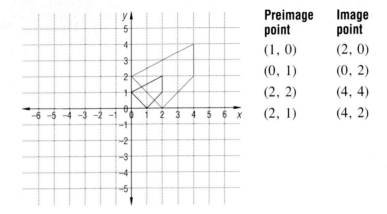

Preimage point	Image point
(1, 0)	(2, 0)
(0, 1)	(0, 2)
(2, 2)	(4, 4)
(2, 1)	(4, 2)

This transformation is called a *size change of magnitude 2*. The image of (x, y) is (2x, 2y). Because the image figure is bigger, this size change is also called an **expansion** of magnitude 2.

Multiplying the coordinates by 3 results in a larger image. Still, each angle and its image have the same measure. Notice that corresponding sides of the preimage and image are parallel. This is a size change or expansion of magnitude 3. The number 3 is the size change factor.

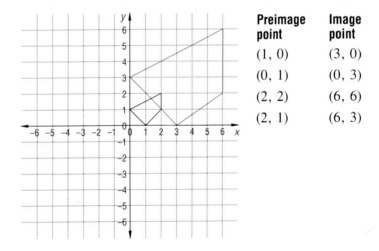

Preimage point	Image point
(1, 0)	(3, 0)
(0, 1)	(0, 3)
(2, 2)	(6, 6)
(2, 1)	(6, 3)

In general, under a size change of magnitude 3, the image of (x, y) is (3x, 3y).

Pictured below is a size change of magnitude 2.25. Each coordinate of the preimage has been multiplied by 2.25.

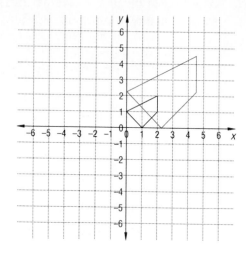

Preimage point	Image point
(1, 0)	(2.25, 0)
(0, 1)	(0, 2.25)
(2, 2)	(4.5, 4.5)
(2, 1)	(4.5, 2.25)

With a size change of magnitude 2.25, the image of (x, y) is $(2.25x, 2.25y)$.

In general, under a **size change of magnitude k,** the image of (x, y) is (kx, ky).

When two figures have the same shape, they are called **similar figures.** In a size change, the preimage and the image are always similar.

The idea of size change can involve quantities other than lengths.

Example 2   John weighed 6.3 pounds at birth. At age 1, his weight had tripled. How much did he weigh at age 1?

Solution   "Tripled" means a size change of magnitude 3. Multiply his weight by 3. He weighed $3 \cdot 6.3$ pounds, or 18.9 pounds.

Example 3   Maureen works in a store for $5 an hour. She gets time-and-a-half for overtime. What does she make per hour when she works over-time?

Solution   "Time-and-a-half" means to multiply by $1\frac{1}{2}$ or 1.5. Working overtime, she makes $1.5 \cdot \$5.00$, or $7.50.

1. **a.** Copy this horizontal segment. ─────────────
   b. If this segment has length L, draw a segment of length $2L$.
   c. Draw a segment of length $3L$.
   d. Draw a segment of length $3.5L$.

2. Draw a line segment that is 1.5 times as long as the segment at left.

3. **a.** Graph the quadrilateral with vertices (1.5, 4), (4, 0) (2, 1), and (1, 2). **b.** Find the image of this quadrilateral under an expansion of magnitude 2. **c.** How do lengths of the sides of the image compare with lengths of sides of the original quadrilateral? **d.** How do the measures of the angles in the preimage and image compare?

4. Figures with the same shape are called __?__ figures.

5. Under a size change, a figure and its image are __?__.

6. *True or false?*   Under a size change, a side of a preimage is parallel to the corresponding side of its image.

7. A triangle has vertices (1, 4), (2, 3), and (1, 2). Graph it and its image under a size change with magnitude 3.

8. Under a size change with magnitude k, the image of (x, y) is __?__.

9. Suzanne saved $25.50. After doing three magic shows, she tripled this amount. **a.** What size change factor is meant by the word "tripled"? **b.** How much money does she have now?

10. David gets $1.50 an hour for babysitting. After 10 P.M., he gets time-and-a-half for overtime. **a.** What does he make per hour after 10 P.M.? **b.** What will David earn for babysitting from 7 P.M. to 11 P.M.?

11. A microscope lens magnifies 150 times. Some human hair is about 0.1 mm thick. How thick would the hair appear under this microscope?

12. The bookcase in the picture is 1/40 of the actual size. This means that the actual bookcase is 40 times as wide. Will the actual bookcase fit into a space 5 feet wide?

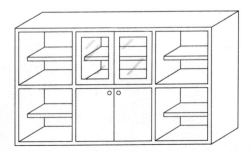

13. An object is 4 cm long. A picture of the object is 12 cm long. The image of the object is ___?___ times actual size.

In 14–17, each word suggests an expansion of what magnitude?

14. doubled

15. quintupled

16. octupled

17. quadrupled

Review

18. Simplify mentally: $3.95 + $3.95 + $3.95 + $3.95 + $3.95 + $3.95 + $3.95 + $3.95 + $3.95 + $3.95 *(Lesson 9-5)*

19. The product of a number and its reciprocal is ___?___. *(Lesson 9-5)*

20. The reciprocal of $\frac{1}{100}$ is ___?___. *(Lesson 9-5)*

21. Suppose a city block is 200 meters long and 50 meters wide. **a.** If you walked around this block, how far would you have to walk? **b.** What is the perimeter of this block? **c.** What is its area? *(Lesson 9-4)*

22. A box is 9″ long, 10″ wide, and 15″ high. *(Lessons 9-2, 9-3)*
   a. What is its surface area?
   b. What is its volume?

In 23–25, name the general property for the given instance. *(Lessons 9-3, 9-1, 1-10)*

23. $50\% \cdot (375 \cdot 63) = (50\% \cdot 375) \cdot 63$

24. $3(ab) = 3(ba)$

25. $7/13 = 28/52$

26. Solve $3.8 = E - 0.09$. *(Lesson 7-4)*

Exploration

27. What is the magnitude of a size change you might find in an electron microscope?

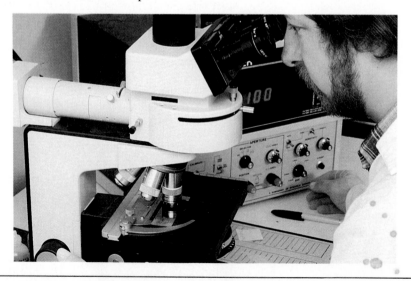

412

Size Changes— Contractions

In Lesson 9–6, all of the size change factors were numbers bigger than 1. This results in products with larger absolute value. In this lesson, we multiply by numbers between 0 and 1. This results in numbers with smaller absolute value. For instance, if 8 is multiplied by 0.35, the product is 2.8. The number 2.8 is smaller than 8.

This can be pictured. $AB = 8$ cm. $CD = 0.35 \cdot 8$ cm $= 2.8$ cm. $\overline{CD}$ is shorter.

A ——————————— 8 cm ——————————— B

C —— 2.8 cm —— D $0.35 \cdot 8 = 2.8$

Think of $\overline{AB}$ as having been reduced in size to 2.8 cm by a shrinking, or a **contraction**. A contraction is a size change with a magnitude whose absolute value is between 0 and 1. In the situation above, the *magnitude of the contraction* is 0.35.

Below is a two-dimensional picture of a contraction. The preimage is the black pentagon. We have multiplied the coordinates of all its vertices by 1/2. Since 1/2 is between 0 and 1, the resulting image is smaller than the original. Again the preimage and image are similar figures. In this case, sides of the image have 1/2 the length of sides of the preimage. Corresponding angles on the preimage and image have the same measure.

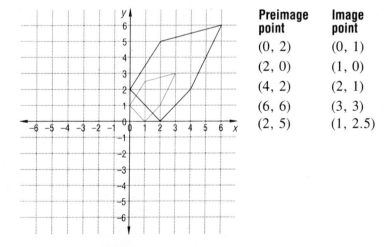

Preimage point	Image point
(0, 2)	(0, 1)
(2, 0)	(1, 0)
(4, 2)	(2, 1)
(6, 6)	(3, 3)
(2, 5)	(1, 2.5)

In general, under a size change of magnitude $\frac{1}{2}$, the image of (x, y) is $(\frac{1}{2}x, \frac{1}{2}y)$.

Expansions and contractions are types of size changes. The general idea is an important model for multiplication.

Size Change Model for Multiplication:

> If a quantity x is multiplied by a size change factor k, then the result is a quantity k times as big.

If k is bigger than 1, then the size change is an expansion. If k is between 0 and 1, the size change is a contraction.

Contractions also occur with quantities that are not lengths.

Example 1 A person buys an airplane ticket. Sometimes a spouse can travel for 2/3 the price and a child under 12 can travel for 1/2 price. On this plan, what will it cost a married couple and their 11-year-old child to fly if the normal price of a ticket is $150?

Solution It will cost one of the adults $150.
It will cost the spouse 2/3 of $150. This can be calculated by using the decimal 0.6666666 for 2/3. Then, multiplying gives $99.99999, which rounds to $100.

It will cost the child 1/2 of $150. That is $0.5 \cdot \$150$, or $75.
The total cost will be $150 + $100 + $75, or $325.

In Example 1, the size change factors are 2/3 and 1/2. Size change factors for contractions are often written as fractions or percents. You have seen the idea in Example 2 before. Now you can think of it as an example of size change multiplication.

Example 2 About 1% of the population of the United States is 85 or older. If the U.S. population is about 243,000,000, how many people are 85 or older?

Solution The size change factor is 1%, or 0.01.
$0.01 \cdot 243{,}000{,}000$ people $= 2{,}430{,}000$ people.

1. a. Measure the length of the segment below to the nearest half cm.

t

   b. If the segment has length *t*, draw a segment with length 0.3*t*.
   c. What is the magnitude of the contraction?

2. Any positive number between __?__ and __?__ can be the magnitude of a contraction.

In 3–5, give the image of the point (6, 4) under the contraction with the given magnitude.

3. 0.5   **4.** 0.75   **5.** $\frac{1}{4}$

6. a. Graph the pentagon with vertices (10, 10), (10, 5), (0, 0), (0, 5), (5, 10). **b.** Graph its image under a contraction with magnitude 0.8. **c.** How do the lengths of the corresponding sides of the preimage and image compare? **d.** How do the measures of corresponding angles in the preimage and image compare?

7. State the Size Change Model for Multiplication.

8. Repeat Example 1 if the cost of a ticket for an adult is $210.

9. About 7.7% of the U.S. population is of Spanish origin. If the population is 240,000,000, about how many people in the U.S. are of Spanish origin?

10. In Question 9, what is the size change factor?

11. The actual damselfly is half the size of the damselfly pictured at left. How long is the actual damselfly?

12. In doing Question 11, some students measure lengths of this insect in centimeters. Others measure in inches. If they measure accurately, will they get equal values for the length of the damselfly?

13. What is the image of (12, 5) under a contraction with magnitude *k*?

14. *Multiple choice* A car was priced at $7000. The salesperson offered a discount of $350. What size change factor, applied to the original price, gives the discount?
  (a) 0.02   (b) 0.05   (c) 0.20   (d) 0.245

15. *Multiple choice*   A car was priced at $7000. The salesperson offered a discount of $350. What size change factor, applied to the original price, gives the offered price?
(a) 0.05   (b) 0.20   (c) 0.80   (d) 0.95

16. A size change of magnitude 1/2 was applied to a pentagon in this lesson. Suppose the preimage and image were switched.
  a. What magnitude size change would now be pictured?
  b. Generalize the idea of this question.

Review

In 17–19, use properties of multiplication to simplify in your head. *(Lessons 9-1, 9-5)*

17. $1000 \cdot m \cdot 0.01$ **18.** $3 \cdot 20 \cdot \frac{1}{3} \cdot 5 \cdot 3$

19. $m + m + \text{-}m + m + 4m \cdot .25 + \text{-}m$

In 20–24, find each number. *(Lessons 5-4, 9-5)*

20. the multiplicative inverse of 40

21. the additive inverse of 40

22. the reciprocal of 40

23. the multiplicative identity

24. the product of 40 and its reciprocal

25. *Multiple choice*   When $x + y = 180$, which is not equal to y? *(Lesson 5-8)*
(a) $180 - x$ (b) $180 + \text{-}x$ (c) $\text{-}180 + x$ (d) $\text{-}x + 180$

26. **a.** Simplify $-\frac{14}{5} - -\frac{3}{10} - \frac{2}{15} - \text{-}50$.
  b. State and name the property that enables all subtractions to be converted to additions. *(Lesson 7-2)*

27. If the high temperature for the day was 20° and the low temperature was -2°, how much did the temperature drop? *(Lesson 7-3)*

28. *R* is a positive number. Which is larger, $R + 0.8$ or $0.8R$? *(Lesson 6-7)*

29. Each edge of a cube has length 7 cm. **a.** Find its volume. **b.** Find its surface area. **c.** Find the total length of all its edges. *(Lessons 3-8, 9-2, 9-3)*

Exploration

30. A map (like a roadmap or a map of the United States) is a drawing of a contraction of the world. The *scale* of the map is the size change factor. For instance, if 1″ on the map is 1 mile on Earth, then the scale is 1″/1mi.
Now 1 mile = 5280 feet = 5280 · 12 inches = 63,360 inches. So the scale on such a map is 1/63,360. Find a map and determine its scale.

31. Below is a drawing. Make a drawing that is similar and 2.5 times the size.

Multiplying by $\frac{1}{n}$

Suppose you make $6.50 an hour but you work for only 1/2 hour. Do you divide $6.50 by 2 to find out how much you make for that half hour? If so, then you are using a basic connection between multiplication, reciprocals, and division.

To multiply by $\frac{1}{2}$, you can divide by 2.

A pizza is to be split equally among 7 people. Each person will get 1/7 of the pizza. This is the same idea.

To divide by 7, you can multiply by $\frac{1}{7}$.

The general principle is called the **Mult-Rec Property of Division**. (Rec is for reciprocal.)

Mult-Rec Property of Division:

For any numbers a and b, when $b \neq 0$,

$$\frac{a}{b} = a \cdot \frac{1}{b}.$$

In words, dividing by b is the same as multiplying by the reciprocal of b.

As a simple instance, $\frac{5}{4} = 5 \cdot \frac{1}{4}$. And because of the Commutative Property of Multiplication, $\frac{5}{4}$ also equals $\frac{1}{4} \cdot 5$. Notice how the Mult-Rec Property is used in the next example.

■ ■ ■ ■ ■ ■ ■ ■ ■

Example 1   A picture is to be reduced to 1/3 its original size. If an original length on the picture was 11 cm, what will be the new length?

Solution   The new length will be $\frac{1}{3} \cdot 11$ cm.
Using the Mult-Rec Property, this equals $\frac{11}{3}$ cm, or $3.\overline{6}$ cm.

Remember that the area of a rectangle can picture products of numbers. To picture ab, draw a rectangle with length a and width b. The area is ab.

Example 2   Picture 2 · 3.

Solution   Draw a rectangle with dimensions 2 and 3.

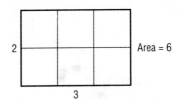

The area of this rectangle is 6, which is 2 · 3.

Using this same idea, multiplication by $\frac{1}{n}$ can be pictured.

Example 3   Picture $2 \cdot \frac{1}{4}$.

Solution   Draw a rectangle with dimensions 2 and $\frac{1}{4}$. (A unit square split into 4 is drawn as a guide.) The area of this rectangle is $2 \cdot \frac{1}{4}$. You can see also that the area equals $\frac{2}{4}$ of the original unit square.

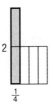

The fractions $\frac{1}{2}$, $\frac{1}{3}$, $\frac{1}{4}$, and so on, are **unit fractions.** A unit fraction is a fraction with 1 in its numerator and a natural number in its denominator. The Mult-Rec Property shows how to multiply any decimal by a unit fraction $\frac{1}{n}$. Here is a situation that requires multiplying two unit fractions together.

Example 4   Five scouts have to stuff envelopes. They divide the job equally. But one of the scouts finds two other friends to help. These three divide their work equally. How much of the entire job did this scout do?

Solution   The scout originally had $\frac{1}{5}$ of the job to do. By dividing the job among three people, the problem is to calculate
$\frac{1}{5}$ divided by 3.

By the Mult-Rec Property, this equals $\frac{1}{5} \cdot \frac{1}{3}$. Now let's figure that out.

Again, draw a rectangle. This time one dimension should be $\frac{1}{5}$ and the other dimension $\frac{1}{3}$. The big square here is a unit square.

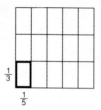

The area of the small outlined rectangle is $\frac{1}{5} \cdot \frac{1}{3}$. But the area is also $\frac{1}{15}$ of the unit square. (There are 15 congruent rectangles in the unit square.) So $\frac{1}{5} \cdot \frac{1}{3} = \frac{1}{15}$. The scout did $\frac{1}{15}$ of the work.

Here is the generalization of Example 4.

Product of Reciprocals Property:

If a and b are not zero, then $\dfrac{1}{a} \cdot \dfrac{1}{b} = \dfrac{1}{ab}$

From the Product of Reciprocals Property, we see that half of a third is a sixth. That is, $\frac{1}{2}$ times $\frac{1}{3}$ equals $\frac{1}{6}$. Also $\frac{1}{10}$ times $\frac{1}{10}$ equals $\frac{1}{100}$.

An important application of this property is in situations involving chance.

■ ■ ■ ■ ■ ■ ■ ■■

Example 5 Slips of paper with the 10 digits 0 through 9 are put in a hat. In another hat are slips for the 26 letters of the alphabet. One slip is taken from each hat. What are your chances of guessing *both* the digit and the letter?

Solution Your chances of guessing the digit are 1 in 10, or 1/10. Your chances of guessing the letter are 1 in 26, or 1/26. Since the guesses do not affect one another, your chances of guessing both is the product of 1/10 and 1/26.

$$\tfrac{1}{10} \cdot \tfrac{1}{26} = \tfrac{1}{260}$$

So the chances of guessing both are 1/260, or 1 in 260. (Most people think the chances are better than that.)

Check For each of the 10 numbers there are 26 letters to choose from. So there are $10 \cdot 26 = 260$ possible number-letter pairs. Only one of these pairs is correct. So the chances of guessing that pair are 1/260.

1. You can find half of a number by dividing that number by __?__.

2. You can find $\frac{1}{n}$ of a number by dividing that number by __?__.

In 3–6, simplify.

3. $2 \cdot \frac{1}{3}$ **4.** $a \cdot \frac{1}{b}$ **5.** $\frac{1}{8} \cdot 16$ **6.** $\frac{1}{x} \cdot 5$

7. A picture of an elephant is 1/10 actual size. If the elephant is 5 meters tall, how tall is the picture of the elephant?

In 8–11, simplify.

8. $\frac{1}{3} \cdot \frac{1}{4}$ **9.** $\frac{1}{5} \cdot \frac{1}{5}$ **10.** $\frac{1}{40} \cdot \frac{1}{x}$ **11.** $\frac{1}{a} \cdot \frac{1}{b}$

12. You are doing 1/4 of a job. You find a friend to help you do your part. You share your part equally with this friend. **a.** How much of the total job will your friend do? **b.** If the total job pays $100, how much should your friend receive?

13. One hat contains 50 pieces of paper. One of these pieces wins a prize. A second hat contains 75 pieces and one of those pieces wins a prize. Without looking, you pick a piece of paper from each hat. What are your chances of winning: **a.** the first prize? **b.** the second prize? **c.** both prizes?

14. What is a unit fraction?

15. A pie is divided into 6 pieces. Each piece is split into three congruent smaller pieces. Each smaller piece is what part of the whole pie?

16. Four shirts are in one drawer and five pair of slacks are on hangers. In the dark, you pick out a shirt and a pair of slacks. What are the chances of choosing the particular shirt and pair of slacks you want?

17. D shirts are in a drawer. H pair of slacks are on hangers. In the dark, you pick out one shirt and one pair of slacks. What are the chances of selecting both the particular shirt and the pair of slacks you want?

18. How much of a will does a person receive if the will is split into: **a.** 2 equal shares; **b.** 6 equal shares; **c.** n equal shares?

19. In a will, five people are left W dollars to share equally. How much should each person expect to receive?

20. *Multiple choice* Which of (a) to (c) is not equal to $\frac{3}{8}$?
(a) 3 divided by 8 (b) 3 times the reciprocal of 8
(c) 8 times the reciprocal of 3 (d) All are equal to $\frac{3}{8}$.

21. **a.** Give the fraction that is the product of 1/7 and 1/23.
    b. Convert your answer to a decimal.
    c. Multiply the decimal for 1/7 by the decimal for 1/23.
    d. Explain why the answers to parts **b** and **c** should be equal.

22. Use rectangles to picture the product $\frac{1}{3} \cdot \frac{1}{4} = \frac{1}{12}$.

23. Use rectangles to picture the product of 3 and $\frac{1}{5}$.

24. Calculate: $\frac{1}{2} \cdot \frac{1}{3} \cdot \frac{1}{4}$.

25. What is half of a half of a half of a half?

26. A contraction has magnitude $\frac{1}{4}$. You can divide lengths on the preimage by __?__ to get lengths on the image.

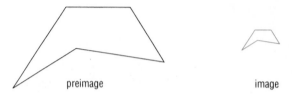

preimage   image

Review

27. **a.** Order from smallest to largest: $\frac{1}{3}$ $\frac{3}{8}$ $\frac{8}{30}$.
    b. Order from smallest to largest: $-\frac{1}{3}$ $-\frac{3}{8}$ $-\frac{8}{30}$. *(Lesson 1-8)*

In 28 and 29, simplify. *(Lesson 9-5)*.

28. $3a + a$ 29. $3a - a$

30. A room is rectangularly shaped with length 5.1 meters and width 6.2 meters. To the nearest square meter, what is its floor area? *(Lesson 9-1)*

31. Which can be measured in yards: perimeter, area, volume, or surface area? *(Lesson 9-2)*

32. Two figures with the same shape are called __?__. *(Lesson 9-6)*

Exploration

33. The dimensions of a rectangular solid, *to the nearest cm*, are 9 cm, 15 cm, and 20 cm. These dimensions are rounded values. To the nearest cubic centimeter, give the smallest and largest volume the rectangular solid can have.

23. A size change has magnitude $\frac{5}{6}$. Is it a contraction or an expansion? *(Lessons 9-6, 9-7)*

In 24 and 25, given that $\overline{PQ} \parallel \overline{ST}$ and angle measures as shown on the figure:

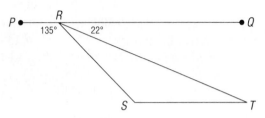

24. Find the measures of the three angles of triangle *RST*. *(Lessons 7-8, 7-10)*

25. Trace the figure and draw the reflection image of $\triangle RST$ over the line containing $\overline{PQ}$. *(Lesson 8-6)*.

26. Find **a.** the surface area and **b.** the volume of a rectangular box 50 cm high, 40 cm wide, and 36 cm deep. *(Lessons 9-2, 9-3)*

Exploration

27. Make up a situation with a question that can be answered by multiplying the fractions $\frac{2}{3}$ and $\frac{1}{6}$.

Summary

Given the dimensions, multiplication helps to find the area of a rectangle, the number of elements in a rectangular array, and the volume of a rectangular solid. By adding six areas, the surface area of a rectangular solid can be found.

Multiplication arises also from size change situations. Multiplying by a number greater than 1 can be pictured by an expansion. Multiplying by a number less than 1 can be pictured by a contraction. In either case, the figure and its image are similar.

If the same number x is an addend n times, then the total sum is nx. In this way, multiplication arises from repeated addition. Instead of dividing by n, you can multiply by $1/n$. In this way, multiplication is related to division.

The properties of multiplication are like those for addition: Multiplication is commutative and associative. There is an identity (the number one) and every number but zero has an inverse (its reciprocal). From these properties, other properties show how to multiply fractions.

Vocabulary

You should be able to give a general description
and a specific example for each
of the following ideas.

Lesson 9–1
Area Model for Multiplication
rectangular array, row, column, dimensions
Commutative Property of Multiplication

Lesson 9–2
rectangular solid, faces
surface area

Lesson 9–3
volume
Associative Property of Multiplication

Lesson 9–5
Repeated Addition Model for Multiplication
perimeter of rectangle
Multiplicative Identity Property of One
multiplicative inverse, reciprocal
Property of Reciprocals

Lesson 9–6
size change factor
size change of magnitude k
expansion
similar figures

Lesson 9–7
contraction
Size Change Model for Multiplication

Lesson 9–8
Mult-Rec Property of Division
unit fraction
Product of Reciprocals Property

Lesson 9–9
Multiplication of Fractions Property

Progress Self-Test

Take this test as you would take a test in class. Then check your work with the solutions in the Selected Answers section in the back of the book.

In 1–4, simplify.

1. $\frac{3}{5} \cdot \frac{2}{5}$

2. $-y + y + y + 3 + y + y$

3. $4 \cdot \frac{1}{3} \cdot \frac{5}{4}$

4. $\frac{1}{x} \cdot \frac{7}{16}$

In 5 and 6, name the general property.

5. $(12 \cdot 43) \cdot 225 = 12 \cdot (43 \cdot 225)$

6. $m \cdot \frac{1}{m} = 1$

7. An auditorium has r rows and s seats in each row. Five seats are broken. How many seats are there to sit in?

8. Give the area and perimeter of a rectangle with length 17.3 meters and width 6.8 meters.

9. How much cardboard is needed to make the closed carton pictured at right?

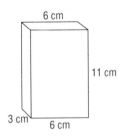

6 cm
11 cm
3 cm
6 cm

10. What is the volume of a rectangular solid with dimensions 3 feet, 4 feet, and 5 feet?

11. If the shoreline of a lake is measured in km, in what unit would you expect to measure the amount of room for fishing?

12. Give dimensions for two noncongruent rectangles whose area is 16.

13. Round the reciprocal of 38 to the nearest thousandth.

14. You buy 3 half gallons of milk at $1.29 a half gallon. Show two different ways of calculating the total cost.

15. What multiplication of fractions is pictured below?

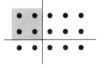

16. What is the image of (8, 2) under an expansion of magnitude 4?

17. Bess earns $5.80 per hour. She gets time-and-a-half for overtime. How much does she make per hour of overtime?

18. A parallelogram has vertices (2, 6), (6, 8), (8, 2), and (4, 0). Graph this parallelogram and its image under a size change of magnitude $\frac{1}{2}$.

19. In Question 18, the size change is called a __?__. The image and preimage are said to be __?__.

20. 3/25 of Howdy High students are in the band. There are 850 students at Howdy High. How many students are in the band?

21. Larry earned a scholarship which pays for 2/3 of his $8400 college tuition. How much is his scholarship?

22. You have a one in ten chance of guessing a correct digit. What are your chances of correctly guessing three digits in a row?

23. You feel you have a 2 in 3 chance of getting an A on a history test, and a 2 in 5 chance of getting an A on your upcoming math test. What are your chances of doing both?

24. Draw a rectangle with very little area for its perimeter.

25. *Multiple choice* Which number is the reciprocal of 1.25?
(a) 0.125   (b) -1.25   (c) 0.8   (d) 0.75

Chapter Review

Questions on **SPUR** Objectives

SPUR stands for **S**kills, **P**roperties, **U**ses, and **R**epresentations. The Chapter Review questions are grouped according to the SPUR Objectives for this chapter.

SKILLS deal with the procedures used to get answers.

Objective A: *Multiply fractions. (Lessons 9-8, 9-9)*

1. Multiply 3 by 1/6 and write the answer in lowest terms.

2. Multiply 4/5 by 4/3 and write the answer in lowest terms.

3. Multiply $100 \cdot \frac{3}{8}$.

4. Multiply $\frac{2}{5} \cdot \frac{2}{5} \cdot \frac{2}{5}$.

5. Multiply $10\frac{1}{8} \cdot 10$.

6. Multiply $2\frac{1}{2} \cdot 3\frac{2}{3}$.

Objective B: *Find the area and perimeter of a rectangle, given its dimensions. (Lesson 9-1)*

7. What are the area and perimeter of a rectangle with length 7 and width 3.5?

8. What are the area and perimeter of a rectangle with length 5 and width w?

Objective C: *Find the surface area and volume of a rectangular solid, given its dimensions. (Lessons 9-2, 9-3)*

9. Give the surface area and volume of the rectangular solid pictured below.

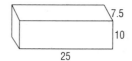

10. Give the surface area and volume of the rectangular solid with dimensions x, y, and z.

PROPERTIES deal with the principles behind the mathematics.

Objective D: *Identify properties of multiplication. (Lessons 9-1, 9-3, 9-5, 9-8)*

11. Write in symbols: The product of a number and the multiplicative identity is that number.

12. What property justifies that $\frac{1}{5}$ divided by 2 equals $\frac{1}{5}$ times $\frac{1}{2}$?

13. What is the reciprocal of $\frac{2}{3}$?

14. What property justifies that $(78 \cdot 4) \cdot 25 = 78 \cdot (4 \cdot 25)$?

Objective E: *Use properties to simplify expressions. (Lessons 9-1, 9-3, 9-5, 9-8)*

15. Simplify: $ab - ba$.

16. Simplify: $x + y + -x + 1$.

17. Simplify: $m + m + m + m + m + -m$.

18. Simplify: $\frac{1}{2} \cdot \frac{1}{5} \cdot 5 \cdot x$.

Objective F: *Use properties to check calculations.* *(Lessons 9-1, 9-5, 9-9)*

19. Using the commutative property, check whether $2.48 \cdot 6.54 = 16.1292$.

20. Check whether $5 \cdot \$7.98 = \$39.90$ by using repeated addition.

21. Find the product of $\frac{1}{8}$ and $\frac{1}{5}$. Check by converting the fractions to decimals.

USES deal with applications of mathematics in real situations.

Objective G: *Pick appropriate units in measurement situations.* *(Lessons 9-1 through 9-4)*

22. The perimeter of a vegetable garden is measured in feet. In what unit would you expect to measure the amount of space you have for planting?

23. If the dimensions of a rectangular solid are measured in inches, in what unit would the surface area most probably be measured?

24. Name two units of volume.

Objective H: *Find areas of rectangles and numbers of elements in rectangular arrays in applied situations.* *(Lesson 9-1)*

25. The flag of the United States has as many stars as states. How many states did the U.S. have when the flag below was in use?

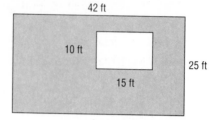

42 ft
10 ft
15 ft
25 ft

26. The smaller rectangle above is the space for a kitchen in a small restaurant. The larger rectangle is the space for the restaurant. The shaded region is space for seating. What is the area of the shaded region?

Objective I: *Find the surface area or volume of a rectangular solid in real contexts.* *(Lessons 9-2, 9-3, 9-4)*

27. A stick of margarine is approximately 11.5 cm long, 3 cm wide, and 3 cm high. To wrap the margarine in aluminum foil, at least what area of foil is needed?

28. What is the volume of the margarine in Question 27?

29. The mattress of a water bed is $7'$ long, $6'$ wide, and 3/4' high. Can a quilt with an area of 48 square feet cover the top and all sides of the mattress?

30. A plastic container has a base with area 72 square centimeters and height 14 cm. Can it hold a liter of soup?

Objective J: *Apply the Size Change Model for Multiplication in real situations.*

(Lessons 9-6, 9-7)

31. Mrs. Kennedy expects to save 1/4 of her weekly grocery bill of $150 a week by using coupons. How much money does she expect to save?

32. On the average, costs of items in the U.S. tripled from 1967 to 1985. If an item cost x dollars in 1967, what did it cost in 1985?

33. If you make $3.50 an hour, what will you make per hour of overtime, if you are paid time-and-a-half?

34. Mr. Jones tithes. That is, he gives one-tenth of what he makes to charity. If he makes $500 a *week*, how much does he give every *year* to charity?

Objective K: *Calculate probabilities of independent events. (Lessons 9-8, 9-9)*

35. On the TV show, "Let's Make a Deal," there are three doors with prizes. One door has a very valuable prize. What is the chance that a contestant picks the door with the valuable prize twice in a row?

36. Five of seven days are weekdays. Resttown gets hit by a tornado about once every 25 years. What are the chances of Resttown being hit by a tornado next year on a weekday?

REPRESENTATIONS deal with pictures, graphs, or objects that illustrate concepts.

Objective L: *Picture multiplication using arrays or area. (Lessons 9-1, 9-8, 9-9)*

37. Show that $5 \cdot 4 = 20$ using a rectangular array.

38. Show that $6.5 \cdot 3$ is larger than $6 \cdot 3$ using rectangles with accurate length and width. (Use centimeters as the unit.)

39. Picture the product of $\frac{1}{2}$ and $\frac{2}{7}$ using the area of rectangles.

40. Picture the product of $\frac{1}{2}$ and $\frac{2}{7}$ using arrays.

Objective M: *Perform expansions or contractions on a coordinate graph. (Lessons 9-6, 9-7)*

41. Graph the triangle with vertices $(0, 5)$, $(6, 2)$, and $(4, 4)$ and its image under an expansion of magnitude 2.5.

42. What is the image of (x, y) under an expansion of magnitude 1000?

43. Is a size change of magnitude $\frac{3}{7}$ an expansion or a contraction?

44. Graph the segment with endpoints $(4, 9)$, and $(2, 3)$. Graph its image under a size change of magnitude $\frac{1}{3}$.

More Multiplication Patterns

Figure A below, with black lines, is the original. The figure named 2A is an expansion of A with magnitude 2. The figure 0.6A is a contraction of A with magnitude 0.6. The two figures called -2A and -0.6A are found by multiplying the coordinates of points on A by negative numbers. The multiplication by negatives reverses directions. As a result, the figures -2A and -0.6A look upside down. They are the figures 2A and 0.6A rotated 180° around the origin. In this chapter you will study this and other applications of multiplication.

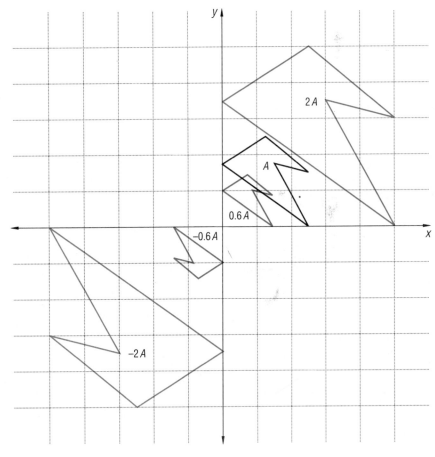

10-1

Solving
$ax = b$

Early pioneers in aviation used the trial and error method in their quest to learn more about aerodynamics.

In each equation shown below, a number is multiplied by an unknown number, x. The result is another number. These are **equations of the form $ax = b$,** where x is the unknown.

$$3x = 12 \qquad 405 = .38x \qquad \tfrac{3}{5} \cdot x = \tfrac{1}{2}$$

The letter x does not have to be used for the unknown. Here are equations of the form $ax = b$ where a different letter is the unknown.

$$862 = \tfrac{35}{71}m \qquad -6 = 2t \qquad \text{Solve for } v: \ uv = w.$$

Many common methods exist for solving these equations. Three methods are given here. A fourth method is in the next lesson.

Example 1   (Substitution) Is 8 a solution to $5 = 40m$?

     Solution   Substitute 8 for m. Since $5 \neq 40 \cdot 8$, 8 is not a solution.

Example 2   (Trial and error) Solve $3x = 12$.

     Solution   You know that $3 \cdot 4 = 12$. So 4 works. Since these equations almost always have only one solution, $x = 4$.

Trial and error works best on the simplest equations. Substitution is the best way to check the other methods.

In Example 2, we used the fact that $3 \cdot 4 = 12$. You also know that $12/4 = 3$ and $12/3 = 4$. These are *related facts*.

Numbers do not have to be simple to be involved in related facts. Suppose you multiply 72 by 35.9 and you get 2584.8 as the product. You can check this by using related facts. Divide 2584.8 by one of the factors. You should get the other factor. That is, if $72 \cdot 35.9 = 2584.8$, then:

$$\frac{2584.8}{72} \text{ should equal } 35.9.$$

$$\frac{2584.8}{35.9} \text{ should equal } 72.$$

The general property is very important to know. We let the letter P stand for the product. In this property, P cannot be zero.

Related Facts Property of Multiplication and Division:

If $xy = P$, then $\frac{P}{x} = y$ and $\frac{P}{y} = x$.

The method of related facts works well on equations involving decimals.

Example 3   (Related facts) Solve $2000 = 8y$.

Solution
Use the Related Facts Property of Multiplication and Division.
Since $8y = 2000$, 2000 divided by 8 equals y.
$$y = \frac{2000}{8}$$
Do the division.
$$y = 250$$

Check   Substitute 250 for y in the original equation.
Does $2000 = 8 \cdot 250$? Yes.

Example 4   Solve $.38t = 405$ to the nearest tenth.

Solution   Use related facts.
When $.38 \cdot t = 405$, then 405 divided by .38 equals t.
$$t = \frac{405}{.38}$$
$$\approx 1065.8 \quad \text{(Use a calculator for the division; then round.)}$$

Check   Substitute 1065.8 for t in the original equation.
$.38 \cdot 1065.8 = 405.004$.
This is good enough since 1065.8 is only an estimate.

A situation is given in Lesson 10-3 that leads to the equation of Example 4.

Questions

Covering the Reading

1. *Multiple choice* Which equation is not of the form $ax = b$?
   (a) $5/x = 3$ (b) $3 = 5x$ (c) $5t = 3$ (d) $-5x = 3$

2. When is an equation in the form $ax = b$?

3. Is 4 a solution to the equation? **a.** $7x = 28$; **b.** $7 = y \cdot 28$;
   c. $28t = 7$; **d.** $.28 = 0.7m$; **e.** $7 + x = 28$.

In 4–6, solve mentally.
   4. $36 = 18C$ 5. $.798x = .798$ 6. $3a = 150$

7. What two division facts are related to $8 \cdot 9 = 72$?

8. What two division facts are related to $37 \cdot 0.46 = 17.02$?

9. State the Related Facts Property of Multiplication and Division.

10. **a.** What two division facts are related to $53t = 901$?
    b. Solve $53t = 901$ and check your answer.

11. Solve $0.8n = 6$ by related facts and check your answer.

12. Solve $0.7n = 6$ to the nearest hundredth by related facts and
    check your answer.

Applying the Mathematics

In 13–16, check whether the product is correct by doing a division involving related facts.

13. $684 \cdot 325 = 222{,}300$

14. $0.4 \cdot 0.3 = 1.2$

15. 72% of $1600 = 1152$

16. $3/4 \cdot 12 = 9$

17. **a.** Perform this key sequence on your calculator.

    $$4.2 \; \boxed{\div} \; 3.8 \; \boxed{=}$$

    What is shown in the display?
    b. Round the display answer to the nearest hundredth.
    c. What equation of the form $ax = b$ does this key sequence
    solve?

18. Solve $x + x + x = 801$.   **19.** Solve $t + t = 4.5$.

Review

20. Why should you not check a problem by doing it the same way
    you did it the first time? *(Lesson 9-5)*

21. What is the reciprocal of: **a.** 6; **b.** 5/12? *(Lesson 9-9)*

22. If x and y are reciprocals, what is the value of $3xy + 5$? *(Lesson 9-9)*

23. Simplify: $4 \cdot x \cdot \frac{1}{4}$. *(Lesson 9-9)*

24. a. To solve $\frac{31}{6} + m = -\frac{5}{8}$, what number can be added to both sides?
b. Solve $\frac{31}{6} + m = -\frac{5}{8}$. *(Lesson 5-8)*

25. Which of these terms are synonyms (mean the same thing)? reciprocal; additive inverse; opposite; multiplicative inverse. *(Lessons 5-4, 9-5)*

26. By the end of 1988, about 40% of households had VCRs. If a town has H households, about how many VCRs would there be? *(Lessons 6-7, 9-7)*

27. A rectangle has length L feet and width 6 feet. **a.** What is its area? **b.** What is its perimeter? *(Lessons 9-1, 9-5)*

28. With a protractor, measure $\angle ABC$ to the nearest degree. *(Lesson 3-5)*

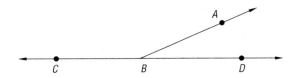

29. Simplify: $1 - 5 - 4$. *(Lesson 7-2)*

30. Write one millionth **a.** as a decimal and **b.** as a power of 10. *(Lessons 1-2, 2-8)*

Exploration

31. A rectangle has a width of one inch and an area of one square foot. What is its length?

The Multiplication Property of Equality

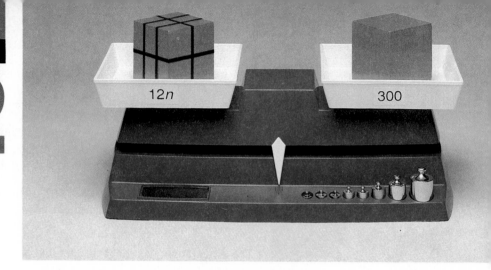

12n   300

Equal numbers may not look equal. For instance:

$$50\% = \tfrac{1}{2}.$$

Now multiply both sides by 6. Are the products equal? Yes, because $\tfrac{1}{2}$ can always be substituted for 50%. The general idea working here is the substitution principle. You can verify the equality by doing the multiplication.

$$6 \cdot 50\% = 6 \cdot \tfrac{1}{2}$$
$$300\% = 3$$

It makes no difference what number you multiply by. The products will still be equal. This special use of the substitution principle is so important that it has its own name.

Multiplication Property of Equality:

If $x = y$, then $ax = ay$.

The most important application of this property is in solving equations.

■ ■ ■ ■ ■ ■ ■ ■■

Example 1   Solve $12n = 300$ using the Multiplication Property of Equality.

Solution   First write down the equation. Leave room for work below it.

$$12n = 300$$

The Multiplication Property of Equality allows both sides of an equation to be changed without affecting the solutions. We pick a number that will leave n by itself on the left side. That number is $\tfrac{1}{12}$, the reciprocal of 12.

$$\tfrac{1}{12} \cdot (12n) = \tfrac{1}{12} \cdot 300$$

Because all numbers at the left are multiplied, there is no need to worry about parentheses. (That's the Associative Property of Multiplication.)

$$\tfrac{1}{12} \cdot 12n = \tfrac{1}{12} \cdot 300$$

The hard part is done. All that is left is to simplify. The names of the properties that are used are given at right. (You don't have to write the names down unless asked by your teacher.)

$$1 \cdot n = \tfrac{300}{12} \qquad \text{(Property of Reciprocals)}$$

$$n = 25 \qquad \text{(Multiplication Property of 1)}$$

Check Substitute 25 for n in the original equation $12n = 300$. It is true that $12 \cdot 25 = 300$.

The Multiplication Property of Equality is very much like the Addition Property of Equality. It can also be adapted to work with inequalities. For these reasons, many teachers prefer students to use the Multiplication Property of Equality rather than related facts in solving equations of the form $ax = b$.

The Multiplication Property of Equality is particularly effective in solving equations where there are fractions.

- - - - - - ■ ■ ■ ■

Example 2 Solve $\quad \tfrac{3}{5} \cdot A = \tfrac{1}{4}$.

Solution We want to multiply both sides by a number that will leave A by itself on the left side. That number is $\tfrac{5}{3}$, the reciprocal of $\tfrac{3}{5}$.

$$\tfrac{5}{3} \cdot (\tfrac{3}{5} \cdot A) = \tfrac{5}{3} \cdot \tfrac{1}{4} \qquad \text{(Multiplication Prop.of Equality)}$$

The only thing left is to simplify. Here are all the steps.

$$(\tfrac{5}{3} \cdot \tfrac{3}{5}) \cdot A = \tfrac{5}{3} \cdot \tfrac{1}{4} \qquad \text{(Associative Property of Mult.)}$$

$$1 \cdot A = \tfrac{5}{3} \cdot \tfrac{1}{4} \qquad \text{(Property of Reciprocals)}$$

Multiplying the fractions on the right side, and using $1 \cdot A = A$,

$$A = \tfrac{5}{12} \qquad \text{(Multiplication Property of 1 and Multiplication of Fractions Prop.)}$$

Check Substitute $\tfrac{5}{12}$ for A in the original equation.

Does $\qquad \tfrac{3}{5} \cdot \tfrac{5}{12} = \tfrac{1}{4}$?

Multiplying the fractions, the left side is $\tfrac{3}{12}$. In lowest terms, this is $\tfrac{1}{4}$. So $\tfrac{5}{12}$ is the solution.

The equation in Example 2 looks hard. But with the Multiplication Property of Equality, it becomes easy to solve. On the next page is another question that seems hard. But it too is easy to answer by solving an equation.

■ ■ ■ ■ ■ ■ ■ ■

Example 3 Six percent of a number is 30. What is the number?

Solution First translate into an equation. Let the number be n.

$$\underline{\text{Six percent}} \quad \underline{\text{of}} \quad \underline{\text{a number}} \quad \underline{\text{is}} \quad \underline{\text{30.}}$$
$$\downarrow \qquad\quad \downarrow \qquad\quad \downarrow \qquad \downarrow \quad\ \downarrow$$
$$.06 \qquad\quad \cdot \qquad\quad n \qquad = \quad 30$$

Here we solve using the Multiplication Property of Equality. Multiply both sides by the reciprocal of .06.

$$\tfrac{1}{.06} \cdot .06n = \tfrac{1}{.06} \cdot 30$$

Now simplify. $n = \tfrac{30}{.06}$

$$n = 500$$

Check 6% of 500 = .06 × 500 = 30

To use the Multiplication Property of Equality, you need to know how to find reciprocals, how to multiply fractions, and how to find equal fractions. Now you can see why these ideas were discussed in past chapters! But you should still wonder when these equations are solved outside of mathematics classes. That is the subject of the next lesson.

Questions

Covering the Reading

1. If $x = y$, then $6x = \underline{\ ?\ }$.

2. What property is needed to answer Question 1?

3. **a.** To solve $5x = 80$ using the Multiplication Property of Equality, by what number should you multiply both sides? **b.** Solve $5x = 80$.

4. **a.** To solve $\tfrac{6}{25} \cdot A = \tfrac{2}{9}$, it is most convenient to multiply both sides by what number? **b.** Solve this equation.

5. **a.** To solve $3x = 0.12$ using the Multiplication Property of Equality, by what number should both sides be multiplied?
   b. Solve $3x = 0.12$ using the Multiplication Property of Equality.
   c. Solve $3x = 0.12$ using a related fact.

6. Delilah said the solution to $\tfrac{2}{3}x = 5$ is $\tfrac{15}{2}$. Is she correct?

7. Seven times a number is 413. What is the number?

8. Seven percent of a number is 84. What is the number?

9. 40% of what number is 25?

10. Ten-thirds of a number is 30. What is the number?

11. Give the property telling why each step follows from the previous one.

$$\frac{7}{4} \cdot A = \frac{1}{5}$$

Step 1: $\frac{4}{7} \cdot (\frac{7}{4} \cdot A) = \frac{4}{7} \cdot \frac{1}{5}$

Step 2: $(\frac{4}{7} \cdot \frac{7}{4}) \cdot A = \frac{4}{7} \cdot \frac{1}{5}$

Step 3: $1 \cdot A = \frac{4}{7} \cdot \frac{1}{5}$

Step 4: $A = \frac{4}{35}$

12. Consider the equation $x/6 = 4/25$. **a.** Rewrite this equation using the Mult-Rec Property of Division. **b.** Solve. **c.** Check.

In 13–15, solve and check.

13. $16.56 = 7.2y$ **14.** $\frac{2}{3}k = 62\%$ **15.** $3.2 + 4.8 = (3.6 + 2.4)x$

16. *Multiple choice*   Which equation does not have the same solution as the others?
(a) $0.2x = 18$ (b) $\frac{1}{5}x = 18$ (c) $.2 = 18x$ (d) $18 = 20\%x$

17. Seven less than a number is 50. What is the number? *(Lesson 7-4)*

18. Seven decreased by a number is 50. What is the number? *(Lesson 7-6)*

19. Three sides of a pentagon have length H meters. The other two sides are each 10 meters long. What is the perimeter of the pentagon? *(Lesson 9-5)*

20. Find the value of 1.08^n when $n = 1, 2, 3, 4,$ and 5. *(Lesson 2-2)*

21. Write 3.2×10^{11} as a decimal. *(Lesson 2-3)*

22. In August of 1985, some major car dealers were offering 7.7% financing on a new car. What simple fraction is this? *(Lesson 2-7)*

23. A model airplane is 1/100 actual size. If an airplane wingspan is 80 meters long, how many centimeters long will the wingspan be on the model? *(Lessons 2-4, 9-7)*

24. How many sides does a decagon have? *(Lesson 5-9)*

25. Estimate the product of 1.0123456789876 and 5.4321012345678 to the nearest thousandth. *(Lesson 1-4)*

Exploration

26. 144 seats can be arranged in a rectangular array with 6 rows and 24 seats in each row. What other rectangular arrays are possible for 144 seats?

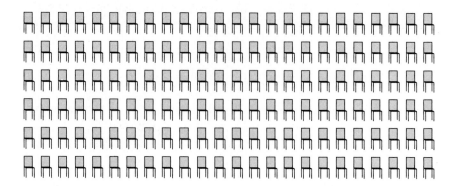

Using $ax = b$

In this and earlier chapters you have learned a variety of applications of multiplication.

> areas of rectangles
> arrays
> volumes of rectangular solids
> repeated addition
> expansions (times as many)
> contractions (part of)
> percents of

Any of these types of applications can lead to an equation of the form $ax = b$. You have already done some problems of this kind. Here are some other examples.

Example 1   Claus' Clothes has 60 feet of frontage as shown in the diagram. The store must be split into selling space and storage space by a partition. Mrs. Claus wants 4200 square feet for selling space. Where should the partition be located?

Front view

Solution   The selling space is a rectangle. One dimension of the rectangle is known to be 60′. The area is to be 4200 square feet. Now apply the formula (on the next page) for the area of a rectangle.

top view

storage

60'

selling space ℓ

w

front of store

You know that $\qquad A = \ell w$

Here $A = 4200$ square feet and $w = 60$ feet.
Substitute for A and w.

$$4200 = \ell \cdot 60$$

Solve this equation either by related facts or by using the
Multiplication Property of Equality. The solution is

$$\ell = \frac{4200}{60} \text{ feet.}$$

Divide. $\qquad\qquad\qquad\qquad \ell = 70$ feet

The partition should be 70 ft from the front of the store.

Check   You should always check answers with the *original
question*. If the depth (length) of the selling space is 70 feet,
will there be 4200 square feet of selling space? Yes, because
$60 \cdot 70 = 4200$.

The next example is of the size change type. Before you begin,
read the question carefully to make certain you understand it.
Without solving anything, you should know whether the answer
will be greater than $12.60 or less than $12.60.

Example 2   A worker receives time-and-a-half for overtime. If a worker gets
$12.60 for an overtime hour, what is the worker's normal hourly
wage?

Solution   Recall that time-and-a-half means the worker's normal
wage is multiplied by $1\frac{1}{2}$ to calculate the overtime wage. Let W be
the normal hourly wage. Then

$$1\frac{1}{2} \cdot W = \$12.60.$$

Now the job is to solve this equation. First change the fraction to a
decimal.

$$1.5W = \$12.60$$

Solve. $\qquad\qquad\qquad W = \dfrac{\$12.60}{1.5}$

Do the arithmetic. $\qquad\quad W = \$8.40$

Check   Ask: If a worker makes $8.40 an hour, will that worker get
$12.60 for overtime? Yes, because half of $8.40 is $4.20, and that
half added to $8.40 equals $12.60.

446

In answering any of these questions, the steps are the same.

(1) Read carefully. Determine what is to be found and what is given.
(2) Let a variable equal the unknown quantity.
(3) Write an equation.
(4) Solve the equation.
(5) Check your answer back in the original question.

Example 3 In a small-town election, it was reported that Phineas Foghorn got 38% of the votes. It was also reported that he received 405 votes. How many people voted?

Solution Let v be the number of people who voted. Then 38% of v equals 405.

$$.38v = 405$$

This is the equation that was solved in Example 4 of Lesson 10-1, page 437. Only the letter v is different. So it has the same solution, $v \approx 1065.8$. There were approximately 1066 voters.

Check Ask: Is 38% of 1066 votes equal to 405 votes? Since 38% of 1066 is 405.08, the answer checks.

Example 4 Dollhouse models are often 1/12 actual size. A window that is 18 mm wide on the model is how wide in reality?

Solution Let w be the real width of the window. Then

$$\tfrac{1}{12}w = 18 \text{ mm}.$$

Multiplying both sides by 12, $w = 216$ mm.

The real width is 216 mm.

Check 1/12 of 216 is 18.

Questions

Covering the Reading

1. What is the first step you should do in solving a problem like those in this lesson?

2. You solve a problem using an equation. Why should you first check the equation's solution in the problem, not in the equation?

3. An artist living in a loft wants to split the loft into a living room and a working space. The loft is diagrammed below. The artist needs 330 square feet for working space. The working space is 22 feet wide. What should be the other dimension of the working space?

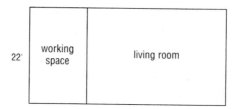

22' | working space | living room

4. Some dollhouse furniture is 1/12 actual size. If a dollhouse table is 3.25 inches long, how long is the actual table?

5. Stacey gets paid time-and-a-half for each hour she babysits after midnight. She made $3.60 per hour after midnight on New Year's eve. How much did she make for each hour before midnight?

6. In the 1984 presidential election, Ronald Reagan got 51% of the votes in Massachusetts. He received 1,297,737 votes there. To the nearest ten thousand, how many people in Massachusetts voted?

Applying the Mathematics

7. The tallest building in the world is the Sears Tower in Chicago. The gift shop at the top of the tower sells models of the tower that are 0.0002 times actual size. The height of the model is 11 cm.
   a. In centimeters, how tall is the tower?
   b. How many meters is this?

8. A newborn giraffe is 1/3 the height of an adult giraffe. If the newborn is 6 feet tall, how much taller is the adult? (Be careful.)

9. The volume of a box needs to be 600 cubic centimeters. The base of the box has dimensions 8 cm and 10.5 cm. How high must the box be?

10. A sofa is on sale at 70% of the original price. The sale price is $489.95. What was the original price?

11. A ballplayer earned three times as much this year as last year. This year the salary was $110,000. To the nearest thousand dollars, what was last year's salary?

12. If $x + x + x + x + x = 32$, what is x?

13. An array has 3000 dots. If there are 75 rows, how many columns are in the array?

14. In the election of Example 3, Wanda Fulperson received 41% of the vote. How many votes did she get?

Review

15. Simplify $40 - 20 \cdot 3 + 200/5 + 5/1$. *(Lesson 4-1)*

16. Since 1 inch = 2.54 cm, 1 foot is how many centimeters? *(Lesson 3-4)*

17. Arrange these terms from most general to most specific: rectangle; square; parallelogram; polygon; quadrilateral. *(Lesson 7-9)*

18. a. Carefully graph the polygon with vertices (0, 6), (0, 0), (6, 0), and (12, 6). **b.** Graph the image of this polygon under an expansion with magnitude $\frac{3}{2}$. *(Lesson 9-6)*

19. The length of a rectangle is π cm and the width is 2 cm. Find its area to the nearest square centimeter. *(Lessons 1-2, 9-1)*

20. Pictured is one level of fruit in a crate. How many pieces are in this level? *(Lesson 9-1)*

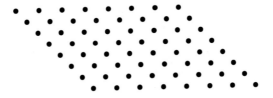

Exploration

21. If 4/3 of a number is 1200, what is 3/4 of that number?

22. The area of a rectangularly shaped farm is 240 acres, or 3/8 of a square mile. What might be the dimensions of the farm?

The Rate Factor Model for Multiplication

SPEED
LIMIT
55

Here are some examples of **rates.** Every rate has a **rate unit.** The rate unit is in italics.

> 55 *miles per hour* (speed limit)
>
> 25.3 *students per class* (average class size)
>
> 70 *centimeters* of snow *per year* (average snowfall in Chicago)
>
> $2\frac{1}{2}$ *pieces for each student* (result of splitting up a pizza)

A quantity is a rate when its unit contains the word "per" or "for each" or some synonym. When used in an expression, the slash / or horizontal bar — means "per." Notice how the above rate units are written in fraction notation.

Using the slash	=	**Using the bar**
55 mi/hr	=	$55 \frac{\text{mi}}{\text{hr}}$
25.3 students/class	=	$25.3 \frac{\text{students}}{\text{class}}$
70 cm/yr	=	$70 \frac{\text{cm}}{\text{yr}}$
$2\frac{1}{2}$ pieces/student	=	$2\frac{1}{2} \frac{\text{pieces}}{\text{student}}$

Suppose a woman gains 2 pounds per month (perhaps during pregnancy). Her rate of weight gain is then

$$2 \frac{\text{pounds}}{\text{month}}.$$

Suppose she keeps this rate up for 5 months. Multiplication gives the total she gains.

$$5 \text{ months} \cdot 2 \frac{\text{pounds}}{\text{month}} = 10 \text{ pounds}$$

Look at the units in the above multiplication. They work as if they were factors in fractions. The unit "months" at left cancels the unit "month" in the denominator. The unit that remains is pounds. You can see where the 10 comes from.

In the next example there are two rates that are multiplied.

■ ■ ■ ■ ■ ■ ■ ■

Example 1 A secretary has 8 letters to type. Each letter is 4 pages long. Each page takes 6 minutes to type. About how long will it take to type the letters?

Solution Think rates. There are 4 pages per letter. There are 6 minutes per page.

$$8 \text{ letters} \cdot 4 \tfrac{\text{pages}}{\text{letter}} \cdot 6 \tfrac{\text{minutes}}{\text{page}}$$
$$= \quad 32 \text{ pages} \quad \cdot 6 \tfrac{\text{minutes}}{\text{page}}$$
$$= \quad\quad 192 \text{ minutes}$$

The general idea behind Example 1 is the **rate factor model for multiplication**.

Rate Factor Model for Multiplication:

When a rate is multiplied by another quantity, the unit of the product is the "product" of units multiplied like fractions. The product has meaning whenever its unit has meaning.

Some multiplications from earlier lessons can be thought of as rate factor multiplications.

■ ■ ■ ■ ■ ■ ■ ■

Example 2 (Array) An auditorium contains 12 rows and 19 seats per row. How many seats are in the auditorium?

Solution $12 \text{ rows} \cdot 19 \tfrac{\text{seats}}{\text{row}} = 228 \text{ seats}$

■ ■ ■ ■ ■ ■ ■ ■

Example 3 (Repeated addition) A person buys 7 cans of tuna at $1.39 per can. What is the total cost?

Solution Here is the way it looks with all units included.

$$7 \text{ cans} \cdot 1.39 \tfrac{\text{dollars}}{\text{can}} = 9.73 \text{ dollars}$$

Here is how it looks using the usual dollar signs and a slash.

$$7 \text{ cans} \cdot \$1.39/\text{can} = \$9.73$$

A special kind of rate factor is the **conversion factor.**
Start with a formula for converting from one unit to another.
Here is an example.

$$1 \text{ mile} = 5280 \text{ feet}$$

Since the quantities are equal, dividing one by the other gives
the number 1.

$$\frac{1 \text{ mile}}{5280 \text{ feet}} = 1 \quad \text{and} \quad \frac{5280 \text{ feet}}{1 \text{ mile}} = 1$$

You could say there is 1 mile for every 5280 feet or there are
5280 feet for every mile.

Example 4   (Conversion) 40,000 feet equals how many miles?

Solution   Multiply 40,000 feet by the conversion factor
with miles in its numerator and feet in its denominator.

$$40{,}000 \text{ feet} \cdot \frac{1 \text{ mile}}{5280 \text{ feet}} = \frac{40{,}000}{5280} \text{ miles}$$
$$= 7.\overline{57} \text{ miles}$$

Example 5   (Conversion) 26.2 miles (the approximate length of a marathon) is
how many feet?

Solution   Use the conversion factor with miles in its denominator.

$$26.2 \text{ miles} \cdot \frac{5280 \text{ feet}}{1 \text{ mile}} = 138{,}336 \text{ feet}$$

Questions

Covering the Reading

In 1 and 2: **a.** Copy the sentence and underline the rate.
b. Write the rate with its unit in fraction notation using the slash.
c. Write the rate with its unit in fraction notation using the fraction bar.

  1. For the game only 4 tickets per student are available.

  2. The speed limit there is 45 miles per hour.

In 3–6: **a.** Do the multiplication. **b.** Make up a question that leads to
the multiplication.

  3. 3 hours $\cdot$ 50 $\frac{\text{miles}}{\text{hr}}$

  4. 8.2 pounds $\cdot$ \$2.29/pound

  5. 2 $\frac{\text{games}}{\text{week}} \cdot$ 8 $\frac{\text{weeks}}{\text{season}}$

  6. 30,000 ft. $\cdot \dfrac{1 \text{ mile}}{5280 \text{ ft}}$

7. If an animal gains 1.5 kg a month for 7 months, how many kg will it have gained in all?

8. A typist can type 40 words a minute. At this rate, how many words can be typed in 20 minutes?

9. An airplane flying 35,000 feet up is how many miles up?

10. A section of a football stadium has 50 rows and has 20 seats in each row. How many people can be seated in this section?

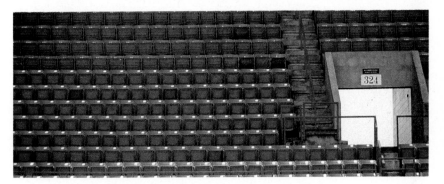

11. What is the Rate Factor Model for Multiplication?

Applying the Mathematics

In 12 and 13, follow the directions of Questions 3-6.

12. 5 classes $\cdot$ 25 $\frac{\text{students}}{\text{class}}$ $\cdot$ 30 $\frac{\text{questions}}{\text{student}}$

13. $\frac{1.06 \text{ quarts}}{\text{liter}}$ $\cdot$ 6 liters

14. Recall that 1 inch = 2.54 cm. Convert 10 cm to inches.

15. If a heart beats 70 times a minute, how many times will it beat in a day?

16. Solve for x: 4 hours $\cdot$ x = 120 miles.

17. When the twins went to France they found that 9 francs were worth 1 dollar. In Spain the next day they found that 1 franc was worth 8 pesetas. How many pesetas could they get for $10?

18. A Chevrolet has a 14-gallon tank and can get about 25 miles per gallon. What do you get when you multiply these quantities?

Review

19. Seventy-four times a number is equal to forty-seven. To the nearest tenth, what is the number? *(Lesson 10-3)*

20. A 30% discount will save you $12 on that item. What was the original cost of the item? *(Lesson 10-3)*

21. The length of this paper clip has been enlarged 1.6 times. Find the length of the actual clip to the nearest mm. *(Lesson 10-3)*

22. Solve for t: $\frac{2}{5}t = 44$. *(Lesson 10-2)*

23. What number is $\frac{2}{3}$ less than $-\frac{2}{3}$? *(Lesson 7-2)*

In 24–26, give an abbreviation for the unit. *(Lessons 3-2, 3-3)*

24. pound   **25.** kilogram   **26.** milliliter

27. How many feet must you go down to get from 25 feet above ground level to 30 feet below? *(Lesson 7-3)*

28. Evaluate $-|x + 5|$ when $x = -3$. *(Lesson 5-5)*

29. Graph the set of ordered pairs that satisfy $x = y + 4$. *(Lesson 8-3)*

30. If x stands for this year, what expression stands for: **a.** next year; **b.** last year; **c.** ten years ago? *(Lesson 4-3)*

Exploration

31. Depending on the number of words it contains, a work of prose is often classified as a short story, a novelette, or a novel. For example, a short story is usually less than 10,000 words. To find the number of words per book, editors rarely count them all, but use a rate factor model.
  a. Describe how you might estimate the number of words in a book.
  b. Estimate the number of words in this chapter.

10-5

Multiplication with Negative Numbers

Rates can be negative. Suppose a man loses 2 pounds per month on a diet. His rate of change in weight is then

$$-2 \, \frac{\text{pounds}}{\text{month}}.$$

If he keeps losing weight at this rate for 5 months, multiplying gives the total loss.

$$5 \text{ months} \cdot -2 \, \frac{\text{pounds}}{\text{month}} = -10 \text{ pounds}$$

Ignoring the units, a positive and a negative number are being multiplied. The product is negative.

$$5 \cdot -2 = -10$$

The number of months does not have to be a whole number. The rate does not have to be an integer. So this example verifies that when a positive number is multiplied by a negative number, the product is negative.

> positive · negative = negative

Multiplication is commutative. So the multiplication can be reversed.

> negative · positive = negative

You already know that the product of two positive numbers is positive.

> positive · positive = positive

Putting these two things together, we have the following important property.

> When a number is multiplied by a positive number, its sign (positive or negative) is not affected.

The next example shows three different ways of finding the product of a positive and a negative number. Of course, all ways lead to the same answer.

Example 1 What is $5 \cdot -4.8$?

Solution 1 Think of this as a loss of 4.8 pounds per month for 5 months. The result is a loss. So the answer is negative. Since $5 \cdot 4.8 = 24$, $5 \cdot -4.8 = -24$.

Solution 2 -4.8 is multiplied by the positive number 5, so its sign is not affected. Since -4.8 is negative, the product is negative. Since $5 \cdot 4.8 = 24$, $5 \cdot -4.8 = -24$.

Solution 3 By repeated addition,
$5 \cdot -4.8 = -4.8 + -4.8 + -4.8 + -4.8 + -4.8 = -24$.

Example 2 What is $-7 \cdot 4$?

Solution Since -7 is multiplied by the positive number 4, the product is negative.
$-7 \cdot 4 = -28$

What happens if both numbers are negative? Again think of the weight-loss situation. A person loses 2 pounds a month. At this rate, 5 months *from now* the person will weigh 10 pounds less. You have already seen this multiplication.

$$5 \text{ months from now} \cdot -2 \tfrac{\text{pounds}}{\text{month}} = 10 \text{ pounds less} = -10 \text{ pounds}$$

Ignoring the units: $5 \cdot -2 = -10$

But also at this rate, 5 months *ago* the person weighed 10 pounds more. Going back is the negative direction for time. So here is the multiplication for this situation.

$$5 \text{ months ago} \cdot -2 \tfrac{\text{pounds}}{\text{month}} = 10 \text{ pounds more} = 10 \text{ pounds}$$

$$-5 \text{ months} \cdot -2 \tfrac{\text{pounds}}{\text{month}} = 10 \text{ pounds}$$

Ignoring the units: $-5 \cdot -2 = 10$

$$\text{negative} \cdot \text{negative} = \text{positive}$$

When a number is multiplied by a negative number, its sign (positive or negative) is changed.

Example 3   What is $-4 \cdot -1.5$?

Solution 1   Think: Multiplication by a negative changes sign. Multiplying -1.5 by -4 changes its sign to positive.
Since $4 \cdot 1.5 = 6$, $-4 \cdot -1.5 = 6$.

Solution 2   Think: 4 months ago $\cdot$ 1.5 pound loss per month. The person weighed more 4 months ago, so the answer is positive.
$4 \cdot 1.5 = 6$.

Questions

Covering the Reading

1. Copy the sentence and underline the negative rate in this sentence: A woman loses 3.8 pounds per month for 3 months.

In 2–4: **a.** What multiplication problem involving negative numbers is suggested by the situation? **b.** What is the product and what does it mean?

2. A person loses 3 pounds a month for 2 months. How much will the person lose in all?

3. A person loses 5 pounds a month. How will the person's weight 4 months from now compare with the weight now?

4. A person has been losing 6 pounds a month. How does the person's weight 2 months ago compare with the weight now?

5. Multiplying by a negative number __?__ the sign of the other number.

6. Multiplying by a positive number __?__ the sign of the other number.

In 7–12, simplify.

7. $-4 \cdot 8$ 8. $73 \cdot -45$ 9. $-6 \cdot -3$

10. $-1 \cdot 2.9$ 11. $8 \cdot -8$ 12. $-5 \cdot -100$

In 13–16, tell whether xy is positive or negative.

13. x is positive and y is positive.

14. x is positive and y is negative.

15. x is negative and y is positive.

16. x is negative and y is negative.

Applying the Mathematics

17. Find the value of $-5x$ when x is:
a. 2; **b.** 1; **c.** 0; **d.** -1; **e.** -2.

18. Evaluate $3 + -7a + 2b$ when $a = -4$ and $b = -10$.

In 19–21, simplify.

19. $-3 \cdot 4 \cdot -5$ **20.** $-6 \cdot -6 \cdot -6 \cdot -6$ **21.** $-\frac{2}{3} \cdot -\frac{9}{10}$

22. *Multiple choice* Morry is now in debt for $2500 and has been spending money at the rate of $200/week. Which expression tells how he was doing 5 weeks ago?
(a) $2500 - 5 \cdot 200$ (b) $-2500 + -200 \cdot -5$ (c) $-2500 + 5 \cdot -200$

Review

23. Solve $2400x = 60$. *(Lesson 10-1)*

24. Solve $\frac{1}{2}y = 54$. *(Lesson 10-2)*

25. Sliced roast beef is advertised in a store for $5.98/pound. How much should 0.45 pounds of roast beef cost? *(Lesson 10-3)*

26. Real estate agents in some places earn 3% of the sale value of a house for helping a person sell the house. This is called the *commission.* **a.** What is the commission on the sale of a house for $80,000? **b.** How much has to be sold in order for the agent to earn $25,000 from commissions? *(Lessons 2-6, 10-3)*

27. Graph all solutions to $x > 5$ on a number line. *(Lesson 4-9)*

28. Write these rates using fraction notation and abbreviations:
a. kilometers per second; **b.** grams per cubic centimeter.
(Lesson 10-4)

29. Give an example of a positive number and a negative number whose sum is positive. *(Lesson 5-3)*

30. What are supplementary angles? *(Lesson 7-7)*

Exploration

31. Find an example of a rate in a newspaper or magazine.

10-6

Picturing Multiplication with Negative Numbers

mathematics

Remember that multiplication can be pictured by expansions or contractions. In Chapter 9, the coordinates of preimage points were positive. Now that we have discussed multiplication with negative numbers, the coordinates can be any numbers. So the preimage can be anywhere. Here the preimage is a quadrilateral with a shaded region near one vertex.

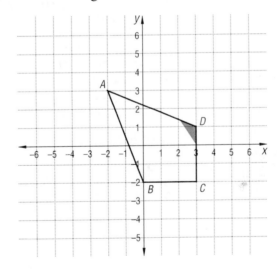

Preimage vertices
$A = (-2, 3)$
$B = (0, -2)$
$C = (3, -2)$
$D = (3, 1)$

First we multiply all coordinates by 2. You know what to expect.

1. The image is similar to the preimage.
2. The sides of the image are 2 times as long as the sides of the preimage.
3. The sides on the image are parallel to corresponding sides on the preimage.

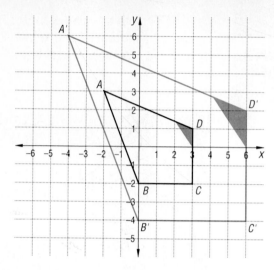

Expansion,
magnitude 2

Preimage point

$A = (-2, 3)$
$B = (0, -2)$
$C = (3, -2)$
$D = (3, 1)$

Image point

$A' = (-4, 6)$
$B' = (0, -4)$
$C' = (6, -4)$
$D' = (6, 2)$

Notice also:
  4. The line containing a preimage point and its image also contains (0, 0).
  5. Image points are 2 times as far from (0, 0) as preimage points.

Now we find the image of the same quadrilateral under an expansion with the negative magnitude, -2. This is done by multiplying all coordinates by -2. We call the image $A''B''C''D''$. (Read this "A double prime, B double prime,...")

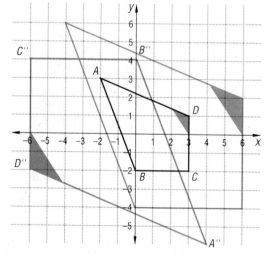

Expansion,
magnitude -2

Preimage point

$A = (-2, 3)$
$B = (0, -2)$
$C = (3, -2)$
$D = (3, 1)$

Image point

$A'' = (4, -6)$
$B'' = (0, 4)$
$C'' = (-6, 4)$
$D'' = (-6, -2)$

Again
  1. the preimage and image are similar.
  2. The sides of $A''B''C''D''$ are 2 times the length of the sides of $ABCD$.
  3. Preimage and image sides are parallel.
  4. The line through a preimage and image point contains (0, 0).
  5. Image points are 2 times as far from (0, 0) as preimage points.

But one new thing has happened.

6. The figure has been rotated 180°. It has been turned upside down. What was right is now left. What was up is now down.

Multiplication by a negative number reverses directions.

Multiplying the coordinates of all points on a figure by the number k yields the transformation known as a *size change of magnitude k*. The number k may be positive or negative. But in all cases:

1. The resulting figure (the image) will be similar to its preimage.
2. Lengths of sides of the resulting figure will be |k| times lengths of sides of the preimage.
3. Corresponding sides will be parallel.
4. Preimage and image points will lie on a line that goes through the origin.
5. Image points will be |k| times as far from the origin as preimage points.
6. If k is negative, the figure will be rotated 180°.

The examples have pictured what happens when $k = 2$ and when $k = -2$.

Questions

Covering the Reading

1. In a size change of magnitude -2, the image of (4, 5) is (__?__).

2. In a size change of magnitude -5, the image of (-10, 7) is (__?__).

3. In any size change, a figure and its image are __?__.

4. In a size change of magnitude -3, lengths on an image will be __?__ times the corresponding lengths on the preimage.

5. In any size change, a segment and its image are __?__.

6. What is the major difference between a size change of magnitude -3 and one of magnitude 3?

7. Let $A = (-2, -2)$, $B = (2, -2)$, and $C = (-2, 0)$. Graph $\triangle ABC$ and its image under an expansion of magnitude -3.

8. Multiplication by a negative number __?__ directions.

9. A size change of magnitude -2 is like one of magnitude 2 followed by a rotation of what magnitude?

LESSON 10-6 *Picturing Multiplication with Negative Numbers* 461

10. A triangle has vertices $P = (4, 8)$, $Q = (-4, 6)$, and $R = (2, -8)$. Graph this triangle and its image under a contraction of magnitude $-\frac{1}{2}$.

11. Let $P = (3.45, -82)$. Suppose that P' is the image of P under a size change of magnitude -10.
True or false? $\overleftrightarrow{PP'}$ contains $(0, 0)$.

12. a. Are the figures $A'B'C'D'$ and $A''B''C''D''$ on page 460 congruent?
b. If so, why? If not, why not?

13. Recall that the four parts of the coordinate plane can be numbered from 1 to 4, as shown below. Consider a size change with magnitude -2.3. If a preimage is in quadrant 4, in what quadrant is its image?

$$
\begin{array}{c|c}
2 & 1 \\
\hline
3 & 4
\end{array}
$$

14. Translate each phrase into a numerical expression or equation:
a. spending $50 a day
b. 4 days from now
c. 4 days ago
d. If you spend $50 a day for 4 days, you will have $200 less than you have now.
e. If you have been spending $50 a day, 4 days ago you had $200 more than you have now. *(Lesson 10-5)*

15. What is the area of a sheet of 8″ by 10.5″ notebook paper? Ignore the holes. *(Lesson 9-1)*

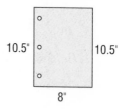

16. Drawn below is a square and one of its diagonals. Copy the figure and draw all of its lines of symmetry. *(Lesson 8-7)*

17. Find the value of $-5x + 6$ when $x = -9$. *(Lesson 4-4)*

18. Find the value of $3a + 2a$ when $a = -7$. *(Lesson 4-4)*

19. Solve for y: $\frac{y}{7} = 30$. *(Lesson 10-2)*

20. Twelve hundred sixty is three-fourths of what number? *(Lesson 10-3)*

21. Twelve hundred sixty is 75% of what number? *(Lesson 10-3)*

22. One thousand two hundred sixty students were asked whether they thought Hardnox High would win its next football game. Seventy-five percent thought it would win. How many students is this? *(Lesson 2-6)*

23. Write 5^{10} as a decimal. *(Lesson 2-2)*

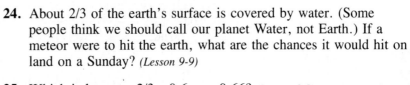

24. About 2/3 of the earth's surface is covered by water. (Some people think we should call our planet Water, not Earth.) If a meteor were to hit the earth, what are the chances it would hit on land on a Sunday? *(Lesson 9-9)*

25. Which is largest; -2/3, -0.6, or -0.66? *(Lesson 1-5)*

26. Three instances of a pattern are given. Describe the pattern using one variable. *(Lesson 4-2)*
$$-3 \cdot 5 + 4 \cdot 5 = 5$$
$$-3 \cdot 7.8 + 4 \cdot 7.8 = 7.8$$
$$-3 \cdot -1 + 4 \cdot -1 = -1$$

Exploration

27. Here are four true statements given in a particular order.
$$4 \cdot -4 = -16$$
$$3 \cdot -4 = -12$$
$$2 \cdot -4 = -8$$
$$1 \cdot -4 = -4$$

  a. Keeping the pattern going, what are the next five statements?
  b. Are your next five statements all true?

28. **a.** Verify the pattern of Question 27 using this computer program.

```
10 FOR X = 4 TO -10 STEP -1
20    PRINT X "TIMES -4 EQUALS", -4*X
30 NEXT X
40 END
```
  b. Modify the program to print different products of positive and negative numbers.

10-7

Multiplication by 0 and -1

Notice what happens when the number 5 is multiplied by positive numbers that get smaller and smaller.

$$
\begin{aligned}
5 \cdot 2 &= 10 \\
5 \cdot 0.43 &= 2.15 \\
5 \cdot 0.07 &= 0.35 \\
5 \cdot 0.000148 &= 0.00074
\end{aligned}
$$

The smaller the positive number, the closer the product is to zero. You know what happens when 5 is multiplied by 0. The product is 0.

$$5 \cdot 0 = 0$$

There is a similar pattern if you begin with a negative number. Multiply -7 by the same numbers as above.

$$
\begin{aligned}
-7 \cdot 2 &= -14 \\
-7 \cdot 0.43 &= -3.01 \\
-7 \cdot 0.07 &= -0.49 \\
-7 \cdot 0.000148 &= -0.001036
\end{aligned}
$$

The products are all negative. But again they get closer and closer to zero. You can check the following multiplication on your calculator.

$$-7 \cdot 0 = 0$$

These examples are instances of an important property of zero.

Multiplication Property of Zero:

For any number x, $x \cdot 0 = 0$.

Since multiplication is commutative, $0 \cdot x$ is also equal to zero. As a special case, $0 \cdot 0 = 0$. All of this makes it tricky to solve equations of the form $ax = b$ when a or b equals zero. Here are the three possibilities.

Example 1   Solve $0 \cdot A = 0$.

Solution   Every number works! So *any number* is a solution.

Example 2   Solve $0 \cdot B = 5$.

Solution   No number works. So there is *no solution*.

Example 3   Solve $3 \cdot B = 0$.

Solution   Multiplying both sides by $\frac{1}{3}$, we find $B = 0$. (You could also find that solution mentally.) So there is *one solution*, the number 0.

Some people confuse "no solution" with "0 is a solution." Notice the difference in the graphs of the solutions.

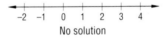

No solution

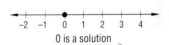

0 is a solution

You already know how to multiply by -1. Here are three instances of the general pattern.

$$-1 \cdot 53 = -53$$
$$-1 \cdot -4 = 4$$
$$-1 \cdot \tfrac{2}{3} = -\tfrac{2}{3}$$

In words, multiplication by -1 changes a number to its opposite. Here is a description with variables.

Multiplication Property of -1:

For any number x, $-1 \cdot x = -x$.

Using the multiplication property of -1, you can turn opposites into multiplications. This enables many expressions to be simplified.

Example 4 Simplify: $-x \cdot -y$.

Solution

$$-x \cdot -y = (-1 \cdot x) \cdot (-1 \cdot y) \quad \text{Multiplication Property of -1}$$
$$= -1 \cdot x \cdot -1 \cdot y \quad \text{Multiplication is associative.}$$
$$= -1 \cdot -1 \cdot xy \quad \text{Multiplication is commutative.}$$
$$= 1 \cdot xy \quad \quad -1 \cdot -1 = 1$$
$$= xy \quad \quad \text{1 is the identity for multiplication.}$$

Example 4 shows that the product of two opposites equals the product of the original numbers. So an even number of opposites being multiplied will equal the product of the numbers without the opposites.

Example 5 Is $-2 \cdot -5 \cdot 3 \cdot -4 \cdot 6 \cdot -2 \cdot -1 \cdot -3$ positive or negative?

Solution There are 6 negative numbers being multiplied. This is an even number; so the product is positive.

Caution: This kind of analysis should only be done when all numbers are multiplied.

Another way of thinking of Example 5 is that multiplication by a negative switches direction. So multiplication by two negatives switches back. An odd number of switches is just like one switch.

Example 6 Tell whether $-1 \cdot -2 \cdot -3 \cdot -4 \cdot -5 \cdot -6 \cdot -7$ is positive or negative.

Solution The product is negative because there are 7 opposites. (Multiplication shows that the product is -5040.)

Questions

Covering the Reading

1. Describe the multiplication property of 0 using variables.

2. Describe the multiplication property of -1 using variables.

In 3–8, simplify.

3. $-1 \cdot -7$ 4. $8 \cdot -1$ 5. $-1 \cdot -1 \cdot -1$

6. $0 \cdot -6$ 7. $0 \cdot -1$ 8. $-3 \cdot -2 \cdot -1 \cdot 0$

10-9

Solving
$ax + b = c$

French fries have about 11 calories apiece. If you eat F french fries, you will have taken in about $11F$ calories. A plain 4-oz hamburger with a bun has about 500 calories. So together the hamburger and french fries have about $500 + 11F$ calories.

> How many french fries can you eat with this hamburger and bun for 800 total calories?

The answer is given by solving the following equation.

$$500 + 11F = 800$$

To solve this equation, first add -500 to both sides and simplify.

$$-500 + 500 + 11F = -500 + 800$$
$$0 + 11F = 300$$
$$11F = 300$$

You've solved many equations like this one. Multiply both sides by $\frac{1}{11}$ and simplify.

$$\tfrac{1}{11} \cdot 11F = \tfrac{1}{11} \cdot 300$$

$$F = \tfrac{300}{11} \approx 27$$

Approximately 27 french fries with the hamburger will give you 800 calories.

In the equation $500 + 11F = 800$, the unknown F is multiplied by a number. Then a second number is added. We call this an **equation of the form $ax + b = c$.** All equations of this type can be solved with two major steps. First add $-b$ to both sides. This step gets the term with the variable alone on one side. Then multiply both sides by $\frac{1}{a}$.

Example 1   Solve $4x + 35 = 91$.

Solution   Add -35 to both sides. This will leave $4x$ alone on one side.

$$4x + 35 = 91$$
$$4x + 35 + \text{-}35 = 91 + \text{-}35$$
$$4x + \quad 0 \quad = \quad 56$$
$$4x \quad = \quad 56$$

Multiply both sides by $\frac{1}{4}$.

$$\tfrac{1}{4} \cdot 4x = \tfrac{1}{4} \cdot 56$$
$$x = 14$$

Check   As usual, substitute 14 for x in the original sentence.
Does $4 \cdot 14 + 35 = 91$?
Yes, $4 \cdot 14 + 35 = 56 + 35 = 91$.

Look again at Example 1. By adding -35 to both sides, the equation that results is $4x = 56$. This is an equation of a type you have solved before. This illustrates a fundamental strategy true of all sentence-solving.

If you cannot solve a sentence, convert it into one you can solve.

Example 2 illustrates this strategy. The sentence may look complicated, but it is easy to change it to a sentence that can be solved.

Example 2   Solve $10 + 6h - 14 = 32$.

Solution   First simplify the left side. You may not need to write all the steps that are shown here.

$$10 + 6h - 14 = 32$$
$$10 + 6h + \text{-}14 = 32 \quad \text{(Add-Opp Property of Subtraction)}$$
$$10 + \text{-}14 + 6h = 32 \quad \text{(Assoc. and Comm. Properties of Addition)}$$
$$\text{-}4 + 6h = 32 \quad \text{(Simplify)}$$

This is an equation like the one solved in Example 1. Add 4 to both sides.

$$4 + \text{-}4 + 6h = 4 + 32 \quad \text{(Addition Property of Equality)}$$
$$6h \quad = 36 \quad \text{(Simplify)}$$

You can solve this equation in your head. If not, multiply both sides by $\frac{1}{6}$.

$$h = 6$$

Check Substitute: Does $10 + 6 \cdot 6 - 14 = 32$?

$$10 + 36 - 14 = 32?$$
$$46 - 14 = 32? \text{ Yes.}$$

Equations of the type $b - ax = c$, where the variable term is subtracted, can be solved with just one extra step.

Example 3 Solve $17 = 63 - 2t$.

Solution The extra step is to convert everything to addition using the Add-Opp Property of Subtraction.

$$17 = 63 - 2t$$
$$17 = 63 + \text{-}2t$$

Now add -63 to both sides. This leaves -2t alone.

$$\text{-}63 + 17 = \text{-}63 + 63 + \text{-}2t$$
$$\text{-}46 \quad = \quad 0 + \text{-}2t$$
$$\text{-}46 \quad = \quad \text{-}2t$$

Now solve as you have done before. Multiply both sides by $-\frac{1}{2}$.

$$-\frac{1}{2} \cdot \text{-}46 = -\frac{1}{2} \cdot \text{-}2t$$
$$23 = t$$

Check This solution checks because $17 = 63 - 2 \cdot 23$.

Questions

Covering the Reading

1. **a.** To solve the equation $4x + 25 = 85$, first add __?__ to both sides.
   b. Solve $4x + 25 = 85$.

2. **a.** To solve the equation $3v - 8 = \text{-}50$, first add __?__ to both sides.
   b. Solve $3v + 8 = \text{-}50$.

3. What fundamental strategy of sentence-solving is given in this lesson?

4. **a.** What should be the first step in solving $3 + 4x + 5 = 6$?
   b. Solve this sentence.

In 5–8, solve:

5. $2y + 7 = 41$

6. $300 + 120t = -1500$

7. $60 - 9x = 48$

8. $17 + 60m + 3 = 100$

In 9–13, use this information. A hamburger has about 80 calories per ounce. A bun has about 180 calories. A typical french fry has about 11 calories.

9. How many calories are in a plain 4-oz hamburger, bun, and 10 french fries?

10. How many calories are in a plain 4-oz hamburger, bun, and F french fries?

11. If you order a plain 4-oz hamburger with a bun, how many french fries can you eat for a total of 900 calories?

Applying the Mathematics

12. How many calories are in h ounces of hamburger without the bun and F french fries?

13. Suppose you ate 20 french fries. How large a hamburger could you eat with a bun and have a total of 1000 calories?

14. a. To solve $mx + n = p$ for x, what could you add to both sides?
b. Solve this equation.

15. Is -17 the solution to $400 - 12x = 196$?

16. Solve and check: $2y + 1 = 0$.

17. Solve and check: $\frac{3}{2} + 14z + \frac{7}{8} = 0$.

18. Meticulous Matilda likes to put in every step in solving equations. Here is her solution to $5m + 7 = -3$. Give a reason for each step.
a. $(5m + 7) + \text{-}7 = -3 + \text{-}7$ **e.** $\frac{1}{5} \cdot (5m) = \frac{1}{5} \cdot \text{-}10$
b. $5m + (7 + \text{-}7) = -3 + \text{-}7$ **f.** $(\frac{1}{5} \cdot 5)m = \frac{1}{5} \cdot \text{-}10$
c. $5m + 0 = -3 + \text{-}7$ **g.** $1 \cdot m = \text{-}2$
d. $5m = \text{-}10$ **h.** $m = \text{-}2$

Review

19. Solve: $\text{-}\frac{2}{3}t = \frac{5}{4}$. *(Lesson 10-8)*

20. Trace the figure below and draw its lines of symmetry. *(Lesson 8-7)*

21. 1 meter $\approx$ 39.37 inches. Then 25 inches is about how many meters? *(Lesson 10-4)*

22. Simplify $\text{-}4(3 + \text{-}2 \cdot 6 + 1)$. *(Lesson 10-5)*

23. Simplify $1 \cdot x + 0 \cdot y + -1 \cdot -2z$. *(Lesson 10-7)*

24. Zero times a certain number is one. What is the number? *(Lesson 10-7)*

25. In the Georgia primary of March, 1988, the Reverend Jesse Jackson received about 248,000 votes. This was about 39% of the total. In all, about how many people voted? *(Lesson 10-3)*

26. a. Simplify: $350 \frac{\text{words}}{\text{page}} \cdot 175 \frac{\text{pages}}{\text{book}}$

    b. Make up a problem that the multiplication of part **a** could answer. *(Lesson 10-4)*

27. On January 1 there were about 2500 deer in the White Forest. During the year, D deer died, B were born, and S were shot. At the end of the year there were about 2300 deer in the forest. Give a relationship among all of these numbers and variables. *(Lessons 5-1, 7-1)*

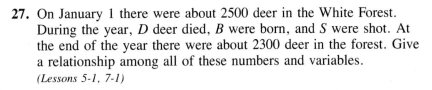

28. You wish to carpet a room that is 9′ by 12′. The carpet you want costs $10.95 per square *yard*. How much will it cost for the carpet? *(Lessons 9-1, 10-4)*

29. First-class postage in 1988 cost 25¢ for the first ounce and 20¢ for each additional ounce. At these rates, give the cost of mailing a letter that weighs: **a.** 2 ounces; **b.** 3 ounces; **c.** 4 ounces; **d.** n ounces. *(Lesson 6-5)*

30. A projectile is shot upward from the ground at a velocity of 128 ft/sec. Ignoring air resistance (but not ignoring gravity), its velocity t seconds after being thrown will be $(-32t + 128)$ ft/sec. *(Lessons 10-5, 10-6)*

    a. What is its velocity 1 second after being thrown?

    b. What is its velocity 2 seconds after being thrown?

    c. Five seconds after being thrown, the projectile's velocity is negative. What does this mean?

Exploration

31. Look in a newspaper for the prices of stocks on the New York Stock Exchange. What fractions are used in describing these prices?

Summary

In Chapter 9, you learned that a size change can picture multiplication by a positive number. In this chapter, size changes picture multiplication by negative numbers. They show that multiplying by a negative changes direction as well as size. So negative · positive = negative, and negative · negative = positive.

Multiplying any number by 0 gives a product of 0. Multiplying by -1 changes a number to its opposite.

An important use of multiplication involves rate factors. Examples of rate factors are the quantities 600 miles/hour, $2.50 per bottle, 27.3 students per class, and -3 kg/month. When rate factors are multiplied by other quantities, the units are multiplied like fractions. Rate factors like 5280 feet/mile can be used to convert units.

These uses, and the area, volume, array, and repeated addition uses you learned in Chapter 9, often lead to equations to be solved. You may know one factor a and the product b, but not know the other factor. Then you have a situation of the type $ax = b$. There are at least three ways to solve these equations: substitution mentally, by related facts, and using the Multiplication Property of Equality. If $a \neq 0$, the solution to $ax = b$ is $x = \frac{b}{a}$.

Equations of the form $ax + b = c$ can be solved by first adding $-b$ to both sides. This gives an equation you already know how to solve.

Vocabulary

You should be able to give a general description and a specific example for each of the following ideas.

Lesson 10–1
equation of the form $ax = b$
Related Facts Property of Multiplication and Division

Lesson 10–2
Multiplication Property of Equality

Lesson 10–4
rate, rate unit, rate factor
Rate Factor Model for Multiplication
conversion factor

Lesson 10–7
Multiplication Property of Zero
Multiplication Property of -1

Lesson 10–9
equation of the form $ax + b = c$

Progress Self-Test

Take this test as you would take a test in class. Then check your work with the solutions in the Selected Answers section in the back of the book. Use graph paper and a ruler for Question 15.

1. The product of $\frac{3}{5}$ and another number is 15. Find the other number.

2. State the Multiplication Property of Equality.

3. The area of a rectangle is 5 square feet. Its length is 10 feet. What is its width?

4. A person made $2000 more this year than last. This increase is 8% of last year's income. What was last year's income?

5. Solve $13x = 1001$ by related facts.

6. Solve $13x = 1001$ using the Multiplication Property of Equality.

7. A person makes $8.50 an hour and works 37.5 hours a week. Multiply the two rates in this situation. What is the result?

8. What multiplication with negative numbers is suggested by the following situation?
For four hours, the flood waters receded three centimeters an hour.

In 9–11, calculate:

9. $5 \cdot \text{-}9$

10. $\text{-}3 \cdot \text{-}3 + \text{-}2 \cdot \text{-}2$

11. $2 \cdot \text{-}3 \cdot 4 \cdot \text{-}5 \cdot 6 \cdot \text{-}7$

12. Evaluate $6x - 3yz$ when $x = 0$, $y = \text{-}1$, and $z = 5$.

13. Simplify: $a + 1 \cdot a + b + 0 \cdot b + \text{-}1 \cdot c + c$.

14. If $de = f$, e is negative, and f is negative, what can you say about d?

In 15 and 16, a triangle has vertices $(12, \text{-}24)$, $(0, 6)$, and $(\text{-}24, 24)$.

15. Graph this triangle and its image under an expansion of magnitude $\text{-}2.5$.

16. Name one thing that is the same about the preimage and image and one thing that is different.

17. Which expression does not equal the others, or are they all equal?
$a - b \qquad a + \text{-}1 \cdot b \qquad a + \text{-}b \qquad a - 1 \cdot b$

In 18 and 19, use the fact that 1 meter ≈ 39.37 inches.

18. What two conversion factors arise from this relationship?

19. Use the appropriate conversion factor to convert 1200 inches to meters.

In 20–25, solve.

20. $\text{-}x = 4$

21. $35.1 = \text{-}9t$

22. $\text{-}\frac{2}{5}m = \text{-}\frac{3}{4}$

23. $0k = 0$

24. $2 + 3A = 17$

25. $12 - 4h - 15 = 10$

Chapter Review

Questions on **SPUR** Objectives

SPUR stands for **S**kills, **P**roperties, **U**ses, and **R**epresentations.
The Chapter Review questions are grouped according to the
SPUR Objectives for this chapter.

SKILLS deal with the procedures used to get answers.

■ **Objective A:** *Multiply positive and negative numbers. (Lesson 10-5)*

1. Simplify $-8 \cdot -2$.
2. Simplify $3 + -10 \cdot 4$.
3. Simplify $5 \cdot -5 \cdot 4 \cdot -4$.
4. If $x = -3$ and $y = -16$, what is the value of $5x + 2y$?

■ **Objective B:** *Solve and check equations of the form $ax = b$ mentally or by substitution. (Lesson 10-1)*

5. Solve $24 = 8h$ mentally.
6. Solve $-15z = 15$ mentally.
7. Solve for x: $-x = 7$.
8. Name all solutions to $10y = 0$.
9. Is the solution to $-2.6845 = -32.5m$ positive or negative?
10. Is $\frac{1}{3}$ the solution to $\frac{3}{8}m = 8$?

■ **Objective C:** *Solve and check equations of the form $ax = b$ using the Multiplication Property of Equality. (Lessons 10-2, 10-8)*

In 11–16, solve and check.

11. $40t = 3000$
12. $-22 = 4A$
13. $0.02v = 0.8$
14. $\frac{2}{3}x = 18$
15. $-49 = -7y$
16. $2.4 + 3.6 = (5 - 0.2)x$

■ **Objective D:** *Solve and check equations of the form $ax + b = c$. (Lesson 10-9)*

In 17–20, solve and check.

17. $8m + 2 = 18$
18. $-2.5 + .5y = 4.2$
19. $11 - 6u = -7$
20. $23 + 4x + 10 = -39$

PROPERTIES deal with the principles behind the mathematics.

■ **Objective E:** *Apply the Multiplication and Addition Properties of Equality. (Lessons 10-2, 10-9)*

21. To solve $\frac{11}{3}y = \frac{2}{9}$, by what number can you multiply both sides of the equation?
22. To solve $-17r + 12 = 50$, what could you add to both sides of the equation?

■ **Objective F:** *Apply the Multiplication Properties of 0 and -1. (Lesson 10-7)*

23. Simplify: $-1 \cdot -x$.

24. Simplify: $0 \cdot a + 1 \cdot b + -1 \cdot c$.
25. Solve: $0x = 3$.

■ **Objective G:** *Use the Related Facts Property of Multiplication and Division. (Lesson 10-1)*

26. What two division facts are related to $16 = 6.4t$?
27. Check whether $48.4 \cdot 274 = 13,261.6$ by using related facts.
28. Solve $9x = 819$ by related facts.

Objective H: *Apply the Rate Factor Model for Multiplication.* (*Lessons 10-4, 10-5*)

In 29 and 30, **a.** do the multiplication, and **b.** make up a question that leads to this multiplication.

29. $2 \frac{\text{cookies}}{\text{day}} \cdot 365 \frac{\text{days}}{\text{year}}$

30. 5 hours $\cdot 25 \frac{\text{miles}}{\text{hour}}$

31. A person makes $10.50 an hour and works 37.5 hours a week. How much does the person earn per year?

32. Fire laws say there is a maximum of 60 people per small conference room. There are 6 small conference rooms. Altogether, how many people can meet in them?

33. If Lois has been losing weight at the rate of 2.3 kg per month, how did her weight 4 months ago compare with her weight now?

Objective I: *Use conversion factors to convert from one unit to another.* (*Lesson 10-4*)

34. Name the two conversion factors from the equality 1 foot = 30.48 cm.

35. 500 cm equals about how many ft?

36. 150 hours equals how many days?

Objective J: *Find unknowns in area, volume, or array situations involving multiplication.* (*Lesson 10-2, 10-3*)

37. A movie theater has 500 seats and 20 rows. There are the same number of seats in each row. How many seats are there per row?

38. A store is in the shape of a rectangle. Find the depth of the store if the area of the store is 3500 sq ft and the width is 40 ft.

39. Find the height of this box if its volume is 2400 cubic centimeters.

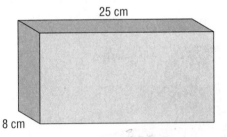

Objective K: *Find unknowns in size change situations involving multiplication.* (*Lesson 10-3*)

40. 6 times a number is 1/3. What is the number?

41. 12% of what number is 240?

42. A sweater is on sale at 80% of the original price. The sale price is $40. What was the original price?

43. When Jed works overtime at time-and-a-half, he makes $12 an hour. What is his usual hourly wage?

44. Seven-eighths of a number is 112. What is the number?

Objective L: *Picture multiplication by negative numbers using size changes.* (*Lesson 10-6*)

45. What is the image of (40, -80) under a size change of magnitude -0.2?

46. Under a size change of magnitude -5, how will a quadrilateral and its image be the same and how will they be different?

47. Let $A = (-4, 5)$, $B = (2, 0)$, and $C = (0, -3)$. Graph $\triangle ABC$ and its image under a size change of magnitude -2.

48. A size change of magnitude -12 is like a size change of magnitude 12 followed by a rotation of what magnitude?

Patterns Leading to Division

Each of the eight questions on this page can be answered by dividing 20 by 7. This chapter is concerned with these and other situations that lead to division.

A. Solve for x. $7x = 20$

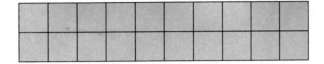

B. Above is pictured a subdivision of land for farming. Split it equally among 7 people. How much will each person get?

C. In 1982, there were 20,000 El Salvadorean refugees living in Honduras and 7000 refugees living in Belize. How many times more refugees were in Honduras than in Belize?

D. You expect 20 people at a dinner meeting. Seven can be seated around each of the tables you have. How many tables are needed?

E. Mr. & Mrs. Torrence have 3 daughters, 4 sons, and 20 grandchildren. On the average, how many children do each of their children have?

F. If $WX = 7$ cm, how long is $\overline{WZ}$?

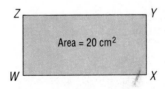

G. If you run at a rate of 7 mi/hr, how long will it take you to run 20 miles?

H. What is the magnitude of the expansion that changed the smaller pentagon below into the larger pentagon?

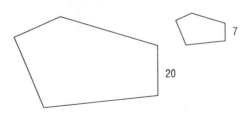

11-1

The Rate Model for Division

Here are some examples of **rates**.

55 miles per hour   1.9 children per family $1.95 for each gallon

The **rate units** can be written as fractions.

$$\frac{miles}{hour} \qquad \frac{children}{family} \qquad \frac{dollars}{gallon}$$

In Chapter 10 you studied the Rate Factor Model for Multiplication. Then you were always given the rate. (You may not have realized this at the time.) You never had to calculate rates. The fraction in rate units suggests that rates can be calculated by dividing. This is exactly the case.

Example 1 A car is driven 250 miles in 5 hours. What is the average rate?

Solution $\dfrac{250 \text{ miles}}{5 \text{ hours}} = 50 \dfrac{miles}{hour}$

People do Example 1 so easily that sometimes they do not realize they divided to get the answer. Example 2 is of the same type. But the numbers are not so simple.

Example 2 A car goes 283.4 miles on 15.2 gallons of gas. How many miles per gallon is the car getting?

Solution $\dfrac{283.4 \text{ miles}}{15.2 \text{ gallons}} \approx 18.6 \dfrac{miles}{gallon}.$
The car is getting about 19 miles per gallon.

Do not let the numbers in rate problems scare you. If you get confused, try simpler numbers and examine how you got the answer.

Examples 1 and 2 are instances of the Rate Model for Division.

Rate Model for Division:

If *a* and *b* are quantities with different units, then *a/b* is the amount of quantity *a* per quantity *b*.

One of the most common examples of rate is **unit cost.**

Example 3 A 6-oz can of peaches sells for 89¢. An 8-oz can sells for $1.17. Which is the better buy?

Solution Calculate the cost per ounce. To do this, divide the total cost by the number of ounces.

Cost per ounce for 6-oz can: $\frac{89¢}{6 \text{ oz}}$ = 14.83... cents per ounce

Cost per ounce for 8-oz can: $\frac{117¢}{8 \text{ oz}}$ = 14.625 cents per ounce

The cost per ounce is called the *unit* cost. The 8-oz can has a slightly lower unit cost. So it is the better buy. But the unit costs do not differ by much. In this case, you should probably choose based on how much you need, not on the cost per can.

Example 4 Eleven people in the scout troop must deliver flyers to 325 households. If the job is split equally, how many flyers will each scout deliver? How many will be left over?

Solution Think: flyers per scout. This means to divide the number of flyers by the number of scouts.

$$\frac{325 \text{ flyers}}{11 \text{ scouts}} = 29.54... \text{ flyers/scout}$$

Each scout will have to deliver 29 flyers. Since 29 · 11 = 319, this would mean that 6 flyers would still not be delivered. The job could be finished if six of the scouts delivered 30 flyers.

Notice in Example 4 that the unit is *flyers per scout*. The number of flyers is a whole number because flyers is a count. But the number of flyers per scout is a rate. Rates do not have to be whole numbers. As you will see in the next two lessons, rates may involve fractions or negative numbers.

Of course, rates can involve variables.

Example 5   Hal typed *W* words in *M* minutes. What is his typing speed?

Solution   The usual unit of typing speed is *words per minute*. So divide the total number of words by the number of minutes.

His typing speed is *W/M* words per minute.

Questions

Covering the Reading

In 1–4, calculate a rate suggested by each situation.

1. The family drove 400 miles in 8 hours.

2. The family drove 400 miles in 8.5 hours.

3. The family drove 600 kilometers in 9 hours.

4. The animal traveled *d* meters in *m* minutes.

In 5–7, calculate a rate suggested by each situation.

5. There were 28 boys and 14 girls at the party.

6. 150 students signed up for 7 geometry classes.

7. Six people live on 120 acres.

8. State the rate model for division.

9. The Smith family went to the grocery store. Boxes of cornflakes were being sold in two different sizes. A 12-oz box cost $1.29 and an 18-oz box cost $1.73.
   a. To the nearest tenth of a cent, give the unit cost of the 12-oz box.
   b. To the nearest tenth of a cent, give the unit cost of the 18-oz box.
   c. Based on unit cost, which box is the better buy?

Applying the Mathematics

10. Nine nannies need to nail one hundred nineteen nails into a nook.
    a. If the job is split evenly, how many nails will each nanny nail?
    b. How many nails will be left over?

11. If in *h* hours you travel *m* miles, what is your rate in miles per hour?

12. A person earns $222 for working 34 hours. How much is the person earning per hour? (Answer to the nearest penny.)

13. In one country a laborer may earn $20 for working 80 hours. How much is this person earning per hour?

14. According to the *1988 World Almanac*, Hawaii had 2743 medical doctors and a population of 964,691 in 1985. California had 72,089 doctors for a population of 23,667,764. Which state had more doctors *per capita*? (The phrase *per capita* means per person. It comes from the Latin words meaning "per head.")

15. The school nurse used 140 bandages in 3 weeks. On the average, how many bandages were used per school day?

16. Susannah calculated that she used an average of $8\frac{2}{5}$ sheets of paper per day. How many sheets of paper could she have used in how many days to get this rate?

Review

17. a. Convert $7\frac{1}{6}$ to a simple fraction. *(Lesson 5-2)*
   b. Give its reciprocal. *(Lesson 9-9)*

18. State the Mult-Rec Property of Division. *(Lesson 9-8)*

19. Solve $-5 + 5m = 5$. *(Lesson 10-9)*

20. If $a = -2$, $b = 5$, and $c = 1$, what is $|a + b + c| - |a|$?
   (Lessons 5-5, 7-2)

In 21–24, lines m and n are parallel. *(Lesson 7-8)*

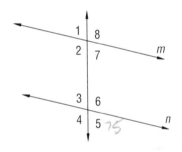

21. Name all pairs of alternate interior angles.

22. Name all pairs of corresponding angles.

23. If $m\angle 5 = 75°$, what is $m\angle 1$?

24. If $m\angle 4 = x$, what is $m\angle 7$?

25. An octagon has ___?___ sides, ___?___ angles, and ___?___ diagonals.
   (Lessons 5-9, 6-3)

Exploration

26. Look in an almanac or other book to find at least one of these rates.
   a. the minimum number of grams of protein per day recommended in a diet for someone your age
   b. the number of people per square mile in the United States
   c. the number of miles per gallon you should expect to get from a certain car
   d. the number of sunny days per year you can expect in El Paso, Texas (nicknamed the "Sun City")

11-2

Division of Fractions

If quantities are given in fractions, then rate situations can lead to division of fractions.

Example 1 Suppose you make $8 for baby-sitting 1 hour 40 minutes. How many dollars have you made per hour?

Solution 40 minutes is $\frac{40}{60}$ or $\frac{2}{3}$ of an hour.
Change the 1 hour 40 minutes to $1\frac{2}{3}$ hours.
Then rewrite $1\frac{2}{3}$ as the simple fraction $\frac{5}{3}$.

Dollars per hour is a rate. Division gives the answer.

$$\text{salary per hour} = \frac{8 \text{ dollars}}{1 \text{ hour } 40 \text{ min}} = \frac{8 \text{ dollars}}{\frac{5}{3} \text{ hours}}$$

To divide 8 by $\frac{5}{3}$, use the Mult-Rec Property of Division:

x divided by $y = x$ times the reciprocal of y.
So, 8 divided by $\frac{5}{3} = 8$ times $\frac{3}{5}$

$$\frac{8}{\frac{5}{3}} = 8 \cdot \frac{3}{5}$$

$$= \frac{24}{5}$$
$$= 4.8$$

The wages per hour are $4.80.

The same idea can be used to divide one fraction by another.

Example 2 What is $\frac{6}{5}$ divided by $\frac{3}{4}$?

Solution By the Mult-Rec Property of Division,
$\frac{6}{5}$ divided by $\frac{3}{4} = \frac{6}{5}$ times $\frac{4}{3}$.

$$\frac{\frac{6}{5}}{\frac{3}{4}} = \frac{6}{5} \cdot \frac{4}{3} = \frac{24}{15} = \frac{8}{5}$$

Check To check that $\frac{8}{5}$ is the answer, you can change the fractions to decimals. $\frac{6}{5} = 1.2$ and $\frac{3}{4} = 0.75$

$$\frac{\frac{6}{5}}{\frac{3}{4}} = \frac{1.2}{0.75} = 1.6$$

Since $\frac{8}{5} = 1.6$, the fraction answer checks.

Example 3 Simplify $\frac{2}{3}$ divided by 15.

Solution $\frac{2}{3}$ divided by $15 = \frac{2}{3} \cdot \frac{1}{15} = \frac{2}{45}$

The next example shows how powerful division of fractions can be.

Example 4 Three-fourths of the way through the season, the Yankees had won 64 games. At this rate, how many games would they win in the entire season?

Solution Games won per entire season $= \dfrac{64 \text{ games}}{\frac{3}{4} \text{ season}}$

$$= 64 \cdot \frac{4}{3} \frac{\text{games}}{\text{season}}$$

$$= \frac{256}{3} \frac{\text{games}}{\text{season}}$$

$$\approx 85.3 \frac{\text{games}}{\text{season}}$$

At this rate, they would win approximately 85 games in the season.

Questions

Covering the Reading

1. A person makes $12 for working two and a half hours. What is the person's wage per hour?

2. State the Mult-Rec Property of Division.

In 3–5, simplify.

3. $\dfrac{\frac{8}{9}}{\frac{4}{3}}$

4. $\dfrac{\frac{2}{5}}{7}$

5. $\dfrac{\frac{17}{6}}{\frac{2}{3}}$

6. Two-thirds of the way into the season, the Dodgers have won 66 games. At this rate, how many games will they win in the entire season?

7. With one-fifth of the season gone, the Sox have lost 12 games. At this rate, how many games will they lose in the season?

Applying the Mathematics

8. a. Divide $4\frac{1}{4}$ by $3\frac{2}{5}$.
   b. The answer you get to part **a** should be bigger than 1. How could you tell this before you did any division?
   c. Check the answer you get to part **a** by changing each fraction to a decimal, dividing the decimals, and comparing the answers.

9. a. Divide $1\frac{2}{3}$ by $5\frac{4}{7}$.
   b. The answer you get to part **a** should be less than 1. How could you tell this before you did any division?
   c. Check the answer you get to part **a** by changing each fraction to a decimal, dividing the decimals, and comparing the answers.
   d. In this question, what advantage do the fractions have over the decimals?

10. Jay walked $\frac{1}{3}$ of a mile in 10 minutes. Ten minutes $= \frac{1}{6}$ hour.
   a. What is Jay's rate in miles per hour?
   b. At this rate, how far will Jay walk in an hour?

In 11 and 12, simplify.

11. $\dfrac{\frac{2}{x}}{\frac{1}{y}}$ **12.** $\dfrac{\frac{a}{b}}{\frac{c}{d}}$

13. Seven and one-half times a number is 375. What is the number?

Review

14. What is the hourly wage if you make $21.12 in 3.3 hours? *(Lesson 11-1)*

In 15–17, solve.

15. $-4 + G = -3$ *(Lesson 7-4)*

16. $-4 - G = -3$ *(Lesson 7-6)*

17. $-4G = -3$ *(Lesson 10-8)*

In 18–20, let $x = \frac{5}{4}$ and $y = \frac{1}{2}$. Write as a simple fraction.

18. $x + y$ *(Lesson 5-2)*

19. $x - y$ *(Lesson 7-2)*

20. $8xy$ *(Lesson 9-9)*

21. Suppose the probability of a hole-in-one on a particular golf hole is 1 in 10,000. What would then be the probability of making two holes-in-one in a row? *(Lesson 9-8)*

In 22–24, use the rectangular solid pictured below. Find the:

22. volume; *(Lesson 9-3)*

23. surface area; *(Lesson 9-2)*

24. perimeter of the largest face. *(Lessons 5-10, 9-4)*

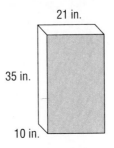

21 in.

35 in.

10 in.

25. Here is a famous puzzler. If a hen and a half can lay an egg and a half in a day and a half, at this rate how many eggs can be laid by two dozen hens in two dozen days?

Division with Negative Numbers

Remember that any division can be converted to a multiplication. Instead of dividing by x, multiply by $\frac{1}{x}$. So, if you can multiply with negative numbers and find reciprocals of them, then you can divide with them.

Example 1   What is -10 divided by 2?

Solution 1   Dividing by 2 is the same as multiplying by $\frac{1}{2}$.

$$\frac{-10}{2} = -10 \cdot \frac{1}{2} = -5$$

Solution 2   Think of a negative rate. A gambler loses 10 dollars in 2 hours. What is the loss rate?

$$\frac{\text{loss of 10 dollars}}{2 \text{ hours}} = \text{loss of 5 dollars per hour}$$

Translate the loss into a negative number.

$$\frac{-10 \text{ dollars}}{2 \text{ hours}} = -5 \frac{\text{dollars}}{\text{hour}}$$

Either way the answer is -5.

In general, if a negative number is divided by a positive number, the quotient is negative. Another example is on the next page.

Example 2 On five consecutive days, the low temperature in a city was 3°, -4°, -6°, -2°, and 0°C. What was the mean low temperature for the five days?

Solution The **mean** (or **average**) temperature is found by adding up the numbers and dividing by 5.

$$\frac{3 + \text{-}4 + \text{-}6 + \text{-}2 + 0}{5} = \frac{\text{-}9}{5} = \text{-}1.8$$

The mean temperature was -1.8°C, or about -2°C. On the Celsius scale, that is a little below freezing.

In Example 3, a positive number is divided by a negative number. The quotient is again negative.

Example 3 What is 10 divided by -2?

Solution 1 Dividing by -2 is the same as multiplying by $\text{-}\frac{1}{2}$, the reciprocal of -2.

$$\frac{10}{\text{-}2} = 10 \cdot \text{-}\frac{1}{2} = \text{-}5$$

Solution 2 Think of the gambler of Solution 2 in Example 1, but go back in time for the 2 hours. The gambler had $10 more 2 hours ago. What is the loss rate?

$$\frac{10 \text{ dollars more}}{2 \text{ hours ago}} = \frac{10 \text{ dollars}}{\text{-}2 \text{ hours}} = \text{-}5 \frac{\text{dollars}}{\text{hour}}$$

Here are two negatives. Is what will happen obvious?

Example 4 What is -150 divided by -7?

$$\frac{\text{-}150}{\text{-}7} = \text{-}150 \cdot \text{-}\frac{1}{7} \quad \text{(Now we know the answer will be positive.)}$$
$$= \frac{150}{7}$$
$$= 21\frac{3}{7}$$
$$\approx 21.43$$

Division with two negative numbers can also be thought of using the rate model. Suppose you lift 14 kg more after 3.5 months' work. You have gained strength at the rate of 4 kg per month.

$$\frac{14 \text{ kg more}}{3.5 \text{ months later}} = \frac{4 \text{ kg}}{\text{month}} \text{ gain}$$

Another way of looking at the situation is that 3.5 months ago you lifted 14 kg less.

$$\frac{14 \text{ kg less}}{3.5 \text{ months ago}} = \frac{4 \text{ kg}}{\text{month}} \text{ gain}$$

Thus $$\frac{14 \text{ kg more}}{3.5 \text{ months later}} = \frac{14 \text{ kg less}}{3.5 \text{ months ago}}.$$

Ignoring the units but using negative numbers:

$$\frac{14}{3.5} = \frac{^-14}{^-3.5}$$

Changing the sign in both numerator and denominator of a fraction is like multiplying the fraction by $\frac{^-1}{^-1}$. This keeps the value of the fraction the same.

For instance, begin with $\frac{^-10}{2}$. Multiplying both numerator and denominator by -1 yields the equal fraction $\frac{10}{^-2}$.

Altogether, the rules for dividing with negative numbers are just like those for multiplying. If both divisor and dividend are negative, the quotient is positive. If one is positive and one is negative, the quotient will be negative. These properties can be stated with variables.

For all numbers a and b, except when $b = 0$:
$$\frac{a}{b} = \frac{^-a}{^-b}$$
$$\frac{^-a}{b} = \frac{a}{^-b} = -\frac{a}{b}$$

If you forget how to do operations with negative numbers, there are two things you can do. (1) Change subtractions to additions; change divisions to multiplications. (2) Think of a real situation using the negative numbers. Use the situation to help you find the answer.

Questions

Covering the Reading

In 1–4, simplify.

1. $\frac{-14}{7}$

2. $\frac{-100}{300}$

3. $\frac{-56}{-8}$

4. $\frac{60}{-2}$

In 5–7, find the mean of each set of numbers.

5. 40, 60, 80, 100

6. -40, -60, -80, -100

7. -11, 14, -17, -20, 6, -30

In 8–11, tell whether the number is positive or negative.

8. $\frac{-2.5}{6} \cdot -4$

9. $-\frac{-100}{300}$

10. $-\frac{-54}{-81}$

11. $\frac{53}{-2} \cdot \frac{55}{-2}$

12. Separate the numbers given here into two collections of equal numbers.

$$-\frac{1}{2} \qquad \frac{-1}{2} \qquad \frac{+1}{+2} \qquad \frac{1}{-2} \qquad -\frac{+1}{+2} \qquad \frac{1}{2} \qquad +\frac{+1}{2}$$

13. Julie lost 4 pounds on a two-day crash diet.
   a. Calculate a rate from this information.
   b. What division problem with negative numbers gives this rate?
   c. Copy and complete: __?__ days ago, Julie weighed __?__ pounds __?__ than she does now.
   d. What division problem is suggested by part **c**?

14. In the twenty years from 1950 to 1970, California's population rose by 9,000,000.
   a. Calculate a rate from this information.
   b. Copy and complete: __?__ years before 1970 California's population was nine million __?__ than it was in 1970.
   c. What division problem is suggested by part **b**? What is the quotient?

15. What two things can you do if you forget how to calculate with negative numbers?

In 16–19, calculate $x + y$, $x - y$, xy, and $\frac{x}{y}$ for the given values of x and y.

16. $x = -10$ and $y = 5$

17. $x = -6$ and $y = -9$

18. $x = 1$ and $y = -1$

19. $x = -12$ and $y = -12$

20. Use $C = 5(F - 32)/9$ to convert $-40°$ Fahrenheit to Celsius.

21. Multiply $\frac{15}{-8}$ by $\frac{2}{-3}$.

22. Round $\frac{350}{-6}$ to the nearest integer.

23. The *center of gravity* of a set of given points is the point whose first coordinate is the mean of the first coordinates of the given points and whose second coordinate is the mean of the second coordinates of the given points.
  a. Find the coordinates of the center of gravity of the four points given at left.
  b. Copy the drawing and graph the center of gravity on your drawing.

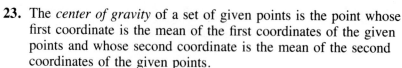

24. a. What simple fraction in lowest terms equals $\frac{10}{3}$ divided by $\frac{5}{6}$?
  b. Check your answer by converting the fractions to decimals and dividing the decimals with a calculator. *(Lesson 11-2)*

25. Begin at the point $(14, 6)$. Move 20 units to the left and 3 units down. What are the coordinates of the image point? *(Lesson 8-5)*

26. In $3\frac{1}{2}$ days, the long-distance runner ran 100 miles. How many miles did the runner run per day? *(Lessons 11-1, 11-2)*

27. a. Write 44% as a decimal. *(Lesson 5-2)*
  b. Write 44% as a simple fraction in lowest terms. *(Lesson 2-7)*

28. What is 40% of 500? *(Lesson 2-6)*

29. 40% of a number is 500. What is the number? *(Lesson 10-3)*

30. a. Press 5 ÷ 0 on your calculator. What does the display show?
  b. Press 5 ÷ 0.001 on your calculator. What is displayed?
  c. Press 5 ÷ 0.001 ± on your calculator. What is displayed?
  d. Divide 5 by other numbers near zero. Record your results. Explain what happens.

11-4

The Ratio Comparison Model for Division

In a certain city, it rained 70 of the 365 days last year. Dividing 70 by 365 indicates how often it rained.

$$\frac{70}{365} \approx .19$$

The answer is often converted to a percent. It rained about 19% of the time.

Notice what happens when the units are put into the numerator and denominator.

$$\frac{70 \text{ days}}{365 \text{ days}}$$

The units are the same. They cancel in the division, so the answer has no unit. Therefore, this is not an example of rate. The answer is called a **ratio.** Ratios have no units. Because the 70 days is being compared to the 365 days, this use of division is called **ratio comparison.**

Ratio Comparison Model for Division:

If a and b are quantities with the same units, then $\frac{a}{b}$ compares a to b.

Example 1 Suppose the tax is $0.42 on a $7.00 purchase. What is the tax rate? (It's called a tax rate even though it is technically a ratio.)

Solution Divide $0.42 by $7.00 to compare them.

$$\frac{\$0.42}{\$7.00} = \frac{0.42}{7.00} = .06$$

.06 = 6%, so the tax rate is 6%.

Check A tax of 6% is 6¢ for every dollar. So for $7, the tax should be 7 · 6¢, or 42¢.

Example 2   Compare the 1986 estimated populations of the United States (245,000,000 people) and Canada (26,000,000 people).

Solution   The units (people) are the same. Divide one of the numbers by the other to compare them.

$$\frac{245,000,000}{26,000,000} \approx 9.4 \leftarrow \text{The population of the U.S. is about 9.4 times that of Canada.}$$

Dividing in the other order gives the reciprocal.

$$\frac{26,000,000}{245,000,000} \approx .11 \leftarrow \text{Canada has about 11\% of the population of the U.S.}$$

Either answer is correct. Comparisons can often be done in either order.

■ ■ ■ ■ ■ ■ ■ ■ ■

Example 3   5 is what percent of 40?

Solution   This problem asks you to compare 5 to 40. So divide, then convert to percent.

$$\frac{5}{40} = 0.125 = 12.5\%$$

Therefore, 5 is 12.5% of 40.

Check   Calculate 12.5% of 40.
$$12.5\% \text{ of } 40 = 0.125 \cdot 40 = 5$$

Questions

Covering the Reading

1. In a city, it rained 12 of the 30 days in a month. What percent of the time is this?

2. A store charges $0.64 tax on a $16.00 purchase. What is the tax rate?

3. There is a tax of 35¢ on a purchase of $5.83.
   a. What is the sales tax rate?
   b. 35 is what percent of 583?

4. According to the ratio comparison model of division, what can you do to compare the numbers 6 and 25?

5. 6 is what percent of 25?

6. What percent is 6 of 12?

7. What percent is 6 of 6?

8. 6 is what percent of 3?

In 9 and 10, answer to the nearest whole number percent.

9. 41 is what percent of 300?

10. 250 is what percent of 300?

11. The population of Canton, Ohio (home of the pro football Hall of Fame) is 90 thousand. The population of Canton, China (from which we get the name Cantonese food) is about 3 million.
   a. Then Canton, Ohio has __?__ percent the number of people of Canton, China.
   b. Canton, China has __?__ times as many people as Canton, Ohio.

12. What is the difference between a rate and a ratio?

Applying the Mathematics

13. 14 of the 25 students in the class are boys.
   a. What percent is this?
   b. What percent are girls?

14. What number is 12 percent of 90?

15. a. Banner H. S. has won 36 of its last 40 games. What percent is this?
   b. What is 36 percent of 40?
   c. 40 is 36 percent of what number?

16. If a $60 jacket is reduced $13.50, what is the percent of discount?

17. If a population of 350,000 increases by 7000, what is the percent of increase?

Review

18. What integer does -6 divided by -2 equal? *(Lesson 11-3)*

19. If $x = \frac{2}{5}$ and $y = \frac{-2}{15}$, write $\frac{x}{y}$ as a simple fraction. *(Lessons 11-2, 11-3)*

20. A person traveled for 2.5 hours at 2.5 miles per hour. How long was the trip? *(Lesson 10-4)*

21. Suppose a person earns time-and-three-quarters for overtime. If the overtime wage is $17.15 per hour, what is the person's normal hourly wage? *(Lesson 10-4)*

22. There are 12 members on the state math team. To send them to the state tournament, it will cost C dollars per team member. $200 has been collected. How much is left to collect? *(Lessons 4-3, 7-1)*

23. If $x = 43$, what does $90 - x$ equal? *(Lesson 4-4)*

24. What simple fraction equals $\frac{3}{5} + \frac{3}{4}$? *(Lesson 5-2)*

25. Let $a = 10$, $b = 20$, $c = 30$, and $d = 40$. What is the value of $\frac{a - c}{b - d}$? *(Lessons 4-7, 7-2, 11-3)*

Exploration

26. The *relative frequency* of an event is the ratio

$$\frac{\text{number of times the event occurs}}{\text{number of times the event could occur}}$$

For instance, suppose it rains exactly 3 days in a week. Since it could rain 7 days in the week, the relative frequency of rain would be $\frac{3}{7}$.
a. Toss a coin 50 times. How many times does it land heads up?
b. What is the relative frequency of heads for your tosses?
c. Change your answer in **b** to a percent.

Properties of Probability

A **probability** is a number from 0 to 1 which tells you how likely something is to happen. A probability of 0 means that the event is *impossible*. A probability of $\frac{1}{5}$ means that you or someone else expects the event to happen 1 in 5 times in the long run. A probability of $\frac{2}{3}$ means that the event is expected to happen about 2 in 3 times. A probability of 1, the highest probability possible, means that the event *must* happen.

The closer a probability is to 1, the more likely the event. Because $\frac{2}{3}$ is greater than $\frac{1}{5}$, an event with a probability of $\frac{2}{3}$ is thought to be more likely than one with a probability of $\frac{1}{5}$. This can be pictured on a number line.

Probabilities can be written as fractions, decimals, or percents, or any way other numbers are written.

Example 1   The weather bureau says there is a 1 in 3 chance of rain tomorrow. It reports a 40% precipitation probability the day after tomorrow. On which day does the weather bureau think rain is more likely?

Solution   The "1 in 3 chance of rain tomorrow" means a probability of $\frac{1}{3}$. To determine whether $\frac{1}{3}$ is larger than 40%, change both numbers to decimals. $\frac{1}{3} = 0.\overline{3}$ and 40% = 0.4, so 40% is larger. So rain is more likely the day after tomorrow.

If there is a $\frac{1}{3}$ probability of rain, then there is a $\frac{2}{3}$ probability that it will not rain. If there is a 40% chance of rain the day after tomorrow, then there is a 60% chance it will not rain.

> If the probability of an event is p, then the probability that the event will not occur is $1 - p$.

There are three common ways that people determine probabilities.

1. Guess. (This is not a great way, but sometimes it is the only thing you can do.)
2. Perform an experiment and take a probability close to the results of that experiment.
3. Assume that some events have certain probabilities and calculate other probabilities from these.

The weather bureau uses a combination of the second and third ways.

Example 2 Perform an experiment to determine the probability that a thumbtack will land up when dropped.

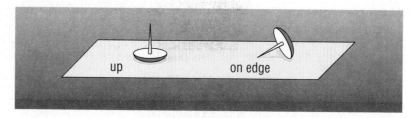

Solution One of the authors found 8 thumbtacks. The author decided to drop all of them 10 times, for a total of 80 dropped tacks. Here are the results.

experiment	1	2	3	4	5	6	7	8	9	10
up	5	3	3	4	5	7	1	5	5	4
on edge	3	5	5	4	3	1	7	3	3	4

Adding the numbers that landed up, a total of 42 tacks landed up. The tacks in the other 38 tosses landed on edge.

The *relative frequency* of a tack landing up was $\frac{42}{80}$. We might pick that number as the probability. However, $\frac{42}{80} = .525$, which is rather close to .5. We might take the probability to be $\frac{1}{2}$.

In Example 2, suppose the experiment had stopped after 8 tacks were thrown. Then the relative frequency of landing up would have been $\frac{5}{8}$, or .625, quite a bit larger than .525. The more times an experiment is repeated, the surer you can be about a probability. But you can never be exactly sure.

Some situations involving probability are similar to the picking of pieces of paper out of a hat. If there are 25 pieces numbered 1 through 25, what is the probability of picking the piece numbered 8? It is reasonable to assume that there is the same probability for picking each of the pieces. Since the total probability is 1, each individual probability is $\frac{1}{25}$. So the probability of picking an 8 is $\frac{1}{25}$.

■ ■ ■ ■ ■ ■ ■ ■■

Example 3   Suppose 25 pieces of paper in a hat are numbered 1 through 25. Assume the probability of picking each is equal. When a piece is picked, what is the probability that its number is prime?

Solution   The prime numbers less than 25 are 2, 3, 5, 7, 11, 13, 17, 19, and 23. There are 9 of them. So the probability of picking a prime number is $\frac{9}{25}$, or 0.36, or 36%.

Example 3 illustrates the following general principle.

> If a situation has n equally likely outcomes and an event includes s of these, then the probability of the event is $\frac{s}{n}$.

For instance, suppose you have 10 pairs of socks in a drawer and you pick one pair without looking. If the pairs are folded together, there are 10 possible outcomes. If 3 are red, then the event of picking a red pair has 3 of these outcomes. If each outcome is equally likely, the probability of picking a red pair is $\frac{3}{10}$.

Questions

Covering the Reading

1. A probability can be no larger than __?__ and no smaller than __?__.

2. If an event is impossible, its probability is __?__.

3. What is the probability of a sure thing?

4. Suppose event A has a probability of $\frac{1}{2}$ and event B has a probability of $\frac{1}{3}$. Which event is more likely?

5. The weather bureau reports a 70% precipitation probability for tomorrow and a $\frac{3}{5}$ chance of thunderstorms the day after tomorrow. Which is more likely, precipitation tomorrow or thunderstorms the day after?

6. Suppose the probability that your teacher gives a test next Friday is 80%. What is the probability your teacher does not give a test next Friday?

7. You listen to a radio station for an hour. You estimate that $\frac{1}{10}$ is the probability that your favorite song will be played. What is the probability that your favorite song will not be played?

8. If the probability that an event occurs is x, what is the probability it does not occur?

9. Identify two common ways in which people determine probabilities.

10. According to the experiment in this lesson, what is a reasonable probability to assume for that thumbtack landing up?

In 11 and 12, imagine a situation where fifty raffle tickets are put in a hat. Each ticket has the same probability of being selected.

11. If you have one of these tickets, what is the probability you will win the raffle?

12. If you and two friends have one ticket apiece, what is the probability that one of you will win the raffle?

Applying the Mathematics

13. A person says, "There is a negative probability that my uncle will leave me a million dollars." What is wrong with that statement?

14. *Multiple choice*   The probability that a coin will land heads up is often given as $\frac{1}{2}$. How is this number determined?
   (a) The coin was tossed 100 times and it came down heads 50 times.
   (b) The two sides of the coin are assumed to be equally likely.
   (c) A good guess is $\frac{1}{2}$.

15. A spinner in a game is pictured below. Assume all positions of the spinner are equally likely.

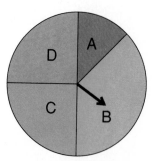

   a. If the angle which forms region A has measure 45°, what is the probability that the spinner will land in region A?
   b. Determine the probabilities of landing in the other regions. Assume radii that look perpendicular are.

16. Suppose in Example 2 that, in 60 of the 80 tosses, the thumbtack landed up. What number might be picked to be the probability that the tack lands up?

17. An organization has a raffle and *n* people buy tickets. You buy 5 tickets. What is the probability that you will win the raffle?

18. What way of determining probability is being used:
a. in Question 16? **b.** in Question 17?

19. Slips of paper numbered from 1 to 100 are put into a hat. A slip is taken from the hat. What is the probability that the number is prime and ends in a 3?

Review

20. Carla's Car Place had 50 used cars for sale a week ago. Today only 36 of these are left. How many cars have been sold per day? *(Lesson 11-1)*

21. In the Maple Ridge School, 35 third-graders are boys and 47 are girls. What percent of the third-graders are boys? *(Lesson 11-4)*

22. a. What is 3% of 32? *(Lesson 2-6)*
b. 3 is what percent of 32? *(Lesson 11-4)*
c. 3 is 32% of what number? *(Lesson 10-2)*

23. When $x = 5$ and $y = -3$, what is the value of $\dfrac{-9x}{y}(x + 2)$? *(Lessons 4-1, 10-5, 11-3)*

24. Write $2 \cdot 3^4$ as a decimal. *(Lesson 2-2)*

Exploration

25. Find a thumbtack or some other object that has more than one side on which it can land after dropped. Drop the object 50 times. Estimate the probability that the object will land on each of its possible sides.

26. a. Pick a page of a local residential phone directory. Calculate the probability that the last digit of a phone number on that page is 0.
b. Do part **a**, but use the yellow pages.
c. Do commercial and residential phone numbers have about the same probability of having a last digit of zero?

Proportions

Remember that the fraction $\frac{a}{b}$ is the result of dividing a by b. This means that every use of division gives rise to fractions. For instance, when 9 out of 12 students in a class ride a bus to school, then $\frac{9}{12}$ of the class ride the bus.

You know that $\frac{9}{12}$ is equal to $\frac{3}{4}$. In this case you could say that 3 of 4 students ride a bus to school. Equal fractions mean equal ratios.

Now consider a rate. A car goes 9 miles in 12 minutes. The fraction

$$\frac{9 \text{ miles}}{12 \text{ minutes}}$$

is the car's rate. This rate is $\frac{9}{12}$ miles per minute. Simplify the fraction.

$$\frac{9 \text{ miles}}{12 \text{ minutes}} = \frac{3 \text{ miles}}{4 \text{ minutes}}$$

Going 9 miles in 12 minutes is the same rate as going 3 miles in 4 minutes. Equal fractions mean equal rates.

A **proportion** is a statement that two fractions are equal. Here are three examples.

$$\frac{730}{365} = \frac{2}{1} \qquad \frac{12ab}{3b} = \frac{4ab}{b} \qquad \frac{3 \text{ miles}}{4 \text{ minutes}} = \frac{11 \text{ miles}}{y \text{ minutes}}$$

Some equations with fractions are not proportions. Examine these two equations.

$$\frac{x + 5}{8} = \frac{x}{2} \qquad\qquad \frac{x}{8} + \frac{5}{8} = \frac{x}{2}$$

a proportion   not a proportion

The left equation is a proportion because on each side there is one fraction. The right equation is equivalent to the left equation. But it is not a proportion because its left side is not a single fraction.

Like other equations, proportions can be true or false.

$$\frac{30}{100} = \frac{1}{3} \qquad\qquad \frac{320}{100} = \frac{16}{5}$$

False   True

When a proportion has variables in it, the question is often to **solve the proportion.** That means to find the values that make the proportion true. For example:

$$\frac{320}{100} = \frac{16}{x} \text{ has the solution } x = 5, \text{ because } \frac{320}{100} = \frac{16}{5}.$$

Solving a proportion is just like solving any other equation. No new properties are needed. But it may take more steps.

■ ■ ■ ■ ■ ■ ■ ■

Example 1 Solve for m: $\dfrac{32}{m} = \dfrac{24}{25}$

Solution Multiply both sides by $25m$. This yields an equation with no fractions.

$$25m \cdot \frac{32}{m} = \frac{24}{25} \cdot 25m$$

We put in a step here that you may not need to write. It shows what is going on.

$$\frac{25m \cdot 32}{m} = \frac{24 \cdot 25m}{25}$$

Now simplify the fractions.

$$25 \cdot 32 = 24m$$
$$800 = 24m$$
$$\frac{800}{24} = m$$

Rewrite the fraction in lowest terms.
$$\frac{100}{3} = m$$

There are many ways to check the result of Example 1.

Check 1 The roughest check is to change $\frac{100}{3}$ to a decimal and substitute in the original sentence.

$$\frac{100}{3} = 33.3 \ldots$$

Does it look right? Does $\frac{32}{33.3}$ seem equal to $\frac{24}{25}$? It seems about right, because in each fraction the numerator is just slightly less than the denominator.

Check 2 A better check is to perform the divisions. $\frac{32}{33.3} \approx .961$, while $\frac{24}{25} = .96$. That's close enough, given the estimate for $\frac{100}{3}$.

Check 3 To do an exact check, substitute $\frac{100}{3}$ for m in the original proportion.

$$\text{Does } \frac{32}{\frac{100}{3}} = \frac{24}{25}?$$

Work out the division of fractions on the left side.

$$\frac{32}{\frac{100}{3}} = 32 \cdot \frac{3}{100} = \frac{96}{100}$$

Since $\frac{96}{100}$ simplifies to $\frac{24}{25}$ (the right side), the answer checks.

Many real situations lead to having to solve proportions.

Example 2 If you can stuff 100 envelopes in 8 minutes, how many could you stuff in 30 minutes? Assume that you can keep up the same rate all this time.

Solution Let N be the number of envelopes you can stuff in 30 minutes. Since the rates are equal,

100 envelopes in 8 minutes = N envelopes in 30 minutes.

$$\frac{100 \text{ envelopes}}{8 \text{ minutes}} = \frac{N \text{ envelopes}}{30 \text{ minutes}}$$

$$\frac{100}{8} = \frac{N}{30}$$

Multiply both sides by $30 \cdot 8$ to get rid of all fractions.

$$30 \cdot 8 \cdot \frac{100}{8} = \frac{N}{30} \cdot 30 \cdot 8$$

$$30 \cdot 100 = N \cdot 8$$

$$3000 = 8N$$

$$375 = N$$

Check $\frac{100}{8} = 12.5$, which equals $\frac{375}{30}$.

Thus at this rate, 375 envelopes can be stuffed in 30 minutes.

Questions

Covering the Reading

1. Suppose 20 out of 60 students in a class are boys. In lowest terms, __?__ out of __?__ students are boys.

2. Suppose you type 300 words in 10 minutes. At this rate, you would type __?__ words in 20 minutes.

3. Define: proportion.

4. *Multiple choice* Which proportion is not true?
   (a) $\frac{100}{7} = \frac{50}{3.5}$ 　　　(b) $\frac{1}{3} = \frac{33}{100}$ 　　　(c) $\frac{24}{60} = \frac{14}{35}$

5. *Multiple choice* Which equation is not a proportion?
   (a) $\frac{x}{5} = \frac{3}{4}$ 　　　(b) $\frac{1}{9} = \frac{15}{23}$ 　　　(c) $\frac{1}{2} + \frac{2}{2} = \frac{3}{2}$

6. Consider the equation $\frac{40}{t} = \frac{21}{15}$.
   a. By what can you multiply both sides to get rid of fractions?
   b. What equation results after that multiplication?
   c. Solve this equation.
   d. Check your answer.

508

In 7–9, solve.

7. $\dfrac{8}{7} = \dfrac{112}{Q}$ **8.** $\dfrac{200}{8} = \dfrac{x}{22}$ **9.** $\dfrac{L}{24} = \dfrac{0.5}{4}$

10. Jennifer can assemble 3 cardboard boxes in 4 minutes. At this rate, how many boxes can she assemble in 24 minutes?

11. Victor can assemble 5 cardboard boxes in 6 minutes. At this rate, how many boxes can he assemble in 45 minutes?

Applying the Mathematics

12. In the book *Big Bucks for Kids,* the author says that a kid can earn $25 for singing 20 minutes at a wedding. At this rate, what should the fee be for singing 45 minutes?

13. One car can travel 300 km on 40 liters of gas. To travel 450 km, will a tank of 50 liters be enough?

14. A recipe says to use $\frac{2}{3}$ of a teaspoon of salt for 6 people. In using this recipe for 25 people, how many teaspoonsful should be used?

15. At the end of the 1987-88 season, hockey player Wayne Gretsky had scored 583 goals in 696 games in his career. At this rate, in what game would he score his 600th goal?

16. Mozart wrote 41 symphonies in a lifetime of only 35 years. At this rate, how many symphonies would he have written, had he lived to 70?

Review

17. Pieces of paper numbered from 1 to 80 are put into a hat. A piece of paper is taken out. Assume each piece is equally likely. Mike's favorite number is 7. What is the probability that the number chosen has a 7 as one of its digits? *(Lesson 11-5)*

18. What percent of 15 is 30? *(Lesson 11-4)*

19. What percent of 30 is 15? *(Lesson 11-4)*

20. Felice and Felipe folded fancy napkins for a Friday feast. In $\frac{2}{3}$ of an hour Felice had folded 32 napkins. In 25 minutes Felipe folded 20 napkins. Who is folding faster? *(Lessons 11-1, 11-2)*

21. The amount of material needed to make a cubical box with edge of length s is $6s^2$. What is the amount of material needed for a cubical box where $s = 30$ cm? *(Lesson 4-1)*

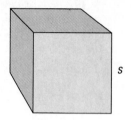

Exploration

22. Suppose a 10″ pizza costs $5.

 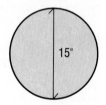

    a. Using proportions, what should a 15″ pizza cost?

    b. Most pizza places charge more for a large pizza than what would be calculated by proportions. Why must they charge more?

    c. Find a menu from a place that sells pizza. Do the larger pizzas cost more per inch of diameter?

11-7

The Means-Extremes Property

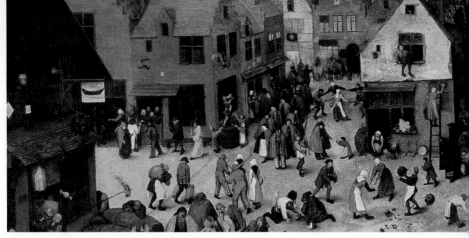

In the Middle Ages, students used a shortcut called the Rule of Three to solve proportions. See Example 2.

Here is a true proportion. $\dfrac{4}{10} = \dfrac{6}{15}$

In some places in the world, this proportion is written

$$4:10 = 6:15.$$

In the United States, the colon sign means "ratio."
We say "the ratio of 4 to 10 equals the ratio of 6 to 15."
Or, we say "4 is to 10 as 6 is to 15."

Look again at $4:10 = 6:15$. The numbers 4 and 15 are on the outside and are called the **extremes** of the proportion. The numbers 10 and 6 are in the middle and are called the **means**. Notice that 4 times 15 equals 10 times 6. The product of the means equals the product of the extremes.

Here is another true proportion. The means are 23 and 3. The extremes are 34.5 and 2.

$$\underset{\text{means}}{\underbrace{\dfrac{34.5}{23}}} \diagdown \overset{}{=} \diagup \underset{\text{extremes}}{\underbrace{\dfrac{3}{2}}}$$

Again the product of the means equals the product of the extremes.

$$23 \cdot 3 = 34.5 \cdot 2$$

This happens because of the Multiplication Property of Equality. Suppose

$$\frac{a}{b} = \frac{c}{d}.$$

Now multiply both sides of the proportion by bd.

$$bd \cdot \frac{a}{b} = bd \cdot \frac{c}{d}$$
$$da = bc$$

On the right side of $da = bc$ is the product of the means. On the left side is the product of the extremes. This is an important property.

Means–Extremes Property:

In any proportion, the product of the means equals the product of the extremes.

The Means–Extremes Property can be used as a shortcut in solving proportions.

Example 1 Solve $\dfrac{2}{3} = \dfrac{12}{x}$.

Solution You may be able to solve this equation in your head. But if you cannot, here is how to use the Means–Extremes Property.

The means are 3 and 12. The extremes are 2 and x. By the property:
$$3 \cdot 12 = 2 \cdot x.$$
$$36 = 2x$$

Solve this equation either mentally or by multiplying both sides by $\frac{1}{2}$.
$$18 = x$$

Check Use substitution.
Does $\frac{2}{3} = \frac{12}{18}$? Yes, because the right fraction simplifies to the left.

In the Middle Ages, students who wanted to solve proportions used a shortcut called the Rule of Three. Here is a typical problem of that time.

Example 2 Suppose 6 bags of wheat cost 11 silver pieces. How much should 10 bags cost?

Solution 1 Clearly the answer involves the numbers 6, 11, and 10. Students were taught just to memorize: Multiply 10 by 11, then divide by 6. You get the right answer, $\frac{110}{6}$. But how do you remember which two numbers to multiply? Students were usually confused. A poem written in the late Middle Ages indicates the confusion.

Multiplication is vexation,
Division is as bad,
The Rule of Three
Does puzzle me
And practice drives me mad. (Writer anonymous.)

Solution 2 Set up the two equal rates. $\dfrac{11 \text{ pieces}}{6 \text{ bags}} = \dfrac{p \text{ pieces}}{10 \text{ bags}}$

Now use the Means–Extremes Property.

$$6p = 110$$

Multiply both sides by $\frac{1}{6}$.

$$p = \frac{110}{6}$$
$$= 18\frac{2}{6}$$
$$= 18\frac{1}{3}$$

The 10 bags should cost a little more than 18 silver pieces.

Good problem solvers try to find shortcuts like the Means–Extremes Property, or even the Rule of Three. But they also try to understand why the shortcuts work. A shortcut in which you have to guess what to do is no good at all. And with shortcuts, it is essential to check answers.

Here is a check for Example 2. Does $\frac{11}{6} = \frac{18.\overline{3}}{10}$? Yes, each equals $1.8\overline{3}$. Here is another check. Since 6 bags cost 11 pieces, 12 bags will cost twice as many, 22 pieces. Ten bags should cost something in between 11 and 22 pieces, which they do.

Questions

Covering the Reading

In 1–4, consider the proportion $\dfrac{15}{t} = \dfrac{250}{400}$.

1. Identify the means.

2. Identify the extremes.

3. According to the Means–Extremes Property, what equation will help you solve this proportion?

4. **a.** Solve this proportion for t.
   b. Check the answer you found in part **a**.

5. Consider this situation. Eight cans of grapefruit juice cost $1.79. You want to know how much ten cans might cost.
   a. Write a proportion that will help answer the question.
   b. Solve the proportion using the Means–Extremes Property.
   c. Check the answer you found.

6. Write down how the proportion $2:3 = 6:9$ is read.

7. Why did the Rule of Three puzzle students in the Middle Ages?

8. Cyril went to market and found that 5 bags of salt cost 12 silver pieces. How much should he pay for 8 bags?

9. What should you be sure to do when you use a shortcut to solve a proportion?

In 10–13, consider the proportion $\frac{a}{b} = \frac{c}{d}$. *True or false?*

10. $ad = bc$ **11.** $ab = cd$

12. $ac = bd$ **13.** $da = cb$

14. Lannie tried to solve the proportion of Question 1 by multiplying both sides by $400t$. Will this work?

15. On the first two days of the week-long hunting season, 47 deer were bagged. **a.** At this rate, how many deer will be killed during the week? **b.** Why might it be incorrect to assume the rate will stay the same all week?

16. If small cans of grapefruit juice are 5 for $1.69, how many cans can be bought for $10?

17. Why won't the Means−Extremes Property work on the equation $x + \frac{2}{3} = \frac{4}{5}$?

In 18–20, a television survey was done in a small town. Of 240 households called on the phone, 119 were watching television at the time.

18. To the nearest hundredth, what percent of households were watching television? *(Lesson 11-4)*

19. Of 25,000 households in this town, how many would you expect to have been watching TV? *(Lesson 11-6)*

20. What number might you choose as the probability that someone in a household was watching television? *(Lesson 11-6)*

In 21–24, simplify. *(Lessons 1-10, 11-3)*

21. $\frac{12}{18}$ **22.** $\frac{12}{-18}$

23. $\frac{-12}{-18}$ **24.** $\frac{-12}{18}$

25. Robert Wadlow of Alton, Illinois, was $5\frac{1}{3}$ feet tall at the age of 5 and $8\frac{2}{3}$ feet tall at the age of 21. On the average, how fast did he grow in these years? *(Lessons 11-1, 11-2)*

Each problem on this page involves both multiplication and addition. Each problem can be done in two ways. In one of these ways, you add before multiplying. In the other way, you do two multiplications before adding. Try to answer each question these two ways.

A. How many dots are there in all?   B. What is the total area?

C. 7 + 11 + 7 + 11 + 7 + 11 + 7 + 11 + 7 + 11 = ?

D. How many segments will join a dot in the top row with a dot in one of the two bottom rows?

E. Pencils cost 5¢. If you buy 7 pencils one day and 11 the next, what is the total amount you have spent?

F. If $a = 5$, $b = 7$, and $c = 11$, what is the value of $ab + ac$?

Each of these questions leads to $5(7 + 11) = 5 \cdot 7 + 5 \cdot 11$, an instance of the **Distributive Property of Multiplication over Addition.** The Distributive Property is the basic property that combines multiplication with addition or subtraction. Such combinations of operations are useful in many situations.

12-1

The Distributive Property

Consider this question:

> Steve wants to buy his sister 21 long-stem roses for her 21st birthday. If the roses cost $2.50 apiece, what will be the total cost?

The answer can be found by a rate factor multiplication.

$$21 \text{ roses} \cdot \frac{\$2.50}{\text{rose}}$$

This multiplication can be done mentally. Ten roses cost $10 \cdot \$2.50$, which is $25. Another ten cost $25, making $50. The last rose costs $2.50, for a grand total of $52.50.

Suppose one rose cost x. Then the cost of 21 roses is $21x$. You could use the same idea to calculate the cost of 21 roses. The cost of 10 roses is $10x$. Another 10 cost another $10x$. The last rose costs x. So $21x = 10x + 10x + x$.

Here's another situation. Find the total area of these rectangles.

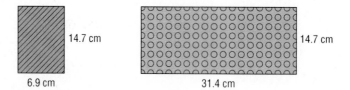

14.7 cm

14.7 cm

6.9 cm

31.4 cm

The obvious way is to multiply $6.9 \cdot 14.7$, then $31.4 \cdot 14.7$, and add the two products. But there is a way to do it with a simpler addition and only one multiplication.
Join the rectangles.

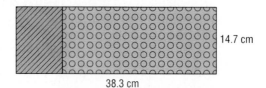

14.7 cm

38.3 cm

One dimension is still 14.7 cm. The other dimension is 6.9 cm + 31.4 cm, or 38.3 cm. Multiplying the two dimensions, 14.7 cm and 38.3 cm, gives the area. This shows

$$6.9 \cdot 14.7 + 31.4 \cdot 14.7 = (6.9 + 31.4) \cdot 4.7.$$

The general pattern is:
$$a \cdot x + b \cdot x = (a + b) \cdot x.$$

These two situations illustrate an important property connecting multiplication and addition.

The Distributive Property of Multiplication over Addition:

For any numbers a, b, and x: $ax + bx = (a + b)x$.

Example 1   Simplify $2m + 5m$.

Solution
Think: The cost of 2 roses + the cost of 5 roses
Write: $2m + 5m = (2 + 5)m = 7m$

Check   Substitute some number for m, say 4.
Does $2 \cdot 4 + 5 \cdot 4 = 7 \cdot 4$? Remember to follow order of operations.
$8 + 20 = 28$, so the answer checks.

Example 2   Simplify $4y - 3y$.

Solution   Think: The cost of 4 roses minus the cost of 3 roses is the cost of one rose.
Putting in all steps, we write:

$$
\begin{aligned}
4y - 3y &= 4y + \text{-}3y \\
&= (4 + \text{-}3)y \\
&= 1y \\
&= y
\end{aligned}
$$

There are too many steps in Example 2. It's easier to use a general property.

The Distributive Property of Multiplication over Subtraction:

For any numbers a, b, and x: $ax - bx = (a - b)x$.

Example 3 Simplify $43.7x + 2x - 19.8x$.

Solution
$$43.7x + 2x - 19.8x$$
$$= (43.7 + 2)x - 19.8x$$
$$= 45.7x - 19.8x$$
$$= (45.7 - 19.8)x$$
$$= 25.9x$$

Check Again, substitute some number for x, say 10. You should find that $43.7 \cdot 10 + 2 \cdot 10 - 19.8 \cdot 10 = 25.9 \cdot 10$.

The name *distributive property* comes from the fact that the final multiplication (in Example 3, it is $25.9x$) was *distributed over* additions or subtractions. The names of these two properties are long, so we call them each just the **Distributive Property,** or even shorter, **distributivity.**

Example 4 Simplify $2t + 3t + 7$.

Solution Using distributivity,
$$2t + 3t + 7$$
$$= \quad 5t + 7$$

This cannot be simplified any more. Think of adding 7 dollars to the cost of 5 roses. There is no number being distributed over the additions.

You could think of Example 4 as coming from the cost of 2 roses at t dollars each, 3 more at t dollars each, and 7 dollars for a vase. The total is 5 roses at t dollars each plus the cost of the vase.

Questions

Covering the Reading

1. **a.** The cost of 21 roses equals the cost of 10 roses plus __?__.
   b. $21 \cdot 3.75 = 10 \cdot 3.75 + $ __?__.
   c. $21x = 10x + $ __?__.

2. **a.** What is the total area of these rectangles?

45   25

   b. How can you check your answer to part **a**?

3. Draw a picture with rectangles to show that $3x + 5x = (3 + 5)x$.

4. The equality of Question 3 is an instance of what property?

5. Fred believes that $6m - m = 5m$. Nell believes that $6m - m = 6$. Who is correct and how can you tell?

In 6–13, simplify.

6. $3x + 5x$

7. $4y + 6y + 8$

8. $2.4v + 3.5v + v$

9. $4b + 6b + 8$

10. $v + v$

11. $9m - 7m + 3m$

12. $t + 6.34t - 2.12t$

13. $60h + 40 - 30h$

14. Give an instance of the Distributive Property of Multiplication over Subtraction.

Applying the Mathematics

15. A hamburger costs x cents. Dave bought 3 hamburgers. Sue bought 2. How much did they spend altogether?

In 16 and 17, work mentally to simplify.

16. $994 \cdot 68 + 6 \cdot 68$

17. $12 \cdot \$3.75 - 2 \cdot \$3.75$

18. Suppose you buy 4 tapes at $7.99 each. You can figure out $\$7.99 \cdot 4$ by first multiplying $8 by 4 and then doing what?

19. I don't know how many bushels of corn an acre of land will yield. So I'll call it B. Liz has 40 acres planted. Orville planted 15.5 acres. Nancy planted 24 acres. How many bushels of corn can the three expect to harvest altogether?

20. Solve for x.
    $2x + 3x = 600$

21. Solve for y.
    $7y + y = 12.6$

22. a. On a calculator, how many presses of *operation* keys are needed to evaluate $ax + bx$?
    b. How many presses of operation keys are needed to evaluate $(a + b)x$?
    c. Which of these expressions would be more quickly evaluated by a computer?

23. Try two special cases to check whether or not
$a(b + c) = ab + ac$. *(Lesson 6-6)*

24. What is the measure of a supplement to an angle with a measure
of 55°? *(Lesson 7-7)*

25. a. Dividing by 3 is the same as multiplying by __?__.
b. Divide $\frac{12}{5}$ by 3. *(Lessons 9-8, 11-2)*

26. $AB = 40$ and $BC = 25$. **a.** Draw a picture. **b.** What are the
smallest and largest possible values of AC? *(Lessons 6-3, 6-6)*

In 27 and 28, rewrite in lowest terms. *(Lesson 1-10)*

27. $\frac{16}{56}$ **28.** $\frac{105}{235}$

29. Find a fraction equal to $\dfrac{3.14}{4}$ with whole numbers in its numerator
and denominator. *(Lesson 2-7)*

30. On the first page of this lesson, the Distributive Property of
Multiplication over *Addition* was pictured by using areas of
rectangles. Picture $35 \cdot 80 - 23 \cdot 80 = 12 \cdot 80$, an instance of
the Distributive Property of Multiplication over *Subtraction*,
by using rectangles.

12-2

Fractions for Repeating Decimals

Decimals either stop or go on forever. Those that stop are called *terminating* or **finite decimals.**

$$2.3 \qquad 5.04 \qquad -0.00002187 \qquad 7890 \qquad 636.2$$

Recall that those that go on forever are called *infinite decimals.* Some infinite decimals repeat. Here are three examples of infinite repeating decimals.

$0.\overline{142857}$	(the entire decimal part repeats)
$0.5\overline{148}$	(only the 148 repeats)
$34.\overline{54}$	(only the 54 repeats)

Every repeating decimal equals a simple fraction. You may remember that $0.\overline{142857}$ equals $\frac{1}{7}$. But how could you know that $0.5\overline{148} = \frac{139}{270}$? The way to find these fractions uses the Distributive Property in a surprising way.

Example 1 Find a simple fraction that equals $0.5\overline{148}$.

Solution
Step 1: Let $x = 0.5\overline{148}$. Write x with a few repetitions of the repetend.

$$x = 0.5148148148\ldots$$

Step 2: The repetend has 3 digits, so multiply x by 1000. This moves the decimal point 3 digits to the right.

$$1000x = 514.8148148148\ldots$$

Step 3: Rewrite $1000x$ with the repetend bar, starting the bar as in x. Subtract.

$$1000x - x = 514.8\overline{148} - 0.5\overline{148}$$

Step 4: Use the Distributive Property on the left. Subtract on the right.

$$(1000 - 1)x = 514.8\overline{148} - 0.5\overline{148}$$
$$999x = 514.3$$

Step 5: Solve the equation.

$$x = \frac{514.3}{999} = \frac{5143}{9990}$$

Dividing numerator and denominator by 37, this fraction equals $\frac{139}{270}$. Therefore,

$$0.5\overline{148} = \frac{139}{270}$$

Check Convert $\frac{139}{270}$ to a decimal using your calculator.
It equals $0.5\overline{148}$.

Example 2   Find a simple fraction equal to $5.0\overline{3}$.

Solution

Step 1: Let $\qquad x = 5.033333333...$

Step 2: The repetend has 1 digit, so multiply x by 10. This moves the decimal point one digit to the right.

$$10x = 50.33333333...$$

Step 3: Subtract. $10x - x = 50.3\overline{3} - 5.0\overline{3}$

Step 4: Simplify. $\qquad 9x = 45.3$

Step 5: Solve. $\qquad x = \dfrac{45.3}{9} = \dfrac{453}{90} = \dfrac{151}{30}$

Example 3   Cleo had just done a division on her calculator when she was distracted. When she returned to her work she realized she had forgotten which numbers she had divided! The display on the calculator read $\boxed{187.54545}$.

What numbers might she have divided?

Solution   The display is probably a rounding of the repeating decimal $187.\overline{54}$. To find out, use the method of this lesson.

Step 1: Let $\qquad x = 187.\overline{54}$

Step 2: Multiply by 100. $\qquad 100x = 18754.\overline{54}$

Step 3: Subtract. $\qquad 100x - x = 18754.\overline{54} - 187.\overline{54}$

Step 4: Simplify. $\qquad 99x = 18567$

Step 5: Solve. $\qquad x = \dfrac{18567}{99} = \dfrac{2063}{11}$

So Cleo may have divided 2063 by 11. Or, she divided any two numbers which make a fraction equal to 2063/11.

Check $2063 \boxed{\div} 11 \boxed{=} \boxed{187.54545}$

Questions

Covering the Reading

In 1–4, classify the decimal as repeating, terminating, or cannot tell.

1. 3.04444

2. $3.0\overline{4}$

3. 3.040404…

4. $3.\overline{04}$

5. Which of the decimals in Questions 1–4 are finite, which infinite?

6. a. If $x = 0.\overline{24}$, then $100x = \underline{\quad?\quad}$
   b. Find a simple fraction equal to $0.\overline{24}$.

7. Find a simple fraction equal to $5.\overline{24}$.

8. Name two numbers other than 2063 and 11 which could have given Cleo's calculator display in Example 3.

Applying the Mathematics

9. Find a simple fraction equal to $0.8\overline{10}$.

10. A hat contains less than 10 marbles. Some marbles are green and the rest are yellow. Without looking you are to reach into the hat and pull out a marble. You are told that the probability of getting a green marble is $0.\overline{2}$.
   a. Rewrite the probability of getting a green marble as a simple fraction.
   b. Use your answer to part **a** to tell how many marbles are in the hat.
   c. How many of the marbles are green?

11. Convert $3.0\overline{405}$ to a fraction.

In 12 and 13, refer to this calculator display: [58.833333]

12. If the 3 repeats forever, name a division problem which would give this display.

13. If this display is the entire decimal, name a division problem which could have given it.

14. Use the method of this section to show that $1 = 0.\overline{9}$.

15. Write $99.\overline{4}\%$ as a simple fraction.

16. Simplify: $4x + 3y + 2x + y + 0x + -1y$. *(Lessons 10-7, 12-1)*

17. Solve $10x - 1 = 30$. *(Lesson 10-9)*

18. To the nearest hundred, how many feet are in a mile?
(Lessons 3-2, 1-4)

In 19 and 20, use this drawing.

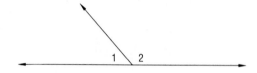

19. If the measure of angle 1 is $48\frac{2}{5}^{\circ}$, what is the measure of angle 2?
(Lessons 5-5, 7-7)

20. If angle 1 has measure x and angle 2 has measure $2x$, what is the value of x? *(Lessons 7-8, 12-1)*

In 21 and 22, use the figure below.

21. How many lines of symmetry does the figure have? *(Lesson 8-7)*

22. Trace the figure and draw a tessellation using it as the fundamental region. *(Lesson 8-8)*

23. What fraction with 1 in its numerator and a two-digit integer in its denominator equals $0.\overline{012345679}$?

24. a. What decimal is the sum of $0.\overline{12}$ and $0.\overline{345}$?
b. What simple fraction is the sum?

12-3

Situations Leading to Linear Expressions

Finding the total cost of a store's stock is a situation leading to a linear expression.

An ounce of hamburger has about 80 calories. If you eat h ounces, you will take in about $80h$ calories. Here is the rate factor multiplication.

$$h \text{ ounces} \cdot 80 \frac{\text{calories}}{\text{ounce}} = 80h \text{ calories}$$

Now suppose you eat f french fries. Recall that a typical french fry may have about 11 calories. Using rate factor multiplication, you will take in about $11f$ calories. The total from the f french fries and h ounces of hamburger is

$$80h + 11f \text{ calories}.$$

The expression $80h + 11f$ involves four different numbers. Unlike $80h + 11h$, $80h + 11f$ *cannot be simplified* using the Distributive Property.

You can think of $80h$ as a multiple of h, and $11f$ as a multiple of f. Then $80h + 11f$ is a sum of multiples of different numbers. The expression $80h + 11f$ is a *linear expression*. A **linear expression** is one in which variables, numbers, or multiples of variables are added or subtracted. $3x - 5$ is a linear expression, but $8xy$ and $5t^2$ are not. Linear expressions arise from many everyday situations.

Example 1 A shoe store owner buys 120 pair of shoes at $11 a pair and 80 pair at $15/pair. What is the total cost to the owner?

Solution The total cost is

$$120 \text{ pair} \cdot 11 \frac{\text{dollars}}{\text{pair}} + 80 \text{ pair} \cdot 15 \frac{\text{dollars}}{\text{pair}}$$
$$= \quad \$1320 \quad + \quad \$1200$$
$$= \quad \$2520$$

Often you know how many things you want but you do not know the price. Then the arithmetic in Example 1 becomes the algebra of Example 2.

Example 2   A store owner buys 120 pair of shoes at x dollars a pair and 80 pair at y dollars a pair. What is the total cost to the store owner?

Solution   The total cost is now

$$120 \text{ pair} \cdot x \, \frac{\text{dollars}}{\text{pair}} + 80 \text{ pair} \cdot y \, \frac{\text{dollars}}{\text{pair}}$$
$$= \qquad \$120x \qquad + \qquad \$80y$$

The expression $120x + 80y$ cannot be simplified.

In the linear expression $120x + 80y$, $120x$ and $80y$ are called **terms**. Terms are numbers or expressions that are added or subtracted. The number 120 is called the **coefficient** of x. The number 80 is the coefficient of y.

The linear expression $6A + 4B - 5A$ has three terms. The terms $6A$ and $5A$ (or $-5A$, if you like to think of addition) are called **like terms** because they involve the same variable. $6A$ and $4B$ are called **unlike terms.** Like terms can be simplified using the Distributive Property. Unlike terms cannot be simplified.

Example 3   Name the coefficients of w, x, y, and z in $4w - 3x + y - z$.

Solution   In naming coefficients, think of all terms as being added. For instance, instead of subtracting $3x$, think of adding $-3x$. The expression becomes $4w + -3x + y + -z$. The coefficient of w is 4 and the coefficient of x is -3. Since $y = 1 \cdot y$, the coefficient of y is 1. Since $-z = -1 \cdot z$, the coefficient of z is -1.

Example 4   Simplify $3x + 2y - 5x + 6y + 40$.

Solution   Because there are some like terms, you can simplify. First, change subtractions mentally to adding the opposite ($3x + 2y + -5x + 6y + 40$). Then reorder to have the like terms next to each other.

$$= 3x + -5x + 2y + 6y + 40$$
$$= (3 + -5)x + (2 + 6)y + 40$$
$$= \quad -2x \quad + \quad 8y \quad + 40$$

Check Substitute one number for x and a different number for y in the original expression. We use $x = 7$ and $y = 8$. Then the value of the original expression is

$$3 \cdot 7 + 2 \cdot 8 - 5 \cdot 7 + 6 \cdot 8 + 40$$
$$= 21 + 16 - 35 + 48 + 40$$
$$= 90.$$

The value of the answer $(-2x + 8y + 40)$ is $-2 \cdot 7 + 8 \cdot 8 + 40$, which is $-14 + 64 + 40$, which is 90. The two values are the same, so the answer checks.

Questions

Covering the Reading

1. Steve went to the graduating class bake sale. He bought 5 cookies for 20¢ each and 4 brownies at 30¢ each. How much did he spend?

2. Ashley went to the same bake sale as Steve in Question 1. But she did not know how many she wanted. What would it cost her for c cookies and b brownies?

3. Give an example of a linear expression using m and n.

4. Consider the expression $4r + 3s$.
   a. What is the coefficient of r?
   b. What is the coefficient of s?
   c. Simplify the expression.

5. Consider the expression $5t - 4m + 2t + q$.
   a. How many terms are in this expression?
   b. Name two like terms.
   c. Name two unlike terms.
   d. What is the coefficient of m?
   e. What is the coefficient of q?
   f. Simplify the expression.

In 6–9, simplify as much as you can. Check your answer.

6. $12a + 5a + 3b$

7. $-4x - y + y - 2$

8. $3t - 3a - a - t$

9. $-6 + 4v - 6 + -4v + v$

In 10–13, simplify if possible.

10. $3t + 6u + 9v$

11. $3t + 6t + 9$

12. $3 - 6t + 9$

13. $3t + 6u - 9u - 12t$

Applying the Mathematics

14. A decagon has six sides of length L and all other sides of length M. What is its perimeter?

15. Use the information from this lesson. A hamburger bun has about 200 calories.
  a. If a person eats 4 oz of hamburger, a bun, and 20 french fries, how many calories will have been taken in?
  b. If a person eats 4 oz of hamburger, a bun, and f french fries, how many calories will have been consumed?

16. At many schools, a grade of C is worth 2 points, B is worth 3 points, and A 4 points.
  a. If you have 6 courses with Cs, 8 with Bs, and 5 with As, how many total points do you have?
  b. If you have c courses with Cs, b with Bs, and a with As, how many total points do you have?

17. Give the value of $3x + 4y$ to the nearest integer when $x = 1/2$ and $y = 1/3$.

18. Simplify: $(a + 2b) + (3a + 4b) + (5a + 6b)$.

19. Simplify: $(3a + 5a)x$.

Review

20. Solve $14x = \frac{2}{7}$. *(Lesson 10-2)*

21. Write $0.2\overline{3}$ as a simple fraction. *(Lesson 12-2)*

22. Add $\frac{a}{2} + \frac{b}{2}$. *(Lesson 5-2)*

23. The box pictured below is open at the top. Find its surface area and volume. *(Lessons 9-2, 9-3)*

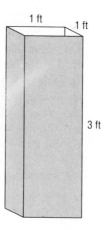

1 ft

1 ft

3 ft

24. Graph all solutions to $x + y = 7$. *(Lesson 8-3)*

25. A line m is perpendicular to the line n drawn here. Line m also contains point P. Trace n and P and draw m. *(Lesson 3-6)*

P

n

13. Multiply 732 by 999,999,999,999,999.

14. Betty bought three outfits. Each outfit consisted of a jacket costing $69.95, a skirt costing $40.75, and a blouse costing $15.50. How can she calculate the total cost with only one multiplication? What did she spend?

15. Phil, Gil, and Will each bought a turntable costing t dollars, an amplifier costing a dollars, and speakers costing s dollars. How much did they spend altogether?

16. Rosalie needs to paint three walls. Each wall is 8 feet high. The width of the first wall is 11 feet 3 inches. The width of the second wall is 7 feet 7 inches. The width of the third wall is 6 feet 2 inches. Altogether, how much area must be painted?

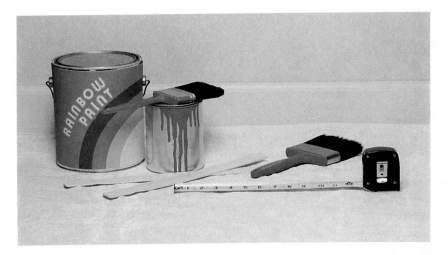

In 17 and 18, use the distributive property. Then simplify if possible.

17. $-2(3 + x) + 5(0.4x)$

18. $\frac{1}{3}(3m + n) + \frac{1}{3}(3m - n)$

19. $4x + 72 = 4(x + \underline{\ ?\ })$

20. $16x - 8y + 56 = 8(\underline{\ ?\ })$

21. Simplify $100m + 81m + 64$. *(Lesson 12-3)*

22. A pizza cost C dollars plus 50¢ for each additional ingredient. How much will a pizza with A additional ingredients cost? *(Lessons 12-3, 6-5)*

In 23–26, name the quadrilateral. *(Lesson 7-9)*

23. It has all sides the same length and all angles the same measure.

24. It has all sides the same length.

25. All its angles are the same measure.

26. It has two pairs of parallel sides.

27. When Jean walks to school, she has two routes. She can either walk along roads or take a shortcut through a field. The choices are pictured below.

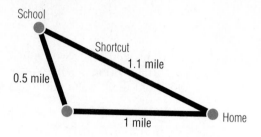

a. Walking along roads at 4 miles per hour, how long does it take her to get from home to school? *(Lesson 10-4)*
b. At this rate, how much time could she save by taking the shortcut? *(Lesson 7-3)*

28. A box with dimensions 20 cm, 15 cm, and 10 cm is filled with sand. 200 cubic centimeters of sand are removed.
a. What percent of the sand was removed? *(Lessons 9-3, 11-4)*
b. How much sand remains? *(Lesson 7-3)*

Exploration

29. Consider the pattern:

$$1 - (2 - 3) = 2$$
$$1 - (2 - (3 - 4)) = -2$$
$$1 - (2 - (3 - (4 - 5))) = 3.$$

Write the next two lines of this pattern.

30. One way to express the area of this figure is $(a + b)(c + d)$. What is another expression for the area?

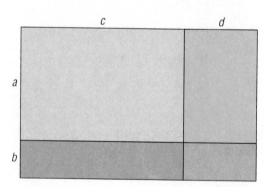

LESSON

12-5

Solving $ax + b = cx + d$

Finding Jamie's age is easy when you know how to solve an equation of the form $ax + b = cx + d$. See Example 3.

The Distributive Property can be applied to solve equations with the same variable on both sides.

Example 1   Solve $3x + 5 = 10x + 26$.

Solution   It takes only one step more to solve this equation than one of the form $ax + b = c$. That step is to add a quantity that will get rid of a variable on one side of the equation. Here we add -10x to both sides. It will get rid of the variable on the right side.

$$-10x + 3x + 5 = -10x + 10x + 26$$

Simplify.

$$-7x + 5 = 26$$

Now add -5 to both sides.

$$-7x + 5 + -5 = 26 + -5$$

Simplify.

$$-7x = 21$$

Multiply both sides by $-\frac{1}{7}$.

$$x = -3$$

Check   Substitute -3 for x every place it occurs in the original equation. Does $3 \cdot -3 + 5 = 10 \cdot -3 + 26$? Yes, both sides equal -4.

The equation in Example 2 is not solved for L because there is an L on the right side. The method of Example 1 also works to solve equations of this type.

Example 2   Solve $L = 15 - 4L$.

Solution   First add $4L$ to both sides.

$$L + 4L = 15 - 4L + 4L$$

Simplify.

$$5L = 15$$

Do in your head.

$$L = 3$$

Check   Does $3 = 15 - 4 \cdot 3$? Yes.

Example 3   In 8 years, Benjamin's sister Jamie will be 3 times as old as she is now. How old is she now?

Solution   Let J = Jamie's age now. Then 8 years from now she will be $J + 8$.

So $$J + 8 = 3J$$

Solve this equation. First add $-J$ to both sides.
$$-J + J + 8 = -J + 3J$$

Simplify. $$8 = 2J$$

Solve. $$4 = J$$

Benjamin's sister is 4 years old.

Check   If Jamie is 4 now, in 8 years she will be 12. That is 3 times her age now.

The next example combines a number of ideas from this and the last chapter.

Example 4   Solve: $$\frac{x - 2}{2} = \frac{x + 3}{4}.$$

Solution   First use the Means-Extremes Property.
$$4(x - 2) = 2(x + 3)$$

Now use the Distributive Property.
$$4x - 4 \cdot 2 = 2x + 2 \cdot 3$$
$$4x - 8 = 2x + 6$$

In this form the equation is easy to solve. Add $-2x$ to both sides.
$$-2x + 4x - 8 = -2x + 2x + 6$$
$$2x - 8 = 6$$

Add 8 to both sides and simplify.
$$2x = 14$$

Multiply both sides by $\frac{1}{2}$. $$x = 7$$

Check   Substitute. Does $\dfrac{7 - 2}{2} = \dfrac{7 + 3}{4}$?

Does $\dfrac{5}{2} = \dfrac{10}{4}$? Yes.

Questions

Covering the reading

1. To solve $s = 18 - 35s$, first add __?__ to both sides.

2. **a.** To solve $3x + 2 = 9x + 5$, what could you add to both sides to get rid of the variable on one side of the equation?
   b. Solve the equation in part **a**.

3. In fourteen years Jamie's brother will be three times as old as he is now. How old is Jamie's brother?

In 4–7, solve and check.

4. $4 - y = 6y - 8$

5. $2(n - 4) = 3n$

6. $\dfrac{t - 2}{4} = \dfrac{t - 6}{12}$

7. $0.6m + 5.4 = \text{-}1.3 + 2.6m$

Applying the Mathematics

8. Twice a number is 500 more than six times the number. What is the number?

9. Under rate plan 1 a new car costs $1000 down plus $200 per month. Under rate plan 2 the car costs $750 down and $250 per month.
   a. Write an expression for the amount paid after n months under plan 1.
   b. Write an expression for the amount paid after n months under plan 2.
   c. After how many months will the amount paid be the same for both plans?

In 10 and 11, solve and check.

10. $11p + 5(p - 1) = 9p - 12$

11. $\text{-}n + 4 - 5n + 6 = 21 + 3n$

12. In $\triangle PIN$, the measure of angle N is $4x + 36$. The measure of angle P is $10x$. If the measure of $\angle N$ equals the measure of $\angle P$, find the measures of all three angles in the triangle.

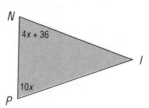

13. The formula for converting degrees Fahrenheit F to degrees Celsius C is $C = \frac{5}{9}(F - 32)$. Substitute an F for C in the formula and solve to find out what temperature reads the same in both systems.

14. Hasty Harry wrote the following solution to $5x - 1 = 2x + 8$. When he checked the answer, it didn't work.
a. In which step did Harry make a mistake?
b. What is the correct solution?

Step 1: $-2x + 5x - 1 = -2x + 2x + 8$
Step 2: $\qquad 3x - 1 = 0 + 8$
Step 3: $\qquad\quad 3x = 8 - 1$
Step 4: $\qquad\quad 3x = 7$
Step 5: $\qquad\quad\ \ x = \frac{7}{3}$

Review

15. Sixteen girls in the chorus each bought a blouse costing b dollars, a skirt costing s dollars, and a vest costing \$12. How much did they spend altogether? *(Lesson 12-4)*

16. What is the total area of these three rectangles? *(Lesson 12-1)*

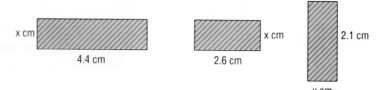

In 17–19, rewrite as a simple fraction in lowest terms. *(Lessons 2-7, 12-2)*

17. 0.92 **18.** $4.\overline{3}$ **19.** $6.\overline{36}$

20. Draw a cube. *(Lesson 3-8)*

21. Simplify: $1.3y + -4z - y - -2.7z + 8$. *(Lessons 7-2, 12-1)*

22. Graph all pairs of solutions to $x + y = 4$. *(Lesson 8-3)*

23. In 1988 there were approximately two million, one hundred sixty thousand farms in the United States. *(Lessons 1-1, 2-3)*
a. Write this number as a decimal.
b. Write this number in scientific notation.

24. Trace the figure below. What word results when the figure is reflected through the given line? *(Lesson 8-6)*

25. In 1930 there were about 295% as many farms as in 1988 (refer back to Question 23). About how many farms were there in the U.S. in 1930? *(Lesson 2-6)*

26. Paula wanted to solve $4x + 7 = 2x - 3$, but did not know the method of this lesson. She knew she wanted the value of the left side to equal the value of the right side. So she substituted a 2 for x to see what happened.

Left side   *Right side*
$4 \cdot 2 + 7 = 15$ $2 \cdot 2 - 3 = 1$

The left side was bigger than the right. Then Paula tried -10.

$4 \cdot -10 + 7 = -33$ $2 \cdot -10 - 3 = -23$

Now the right side was bigger than the left. She figured that the solution must be some number between -10 and 2.
a. Find the value that makes the two sides of the equation equal.
b. Use Paula's method to solve $5x - 7 = 3x + 9$.

12-6

Graphing Lines

The costs of mailing a first-class letter in 1988 are in the table below. At right, the pairs of numbers—the weight and cost—are graphed.

weight in ounces	cost in cents
1	25
2	45
3	65
4	85
5	105
6	125
7	145
8	165
9	185
10	205

Call the weight w and the cost c. The table shows a simple pattern connecting w and c. If you multiply w by 20 and add 5, you get c.

$$c = 20w + 5$$

You might say that it costs 5¢ to mail anything, and then add 20¢ for each ounce. For instance, suppose you want to mail some papers weighing 6.3 ounces. For the post office, the weight is 7 ounces. (Weights are rounded up to the next ounce.) So $w = 7$. Substituting in the formula:

$$c = 20 \cdot 7 + 5$$
$$c = 145.$$

This is in pennies. Dividing by 100 converts the pennies to dollars. The cost to mail these papers is $1.45. The table gives the same cost.

On page 556 are three ways to display postal rates: in a table, by a formula, and with a graph. The table is easiest to understand. The formula is shortest. The formula allows for values not in the table. Also, the formula can be used by a computer. The graph pictures the rates. It shows that they go up evenly. For a situation like this, the graph is not needed. But look at the graph below. The postal rates for 1965, 1975, and 1988 are compared. The picture displays the changes over time in a way that is easy to understand.

Postal rates
w = weight in ounces
c = cost in pennies

1965: $c = 5w$

1975: $c = 11w + 2$

1988: $c = 20w + 5$

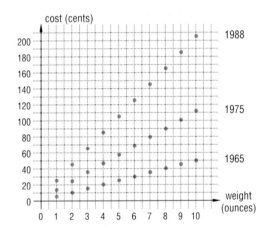

Each formula yields points on a line. The line $c = 5w$ is the lowest line. (The 1965 costs were lowest.)
The line $c = 11w + 2$ is in the middle.

The equation $c = 11w + 2$ is a **linear equation.** The name *linear* arose because its graph is a line. Below is another example of a linear equation. Notice that you may have to solve equations to find points on the line.

Example Graph the line with equation $2x - y = 8$.

Solution Pairs of values that work are needed.
When $x = 5$, then $2 \cdot 5 - y = 8$
Solve for y. $y = 2$
So $(5, 2)$ is on the line.

When $x = 0$, then $2 \cdot 0 - y = 8$.
Solve for y. $y = -8$
So $(0, -8)$ is on the line.

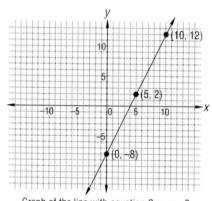

Graph of the line with equation $2x - y = 8$.

Two points determine the line. But find a third point to check.
When $x = 10$, $2 \cdot 10 - y = 8$.
Then $y = 12$.
So $(10, 12)$ is on the line.

Questions

Covering the Reading

In 1–4, use the first-class postal rates for 1988.

1. What formula relates the weight of a letter and the cost to mail it?

2. What is the cost of mailing a letter that weighs 6 ounces?

3. What is the cost of mailing a letter that weighs 2.4 ounces?

4. What letters cost 45¢ to mail?

5. Convert 185¢ to dollars.

6. What is a general rule for converting cents to dollars?

7. What is an advantage of displaying postal rates in a table?

8. What is an advantage of having a formula for postal rates?

9. What is an advantage of graphing postal rates?

In 10–14, use the first-class postal rates for 1965, 1975, and 1988.

10. What was the cost of mailing a 2-oz letter in 1965?

11. In 1965, what was the cost of mailing a letter weighing 9.2 oz?

12. You could mail a 3-oz letter in 1975 for what it cost to mail a ___?___-oz letter in 1965.

13. What is the lowest cost for mailing a letter in:
  a. 1965;
  b. 1975;
  c. 1988?

14. In 1975, by how much did the rate go up for each extra ounce of weight?

15. The line $2x - y = 8$ is graphed in this lesson. Give the coordinates of two points on this line that are not identified on the graph.

16. Find three points on the line $y = -3x + 5$. Graph this line.

17. Find three points on the line $2x - 3y = 12$. Graph this line.

18. *Multiple choice*   Which line could be the graph of $5x - y = 10$?
  (a) (b) (c) (d)

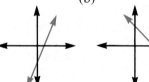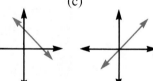

19. Today there are 400 packages of duplicating paper at the school. Each week about 12 packages are used.
  a. Make a table with two columns, "weeks from now" and "number of packages left."
  b. Graph six pairs of numbers in the table. Let w, the number of weeks, be graphed on the x-axis. L, the number of packages left, should be graphed on the y-axis.
  c. w and L are related by the equation $L = 400 - 12w$. Find the value of w when $L = 0$.
  d. What does this value mean?

20. a. Coordinates of points on what line are found by this program?

```
10 PRINT "X", "Y"
20 FOR X = 1 TO 10
30    Y = 11*X + 2
40    PRINT X, Y
50 NEXT X
60 END
```

b. Modify the program so that it will find 100 points on the line of Question 16.

Review

In 21–23, solve and check. *(Lessons 12-4, 12-5)*

21. $11 + 2y = 8y + 5$

22. $3(5n + 22) = 5n + 6 + 19n$

23. $\dfrac{x - 9}{2} = \dfrac{x + 4}{3}$

24. Alvin ate about $\frac{1}{4}$ of the tossed salad. Betty ate half of what was left. How much now remains? *(Lesson 9-8)*

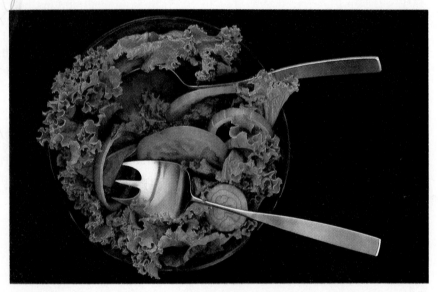

25. Diana gave P plants $\frac{1}{2}$ cup water each and Q plants $\frac{3}{4}$ cup water each. How much water did she use altogether? *(Lesson 12-3)*

26. A salesperson keeps a record of miles traveled for business. A car was driven 18,000 miles last year and 65% of this was for business. The salesperson gets 22¢ per mile traveled back from the company. How much should the salesperson get back from the company? *(Lessons 2-6, 10-4)*

27. Simplify: *(Lessons 5-5, 7-2, 10-5, 11-3)*
   a. -5 + -3   **b.** -5 − -3
   c. -5 · -3   **d.** $\frac{-5}{-3}$

28. Solve: $\dfrac{42}{5} = \dfrac{7x}{10}$. *(Lessons 11-5, 10-1)*

29. Use $\triangle BCD$. Find m$\angle BCD$. *(Lessons 7-7, 7-10)*

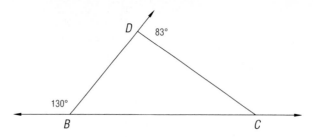

30. Consider the equation $y = |x|$.
  a. When $x = 5$, $y =$ __?__.
  b. When $x = -2$, $y =$ __?__.
  c. When $x = 0$, $y =$ __?__.
  d. The answers to **a, b,** and **c** give three points on the graph of $y = |x|$. Graph these points.
  e. Graph seven other points that satisfy $y = |x|$. Make sure you pick some negative values for x.
  f. The points do not lie on the same line. What figure do they form?

3(x+9) = 2(x+4)
3x + 27 = 2x+6
= 2x + 2x+8
1x + 27 + 27 = 8 + 27
= 35

$\frac{42}{6} = \frac{7x}{10}$

Summary

The main concern of this chapter is the Distributive Property and its applications. This property involves combining multiplication and addition (and subtraction). There are four main versions of the Distributive Property.

$(a + b)x = ax + bx$ $x(a + b) = xa + xb$
$(a - b)x = ax - bx$ $x(a - b) = xa - xb$

A repeating decimal x can be multiplied by a power of 10 so that the product has the same repetend. Then, when the two numbers are subtracted (using the distributive property), an equation of the form $ax = b$ results. Solving this equation for x gives the simple fraction for that repeating decimal.

The Distributive Property can be used to solve equations of the form $ax + b = cx + d$. After getting the variable terms all on one side of the equation, they can be combined. Then the equation is in a form you already know how to solve.

The linear expression $ax + by$ is a sum of multiples of different numbers. The points (x, y) that work in $ax + by = c$ lie on a line. These lines arise from the many situations that involve both addition and multiplication.

Vocabulary

You should be able to give a general description and a specific example for each of the following ideas.

Lesson 12-1
Distributive Property of Multiplication over
  Addition
Distributive Property of Multiplication over
  Subtraction
distributivity

Lesson 12-2
finite decimal, infinite decimal

Lesson 12-3
linear expression
terms, like terms, unlike terms
coefficient

Lesson 12-5
equation of the form $ax + b = cx + d$

Lesson 12-6
linear equation

Progress Self-Test

Take this test as you would take a test in class. Then check your work with the solutions in the Selected Answers section in the back of the book. You will need graph paper and ruler.

In 1–3, simplify.

1. $m - 3m$

2. $4x + 1 + 3x$

3. $7m + 2n + 4m + n$

4. Write the Distributive Property of Multiplication over Addition.

In 5–8, solve.

5. $1 - 9x = 13 + 3x$

6. $2(y - 3) = 12y$

7. $\dfrac{2t + 7}{4} = \dfrac{t - 8}{5}$

8. $0.2m + 6 = \text{-}m + 2 + 0.4m$

9. In 7 years Lee will be 1.5 times as old as he is now. How old is Lee?

10. A bookstore sells T books at \$3.95, F books at \$4.95, and V books at \$5.95. How much money is taken in from these sales?

11. Write the perimeter of the hexagon below in simplest form.

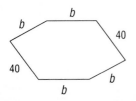

12. A hamburger has about 80 calories per ounce. A bun has about 180 calories. A typical french fry has about 11 calories. If you eat H 4-oz hamburgers with buns, and F french fries, how many total calories will you have eaten?

13. A point is on the line $5x - 2y = 10$. The first coordinate of this point is 3. What is the second coordinate?

14. Find three points on the line $y = 3x - 2$.

15. Graph the line with equation $x + 3y = 6$.

16. Write $0.\overline{81}$ as a simple fraction.

17. Write $1.02\overline{8}$ as a simple fraction.

18. Explain how the Distributive Property can be used to calculate $49 \cdot 7$ mentally.

19. The Distributive Property is used here in going from what line to what line?

Line 1 $ax + b = cx + d$
Line 2 $\text{-}cx + ax + b = \text{-}cx + cx + d$
Line 3 $\text{-}cx + ax + b = 0 + d$
Line 4 $(\text{-}c + a)x + b = 0 + d$
Line 5 $(\text{-}c + a)x + b = d$

20. Find the total area of these rectangles.

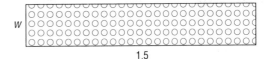

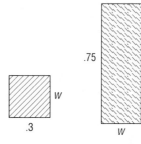

Chapter Review

Questions on **SPUR** Objectives

SPUR stands for **S**kills, **P**roperties, **U**ses, and **R**epresentations.
The Chapter Review questions are grouped according to the
SPUR Objectives for this chapter.

SKILLS deal with the procedures used to get answers.

■ **Objective A:** *Simplify linear expressions when possible, using distributivity.*
(Lessons 12-1, 12-3, 12-4)

1. Simplify $2v + 8v$.

2. Simplify $5x - x - 2x$.

3. Simplify $13a + 4b + 7a$.

4. Simplify $-9 + 5m + 2 - 3m + m$.

5. Simplify $-6r + 3t + {}^{-}8t + 7 + {}^{-}8r$.

6. Simplify $m(1 + n) - m$.

7. Multiply $6(a - b + 2c)$.

■ **Objective B:** *Convert repeating decimals to fractions. (Lesson 12-2)*

8. Find a simple fraction equal to $5.\overline{7}$.

9. Find a simple fraction equal to $0.89\overline{2}$.

10. Find a simple fraction equal to $6.\overline{54}$.

11. Find a simple fraction equal to $0.\overline{393}$.

■ **Objective C:** *Solve and check equations of the form $ax + b = cx + d$. (Lesson 12-5)*

12. Solve and check: $15x + 8 = 7x + 32$.

13. Solve and check:
$2 - 35m = 10m + 19 - 6m$.

14. Solve and check: $\dfrac{E - 9}{6} = \dfrac{3E + 5}{3}$.

15. Solve and check:
$7(y - 3) = 2y + 9 + 6y$.

PROPERTIES deal with the principles behind the mathematics.

■ **Objective D:** *Recognize and use the Distributive Property. (Lessons 12-1, 12-4)*

16. The Distributive Property is used here in going from what line to what other line?

Line 1	$3x - x$
Line 2	$= 3x - 1 \cdot x$
Line 3	$= (3 - 1)x$
Line 4	$= 2x$

17. Explain how the Distributive Property can be applied to calculate $\$19.95 \cdot 4$ mentally.

18. How can the Distributive Property be applied to simplify $5 \cdot 39 + 5 \cdot 39$?

USES deal with applications of mathematics in real situations.

▮ **Objective E:** *Translate real situations involving multiplication, addition, and subtraction into linear expressions and linear equations.*
(Lessons 12-3, 12-4, 12-5)

19. A tablespoon of butter has about 100 calories. A piece of white bread has about 70 calories. How many calories are there in T tablespoons of butter and P pieces of white bread?

20. Julie bought r records at $7.99 each and a record brush for $4.95. How much did she spend before tax?

21. E rows have 11 seats and T rows have 12 seats. How many seats are there altogether?

22. In 21 years Elijah will be 2.5 times as old as he is now. How old is he?

23. 5 more than $\frac{2}{3}$ a number is 4 more than $\frac{3}{4}$ the number. What is the number?

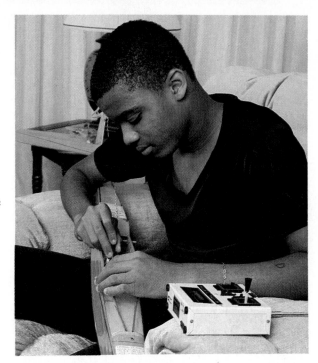

REPRESENTATIONS deal with pictures, graphs, or objects that illustrate concepts.

▮ **Objective F:** *Represent the Distributive Property by areas of rectangles.* *(Lessons 12-1, 12-4)*

24. What instance of the Distributive Property is pictured here?

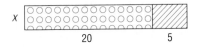

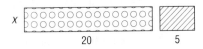

25. Using rectangles, show that $8.2 \cdot 13.6 + 9 \cdot 13.6 = (8.2 + 9) \, 13.6$.

▮ **Objective G:** *Graph solutions to linear equations.* *(Lesson 12-6)*

26. Find three points on the line with equation $y = 4x - 5$.

27. Find three points on the line with equation $2x + 5y = 10$.

28. Graph the line with equation $x - 2y = 11$.

29. Graph the line with equation $4x + 6y = 10$.

Measurement Formulas and Real Numbers

The figure below consists of a big circle, part of a smaller circle, and a right triangle. The bigger circle has center *B*. The smaller circle has center *M*. The portion of the smaller circle that is not part of the larger circle is called a *lune*. (It is the orange region.)

Which region has the greater perimeter, the lune or the triangle?

Which region has the greater area, the lune or the triangle?

These are hard questions. Even with an accurate drawing, you may not be able to answer them by just looking. In this chapter, you will learn how to calculate areas and perimeters of triangles, circles, and other figures. Along the way, you will meet some of the most famous numbers and formulas in all of mathematics.

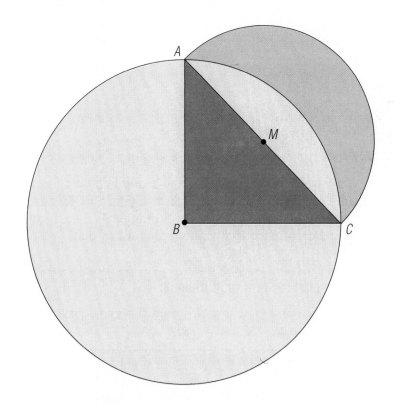

Area of a Right Triangle

A triangle is made up of only the three segments you see. A **triangular region** consists of a triangle and the space inside it. To be precise, we should talk about the area of a triangular region. But everyone talks about the area of a triangle.

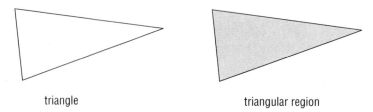

triangle   triangular region

In area, it is easy to see that every *right* triangle is half a rectangle.

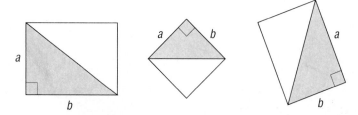

The two sides of a right triangle that help to form the right angle are called the **legs** of the right triangle. The legs in each picture above have lengths a and b. So the area of each rectangle is ab. The area of each right triangle is half of that.

Area formula for a right triangle:

Let A be the area of a right triangle with legs of lengths a and b. Then $A = \frac{1}{2} ab$.

The longest side of a right triangle is called its **hypotenuse.** In each right triangle above, the hypotenuse is a diagonal of the rectangle. You should ignore the hypotenuse when calculating area.

Example 1 Find the area of a right triangle with sides of lengths 3 cm, 4 cm, and 5 cm.

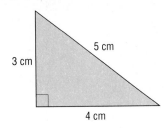

Solution The hypotenuse is the longest side. It has length 5 cm. So the legs have lengths 3 cm and 4 cm. Thus

$A = \frac{1}{2}ab$
$= \frac{1}{2} \cdot 3 \text{ cm} \cdot 4 \text{ cm}$
$= 6 \text{ cm}^2.$

By joining or cutting out right triangles, areas of more complicated figures can be found.

Example 2 A small garden is cut out of a larger garden as in the drawing. Both gardens are shaped like right triangles. What is the area of the shaded region that remains?

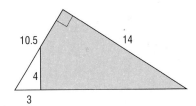

Solution The area of the large garden is $\frac{1}{2} \cdot 10.5 \cdot 14$, or 73.5.

The area of the small garden is 6, as found in Example 1. Take away the 6 from 73.5, and you have the area of the remaining region. The answer is 67.5.

In Example 2 no unit is named. You can assume then that the same unit applies to all lengths of sides. The area is still in square units. For instance, if the legs of the big garden are 10.5 feet and 14 feet, the area of the shaded region is 67.5 square feet. If the legs are 10.5 meters and 14 meters, the area of the shaded region is 67.5 square meters. Area is measured in square units even when the figures are not squares or rectangles.

1. What is the difference between a triangle and a triangular region?

2. Most precisely, people should talk about the area of a __?__. But people usually speak of the area of a __?__.

In 3–6, consider the right triangle with sides of lengths 9, 40, and 41.

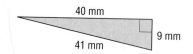

3. What are the lengths of the legs of this triangle?

4. What is the length of its hypotenuse?

5. What is its area?

6. What is its perimeter?

7. Repeat Question 3–6 for the right triangle ABC.

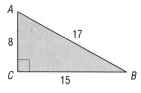
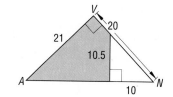

8. Find the area of the shaded region in the figure drawn above at right.

9. What is the area of a right triangle with legs of lengths *a* and *b*?

10. A tree is in the middle of a garden. Around the tree there is a square region where nothing will be planted. The dimensions of the garden are shown in the drawing below. How much area can be planted?

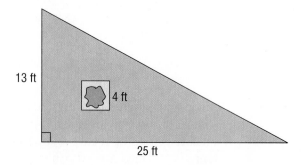

11. *RECT* is a rectangle with length 6 and height *h*.

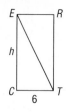

    a. What is the area of triangle *ECT*?
    b. What is the area of triangle *ERT*?

In 12 and 13, use the drawing of the flag of the Caribbean island Bonaire.

12. The dimensions of a real flag are to be 20″ by 30″. The bottom right triangle of the flag is blue. What is the area of the blue part?

13. The small right triangle is yellow. The sides of this triangle are 2/5 the length and width of the whole flag. What is the area of the yellow part?

14. Find the area of △*RST*.

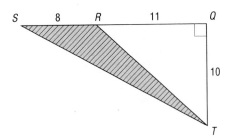

15. The area of a right triangle is 48 cm^2 and the length of one leg is 6 cm. What is the length of the other leg?

16. a. Draw a right triangle with legs of length 1″ and 2″.
    b. What is the area of this triangle?
    c. To the nearest eighth of an inch, measure the length of its hypotenuse.

17. Find the area of △*ELF*. *EA* = 8, *FA* = 6.4, *EL* = 6, and *EF* = 4.8.

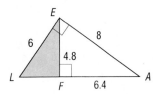

18. Simplify $\frac{1}{3} \cdot \frac{1}{3}$. *(Lesson 9-8)*

19. What is the volume of a cube with each edge of length 1/3 meter? *(Lessons 3-8, 9-8)*

20. What is the opposite of the reciprocal of 3/8? *(Lessons 1-5, 9-9)*

21. What simple fraction in lowest terms equals 0.41666666... (6 repeating)? *(Lesson 12-2)*

22. *Multiple choice* A drawing is put in a copy machine. The machine reduces dimensions of figures by 1/5. A copy is made of the copy. How will the dimensions of the second copy compare with the original?
(a) They will be 1/25 the size of the original.
(b) They will be 60% of the size of the original.
(c) They will be 64% of the size of the original.
(d) They will be 80% of the size of the original.
(Lessons 2-7, 9-7, 9-8)

23. Here are three instances of a pattern. Describe the general pattern using four variables. *(Lesson 4-2)*
$(40 + 13)(12 + 81) = 40 \cdot 12 + 40 \cdot 81 + 13 \cdot 12 + 13 \cdot 81$
$(6 + 3)(6 + \text{-}4) = 6 \cdot 6 + 6 \cdot \text{-}4 + 3 \cdot 6 + 3 \cdot \text{-}4$
$(30 + 5)(30 + 5) = 30 \cdot 30 + 30 \cdot 5 + 5 \cdot 30 + 5 \cdot 5$

24. Solve $11 - 5x = 511$. *(Lesson 10-9)*

25. Evaluate $a^2 + b^2$ when $a = 7$ and $b = 10$. *(Lessons 2-2, 4-4)*

26. The United States flag has 7 red stripes and 6 white ones. The stripes all have the same thickness. The upper left corner is blue with 50 white stars. Dimensions of a big flag are shown below.
a. What percent of the flag is red?
b. What percent of the flag is made up of white stripes?
c. What percent of the flag is blue with white stars?

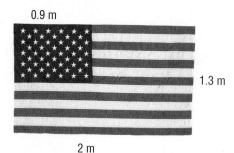

0.9 m

1.3 m

2 m

13-2

Square Roots

Here are two squares and their areas.

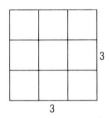
3
3

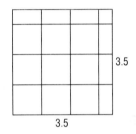
3.5
3.5

Area = 3 · 3 = 3² = 9   Area = 3.5 · 3.5 = 3.5² = 12.25

As you know, 9 is called the *square* of 3. We say that 3 is a **square root** of 9. Similarly, 12.25 is the square of 3.5 and we say that 3.5 is a square root of 12.25.

If $A = s^2$, then s is called a *square root* of A.

Since -3 · -3 = 9, (-3)² = 9. So -3 and 3 are both square roots of 9. *Every positive number has two square roots*. The two square roots are opposites of each other. The symbol for the positive square root is $\sqrt{}$, called the **radical sign**. We write $\sqrt{9} = 3$. The negative square root of 9 is $-\sqrt{9}$, or -3.

All scientific calculators have a square root key $\boxed{\sqrt{}}$. This key gives or estimates the positive square root of a number. For instance, enter 12.25 into your calculator and then press the square root key. You should see 3.5 displayed. This tells you that the square roots of 12.25 are 3.5 and -3.5.

Notice what happens when you use a calculator to try to find $\sqrt{2}$.

Key sequence: 2

Display:

The actual decimal for $\sqrt{2}$ is infinite and does not repeat. The number 1.4142136 is an estimate of $\sqrt{2}$. To check that 1.4142136 is a *good* estimate for $\sqrt{2}$, multiply it by itself. Our calculator shows that

$$1.4142136 \cdot 1.4142136 \approx 2.0000001$$

The negative square root of 2 is about -1.4142136.

It is easy to find a segment whose length is $\sqrt{2}$. The square below has area 2. (The four parts can be rearranged to fit 2 square units.) Let s be a side of this square. Then $s^2 = 2$. So $s = \sqrt{2}$.

Square roots of positive integers are either integers or infinite non-repeating decimals. If a square root is an integer, you should be able to find it without a calculator. If a square root is not an integer, then you should be able to estimate it without a calculator.

Example   Between what two whole numbers is $\sqrt{40}$?

Solution   Write down the squares of the whole numbers from 1 through 7.

$$1 \cdot 1 = 1$$
$$2 \cdot 2 = 4$$
$$3 \cdot 3 = 9$$
$$4 \cdot 4 = 16$$
$$5 \cdot 5 = 25$$
$$6 \cdot 6 = 36$$
$$7 \cdot 7 = 49$$

This indicates that $\sqrt{36} = 6$ and $\sqrt{49} = 7$. You know that $\sqrt{40}$ must be between $\sqrt{36}$ and $\sqrt{49}$. So $\sqrt{40}$ is between 6 and 7.

A better decimal approximation to $\sqrt{40}$ can be found without using a square root key. Beginning with 6.1, square the one-place decimals between 6 and 7. Stop as soon as you have a square greater than 40.

$$6.1 \cdot 6.1 = 37.21$$
$$6.2 \cdot 6.2 = 38.44$$
$$6.3 \cdot 6.3 = 39.69$$
$$6.4 \cdot 6.4 = 40.96$$

From this list, $\sqrt{39.69} = 6.3$ and $\sqrt{40.96} = 6.4$. So $\sqrt{40}$ must be between 6.3 and 6.4. By squaring decimals between 6.3 and 6.4 (not hard with a calculator), you can get a better decimal estimate to $\sqrt{40}$. However, anyone who needs to estimate square roots frequently should use a calculator with a $\sqrt{\ }$ key.

The idea of square root was known to the ancient Egyptians. The ancient Greeks discovered that square roots of many numbers cannot be simple fractions. The $\sqrt{\ }$ sign was invented in 1525 by the German mathematician Christoff Rudolff.

The bar of the radical sign is a grouping symbol. It is like parentheses. You must work under the bar before doing anything else. For example, to simplify

$$\sqrt{36 + 49},$$

you must add 36 and 49 first. Then take the square root.

$$\sqrt{36 + 49} = \sqrt{85} \approx 9.21954$$

Questions

Covering the Reading

1. Because $100 = 10 \cdot 10$, 10 is called a __?__ of 100.

2. When $A = s^2$, A is called the __?__ of s and s is called a __?__ of A.

3. $6.25 = 2.5 \cdot 2.5$. Which number is a square root of the other?

4. The two square roots of 9 are __?__ and __?__.

In 5–7, calculators are not allowed. Give the square roots of each number.

   5. 81   **6.** 4   **7.** 25

8. The $\sqrt{\ }$ sign is called the __?__ sign.

In 9–11, calculators are not allowed. Simplify.

   9. $\sqrt{64}$ **10.** $\sqrt{1}$ **11.** $-\sqrt{49}$

12. **a.** Approximate $\sqrt{300}$ using your calculator.
    b. How can you check that your approximation is correct?
    c. Round the approximation to the nearest hundredth.

13. Approximate $\sqrt{2}$ to the nearest thousandth.

14. *Multiple choice* The decimal for $\sqrt{2}$ is:
    (a) finite
    (b) infinite and repeating
    (c) infinite and nonrepeating.

15. The area of a square is 400 square meters.

Area
400 m²

a. Give the length of a side of the square.
b. What is the positive square root of 400?
c. Simplify: $-\sqrt{400}$.

16. A square has area 8. To the nearest tenth, what is the length of a side of the square?

In 17–22, simplify.

17. $\sqrt{25} + \sqrt{16}$　　**18.** $\sqrt{25} - \sqrt{16}$　　**19.** $\sqrt{25 + 16}$

20. $\sqrt{25} \cdot \sqrt{25}$　　**21.** $\sqrt{25 - 16}$　　**22.** $\sqrt{5^2 + 4^2}$

23. $\sqrt{50}$ is between what two whole numbers?

Applying the Mathematics

24. A side of a square has length $\sqrt{10}$. What is the area of the square?

25. Which is larger, $\sqrt{2}$ or 239/169?

26. The length of each side of the little squares below is 1 unit.

a. What is the area of the big tilted square?
b. What is the length of a side of this square?

In 27–30, use the table of numbers and squares at right. Do not use a calculator. According to the table:

27. What is a square root of 268.96?

28. $\sqrt{285.6}$ is about __?__.

29. $\sqrt{270}$ is between __?__ and __?__.

30. $\sqrt{250}$ is less than __?__.

Number	Square
16.0	256.00
16.1	259.21
16.2	262.44
16.3	265.69
16.4	268.96
16.5	272.25
16.6	275.56
16.7	278.89
16.8	282.24
16.9	285.61
17.0	289.00

31. A right triangle has sides of lengths 26 meters, 24 meters, and 10 meters. What is the area of the triangle? *(Lesson 13-1)*

32. Find the area of triangle *ABC*. *(Lesson 13-1)*

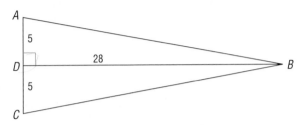

33. *Multiple choice*   Which line could be the graph of $2x - y = 4$? *(Lesson 8-3)*

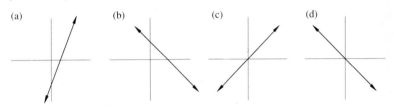

(a) (b) (c) (d)

34. Simplify: $3x + 4y + 5x + 6y + 7x + 8y$. *(Lesson 12-1)*

35. *Multiple choice*   An item costs *C* dollars. The price is reduced by *R* dollars. You buy the item at the reduced price and pay *T* dollars tax. How many dollars must you pay for the item?
(a) $R - C + T$ (b) $C - R + T$
(c) $C - R - T$ (d) $R - C - T$ *(Lessons 5-3, 7-2)*

36. a. Using your calculator, write down the square roots of the integers from 1 to 15.
   b. Verify that the product of $\sqrt{2}$ and $\sqrt{3}$ seems equal to $\sqrt{6}$.
   c. The product of $\sqrt{3}$ and $\sqrt{5}$ seems equal to what square root?
   d. Write the general pattern using variables.

37. To estimate $\sqrt{}$ with a computer, you can type in ?SQR( ).
   a. What does a computer print when ?SQR(150) is entered?
   b. You can do Question 36 with the help of the following program.

```
10 FOR N = 1 TO 15
20    PRINT N, SQR(N)
30 NEXT N
40 END
```

   Type and run this program.
   c. If you have only one square root to calculate, a calculator is faster than a computer. If you have to calculate the square roots of whole numbers from 1 to 1000, using the above program and a computer would be faster. Assuming you have both a calculator and a computer, how many square roots would you think you would have to calculate before you would use the computer?

13-3

The Pythagorean Theorem

The Pythagorean Theorem is a formula relating the lengths of the three sides of a right triangle. Here is the idea. Suppose a right triangle has legs of length 4 and 5. Such a triangle is pictured below. We want to find c, the length of the hypotenuse.

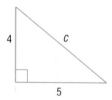

The idea is to form two squares by making copies of this triangle. Below the triangle is copied and rotated three times. This forms a large square with side 9 and a tilted square in the middle with side c.

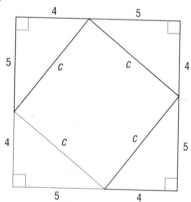

We find the length c by finding the area of the tilted square. The area of the big square is $9 \cdot 9$, or 81. The area of each corner right triangle is $1/2 \cdot 4 \cdot 5$, or 10. Cut off the four right triangles from the big square and you've cut off an area of 40. The remaining area, the area of the tilted square, is 41.

Since $c^2 = 41$, $c = \sqrt{41}$. The numbers 4, 5, and $\sqrt{41}$ are related in a simple but not obvious way.

$$4^2 + 5^2 = (\sqrt{41})^2$$

That is, add the squares of the two legs. The sum is the square of the hypotenuse. The Pythagorean Theorem is the general pattern. It is simple, surprising, and elegant.

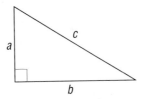

Pythagorean Theorem:

Let the legs of a right triangle have lengths a and b. Let the hypotenuse have length c. Then

$$a^2 + b^2 = c^2.$$

Example 1 What is the length of the hypotenuse of the right triangle drawn below?

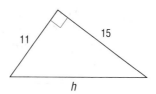

Solution To answer this question, use the formula of the Pythagorean Theorem. From the formula,

$$11^2 + 15^2 = h^2$$

So $121 + 225 = h^2$

$$346 = h^2$$

$h = \sqrt{346}$ or $-\sqrt{346}$. But we know h is positive.

So $h = \sqrt{346}$. A calculator shows that $\sqrt{346} \approx 18.60$.

Check Draw a right triangle with legs 11 and 15 units. Then measure the hypotenuse. It should be about 18.6 units.

When you know the lengths of *any* two sides of a right triangle, the Pythagorean Theorem can help get the length of the third side. Example 2 shows how to use this theorem to find lengths that cannot be measured.

Example 2   The bottom of a 12-foot ladder is 3 feet from a wall. How high up does the top of the ladder touch the wall?

Solution   First draw a picture.

According to the Pythagorean Theorem,

$$3^2 + x^2 = 12^2.$$

Now solve the equation.
First simplify. $9 + x^2 = 144$
Add -9 to both sides. $x^2 = 135$

Now, use the definition of square root.

$$x = \sqrt{135} \text{ or } -\sqrt{135}$$

But we know x cannot be negative. So

$$x = \sqrt{135}.$$

A calculator shows that $\sqrt{135} \approx 11.6$. This seems correct because the ladder must be less than 12 feet up on the wall.

A *theorem* is a statement that follows logically from other statements known or assumed to be true. The Pythagorean Theorem is the most famous theorem in all geometry. This theorem was known to the ancient Chinese and ancient Egyptians. But it gets its name from the Greek mathematician Pythagoras. Pythagoras was born about 572 B.C. He and his followers may have been the first people in the Western World to know that this amazing theorem is true for any right triangle.

Caution:
The Pythagorean Theorem only works for right triangles.
It does not work for any other triangles.

Questions

Covering the Reading

1. What is a theorem?

2. *Multiple choice*   Pythagoras was an ancient
(a) Chinese   (b) Greek   (c) Egyptian   (d) Babylonian

3. State the Pythagorean Theorem.

In 4 and 5, use the drawing below.

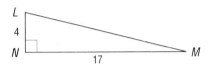

4. a. What relationship exists between 8, 9, and *y*?
   b. Find *y*.

5. a. What relationship exists between *x*, 8, and 10?
   b. Find *x*.

6.

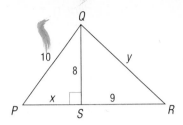

Lee had to find *LM* in the above triangle. She forgot the Pythagorean Theorem. Take Lee through steps which will lead her to find *LM*.
   a. Draw △*LMN*. Then draw three copies of the triangle which will form a large square and a tilted square in the middle.
   b. Find the area of the large square.
   c. Find the area of △*LMN*.
   d. Find the area of the tilted square in the middle.
   e. Find *LM*.

7. The bottom of a 3-meter ladder is 1 meter away from a wall. How high up on the wall will the ladder reach?

8. A right triangle has legs with lengths 6″ and 7″. Find the length of its hypotenuse, to the nearest tenth.

9. On what type of triangle can the Pythagorean Theorem be used?

10. *Multiple choice* On which of the following triangles can the Pythagorean Theorem be used?

(a)   (b)   (c)

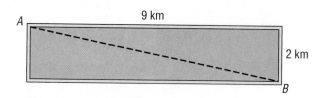

11. A farm is pictured below. It is 9 km long and 2 km wide. Danny wants to go from point *A* to point *B*.

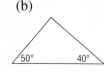

a. How long is the trip going along the roads that surround the farm?
b. How long is it by tractor directly through the farm?
c. How much shorter is it directly through the farm than going along the roads?

12. In the graph at left, point *C* has coordinates (1, 2). Point *D* has coordinates (3, 1). What is the distance between these points? (Hint: Use a right triangle with hypotenuse $\overline{CD}$.)

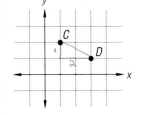

13. Typing paper is an 8.5″ by 11″ rectangle. Find the length of a diagonal of the rectangle:
a. by measuring with a ruler;
b. by using the Pythagorean Theorem.

14. *Multiple choice* There was no year 0. What year is 2500 years after the estimated year of Pythagoras' birth?
(a) 1928   (b) 1929   (c) 1972   (d) 2072

15. Simplify: $\sqrt{225 - 144}$. *(Lesson 13-2)*

16. Simplify: $\sqrt{2^2 + 3^2}$. *(Lesson 13-2)*

17. *True or false?* $\sqrt{9} + \sqrt{16} = \sqrt{25}$. *(Lesson 13-2)*

18. a. The square of what number is 0?
b. Simplify: $\sqrt{0}$. *(Lesson 13-2)*

19. To the nearest integer, what is 2.5^7? *(Lesson 2-2)*

20. Solve: $5000 = 50 + x - 25$. *(Lessons 5-8, 7-2)*

21. In the first 40 games of the baseball season, Homer had 31 hits. At this rate, how many hits will he have for the entire 125-game season? *(Lesson 11-2)*

22. *Multiple choice* $0 + (x + 1) = 0 + (1 + x)$ is an instance of what property? *(Lessons 5-4, 5-7)*
(a) Commutative Property of Addition
(b) Associative Property of Addition
(c) Addition Property of Zero
(d) Addition Property of One

23. At 35 miles per hour, how long will it take to go 10 miles? *(Lesson 11-5)*

Exploration

24. The Pythagoreans worshiped numbers and loved music. They discovered relationships between the lengths of strings and the musical tones they give.

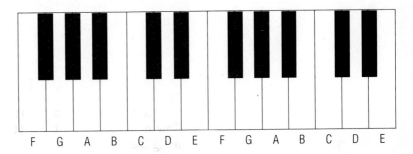

Look in an encyclopedia to find out one of the relationships discovered by the Pythagoreans.

Area of Any Triangle

If the proper information is given, you already know enough to get the area of any triangle.

∎ ▪ ▪ ▪ ▪ ▪ ▪ ▪

Example 1 Find the area of △ABC.

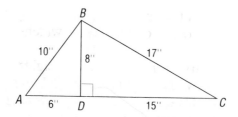

Solution Separate △ABC into the two right triangles ABD and BDC.

Area of △ABD = $\frac{1}{2} \cdot 6 \cdot 8$ square in.

Area of △BDC = $\frac{1}{2} \cdot 8 \cdot 15$ square in.

Add the areas to get the area of the big triangle ABC.

$$\text{Area of } \triangle ABC = \frac{1}{2} \cdot 6 \cdot 8 + \frac{1}{2} \cdot 8 \cdot 15$$
$$= \quad 24 \quad + \quad 60$$
$$= 84 \text{ square inches}$$

(The 10″ and 17″ lengths are not needed here for the area.)

By using the Distributive Property, this idea can be generalized. The result is a formula for the area of any triangle. Start with any triangle ABC.

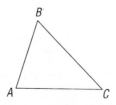

Draw the perpendicular segment from B to $\overline{AC}$. We call its length h, since it is the **height** of the triangle. This splits $\triangle ABC$ into two right triangles. It also splits $\overline{AC}$ into two segments with lengths we call x and y.

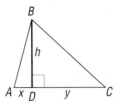

$$\text{Area of } \triangle ABC = \text{Area of } \triangle ABD + \text{Area of } \triangle BDC$$
$$= \tfrac{1}{2}hx + \tfrac{1}{2}hy$$

Now use the Distributive Property.

$$= \tfrac{1}{2}h(x + y)$$
$$= \tfrac{1}{2}h \cdot AC$$

Thus the area of this triangle is one-half times its height times the length of the side to which the height is drawn.

Every triangle has three heights. It depends to which side you draw the perpendicular. Below are three copies of $\triangle ABC$. The three heights are drawn with a heavy line. Also drawn are three rectangles. The area of the triangle is always one-half the area of the rectangle. That is, the area of the triangle is $\tfrac{1}{2}hb$.

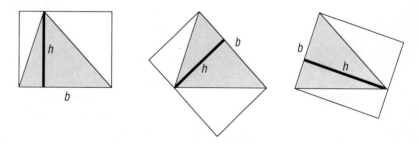

Another name for height is **altitude**. The side to which the altitude is drawn is called the **base** for that altitude. Using these words, the area of a triangle is half the product of any of its bases and the altitude to that base.

Area formula for any triangle:

Let b be the length of a side of a triangle with area A.
Let h be the length of the altitude drawn to that side.

$$\text{Then } A = \tfrac{1}{2}hb.$$

Example 2 $\overline{VY}$ is perpendicular to $\overline{XZ}$. Find the area of $\triangle XYZ$.

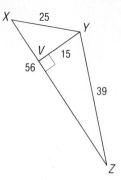

Solution   Think of $\overline{XZ}$ as the base of the triangle. Then $\overline{VY}$ is the altitude to that base.

$$\text{Area} = \frac{1}{2} \cdot hb$$
$$= \frac{1}{2} \cdot VY \cdot XZ$$
$$= 0.5 \cdot 15 \cdot 56$$
$$= 420$$

Questions

Covering the Reading

1. Find the area of $\triangle DEF$.   **2.** Find the area of $\triangle ABC$.

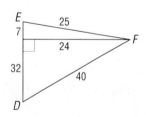

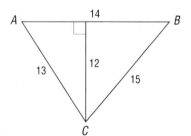

3. Trace $\triangle XYZ$.

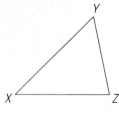

a. Draw the altitude from Y to side $\overline{XZ}$.
b. Draw the altitude from X to side $\overline{YZ}$.
c. Draw the altitude from Z to side $\overline{XY}$.

4. Give another name for: **a.** altitude; **b.** the side of a triangle to which the altitude is perpendicular.

5. Give a formula for the area of a triangle.

6. The squares in the grid below are 1 unit on a side. Find the area of $\triangle MNP$.

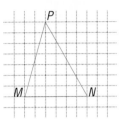

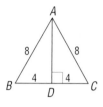

7. In an *equilateral* triangle, all sides have the same length. Drawn at left is equilateral triangle ABC with sides of length 8 cm.
  a. Find the length of the altitude $\overline{AD}$.
  b. Find the area of $\triangle ABC$.

8. The triangle below has a base with length 40 cm and an area of 300 cm². What is the length of the altitude to that base?

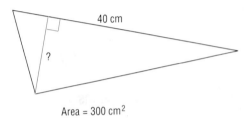

40 cm

?

Area = 300 cm²

9. Below is a photograph of two of the great pyramids of Giza in Egypt. Each face of the largest pyramid has a base about 230 meters long. The height of each face is about 92 meters. What is the area of a face?

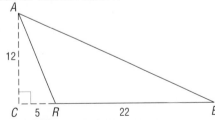

10. Find the area of $\triangle EAR$ below.

11. Evaluate $3x + 14x + 2x + x$ when $x = 5.671$. *(Lesson 12-1)*

12. Multiply $a(a + 2)$. *(Lesson 12-4)*

13. Solve: $x - 0.4 = 3.02$ *(Lesson 7-4)*

14. Round $\frac{440}{-6}$ to the nearest integer. *(Lessons 1-4, 11-3)*

15. Order from smallest to largest: $\sqrt{3}$, 3%, $0.\overline{3}$, $\frac{3}{10}$. *(Lessons 1-8, 2-5, 13-2)*

16. Add: $\frac{2}{5} + \frac{1}{3} + \frac{1}{4}$. *(Lesson 5-2)*

17. What is the value of $-4m$ when $m = -4$? *(Lessons 4-4, 10-5)*

18. Translate into English: 345.29. *(Lesson 1-2)*

19. Ignoring air resistance, it takes about $0.25\sqrt{s}$ seconds for an object to fall s feet. A dime is dropped from the top of the Sears Tower, 1454 feet above the ground. To the nearest second, about how long will it take the dime to reach the ground? *(Lesson 13-2)*

20. How many two-digit numbers satisfy both of the following conditions?
   (1) The first digit is 1, 3, 5, or 7.
   (2) The second digit is 2, 4, or 6. *(Lessons 6-1, 9-1)*

21. Find the simple fraction in lowest terms equal to $\dfrac{0.46}{9.2}$. *(Lesson 1-10)*

22. By drawing an altitude and measuring lengths, find the area of this triangle to the nearest square inch.

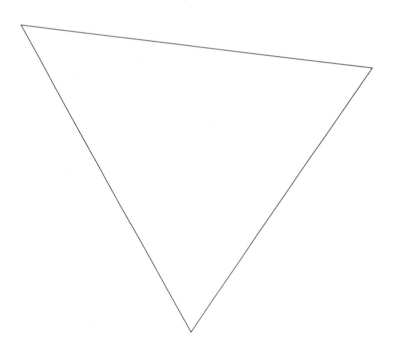

13-5

Areas of Polygons

Pentagon *ABCDE* is split into three triangles.

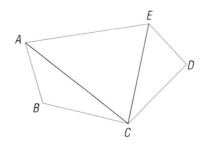

To find the area of *ABCDE*, you could add the areas of the triangles. This is one reason why you learned how to find the area of a triangle. *Any* polygon can be split into triangles.

If the triangles have the same altitude, then the areas can be added using the Distributive Property. A simple formula can be the result. Here is an example using a **trapezoid**. A trapezoid is a quadrilateral that has at least one pair of parallel sides.

Example Find the area of trapezoid *TRAP*.

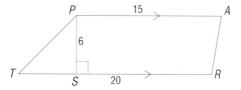

Solution Draw the diagonal $\overline{PR}$. This splits the trapezoid into two triangles, *PAR* and *PRT*. Each triangle has altitude 6.

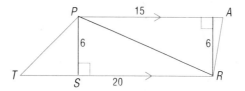

Area of trapezoid *TRAP* = Area of △*PAR* + Area of △*PRT*

$$= \quad \tfrac{1}{2} \cdot 6 \cdot 15 \quad + \quad \tfrac{1}{2} \cdot 6 \cdot 20$$
$$= \qquad 45 \qquad + \qquad 60$$
$$= \qquad\qquad 105$$

The parallel sides of a trapezoid are called its **bases**. The distance between the bases is the **height** or **altitude** of the trapezoid. The example shows that you only need the lengths of the bases and the height to find the area of a trapezoid.

To find a general formula, replace the specific lengths with variables. Let the bases have lengths b and B. Let the height be h.

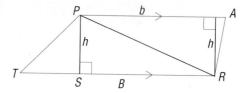

Area of trapezoid $TRAP$ = Area of $\triangle PAR$ + Area of $\triangle PRT$

$$= \tfrac{1}{2} \cdot h \cdot b + \tfrac{1}{2} \cdot h \cdot B$$

Now use the Distributive Property. The following formula is the result.

Area formula for a trapezoid:

Let A be the area of a trapezoid with bases B and b and height h. Then
$$A = \tfrac{1}{2} \cdot h(b + B).$$

Some people prefer the formula in words.

The area of a trapezoid is one-half the product of its height and the sum of the lengths of its bases.

Trapezoids come in many different sizes and shapes. Here are some trapezoids with bases drawn darker. Heights are dotted. In the trapezoid at right, the trapezoid is quite slanted. So one base has to be extended to meet the height.

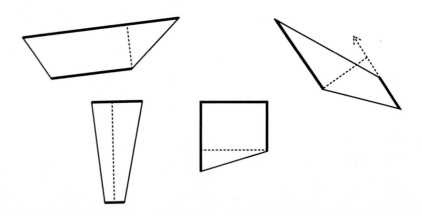

Rectangles, squares, rhombuses, and parallelograms have parallel sides. So they are trapezoids. This makes trapezoids important. Whatever is true for all trapezoids is true for all rectangles, squares, rhombuses, and parallelograms. The area formula for a trapezoid works for all these other figures also.

There is no general formula that works for the area of all polygons.

Questions

Covering the Reading

1. Why is the area formula for a triangle so important?

2. How can you tell if a figure is a trapezoid?

In 3–7, *true or false*.

3. All quadrilaterals are trapezoids.

4. All squares are trapezoids.

5. All trapezoids are rectangles.

6. The formula for the area of a trapezoid can be used to find the area of a parallelogram.

7. There is a formula for the area of any polygon.

8. Use the trapezoid below.

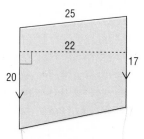

a. Give the lengths of its bases.
b. Give its height.
c. Give its area.

9. a. Draw a trapezoid with bases of length 4 cm and 5 cm and a height of 2 cm.
b. Find the area of this trapezoid.

10. A trapezoid has bases b and B and height h. What is its area?

11. In words, state the formula for the area of a trapezoid.

12. Draw a trapezoid with exactly two sides of equal length.

13. Find the area of the parallelogram drawn below.

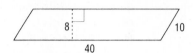

14. The shape of Egypt roughly approximates a trapezoid. The north edge of Egypt is about 900 km long, the south edge about 1100 km long, and the height is about 1100 km. What is the approximate area of Egypt?

15. A trapezoid has area 60 square meters. Its height is 10 square meters. One of the bases has length 5 meters. What is the length of the other base?

16. Order these seven terms from most general to most specific.
polygon   square   trapezoid   figure
rectangle   quadrilateral   parallelogram

17. Draw an altitude of trapezoid *ABCD*.

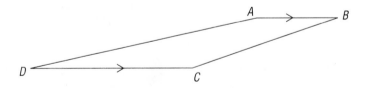

18. The diagonal of a rectangle is drawn. This splits the rectangle into two right triangles. *True or false:* The perimeter of each right triangle is one-half the perimeter of the rectangle. *(Lesson 5-10)*

19. Find the area of a right triangle with sides of lengths 12 ft, 16 ft, and 20 ft. *(Lesson 13-1)*

20. Find the length of the hypotenuse of △*ABC* below. *(Lesson 13-3)*

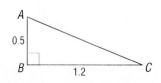

21. *True or false?* $\sqrt{\frac{1}{2}} > \frac{1}{2}$. *(Lesson 13-2)*

22. Solve: $2t + 5 = 9 + 8t$. *(Lesson 12-5)*

23. Solve: $3(2u - 5) = 27$. *(Lessons 10-9, 12-5)*

24. To the nearest integer, what is the sum of the mixed numbers $2\frac{1}{3}$, $3\frac{1}{4}$, and $4\frac{1}{5}$? *(Lesson 5-2)*

25. Two-thirds of an amount of cloth was used. The starting amount was A. How much is left? *(Lesson 10-3)*

26. Find the simple fraction equal to $8.\overline{2}$. *(Lesson 12-2)*

Exploration

27. Words often have many meanings. Sometimes those meanings do not agree with each other. One of the meanings of trapezoid is "trapezium."
a. Look in a dictionary to find another meaning of "trapezium."
b. Draw a trapezium.

The Number π

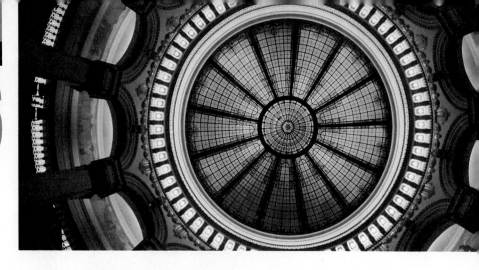

Suppose you put a tape measure around your waist. Then you can measure the perimeter of your waist. You can do this even though your waist is curved.

The same idea works for circles. The perimeter of a circle can be measured. It is the distance around the circle, the distance you would travel if you walked around the circle.

A **circle** is the set of points at a certain distance (its **radius**) from a certain point (its **center**). The distance across the circle is twice the length of its radius. That distance is the circle's **diameter**.

The plural of radius is *radii*. Both radii and diameters may be segments or distances. The circle at left below has center C. One radius of the circle is $\overline{CD}$. The radius of this circle is 5. One diameter of the circle is $\overline{DE}$. The diameter is 10.

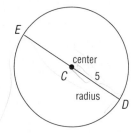

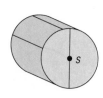

The top of the tin can pictured at right is a circle with diameter s. Think of the distance around this circle. (It is how far an electric can opener turns in opening the can.) The amount needed can be estimated by unraveling the circle. We draw the circle with different thicknesses so you can see the unraveling.

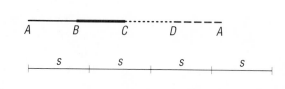

The unraveled circle is not 4 times the length of the diameter. It is just a little more than 3 times the diameter, as the picture shows. In fact, the unraveled length, called the **circumference** of the circle, is exactly 3.1415926535... times the diameter. You have seen this number before. It is called π (pi) and its decimal never repeats or ends.

The circumference of a circle is the circle's perimeter. Don't be fooled just because the word is long and different.

In a circle, the diameter d and circumference C are related by the formula $C = \pi d$.

■ ■ ■ ■ ■ ■ ■ ■ ■

Example To the nearest inch, what is the circumference of a tin can with a 4″ diameter?

4 in.

Solution $C = \pi \cdot 4 = 4\pi$ inches exactly.
To approximate C to the nearest inch, use 3.14 for π.
$C \approx 3.14 \cdot 4 = 12.56$ inches, so C is about 13″.

The number π is so important that scientific calculators almost always have a $\boxed{\pi}$ key. Pressing that key will give you many decimal places of π. Without a calculator, people use various approximations. For rough estimates, you can use 3.14 or $\frac{22}{7}$. Use more decimal places if you want more accuracy.

Because $C = \pi d$, $\pi = \dfrac{C}{d}$. That is, π is the ratio of the circumference of a circle to its diameter. $\dfrac{C}{d}$ looks like a simple fraction. However, the numbers C and d cannot both be whole numbers and still have the ratio equal π.

A number that *can* be written as a simple fraction is called a **rational number.** Finite decimals, repeating decimals, and mixed numbers all represent rational numbers. A number that *cannot* be written as a simple fraction is called an **irrational number**. Irrational numbers are exactly those numbers whose decimals are infinite and do not repeat. When the square root of a positive integer, like $\sqrt{2}$, is not an integer, then it is irrational.

Irrational numbers are very important in many measurement formulas. Square roots often appear as lengths of sides of right triangles. With circles, all formulas for area and circumference involve π. As you study more mathematics, you will learn about many other irrational numbers.

A number that can be written as a decimal is called a **real number**. All of the numbers discussed in this book have been real numbers. (There are other numbers. You will learn about them in future mathematics courses.) Every real number is either rational or irrational. The chart shows how various kinds of numbers are related.

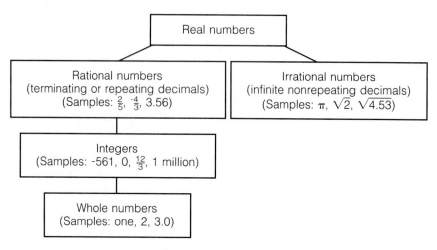

Questions

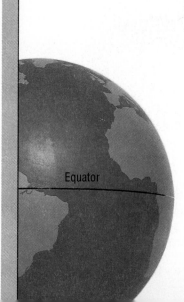

Equator

1. What is a circle?

2. The distance across a circle at its center is called the __?__ of the circle.

3. The perimeter of a circle is called the __?__ of the circle.

4. A circle has diameter 10 cm. To the nearest cm, what is its circumference?

5. The circumference of a circle with diameter s is __?__.

6. A simple fraction that is used as an approximation to π is __?__.

7. A calculator shows π to be 3.141592654.
   a. Is this an exact value or an estimate?
   b. Round this number to the nearest hundredth.
   c. Round this number to the nearest hundred thousandth.
   d. What does your calculator show for π?

8. The equator of the earth is approximately a circle whose diameter is about 7920 miles. What is the distance around the earth at its equator?

9. Name the two division facts related to $C = \pi d$. $\pi = \frac{C}{d}$ $d = \frac{C}{\pi}$

10. When is a number rational? *simple fraction*

11. When is a number irrational?

In 12–17, tell whether the number is rational or irrational.

12. $\frac{2}{3}$ **13.** π **14.** $6.\overline{87}$

15. $\sqrt{5}$ **16.** $5\frac{1}{2}$ **17.** 0.0004

18. What is a real number?

19. Which of the numbers of Questions 12–17 are real numbers? *all*

20. Are there any numbers that are not real numbers? *yes*

Applying the Mathematics

0.6"

In 21–22, use the fact that the diameter of a circle is twice its radius.

21. The circle at left has radius 0.6″. What is its circumference? 1.2π

22. A circle has radius r. What is its exact circumference? $2r\pi$

23. To protect a city from attack, fortifications are built in the shape of a circle. The center of the circle is the center of the city. The radius of the circle is 12 miles. What is the length of the fortifications? *75*

24. A plastic tube 50″ long is bent to make a hoop. To the nearest inch, what is the diameter of the hoop? *16 in*

25. Some bicycle wheels are 24″ in diameter. How far will the bike go if the wheels turn 10 revolutions? *754 in*

26. The number $\frac{355}{113}$ is a good estimate for π. Which is a better approximation to π, $\frac{355}{113}$ or $\frac{22}{7}$? $\frac{365}{113}$

27. Which is larger, π or $\sqrt{10}$?

28. Approximate $\pi + 1$ to the nearest tenth. *4.1*

29. Each side of polygon *ABCD* has exactly one point in common with circle *O*. The radius of that circle to that point is perpendicular to the side. If the radius is 6, what is the area of *ABCD*? (Hint: Split the area into triangles *OAB*, *OBC*, *OCD*, *ODA*.)

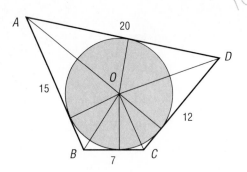

Review

30. What is the perimeter of the quadrilateral *ABCD* of Question 29? *(Lesson 5-10)*

31. Simplify $\sqrt{841} - \sqrt{400}$. *(Lesson 13-2)*

32. Find the area of the trapezoid below. *(Lessons 13-3, 13-5)*

33. Evaluate $5\sqrt{3}$ to the nearest integer. *(Lesson 13-2)*

34. Evaluate $|2 - n|$ when $n = 5$. *(Lesson 5-5)*

35. Evaluate $9x^3 - 7x^2 + 12$ when $x = 6$. *(Lesson 4-4)*

36. Olivia biked *m* miles at 20 miles per hour. How many hours did it take her to do this? *(Lessons 6-7, 11-5)*

37. 6% of what number is 30? *(Lesson 10-3)*

38. 6 is what percent of 30? *(Lesson 11-4)*

39. The Greek mathematician Archimedes knew that π was between $3\frac{1}{7}$ and $3\frac{10}{71}$. (Archimedes lived from about 287 B.C. to 212 B.C. and was one of the greatest mathematicians of all time.)

  a. Calculate the decimal equivalents of these mixed numbers.

  b. Why didn't Archimedes have a decimal equivalent for π?

  c. How old was Archimedes when he died?

  d. What were the sad circumstances that led to the death of this famous man? (Use references from your school library.)

40. a. Run this program, putting a large number in the blank.

```
10 SUM = 0
20 FOR N = 1 TO ____
30    TERM = 1/(N*N)
40    SUM = SUM + TERM
50    NEARPI = SQR(6*SUM)
60    PRINT N, NEARPI
70 NEXT N
80 END
```

Write down the last line the computer prints.

  b. What does the program do?

  c. Try a larger number in the blank and see what happens.

13-7

Circles and Sectors

All formulas for area or volume of circles and spheres involve the number π. The most famous of these is for the area of a circle.

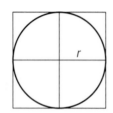

At left are four little squares, each with side r. So their total area is $4r^2$. This shows that the area of the circle is less than $4r^2$. But it does not show the exact area of the circle. To figure that out requires more advanced mathematics. But it does seem that the area of the circle equals a little more than 3 of the 4 squares. In fact, the area equals 3.14159... of the squares.

Area formula for a circle:

Let A be the area of a circle with radius r.
Then $A = \pi r^2$.

Example 1   Find the area of a circle with a radius of 5 inches, to the nearest square inch.

Solution $A = \pi \cdot (5 \text{ in.})^2 = 25\pi \text{ in.}^2$
$$\approx 25 \cdot 3.1416 \text{ in.}^2$$
$$\approx 78.54 \text{ in.}^2$$
$$\approx 79 \text{ in.}^2$$

Check   Notice that a square with side 10″ would cover the circle. The area of the square is 100 square inches. So an area of about 79 square inches for the circle seems about right.

10 inches

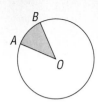

In the figure at left, angle *AOB* is called a *central angle* of circle *O*. A **central angle** is an angle with its vertex at the center. The part of the circle that looks like a slice of pie is called a **sector.**

The area of a sector depends on the size of the central angle.

Example 2 Below a sector is pictured. Angle *VCR* is a right angle. *VC* = 8. Find the area of the sector.

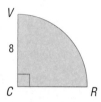

Solution A right angle has measure 90°. This is $\frac{90}{360}$, or $\frac{1}{4}$ of a revolution. So the sector has $\frac{1}{4}$ the area of the circle.
$A = \frac{1}{4} \cdot \pi \cdot 8^2 = 16\pi$

Check Notice that $16\pi \approx 16 \cdot 3.14 \approx 50$. A square with sides $\overline{VC}$ and $\overline{CR}$ has area 64. This is larger than the area of the sector, as it should be.

Example 3 Consider the figure below. *AG* = 1 cm. The measure of angle *BAG* is 45°. Find the area of sector *BAG*.

Solution 45 degrees is 45/360 = 1/8 of a revolution. The area of circle *A* is $\pi \cdot 1^2 = \pi$ cm². So the area of sector *BAG* is $\frac{1}{8}$ of π or approximately 0.4 cm².

The area of a sector of a circle is generalized in this formula.

Area formula for a sector:

Let *A* be the area of a sector of a circle with radius *r*. Let *m* be the measure of the central angle of the sector in degrees. Then $A = \frac{m}{360} \cdot \pi r^2$.

Questions

1. What is the area of a square with side length 8?

2. What is the area of a circle with radius r?

3. To the nearest integer, what is the area of a circle with radius 4?

4. Without calculating, how can you know that the answer to Question 3 must be less than the answer to Question 1?

5. What is the area of one half of a circle with radius 6?

6. What is a central angle of a circle?

In 7–10, use the figure at right.

7. What is the name of this figure?

8. What is the measure of angle *GHI*?

9. What part of a circle is pictured?

10. If *HI* = 10, what is the area of this figure?

11. A quarter has radius 12.15 mm. What is the area of one of its faces?

12. What calculator key sequence will give you an estimate to the area of a circle with radius 50?

13. A central angle of a sector has measure 50°. If the area of the circle is 180 square meters, what is the area of the sector?

14. Assume that the smaller circle at left has radius 0.5 inches, and the larger circle has radius 0.75 inches.
a. What is the area of the ring?
b. Which has more area, the smaller circle or the shaded ring?

15. Clyde decided to plant a circular flower garden. He wanted equal-sized plots of ground for each of three flower types. Below is his landscape plan.

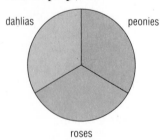

a. What is the measure of the central angle of each sector of Clyde's garden?
b. If the diameter of the garden is to be 14 feet, what is the area of each sector of the garden?

602

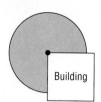

Building

16. Lisa read that there were about 10 calories per square inch of a 12-inch diameter cheese pizza. If she ate $\frac{1}{8}$ of a pizza, about how many calories would she consume?

17. A dog is on a leash tied to the corner of a building. This enables the dog to travel in a sector of the circle, as shown at left. If the leash is 9 meters long, what is the area of land on which the dog may roam?

Review

18. To the nearest tenth of an inch, find the circumferences of the two circles in Question 14. *(Lesson 13-6)*

19. The hypotenuse of a right triangle has length 50. One leg has length 14. What is the length of the other leg? *(Lesson 13-3)*

20. Find the area of $\triangle NOW$. *(Lesson 13-4)*

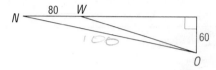

21. When does a decimal represent an irrational number? *(Lesson 13-6)*

22. A plant called the lichen grows 0.01 inch in a year. How many inches will it grow in a century? *(Lesson 10-4)*

23. The triangles below are similar and tilted the same way. Find *PR*. *(Lesson 11-7)*

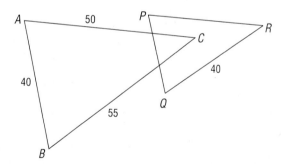

24. Simplify: $5(x - y + 12) + 6(y + x - 8)$. *(Lessons 12-3, 12-4)*

Exploration

25. Take two pieces of string of equal length. Form the first string into a circle. Form the second string into a square.
   a. Which figure has the greater area?
   b. Does the answer to part **a** depend on the length of the string?

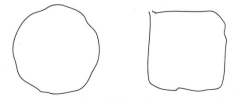

13-8

Circle Graphs

Sectors of circles are commonly found in **pie** or **circle graphs**. A circle graph pictures a whole quantity that has been split up. For example, suppose 80 students were asked to choose one dessert at a carnival. At left this information is given in a table. At right the same information is displayed in a circle graph.

Choice	Number of Students Picking that Choice
Ice Cream	40
Popcorn	20
Fruit	15
None	5

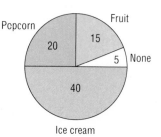

Here is how the circle graph is made.

$\frac{40}{80}$ of the students picked ice cream. This is $\frac{1}{2}$ of the students. So the sector for ice cream is half a circle, a **semicircle**.

Popcorn was picked by $\frac{20}{80}$ or $\frac{1}{4}$ of the students. So the sector for popcorn is $\frac{1}{4}$ of the circle.

Fruit was picked by 15/80 of the students. Since a revolution is 360°, $\frac{15}{80} \cdot 360°$ is the measure of the central angle of the fruit sector. That turns out to be 67.5°.

No dessert was picked by $\frac{5}{80}$ of the students. The sector for "none" has a central angle of magnitude $\frac{5}{80} \cdot 360°$. That is 22.5°.

■ ■ ■ ■ ■ ■ ■ ■ ■

Example The top six wheat producing countries in 1985 were the U.S.S.R., the U.S., China, India, Canada, and France. The chart below at left lists estimated production for each of these countries in millions of bushels. Make a circle graph to display this information.

Solution First find the total production. This is 330 million bushels. Now find what part of the total each country produced. Just divide 330 into the country's production. This is recorded in the table below at right in the column labeled $\frac{w}{330}$, where w stands for a country's wheat production.

1985 Leading wheat producers	
China	85
U.S.S.R	80
U.S.	65
India	45
France	30
Canada	25
Total	330

Country	$\frac{w}{330}$	$\frac{w}{330} \cdot 360°$
China	.26	94°
U.S.S.R.	.24	87°
U.S.	.20	72°
India	.14	50°
France	.09	32°
Canada	.07	25°

Finally, calculate the central angle of the sector for each country. This is simply the fraction in the second column times 360°. These results are recorded in the last column of the table on the right above.

The last step is to draw a circle and sectors with central angles equal to those calculated.

1985 Leading wheat producers

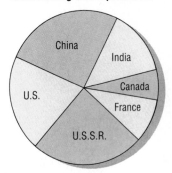

Check There are two things you can do to check your work. First, add all the fractions in the $\frac{w}{330}$ column. The sum should be very near 1. Since .26 + .24 + .20 + .14 + .09 + .07 = 1.00, the sum checks.

Next, add all the central angles in the $\frac{w}{330} \cdot 360°$ column.

The sum should be 360°, the number of degrees in a revolution. 94° + 87° + 72° + 50° + 32° + 25° = 360°, so this checks too.

The first circle graphs were done by William Playfair in the late 1700s. Today circle graphs are found in many newspapers and magazines. There is software for most computers that will automatically construct circle graphs.

Questions

Covering the Reading

1. Who drew the first circle graphs, and when?

2. What is another name for circle graph?

3. The central angle of a semicircle measures ___?___. *180*

In 4 and 5, use the circle graph of dessert choices.

4. The total number of people choosing to have dessert is ___?___. *75*

5. What fraction of people wanted popcorn?

Applying the Mathematics

In 6 and 7, use the circle graph of wheat production.

6. Which country produced more wheat, Canada or India?

7. What fraction of wheat was produced in the United States?

8. *True or false* The sum of the central angles of all sectors in a circle graph could be 390°.

In 9–12, use the circle graph at left. It shows how many days the Williams family spent on their recent vacation in four states.

9. a. What percent of the time did they spend in Utah? *20*
   b. What is the measure of the central angle for the Utah sector? *72*

10. Give the measure of the central angle for the Colorado sector. *108*

11. Give the measure of the central angle for the Wyoming sector. *144*

12. *True or false* The Colorado sector has 3 times as much area as the Montana sector.

13. From the circle graph below:
   a. Which age bracket has the fewest people?
   b. Which age bracket has the most people?
   c. Which age is missing?
   d. How many people are between the ages of 6 and 19?

Utah 2 days
Colorado 3 days
Montana 1 day
Wyoming 4 days

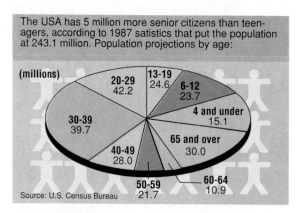

The USA has 5 million more senior citizens than teenagers, according to 1987 satistics that put the population at 243.1 million. Population projections by age:

(millions)
20-29 42.2
13-19 24.6
6-12 23.7
4 and under 15.1
30-39 39.7
65 and over 30.0
40-49 28.0
60-64 10.9
50-59 21.7
Source: U.S. Census Bureau

14. For their elective course, the students at Pumpkin Junction High School signed up as follows: 20 took Music, 10 took Woodshop, 5 took Drawing, and 15 took Typing.

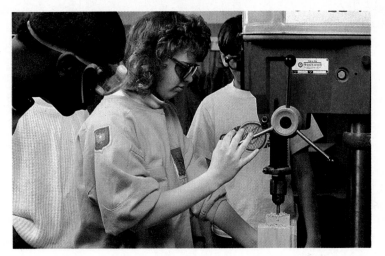

a. What percent of students took Typing?

b. What is the fraction of students who took either Music or Drawing?

c. Make a circle graph to display the given information.

Review

15. In the middle of a circular fountain 30 feet in diameter is a square structure supporting a statue. A side of the square is 3.5 feet. What is the surface area of the water around the structure? *(Lesson 13-7)*

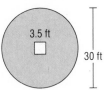

16. *Multiple choice* Which proportion is *not* true? *(Lessons 11-5, 12-5)*

(a) $\frac{2}{15} = \frac{6}{45}$ (b) $\frac{x-4}{2} = \frac{3x-12}{6}$ (c) $\frac{75}{8} = \frac{4}{.32}$

17. Solve $3.5x + 4 = 9x - 1$. *(Lesson 12-4)*

In 18 and 19, use the figure below.

18. If $LB = .5''$ and $LI = 1''$, find IB. *(Lesson 13-3)*

19. If $LB = .5''$, $GL = .5''$ and $IL = 1.5''$, find the area of $\triangle GIB$. *(Lesson 13-4)*

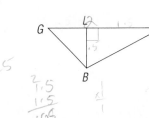

20. The distance from the earth to the moon averages about two hundred thirty-nine thousand miles. Write this number in scientific notation. *(Lessons 1-1, 2-3)*

In 21 and 22, simplify. *(Lessons 12-1, 12-4)*

21. 3(5m + 6t − 4)

22. 8.7(4.2 − r) + r

23. What is the result of a -23° turn followed by a 14° turn? *(Lesson 5-5)*

24. Approximate $4\pi(2)^2$ to the nearest tenth. *(Lesson 13-6)*

25. George Polya died in September of 1985. He was born in December of 1887.
a. How old was he when he died? *(Lesson 7-1)*
b. What are his four steps to successful problem solving? *(Lesson 6-1)*

Exploration

26. Find a circle graph in a newspaper or magazine or make one up yourself. Bring the graph to class.

27. There is software that enables a computer to display a circle graph on a monitor. If you have access to a computer, find the name of such software. If the software is available, use it to draw the circle graph on the first page of this lesson.

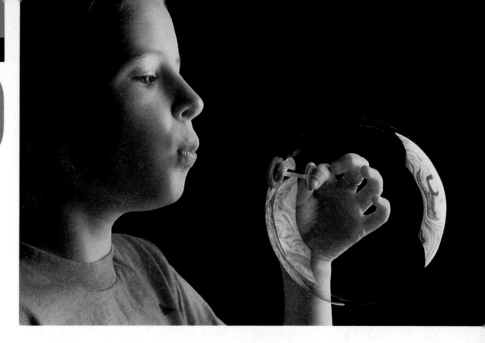

LESSON 13-9

Spheres

A **sphere** is the set of points *in space* at a given distance (its *radius*) from a given point (its *center*). Drawn below is a sphere with radius *r*. Planets and moons in space, baseballs, marbles, and many other objects are in the shape of spheres. In mathematics, a sphere is like a soap bubble. It doesn't include any points inside. Even the center *C* of a sphere is not a point on the sphere.

The formulas for the surface area and volume of a sphere were first discovered by Archimedes.

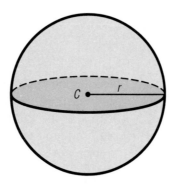

Surface area and volume formulas for a sphere:

In a sphere with radius *r*, surface area *S*, and volume *V*:
$$S = 4\pi r^2$$
$$\text{and} \quad V = \tfrac{4}{3}\pi r^3.$$

When computing surface areas and volumes of spheres, it helps to have a calculator.

■ ■ ■ ■ ■ ■ ■ ■

Example 1   The Earth is nearly a sphere with radius 3960 miles. What is its surface area?

Solution   The formula for surface area is $S = 4\pi r^2$. Substitute 3960 for r. Here is a key sequence that will work on many calculators.

$$4 \boxed{\times} \boxed{\pi} \boxed{\times} 3960 \boxed{x^2} \boxed{=}$$

(By using the $\boxed{x^2}$ squaring key, 3960 does not have to be entered twice.)

The calculator should display a result close to 197,000,000 square miles.

■ ■ ■ ■ ■ ■ ■ ■

Example 2   Find the volume of a sphere with radius 6.

Solution 1   Let V be the volume. $V = \frac{4}{3}\pi r^3 = \frac{4}{3}\pi \cdot 216 = 288\pi$

288π is the exact value. To get an approximate value, substitute an estimate for π, say 3.14. Then $V \approx 288 \cdot 3.14 \approx 904$.

Solution 2   Use a calculator to get an estimate. Here is a key sequence that usually will work.

$$4 \boxed{\div} 3 \boxed{\times} \boxed{\pi} \boxed{\times} 6 \boxed{y^x} 3 \boxed{=}$$

To the nearest hundredth, a calculator will give 904.78. This differs from the answer of Solution 1 because a different estimate is used for π.

Remember that volume is measured in cubic units. Surface area is measured in square units (just as any other area). For instance, suppose the radius of a sphere is given in centimeters. Then the surface area is in square centimeters and the volume is in cubic centimeters.

The formulas for measuring spheres contain both rational and irrational numbers. They combine the three themes of this book: arithmetic, algebra, and geometry. We think it is nice to finish this book by discussing a topic that combines so much. But it is even nicer to finish with spheres, because the sphere is among the most beautiful of all figures.

1. What is a sphere?

2. Give a formula for the surface area of a sphere.

3. Calculate the surface area of a sphere with radius 12 cm.

4. Give a formula for the volume of a sphere.

5. Calculate the volume of a sphere with radius 12 cm.

6. Who discovered the formulas for the surface area and volume of a sphere?

7. What calculator sequence will yield the volume of a sphere with radius 7?

In 8–11, tell whether the idea is more like surface area or volume.

8. how much land there is in the United States

9. how much material in a bowling ball

10. how much material it takes to make a basketball

11. how much material in a marble

For 12 and 13, a bowling ball is approximately 8.59 inches in diameter.

12. How much surface does a bowling ball have?

13. How much material does it take to make a bowling bowl? (Ignore the holes.)

14. The moon is approximately a sphere with radius 1080 miles.
   a. Estimate the surface area of the moon to the nearest million square miles.
   b. How many times more surface area does the earth have than the moon?

15. A 12 cm diameter ball is put snugly into a box. What percent of the box is filled by the ball? (The answer surprises most people.)

16. Make a circle graph from the information provided here.
   Of all adults: 22% sleep 6.5 hours or less
             26% sleep over 6.5 to 7.5 hours
             37% sleep over 7.5 to 8.5 hours
             9% sleep over 8.5 to 9.5 hours
             6% sleep 9.5 hours or more
   (Hint: Take percents of 360° to determine the number of degrees in each central angle.) *(Lesson 13-8)*

17. From the top of a tall building, a person can see 15 miles away in any direction. How many square miles are then visible? *(Lesson 13-7)*

18. The surface area of the world is given in this lesson. Only about 29.4% of the surface area is land.
   a. To the nearest million square miles, what is the total land area of the earth? *(Lesson 2-6)*
   b. The area of the United States is approximately 3,540,000 square miles. What percent of the total land area of the earth is in the United States? *(Lesson 11-4)*

   c. What three countries of the world have more land area than the United States? (Look in an almanac for this information, or look at a globe.)

19. Consider the drawing at the beginning of this chapter.
   a. What is the area of triangle *ABC*?
   b. What is the area of the lune?
   c. Which area is larger, or are they equal?

612

Summary

This book began by discussing decimals. Numbers that can be represented as decimals are called *real numbers*. Real numbers are very important in measurement and are found in almost all measurement formulas. A formula is algebra, measurement is geometry, and numbers are arithmetic. So this chapter is about arithmetic, algebra, and geometry. It uses many of the ideas of earlier chapters and thus is a nice way to end this course.

The important arithmetic in this chapter is the use of irrational numbers. They are numbers with infinite decimals that do not repeat. If a square root of a positive integer is not an integer, the square root is irrational. So is π. Lengths, areas, and volumes may be rational or irrational.

The geometry of this chapter is concerned with length, area, and volume. Missing lengths of sides of a right triangle can be found using the Pythagorean theorem. From the area of a rectangle comes the area of a right triangle. Two right triangles can be combined to find the area of any triangle. Triangles may be combined to find areas of trapezoids and other polygons.

Formulas for the areas of these figures show the power of algebra. Other formulas give the circumference of a circle, the area of a circle, and the surface area and volume of a sphere. The area of a circle can be split up to make a circle graph display.

Vocabulary

You should be able to give a general description
and a specific example for each
of the following ideas.

Lesson 13-1
triangular region
legs, hypotenuse of a right triangle

Lesson 13-2
square root
radical sign, $\sqrt{}$

Lesson 13-3
Pythagorean Theorem, Pythagoras
theorem

Lesson 13-4
height, altitude of a triangle
base of a triangle
equilateral triangle

Lesson 13-5
trapezoid
bases, height of a trapezoid

Lesson 13-6
circle
center, radius, diameter of circle
circumference
π, approximations to π
rational number, irrational number
real number

Lesson 13-7
central angle, sector

Lesson 13-8
pie graph, circle graph
semicircle

Lesson 13-9
sphere
center, radius, diameter of sphere

Progress Self-Test

Take this test as you would take a test in class. Then check your work with the solutions in the Selected Answers section in the back of the book.

1. A circle has radius $\frac{3}{8}''$. Find its circumference to the nearest tenth.

2. What is the area of a square if one side has length $\sqrt{3}$?

3. If a square has area 10, what is the exact length of a side?

4. Estimate $\sqrt{30} + \sqrt{51}$ to the nearest integer.

5. Find x.

6. Find the length of $\overline{AB}$.

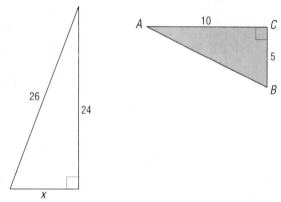

7. Which number is rational?
$\sqrt{24}$ $\sqrt{25}$ $\sqrt{27}$

In 8–10, give the area of each figure.

8. **9.** **10.**

11. Name the hypotenuse and the two legs in the right triangle of Question 6.

12. The area of a triangle is 400 square inches. The height is 25 inches. What must be the length of the base?

13. Which is not always a trapezoid? quadrilateral; rectangle; square; parallelogram

14. To the nearest integer, what is the circumference of a 7″ diameter record?

15. A circle has radius 16. What is its exact area?

16. When does a decimal represent an irrational number?

17. A basketball is hollow with a radius of about 12 cm. About how much material is needed to make it?

18. What is the volume of a sphere with radius 9, to the nearest cubic unit?

19. The circle graph below tells about the number of players in a string orchestra. What percent of the orchestra are cellos (pictured below)?

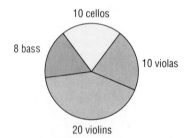

10 cellos

8 bass

10 violas

20 violins

20. A circle has diameter 8 cm. What is the area of a sector of the circle having a central angle of 60°?

Chapter Review

Questions on **SPUR** Objectives

SPUR stands for **S**kills, **P**roperties, **U**ses, and **R**epresentations.
The Chapter Review questions are grouped according to the
SPUR Objectives for this chapter.

SKILLS deal with the procedures used to get answers.

■ **Objective A:** *Find the area of any triangle.*
(Lessons 13-1, 13-4)

1. Find the area of △*CAT*.

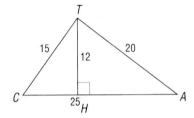

2. Find the area of △*NOW*.

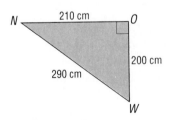

3. Find the area of △*BUI*.
4. Find the area of △*BIG*.

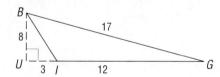

■ **Objective B:** *Estimate square roots of a number without a calculator.* *(Lesson 13-2)*

5. Between what two integers is $\sqrt{80}$?
6. Between what two integers is $-\sqrt{3}$?
7. Simplify $\sqrt{144 + 256}$.
8. Name the two square roots of 36.

■ **Objective C:** *Use the Pythagorean Theorem to find lengths of third sides in right triangles.*
(Lesson 13-3)

9. Find *BI* in the figure for Questions 3 and 4.
10. Find *HA* in the figure for Question 1.
11. The legs of a right triangle have lengths 20 and 48. What is the length of the hypotenuse of this triangle?
12. Find *y* in the figure below.

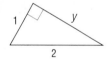

■ **Objective D:** *Find the area of a trapezoid.*
(Lesson 13-5)

13. If *ZY* = 350, find the area of *WXYZ*.
14. If *ZY* = 350, find the area of parallelogram *WEYZ*.
15. If *ZD* = 110, find the area of *WXDZ*.

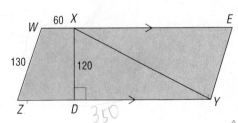

16. What is a formula for the area of a trapezoid?

Objective E: *Find the circumference or area of a circle or sector, given its radius or diameter.* (*Lessons 13-6, 13-7*)

17. Find the circumference and area of a circle with radius 10.

18. To the nearest whole number, find the circumference and area of a circle with diameter 2 meters.

19. Give the area of a 90° sector of a circle with radius 10.

20. Give the area of a 100° sector of a circle with radius 6, to the nearest square unit.

Objective F: *Find the surface area or volume of a sphere, given its radius or diameter.* (*Lesson 13-9*)

21. A sphere has diameter 10. Give its exact surface area.

22. To the nearest cubic inch, give the volume of a sphere with radius 4″.

PROPERTIES deal with the principles behind the mathematics.

Objective G: *Identify numbers as rational, irrational, or real.* (*Lesson 13-6*)

23. Which of these numbers are rational?
    π 3.14 $\frac{22}{7}$ $3\frac{1}{7}$

24. Which of these numbers are irrational?
    $\sqrt{2}$ $\sqrt{3}$ $\sqrt{4}$ $\sqrt{5}$

25. When does a decimal represent a real number?

USES deal with applications of mathematics in real situations.

Objective H: *Apply area formulas in real situations.* (*Lessons 13-1, 13-4, 13-7, 13-9*)

26. An 8″ by 10.5″ rectangular sheet of paper is cut in half at its diagonal. What is the area of each half?

27. A triangular sail (in gold below) is 3 meters high and 1.8 meters across. How much material does it take to make this sail?

28. A child is lost in a forest. Police decide to search every place within 2 miles of the place the child was last seen. To the nearest square mile, how much area must be searched?

29. What is the surface area of a ball 20 cm in diameter?

30. Pearl is making a color wheel for school. She wants to put 12 equal-sized sectors on the wheel. What is the area of one of those sectors if the wheel is to be 18″ in diameter?

Objective I: *Apply formulas for the circumference of a circle and volume of a sphere in real situations.* (*Lessons 13-6, 13-9*)

31. To keep a famous statue from being touched, a rope is placed in a circle around the statue. Each point on the rope is 10 feet from the center of the statue. How long is the rope?

32. The Earth goes around the sun in an orbit that is almost a circle with radius 150,000,000 km. How far does Earth travel in one year in its orbit?

33. How much clay is needed to make a ball 4″ across?

34. To the nearest cubic centimeter, what is the volume of a soap bubble with a radius of 1.5 centimeters?

REPRESENTATIONS deal with pictures, graphs, or objects that illustrate concepts.

■ **Objective J:** *Know how square roots and geometric squares are related. (Lesson 13-2)*

35. A square has area 50. What is the exact length of a side?

36. A side of a square has length $\sqrt{4.9}$. What is the area of the square?

37. If the big square below has area 4, what is the length of a side of the tilted square?

■ **Objective K:** *Read, make, and interpret circle graphs. (Lesson 13-8)*

In 38 and 39, the graph pictures the spending of $27.

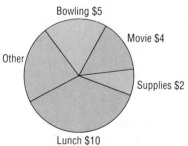

Money Spent Last Week

38. How much was spent on "other" things?

39. How can you tell that more than 25% of the money spent was for lunch?

40. The table below gives approximations in billions of dollars of the top four areas of 1988 U.S. government expenses. Make a circle graph to display this information.

<u>**1988 U.S. Government Expenses**</u>

Income Security	125
National Defense	295
Interest on national debt	140
Social Security and Medicare	280

LESSON 1-1 (pp. 4–7)
11. 90 **13.** 8 **15.** 2 **17.** 6 **19.** No **25. a.** 50 **b.** stars
27. a. Appleton-Oshkosh, Wisconsin **b.** McAllen-Edinburg,
Texas **29.** 600,000,000 **31.** 506 **33.** 9999

LESSON 1-2 (pp. 8–13)
1. 21 and 22 **3.** 3 **5.** 3 **7.** 2 **9.** 6 **15.** largest, 0.033;
smallest, 0.015 **17.** largest, 0.98; smallest, 0.8 **19. a.** π
b. 14159 **21.** K **23.** S **27.** five and nine tenths
29. twenty-four thousandths **31.** 2 **33.** $3.20 **35.** three
millionths, three thousandths, four thousandths **37.** faster
39. 31,068 **41.** Miami **43.** count: 76; counting unit:
trombones

LESSON 1-3 (pp. 14–17)
5. 1800 **7.** 34¢ **9.** 0.012345 **11.** 0.97531246 **13. a.** 6000
b. 5000 **15. a.** $40 **b.** $30 **17.** high **19.** low **21.** 5.001,
5.01, 5.1 **23.** .086 **25.** Answers will vary. 5.9_, where
any digit except 0 can be put in the blank. **27. a.** Q **b.** R
c. Y

LESSON 1-4 (pp. 18–21)
1. a. 50 **b.** 40 **c.** 40 **3. a.** 88.89 **b.** 88.9 **c.** 89 **d.** 90
e. 100 **5.** $5.00 **7.** 200,000 miles per second **9.** 0.053 or
0.052 **11. a.** $89 **b.** $166 **c.** $101 **d.** $5324 **13.** 328
15. 12.53 **17. a.** 11 **b.** Sample: round to the nearest tenth
or hundredth **19.** $6 **21.** 5 **23.** Answers will vary. 3.2_ or
3.3_, where the blank can be filled by any digit but 0.
25. There are none. These numbers are equal. **27.** count:
12; counting unit: eggs. (Dozen is a collective, just like
hundred or score.) **29. a.** 1.01 **b.** 1.00 **31.** 7

LESSON 1-5 (pp. 22–25)
1. negative four, opposite of four **3.** behind **5.** below
7. See below. 9. Tomorrow is positive, yesterday was
negative, today is zero. **11.** . . . , -3, -2, -2, -1, 0, 1, 2,
3, . . . **15.** Samples: -1.5, -π, -2.36 **17. a.** 3 **b.** -10 **c.** 0
19. Q **21.** none **23.** -1, 0, $\frac{1}{2}$ **25.** -4 **27.** -1 **29.** 5.067,
5.60, 5.607, 5.67 **31.** 4 **33. a.** $29 **b.** $28 **c.** $28

7.

LESSON 1-6 (pp. 26–29)
5. 6 > -12 **7.** -2 < 0 < 2 or 2 > 0 > -2 **9.** 0 < 18
11. Negative three is less than three. **13.** Negative three is
greater than negative four and less than negative two.
15. 7'4" > 7'2" **19.** $8000 > -$2000 **21.** > **23.** >
25. < **27.** 0.621 < 6.21 < 62.1, or 62.1 > 6.21 > 0.621
29. 99.2 < 99.8 < 100.4, or 100.4 > 99.8 > 99.2
31. 0.07243, 0.07249, 0.0782 **33.** -3, -2, -1, 0, 1, 2 **35.** 77
37. 6.283

LESSON 1-7 (pp. 30–33)
3. On a scientific calculator, the blanks will be filled in with
8, 8, 7.2, 7.2, 10, 80. On a non-scientific calculator, the
blanks will be filled with 8, 8, 7.2, 15.2, 10, 152. **5.** If the
calculator displays 3.1415926 or 3.141592653, it truncates.
If it displays 3.1415927 or 3.141592654, it rounds to the
nearest. If it displays 3.14159265, you can't tell. **7.** On
many calculators the number of decimal places equals the
last digit in the display. **9.** 2.889 **11.** 206 **13.** Answer
depends on the calculator; sample: 99,999,999 or
9,999,999,999. **15.** usually the opposite of the answer to
Question 13: sample: -99,999,999. **17.** usually C̲, C̲E̲, or
C̲E̲/̲C̲ **19. a.** -2, -1.5, -1 **b.** -2 < -1.5 < -1, or -1 > -1.5 >
-2 **21.** > **23.** 54 seconds **25.** Answers will vary. -4.631_,
where the blank can be filled by any digit but 0. **27.** 5

LESSON 1-8 (pp. 34–38)
1. a. 15 **b.** 8 **c.** – **d.** $\frac{15}{8}$ **e.** No **f.** Yes **g.** 8 **h.** 15
i. 1.875 **7.** 1.15 **9.** .$\overline{571428}$ **11.** 27 **13.** 9.8777777777
15. -5.4444444444 **17.** $\frac{2}{5}$ or $\frac{4}{10}$ **19.** $\frac{1}{3}$ **21.** $\frac{7}{10}$ **23.** factor
25. 1, 2, 3, 5, 6, 10, 15, 30 **27.** .071 **29.** $\frac{2}{11}$, $\frac{2}{9}$, $\frac{2}{7}$
31. 34.0079 **33.** 99.6°

LESSON 1-9 (pp. 39–41)
1. a. 10 and 11 **b.** 10 **c.** 10.75 **d. See below. 3.** Fourths
are quarters, a term used in money. **5.** 7.4 **7.** 17.8$\overline{3}$
9. 12.1875 **11.** 20.5$\overline{3}$ **13.** $4.25 **15.** 2$\frac{3}{5}$, 3$\frac{3}{5}$, 5$\frac{2}{3}$ **17.** 12.533
19. longer **21.** 1 **23.** 999,999 **25. a.** -4.3 **b.** Answers
will vary, -4.3_, where the blank can be filled in by any
digit but 0. **27.** 100 **29.** -9.99 < 9 < 9.99 **31.** 4
33. 1, 3, 13, 39

1. d.

LESSON 1-10 (pp. 42–46)
1. b **3.** All are equal. **5.** Sample: $\frac{42}{24}$ **7. a.** 1, 2, 3, 4, 6, 8,
12, 16, 24, 48 **b.** 1, 2, 3, 4, 5, 6, 10, 12, 15, 20, 30, 60
c. 1, 2, 3, 4, 6, 12 **d.** 12 **e.** $\frac{4}{5}$ **9. a.** 5 **b.** $\frac{3}{4}$ **11. a.** Sample: 24

b. $\frac{10}{3}$ **13.** Sample: $37\frac{6}{14}$ **15. See right.** **17.** $\frac{24}{3}$
19. $\frac{75}{100} = \frac{3}{4}$ **21.** .01 **23.** Examples: $-\frac{1}{2}$, -.2, -.05
25. $4062 \times .003 \approx 12.2$ **27.** 19.6 **29. a.** .4 **b.** .625
c. .75 **d.** $.\overline{3}$ **e.** $.8\overline{3}$ **31.** 1, 3, 17, 51

15.

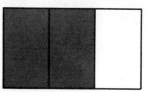

CHAPTER 1 PROGRESS SELF-TEST (p. 48)

1. 700,000 **2.** 45.6 **3.** 0.25 **4.** $15\frac{13}{16} = 15 + \frac{13}{16} = 15 +$
$0.8125 = 15.8125$ **5.** 6 **6.** three thousandths
7. Remember that $.\overline{6} = .666 \ldots$, $.66 = .660$, and $.6 =$
.600. This indicates that $.\overline{6}$ is the largest. **8.** Change each
fraction to a decimal. $\frac{1}{2} = .5$, $\frac{2}{5} = .4$, $\frac{3}{10} = .3$ and $\frac{1}{3} =$
.333 . . . So $\frac{3}{10}$ is smallest. **9.** 98.7 **10.** 99 **11.** -80 ft >
-100 ft; the negative numbers are below sea level and the >
sign means "is higher than." **12.** Each tick mark to the
right of 0 is $\frac{1}{4}$. M is $\frac{2}{4}$ or $\frac{1}{2}$. **13.** Each tick mark to the left
of 0 is a decrease of 0.25. F corresponds to -1.25.
14. Rewrite the numbers as 16.50 and 16.60. Any decimal
beginning with 16.5 . . . is between. **15.** Rewrite the numbers as -2.3900 and -2.3910. Any decimal beginning with
-2.390 . . . is between. **16.** < **17.** =; Adding zeros to the
right of a number and the right of a decimal point does not
affect the value of the number. **18.** > **19.** $\frac{6}{10}$ or $\frac{3}{5}$
20. Any number other than 0, 1, 2, -2, etc. For example, $\frac{1}{2}$,
0.43, or 7.6. **21.** The store will round up. You will
pay 18¢. **22.** $3 + 9 = 12$ **23.** 3.456 $\boxed{\times}$ 2.345 $\boxed{=}$

24. 6 $\boxed{\times}$ $\boxed{\pi}$ $\boxed{=}$ is a calculator sequence that will yield
18.8495 . . . Round to the nearest integer, the answer is 19.
25. 7 **26.** On the graph below each tick mark represents
0.1. **See below.** **27. See below.** **28.** Sample: the number of
people who watched a particular TV program **29.** Sample:
Twelve <u>elephants</u> marched in the circus parade. **30.** The
numbers are 0.1, 0.000001, 0.000000001, and .001. Of
these 0.1 is largest. **31.** 1, 2, 3, 6, 9, 18. **32.** Multiply the
numerator and denominator of $\frac{6}{1}$ by 5. This gives $\frac{30}{5}$.
33. 3 is a factor of both 12 and 21. So $\frac{12}{21} = \frac{4}{7}$. **34.** b,
around 800 A.D.

26.

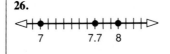

7 7.7 8

27.

5
3
1
0
-1
-3
-4
-5
-7

The chart below keys the **Progress Self-Test** questions to the objectives in the **Chapter Review** on pages 49–51 or to the **Vocabulary**
(Voc.) on page 47. This will enable you to locate those **Chapter Review** questions that correspond to questions you missed on the
Progress Self-Test. The lesson where the material is covered is also indicated in the chart.

Question	1	2	3	4	5	6	7–8	9	10	11
Objective	A	A	H	G	A	A	B	D	D	N
Lesson	1-1	1-2	1-8	1-9	1-1	1-2	1-8	1-3	1-4	1-6

Question	12	13	14	15	16–18	19	20	21	22	23
Objective	P	P	C	C	I	H	Voc.	L	E	Q
Lesson	1-2	1-5	1-2	1-5	1-6	1-8	1-5	1-4	1-4	1-7

Question	24	25	26	27	28	29	30	31–33	34
Objective	F	J	O	O	M	Voc.	B	K	R
Lesson	1-7	1-8	1-2	1-5	1-3	1-1	1-2	1-10	1-1

CHAPTER 1 REVIEW (pp. 49–51)

1. 4003 **3.** 120,000,000 **5.** five hundred thousand four
hundred **7.** 400,000,001 is largest; 0.4 is smallest
9. -586.363, -586.36, -586.34 **11.** $\frac{6}{10}$, 0.66, $\frac{2}{3}$ **13.** 4.33,
5.3, $5.\overline{3}$ **15.** -1.__, where anything other than 0 can be

put in the blank. **17.** Samples: 3.401, 3.402, 3.403
19. 5.84 **21.** 0.595959 **23.** 6.8 **25.** 62 **27.** 4402.912
29. 69.8584 **31.** $-5.\overline{3}$ **33.** 5.25 **35.** $0.\overline{6}$ **37.** $.1\overline{6}$ **39.** $\frac{1}{3}$
41. > **43.** $.6 < \frac{2}{3} < .667$ or $.667 > \frac{2}{3} > .6$ **45.** $468.5\overline{68}$
47. 1, 2, 3, 6, 7, 14, 21, 42 **49.** 29,000 **51.** 50¢

53. Example: number of minutes of travel time to school
55. $-75,000 < 10,000$ **57. See right. 59. See right.**

61. 46 **63.** $7\frac{1}{5}$ **65.** $77 \boxed{\div} 8.2 \boxed{=}$ **67.** c

57.

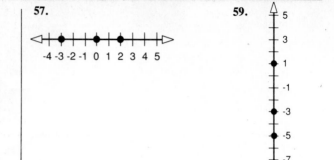

-4 -3 -2 -1 0 1 2 3 4 5

59.

5

3

1

-1

-3

-5

-7

LESSON 2-1 (pp. 54–57)
1. 10 **3.** 24 **5.** 472.1 **7.** Move the decimal point two places to the right. **9.** 5 **11.** 630.1 **13.** Move the decimal point four places to the right. **15.** 32,000 **17.** 950 **25.** 1,350,000 **27.** Round 46.314 to 46 or 47. The answer should be between 46,000 and 47,000. **29.** 2.4 billion or 2.5 billion; 2,400,000,000 or 2,500,000,000 **31.** 3.7 billion or 3.8 billion; 3,700,000,000 or 3,800,000,000 **33.** 230 million **35.** 26.5 trillion **37. a.** 0.5 **b.** 0.1 **c.** G

LESSON 2-2 (pp. 58–61)
1. a. 4 **b.** 6 **c.** 4, 6, power **5.** 1,048,576; 400
7. 1.259712 **13.** 500 **17. a.** 4 **b.** 4^4, 4^3, 4^2, _ or 2^8, 2^6, 2^4, _. **19.** 3^2 **21.** seventh **23. a.** 96 or 7776 **b.** If the answer was 96, the calculator took the power first. If the answer was 7776, the calculator multiplied first.
25. Forty-three quintillion, two hundred fifty-two quadrillion, three trillion, two hundred seventy-four billion, four hundred eighty-nine million, eight hundred fifty-fix thousand **27.** 3×7 **29.** $44.\overline{4}$ **31. a.** 1,000,000
b. 1,800,000 **c.** 8000

LESSON 2-3 (pp. 62–66)
1. 26,000,000,000,000 miles **5.** 8.04×10^2 **7.** 5.88×10^{21} **9.** $\$1.2 \times 10^{12}$ **11.** 7.654×10^2
13. $\boxed{4.9\ 15}$ or equivalent **15.** $\boxed{3.8\ 12}$ or equivalent
17. 31,536,000 **19.** 1×10^{10} **21.** 6 **23.** $14.6 = 14\frac{3}{5}$,
$14.\overline{61}$, $14.\overline{6}$ **25. a.** q **b.** e **c.** s **d.** c **27. a.** 1,000,000,000
b. one billion

LESSON 2-4 (pp. 67–69)
5. Move the decimal point one place to the left. **7.** Move the decimal point two places to the left. **9.** 4.6 **11.** 4.6
13. .06 **15.** 7.7 **17.** .0052 **21.** $\frac{1}{10,000} \times 15.283 =$ 0.0015283; $\frac{1}{100,000} \times 15.283 = 0.00015283$; $\frac{1}{1,000,000} \times$ $15.283 = 0.000015283$ **23.** Sample: $7 \times 10 = 70$ and $70 \times .1 = 7$ **25.** 9 pounds **27.** 9,690,000; 14,670,000; 12,500,000 **29. a.** 59 and 60 **b.** $59.\overline{45}$ **c.** 59.454545
31. 3.9×10^7 **33. a.** .2 **b.** .5 **c.** $.\overline{6}$ **d.** $.8\overline{3}$

LESSON 2-5 (pp. 70–73)
5. .8 **7.** .05 **9.** .015 **11.** 3.00 **13.** 1.05 **15.** .085 **17.** .25;
$\frac{1}{4}$ **19.** $.2; \frac{1}{5}$ **21.** $.\overline{3}; \frac{1}{3}$ **23.** $.875; \frac{7}{8}$ **25.** $\frac{2}{3}$ **27.** .5; 50%
29. $.875; 87\frac{1}{2}\%$ **33.** $\frac{3}{2}$, $1\frac{1}{2}$, or 1.5 **35.** b **37.** 0 and 1
39. $.04 = 4\%$ **41. a.** 2300 **b.** 23 **c.** 23,000 **d.** .023 **e.** .00023 **43.** 9×10^4

LESSON 2-6 (pp. 74–78)
3. a. True **b.** True **c.** True **7.** 12 **9.** 45 **11.** $2.75
13. Let's split it equally, half for you, half for me.
15. 4,000,000 people **17.** store A **19.** half price **21.** $15
23. a. 29,028 feet **b.** 29,000 feet **c.** 29,000 feet **d.** 30,000 feet **25.** 0.7853 **27. a.** 25% **b.** $33\frac{1}{3}\%$ **c.** 125% **29.** $\frac{12}{25}$

LESSON 2-7 (pp. 79–82)
1. a. eight and twenty-seven hundredths **b.** $8\frac{27}{100}$
3. a. one thousandth **b.** $\frac{1}{1000}$ **5.** 72.4% **7.** $3\frac{14}{100}$ or $3\frac{7}{50}$ or $\frac{157}{50}$
9. 25% **11.** $\frac{105}{26}$ **13.** $\frac{675}{10,000}$ or $\frac{27}{400}$ **15.** $3\frac{1}{5}$; 320% **17.** $\frac{27}{100}$; 27%
19. $\frac{1}{3}$ off **21.** 32.34 **23.** one billion **25.** $\frac{1}{100}$; .011; $\frac{1}{10}$
27. 2.78784×10^7 **29.** $1.50 **31.** 240,000

LESSON 2-8 (pp. 83–86)
1. 7^3 **5.** $10^0 = 1$ **7. a.** positive **b.** positive **13.** .000345
15. .004 **17.** .000005 **19.** (f) **21.** .000001 **23.** 0, 10^{-5}, 1, 10^2 **25. a.** $12\frac{45}{100}$ or $12\frac{9}{20}$ **b.** 1245% **27.** They are the same price. **29. a.** .3 **b.** $\frac{3}{10}$ **31.** 9.3×10^7

LESSON 2-9 (pp. 87–90)
5. 6.008×10^{-5} **7.** 2.8×10^{-1} **11.** .00000 02 m
13. .009803; some calculators may put this small a number into scientific notation. **15.** .05 **17.** = **19. a.** 10^6 **b.** 10^{-6}
21. The team lost more often. **23.** .03 **25.** 1.50
27. a. $.001 **b.** $.0001 **c.** $.0111 **d.** $.01 **29.** low
31. $\frac{-2}{3}$, -.666, -.66, -.656, -.6

CHAPTER 2 PROGRESS SELF-TEST (p. 92)

1. Move the decimal point 8 places to the right.
2,351,864,000 **2.** $0.34 \times 600 = 204$ **3.** $32 \times 10^{-9} = 0.00000 0032$ **4.** Move the decimal point 5 places to the left. 0.0082459 **5.** $0.001 \times 77 = 0.077$ **6.** Move the decimal point 5 places to the right. 345,689,100

7. Move the decimal point 3 places to the left. 0.002816
8. 0.00000 01 **9.** $8\% = 8 \times .01 = .08$ **10.** 216 **11.** base; exponent **12.** $125 \boxed{y^x} 6 \boxed{=}$ **13.** $\boxed{3.8146972\ \ 12}$
14. 3,814,700,000,000 **15.** Start between the 2 and 1. You must move the decimal point 10 places to the right to get the given number. So the answer is 2.107×10^{10}. **16.** Start to the right of the 8. Move the decimal point 8 places to the

left to get the given number. So it equals 8×10^{-8}.
17. 4.5 [EE] 13 **18.** First write in scientific notation: 1.23456 [EE] 7 [±]. **19.** In the order given, the numbers equal 256, 125, and 243. So from smallest to largest, they are: 5^3, 3^5, 4^4. **20.** First change to a decimal. 40% = 0.40. This number is between 0 and 1. **21. a.** $4.73 = \frac{4.73}{1} = \frac{473}{100}$; **b.** $\frac{473}{100} = 473\%$ **22.** $\frac{1}{3}$ **23.** 30% $\times$ 150 = .3 $\times$ 150 = 45

24. You save 0.25 $\times$ \$699 = \$174.75. Subtract that from \$699 to get the sale price, \$524.25. Rounded to the nearest dollar, this is \$524. **25.** $0.8 \times 20 = 16$. This is the number correct. So $20 - 16 = 4$ is the number missed. **26.** 22.4 is not between 1 and 10. **27.** 6, since $10^6 = 1,000,000$ **28.** $\frac{3}{5} = 60\%$, $\frac{1}{10} = 10\%$, so fill the blanks with 60 and 10. **29.** 250 billion = 250,000,000,000 = 2.5×10^{11}

The chart below keys the **Progress Self-Test** questions to the objectives in the **Chapter Review** on pages 93–95 or to the **Vocabulary** (Voc.) on page 91. This will enable you to locate those **Chapter Review** questions that correspond to questions you missed on the **Progress Self-Test.** The lesson where the material is covered is also indicated in the chart.

Question	1	2	3	4–5	6	7	8	9	10	11	12–13	14	15
Objective	A	J	B	E	F	F	D	H	C	Voc.	P	C	G
Lesson	2-1	2-6	2-6	2-4	2-2	2-8	2-8	2-5	2-2	2-2	2-3	2-2	2-3

Question	16	17	18	19	20	21	22	23–25	26	27	28	29
Objective	G	P	P	C	H	K	I	N	M	D	L	O
Lesson	2-9	2-3	2-9	2-2	2-5	2-7	2-5	2-6	2-3	2-2	2-6	2-3

CHAPTER 2 REVIEW (pp. 93–95)

1. 320,000 **3.** 25,000 **5.** \$10,000,000,000 **7.** 64 **9.** 100,000 **11.** 0.0001 **13.** twelfth **15.** 0.00000 00273 **17.** 0.075 **19.** 30,000,000 **21.** 7.34 **23.** 4.8×10^5 **25.** 1.3×10^{-4} **27.** 0.15 **29.** 0.09 **31.** 50% **33.** $\frac{3}{10}$ **35.** 75 **37.** 6.2 **39.** Sample: $\frac{57}{10}$ **41.** 86% **43.** 42.8% or 42.9% (either answer is okay) **45.** If two numbers are equal, one can be substituted for the other in any computation without changing the results of the computation. **47.** $\frac{1}{2}$ and .5 **49.** 23 is not between 1 and 10. **51.** \$15.90 **53.** \$42,240 **55.** 5×10^{-3} **57.** 1 [EE] 12 [±] **59.** [3.5184 13] **61.** 3.3516×10^{13} **63.** 3 [EE] 21

LESSON 3-1 (pp. 98–103)

13. $2\frac{1}{8}$ in. **15.** $\frac{3}{4}$ in. **17. a.** 10.1 cm **b.** 4 in. **19.** Answers will vary. **a.** may range from 25.1 cm to 25.3 cm; **b.** may range from 19.5 cm to 20.1 cm **21.** The vertical segment at right has length 3.5 in. **23.** If two numbers are equal, one may be substituted for the other in any computation without changing the results of the computation. **25. a.** improve **b.** 156 **27.** 28,200,000 **29.** $\frac{7}{5}$

LESSON 3-2 (pp. 104–107)

13. 14,000 pounds **15.** 33.2 quarts **17.** 16.5 feet **19.** 1,320 feet **21.** 80 **23.** A gallon is not a unit of length; it is a unit of volume or capacity. **25. a.** 6 in. **b.** $6\frac{1}{4}$ in. **c.** $6\frac{2}{8}$ in. or $6\frac{1}{4}$ in. **27. a.** 5.2 **b.** .0003446 **c.** 1.536 **d.** 6,400,000

LESSON 3-3 (pp. 108–112)

13. .345 liter **15.** 10,000 m **17.** .060 g **19. a.** Sample: height of a doorknob **b.** Sample: 4 football fields **c.** Sample: thickness of a dime **25.** b **27.** Yes **29.** 57,000,000 tons **31. a.** \$.56 **b.** 1349¢ **c.** \$76,000 **33.** 0, 10^{-4}; $\frac{1}{100}$ **35. a.** < **b.** < **c.** < **d.** = **37.** 1.7 cm

LESSON 3-4 (pp. 113–116)

11. b. Sample: using 2.2 lb instead of 1 kg **13.** about 1.9 quarts **15.** 12.7 cm **17.** liter **19.** inch **21. a.** .3125 **b.** .8 cm or 8 mm **23.** about 10.2 miles **25.** 2 **27.** 36 inches **29.** 80 oz **31.** 80 mm **33.** 25

LESSON 3-5 (pp. 117–121)

1. $\overrightarrow{CB}$ (or $\overrightarrow{CA}$) and $\overrightarrow{CD}$ (or $\overrightarrow{CE}$) **3.** (a), (b), (c), (e), (g) **7.** B **9.** 66° **11.** 151° **13.** 90° **17.** $\angle JGH$ **19.** See below. **21. and 23.** See below. **25.** 93 miles **27.** .082 m **29.** quarts or gallons **31.** $\frac{3}{4}$

19.   **21. and 23.**

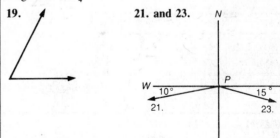

LESSON 3-6 (pp. 122–125)

7. acute **9.** right **11.** acute **13.** obtuse **15.** (c) **17. a.** acute **b.** 87° **19. a.** right **b.** 90° **21. a.** acute **b.** 60° **23. a.** See p. 622. **b.** See p. 622. **25. a.** .0004 inches **b.** 4×10^{-4} inches **27. a.** $3\frac{1}{2}$ in. **b.** $3\frac{1}{4}$ in. **29. a.** > **b.** < **c.** < **d.** < **e.** = **f.** =

23. a.

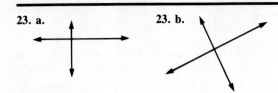

23. b.

LESSON 3-7 (pp. 126–129)
5. Sample: a caution sign on a street 9. 5625 ft²
11. 2.25 in.² 13. 6 in.² 15. a. See right. b. 9 ft²
17. a. square meters b. square feet 19. 21,780 ft²
21. 1,074,000,000 23. a. 60 b. 120, 240, 420 (Do by multiplying by 2, 4, and 7 respectively.)

25. about 200 miles 27. 60,000 g 29. acute

15. a.

LESSON 3-8 (pp. 130–132)
9. 64 cubic inches 11. 343 cubic yards
15. a. 34.328125 cubic feet b. 34.33 cubic feet
17. 241 19. 1000 g or 1 kg 21. a. 17,000,000
b. 34,000,000 copies c. 3.4×10^7 23. a. .00034 b. $\frac{17}{50,000}$
25. 100 cm²

CHAPTER 3 PROGRESS SELF-TEST (p. 134)

1. $2\frac{5}{8}''$ 2. See below. 3. 2.54 cm = 1 in.
4. kilogram 5. $\frac{3}{4}$ mile = $\frac{3}{4}$ × 5280 feet = 0.75 ×
5280 ft. = 3960 ft 6. 1 gallon = 4 quarts 7. 1000 tons
8. 1103 mg = 1103 × .001 g = 1.103 g 9. 5 cm =
5 × .01 m = .05 m 10. 3.2 m ≈ 3.2 × 39.37 in. =
125.984 in. 11. 4 km ≈ 4 × 0.62 mi = 2.48 mi 12. 135°
13. 76° 14. 0°; 90° 15. a right angle 16. See below.
17. Area = 4.5² square inches = 20.25 square inches
18. square centimeters 19. 1000 cubic centimeters = 1 liter

20. Angles B and C are acute, angle A is obtuse, there are no right angles. 21. $V = (5 \text{ cm})^3 = 125 \text{ cm}^3$ 22. 6 ft =
2 yd; (2 yd)² = 4 yd² 23. 1 kilogram ≈ 2.2 pounds
24. 9 liters = 9 × 1 liter ≈ 9 × 1.06 quarts =
9.54 quarts. So 10 quarts is larger. 25. England

2. ───────────────

16.

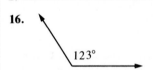

The chart below keys the **Progress Self-Test** questions to the objectives in the **Chapter Review** on pages 135–137 or to the **Vocabulary** (Voc.) on page 133. This will enable you to locate those **Chapter Review** questions that correspond to questions you missed on the **Progress Self-Test.** The lesson where the material is covered is also indicated in the chart.

Question	1	2	3	4	5	6	7	8–9	10–11	12–13	14	15
Objective	A	P	H	J	K	F	G	L	M	B	Voc.	C
Lesson	3-1	3-1	3-4	3-3	3-2	3-2	3-3	3-3	3-4	3-5	3-6	3-6

Question	16	17	18	19	20	21	22	23	24	25
Objective	Q	D	Voc.	G	N	E	O	I	H	R
Lesson	3-5	3-7	3-7	3-8	3-6	3-8	3-7	3-4	3-4	3-1

CHAPTER 3 REVIEW (pp. 135–137)
1. 2 inches 3. 7 cm 5. 63° 7. 36° 9. obtuse 11. 4 cm²
13. m² 15. 53 in.³ 17. 16 oz 19. $\frac{1}{1000}$ or .001 21. 1000
23. 2.54 cm = 1 in. 25. meter 27. 1L ≈ 1.06 qt 29. cm
31. gallons 33. 29.2 qt 35. 1980 ft 37. 5000 m 39. .06 g
41. about 540.64 mi 43. about 220 lb 45. ∠ABC, ∠BEA,
∠BCD, ∠DEC 47. 1728 cm³ 49. See below. 51. See
below. 53. See below. 55. It was the distance from the tip

of the nose of King Henry I of England to the tips of his fingers.

49. ───────────────

51.   53.

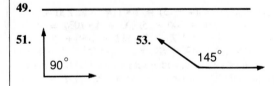

LESSON 4-1 (pp. 140–144)
1. numerical 5. division 7. whichever is to the left 9. 27
11. 10 13. 133 23. 15.2 25. 0.5 27. 14 29. 996 31. (c)
33. 87 + 12 − 3 35. 115° 37. 6.543 × 10⁻¹²
39. 125 cubic inches

LESSON 4-2 (pp. 145–148)
5. Samples: 5% = 5 × .01; 1.2% = 1.2 × .01; 300% =
300 × .01 7. Samples: 3 + 4 = 4 + 3; $\frac{1}{2} + \frac{3}{4} = \frac{3}{4} + \frac{1}{2}$;

0.8 + 6 = 6 + 0.8 13. Samples: 6 • 4 + 13 • 4 = 19 •
4; 6 • 9.7 + 13 • 9.7 = 19 • 9.7; 6 • 100 + 13 • 100 =
19 • 100 15. $a \cdot 0 = 0$ (Any letter can be used.) 17. in n
years we expect $n \cdot 100$ more students and $n \cdot 5$ more teach-
ers. 19. $\frac{a}{3} + \frac{b}{3} = \frac{a+b}{3}$ 21. 55 23. 74 25. 3 27. $\frac{50}{.0001}$;
500,000 29. 3 meters

LESSON 4-3 (pp. 149–153)

3. $n + 3$ or $3 + n$ **5.** $n - 5$ **7.** $n - 7$ **9.** $\frac{n}{9}$ **11.** $11 - n$
13. Sample: five times a number increased by six **15.** Samples: two minus a number; subtract a number from two; two decreased by a number **17.** It could mean $14 - 5 + 3$, with either the addition or the subtraction done first.
19. $6\% \cdot t$ or $.06 \cdot t$ **21. a.** $C + 50$ **b.** $C - 12$ **c.** $C \cdot 3$
23. a. $6 < n$ **b.** $n - 6$ **c.** $6 - n$ **25.** $2\frac{1}{2}$ or $2\frac{4}{8}$ inches
27. $\frac{a}{1} = a$ **29.** 688.2 miles **31.** Examples: **a. See below.**
b. See below. c. See below. 33. a. .00001 **b.** .001%

31. a.   **31. b.**   **31. c.**

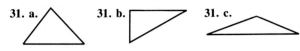

LESSON 4-4 (pp. 154–157)
1. (c) **3.** 3 **5.** 15 **9.** 50¢ **13.** 68 **15.** 5% **17.** 90
19. 254.469 **21. a.** 0 **b.** No, because $xy = yx$ for any numbers. **23. a.** $5n - 8$ **b.** 42 **25. a.** n^3 **b.** 1000
27. $1 \times b = b$ **29.** (a) **31.** (b) and (d)

LESSON 4-5 (pp. 158–162)
1. to change order of operations **3.** True **5.** False **7.** 52
9. 11 **11.** 0 **13.** $2 \boxed{\times} \boxed{(} 5 \boxed{+} 4 \boxed{\times} 8 \boxed{)} \boxed{=}$ **15.** 100
17. 50 **19. a.** $10 - 1$ **b.** 909 **21.** 163 **23.** No
25. $(a + 4)b + 3$ **27.** (d) **29.** 436 **31.** $16 - (8 - 4 - 2) = 14$ **33.** 23 **35.** $n^4 = n \cdot n \cdot n \cdot n$

LESSON 4-6 (pp. 163–166)
3. 4.3 cm² **5.** No **7.** 2.2 cm² **11.** They are the first letters of the quantities they represent. **13.** $2.98 **15.** No, about 1190 are needed. **17.** inside parentheses, then powers, then multiplications or divisions from left to right, then additions or subtractions from left to right **19.** 103 **21.** 8
23. 1000 cm³ **25.** < **27.** <

LESSON 4-7 (pp. 167–171)
7. 16 **9.** $3 \boxed{\times} \boxed{(} 2 \boxed{+} 4 \boxed{\times} \boxed{(} 5 \boxed{-} 2 \boxed{)} \boxed{)} \boxed{=}$ **11.** 9
13. 560 $\boxed{\div} \boxed{(} 7 \boxed{\times} \boxed{(} 6 \boxed{+} 3 \boxed{\times} 4.5 \boxed{)} \boxed{)} \boxed{=}$ **15.** 3
17. $231.\overline{6}$ **19. a.** $58.\overline{3}$ **b.** $91.\overline{6}$ **21.** 1.000 **23.** .200 **25.** 69°
27. $7\frac{2}{3} > 7.65 > 7\frac{3}{5}$ **29.** Sample: depending on the table.

LESSON 4-8 (pp. 172–175)
7. (a) **9.** 5 **11.** .5 **13.** 25 m **15.** Samples: Los Angeles, London, Mexico City, Chicago **17.** eight **19.** Sample: -9
21. 6 **23.** 11 **25.** 4 **27.** 1 **29.** 50,000 mm < 500 m < 5 km, or 5 km > 500 m > 50,000 mm **31. a.** $\frac{5(5 + 1)}{2} = 15$ **b.** $1 + 2 + 3 + 4 + 5 = 15$ **c.** 5050 **33.** 26,127

LESSON 4-9 (pp. 176–179)
7. Yes **9.** True **11.** False **13.** Sample: 5001 **15.** Sample: $6\frac{3}{4}$ **17.** (c) **19.** (b) **21.** (a) **23.** (d) **25. See below.**
27. a. $f > 55$ **b.** Samples: 60, 57, 61 **c. See below.**
29. a. $400 < A \le 500$ **b.** Samples: 490, 421, 439.36
c. See below. 31. $1.92 **33.** Sample: there are $6 \cdot 3$ legs on 3 insects; there are $6 \cdot 108$ legs on 108 insects; there are 6 million legs on 1 million insects **35.** 144

25.

27. c.

29. c.

CHAPTER 4 PROGRESS SELF-TEST (pp. 181–182)

1. $6 + 56 + 9 = 71$ **2.** $35 + 50 = 85$ **3.** 21; Do subtractions from left to right. **4.** $5 + 3 \cdot 16 = 5 + 48 = 53$
5. $\frac{100 + 10}{10 + 5} = \frac{110}{15} = 7.\overline{3} \approx 7$ **6.** $10 + 3 \cdot 100 = 10 + 300 = 310$ **7.** $(3 + 4)(4 - 3) = 7 \cdot 1 = 7$ **8.** $100 + 5[100 + 4(100 + 3)] = 100 + 5[100 + 4 \cdot 103] = 100 = 5[100 + 412] = 100 + 5 \cdot 512 = 100 + 2560 = 2660$ **9.** $(4x)^2 = 64$; $16x^2 = 64$; try 2: $16 \cdot 2^2 = 16 \cdot 4 = 64$. So 2 is a solution. 4, 8, and 16 do not work. The correct answer is (a). **10.** $10 \cdot a = 6 \cdot a + 4 \cdot a$ **11.** $a + b = b + a$ **12.** In p years, we expect the town to grow by $p \cdot 200$ people. **13.** $c = 20 + 5 = 105$¢, or $1.05 **14.** $c = 20 \cdot 9 + 5 = 185$¢, or $1.85 **15.** 12×16 **16.** $47 + 40$
17. $n < 0$ **18.** $\frac{9}{a}$ **19.** p, s, and c **20.** $p = \$45 - \$22.37 =$ $22.63 **21.** $\frac{W}{W + L} = \frac{W}{(W + L)}$; The correct answer is (b)
22. (c) **23.** (b) **24.** $6 \cdot 7 = 42$, so $x = 7$ **25.** Any number between -5 and -4 is a solution. Some are -4.2, -4.9, -4$\frac{1}{2}$.
26. If width is 3 inches and length is 4 feet, the area is not 12 of either unit, even though $A = lw$. **27.** $x = 7 \cdot 3 = 21$
28. See below. 29. all numbers between 4.5 and 6, including 4.5 but not including 6. This is written as $4.5 \le y < 6$.
30. Samples: If you are 10 years old, your sister is $10 - 5$, or 5, years old. If you are 14 years old, your sister is $14 - 5$, or 9, years old. **31.** Samples: $30 \cdot \frac{2}{5} = 6 \cdot 2$; $30 \cdot \frac{8}{5} = 6 \cdot 8$. You can check that both of these are true.

28.

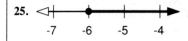

The chart below keys the **Progress Self-Test** questions to the objectives in the **Chapter Review** on pages 183–185 or to the **Vocabulary** (Voc.) on page 180. This will enable you to locate those **Chapter Review** questions that correspond to questions you missed on the **Progress Self-Test.** The lesson where the material is covered is also indicated in the chart.

Question	1	2	3–4	5	6	7	8	9	10–11	12
Objective	A	B	A	A	C	C	C	D	G	I
Lesson	4-1	4-7	4-1	4-7	4-4	4-5	4-7	4-8	4-2	4-2
Question	13–14	15–16	17–18	19	20	21	22	23	24–25	26
Objective	L	J	K	Voc.	L	F	O	Voc.	E	Voc.
Lesson	4-6	4-3	4-3	4-6	4-6	4-7	4-1	4-9	4-8	4-6
Question	27	28	29	30	31					
Objective	C	M	N	H	H					
Lesson	4-4	4-9	4-9	4-2	4-2					

CHAPTER 4 REVIEW (pp. 183–185)

1. 215 **3.** 83 **5.** 31 **7.** 158 **9.** 1966 **11.** 5 **13.** $\frac{14}{65} =$ 0.215 . . . **15.** 24 **17.** 18 **19.** 24 **21.** 184 **23.** $\frac{8}{12} = .\overline{6}$
25. (b) **27.** $x = 4$ **29.** $y = 2$ **31.** powering **33.** (d) **35.** $5 \cdot x + 9 \cdot x = 14 \cdot x$ **37.** $\frac{a}{9} + \frac{b}{9} + \frac{a+b}{9}$ **39.** Sample: $2 + 6 = 1 + 6 + 1$ **41.** If the weight is w ounces, the postage is $s + 20 \cdot w$ cents **43.** $18 + 27$ **45.** $4 \times 20 - 1$
47. $2x + 7$ **49.** $x < 5$ **51.** $127.\overline{27}$ **53.** 72 in.² or .5 ft²

55. See below. **57.** See below. **59.** $y \geq 2$ **61.** See below.
63. **∗∗**, ↑

55.

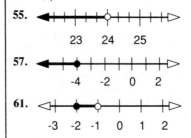

23 24 25

57.

-4 -2 0 2

61.

-3 -2 -1 0 1 2

LESSON 5-1 (pp. 188–192)

5. Sample: If you bike $\frac{1}{4}$ mile and $\frac{1}{2}$ mile, then altogether you have biked $\left(\frac{1}{4} + \frac{1}{2}\right)$ miles. **7.** Both are. If you change the units to pieces of fruit, then Carla is right. If you do not change the units, Peter is right. **9.** (1) 13 pieces (2) 49,050,525 people (3) $3.13 (4) 27% (5) 5.25 lb
11. $15 + r = 43$ **13.** $M + 112 \leq 250$ **15.** 109 oz
17. 2100 g **19.** $b + s + 1$ **21.** No, rain and sun could appear on the same day. **23.** Mountain region **25.** (a), (b), (d), (f) **27.** 3 **29.** True **31.** $\frac{3}{10}$

LESSON 5-2 (pp. 193–197)

1. $\frac{16}{4}$ km or 4 km **3. a.** $\frac{1}{3} + \frac{1}{4}$ **b.** Sample: $\frac{2}{6}, \frac{3}{9}, \frac{4}{12}, \frac{5}{15}, \frac{6}{18}$
c. Sample: $\frac{2}{8}, \frac{3}{12}, \frac{4}{16}, \frac{5}{20}, \frac{6}{24}$ **d.** $\frac{7}{12}$ **5. a.** $\frac{11}{10}$ **b.** $.8 + .3 = 1.1 = \frac{11}{10}$ **7.** $\frac{17}{x}$ **9.** $\frac{41}{40}$ **11.** $\frac{19}{6}$ **13.** $\frac{5}{2}$ km or $2\frac{1}{2}$ km **15.** $\frac{169}{24}$
17. $\frac{961}{44}$ **19.** 20 pieces **21.** 6×10^4 **23. a.** Sample: -3, 0, $\frac{1}{2}$
b. See below.

23. b.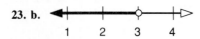

1   2   3   4

LESSON 5-3 (pp. 198–201)

7. twice the length, pointed right **9.** $\frac{6}{5}$ of the length, a little longer than what is drawn, pointed right. **11. a.** See below.
b. -11 **13.** $1 \boxed{\pm} \boxed{+} 8 \boxed{\pm} \boxed{=}$ **15. a.** 250 + -150 **b.** 100

17. a. -50 + -40.27 **b.** -90.27 **19.** Sample: Joe loses seven yards in football and then loses five more; the result is a loss of twelve yards, -12. **21.** It goes 20 km in the opposite direction. **23.** The temperature is -7°. **25.** (a)
27. a. 18% **b.** 128,000 people **29.** 6.2 **31.** Sample: 0 or $\frac{1}{2}$
33. 32,680 feet **b.** 6.189 or $6\frac{25}{132}$

11. a.

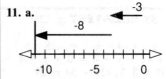

-10   -5   0

LESSON 5-4 (pp. 202–205)

3. -7 **5.** -70 **7.** $\frac{1}{2}$ **13.** Additive Identity Property of Zero
15. Property of Opposites **17.** 0 **19.** $\frac{14}{11}$ **21. a.** 40 + -40 = 0 **b.** Property of Opposites **23.** 6 **25.** -6 **27.** 3
29. a. The temperature is -9°. **b.** -11 + 2 = -9
31. $t + -35 = -60$ **33.** 9.7×10^{-5}; 3.2×10^4; 5.1×10^7 **35. a.** 10,000 lb **b.** 3750 lb **c.** No

LESSON 5-5 (pp. 206–210)

1. (d) **3.** 4.01 **5.** 11 **7.** 20 **9.** 0 **11. a.** positive **b.** 6.2
13. a. positive **b.** 13 **15.** True **17.** False **21.** -14 **23.** -1
25. $\frac{-1117}{30}$ **27.** $\frac{-15}{2}$ **29.** 6 **31.** 4.3 **33.** True **35.** True **37.** 0
39. $\frac{129}{6}$, or 21.5 **41.** $n + -n = 0$ **43.** $2\frac{1}{4}''$ or $2\frac{2}{8}''$

LESSON 5-6 (pp. 211–215)

3. 180° **5.** counterclockwise **9.** 180° **11.** -300° **13.** 125° **15.** -11° **19.** 120° **21. a.** 60° (or -300°) **b.** D **23.** I **25. a.** -30° **b.** -5° **27.** 45 + m = 180 (in minutes), or m + $\frac{3}{4}$ = 3 (in hours) **29.** 0 **31.** 55 **33.** 6000 m **35.** x + y + x = y + (x + x)

LESSON 5-7 (pp. 216–220)

1. Sample: 3 + 2.4 = 2.4 + 3 **3.** Associative Property of Addition **5.** (b) **7.** (c) **11.** 12 **13.** 0 **15.** They are $10.25 over budget. **17.** 1° **19. a.** Sample: (9 − 6) − 2 ≠ 9 − (6 − 2) **b.** Subtraction does not possess the associative property. **21.** (b) **23. a.** 60° **b.** acute **25.** -60° **27.** 8453 g or 8.453 kg **29.** (t − 3) degrees **31.** For any number a, a + -a = 0.

LESSON 5-8 (pp. 221–225)

1. 5 **3. a.** Yes **b.** Yes **c.** Yes **d.** Addition Property of Equality **5. a.** -86 **b.** 144 **c.** 144 + 86 = 230 **7. a.** $\frac{-22}{3}$ **b.** $\frac{158}{3}$ or $52\frac{2}{3}$ **c.** 60 = $\frac{158}{3}$ + $\frac{22}{3}$ **9.** (b) **11.** 5° **13.** 82; 82 + 43 + -5 = 120 **15.** $1025 **17. a.** G + 10 **b.** W + 10 **c.** G = W **d.** If G = W, then G + 10 = W + 10 **e.** Addition Property of Equality **19.** Step 1, Associative Property of Addition; step 2, Commutative Property of Addition; step 3, Associative Property of Addition; step 4, Property of Opposites; step 5, Additive Identity Property of Zero **21. a.** Sample: -4 **b.** Sample: 2 **23.** 30 **25.** See below. **27.** 73 mm **29.** t − 5 **31.** the ray with endpoint A containing B

25.

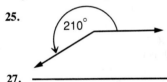

27. ——————————————————

LESSON 5-9 (pp. 226–229)

3. $\overline{FE}$ or $\overline{EF}$ **15.** 26-gon **17.** 12 **19. a.** Sample:

POLYGON, LOPNGY, GNPOLY **b.** hexagon **21.** nonagon **23. a.** $\overline{PR}$, $\overline{PS}$, $\overline{QT}$, $\overline{QS}$, $\overline{TR}$ **b.** 5; See below. **25.** (c) **27.** -22; -22 + 12 = -10 **29.** step 1, Addition Property of Equality; step 2, Property of Opposites; step 3, Additive Identity Property of Zero

23. b.

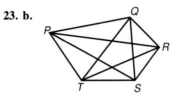

LESSON 5-10 (pp. 230–234)

1. 436 miles **3. a.** line through P and Q **b.** See below. **5. a.** line segment from P to Q **b.** See below. **7.** 8 **9.** x + 3 **13.** (x + 543)ft **15. a.** 9 + 9 + 5 + 5 + x = 30 **b.** 2 **17.** 40 and 20; 30 and 30 **19. a.** Yes **b.** 20 **21.** See below. **23. a.** -22 + t = 10 **b.** 32 **c.** -22 + 32 = 10 **25. a.** 0 **b.** x + y **27.** All are obtuse. **29.** 93° **31.** See below.

3. b.

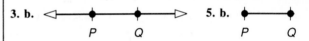

5. b.

P   Q

21.

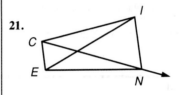

31.

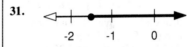

CHAPTER 5 PROGRESS SELF-TEST (p. 236)

1. -7 **2.** -710 **3.** -9.8 + -(-1) = -9.8 + 1 = -8.8 **4.** x + y + -x + 4 = x + -x + y + 4 = 0 + y + 4 = y + 4 **5.** 8 **6.** 2 + 1 + 0 = 3 **7.** -29 + 58 = 29 **8.** |-(-3) + 8| = |3 + 8| = |11| = 11 **9.** Add -43 to both sides; x = -12 **10.** Add 25 to both sides; y = 37 **11.** 8 = z + -7; add 7 to both sides; z = 15 **12.** $\frac{53}{12}$ + $\frac{11}{12}$ = $\frac{(53 + 11)}{12}$ = $\frac{64}{12}$ = $\frac{16}{3}$ **13.** $\frac{5}{x}$ + $\frac{10}{x}$ = $\frac{(5 + 10)}{x}$ = $\frac{15}{x}$ **14.** 9 is the common denominator. So $\frac{8}{3}$ = $\frac{24}{9}$ and $\frac{17}{9}$ + $\frac{24}{9}$ = $\frac{41}{9}$. **15.** Notice that $\frac{2}{16}$ = $\frac{1}{8}$. So 8 is a common denominator and $\frac{2}{8}$ + $\frac{3}{8}$ + $\frac{1}{8}$ = $\frac{6}{8}$ = $\frac{3}{4}$. **16.** 20 **17.** Addition Property of Equality **18.** Associative Property of Addition **19.** One instance is 3 + 0 = 3. There are many others. **20.** hexagon

21. 3 cm + 3 cm + 4 cm + 4 cm + 4 cm = 18 cm **22.** (a); (b) is a segment, (c) is a ray, and (d) is a line **23.** m + n = 50 **24.** -20 + c = 150 **25.** Add 20 to both sides; c = 170 **26.** MP = MA + AP = 16 + 8 = 24 **27.** MA + PA = MP, so 2.3 + PA = 3. Add -2.3 to both sides to get PA = 0.7. **28.** See below. **29.** 5 m + 3 cm = 5 m + .03 m = 5.03 m **30.** Positive, since the absolute value of the second addend is larger than the absolute value of the first addend. **31.** $\frac{360°}{5}$ = 72° **32.** clockwise turn of 72° + 72° has a magnitude of -144° **33.** -50° + 250° = 200° **34.** (b)

28.

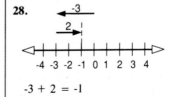

-3 + 2 = -1

The chart below keys the **Progress Self-Test** questions to the objectives in the **Chapter Review** on pages 237–239 or to the **Vocabulary** (Voc.) on page 235. This will enable you to locate those **Chapter Review** questions that correspond to questions you missed on the **Progress Self-Test.** The lesson where the material is covered is also indicated in the chart.

Question	1	2	3	4	5–6	7	8	9–11	12–15	16	17	18
Objective	A	A	C	A	B	C	B	E	A	D	F	F
Lesson	5-5	5-3	5-4	5-3	5-5	5-4	5-5	5-10	5-2	5-8	5-8	5-7

Question	19	20	21	22	23	24	25	26–27	28	29	30	31–33	34
Objective	F	G	E	Voc.	I	K	D	J	M	K	A	L	H
Lesson	5-4	5-9	5-10	5-10	5-8	5-8	5-8	5-10	5-3	5-3	5-5	5-6	5-9

CHAPTER 5 REVIEW (pp. 237–239)

1. -12 **3.** 9.6 **5.** 1 **7.** $\frac{46}{9}$ **9.** $\frac{13}{12}$ **11.** 12 **13.** 8 **15.** -17 **17.** -40 **19.** $\frac{2}{7}$ **21.** 48 **23.** 20 **25.** -3 **27.** 38 **29.** $x = 180 + -y$ **31.** 12 **33.** 15 cm **35.** $12 + 18 + 20 + 7 + x = 82$ **37.** Addition Property of Equality **39.** Commutative Property of Addition **41.** pentagon, convex **43.** *LEAK* **45.** 4, 4 **47.** $1\frac{1}{2} + \frac{3}{5} = M$ **49.** $T = D + M + C$ **51.** $x + 3$

53. a. $\frac{3}{8} + -\frac{1}{4}$ **b.** $\frac{1}{8}$ point **55. a.** -250 + 75 **b.** 175 feet below the surface **57.** 135° **59.** A **61. See below. 63. See below.**

61.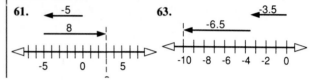

63.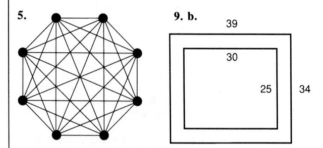

LESSON 6-1 (pp. 242–246)

5. What is 34.2×5.67? **7.** Take your time. **9.** Don't give up. **13.** She gave up instead of trying. **17. 25.** Here is the list:

AA EA IA OA UA
AE EE IE OE UE
AI EI II OI UI
AO EO IO OO UO
AU EU IU OU UU

19. 13 trains **21.** 12 edges **23.** $\frac{55}{42}$ **25.** 13 **27.** $16.\overline{6}$ or $16\frac{2}{3}$ **29.** 51 million

LESSON 6-2 (pp. 247–250)

5. 15 **7.** 7 **9.** 36 **11.** Not enough information is given. **13.** (c) **15.** 39 **17.** 35 **19. See below.** Sides must have same length, angles same measure. **21.** two consecutive odd numbers that are both primes; sample: 29 and 31 **23.** last year **25.** Not enough information given. It depends on which is larger, $b + e + h$ or $c + f + g$. **27.** 0 is the total difference. **29.** 10 **31.** $\overline{BC}$ and $\overline{CD}$

19.

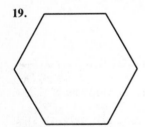

LESSON 6-3 (pp. 251–254)

3. 2 diagonals **5.** 56 games; **See right. 7.** Wanda is youngest. $W < B < J$; $C < J < P$; $W < C$; $B < P$ (known); $B < C$ **9. a.** 110 ft **b.** 146 ft; **See right. 11.** 1, 2, 4, 5, 8, 10, 20, 40 **13.** 16,009 **15.** 41, 43, 47 **17.** If Sarah and Dana have the same amount of money, then they will still have the same amount if each receives $2 more. **19.** 30 **21.** 56.83 **23.** 22 pounds

5.

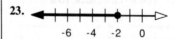

9. b.

```
          39
  ┌──────────────┐
  │      30      │
  │  ┌──────┐    │
  │  │      │    │
  │  │   25 │ 34 │
  └──┴──────┴────┘
```

LESSON 6-4 (pp. 255–258)

3. 5 **5.** 3 **7.** 3 **11.** No **13.** 147, 118, 35 **15.** 13 and 1 **17.** three possible answers: 91 and 37, 82 and 28, or 73 and 19 **19.** Ali **21.** Work inside parentheses, then do powers, then multiplications or divisions from left to right, then additions or subtractions from left to right. **23. See below. 25.** Sample: $(2 + 3) + 7 = 2 + (3 + 7)$ **27.** 32 inches **29. a.** $1.41\overline{42857}$ **b.** 1.414 **c.** 1 and 2

23.

LESSON 6-5 (pp. 259–263)

3. 65 diagonals **5.** $5.47 **7.** $21.67 **9.** The cost of a m-minute call for Francie is $.25 + (m - 1) \cdot .18$ dollars. **11. a. See below. b.** $1.46 + 24 \cdot .82 = $21.14 **c.** $1.42 + (m - 1) \cdot .82 **13.** 43 **15.** $x = 7$ and $y = 3$ **17.** -8 pounds

11. a.

number of minutes	cost
1	$1.46
2	$1.46 + .82
3	$1.46 + 2 \cdot 82
4	$1.46 + 3 \cdot 82
5	$1.46 + 4 \cdot 82

LESSON 6-6 (pp. 264–268)

3. Yes 7. **a.** quadrilateral **b.** Yes 9. **a.** 6 **b.** Yes 11. **See below.** Octagon = 8-gon; 8 − 3 diagonals from each vertex 13. Move the decimal point 3 places to the right. 15. **a.** Yes **b.** Yes **c.** No **d.** No 17. **a.** Sample: if $m = 2$, $-(-2 + 9) = 2 + -9$, True **b.** Sample: if $m = -4$, $-(-(-4) + 9) = -4 + -9$, True **c.** possibly true 19. (b) 21. 10 games 23. **a.** \$4.50 **b.** $\$1.00 + (h − 1).50$

25. $0.\overline{3}$, $33\frac{1}{3}\%$ 27. perimeter

11.

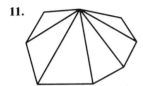

LESSON 6-7 (pp. 269–273)

1. \$10 3. The same operation is used; only the numbers differ. 5. If you cannot do a problem with complicated numbers, try simpler numbers. 7. $\frac{30}{M}$ miles 9. **a.** \$2.45

b. $98k$ cents **c.** ck cents 11. $(R − Z)$ sheets 13. $(G − 49.95)$ dollars 15. 4 places to the left 17. -2 19. 3.5×10^{11} 21. 4025.043 grams 23. 15,625

CHAPTER 6 PROGRESS SELF-TEST (p. 275)

1. any two of dictionary, glossary in a math book, encyclopedia 2. An octagon has 20 diagonals. **See right.** 3. Name the teams A, B, C, D, E and F. Draw all the segments connecting these points. The figure created is a hexagon. The number of games is equal to the number of diagonals plus the number of sides in the hexagon. That is $9 + 6 = 15$ games. **See right.** 4. Use trial and error. The sums of each pair of factors of 24 are: $1 + 24 = 25$; $2 + 12 = 14$; $3 + 8 = 11$ and $4 + 6 = 10$. So 4 and 6 give the smallest sums. 5. If you know an algorithm for an operation, you know how to answer the question. So multiplying fractions is only an exercise, not a problem. 6. 53, 59 7. If one value is positive and one is negative, the pattern will be false. For instance, $|-5| + |3| = 5 + 3 = 8$, but $|-5 + 3| = |-2| = 2$. 8. 2 pounds at \$3 per pound cost \$6, so multiplication gives the answer. \$1.49 per pound • 1.62 pounds = \$2.4138, which rounds up to \$2.42. 9. True 10. By trial and error, $(8 − 3) + (8 − 4) = 5 + 4 = 9$, so 8 is the solution. 11. Read carefully and draw a picture. There must be 6 more dots on the right side between 3 and 10, for a total of 14 dots. **See right.** 12. Use trial and error. A 3-gon has 0 diagonals, a 4-gon has 2 diagonals, a 5-gon has 5 diagonals, a 6-gon has 9 diagonals. 13. Use a special case. $\frac{.05}{.01} = 5$, which means that the decimal point is moved two places to the right. 14. **See right.** 15. After 31 weeks, Phyllis will have $1000 − 31 • 25$ dollars left. That computes to \$225. 16. After you find an answer, you should check your work.

2.

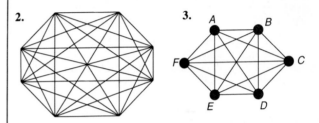

3.

11.

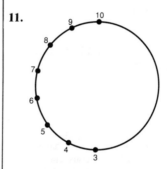

14.

weeks	amount left
1	1000 − 25
2	1000 − 2 • 25
3	1000 − 3 • 25
4	1000 − 4 • 25

The chart below keys the **Progress Self-Test** questions to the objectives in the **Chapter Review** on pages 276–277 or to the **Vocabulary** (Voc.) on page 274. This will enable you to locate those **Chapter Review** questions that correspond to questions you missed on the **Progress Self-Test.** The lesson where the material is covered is also indicated in the chart.

Question	1	2	3	4	5	6	7	8
Objective	D	J	I	B	D	C	G	H
Lesson	6-2	6-3	6-2	6-4	6-2	6-2	6-3	6-7

Question	9	10	11	12	13	14–15	16
Objective	Voc.	B	K	K	F	E	A
Lesson	6-6	6-4	6-3	6-3	6-6	6-5	6-1

CHAPTER 6 REVIEW (pp. 276–277)

1. A good problem solver is flexible by trying different ways to solve a problem. 3. There are several ways to check this answer. She could multiply 309 × 1487 on her calculator, or divide by 309 to see if she gets 1487. 5. (b) 7. 1036 9. prime; only 1 and 47 are factors. 11. 31, 37 13. a number that equals the sum of all its divisors except itself 15. 64, 128, and 256 are the next rows in the table below, so 256 has nine factors. 17. 6, left 19. If $x = 2$ and $y = 3$, then $5x + 5y = 5 \cdot 2 + 5 \cdot 3 = 25$, but $10xy = 10 \cdot 2 \cdot 3 = 60$ 21. Simpler numbers indicate to multiply. Your cost is $8.69. 23. Use a pentagon. 5 diagonals and 5 sides add to 10 games. Since they play twice it is 20 games for the season. **See right.** 25. A diagram helps. **See right.** Pueblo is the farthest south. 27. The decagon has 35 diagonals. **See right.** 29. 7 triangles. **See right.**

15.

2	1, 2
4	1, 2, 4
8	1, 2, 4, 8
16	1, 2, 4, 8, 16
32	1, 2, 4, 8, 16, 32

23.

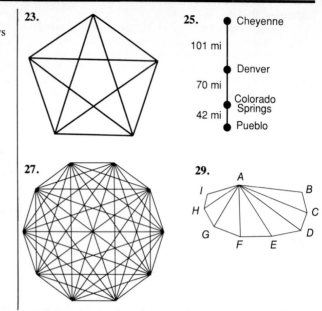

25.
Cheyenne
101 mi
Denver
70 mi
Colorado Springs
42 mi
Pueblo

27.

29.
A B C D E F G H I

LESSON 7-1 (pp. 280–284)

1. 4 rolls 3. 316 passengers 5. the take-away model 7. 81° 9. m∠DBC 11. $b^2 - a^2$ 13. 24.64 square units 15. AB = 113 miles 17. 55% 19. a. $470.75 b. $510.75 - W$ dollars 21. $\frac{3}{5}$ 23. 637 25. 1 milligram = .001 gram (or 1000 mg = 1 g) 27. Sample: let $a = 5$, $b = -2$. Then $-(a + b) = -(5 + -2) = -3$ and $-b + -a = -(-2) + -5 = -3$. It may be true always. 29. Sample: 3.00_, where any digit except 0 can be put in the blank.

LESSON 7-2 (pp. 285–289)

1. 3, 4, left 3. a. $74 - 20$ b. $74 + -20$ c. 54°F 5. a. $72 - 3$ b. $72 + -3$ c. 69 kg 7. 8 9. -53 11. -4 13. 10 15. -3 19. the opposite of A minus negative four 21. a. 3 b. 2 c. 1 d. 0 e. -1 f. -2 23. 2 25. (c) 27. a. True b. True 29. a. $a - b = b - a$ for all numbers a and b b. No 31. $n - 4$ 33. Addition Property of Equality

LESSON 7-3 (pp. 290–294)

1. 4 3. 8 5. 6 lb 7. 540 ft 9. 1° 11. 17 points (His guess was 17 points too high.) 13. -368 15. positive 17. positive 19. negative 21. $x - y = 437,000$ 23. a. from 1950 to 1960, 48; from 1960 to 1970, 6291; from 1970 to 1980, -13,584 b. -7245 c. The population decreased by 7245 from 1950 to 1980. 25. 66 or 67 27. a. 899 b. $J - I - 1$ 29. a. 1410 people b. from 4 to 10 years old 31. 12 in.

LESSON 7-4 (pp. 295–298)

3. a. $x + -14 = -2$ b. 12 5. a. $a + -6 = 9$ b. $a = 15$ 7. No 9. (c) 11. 12.21; $3.01 = 12.21 - 9.2$ 13. a. $s - 3 = -2$ b. 1 c. The team was ahead by one point. 15. -7 feet (7 feet below the surface) 17. -11 19. a. 58 years b. 214° 21. $G < 21$ or $G > 31$ 23. two thousand, three hundred five and 00/100 dollars 25. 70 cm or 0.7 m 27. 1.5 29. 6,340,000 31. .000064

LESSON 7-5 (pp. 299–302)

3. a. III b. -2 5. $4 + 1 = y$ 7. a. $-15 = y$ b. between lines 2 and 3 11. $x = -5$ 13. $y = 10.5$ 15. $80 = 94 - 14$ or $94 - 80 = 14$ 17. $-1 - -5 = 4$ or $-5 = -1 - 4$ 19. $10 = -13 + 23$ 21. (c) 23. $y = 48$ 25. 58 or 59 years old 27. a. -14 b. 88 29. 180° 31. $2n - 3$

LESSON 7-6 (pp. 303–306)

3. t 5. 302; $300 - 302 = -2$ 7. 90; $-45 = 45 - 90$ 9. -53; $-53 - 57 = -110$ 11. a. 3288 b. 3288 tickets have been sold. 13. a. $22,500 - d = 20,250$ b. 2,250 feet c. They came down 2,250 feet. 15. 0 17. 13 19. 1: Add-Opp Property; 2: Addition Property of Equality; 3: Assoc. Property of Addition; 4: Prop. of Opposites; 5: Additive Identity Property of Zero; 6: Addition Property of Equality; 7: Assoc. Property of Addition; 8: Property of Opposites; 9: Additive Identity Property of Zero 21. $A = 28$ 23. **See below.** 25. a. **See below.** b. right angles 27. a. $s - 1.14 = 637.47$ b. 638.61 29. 180°

23.

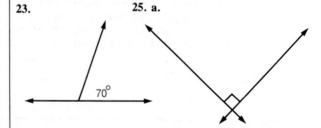

70°

25. a.

LESSON 7-7 (pp. 307–312)

1. straight 3. linear pair 5. 92° 7. supplementary 9. angles 1 and 4, 2 and 3, 3 and 4, 2 and 1 11. m∠2 = 55°, m∠3 = 125°, m∠4 = 55° 13. $x = 135°$ 15. $d = f = 90.5°$, $e = 89.5°$ 17. True 19. 6 21. 71st and South Chicago 23. angles DCA and ACB 25. True 27. True 29. 122° 31. $x + y = 180°$ 33. 157 35. -38 37. $2.60

LESSON 7-8 (pp. 313–317)
1. 118° **3.** 62° **5.** 118° **7.** *p* **9.** angles 1 and 6, 4 and 5, 2 and 8, 3 and 7 **11.** angles 2, 3, 5, and 6 **13.** Yes **15.** m∠1 = m∠6 = m∠8 = 84°, m∠3 = m∠4 = m∠5 = m∠7 = 96° **17.** all of the angles 1 through 8 **19. See below. 21.** // **23.** 90° **25.** m∠1 = 90°, m∠2 = m∠4 = 40°, m∠3 = 140° **27.** 360° **29.** angles 3 and 4; **See below. 31.** $a \cdot 1 = a$ **33.** $c = 180 - a - b$ **35.** $C - W + D$

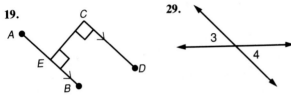

19.   **29.**

LESSON 7-9 (pp. 318–321)
3. a. $TU = TS = SV = UV = 15$ mm **b.** m∠U = m∠S ≈ 100°, m∠T = m∠V ≈ 80° **5.** $\overline{MN}$ and $\overline{QP}$, or $\overline{MQ}$ and $\overline{NP}$ **7.** ∠Q **9.** 110° **11.** all sides equal in length

13. *A, D, E, G* **15.** *A, B, C, D, E, G, H* **17.** rectangles and squares **19.** parallelograms, rhombuses, rectangles, and squares **21.** not enough information **23. a.** 147° **b.** 57° **c.** 123° **d.** 33° **25.** *ABG* **27.** m∠*DBA* = 30°; m∠*CBD* = m∠*FBA* = 150° **29.** ⊥ **31. a.** from 1950 to 1960, 103,932; from 1960 to 1970, -23,952; from 1970 to 1980, -81,160 **b.** -1,180 **c.** from 1950 to 1980 the population decreased by 1180 people

LESSON 7-10 (pp. 322–327)
5. 1° **7.** 40° **9.** If a triangle had two obtuse angles, the sum of their measures would be more than 180°. But the sum of the measures of all three angles is 180°. **11.** 90° **13.** (d) **15.** 146° **17.** $\overline{AD}$ and $\overline{BC}$ are parallel. **19.** m∠B = m∠BCD **21. a.** Line segment *AB* is parallel to ray *CD*. **b. See below. 23. a.** True **b.** True **25.** 910 **27.** 20.4

21. b.

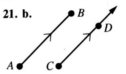

CHAPTER 7 PROGRESS SELF-TEST (p. 329)

1. -6 + -22 = -28 **See below. 2.** 45 + -110 = -65 **3.** 5 − 13 + 2 − -11 = 5 + -13 + 2 + 11 = 5 **4.** $y + -14 = -24$; add 14 to both sides; $y = -10$ **5.** Add *x* to both sides; $x + -50 = 37$; add 50 to both sides; $x = 87$ **6.** $g + -3.2 = -2$; add 3.2 to both sides; $g = 1.2$ **7.** $c + -a = b$; add *a* to both sides; $c = b + a$; add -b to both sides; $c + -b = a$ **8.** Angles *ABE* and *ABD* are a linear pair, so their measures add to 180. So m∠*ABE* + 25 = 180, from which m∠*ABE* = 155. **9.** m∠*CBD* = 90 − m∠*ABD* = 90 − 25 = 65 **10.** ∠5 and ∠6 are corresponding angles, so have the same measure 74°. ∠7 forms a linear pair with ∠6, so 74 + m∠7 = 180, from which m∠7 = 106. **11.** ∠5, a corresponding angle; ∠3, a vertical angle; and ∠4, the vertical angle to ∠5 **12.** Angles 1 and 8 each form a linear pair with ∠5, so are supplementary. Angles 2 and 7, having the same measures as angles 1 and 8, are therefore also supplementary. **13.** The sum of

3 right angles would be 270°, which is greater than triangle-sum of 180°. **14.** 55 + 4 + *x* = 180; 59 + *x* = 180; *x* = 121 **15.** ∠*CBE*, an alternate interior angle **16. See below. 17.** rhombuses, which are parallelograms with all sides of the same length **18.** $x + -y + 5$ **19.** (c); all others are facts related to $x + y = 180$ **20.** Use the comparison model. $V − N = L$, or $N + L = V$. **21.** Use the take-away model. $5 − 0.4 = 4.6$ meters. **22.** Use the comparison model or try simpler numbers. $Z − 67$ inches **23.** Use the slide model. $x° − 7° = -3°$. **24.** Add 7 to both sides. $x = 4°$. **25.** Use the take-away model. Area of outer square = 8^2 square meters. Area of inner square = 4^2 square meters. $8^2 − 4^2 = 64 − 16 = 48$ square meters.

1.   **16.**

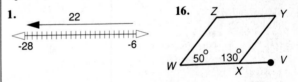

The chart below keys the **Progress Self-Test** questions to the objectives in the **Chapter Review** on pages 330–333 or to the **Vocabulary** (Voc.) on page 328. This will enable you to locate those **Chapter Review** questions that correspond to questions you missed on the **Progress Self-Test**. The lesson where the material is covered is also indicated in the chart.

Question	1	2–3	4	5	6	7	8–9	10	11–12	13	14
Objective	Q	A	B	C	B	C	D	E	K	M	F
Lesson	7-2	7-2	7-4	7-6	7-4	7-6	7-7	7-8	7-8	7-10	7-10
Question	15	16	17	18	19	20	21	22	23	24	25
Objective	K	G	L	H	I	P	N	P	O	B	N
Lesson	7-8	7-9	7-9	7-3	7-5	7-3	7-1	7-3	7-2	7-3	7-1

CHAPTER 7 REVIEW (pp. 330–333)

1. -320 **3.** 13.7 **5.** 72 **7.** -7.2 **9.** $c = e + 45$ **11.** 56

13. $\frac{1}{6}$ **15.** 90° **17.** 180° − *x*° **19.** Angles 7, 1, and 3 **21.** 180° − *y*° **23.** 38° **25.** 50° **27.** Yes, 10 cm **29.** 4 **31.** -3 **33.** $a + c = b$ **35.** 140 **37.** 180° − *x*° **39.** 1, 8,

4, and 5 **41.** 1, 7, 5, and 3 **43.** rectangles and squares
45. all **47.** Yes, the angles could have measures 40°, 60°,
and 80°, which add to 180°. **49.** 5500 square feet **51.** 21
53. 1905 or 1904 **55.** 2.5 million **57.** $F - R = L$ **59. See below.**

59.

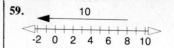

-2 0 2 4 6 8 10

LESSON 8-1 (pp. 336–340)
1. 1 hour **3.** Sample: relaxation time **5.** horizontal **7.** Los
Angeles and Houston **9.** 2 million people **11. a.** 1981
b. -$4.9 billion **13.** vertical **15. a.** Yes **b.** 3 **17. a.** No
b. numbers are not equally spaced **19.** 3.4 and 3.294
21. 100,000 or 200,000 votes **23. See below.**
25. -2,200,000,000 **27.** Lincoln: 1,900,000; Douglas:
1,400,000; Breckinridge: 800,000; Bell: 600,000 **29.** 144

23.

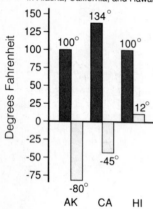

All-time High and Low Temperatures
in Alaska, California, and Hawaii

LESSON 8-2 (pp. 341–347)
1. See below. **3.** E **5.** C **7.** H **9.** F **11.** R **13.** J **15. See
below.** **17.** 14.5° **19.** -3 **23.** 0 **25.** II **27.** III **29.** III and
IV **31.** II and III **33.** III **35.** II **37.** Numbers on the scale
should be 0, 2640, 5280, 7920, 10,560, 13,200, 15,840,
18,480, and 21,120. **39. See below.** **41.** $-\frac{9}{32}$

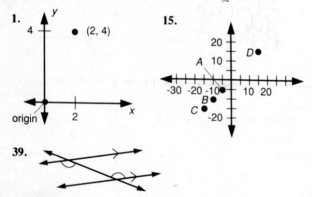

39.

LESSON 8-3 (pp. 348–353)
7. a. -2 **b.** (3, -2) **9.** In these answers, to save space,
graphs of lines are not shown. Instead, some points are
given. Some points on this line: (0, 10), (5, 5), (8, 2)
11. c **13. a.** $x - y = 8$ **b.** some points on this line:
(0, -8), (8, 0), (10, 2) **15. a.** $y = -x - 7$ **b.** Samples:

(0, -7), (2, -9), (-10, 3) **17.** II **19. a.** 25.1% **b.** 0.5%
21. $10.50 **23.** 99

LESSON 8-4 (pp. 354–357)
1. 1987–88 **3. a.** 18° **b.** 20° **c.** -9° **5.** January **7.** 1 day
9. (Dec.24th, -20°) **11.** Graphs can describe drawings and
geometric figures. **13.** circle; **See below.** **15. See below.**
17. some points on the line: (0, -3), (5, 2), (3, 0) **19.** (3, 8)

13.   **15.**

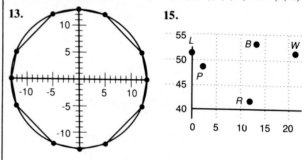

LESSON 8-5 (pp. 358–361)
3. The figure is moved 7 units down. **7.** The image is a triangle with vertices $A' = (3, -5)$, $B' = (7, 2)$, and $C' =
(-5, 4)$. **9.** The graph is moved up k units. **13. See below.**
c. They are congruent. **15. a.** Samples: image of (0, 0) is
(4,-5), image of (3, -1) is (7, -6), image of (-2, 3) is (2, -2)
b. See below. **17.** some points on the line: (2, -2), (-5, 5),
(0, 0) **19. a. See below.** **b.** It is easier to insert additional
points.

13.   **15. b.**   **19. a.**

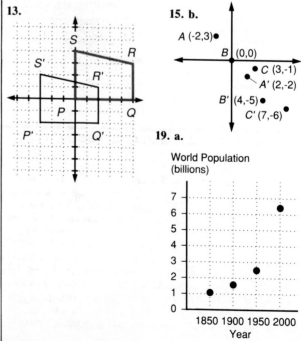

World Population
(billions)

---

9. See below. 11. See below. 13. a.–b. See below.
c. over the *y*-axis 15. TOMATO 17. CHEEK 19. *B* =
(150, 0), *C* = (150, 50), *D* = (50, 50), *E* = (50, 225),
F = (0, 225) 21. a. 5% b. 12% c. $\frac{\text{telephone}}{\text{telegraph}}$

9.

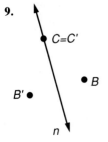

11.

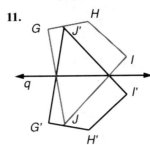

13. a.-b.

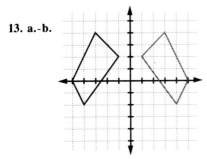

LESSON 8-7 (pp. 367–371)
9. A, H, I, M, O, T, U, V, W, X, Y 11. 8 13. See
below. 15. See below. 17. See below. 19. Sample: See
below. 21. See below. 23. some points on this line:
(-2, -2), (5, -9), and (0, -4) 25. 103

13.

15.

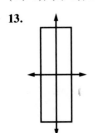
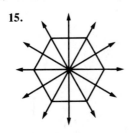

17.

19.

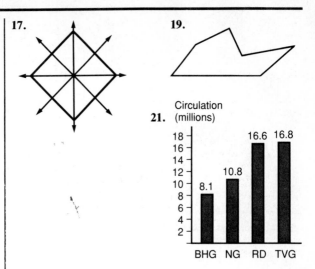

21.

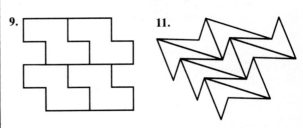

Circulation (millions)

BHG NG RD TVG

LESSON 8-8 (pp. 372–375)
9. Sample: **See below.** 11. Sample: **See below.** 13. See
below. 15. **a.** A sheet of stamps is a tessellation; rectangles
tessellate, so no paper is wasted. 17. square 19. **See below.**
21. There are no symmetry lines. 23. 2×10^{-8} 25. (c)

9.

11.

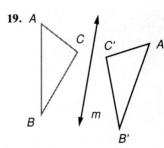

13.

19.

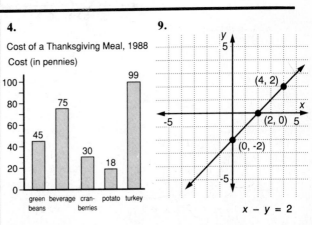

CHAPTER 8 PROGRESS SELF-TEST (p. 377)

1. the week of November 9 2. about 3 million barrels
3. 0.4 million barrels 4. **See right.** 5. a. *E* b. *A* 6. *E*
7. *B*, since -4 + 2 = -2. 8. Add 10 to the second coordinate to get (2, 15). 9. **See right.** 10. *M* is 3 units below
(3, 9), so the first coordinate of *M* is 3 and the second coordinate 9 − 3 or 6. *M* = (3, 6). 11. The hole is directly
above (9, 3) so its first coordinate is 9. Its second coordinate
is halfway between 9 and 12, so is 10.5. Hole = (9, 10.5)
12. Sample: See p. 632. 13. Sample: See p. 632. 14. See
p. 632. 15. See p. 632.16. See p. 632. 17. See p. 632.
18. m∠*V* = m∠*W*; m∠*W* = 72° 19. Sample: graphs can
show a lot of information in a small place. Graphs can picture relationships. 20. when they have the same size and
shape

4.

Cost of a Thanksgiving Meal, 1988
Cost (in pennies)

100 ―
 80 ―   75   99
 60 ―
 45   30
 40 ―   18
 20 ―
  0 ―
    green beverage cran- potato turkey
    beans   berries

9.

x − *y* = 2

(4, 2)
(2, 0)
(0, -2)

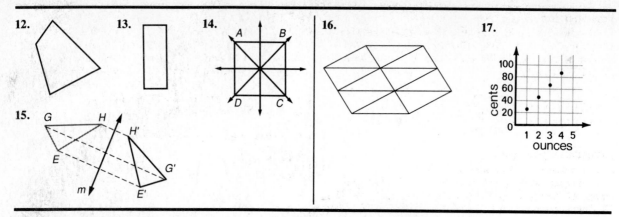

12. **13.** **14.** **16.** **17.**

15.

The chart below keys the **Progress Self-Test** questions to the objectives in the **Chapter Review** on pages 379–381 or to the **Vocabulary** (Voc.) on page 376. This will enable you to locate those **Chapter Review** questions that correspond to questions you missed on the **Progress Self-Test.** The lesson where the material is covered is also indicated in the chart.

Question	1–3	4	5–6	7	8	9	10	11	12–14	15
Objective	F	G	K	L	M	L	K	H	B	A
Lesson	8-1	8-1	8-2	8-3	8-5	8-3	8-2	8-2	8-7	8-6

Question	16	17	18	19	20
Objective	C	I	D	J	E
Lesson	8-8	8-2	8-6	8-4	8-5

CHAPTER 8 REVIEW (pp. 379–381)

1. See below. **3.** See below. **5.** See below. **7.** See right.
9. See right. **11.** 90° **13.** Yes **15.** 2″ **17.** 4′11″
19. 10 calories **21.** 1 million **23.** The number of computer magazines published increased rapidly from 1982 through 1987. **25.** 1978 **27.** See right. **29.** Graphs show trends. Graphs can picture geometric figures. **31.** $B = (-2, 4)$; $C = (-2, 0)$ **33.** See right. **35.** See right. **37.** $x - y = 3$
39. $(-2, -3)$ **41.** $(9, 3); (7, 7); (10, 5)$

7.

9.

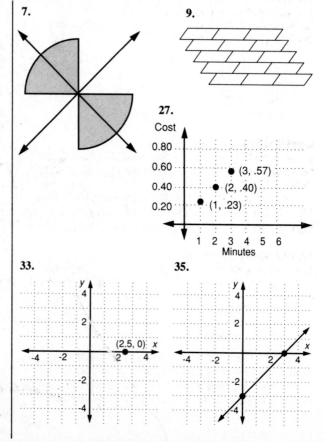

27.

1.

3.

5.

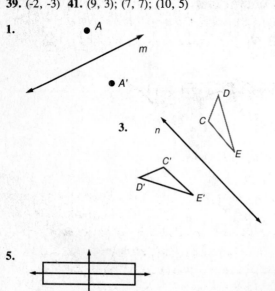

33. **35.**

LESSON 9-1 (pp. 384–388)
5. 2 sq. in. **7. a.** 3 **b.** 20 **c.** 60 **11.** Sample: **See below.**
13. $cr = d$ **15.** b **17.** True **19. a.** Yes **b.** Yes **c.** Yes
21. See below. **23.** -25 **25. a.** 24 miles **b.** 36 square miles
27. 0.270901 cm³

11. 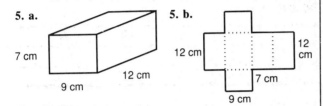 **21.**

LESSON 9-2 (pp. 389–392)
5. a. See below. **b.** See below. **c.** 510 cm²
7. 1116 square inches, or 7.75 square feet **9.** 367 square
inches **11.** Construct a box. **13.** 150 square units **15.** 52
17. Commutative Property of Addition **19.** $34 + 57 = 91$;
$91 - 57 = 34$; $91 - 34 = 57$ **21. a.** $n - 2$ **b.** $2 < n$
c. $2 - n$ **23.** 125 cubic units

5. a. **5. b.**

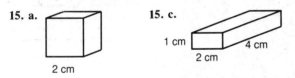

LESSON 9-3 (pp. 393–397)
3. 162 in.³ **5.** 160 cm³ **7.** Ah **9.** Sample: $3 \cdot (4 \cdot 0.5) =$
$3 \cdot 2 = 6$ and $(3 \cdot 4) \cdot 0.5 = 12 \cdot 0.5 = 6$ **11.** 0
13. 864 ft³ **15. a.** See below. **b.** cube **c.** See below.
17. 262,080 dots **19.** -27 **21. a.** 132.678 **b.** 132.678
c. Commutative Property of Multiplication **23.** $<$
25. a. fourth **b.** Sample: $y = x - 5$ **27.** 2600 meters
29. three places to the right

15. a. **15. c.**

LESSON 9-4 (pp. 398–402)
1. cm **3.** cm² **7.** perimeter **9. a.** miles **b.** square miles
11. False (they are only numerically equal). **13.** 35 in.²;
98 in.²; 70 in.² **15.** $\ell + \ell + \ell + \ell + w + w + w +$
$w + h + h + h + h$ **17.** surface area **19.** volume **21.** c
23. 133 square units **25.** 15,840 feet **27.** (8, -14)
29. a. $33.\overline{3}\%$ or $33\frac{1}{3}\%$ **b.** $66.\overline{6}\%$ or $66\frac{2}{3}\%$ **c.** 80%

LESSON 9-5 (pp. 403–407)
1. a. Samples: 67.8 ☒ 3.00 ☐ or 67.8 ☐ 67.8 ☐ 67.8 ☐
b. Yes **3.** $953 + 953 + 953 + 953 = 3812$; the answer
does not check. **7. a.** $\frac{1}{x}$ **b.** $-x$ **c.** $-x$ **d.** $\frac{1}{x}$ **9.** $2\ell + 2w$
11. They can represent the length and width of a rectangle;
the result is the perimeter. **13.** $x + x + z + z + z + z$
15. $\$1.19c$ **17.** c **19.** f **21.** $\frac{25}{2}, \frac{2}{25}$ **23. a.** Associative
Property of Addition **b.** Associative Property of Multiplica-
tion **c.** Add-Opp Property of Subtraction **25. a.** 1 point
b. $w - z$ points **27.** $m\angle 1 = m\angle 3 = m\angle 4 = 145°$;
$m\angle 2 = 35°$

LESSON 9-6 (pp. 408–412)
1. a. 4.4 cm segment; **See below. b.** 8.8 cm segment.
c. 13.2 cm segment. **d.** 15.4 cm segment.
3. a.–b. See below. **c.** They are twice as long. **d.** They
are the same. **7.** See below. **9. a.** 3 **b.** $76.50
11. 15 mm **13.** 3 **15.** 5 **17.** 4 **19.** 1 **21. a.** 500 m
b. 500 m **c.** 10,000 m² **23.** Associative Prop. of Mult.
25. Equal Fractions Property

1. a. ───────────

3. a.–b. **7.**

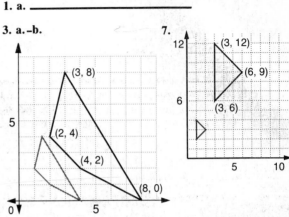

LESSON 9-7 (pp. 413–417)
1. a. 3.5 cm **b.** See below. 1.05 cm **c.** 0.3 **3.** (3, 2)
5. (1.5, 1) **9.** 18,480,000 **11.** about 2.25 cm or .875 in.
13. $(12k, 5k)$ **15.** (d) **17.** $10m$ **19.** $2m$ **21.** -40 **23.** 1
25. (c) **27.** 22° **29. a.** 343 cm³ **b.** 294 cm² **c.** 84 cm

1. b. ───────────

LESSON 9-8 (pp. 418–422)
3. $\frac{2}{3}$ **5.** 2 **7.** 0.5 m **9.** $\frac{1}{25}$ **11.** $\frac{1}{ab}$ **13. a.** $\frac{1}{50}$ **b.** $\frac{1}{75}$
c. $\frac{1}{3750}$ **15.** $\frac{1}{18}$ **17.** $\frac{1}{DH}$ **19.** $\frac{W}{5}$ dollars **21. a.** $\frac{1}{161}$
b. 0.0062112 **c.** $0.142857 \cdot 0.0434783 = 0.0062112$ **d.** A
number may be substituted for its equal without affecting the
answer (Substitution Principle). **23.** See below. $3 \cdot \frac{1}{5} = \frac{3}{5}$
25. $\frac{1}{16}$ **27. a.** $\frac{8}{30}, \frac{1}{3}, \frac{3}{8}$ **b.** $-\frac{3}{8}, -\frac{1}{3}, -\frac{8}{30}$ **29.** $2a$ **31.** perimeter

23.

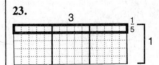

LESSON 9-9 (pp. 423–427)
1. $\frac{12}{45}$ (or $\frac{4}{15}$) **3.** $\frac{1}{2}$ **7.** $12 \cdot 0.75 = 9$ **9.** $\frac{6}{5}$ **11.** $0.625 \cdot 1.6 = 1$
13. $4 \cdot \frac{1}{5} + 3 \cdot \frac{1}{15} = \frac{4}{5} + \frac{1}{5} = 1$ **15.** 3 square miles
17. a. $\frac{1}{2} \cdot \frac{1}{3} \cdot \frac{1}{4} = \frac{1 \cdot 1 \cdot 1}{2 \cdot 3 \cdot 4} = \frac{1}{24}$ **b.** The magnitudes $\frac{1}{3}$ and $\frac{1}{4}$ are
each between zero and one, so they are contractions on $\frac{1}{2}$.
The answer must be less than $\frac{1}{2}$ and therefore less than 1.
21. $\frac{3}{4}$ **23.** contraction (the magnitude is between zero and
one) **25.** See p. 634.

25.

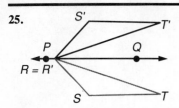

CHAPTER 9 PROGRESS SELF-TEST (pp. 429–430)

1. $\frac{6}{25}$ **2.** $3y + 3$ **3.** $\frac{5}{3}$ **4.** $\frac{7}{16x}$ **5.** Associative Property of Multiplication **6.** Property of Reciprocals **7.** There are rs seats broken or unbroken; there are $rs - 5$ seats to sit in. **8.** Area $= 17.3$ m $\cdot$ 6.8 m $= 117.64$ m²; perimeter $= 2 \cdot 17.3$ m $+ 2 \cdot 6.8$ m $= 34.6$ m $+ 13.6$ m $= 48.2$ m. **9.** $6 \cdot 11 + 6 \cdot 11 + 6 \cdot 3 + 6 \cdot 3 + 3 \cdot 11 + 3 \cdot 11 = 234$ cm² **10.** 3 ft $\cdot$ 4 ft $\cdot$ 5 ft $= 60$ ft³ **11.** square kilometers, because area measures fishing room **12.** Sample: 8 and 2, 16 and 1, 10 and 1.6 **13.** The reciprocal is $\frac{1}{38} = 0.02631 \ldots \approx 0.026$ **14.** $\$1.29 + \$1.29 + \$1.29$ or $3 \cdot \$1.29 = \$3.87$ **15.** $\frac{2}{3} \cdot \frac{2}{5} = \frac{4}{15}$ **16.** $(4 \cdot 8, 4 \cdot 2) = (32, 8)$ **17.** $1.5 \cdot \$5.80 = \$8.70$ **18. See below.** **19.** contraction (the magnitude is between zero and one), similar **20.** $0.12 \cdot 850 = 102$ students **21.** $\frac{2}{3} \cdot \$8400 = \$5600$ **22.** $\frac{1}{10} \cdot \frac{1}{10} \cdot \frac{1}{10} = \frac{1}{1000}$. Your chances are 1 in 1000.

23. $\frac{2}{3} \cdot \frac{2}{5} = \frac{4}{15}$. Your chances are 4 in 15. **24. See below.**
Sample: Make the rectangle very thin as shown here. This rectangle has length 3 in. and width $\frac{1}{8}$ in. for a perimeter of 6.25 in. and an area of $\frac{3}{8}$ sq. in. **25.** $\frac{1}{1.25} = 0.8$, choice (c).

18.

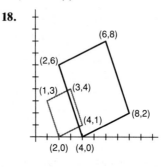

24.

The chart below keys the **Progress Self-Test** questions to the objectives in the **Chapter Review** on pages 431–433 or to the **Vocabulary** (Voc.) on page 428. This will enable you to locate those **Chapter Review** questions that correspond to questions you missed on the **Progress Self-Test.** The lesson where the material is covered is also indicated in the chart.

Question	1–4	2	3–4	5	6	7–8	9	10	11
Objective	A	E	A	D	D	H	I	C	G
Lesson	9-9	9-3	9-9	9-3	9-5	9-1	9-2	9-3	9-4

Question	12	13	14	15	16	17	18	19	20–21
Objective	B	D	F	L	M	J	M	Voc.	J
Lesson	9-1	9-8	9-5	9-9	9-6	9-6	9-7	9-7	9-7

Question	22	23	24	25
Objective	K	K	B	D
Lesson	9-8	9-9	9-1	9-8

CHAPTER 9 REVIEW (pp. 431–433)

1. $\frac{1}{2}$ **3.** $\frac{300}{8}$ or $\frac{75}{2}$ **5.** $\frac{405}{4}$ or $101\frac{1}{4}$ **7.** area $= 24.5$ square units; perimeter $= 21$ units **9.** surface area $= 1025$ square units; volume $= 1875$ cubic units **11.** For any number n, $n \cdot 1 = n$. **13.** $\frac{3}{2}$ **15.** 0 **17.** $4m$ **19.** Multiply in the reverse order. $6.54 \cdot 2.48 \neq 16.1292$; it does not check. **21.** $\frac{1}{40}$; $\frac{1}{5} = 0.2$, $\frac{1}{8} = 0.125$; $\frac{1}{5} \cdot \frac{1}{8} = 0.2 \cdot 0.125 = 0.025$, which equals $\frac{1}{40}$ **23.** square inches **25.** 48 **27.** 156 square

centimeters **29.** No **31.** $37.50 **33.** $5.25 **35.** $\frac{1}{9}$ **37.** See below. **39. See below.** **41. See p. 635.** **43.** contraction

37.

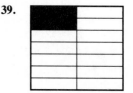

39.

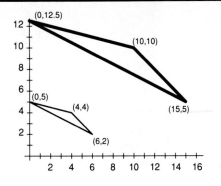

LESSON 10-1 (pp. 434–435)

1. (a) **3. a.** Yes **b.** No **c.** No **d.** No **e.** No **5.** 1 **7.** $\frac{72}{9} = 8$; $\frac{72}{8} = 9$ **11.** 7.5; $0.8 \cdot 7.5 = 6$ **13.** Sample: $\frac{222,300}{325} = 684$; correct **15.** Sample: $\frac{1152}{.72} = 1600$; correct **17. a.** Sample: 1.1052632 **b.** 1.11 **c.** $3.8x = 4.2$ **19.** 2.25 **21. a.** $\frac{1}{6}$ **b.** $\frac{12}{5}$ **23.** x **25.** reciprocal and multiplicative inverse; opposite and additive inverse **27. a.** $6L$ square feet **b.** $12 + 2L$ feet **29.** -8

LESSON 10-2 (pp. 440–444)

1. $6y$ **3. a.** $\frac{1}{5}$ **b.** 16 **5. a.** $\frac{1}{3}$ **b.** $x = 0.12 \cdot \frac{1}{3} = 0.04$ **c.** $x = \frac{0.12}{3} = 0.04$ **7.** 59 **9.** 62.5 **11.** step 1: Multiplication Prop. of Equality; step 2: Associative Prop. of Mult.; step 3: Prop. of Reciprocals; step 4: mult. of fractions and Mult. Identity Prop. of 1 **13.** 2.3; $7.2 \cdot 2.3 = 16.56$ **15.** $\frac{4}{3}$ or $1.\overline{3}$; $3.2 + 4.8 = (3.6 + 2.4) \cdot 1.\overline{3}$ **17.** 57 **19.** $3H + 20$ meters **21.** 320,000,000,000 **23.** 80 cm **25.** 5.499

LESSON 10-3 (pp. 445–449)

3. 15 feet **5.** $2.40 **7. a.** 55,000 cm **b.** 550 m **9.** about 7.14 cm **11.** $37,000 **13.** 40 columns **15.** 25 **17.** Polygon, quadrilateral, parallelogram, rectangle, square **19.** 6 cm²

LESSON 10-4 (pp. 450–454)

1. a. For the game only 4 tickets per student are available. **b.** 4 tickets/student **c.** $4 \frac{\text{tickets}}{\text{student}}$ **3. a.** 150 miles **b.** Sample: how far will a person travel driving at 50 miles per hour for 3 hours? **5. a.** $16 \frac{\text{games}}{\text{season}}$ **b.** Sample: a team plays 2 games a week. There are 8 weeks in the season. How many games will the team play per season? **7.** 10.5 kg **9.** about 6.63 miles **11.** When a rate is multiplied by another quantity, the unit of the product is the "product" of the units, multiplied like fractions. The product has mèaning whenever its unit has meaning. **13. a.** 6.36 quarts **b.** Convert 6 liters to quarts. **15.** 100,800 beats **17.** 720 pesetas **19.** 0.6 **21.** 26 millimeters **23.** $-\frac{4}{3}$ **25.** kg **27.** 55 ft **29.** Three points on the line are (0, -4), (2, -2), and (4, 0).

LESSON 10-5 (pp. 455–458)

1. $-3.8 \frac{\text{pounds}}{\text{month}}$, or loses 3.8 pounds per month

3. a. $-5 \frac{\text{pounds}}{\text{month}} \cdot 4$ months **b.** -20 pounds; the person will be 20 pounds lighter. **5.** changes **7.** -32 **9.** 18 **11.** -64 **13.** positive **15.** negative **17. a.** -10 **b.** -5 **c.** 0 **d.** 5 **e.** 10 **19.** 60 **21.** $\frac{3}{5}$ **23.** 0.025 or $\frac{1}{40}$ **25.** $2.69 **27. See below. 29.** Sample: $-2 + 3 = 1$

27.

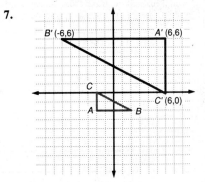

LESSON 10-6 (pp. 459–463)

1. (-8, -10) **7. See below. 9.** 180° **11.** True **13.** 2 **15.** 84 square inches **17.** 51 **19.** 210 **21.** 1680 **23.** 9,765,625 **25.** -0.6

7.

LESSON 10-7 (pp. 464–468)

3. 7 **5.** -1 **7.** 0 **11.** ab **13.** one **15.** none **17.** negative **19.** 0 **21.** $-c$ **23.** $2e$ **27. a.** No **b.** $0 \cdot 0 \neq 1$ **29.** 34 **31.** For any number x, $x + 0 = x$. **33.** 52.4 **35.** 14 **37.** 1250 miles

LESSON 10-8 (pp. 469–472)

1. $-\frac{1}{8}$ or -0.125 **3.** $-\frac{5}{9}$ or $-0.\overline{5}$ **5.** $-\frac{1}{x}$ **7.** -2; $-4 \cdot -2 = 8$ **9.** -70; $-1.2 \cdot -70 = 84$ **11.** $\frac{2}{25}$; Does $-\frac{2}{15} = -\frac{5}{3} \cdot \frac{2}{25}$? Yes, since $-\frac{10}{75} = -\frac{2}{15}$. **15.** about 15 days **17.** $-800m = -4500$; about 5.6 months **19.** y is positive **21.** $-a$

23. 180 students **25.** $\frac{1}{18}$ **27.** m$\angle HEG = 98°$; m$\angle H = 50°$; m$\angle G = 32°$

LESSON 10-9 (pp. 473–477)

1. a. -25 **b.** 15 **5.** 17 **7.** $\frac{4}{3}$ **9.** 610 calories **11.** about

36 French fries **13.** 7.5 ounce hamburger **15.** No **17.** $\frac{19}{112}$; $\frac{3}{2} - 14\left(\frac{19}{112}\right) + \frac{7}{8} = \frac{12}{8} - \frac{19}{8} + \frac{7}{8} = 0$ **19.** -$\frac{15}{8}$ **21.** .635 m **23.** $x + 2z$ **25.** 635,900 people **27.** 2500 $- D + B - S = 2300$ **29. a.** 45¢ **b.** 65¢ **c.** 85¢ **d.** 25 + 20($n - 1$) cents

CHAPTER 10 PROGRESS SELF-TEST (p. 479)

1. $\frac{3}{5}n = 15$; multiply both sides by $\frac{5}{3}$; $n = 25$. **2.** If $x = y$, then $ax = ay$. **3.** $10w = 5$; $w = \frac{1}{2}$ foot **4.** 2000 = .08L; multiply both sides by $\frac{1}{.08}$; $L = \$25,000$

5. $x = \frac{1001}{13} = 77$ **6.** Multiply both sides by $\frac{1}{13}$; $x = \frac{1}{13} \cdot 1001 = 77$. **7.** 37.5 hours $\cdot \frac{\$8.50}{hr} = \$318.75$

8. 4 hours $\cdot -3 \frac{cm}{hr} = -12$ cm **9.** -45 **10.** $9 + 4 = 13$
11. There are three negatives, so the product is negative; $2 \cdot 3 \cdot 4 \cdot 5 \cdot 6 \cdot 7 = 5040$, so the answer is -5040.
12. $6 \cdot 0 - 3 \cdot -1 \cdot 5 = 0 - -15 = 0 + 15 = 15$
13. $a + a + b + 0 + -c + c = 2a + b$ **14.** $d \cdot$ negative $=$ negative, so d must be positive. **15. See right.**
16. Samples: Things the same: Figures have same shape, same angle measures, corresponding sides parallel. Things different: lengths of sides of image are 2.5 times lengths on preimage; preimage is rotated 180° to get image. **17.** all equal **18.** $\frac{39.37 \text{ inches}}{1 \text{ meter}}$, $\frac{1 \text{ meter}}{39.37 \text{ inches}}$ **19.** 1200 inches $\cdot$

$\frac{1 \text{ meter}}{39.37 \text{ inches}} \approx 30.48$ meters **20.** Multiply both sides by -1; $x = -4$. **21.** Multiply both sides by $-\frac{1}{9}$; $t = -3.9$ **22.** Multiply both sides by $-\frac{5}{2}$; $m = \frac{15}{8}$. **23.** Since any number times 0 is 0, k can be any number. **24.** Add -2 to both sides; $3A = 15$. Multiply both sides by $\frac{1}{3}$; $A = 5$. **25.** Simplify the left side; $-4h - 3 = 10$. Add 3 to both sides; $-4h = 13$. Multiply both sides by $-\frac{1}{4}$; $h = -\frac{13}{4}$.

15.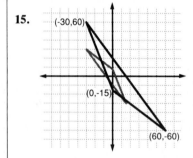

The chart below keys the **Progress Self-Test** questions to the objectives in the **Chapter Review** on pages 480–481 or to the **Vocabulary** (Voc.) on page 478. This will enable you to locate those **Chapter Review** questions that correspond to questions you missed on the **Progress Self-Test.** The lesson where the material is covered is also indicated in the chart.

Question	1	2	3	4	5	6	7	8
Objective	B	Voc.	J	K	G	E	H	L
Lesson	10-1	10-2	10-3	10-3	10-1	10-2	10-4	10-6
Question	9–11	12–14	15–16	17	18–19	20–22	23	24–25
Objective	A	F	L	F	I	C	F	D
Lesson	10-5	10-7	10-6	10-7	10-4	10-8	10-7	10-9

CHAPTER 10 REVIEW (pp. 480–481)

1. 16 **3.** 400 **5.** 3 **7.** -7 **9.** positive **11.** 75; $40 \cdot 75 = 3000$ **13.** 40; $0.02 \cdot 40 = 0.8$ **15.** 7; $-49 = -7 \cdot 7$ **17.** 2; $8 \cdot 2 + 2 = 16 + 2 = 18$ **19.** 3; $11 - 6 \cdot 3 = 11 - 18 = -7$ **21.** $\frac{3}{11}$ **23.** x **25.** no solutions **27.** Is $274 = \frac{13,261.6}{48.4}$? Yes **29. a.** 730 $\frac{\text{cookies}}{\text{year}}$ **b.** If an elf eats 2 cookies per day, how many will it eat in a year?
31. \$20,475 **33.** She weighed 9.2 kg more. **35.** about 16.4 ft
37. 25 seats **39.** 12 cm **41.** 2000 **43.** $\frac{\$8}{hr}$ **45.** (-8, 16)
47. See right.

47.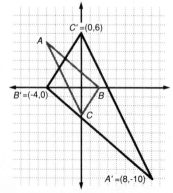

LESSON 11-1 (pp. 484–487)

1. $50 \frac{mi}{hr}$ or 50 mph 3. about $66.7 \frac{km}{hr}$ 5. 2 boys per girl
7. 20 acres per person 9. a. 10.8 cents per ounce
b. 9.6 cents per ounce c. the 18-oz box 11. $\frac{m}{h}$ miles per
hour 13. $0.25 per hour 15. $9\frac{1}{3}$ bandages per day (5-day
week) 17. a. $\frac{43}{6}$ b. $\frac{6}{43}$ 19. $m = -2$ 21. angles 3 and 7;
angles 2 and 6 23. 75° 25. 8, 8, 20

LESSON 11-2 (pp. 488–491)

1. $4.80 per hour 3. $\frac{2}{3}$ 5. $\frac{17}{4}$ or $4\frac{1}{4}$ 7. 60 games 9. a. $\frac{35}{117}$
b. $5\frac{4}{7}$ is greater than $1\frac{2}{3}$ c. $\frac{1.67}{5.57} \approx 0.3 \approx \frac{35}{117}$ d. The decimals are infinite, so it is easier to work with the fractions.
11. $\frac{2y}{x}$ 13. 50 15. 1 17. $\frac{3}{4}$ 19. $\frac{3}{4}$ 21. $\frac{1}{100,000,000}$
23. 2590 square inches

LESSON 11-3 (pp. 492–496)

1. -2 3. 7 5. 70 7. -9.6 9. positive 11. positive
13. a. -2 pounds per day b. $\frac{-4 \text{ pounds}}{2 \text{ days}}$ c. 2, 4, more
d. $\frac{4 \text{ pounds more}}{2 \text{ days ago}} = \frac{4 \text{ pounds}}{-2 \text{ days}} = -2 \frac{\text{pounds}}{\text{day}}$ 17. -15, 3, 54,
$\frac{2}{3}$ 19. -24, 0, 144, 1 21. $\frac{5}{4}$ 23. a. $\left(\frac{1}{4}, 5\right)$ b. See below.
25. (-6, 3) 27. a. 0.44 b. $\frac{11}{25}$ 29. 1250

23. b.
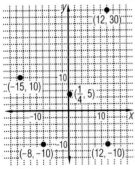

LESSON 11-4 (pp. 497–500)

1. 40% 3. a. 6% b. about 6% 5. 24% 7. 100% 9. 14%
11. a. 3% b. $33.\overline{3}$ or $33\frac{1}{3}$ 13. a. 56% b. 44% 15. a. 90%
b. 14.4 c. $111.\overline{1}$ 17. 2% 19. $\frac{-3}{1}$, or -3 21. $9.80 23. 47
25. 1

LESSON 11-5 (pp. 501–505)

1. 1, 0 3. 1 5. Precipitation tomorrow is more likely.
7. $\frac{9}{10}$ 9. One common way is to guess a probability; another

way is to calculate a probability based on assumptions made
about the probability of an associated event. 11. $\frac{1}{50}$ 13. A
probability cannot be a negative number; probability is a
number from 0 to 1. 15. a. $\frac{45}{360}$ or $\frac{1}{8}$ b. B: $\frac{3}{8}$; C: $\frac{1}{4}$; D: $\frac{1}{4}$
17. $\frac{5}{n}$ 19. $\frac{7}{100}$ 21. 43% 23. 105

LESSON 11-6 (pp. 506–510)

1. 1, 3 5. (c) 7. 98 9. 3 11. 37.5 boxes or 37 boxes
13. No 15. in his 717th game 17. $\frac{17}{80}$ 19. 50%
21. 5400 cm²

LESSON 11-7 (pp. 511–515)

1. t, 250 3. $250t = 400 \cdot 15$ 5. a. $\frac{8}{\$1.79} = \frac{10}{c}$ b. $c =$
$2.2375 \approx $2.24 c. Does $\frac{8}{1.79} = \frac{10}{2.2375}$? Yes 11. False
13. True 15. a. 164 or 165 deer 17. because the equation is
not a proportion 19. about 12,400 households 21. $\frac{2}{3}$ 23. $\frac{2}{3}$
25. $\frac{5}{24}$ feet/year or 2.5 inches/year 27. 27 29. $\frac{1}{64}$ square
inches 31. $\frac{1}{2}$ inch

LESSON 11-8 (pp. 516–520)

3. 27.5 5. Answers will vary. Sample: See below. 7. Answers will vary. Samples: photographs, scale models,
magnifications 9. a. 12 cm long and 9 cm wide b. Yes
c. Yes 11. 12.5 13. (c), (d), (e), (f) 15. $15 17. 3
19. $\frac{56}{25}$ 21. $3.8 \cdot 10^9$ 23. 5.125; $5\frac{1}{8}$

5.
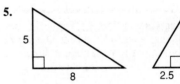

LESSON 11-9 (pp. 521–524)

3. $\frac{2 \text{ cans}}{\$2.50} = \frac{6 \text{ cans}}{\$C}$ 5. True 7. 2 hours 9. 4, 5
11. a. $\frac{120 \text{ miles}}{55 \frac{\text{miles}}{\text{hour}}} = 2.\overline{18}$ b. At 55 mph, you go 110 miles
in 2 hours, 165 miles in 3 hours, so the answer seems right.
13. a. $12,000 \text{ acres} \cdot \frac{1 \text{ square mile}}{640 \text{ acres}} = 18.75$ square miles
b. $\frac{640 \text{ acres}}{1 \text{ sq. mi}} = \frac{12,000 \text{ acres}}{x \text{ sq. mi}}$; from which $x = 18.75$ sq. mi
15. 40 minutes 17. $\frac{\$625}{\text{month}}$ 19. $y = 34.5$ 21. -3 23. about
1428.57 25. $2\frac{6}{7}$ hours

CHAPTER 11 PROGRESS SELF-TEST (p. 526)

1. $\frac{300 \text{ words}}{5 \text{ minutes}} = 60$ words per minute 2. $\frac{m \text{ km}}{h \text{ hours}} =$
$\frac{m}{h}$ kilometers per hour 3. $\frac{4}{3}$ 4. $\frac{7}{4}$ 5. $\frac{3}{5} \cdot \frac{5}{6} = \frac{1}{2}$ 6. $\frac{10}{-1} = -10$
7. Add them, then divide by 3. $\frac{(7 + -17 + 7)}{3} = \frac{-3}{3} = -1$
8. $\frac{a}{b}$ and $\frac{-a}{-b}$ 9. Sample: If you lose 8 kilograms in
2 months, what is the rate at which your weight has changed?
10. $8x = 200$, so $x = 25$ 11. $12p = 15$, so $p = 1.25$
12. $\frac{14}{150} = 0.093 \ldots \approx 9\%$ 13. $\frac{0.30}{4.00} = 0.075 = 7.5\%$
14. $.60x = 30$, so $x = 50$ 15. $\frac{189 \text{ miles}}{45 \text{ mph}} = 4.2$ hours

16. 10,000 sq miles $\cdot \dfrac{640 \text{ acres}}{1 \text{ sq mile}}$ = 6,400,000 acres

17. b and c **18.** If $\dfrac{a}{b} = \dfrac{c}{d}$, then $ad = bc$. **19.** $\dfrac{x}{40} = \dfrac{144}{64}$,

so $64x = 5760$ and $x = 90$ **20.** $\dfrac{180}{y} = \dfrac{144}{64}$, so $144y =$

11,520 and $y = 80$ **21.** $\dfrac{12}{15} = \dfrac{n}{50}$, so $600 = 15n$ and

$n = 40$ **22.** $\dfrac{12}{15} = \dfrac{4}{5}$ **23.** $\dfrac{\frac{1}{3}}{4} = \dfrac{x}{9}$ gives $x = \dfrac{3}{4}$ tsp.

24. $A = 6$. (Do mentally.) **25.** Rewrite as $\dfrac{3}{n} = \dfrac{8}{1}$ if

necessary. $8n = 3$, $n = \dfrac{3}{8}$ or 0.375

The chart below keys the **Progress Self-Test** questions to the objectives in the **Chapter Review** on pages 527–529 or to the **Vocabulary** (Voc.) on page 525. This will enable you to locate those **Chapter Review** questions that correspond to questions you missed on the **Progress Self-Test.** The lesson where the material is covered is also indicated in the chart.

Question	1–2	3	4	5	6	7	8	9	10–11
Objective	G	A	B	A	B	H	E	L	C
Lesson	11-1	11-2	11-3	11-2	11-3	11-3	11-3	11-3	11-6
Question	12–14	15–16	17–18	19–20	21	22	23	24	25
Objective	I	K	D	M	J	F	K	C	C
Lesson	11-4	11-7	11-7	11-8	11-5	11-5	11-9	11-6	11-7

CHAPTER 11 REVIEW (pp. 527–529)

1. 18 **3.** $\dfrac{1}{4}$ **5.** $\dfrac{7}{4}$ **7.** positive **9.** $\dfrac{4}{3}$ **11.** 21 **13.** $bd = ae$
15. The left side is not a single fraction. **17.** negative
19. $\dfrac{1}{3}$ **21.** $\dfrac{5}{16}$ pounds per hamburger **23.** about 12,100

25. -10.5 **27.** 20% **29.** 59% **31.** $\dfrac{1}{5}$ **33.** $\dfrac{b}{b+g}$ **35.** about
35.7 or 36 minutes **37.** \$1.88 **39.** How fast is the crew
going up the road? Answer: $\dfrac{\text{-6 km}}{\text{-3 days}} = \dfrac{2 \text{ km}}{\text{day}}$.
41. 2.5 and 6

LESSON 12-1 (pp. 532–536)

3. The total area of the rectangles is $3x + 5x$. Put them together and the area is $(3 + 5)x$. **See below. 5.** Fred is
correct. $6m - m = 6 \cdot m - 1 \cdot m = (6 - 1)m = 5m$.
You can check by substitution. **7.** $10y + 8$ **9.** $10b + 8$
11. $5m$ **13.** $30h + 40$ **15.** $3x + 2x$, or $5x$ cents
17. \$37.50 **19.** $40B + 15.5B + 24B$ or $79.5B$ **21.** 2.1
23. Samples: $3(4 + 5) = 3 \cdot 4 + 3 \cdot 5$; $-2(8 + -8) = -2 \cdot$
$8 + -2 \cdot -8$ **25. a.** $\dfrac{1}{3}$ **b.** $\dfrac{4}{5}$ **27.** $\dfrac{2}{7}$ **29.** In lowest terms: $\dfrac{157}{200}$

3.

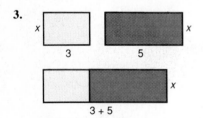

LESSON 12-2 (pp. 537–540)
1. terminating **3.** can't tell **5.** 3.04444 is finite, the rest are
infinite. **7.** $\dfrac{519}{99}$ or $\dfrac{173}{33}$ **9.** $\dfrac{810}{999}$ or $\dfrac{30}{37}$ **11.** $\dfrac{30,101}{9900}$ **13.** Sample:
$\dfrac{58,833,333}{1,000,000}$ **15.** $\dfrac{895}{900}$ or $\dfrac{179}{180}$ **17.** 3.1 or $\dfrac{31}{10}$ **19.** $131\frac{3}{5}$ **21.** none

LESSON 12-3 (pp. 541–545)
1. \$2.20 **3.** Sample: $2m + 3n$ **5. a.** 4 **b.** $5t$ and $2t$
c. Sample: $-4m$ and q **d.** -4 **e.** 1 **f.** $7t - 4m + q$
7. $-4x - 2$ **9.** $v - 12$ **11.** $-3t + 9$ **13.** $-3u - 9t$

15. a. 740 calories **b.** $520 + 11f$ calories **17.** 3 **19.** $8ax$
21. $\dfrac{7}{30}$ **23.** surface area, 13 ft²; volume, 3 ft³
25. See below. 27. 61, 67 **29.** 40

25.

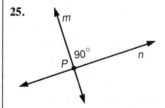

LESSON 12-4 (pp. 546–550)
1.

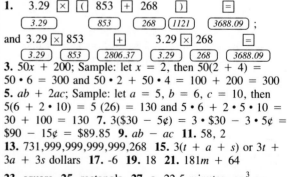

3. $50x + 200$; Sample: let $x = 2$, then $50(2 + 4) =$
$50 \cdot 6 = 300$ and $50 \cdot 2 + 50 \cdot 4 = 100 + 200 = 300$
5. $ab + 2ac$; Sample: let $a = 5$, $b = 6$, $c = 10$, then
$5(6 + 2 \cdot 10) = 5 (26) = 130$ and $5 \cdot 6 + 2 \cdot 5 \cdot 10 =$
$30 + 100 = 130$ **7.** $3(\$30 - 5\text{¢}) = 3 \cdot \$30 - 3 \cdot 5\text{¢} =$
$\$90 - 15\text{¢} = \$89.85$ **9.** $ab - ac$ **11.** 58, 2
13. 731,999,999,999,999,268 **15.** $3(t + a + s)$ or $3t +$
$3a + 3s$ dollars **17.** -6 **19.** 18 **21.** $181m + 64$
23. square **25.** rectangle **27. a.** 22.5 minutes, or $\dfrac{3}{8}$ or
.375 hr **b.** 6 minutes, or .1 hr

LESSON 12-5 (pp. 551–555)
3. 7 years old **5.** -8; 2(-8 − 4) = 3(-8); -24 = -24
7. 3.35; .6(3.35) + 5.4 = -1.3 + 2.6(3.35); 2.01 +
5.4 = -1.3 + 8.71; 7.41 = 7.41 **9. a.** 1000 + 200n

b. 750 + 250n **c.** 5 months **11.** -$\frac{11}{9}$; -$\left(-\frac{11}{9}\right)$ + 4 −
5$\left(-\frac{11}{9}\right)$ + 6 = 21 + 3$\left(-\frac{11}{9}\right)$; 10 + $\frac{66}{9}$ = $\frac{189}{9}$ − $\frac{33}{9}$; $\frac{156}{9}$ =
$\frac{156}{9}$ **13.** -40° **15.** 16(b + s + 12) or 16b + 16s +
192 dollars **17.** $\frac{23}{25}$ **19.** $\frac{70}{11}$ **21.** .3y − 1.3z + 8
23. a. 2,160,000 **b.** 2.16 × 10^6 **25.** 6,372,000 farms

LESSON 12-6 (pp. 556–561)
3. 65¢ **5.** $1.85 **11.** 50¢ **13. a.** 5¢ **b.** 13¢ **c.** 25¢
15. Samples: (4, 0), (2, -4) **17.** Sample points: (0, -4),
(6, 0), (3, -2); **See right.** **19. a. See right.** **b.** The pairs
(1, 388), (2, 376), and so on lie on the same line. **c.** 33$\frac{1}{3}$
d. In about 33 weeks the paper will be used up. **21.** .6 or $\frac{3}{5}$
23. 35 **25.** $\frac{1}{2}P$ + $\frac{3}{4}Q$ cups **27. a.** -8 **b.** -2 **c.** 15 **d.** $\frac{5}{3}$
29. 33°

17.

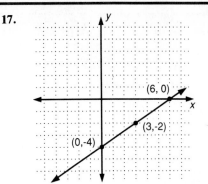

19. a.

weeks from now (w)	number of packages left (L)
1	388
2	376
3	364
4	352
5	340
6	328

CHAPTER 12 PROGRESS SELF-TEST (p. 563)

1. (1 − 3)m = -2m **2.** 4x + 3x + 1 = 7x + 1
3. 7m + -4m + n + -2n = (7 + -4)m + (1 + -2)n =
3m − n **4.** For any numbers a, b, and x, ax + bx =
(a + b)x. **5.** Add 9x to both sides; 1 = 13 + 12x. Add
-13 to both sides; -12 = 12x. Multiply both sides by $\frac{1}{12}$;
-1 = x. **6.** Distribute the 2; 2y − 6 = 12y. Add -2y to
both sides; -6 = 10y. Multiply both sides by $\frac{1}{10}$;
y = $\frac{-6}{10}$ = $\frac{-3}{5}$. **7.** Use the means-extremes property;
5(2t + 7) = 4(t − 8). Distribute; 10t + 35 = 4t − 32.
Add -4t to both sides; 6t + 35 = -32. Add -35 to both
sides; 6t = -67. Multiply both sides by $\frac{1}{6}$; t = -$\frac{67}{6}$.
8. Simplify; .2m + 6 = -.6m + 2. Add .6m to both sides;
.8m + 6 = 2. Add -6 to both sides; .8m = -4. Multiply
both sides by $\frac{1}{.8}$; m = -5. **9.** Let A = Lee's age now.
Then A + 7 = 1.5A. Add -A to both sides; 7 = .5A.
Multiply both sides by $\frac{1}{.5}$; 14 = A. Lee is 14 years old.
10. T books $\cdot \frac{\$3.95}{\text{book}}$ + F books $\cdot \frac{\$4.95}{\text{book}}$ + V books $\cdot$
$\frac{\$5.95}{\text{book}}$ = 3.95T$ + 4.95F$ + 5.95V$ **11.** p = b + b +
40 + b + b + 40 = 4b + 80 **12.** The H 4-oz
hamburgers have 4H ounces and 80 $\cdot$ 4H = 320H calories.
The H buns have 180H calories. The F French fries have
11F calories. Together they have 320H + 180H + 11F =
500H + 11F calories. **13.** 5 $\cdot$ 3 − 2y = 10, 15 − 2y =
10. Add -15 to both sides; -2y = -5. Multiply both sides by
-$\frac{1}{2}$; y = $\frac{5}{2}$ = 2.5. So the second coordinate is 2.5.

14. Sample: when x = 2, y = 3 $\cdot$ 2 − 2 = 4, so (2, 4) is
on the line. When x = 10, y = 3 $\cdot$ 10 − 2 = 28, so
(10, 28) is on the line. Another point is (3, 7). **15. See
below. 16.** Let x = 0.$\overline{81}$. 100x = 81.$\overline{81}$. 100x − x =
81.$\overline{81}$ − 0.$\overline{81}$ = 81. 99x = 81. x = $\frac{81}{99}$ = $\frac{9}{11}$. **17.** Let
x = 1.02$\overline{8}$. 10x = 10.2$\overline{8}$. 10x − x = 10.2$\overline{8}$ −
1.02$\overline{8}$ = 9.26. 9x = 9.26. x = $\frac{9.26}{9}$ = $\frac{926}{900}$ = $\frac{463}{450}$.
18. 49 $\cdot$ 7 = 50 $\cdot$ 7 − 1 $\cdot$ 7 = 350 − 7 = 343 **19.** from
line 3 to line 4 **20.** w(1.5 + .75 + .3) = w(2.55)

15.

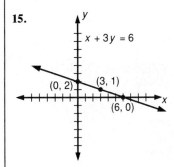

The chart below keys the **Progress Self-Test** questions to the objectives in the **Chapter Review** on pages 564–565 or to the **Vocabulary** (Voc.) on page 562. This will enable you to locate those **Chapter Review** questions that correspond to questions you missed on the **Progress Self-Test.** The lesson where the material is covered is also indicated in the chart.

Question	1–3	4	5–8	9	10	11	12	13–15	16–17
Objective	A	D	C	E	E	F	E	G	B
Lesson	12-1	12-4	12-5	12-4	12-3	12-4	12-3	12-6	12-2

Question	18–19	20
Objective	D	F
Lesson	12-4	12-4

CHAPTER 12 REVIEW (pp. 564–565)

1. $10v$ **3.** $20a + 4b$ **5.** $-5t - 14r + 7$ **7.** $6a - 6b + 12c$
9. $\frac{803}{900}$ **11.** $\frac{131}{333}$ **13.** $-\frac{17}{39}$ **15.** -30 **17.** $\$19.95 \cdot 4 =$
$(\$20.00 - \$0.5) \cdot 4 = \$80.00 - \$.20 = \$79.80$
19. $100T + 70P$ **21.** $11E + 12T$ **23.** 12 **25. See below.**
27. Samples: (5, 0), (0, 2), (10, -2) **29. See right.**

25.

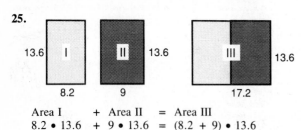

Area I   + Area II   = Area III
$8.2 \cdot 13.6$ + $9 \cdot 13.6$ = $(8.2 + 9) \cdot 13.6$

29.

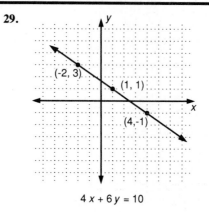

$4x + 6y = 10$

LESSON 13-1 (pp. 568–572)

3. 40 mm, 9 mm **5.** 180 square millimeters **7.** legs 8, 15; hypotenuse 17; area 60 square units; perimeter 40 units
9. $\frac{1}{2}ab$ **11. a.** $3h$ **b.** $3h$ **13.** 48 square inches **15.** 16 cm
17. 8.64 square units **19.** $\frac{1}{27}$ cubic meter **21.** $\frac{5}{12}$ **23.** $(a + b)$ $(c + d) = ac + ad + bc + bd$ **25.** 149

LESSON 13-2 (pp. 573–577)

1. square root **3.** 2.5 is the square root of 6.25 **5.** 9, -9
7. 5, -5 **9.** 8 **11.** -7 **13.** 1.414 **15. a.** 20 m **b.** 20 **c.** -20
17. 9 **19.** $\sqrt{41} \approx 6.4031$ **21.** 3 **23.** 7 and 8 **25.** $\sqrt{2}$
27. 16.4 **29.** 16.4, 16.5 **31.** 120 square meters **33.** (a)
35. (b)

LESSON 13-3 (pp. 578–583)

5. a. $x^2 + 8^2 = 10^2$ **b.** 6 **7.** $\sqrt{8}$ meters **11. a.** 11 km
b. $\sqrt{85}$ or about 9.2 km **c.** about 1.8 km **13. a.** about $13\frac{7}{8}''$
or 13.9" **b.** $\sqrt{193.25}''$ or about 13.9" **15.** 9 **17.** False
19. 610 **21.** 97 **23.** $\frac{10}{35}$ hour or about 17 minutes

LESSON 13-4 (pp. 584–588)

1. 468 square units **3. a.** $\overline{YA}$ **b.** $\overline{XB}$ **c.** $\overline{ZC}$ **See right.**
7. a. $\sqrt{48}$ cm **b.** $4\sqrt{48}$ cm² **9.** 10,580 square meters
11. 113.42 **13.** 3.42 **15.** 3%, $\frac{3}{10}$, $.\overline{3}$, $\sqrt{3}$ **17.** 16

19. 10 seconds **21.** $\frac{1}{20}$
3.

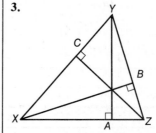

LESSON 13-5 (pp. 589–593)

3. False **5.** False **7.** False **9. a.** Sample: **See below.**
b. 9 cm² **13.** 320 square units **15.** 7 meters **17.** One example of an altitude is the dotted segment. **See p. 641.**
19. 96 square feet **21.** True **23.** 7 **25.** $\frac{1}{3}A$ or $\frac{A}{3}$

9. a. sample:

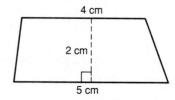

4 cm

2 cm

5 cm

17.

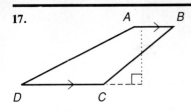

LESSON 13-6 (pp. 594–599)
5. πs **7. a.** estimate **b.** 3.14 **c.** 3.14159 **d.** Answers will vary. Some calculators show 3.1415927. **9.** $\pi = \dfrac{C}{d}$; $d = \dfrac{C}{\pi}$
13. irrational **15.** irrational **17.** rational **19.** all of them
21. 1.2π inches $\approx 3.77''$ **23.** 24π (or about 75) miles
25. about 754 inches or 63 feet **27.** $\sqrt{10}$ **29.** 162 square units **31.** 9 **33.** 9 **35.** 1704 **37.** 500

LESSON 13-7 (pp. 600–603)
1. 64 square units **3.** 50 square units **5.** 18π square units
7. sector **9.** $\frac{1}{4}$ **11.** about 463.77 mm² **13.** 25 square meters

15. a. 120° **b.** $\dfrac{49\pi}{3} \approx 51.3$ square feet **17.** 60.75π or about 191 square meters **19.** 48 **21.** when it is infinite and does not repeat **23.** $36.\overline{36}$

LESSON 13-8 (pp. 604–608)
3. 180° **7.** $\frac{1}{5}$ **9. a.** 20% **b.** 72° **11.** 144° **13. a.** 60–64
b. 20–29 **c.** 5 **d.** 48.3 million **15.** about 695 square feet
17. $\frac{10}{11}$ **19.** .5 square inches **21.** $15m - 18t - 12$ **23.** a -9°
turn **25. a.** 97 **b.** 1) Read the problem carefully.
2) Devise a plan. 3) Carry out the plan. 4) Check work.

LESSON 13-9 (pp. 609–612)
3. 576π or about 1810 cm² **5.** 2304π or about 7238 cm³
7. 4 $\div$ 3 $\times$ π $\times$ 7 y^x 3 $=$ **9.** volume **11.** volume
13. about 332 cubic inches **15.** $\dfrac{\pi}{6} \approx 0.52 = 52\%$ **17.** 225π
or about 707 square miles

CHAPTER 13 PROGRESS SELF-TEST (p. 614)

1. $C = \pi d = \pi(2r)$. So $C = \pi\left(2 \cdot \frac{3}{8}\right) = \pi\left(\frac{3}{4}\right) \approx 2.4$ in.
2. $\sqrt{3} \cdot \sqrt{3} = 3$ **3.** $\sqrt{10}$ **4.** $5.48 + 7.14 \approx 12.62 \approx 13$
5. $x^2 + 24^2 = 26^2$, so $x^2 + 576 = 676$, so $x^2 = 100$,
$x = 10$ or -10. Since x is a length, $x = 10$ **6.** $AB^2 = 10^2 + 5^2 = 125$, so $AB = \sqrt{125}$ **7.** $\sqrt{25}$, which is 5
8. $A = \frac{1}{2} \cdot 24$ cm $\cdot 7$ cm $= 84$ cm² **9.** $A = \frac{1}{2} \cdot 30 \cdot 36 = 540$ **10.** $A = \frac{1}{2} \cdot 8 \cdot (30 + 9) = 156$ **11.** The legs are $\overline{AC}$ and $\overline{BC}$. The hypotenuse is $\overline{AB}$. **12.** Since $A = \frac{1}{2} \cdot bh$,

$400 = \frac{1}{2} \cdot b \cdot 25$, so $400 = 12.5b$, so $b = 32$ inches.
13. quadrilateral **14.** $7\pi \approx 22$ inches **15.** $A = \pi r^2 = \pi \cdot 16^2 = 256\pi$ **16.** when it is infinite and nonrepeating
17. $S = 4\pi r^2 = 4\pi \cdot 12^2 = 576\pi \approx 1810$ cm²
18. $V = \frac{4}{3}\pi r^3 = \frac{4}{3}\pi \cdot 9^3 = \frac{4}{3} \cdot \pi \cdot 729 = 972\pi \approx 3054$ cubic units **19.** The total number of players is 48.
$\frac{10}{48} = 0.208\overline{3} \approx 20.8\%$. **20.** 60° is $\frac{60}{360} = \frac{1}{6}$ of a circle.
The area of the circle is $\pi\left(\frac{8}{2}\right)^2 = \pi \cdot 4^2 = 16\pi$ cm². So
the area of the sector is $\frac{1}{6} \cdot 16\pi = \dfrac{8\pi}{3}$ cm²

The chart below keys the **Progress Self-Test** questions to the objectives in the **Chapter Review** on pages 615–617 or to the **Vocabulary** (Voc.) on page 613. This will enable you to locate those **Chapter Review** questions that correspond to questions you missed on the **Progress Self-Test.** The lesson where the material is covered is also indicated in the chart.

Question	1	2	3	4	5–6	7	8	9	10	
Objective	E	D	J	B	C	G	A	A	D	
Lesson	13-7	13-5	13-2	13-2	13-3	13-6	13-1	13-4	13-5	
Question	11	12	13	14	15	16	17	18	19	20
Objective	Voc.	A	Voc.	I	E	G	H	F	K	E
Lesson	13-1	13-4	13-5	13-6	13-7	13-6	13-9	13-9	13-8	13-7

CHAPTER 13 REVIEW (pp. 615–617)

1. 150 **3.** 12 **5.** 8 and 9 **7.** 20 **9.** $\sqrt{73}$ **11.** 52 **13.** 24,600
15. 10,200 **17.** circumference 20π; area 100π **19.** 25π
21. 100π **23.** all but π **25.** Any decimal represents a real number. **27.** 2.7 square meters **29.** about 1257 cm²
31. 20π or about 63 feet **33.** $\dfrac{32\pi}{3}$ or about 33.5 cubic inches
35. $\sqrt{50}$ **37.** $\sqrt{2}$ **39.** $25\% = \frac{1}{4}$, and the sector for lunch has more than a quarter of the circle's area.

absolute value The absolute value of a positive number or zero is that number. The absolute value of a negative number is the opposite of that number. The absolute value of a number is the distance of a number from zero.

acute angle An angle whose measure is between 0° and 90°.

addend A number to be added.

addition property of equality If $a = b$, then $a + c = b + c$.

additive identity The number 0.

Additive Identity Property of Zero For any number n: $n + 0 = n$.

additive inverse The number, which when added to a number, gives a sum of 0. The additive inverse of n is denoted $-n$. Also called *opposite*.

Add-opp Property of Subtraction For any numbers a and b: $a - b = a + -b$. In words, subtracting b is the same as adding the opposite of b.

algebraic expression An expression that contains a variable alone or with numbers and operation symbols.

algorithm A sequence of steps that leads to a desired result.

alternate interior angles Angles formed by two lines and a transversal that are between the two lines and on opposite sides of the transversal.

altitude of a triangle The perpendicular distance from any vertex of a triangle to the side opposite that vertex. Also called *height*.

angle The union of two rays with the same endpoint.

area Measure of the space inside a two-dimensional figure.

Area Model for Multiplication The area of a rectangle with length ℓ and width w is $\ell \cdot w$ *or* ℓw.

Associative Property of Addition For any numbers a, b, and c: $(a + b) + c = a + (b + c) = a + b + c$.

Associative Property of Multiplication For any numbers a, b, and c: $a(bc) = (ab)c = abc$.

average A number representing a set of other numbers determined by taking the sum of those numbers and dividing by the number of them. Also called *mean*.

bar graph A graph in which information is represented using bars of various lengths to show values of a particular category.

base In the power x^n, x is the base.

base of a triangle The side of a triangle to which an altitude is drawn.

bases of a trapezoid The parallel sides of a trapezoid.

billion A word name for 1,000,000,000 or 10^9.

billionth A word name for 0.000000001 or 10^{-9}.

brackets [ ] grouping symbols which serve the same role as parentheses.

center of a circle The given point from which the set of points of the circle are at a given distance.

center of a sphere The given point from which the set of points of the sphere are at a given distance.

centi- a prefix meaning $\frac{1}{100}$.

centimeter $\frac{1}{100}$ of a meter.

central angle of a circle An angle with its vertex at the center of the circle.

certain event An event with a probability of 1.

circle The set of points in a plane at a certain distance from a certain point.

circle graph A graph in which information is represented using a circle that is cut into sectors to show values of a particular category. Also called *pie graph*.

circumference A circle's perimeter.

clockwise The direction around a circle in which the hands of a clock usually move.

coefficient The number by which a certain variable in a term is multiplied.

coincide To occupy the same position.

column A vertical line of objects in a rectangular array.

common denominator A multiple of all the denominators in a problem.

Commutative Property of Addition For any numbers a and b: $a + b = b + a$.

Commutative Property of Multiplication For any numbers a and b: $ab = ba$.

Comparison Model for Subtraction $x - y$ is how much more x is than y.

composite number Any positive integer exactly divisible by one or more positive integers other than itself and 1.

congruent figures Figures with the same size and shape. Figures which are the image of each other under a reflection, rotation, or translation, or combination of these.

contraction A size change with a magnitude between 0 and 1.

conversion factor A factor by which one unit can be converted to another.

convex polygon A polygon in which no diagonals lie outside the polygon.

coordinate graph A graph displaying points as ordered pairs of numbers.

corresponding angles Any pair of angles in similar locations in relation to a transversal intersecting two lines.

corresponding sides Any pair of sides in the same relative positions in two similar figures.

count A number of particular things.

counterclockwise The direction around a circle opposite from that in which the hands of a clock move.

counting unit The name of the particular things being tallied in a count.

cube A three-dimensional figure with six faces, each face being a square.

cubic units Units for measuring volume.

decagon A ten-sided polygon.

decimal notation The notation in which numbers are written using ten digits and each place stands for a power of 10.

decimal system The system in which numbers are written in decimal notation.

degree A unit of measurement equal to $\frac{1}{360}$ of a complete revolution.

denominator The divisor in a fraction, b in the fraction $\frac{a}{b}$ or a/b.

diagonal of a polygon A segment that connects two vertices of the polygon but is not a side of the polygon.

diameter of a circle A segment connecting two points of a circle and containing its center. The length of that segment.

difference The answer to a subtraction problem.

digit One of the ten symbols, 0 1 2 3 4 5 6 7 8 9, used to write numbers from zero to nine.

dimensions The lengths of the sides of a rectangle. The number of rows and the number of columns in a rectangular array.

display The area on a calculator where numbers appear.

Distributive Property of Multiplication over Addition
For any numbers a, b, and x:
$ax + bx = (a + b)x$ and $x(a + b) = xa + xb$.
Also called *distributivity*.

Distributive Property of Multiplication over Subtraction
For any numbers a, b, and x:
$ax - bx = (a - b)x$ and $(a - b)x = ax - bx$.
Also called *distributivity*.

dividend The number in a quotient which is being divided. a is the dividend in $a \div b$ or $\frac{a}{b}$.

divisor (1) The number by which you divide in a quotient. b is the divisor in $a \div b$ or $\frac{a}{b}$. (2) A number that divides another number exactly. Also called *factor*.

endpoint of a ray The starting point of a ray.

Equal Fractions Property If the numerator and denominator of a fraction are both multiplied (or divided) by the same nonzero number, then the resulting fractions are equal.

equally likely outcomes Outcomes in a situation where each outcome is assumed to occur as often as every other outcome.

equation A sentence with an equal sign.

equation of the form $x + a = b$ An equation in which an unknown number x is added to a known number a, resulting in a known number b.

equation of the form $ax = b$ An equation in which the unknown number x is multiplied by a known number a, resulting in a known number b.

equation of the form $ax + b = c$ An equation in which an unknown number x is multiplied by a known number a, then added to a known number b, resulting in a known number c.

equation of the form $ax + b = cx + d$ An equation in which the same unknown number x is multiplied by numbers a and c and added to known numbers b and d, resulting in equal values.

equilateral triangle A triangle in which all the sides have the same length.

equivalent formulas Formulas in which the same numbers work.

equivalent sentences Sentences that have exactly the same solutions.

estimate A number which is near another number. Also called *approximation*.

Estimation Principle If two numbers are nearly equal, then when one is substituted for the other in a computation, the results of the computation will be nearly equal.

evaluating an expression Finding the value of an algebraic expression by substituting a value for the variable(s).

evaluating a numerical expression Working out the arithmetic in a numerical expression.

event A collection of possible outcomes of an experiment.

exercise A question which you know how to answer.

expansion A size change with magnitude greater than one.

exponent In the power x^n, n is the exponent.

exponential form The form a^b.

exterior angles Angles formed by two lines and a transversal that are not between the two lines.

extremes In the proportion $\frac{a}{b} = \frac{c}{d}$, the numbers a and d.

faces The sides of a solid.

factor A number that divides another number exactly. Also called *divisor*.

finite decimal A decimal that ends. Also called *terminating decimal*.

foot (ft) A unit of length in the U.S. system of measurement equal to 12 inches.

formula A sentence in which one variable is written in terms of other variables.

fraction A number written in the form $\frac{a}{b}$; b is nonzero.

fraction bar A grouping symbol separating the numerator and denominator of a fraction and standing for division.

full turn A turn of 360°. Also called *revolution*.

Fundamental Property of Turns If a turn of magnitude x is followed by a turn of magnitude y, the result is a turn of magnitude $x + y$.

fundamental region A figure which can be used to form a tessellation.

gallon (gal) A unit of capacity in the U.S. system of measurement equal to 4 quarts.

generalization A statement that is true about many instances.

gram A unit of mass in the metric system.

grouping symbols Symbols such as parentheses, brackets, and fraction bars that group numbers and/or variables together.

half turn A turn of 180°.

height of a trapezoid The distance between the bases of a trapezoid.

height of a triangle The perpendicular distance from any vertex of a triangle to the side opposite that vertex. Also called *altitude*.

heptagon A seven-sided polygon.

hexagon A six-sided polygon.

hundredth A word name for 0.01 or 10^{-2}.

hypotenuse of a right triangle The longest side of a right triangle.

image point A point resulting from applying a transformation.

impossible event An event with a probability of 0.

inch (in.) The base unit of length for the U.S. system of measurement.

inequality A sentence with one of the following symbols: $\neq$, $<$, $>$, $\leq$, $\geq$, $=$.

infinite decimal A decimal that goes on forever.

infinite repeating decimal A decimal in which a digit or group of digits to the right of the decimal point repeats forever.

instance An example of a pattern.

integer A number which is a positive whole number, a negative whole number, or zero.

interior angles Angles formed by two lines and a transversal that are between the two lines.

international system of measurement A system of measurement based on the decimal system. Also called *metric system*.

interval on a scale The constant difference between successive tick marks on the scale of a graph.

irrational number A number that cannot be written as a simple fraction. An infinite and nonrepeating decimal.

key in To press keys or enter information into a calculator.

key sequence A set of instructions for what to key in on a calculator to perform a certain operation.

kilo- A prefix meaning 1000.

legs of a right triangle The two sides of a right triangle that form the right angle.

like terms Terms that involve the same variables to the same powers.

linear combination A sum of multiples of different variables to the first power.

linear equation An equation in which the graph of the solutions is a line. An equation equivalent to $ax + b = cx + d$.

linear expression An expression in which the variables are to the first power and are not multiplied or divided.

linear pair Angles that have a common side, and whose non-common sides are opposite rays.

line segment The points A and B along with the points on $\overleftrightarrow{AB}$ between A and B. Also called *segment*.

line symmetry The property of a figure that coincides with its reflection image over a line. Also called *symmetry with respect to a line* or *reflection symmetry*.

liter A volume or capacity in the metric system equal to 1000 cubic centimeters.

lowest terms A fraction written with the smallest possible whole numbers.

mean A number representing a set of other numbers determined by taking the sum of those numbers and dividing by the number of them. Also called *average*.

means In the proportion $\frac{a}{b} = \frac{c}{d}$, the numbers b and c.

means-extremes property In any proportion, the product of the means equals the product of the extremes.

meter The basic unit of length in the metric system.

metric system of measurement A system of measurement based on the decimal system. Also called the *international system of measurement*.

mile (mi) A unit of length in the U.S. system of measurement equal to 5280 feet.

milli- A prefix meaning $\frac{1}{1000}$.

million A word name for 1,000,000.

millionth A word name for 0.000001 or 10^{-6}.

minuend The number a in $a - b$.

mirror A line over which a figure is reflected. Also called *reflecting line*.

mixed numeral A symbol consisting of a whole number with a fraction next to it denoting the sum of those numbers.

mixed number A number written as a mixed numeral.

Multiplication of Fractions Property For all numbers a, b, c, and d with $b \neq 0$ and $d \neq 0$:
$\frac{a}{b} \cdot \frac{c}{d} = \frac{ac}{bd}$.

Multiplication Property of Equality If $x = y$, then $ax = ay$.

Multiplication Property of -1 For any number x: $-1 \cdot x = -x$.

Multiplication Property of Zero For any number x: $x \cdot 0 = 0$.

Multiplicative Identity Property of One For any number n: $n \cdot 1 = 1 \cdot n = n$.

multiplicative inverse The number by which a given number can be multiplied resulting in a product equal to 1. Also called *reciprocal*.

Mult-Rec Property of Division For any numbers a and b, with $b \neq 0$: $\frac{a}{b} = a \cdot \frac{1}{b}$. In words, dividing by b is the same as multiplying by the reciprocal of b.

natural number Any one of the numbers 1, 2, 3, ... Also called *positive integer*. (Some people include 0 as a natural number.)

negative integer Any one of the numbers -1, -2, -3, ...

negative number A number which is the opposite of a positive number.

nested parentheses Parentheses which are inside parentheses.

***n*-gon** A polygon with n sides.

nonagon A nine-sided polygon.

number line A line in which the points in order correspond to numbers in order.

numerator a in the fraction $\frac{a}{b}$.

numerical expression A symbol for a number.

obtuse angle An angle whose measure is between 90° and 180°.

octagon An eight-sided polygon.

open sentence A sentence with variables that can be true or false, depending on what is substituted for the variables.

Op-op Property For any number n: $-(-n) = n$.

opposite The number, which when added to a given number, yields a sum of 0. The opposite of a number n is denoted $-n$. Also called *additive inverse*.

opposite rays Rays that have the same endpoint and together form a line.

ordered pair A pair of numbers or objects (x, y) in which x is the first coordinate and y is the second coordinate.

order of operations Rules for evaluating an expression: work first within parentheses; then calculate all powers, from left to right; then do multiplications or divisions, from left to right; then do additions or subtractions, from left to right.

origin The point where the x- and y-axes intersect denoted by $(0, 0)$.

ounce (oz) A unit of weight in the U.S. system of measurement equal to $\frac{1}{16}$ of a pound.

parallel lines Two lines in a plane are parallel if they have no points in common or are identical.

parallelogram A quadrilateral with two pairs of parallel sides.

parentheses ( ) Grouping symbols which indicate the order of operations that should be followed in evaluating an expression; the work inside them should be done first.

pattern A general form for which there are many examples.

pentagon A five-sided polygon.

percent %, times $\frac{1}{100}$ or .01, one one-hundredth.

perimeter The sum of the lengths of the sides of a polygon.

perimeter of a rectangle $2\ell + 2w$ where ℓ is the length and w is the width of the rectangle.

perpendicular The name given to rays, segments, or lines that form right angles.

pi (π) The ratio of the circumference of a circle to its diameter: approximately $3.1415926535 \ldots$.

pie graph A graph in which information is represented using a circle that has been cut into sectors to show values of a particular category. Also called *circle graph*.

pint A unit of capacity in the U.S. system of measurement equal to one half quart.

place value The number that each digit stands for in a decimal.

polygon A union of segments connected end to end, such that each segment intersects exactly two others at its endpoints.

positive integer Any one of the numbers 1, 2, 3, ... Also called *natural number*.

pound (lb) A unit of weight in the U.S. system of measurement equal to 16 ounces.

power The answer to a problem a^b.

preimage point A point to which a transformation has been applied.

prime number A positive integer whose only positive integer divisors are itself and 1.

probability A number from 0 to 1 which indicates how likely something is to happen.

problem A question which you do not know how to answer.

product The result of doing a multiplication.

Product of Reciprocals Property If a and b are not zero, then $\frac{1}{a} \cdot \frac{1}{b} = \frac{1}{ab}$.

Property of Opposites For any number n: $n + -n = 0$.

Property of Reciprocals For any nonzero number n: $n \cdot \frac{1}{n} = 1$.

proportion A statement that two fractions are equal.

proportional thinking The ability to get or estimate an answer to a proportion without going through the equation-solving process.

protractor An instrument used for measuring angles.

Putting-together Model for Addition If a count or measure x is put together with another count or measure y in the same units, and there is no overlap, then the result has count or measure $x + y$.

Pythagorean theorem In a right triangle with legs a and b, and hypotenuse c, $a^2 + b^2 = c^2$.

quadrant One of the four parts into which the co-ordinate plane is divided by the *x*-axis and *y*-axis.

quadrilateral A four-sided polygon.

quadrillion A word name for 1,000,000,000,000,000.

quadrillionth A word name for 10^{-15}, or .00000 00000 00001 .

quart (qt) A unit of volume in the U.S. system of measurement equal to 2 pints.

quintillion A word name for 1,000,000,000,000,000,000.

quintillionth A word name for 10^{-18}, or .00000 00000 00000 001 .

quotient The result of dividing one number by another.

radius of a circle (plural radii) The distance from the center to any point on the circle.

radius of a sphere The distance from the center to any point on the sphere.

rate A quantity whose unit contains the word ''per'' or ''for each'' or some synonym.

rate factor A rate used in a multiplication.

Rate Model for Division If *a* and *b* are quantities with different units, then $\frac{a}{b}$ is the amount of quantity *a* per quantity *b*.

Rate Factor Model for Multiplication When a rate is multiplied by another quantity, the unit of the product is the ''product'' of units multiplied like fractions. The product has meaning whenever its units have meaning.

rate unit The unit of measurement in a rate.

ratio The quotient of two quantities with the same units.

Ratio Comparison Model for Division If *a* and *b* are quantities with the same units, then $\frac{a}{b}$ compares *a* to *b*.

rational number A number that can be written as a simple fraction. A terminating or repeating decimal.

ray A part of a line which begins at some point and goes forever in a particular direction.

real number A number that can be written as a decimal.

reciprocal A number which, when multiplied by a given number, yields the product 1. Also called *multiplicative inverse*.

rectangle A quadrilateral with four right angles.

rectangular array An arrangement of objects into rows and columns.

rectangular solid A box.

reflecting line The line over which a figure is reflected. Also called *mirror*.

reflection image The image of a figure reflected over a line.

regular polygon A convex polygon whose sides all have the same length and whose angles all have the same measure.

Related Facts Property of Multiplication and Division If $xy = P$, then $\frac{P}{x} = y$ and $\frac{P}{y} = x$.

Repeated Addition Model for Multiplication If *n* is a positive integer, then
$$nx = \underbrace{x + x + \ldots + x.}_{n \text{ addends}}$$

repetend The digits which repeat forever in an infinitely repeating decimal.

revolution A turn of 360°. Also called *full turn*.

rhombus A quadrilateral with all sides of the same length.

right angle An angle whose measure is 90°.

right triangle A triangle with a right angle.

rounding down Making an estimate that is smaller than the exact value.

rounding to the nearest Making an estimate to a particular decimal place by either rounding up or rounding down depending on which estimate the exact value is closest to.

rounding up Making an estimate that is bigger than the exact value.

row A horizontal line of objects in a rectangular array.

scientific calculator A calculator which writes very large or very small numbers in scientific notation and with the powering, factorial, square root, negative, and reciprocal keys.

scientific notation for large numbers A way of writing a large number in terms of a positive integer power of 10 multiplied by a number greater than or equal to 1 and less than 10.

scientific notation for small numbers A way of writing a small number in terms of a negative integer power of 10 multiplied by a number greater than or equal to 1 and less than 10.

sector A part of a circle bounded by two radii and the circle.

segment ($\overline{AB}$) The points A and B along with the points on $\overrightarrow{AB}$ between A and B. Also called *line segment*.

semicircle Half a circle.

short ton A unit of weight in the U.S. system of measurement equal to 2000 pounds.

side One of the segments which makes up a polygon. One of the rays of an angle. One of the faces of a solid.

similar figures Two figures that have the same shape, but not necessarily the same size.

simple fraction A fraction with an integer in the numerator and a nonzero integer in the denominator.

simpler number A number used to more easily solve problems with complicated numbers.

size change factor A number which multiplies other numbers to change their size.

size change of magnitude k A transformation in which the coordinates of the original figure have all been multiplied by k.

Size Change Model for Multiplication If a quantity x is multiplied by a size change factor k, then the result is a quantity k times as big.

slide image The result of adding the same number to the coordinates of the points in a figure. Also called *translation image*.

Slide Model for Addition If a slide x is followed by a slide y, the result is a slide $x + y$.

Slide Model for Subtraction If a quantity a is decreased by an amount b, the resulting quantity is $a - b$.

solution A value of a variable that makes an open sentence true.

solving an open sentence Finding values of the unknown(s) in an open sentence that make it true.

solving a proportion Finding the value of a variable that makes a proportion true.

special case An instance of a pattern used for some definite purpose.

sphere The set of points in space at a given distance from a given point.

square A four-sided figure with four right angles and four sides of equal length. A rectangle with the same length and width.

square root If $A = s^2$, then s is called a square root of A.

square units Units for measuring area.

straight angle An angle whose measure is 180°.

Substitution Principle If two numbers are equal, then one may be substituted for the other in any computation without changing the results of the computation.

subtrahend b in the subtraction $a - b$.

sum The result of an addition.

supplementary angles Two angles whose measures add to 180°.

surface area The sum of the areas of the faces of a solid.

symmetric figure A figure that is symmetric with respect to at least one line.

symmetry with respect to a line The property of a figure that coincides with its reflection image over a line. Also called *line symmetry*.

table An arrangement of data in rows and columns.

Take-away Model for Subtraction If a quantity y is taken away from an original quantity x with the same units, the quantity left is $x - y$.

tenth A word name for 10^{-1} or 0.1.

terminating decimal A decimal that ends. Also called *finite decimal*.

terms Numbers or expressions that are added or subtracted.

tessellation A filling up of a two-dimensional space by congruent copies of a figure that do not overlap.

transformation An operation on a geometric figure by which each point gives rise to a unique image.

translation image The result of adding the same numbers to the coordinates of the points in a figure. Also called *slide image*.

transversal A line that intersects two or more lines.

trapezoid A quadrilateral that has at least one pair of parallel sides.

trial and error A problem-solving strategy in which various solutions are tried until the correct solution is found.

Triangle-Sum Property In any triangle, the sum of the measures of the angles is $180°$.

triangular region A triangle and the space inside it.

trillion A word name for $1,000,000,000,000$.

trillionth A word name for 10^{-12}, or $.000000000001$.

truncate To cut off a number at a particular decimal place.

uniform scale A scale in which numbers that are equally spaced differ by the same amount.

unit cost The cost per given unit of an object.

unit fraction A fraction with 1 in its numerator and a natural number in its denominator.

unknown A variable which is to be solved for in an equation.

unlike terms Terms that involve different variables or the same variable with different exponents.

U.S. system of measurement A measurement system in common use in the United States today, based on inches and pounds. Also called the *customary system of measurement*.

value of a numerical expression The number that is the result of evaluating a numerical expression.

value of an expression The number that is the result of evaluating an algebraic expression.

value of a variable A number that is substituted for a variable.

variable A symbol that can stand for any one of a set of numbers or other objects.

vertex (plural vertices) The point two sides of a polygon have in common. The point of intersection of the sides of an angle.

vertical angles Angles formed by two intersecting lines, but which are not a linear pair.

volume Measurement of the space inside a three-dimensional, or solid figure.

whole number Any of the numbers 0, 1, 2, 3, ...

x-axis The horizontal number line in a coordinate graph.

x-coordinate The first coordinate of an ordered pair.

y-axis The vertical number line in a coordinate graph.

y-coordinate the second coordinate of an ordered pair.

yard (yd) A unit of length in the U.S. system of measurement equal to 3 feet.

terms
of an expression, 542
like, 542
of a sequence, 148
unlike, 542
tessellation, 372–373
test *See* progress self-test.
test a special case *See* problem-solving strategies.
theorem, 580
time, system of measurement of, 107, 118
ton
gross, 105
short, 104
transformations, 363
reflections, 362–363
rotations (turns), 211–212
translations, 358–359
translating expressions, 149–151
addition and subtractions, 149–150
multiplication and division, 150–151
translation, 358–359
image, 358
preimage, 358
transversal, 313
trapezoid, 589
altitude of, 590
area of, 590
base of, 590
height of, 590
trial and error *See* problem-solving strategies.
triangle, 123, 227, 568
altitude of, 585
area of, 585
base of, 585
equilateral, 372, 587
height of, 585
right, 123
sum of angles in, 323
triangle-sum property, 323
triangular region, 568
truncate, 15
try simpler numbers *See* problem-solving strategies.

turn(s), 211–212
fundamental property of, 212
magnitude of, 211
two-step equations, 473–475, 535

unit cost, 485
unit fraction, 419
unit of measure, 8, 398–400
for area, 569
for surface area, 610
for volume, 610
unknown, 173
unlike terms, 542
use an alternate approach *See* problem-solving strategies.
use counterexamples *See* problem-solving strategies.
use a diagram/picture *See* problem-solving strategies.
use estimation *See* problem-solving strategies.
use a formula *See* problem-solving strategies.
use a graph *See* problem-solving strategies.
use logical reasoning *See* problem-solving strategies.
use a mathematical model *See* problem-solving strategies.
use physical models *See* problem-solving strategies.
use proportional thinking *See* problem-solving strategies.
use proportions *See* problem-solving strategies.
use ratios *See* problem-solving strategies.
use a table *See* problem-solving strategies.
use a theorem *See* problem-solving strategies.
U.S. system of measurement *See* customary system of measurement.

Valdes, Manuel Antonio, 34, 139
See history of mathematics.
value
of the expression, 140, 154
of the variable, 154
variable, 145
vectors, 201
vertex
of an angle, 117
of polygon, 226
vertical angles, 308
vertical number line, 22, 27
Viète, François, 146 *See* history of mathematics.
vinculum, 139
volume, 130–131, 393, 399–400
of a cube, 130
of rectangular solid, 393–395
of sphere, 609

whole numbers, 4, 596
Widman, Johann, 139 *See* history of mathematics.
write an equation *See* problem-solving strategies.

x-axis, 343
x-coordinate, 343

yard, 104
y-axis, 343
y-coordinate, 343

zero
absolute value of, 207
division by, 33
equations with, 465
as an integer, 23
multiplying by, 464
opposite of, 203
power, 83

MATHEMATICAL SYMBOLS

$>$	is greater than	$\overleftrightarrow{AB}$	line through A and B
$<$	is less than	AB	length of segment from A to B
$=$	is equal to	$\overrightarrow{AB}$	ray starting at A and containing B
$\neq$	is not equal to	$\overline{AB}$	segment with endpoints A and B
$\leq$	is less than or equal to	$\angle ABC$	angle ABC
$\geq$	is greater than or equal to	$m\angle ABC$	measure of angle ABC
$\approx$	is approximately equal to	$\sqrt{n}$	positive square root of n
$+$	plus sign	π	Greek letter pi; $= 3.141592...$ or $\approx \frac{22}{7}$.
$-$	minus sign		
$\times$, $\bullet$	multiplication signs	?	computer input or PRINT command
$\div$, $\overline{)}$, $/$	division signs	INT ( )	computer command rounding down to the nearest integer
$\%$	percent	2*3	computer command for $2\bullet3$
ft	abbreviation for foot	4/3	computer command for $4 \div 3$
yd	abbreviation for yard	3^5	computer command for 3^5
mi	abbreviation for mile	$> =$	computer command for $\geq$
in.	abbreviation for inch	$< =$	computer command for $\leq$
oz	abbreviation for ounce	$<>$	computer command for not equal to
lb	abbreviation for pound	SQR (N)	computer command for $\sqrt{n}$
qt	abbreviation for quart		
gal	abbreviation for gallon	$\boxed{y^x}$ or $\boxed{x^y}$	calculator powering key
$n°$	n degrees	$\boxed{x!}$	calculator factorial key
( )	parentheses	$\boxed{\sqrt{n}}$	calculator square root key
[ ]	brackets	$\boxed{\pm}$ or $\boxed{+/-}$	calculator negative key
$|x|$	absolute value of x	$\boxed{\pi}$	calculator pi key
$-x$	opposite of x	$\boxed{1/x}$	calculator reciprocal key
$\perp$	is perpendicular to	$\boxed{INV}$, $\boxed{2nd}$, or $\boxed{F}$	calculator second function key
$//$	is parallel to	$\boxed{EE}$ or $\boxed{EXP}$	calculator scientific notation key
$\llcorner$	right angle symbol		
(x, y)	ordered pair x, y		
A'	image of point A		

ACKNOWLEDGMENTS

For permission to reproduce indicated information on the following pages, acknowledgment is made to:

3 Decimal notation table, from a *History of Mathematical Notations* by Florian Cajori, © 1928, Open Court Publishing Company. **73** Information for graph on New Car Sales, from 1988 *Ward's Automotive Yearbook.* **241** Quote from *How to Solve It*, by George Polya, © 1973, Princeton University Press. **338** S & L earnings bar graph, from *USA Today*, January 12, 1984 © 1984. **352** Indoor greenery graph, from *USA Today*, © 1984. **366** Ups & downs of travel cost bar graph, from *USA Today*, © 1984. **377** U.S. oil imports graph, American Petroleum Institute, Washington, D.C. **381** Graph using information from *PC Market Review and Forecast*, Publication #3520, Table 7: Personal Computer Forecast, International Data Corporation, Framingham, Massachusetts.

Extant Materials Unless otherwise acknowledged, all photos are the property of Scott, Foresman and Company. Page positions are as follows: (T)top, (C)center, (B)bottom, (L)left, (R)right, (INS)inset.

4 Jim Whitmer **5** Lee Boltin **7T** Michele & Tom Grimm/After-Image **7B** Reprinted with permission from MATHEMATICS AND HUMOR, copyright 1978 by the National Council of Teachers of Mathematics **8** Focus on Sports **12** Focus on Sports **13** Dennis Hallinan/FPG **14** Eric Carle/Bruce Coleman Inc. **17** Focus on Sports **18** Chuck O'Rear/Woodfin Camp & Associates **23** NASA **25** David Carriere/After-Image **26** Grace Moore/Taurus Photos, Inc. **28** Wolfgang Kaehler **33** David R. Frazier Photolibrary **40** C. W. Schwartz/ANIMALS ANIMALS **51** Thomas Braise/After-Image **52** Dan McCoy/Rainbow **53** Reprinted by permission: Tribune Media Services **54** David Malin/Anglo-Australian Telescope Board **55** Roger Ressmeyer **56** David Carriere/After-Image **57** Jessica Anne Ehlers/Bruce Coleman Inc. **61** Mitchell B. Reibel/Sportschrome, Inc. **62** Eric Meola/The Image Bank **70** Jim Anderson/Woodfin Camp & Associates **71** Holderman Photo/West Stock **74** Spencer Grant/Taurus Photos, Inc. **75** Bil Plummer/The Image Bank **78** Jonathan T. Wright/Bruce Coleman Inc. **79** Everett C. Johnson/After-Image **80** Courtesy Elizabeth Dupee **82** E. R. Degginger/Bruce Coleman Inc. **86** Courtesy Park, Davis & Co. **87** Topham from The Image Works **88** Alec Duncan/Taurus Photos, Inc. **90** D. Mason/West Stock **92** Robert P. Carr/Bruce Coleman Inc. **94** Lee Boltin **96** Alan Becker/The Image Bank **98** Courtesy U.S. Capitol Historical Society, National Geographic Photography, George F. Mobley **100** Mike Douglas/The Image Works **101T** The Granger Collection, New York **101B** Bill Gallery/Stock Boston **105** Spencer W. Jones/Bruce Coleman Inc. **106** Reprinted with special permission of King Features Syndicate, Inc. **108** David R. Frazier Photolibrary **113** David R. Frazier Photolibrary **115** Grant V. Faint/The Image Bank **117** Jonathan T. Wright/Bruce Coleman Inc. **122** Milt & Joan Mann/Cameramann International, Ltd. **124** Vince Streano/After-Image **125** David Madison/Bruce Coleman Inc. **126** Teri Gilman/After-Image **129** Thomas Zimmermann/FPG **132** David R. Frazier Photolibrary **137** National Portrait Gallery, London **138** Stacy Pick/Stock Boston **138INS(C)** The Granger Collection, New York **138INS(R)** The Bettmann Archive **140** Enrico Ferorelli/Dot Picture Agency **142** Steve Solum/Bruce Coleman Inc. **144** Official U.S. Navy Photograph **145 (T)** John Madere/The Image Bank **146** The Granger Collection **149** Bob Daemmrich/The Image Works **150** Michael Heron/Woodfin Camp & Associates **152** John Ficara/Woodfin Camp & Associates **153** Milt & Joan Mann/Cameramann International, Ltd. **154** Milt & Joan Mann/Cameramann International, Ltd. **156** Jeffry W. Myers/Stock Boston **157** Frank Oberle/After-Image **158** Walter Chandoha **162** Alfred Pasieka/Taurus Photos, Inc. **163** Milt & Joan Mann/Cameramann International, Ltd. **166** Audrey Ross/Bruce Coleman Inc. **170** David Madison **174** Film Stills Archive/Museum of Modern Art **178** Don and Pat Valenti **185** Gilbert Grant/Photo Researchers **186** David R. Frazier Photolibrary **188** Ron Thomas/FPG **190** Gabe Palmer/After-Image **191** James W. Kay/After-Image **192** G. Newman Haynes/The Image Works **193** Jean-Claude Lejeune/Stock Boston **196** Jim Whitmer **198** Walter Chandoha **201** Alan Carey/The Image Works **205** Adolf Schmidecker/FPG **206** David W. Hamilton/The Image Bank **211** Joseph Nettis/Photo Researchers **212** Robert Frerck/After-Image **214** Matt Bradley/Bruce Coleman Inc. **219** Milt & Joan Mann/Cameramann International, Ltd. **224** Dan Guravich/Photo Researchers **226** Harald Sund/The Image Bank **228** Peter Gridley **230** Milt & Joan Mann/Cameramann International, Ltd. **232** Baron Wolman/After-Image **233** David Falconer/After-Image **238** Georg Gerster/COMSTOCK INC. **239** Carl Roessler/Bruce Coleman Inc. **240–241** Courtesy Hallmark, Inc. **241T** Copyright 1987, Newsday, Inc. Reprinted by permission. **242** Georg Gerster/COMSTOCK INC. **244** Stanford University **245** Bryan F. Peterson/The Stock Market **246** Dennis Hallinan/FPG **249** Kevin Horan/Stock Boston **253** Larry Reynolds **254** Cezus/FPG **257** Mark Antman/The Image Works **267** Alan Becker/The Image Bank **268** Walter Chandoha **275** David Stoecklein/West Stock **278** Pete Turner/The Image Bank **278INS** Mike Mitchell/After-Image **282** Peter Gridley/FPG **283L** G. & M. Kohier/FPG **283R** Charles Gatewood/The Image Works **285** David Madison **287T** David Madison/Bruce Coleman Inc. **290** Kevin Horan/Stock Boston **292** D. Sucsy/FPG **293** Sullivan Rogers/Bruce Coleman Inc. **294** The Bettmann Archive **295** G. A. Belluche, Jr./FPG **296** Carl Roessler/FPG **298** David R. Frazier Photolibrary **299** David R. Frazier Photolibrary **301** Library of Congress **302** Travelpix/FPG **303** Lawrence Migdale **306** FPG **307** Joanna McCarthy/The Image Bank **312** HERMAN © 1984 Universal Press Syndicate. Reprinted with permission. All Rights Reserved. **318** Coco McCoy/Rainbow **321** Paul H. Henning/Third Coast **322** Reprinted by permission: Tribune Media Services **332** Dennis Hallinan/FPG **333** David R. Frazier Photolibrary **334** David R. Frazier Photolibrary **336** Lawrence Migdale **337** Clyde H. Smith/FPG **339** Library of Congress **340** R. Laird/FPG **341** Brent Jones **348** David Madison **354** Brent Jones **356** John S. Flannery/Bruce Coleman Inc. **357** Travelpix/FPG **361B** © 1988 M. C. Escher Heirs/Cordon Art-Baarn-Holland. Photograph from the Collection of C. V. S. Roosevelt, Washington, D.C. **361T** Mel Digiacomo/The Image Bank **363** P. Pearson/Click/Chicago/Tony Stone **367** Frithfoto/Bruce Coleman Inc. **369L** Lynn M. Stone/Bruce Coleman Inc. **369R** Bruce Coleman Inc. **372** Jeff Foott/Bruce Coleman Inc. **373** © 1988 M. C. Escher Heirs/Cordon Art-Baarn-Holland. **374T** © 1988 M. C. Escher Heirs/Cordon Art-Baarn-Holland. **382** David J. Maenza/The Image Bank **384** Ames Research Center/NASA **393** Rick Browne/Stock Boston **398** Grant Heilman Photography **399** James H. Carmichael/Bruce Coleman Inc. **400** David Madison/Bruce Coleman Inc. **407** Charles Feil/After-Image **408** Terry G. Murphy/ANIMALS ANIMALS **412** Robert Rathe/FPG **413(all)** Des & Jen Bartlett/Bruce Coleman Inc. **416** Timothy O'Keefe/Bruce Coleman Inc. **417** Kevin Galvin/Bruce Coleman Inc. **418** Teri Gilman/After-Image **421** Adolf Schmidecker/FPG **423** John Coletti/Stock Boston **426** Isaac Geib/Grant Heilman Photography **429L** Don and Pat Valenti **429R** David R. Frazier Photolibrary **430** Bob Daemmrich/The Image Works **432** Owen Franken/Stock Boston **433** E. R. Degginger/Earth Scenes **434** Manfred Kage/Peter Arnold, Inc. **436** The Erik Hildes-Heim Collection/Smithsonian Institution **439** Jeffrey Sylvvester/FPG **443** David Carriere/After-Image **445** Mike Mitchell/After-Image **448** David R. Frazier Photolibrary **450** David Lissy/The Picture Cube **453** Janeart Ltd./The Image Bank **457** David Madison/Bruce Coleman Inc. **458** Chad Slattery/After-Image **463** Cameron Davidson/Bruce Coleman Inc. **468** James W. Kay/Bruce Coleman Inc. **471** Grant Heilman Photography **477T** Tom Edwards/ANIMALS ANIMALS **479** Don and Pat Valenti **484** Henley & Savage/After-Image **485** David R. Frazier Photolibrary **486** Tom Tracy/After-Image **487** Joachim Messerschmidt/Bruce Coleman Inc. **488** D. & J. McClurg/Bruce Coleman Inc. **489** Focus On Sports **491** Hans Reinhard/Bruce Coleman Inc. **492** S. L. Craig, Jr./Bruce Coleman Inc. **495** Chael Slattery/After-Image **497** Bryan Peterson/West Stock **499** Norman Myers/Bruce Coleman Inc. **506** David R. Frazier Photolibrary **508** Bob Daemmrich/The Image Works **509** Bob Daemmrich/The Image Works **511** Kunsthistorisches Museum, Vienna/The Bridgeman Art Library from Art Resource, NY **514** Dave Schaefer/The Picture Cube **515** Eunice Harris/The Picture Cube **516** David R. Frazier Photolibrary **522** Franz Kraus/The Picture Cube **523** David R. Frazier Photolibrary **524** Don and Pat Valenti **528** Ken Kaminsky/The Picture Cube **529** Kevin Syms/David R. Frazier Photolibrary **530** Gill C. Kenny/The Image Bank **535** Frank Oberle/Bruce Coleman Inc. **537** David H. Wells/The Image Works **546** John Eastcott/Yva Momatiuk/The Image Works **553** David R. Frazier Photolibrary **555** Gabe Palmer/After-Image **556** David R. Frazier Photolibrary **560** Harry Hartman/Bruce Coleman Inc. **563** Jonathan L. Barkan/The Picture Cube **566** Willie L. Hill, Jr./Stock Boston **566** Kandinsky, Composition VIII, No. 260; July 1923; Collection, Solomon R. Guggenheim Museum, New York. Photo: David Heald. **568** Tim Heneghan/West Stock **569** Walter Chandoha **573** George Dillon/Stock Boston **575** Hirmer Fotoarchiv, Munich **577** Mike Mazzaschi/Stock Boston **578** Norman Owen Tomalin/Bruce Coleman, Inc. **581** Frank Siteman/The Picture Cube **584** Jon Feingersh/Stock Boston **587** Bob Burch/West Stock **588** Cezus/FPG **589** Robert Fried/Stock Boston **593** Jeff Persons/Stock Boston **594** Owen Franken/Stock Boston **597** David Madison/Bruce Coleman Inc. **598** Glenn Short/Bruce Coleman Inc. **599** *Portraits and Lives of Illustrious Men* by Andre Thevet, Keruert et Chaudiere, Paris, 1584 **600** Jon Riley/After-Image **602** Derek Fell **605** D. Dietrich/FPG **607** Will & Deni McIntyre/Aperture Photobook **609** Don Mason/West Stock **610** NASA **611** Rene Sheret/After-Image **612** GEOPIC (TM)/Earth Satellite Corporation **614** Jeff Albertson/Stock Boston **617** Joel W. Rogers/Alaska Photo